"ULSTER WILL FIGHT ..."

Volume 1: Home Rule and the Ulster Volunteer Force 1886-1922

David R. Orr & David Truesdale

Helion & Company

Helion & Company Limited
26 Willow Road
Solihull
West Midlands
B91 1UE
England
Tel. 0121 705 3393
Fax 0121 711 4075
Email: info@helion.co.uk
Website: www.helion.co.uk
Twitter: @helionbooks
Visit our blog http://blog.helion.co.uk/

Published by Helion & Company 2016
Designed and typeset by Mach 3 Solutions Ltd (www.mach3solutions.co.uk)
Cover designed by Paul Hewitt, Battlefield Design (www.battlefield-design.co.uk)
Printed by Gutenberg Press Limited, Tarxien, Malta

Text © David R. Orr 2016
Images © as individually credited
Front cover: On 25 April 1914 the *Innismurray* arrived in Donaghadee with arms and ammunition for the Ulster Volunteer Force. Met by James Craig and the men from Comber and Newtownards areas, who formed the 2nd Battalion, North Down Volunteers, everything was unloaded by 9.00am. (Painting by Peter Dennis © Helion & Company Ltd 2016)

Every reasonable effort has been made to trace copyright holders and to obtain their permission for the use of copyright material. The author and publisher apologize for any errors or omissions in this work, and would be grateful if notified of any corrections that should be incorporated in future reprints or editions of this book.

ISBN 978-1-910777-62-6

British Library Cataloguing-in-Publication Data.
A catalogue record for this book is available from the British Library.

All rights reserved. No part of this publication may be reproduced, stored in a retrieval system, or transmitted, in any form, or by any means, electronic, mechanical, photocopying, recording or otherwise, without the express written consent of Helion & Company Limited.

For details of other military history titles published by Helion & Company Limited contact the above address, or visit our website: http://www.helion.co.uk.

We always welcome receiving book proposals from prospective authors.

The authors would like to dedicate both volumes of this history to those members of their families who enlisted as Irishmen in the Great War, 1914-1918.

Lance Corporal Albert Edward Truesdale, No.19221
D Company, 13th Royal Irish Rifles
Enlisted 19 September 1914, wounded 1 July 1916, gassed 21 March 1918
Medically discharged 26 June 1918
Silver War Badge No.423263

Captain Joseph Orr, No.2021
1st Battalion, Irish Guards
Enlisted 8 September 1904, wounded 2 February 1917
Retired due to wounds 20 March 1920
Later served as Major, King's African Rifles

A/RQMS William John Orr, No.16395
5th Royal Irish Rifles
re-enlisted 18 September 1914 for the duration of the war.
Formerly Colour Sergeant, No.231
1st Royal Irish Rifles
7 July 1882 to 9 July 1908

Rifleman Joseph Totten, No.11/6463
11th Royal Irish Rifles
Enlisted May 1915.
GSW to face and leg, 8 August 1917
GSW to face, right arms and right thigh 21 July 1918
Transferred to Labour Corps 17 November 1918

Rifleman Herbert Totten, No.11/7550
11th Royal Irish Rifles
Enlisted 15 June 1915
Discharged 26 October 1915; aged 16 years

Lieutenant John Richard Orr
Royal Air Force, formerly Royal Flying Corps
Killed in Action 8 August 1918
Formerly 177th Overseas Battalion (Simcoe Foresters),
Canadian Expeditionary Force

Lieutenant William James Orr, No.143568
60 Siege Battery, Royal Garrison Artillery
Enlisted 8 December 1915
Transferred to Supplementary Reserve 8 March 1919
Relinquished Commission 1 April 1920

Contents

Foreword		vi
Introduction		iii
1	The Origins of Home Rule	9
2	Unionists Start to Prepare	31
3	Tensions Mount	61
4	The Ulster Covenant	77
5	Greater Organisation	135
6	Curragh Incident	189
7	Unionist Gun-running	206
8	Volunteers Prepare	230
9	National Volunteers Begin to Arm	236
10	Ulster Stands at the Brink	258
11	The UVF at Home and at War	288
12	Easter Rebellion and the Somme	326
13	Post-war	340
14	Not Forgotten	362
Appendices		
I	Order of Battle	377
II	Principal War-Time Philanthropies and Amounts Raised	383
III	Weapons	385
IV	An example of orders for a UVF camp of instruction	396
V	UVF Special Order – Enlistment for Imperial Forces	398
Bibliography		400
Index		409

Foreword

The character and formation of the 36th (Ulster) Division is inexplicably linked to the events of the preceding years and in particular the tensions around Home Rule for Ireland. The current 'Decade of Centenaries' in Northern Ireland has encouraged many people to re-explore this period of Irish history however the roots of the events of this decade are firmly embedded in the last years of the Nineteenth Century. Randolph Churchill's call in 1886 "That Ulster will fight and Ulster will be right" was to echo in the country in subsequent years.

The actions of the Unionists in Ireland and in particular in the province of Ulster were to lead to defining moments in Irish history. Bolstered by support from the British Conservative party and key members of the British establishment they became more determined in their resistance to Home Rule. The signing of the Ulster Solemn League and Covenant in 1912 declared the signatories unswerving loyalty to the State and their determination to prevent the establishment of rule from Dublin. This stance was reinforced by the formation of the Ulster Volunteer Force to resist any attempts by the British Government to 'impose' Home Rule on Ulster.

It was these men of the Ulster Volunteer Force who would come forward as volunteers to form the nucleus of the 36th (Ulster) Division during the First World War. Those men and women of the Ulster Volunteers left in Ireland would continue their preparations to resist against the possibility of Home Rule.

In order to tell the complete story of the Ulster Division it is important to explore the Home Rule issues which led to men and women from, towns, villages and farms from all over the nine counties of Ulster and beyond, signing the Covenant and joining the Ulster Volunteers. These men were prepared to resist by force of arms if necessary.

The Somme Association is grateful to the authors for their efforts and attention to detail in explaining the issues surrounding Home Rule and the formation of the Ulster Volunteers who in turn provided the core of the 36th (Ulster) Division.

Carol Walker
Director
The Somme Association & Somme Museum

Introduction

To be ignorant of what occurred before you were born is to remain always a child. For what is the worth of human life, unless it is woven into the life of our ancestors by the records of history?

Cicero

What answer from the North?
One Law, one Land, one Throne,
If England drive us forth,
We shall not fall alone.

Kipling

Irish history is littered with innumerable "what ifs". One such significant "what if" surrounds the Ulster Volunteer Force (UVF), the nucleus of the 36th (Ulster) Division and the outbreak of the First World War.

If the Austro-Hungarian heir had not been assassinated and sparked the chain of events which led to the war the Home Rule Bill may not have been delayed, the UVF may have been embroiled in a bloody civil war and as a result there may not have been a republican rising in Dublin. How different would Irish history have evolved? Would there have been an effective Irish parliament? Would there have been partition of the island?

Ironically contrary to many accounts of the period which argue that much of the activities, including the gun-running occurred in 'secret', the Royal Irish Constabulary was continually gathering relevant and often detailed information which was being passed to the government, who choose not to act. What if they had?

The UVF spanned not just the geographic rural and urban Protestant Ulster from the Atlantic coast of Donegal to the shipyards of East Belfast but also the diverse political ideals of individuals.

By the outbreak of the Great War it had become an organisation of armed volunteers, the first to use motorcycle despatch riders and motor transport on a large scale and the first to use armoured lorries in street patrols. It was also one of the first in the twentieth century to recognise the varied role for women in warfare against a backdrop of a rise in women's suffrage in the United Kingdom and the United States of America.

The importance, role and significance of the existence of the UVF are well summed up in Sir Winston Churchill's book, *Great Contemporaries*, that "if Ulster had confined herself simply to constitutional agitation, it is extremely improbable that she would have escaped forcible inclusion in a Dublin Parliament."

Whilst Carson negotiated for the exclusion of the Ulster counties from Home Rule for the duration of the war, it is important to remember that he always primarily sought to maintain the whole island of Ireland within the Union, gradually withdrawing from politics following the Government of Ireland Act (1920) which he saw as a betrayal of Southern loyalists.

Whilst the Rebellion in Ireland in 1916 can be seen as the initial phase of the call for independence across the British Empire over the next 50 years, the actions of the UVF could also be argued as bringing the gun into modern Irish politics and leading the way of unconstitutionalism and resistance.

The strategic importance of Ireland to the defence of the United Kingdom, highlighted by Wilfrid Spender, was recognised by Winston Churchill in a message to JM Andrews, Northern Ireland Prime Minster, in April 1943:

> When you became Prime Minister in December 1940 it was a dark and dangerous hour. We were alone, and had to face single handed the full fury of the German attack, raining down death and destruction on our cities and, still more deadly, seeking to strangle our life by cutting off the entry to our ports of ships which brought us our food and the weapons we sorely needed. That channel remained open because loyal Ulster gave us the full use of the Northern Irish ports and waters, and thus ensured the free working of the Clyde and the Mersey. But for the loyalty of Northern Ireland and its devotion to what has now become the cause of thirty governments or nations we should have been confronted by slavery and death, and the light which now shines so strongly throughout the world have been quenched.

In December 2012 *The Telegraph* newspaper ran an article which quoted a survey carried out in 2011 by Ark, a joint project by Queen's University and the University of Ulster which showed that 52 percent of Northern Ireland's Catholics wished to remain in the United Kingdom, against just 33 percent who wish to have a united Ireland. It compared this result against 48 percent of English people who want to keep the union.[1]

It then compared these figures to 19 percent of Catholics questioned by the same survey team in 1998 who favoured the UK connection, while 49 percent claimed they wanted a united Ireland.[2]

We would like to thank the Somme Museum, Conlig, County Down, for inviting us on their behalf to explore the Irish Home Rule developments and the subsequent creation of the Ulster Volunteer Force, aided in no small part by the ability to draw on their artefacts and archives and providing us with the necessary background.

David R Orr & David Truesdale
11 November 2015

---

1 *The Telegraph* – Northern Ireland Catholics are now more unionist than the English. Can the United Kingdom last? <http://blogs.telegraph.co.uk/news/edwest/100095628/northern-ireland-catholics-are-now-more-unionist-than-the-english-can-the-united-kingdom-last/> (Accessed 28 December 2012).
2 *Belfast Telegraph* – Is Catholic support for a united Ireland on the wane? <http://www.belfasttelegraph.co.uk/news/local-national/northern-ireland/is-catholic-support-for-a-united-ireland-on-the-wane-16013433.html#ixzz2GNeziqjv> (Accessed 28 December 2012).

1

The Origins of Home Rule

A legacy of the seventeenth century was the Irish Ascendancy and the associated plantation of Ulster which in turn at the start of the Twentieth Century led to two armed camps in Ireland, one largely Catholic, containing the extreme nationalists and the other largely Protestant containing extreme unionists.

Since 1264 Ireland had had some kind of parliament until the 1798 rebellion resulted in Britain trying to prevent Napoleonic France from meddling further in Ireland and hence threatening Britain by enacting the Act of Union in 1801.[1]

The irony was that many of the landed Anglo-Irish Protestants were opposed to the Act of Union and the transfer of power to London brought about by Pitt and Lord Castlereagh's use of bribes of office and peerages. One Ulsterman, Colonel Napier was unsure of the rights and wrongs of Union, but was sure of some of the expected side effects, writing in 1799, "The obsequious Unionists' modestly insinuate that a Kingdom derives consequences from having its legislative powers transferred to another country and accumulates wealth from 130 of its richest subjects with their long sequel of Pimps and Parasites, transporting themselves to pursue the trade of Parliament in a distant capital."[2]

Meanwhile many Roman Catholics hoped the Union would bring about reconciliation and regeneration for Ireland and more importantly their emancipation. However it wasn't until the actions of Daniel O'Connell raised massive popular support that London granted Catholic Emancipation[3] in 1829.

In February 1848 John Mitchell, an Ulster Protestant, established the *United Irishman* newspaper advocating "a holy war" to rid English influence from Ireland, going even further by advocating that every man should have arms and promoting their use. He believed that "no good can come from an English Parliament."[4]

On being elected as Liberal Prime Minister in 1868, William Ewart Gladstone is reputed to have uttered the momentous phrase, "My mission is to pacify Ireland".[5] He and the Liberal Party came to power with the slogan "Justice for Ireland", Irish Liberals gaining 65 of the 105 Irish seats at Westminster. He saw his role as to finally pacify Ireland and was the first English statesman to feel that it was an affront to Ireland's dignity and manhood to be ruled by an "alien" minority.[6] The disestablishment of the Anglican Church of Ireland in 1869 was his first step to reducing the control of the minority who would have largely voted Conservative and made all political decisions in Ireland.

---

1   Shearman, Hugh, *Not an Inch: A Study of Northern Ireland and Lord Craigavon* (1942).
2   Lewis, Geoffrey, *Carson: The man who divided Ireland* (2006).
3   Lewis, Geoffrey, *Carson: The man who divided Ireland* (2006).
4   Denman, Terence, *A Lonely Grave: The Life and Death of William Redmond* (1995).
5   Downing, Taylor (ed) *The Troubles* (1990).
6   Lewis, Geoffrey, *Carson: The man who divided Ireland* (2006).

Gladstone's Irish Land Act in 1870 was the first of a series of cautious moves towards fair rents and security of tenure for the Irish peasantry; essentially a movement of power in the Irish countryside from landlord to peasant.[7]

After defecting from the Irish Conservative Party in 1873 Isaac Butt, an Irish Protestant and former Tory[8] formed The Home Rule League. This was an attempt to gain a limited form of freedom from Britain and yet protect and control Irish domestic affairs in the interests of the Protestant landlord class.

The League came more to the foreground when Gladstone unexpectedly called an election in February 1874. Despite having difficulty in finding suitable candidates to represent the Home Rule issue, it succeeded in winning 59 Irish seats, many with ex-Liberals. This result placed Home Rule and its centrepiece of the restoration of an Irish parliament in Dublin back on the national agenda, so with this success behind them 46 members gathered in Dublin and formed themselves into a separate Irish parliamentary party.

William Ewart Gladstone, Prime Minister.

The first Home Rule motion was a very modest proposal intended to give Ireland a separate Parliament in Dublin that would deal with purely domestic matters. It was put to the House of Commons, 30 June 1874 and was defeated by 458 to 461 votes.[9]

However as with many political reforms throughout history a small group of impatient young men, led by Charles Stewart Parnell saw themselves as the genuine "Home-Rulers" and distanced themselves from Isaac Butt's approach and what they believed to be a somewhat ineffective leadership and adopted the method of parliamentary "obstructionism" during 1876-77.

Around the same time in the American west the exploitation of corn-growing plains and improved trans-Atlantic transportation was flooding Europe with cheap grain against which Ireland could not compete, resulting in prices starting to fall and Irish farmers being unable to pay their rents. When this combined with an extremely wet summer in 1877 and an attack of blight on the potato crop reducing it to less than half its usual output there was the threat of a famine. The culmination of these factors was that in 1878 evictions were the highest for over a decade, doubling again by 1880 with about half of Irish peasants living on charity.[10]

The 1880 General Election saw 64 Home Rulers being elected, 27 of them Parnell supporters, which resulted in his nomination as leader of a divided Home Rule Party. With the country on the brink of a land war, he saw that support for land agitation was a means to achieving his objective of self-government. By the end of 1880 Parnell's party was sitting in opposition to Gladstone's new Liberal government and engaging in disruptive tactics in the Commons by keeping 'Ireland' to the fore.[11]

---

7   Denman, Terence, *A Lonely Grave: The Life and Death of William Redmond* (1995).
8   Denman, Terence, *A Lonely Grave: The Life and Death of William Redmond* (1995).
9   Denman, Terence, *A Lonely Grave: The Life and Death of William Redmond* (1995).
10 Denman, Terence, *A Lonely Grave: The Life and Death of William Redmond* (1995).
11 Denman, Terence, *A Lonely Grave: The Life and Death of William Redmond* (1995).

On 6 May 1882, Irish Nationalists, alleged to have been Land Leaguers, murdered Irish Chief Secretary and Under-Secretary, Lord Frederick Cavendish and Thomas Henry Burke, the Permanent Under-Secretary, in Phoenix Park, Dublin.[12] The result of these murders caused many people who although not actively supporting Home Rule at the time but were not prepared to oppose it, to reconsider their position; "People who do these kinds of things could not possibly be entrusted with self-government."[13]

To both British and Irish Unionists the concept of Irish Home Rule would result in the dismemberment of the United Kingdom and perhaps even threaten the very foundation of the British Empire.

In June 1883, the *Northern Whig* declared, "Ulster is not National and cannot be made National … the loyal Ulster electors, Protestant and Catholic, have only to come to an understanding to divide the representation. Under such an arrangement not one nationalist candidate will be returned for Ulster.[14]

However the electoral reforms of 1884-85 extending the franchise to every householder and the redrawing of constituency boundaries gave the Irish party the opportunity to contest seats in many parts of Ulster which previously would have been difficult, if not impossible.[15] The electorate in Ireland increased from 200,000 to 700,000 with Nationalists securing no less than 86 out of a total of 103 seats in the next General Election in 1885.[16]

It led to the formation of groups such as the Irish Loyal and Patriotic Union in 1885 and the Ulster Loyalist Anti-Repeal Union in 1886.[17] At an 1886 meeting of the Irish Loyal and Patriotic Union, of the 28 speakers only two were Roman Catholics and 18 were peers, sons of peers or landed gentry. The Protestant working class was conspicuous by its absence at such events, being politically active in the streets instead.[18]

The Royal Irish Constabulary noted some drilling being organised in the country, for example a maximum of 50 men appear to have been drilled in the Demesne and Temperance Hall in Richill. By identifying 26 of them the constabulary were able to indicate it was a fairly wide cross-section of the rural community.[19]

At the end of 1885, William 'Willie' Redmond, who later died as a Major in the Royal Irish Regiment during the battle for Messines Ridge 1917, was returned as MP for Fermanagh North, the first nationalist to sit for the seat and the first Catholic MP in the area for 200 years. In his victory speech he promised to be a "faithful servant to

William 'Willie' Redmond, who later died as a Major in the Royal Irish Regiment during the battle for Messines Ridge 1917. (Somme Museum)

---

12   Denman, Terence, *A Lonely Grave: The Life and Death of William Redmond* (1995).
13   Crozier, Brig-Gen FP Crozier, CB, CMG, DSO, *Ireland for Ever* (1932).
14   Denman, Terence, *A Lonely Grave: The Life and Death of William Redmond* (1995).
15   Denman, Terence, *A Lonely Grave: The Life and Death of William Redmond* (1995).
16   Hyde, H Montgomery, *Carson* (1953).
17   Hume, David, *"For Ulster and Her Freedom": The story of the April 1914 gun-running* (1989).
18   Muenger, Elizabeth A, *The British Military Dilemma in Ireland: Occupation Politics 1886-1914* (1991).
19   Bowman, Timothy, *Carson's Army: Ulster Volunteer Force, 1910-22* (2007).

Protestants and Catholics alike".[20] He won the seat again in the election of July 1886.

Not all Ulster was against Home Rule, three of the counties, Monaghan, Donegal and Cavan had large Nationalist and therefore Home Rule majorities, whilst two others, Fermanagh and Tyrone were evenly balanced with a slight bias in favour of Nationalists. The remaining counties, whilst having pockets of strong Nationalist opinion, were overwhelmingly anti-Home Rule.[21]

As a result of the General Election of 1885 Parnell's party had 86 seats; the Liberals had 319 and the Conservatives only 247 seats. This disappointing showing by the Conservatives gave the Irish Parliamentary Party the balance of power. Whilst the Liberals had gained most of the 670 seats in the House of Commons, 336 seats were required for a Parliamentary majority.[22]

Parnell used his increased influence and pressed Gladstone to use Home Rule to finally resolve the Irish Question. However there were more than a few Liberals who believed the two countries should maintain political union and were deeply shocked at what they felt was an ignominious surrender on Gladstone's part; one such was Edward Carson.[23]

Sir Edward Carson.
(Somme Museum: 1994-655)

Gladstone though was now converted and committed to granting Home Rule to Ireland, introducing the first Home Rule Bill in 1886. This was in direct response to demands from the Irish Parliamentary Party formed in 1882 by Charles Stewart Parnell, replacing the Home Rule League, as official parliamentary party for Irish Nationalist Members of Parliament (MPs) elected to the House of Commons in Westminster. The central objectives of the Irish Parliamentary Party were legislative independence for Ireland and land reform by proposing a two-level legislature for Ireland with the Lord Lieutenant remaining in Dublin. The Imperial Government in London would still deal with issues affecting the Crown, peace, war, defence, treaties, titles and honours, treason, trade, navigation, coinage and weights. No Irish representatives were to remain in Westminster.[24]

However Gladstone's opponents protested that his coming out in favour of Home Rule for Ireland was a threat to the Empire itself; the Irish crises coincided with unrest in South Africa, Egypt and Afghanistan. His critics often used the terms 'United Kingdom and 'empire' interchangeably in Parliamentary debates.[25]

Whilst many argued that the will of the majority should be respected, the debate was then who was the majority. Those in favour of the Union maintained that it was the majority in the United

---

20 Denman, Terence, *A Lonely Grave: The Life and Death of William Redmond* (1995).
21 Ryan, AP, *Mutiny at the Curragh* (1956)
22 1885 General Election <http://en.wikipedia.org/wiki/United_Kingdom_general_election,_1885> (Accessed 23 November 2014).
23 Hyde, H Montgomery, *Carson* (1953).
24 Denman, Terence, *A Lonely Grave: The Life and Death of William Redmond* (1995).
25 Kenny, Kevin (ed), *Ireland and the British Empire* (2004).

Kingdom who could determine repealing the Act of Union. Lord Rosebery at one time held the view that a majority in Great Britain alone was the 'predominant partner' whilst Irish Nationalists claimed that only a majority in Ireland as a distinct unit was relevant. Ulster agreed with the general Unionist position, but contended that her majority also deserved to have a say.[26]

The Orange Order was founded in 1795 following a planned confrontation at a crossroads known as "The Diamond", near Loughgall, County Armagh, between the Catholic Defenders and the Protestant Peep o' Day Boys on 21 September 1795. Lord Cushendun, an eminent Unionist leader of his time, described its past and growth as follows:

> The Loyal Orange Institution founded at the end of the eighteenth century to commemorate and to keep alive the principles of the Whig Revolution of 1688, had fallen into not unmerited disrepute prior to 1886. Few men of education or standing belonged to it, and the lodge meetings and anniversary celebrations had become little better than occasions for conviviality wholly inconsistent with the irreproachable formularies of the Order. But its system of local lodges, affiliated to a Grand Lodge in each county, supplied the ready-made framework of an effective organisation. Immediately after the introduction of Gladstone's first bill in 1886, it received an immense accession of strength. Large numbers of country gentlemen, clergymen of all Protestant denominations, businessmen and professional men, farmers, and the better class artisans in Belfast and other towns, joined the local lodges, the management of which passed into capable hands; the character of the Society was thereby completely and rapidly transformed, and, instead of being a somewhat disreputable and obsolete survival, it became a highly respectable as well as an exceedingly powerful political organisation, the whole weight of whose influence was on the side of the Union.[27]

This great revival of the Orange Order in the northern Irish province of Ulster which reached across all social divides appealing to both working class and aristocracy alike left no doubt in everyone's mind that Ulster Protestants would resist any attempted Home Rule or as it was perceived, "Rome Rule", by force if necessary. This stance was somewhat encouraged by a leading Conservative, Lord Randolph Churchill, who described Gladstone's first Home Rule Bill as plunging the knife into the heart of the British Empire. At a public address in Belfast, February 1886 he told the Belfast crowds that if Ulster chose to fight, then "there will not be wanting to you those of position and influence in England who are willing to cast in their lot with you – whatever it may be – and who will share in your fortune."[28] Such rhetoric was set to encourage those in Ireland opposing Irish Home Rule.

He arrived at Larne in 1886 and was later described by his son Winston as being 'welcomed like a King'. During Churchill's 90 minute address in the Ulster Hall, 22 February 1886, he recommended that "Ulster should wait, and watch, and organise, and prepare"[29] The words which he used in a speech when later leaving Larne would become the clarion call for the Ulster Movement, "Ulster will fight and Ulster will be right!" the next line of his speech at Larne held a prophecy for the movement, "Ulster will emerge victorious."[30] At this stage no one could possibly have guessed the direction future events would take.

---

26 McNeill, Ronald, *Ulster's Stand for Union* (1922).
27 Shearman, Hugh, *Not an Inch: A Study of Northern Ireland and Lord Craigavon* (1942) and McNeill, Ronald, *Ulster's Stand for Union* (1922).
28 Downing, Taylor, (ed) *The Troubles* (1990).
29 Ingram, Rev Brett, *Covenant and Challenge* (1989).
30 Ingram, Rev Brett, *Covenant and Challenge* (1989).

The Ulster Hall was an obvious choice of venue, opened in 1862 it was one of the largest music halls in the British Isles with seating for an audience of 2,000 and space for 250 performers. It was also frequently used for public political meetings so long as they met with the Belfast Unionist stance.[31]

Unionist article describing Lord Randolph Churchill's visit to Belfast. (PRONI T2917/3)

---

31 Leslie and Quail, *Old Belfast* (2013).

THE ORIGINS OF HOME RULE 15

The Ulster Hall, Belfast. On its opening night on 12 May 1862, the hall was described by *The Belfast News Letter* as: " stand[ing] unexcelled, and all but unrivalled, as an edifice for the production of musical works. ... the hall is a great and unmingled success, and the public, no less than the proprietors, may feel the utmost gratification at a result at once so pleasant and so rare. (D.R. Orr)

In a subsequent letter which displayed a similar approach, but one not as violent or histrionic as the Ulster Hall speech, Randolph Churchill set out the Ulster position, "If political parties and political leaders, not only parliamentary but local, should be so utterly lost to every feeling and dictate of honour and courage as to hand over coldly and for the sake of purchasing a short and illusory parliamentary tranquillity, the lives and liberties of the loyalists of Ireland to their hereditary and most bitter foes, make no doubt on this point – Ulster will not be a consenting party; Ulster at the proper moment will resort to the supreme arbitrament of force; Ulster will fight, Ulster will be right; Ulster will emerge from the struggle victorious, because all that Ulster represents to us Britons will command the sympathy and support of an enormous section of our British community, and also, I feel certain, will attract the admiration and the approval of free and civilised nations."[32]

This public support belied a more complicated relationship. Churchill had a short time before complained to Lord Salisbury that "these foul Ulster Tories have always ruined our party", whilst Colonel Saunderson, leader of the Irish Unionist Party in Westminster, told Churchill[33] that they distrusted him more than any of his colleagues.

After a long and fierce debate the bill was defeated in June 1886 by 311 to 341 votes. It was heavily defeated in the Commons and was heavily opposed by Irish Protestants as well as the majority of the British public.[34]

However it didn't go quietly and the bill caused serious riots in Belfast during the summer and autumn of 1886 during which many were killed.

---

32 Shearman, Hugh, *Not an Inch: A Study of Northern Ireland and Lord Craigavon* (1942).
33 Stewart, ATQ, *The Ulster Crises* (1967).
34 Denman, Terence, *A Lonely Grave: The Life and Death of William Redmond* (1995).

How the *Illustrated London News* depicted 'The Riots in Belfast' in 1886. The rioting persisted throughout June and into July fuelled by rumours and suspicion. The disturbances did not die down until mid-September when the final death toll is thought to have been 50. (PRONI T2125/3/20)

The accompanying speeches and the nature of newspaper reports inflamed a city with unemployment and social distress which were already stoking sectarian unrest. In the docks on 5 June, Catholic workers were attacked by Protestant colleagues, resulting in a young 17-year old boy drowning when forced into the sea.[35]

The day after the Home Rule Bill was rejected the inhabitants of the strongly Protestant working class district of Shankill lit bonfires to celebrate. The police attempted to stamp them out, infuriating the crowd who attacked the police with missiles including ripped-up paving stones. The police fired back causing casualties. At the subsequent coroner's jury the verdict of wilful murder was brought against the Royal Irish Constabulary who, after the events, became popularly known as 'Morley's Murderers' (after the Chief Secretary at the time, Liberal John Morley). The Catholics residents of the Nationalist Falls Road area joined in the disorder, leaving the city in a virtual state of siege with the dead being secretly buried in back yards. At the time the Ulster Unionists lacked a leader who could rally the populace and exercise a degree of restraint. It was the appointment of the new Lord Lieutenant and a new Chief Secretary which led to a subsidence of the Belfast riots and a return to peaceful streets.[36]

---

35 Lewis, Geoffrey, *Carson: The man who divided Ireland* (2006).
36 Hyde, H Montgomery, *Carson* (1953).

THE ORIGINS OF HOME RULE 17

A party of Royal Irish Constabulary at Furlough, Co.Mayo about 1890 (Police Museum)

TM Healy later reported that on the day he lost his seat in South Derry in July 1886, he came upon on a police party "sheltering from a rain shower behind a gable in Magherafelt." Whilst an Orange mob were jeering and howling at his heels the constables came to the salute as he passed. He said "could any beaten man in such an hour forget this homage by the R.I.C. to the Cause of Ireland?"[37]

A split within the Liberal Party for the second reading of the Home Rule Bill on 8 June occurred when the rebels led by Joseph Chamberlain defected to the Conservative party which relabelled itself the Unionist Party to receive them[38] and resulted in the defeat of the bill by 30 votes,[39] bringing down Gladstone's government. His resignation caused another General Election in 1886. The outcome of this General Election found the Conservatives as the largest party who formed a minority government with the support of the Liberal Unionist Party who were opposed to Home Rule; combined they held 394 seats, against the Liberals' 191 seats and Irish Parliamentary Party, 85.[40]

---

37 TM Healy <http://indigo.ie/~kfinlay/Tim%20Healy/ First Home Rule Bill (1886). – antrim Militai.htm> (Accessed 24 November 2001).
38 Beatty, Jack, *The Lost History of 1914: How the Great War was not inevitable* (2012).
39 Lewis, Geoffrey, *Carson: The man who divided Ireland* (2006).
40 1886 General Election <http://en.wikipedia.org/wiki/United_Kingdom_general_election,_1886> (Accessed 23 November 2014).

Gladstone had not given much consideration to the Protestant, largely Presbyterian, majority in the north east of Ulster. It had a prosperous farming community whose tenants had a better security of tenure than elsewhere in Ireland, but perhaps more importantly had developed a thriving industrial base, founded on the spinning, bleaching, weaving and finishing of linen cloth. By the second half of the nineteenth century linen had boomed in this part of Ireland leading to the development of machinery in Belfast to aid this linen expansion. The census of 1891 showed that Belfast had overtaken Dublin as the most populated city in Ireland. By 1910 Harland and Wolff in Belfast would be the largest shipyard in the world, employing 12,000 men.[41]

Whilst considered a Protestant city, there was a large minority of Catholics who had been attracted to the city by its demand for labour, but were divided from the Protestants by both street plan and class. Below a layer of wealthy Protestant professionals and business men were the urban working class, both Protestant and Catholic. By this attempt at Home Rule the sectarian divisions between the Catholic Falls and Protestant Shankill living cheek to jowl had already emerged.[42]

Ulster Presbyterians who were traditionally Liberal found themselves becoming Liberal Unionists and found a common cause with the Anglican gentry, a group with whom they had often disagreed in the past.

In the early eighteenth century there was rivalry between the established Church supported by the Anglo-Irish, and the Presbyterian Church being largely Scottish anti-episcopal and including socially inferior Dissenters. Following the introduction of the penal laws against Catholics in the 1690s the Anglo-Irish had started to legislate against Presbyterians, an emerging rival for power.[43]

This emerging alliance between the Ulster Presbyterians and Anglicans was at the root of the emergence of modern organised Unionism and was as a direct consequence of the introduction of Gladstone's Home Rule Bill in 1886.

Six years later in the 1892 General Election the Conservatives and Liberal Unionists failed to secure and achieve enough seats to form a majority Government; 268 Conservative and 45 Liberal Unionists – 23 seats short of a majority. This led to Gladstone forming a minority government which was dependent on Irish Nationalist support and enabled him to become Prime Minister and once again attempt to introduce Home Rule for Ireland. The Liberals had 272 seats and the Irish Parliamentary Party 81.[44] Gladstone introduced his second Home Rule Bill on 13 February 1893.[45]

Whilst the Unionists in Ireland had gained slightly in the election it was still insufficient to prevent Gladstone's plans regarding Home Rule.

The 1893 Home Rule Bill, introduced by the Liberals, was essentially the same as that proposed in 1886, however this time it was passed by the House of Commons on 2 September 1893 but was decisively rejected by the House of Lords a week later,[46] which had the power to veto legislation passed by the lower house.

The rejection of the first two Home Rule Bills in 1886 and 1893 by Parliament was a result of concerted pressure from Unionists in both Great Britain and Ireland.

Unionists in Ireland had heeded the previous advice from Churchill and had started to organise themselves.

---

41 Lewis, Geoffrey, *Carson: The man who divided Ireland* (2006).
42 Lewis, Geoffrey, *Carson: The man who divided Ireland* (2006).
43 Kenny, Kevin (ed)., *Ireland and the British Empire* (2004).
44 General Election 1892 <http://en.wikipedia.org/wiki/United_Kingdom_general_election,_1892> (Accessed 26 November 2014).
45 Lewis, Geoffrey, *Carson: The man who divided Ireland* (2006).
46 Denman, Terence, *A Lonely Grave: The Life and Death of William Redmond* (1995).

THE ORIGINS OF HOME RULE 19

Unionist Convention, Caledonia Street (Now Rugby Road) June 1892 when 12,000 delegates elected by Unionist Associations across the province met in specially constructed halls near Strandmillis to voice their opposition to the second Home Rule Bill. Note the patriotic sign in Irish "Erin Go Bragh". (Ulster Museum)

The strength of opposition to Home Rule was manifested in June 1892 by a massive popular demonstration in Belfast. The Ulster Convention was organised by Thomas Sinclair[47] and chaired by the Duke of Abercorn, attracting some 20,000 opponents of Home Rule from throughout Ulster;[48] the delegates being democratically elected through a series of preliminary meetings on the basis of the constituencies of Ulster.[49]

Sinclair, born in 1838, was educated at Royal Belfast Academical Institution (RBAI) and Queen's University, becoming a leading figure in the business community in Belfast and was a generous philanthropist and prominent lay member of the Presbyterian Church. Whilst he declined electoral office, he played a key role within the Liberal party and then following the split, the Liberal Unionists.[50]

Such was the scale of the meeting for Unionists from all over Ireland that there was no hall large enough to accommodate them so they built a venue to host the event, dismantling it again afterwards. Embellished with the Gaelic motto "*Erin Go Bragh*!", most often translated as "Ireland Forever", those attending heard speeches delivered by the Duke of Abercorn and the great Irish linen magnate, Sir William Ewart.[51]

---

47   Belfast Covenant Trail – Ulster Historical Foundation.
48   http://www.proni.gov.uk/index/search_the_archives/ulster_covenant/background_to_the_covenant.htm
49   McNeill, Ronald, *Ulster's Stand for Union* (1922).
50   Belfast Covenant Trail – Ulster Historical Foundation.
51   Ingram, Rev Brett, *Covenant and Challenge* (1989).

The theme of the conference on 19 June[52] was simple, 'We resolve to retain our present position as an integral part of the United Kingdom'. The badge manufactured for this Unionist convention was a Harp for Ireland, the Union flag of the United Kingdom, the Red Hand in an orange field surrounded by nine shamrocks, each one representing one of the counties of Ulster.[53] The specially built venue to house the delegates was a pavilion, the largest ever used for a political meeting and was constructed close to the Botanical Gardens, Belfast. It covered 33,000 square feet and costing £3,000 it was constructed in three weeks.[54]

During the Convention, the Duke of Abercorn declared "We won't have Home Rule", though the principal Resolution was:

> That we express the devoted loyalty of Ulster Unionists to the Crown and Constitution of the United Kingdom; that we avow our fixed resolve to retain our present position as an integral portion of the United Kingdom, and protest in the most unequivocal manner against the passage of any measure that would rob us of our inheritance in the Imperial Parliament, under the protection of which our capital has been invested and our homes and rights safeguarded…

Also in 1892 a young Belfast engineer called Fred Crawford who began life as a premium apprentice in Harland and Wolf's shipyard,[55] formed a secret society known as Young Ulster with the purpose of fighting Home Rule.[56] However it doesn't appear to have survived past 1893.[57] One of the conditions of membership was that each member had to possess either a revolver, a Martini-Henry with a sword bayonet, a Winchester cavalry carbine or a .455 revolver along with 100 rounds of ammunition.[58] With the legal restrictions on arms at the time this often meant that members had to prepare their ammunition in secret; it was not uncommon for individuals to melt down lead into bullet moulds in the heating furnaces of certain Presbyterian churches.[59]

In October 1893 the Ulster Defence Union was formed with 600 members in the Central Assembly, their list of names being printed in the Belfast Weekly News. The newspaper articles of the time stated that the members were selected with great care and chosen from every class and creed and were to be 'fully representative of the Unionism of the Imperial Province'. It was to meet for the first time in the Ulster Hall, 24 October, when along with other business they were to elect a council of 40.[60] One of the founding members was Colonel Edward James Saunderson PC, JP, DL who having served in the Cavan militia (4th Battalion Royal Irish Fusiliers) was Member of Parliament for Cavan and leader of the Irish Unionist Party in the House of Commons. He was also the first leader of the Irish Unionist Alliance in 1891, a political party which sought to unite the unionist movement across Ireland, a position he held until his death.[61]

---

52 McNeill, Ronald, *Ulster's Stand for Union* (1922).
53 Ingram, Rev Brett, *Covenant and Challenge* (1989).
54 McNeill, Ronald, *Ulster's Stand for Union* (1922).
55 McNeill, Ronald, *Ulster's Stand for Union* (1922).
56 Shearman, Hugh, *Not an Inch: A Study of Northern Ireland and Lord Craigavon* (1942).
57 Bowman, Timothy, *Carson's Army: Ulster Volunteer Force, 1910-22* (2007).
58 Haines, Keith, *Fred Crawford: Carson's Gunrunner* (2009).
59 Shearman, Hugh, *Not an Inch: A Study of Northern Ireland and Lord Craigavon* (1942).
60 Belfast Weekly News – 21 October 1893.
61 Edward James Saunderson <http://en.wikipedia.org/wiki/Edward_James_Saunderson> (Accessed 24 November 2014).

Ulster Defence Union membership card. The UDU was formed in October 1893.

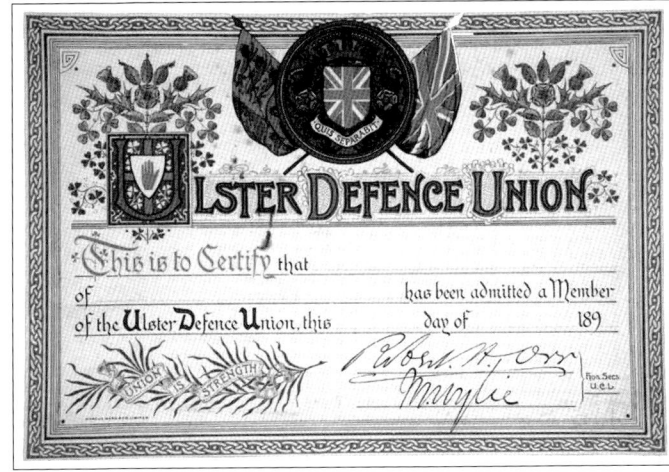

Another signatory was Boughey William Dolling Montgomery,[62] a member of the Ulster Club and a prominent Freemason, who became Secretary of the Belfast Unionist Club.[63] Montgomery would later be credited with conceiving the format of the Ulster Covenant.

Opposition was also evident from authors, such as Francis Frankfort Moore, brother-in-law to Bram Stoker of *Dracula* fame. Moore, the son of a successful Limerick Jeweller, his parents were Presbyterians and was educated in Belfast. He joined the *Belfast News Letter* as a journalist before moving to London and later reported on the Berlin Congress 1878 which ended the Russo-Turkish War and also the Zulu War in 1879. He was a great satirist and, disliking Home Rule, he penned three books under the pseudonym, Bernard O'Hea; *Diary of an Irish Cabinet Minister* (1892), *The Viceroy of Muldoon* (1893), and *Rise and Fall of Larry O'Lannigan JP* (1892).[64]

"The Viceroy Muldoon: his court and courtship" imagines an Ireland of 1895 when Gladstone's Home Rule Bill has been implemented. Michael Muldoon, a "spirit grocer in the thriving centre of Ballynamuck", is elected Lord Lieutenant by the newly constituted Irish parliament, largely on account of his ability to play the flute. Chaos and disorder follow, and the pamphlet ends with Balfour being called in to restore order, pending the passing of a "Re-Union Bill".[65]

Also in 1893 to reinforce the opposition Viscount Templetown established Unionist Clubs over the province, the first being formed at his own home, Castle Upton in Templepatrick.[66] The purpose of the clubs was to provide Unionism with a local focal point and network where men learnt drill and military tactics,[67, 68] though by 1896, these had been suspended though the leadership appear to have wanted them to remain intact for future use.[69]

---

62 ,http://clydesburn.blogspot.co.uk/2012/04/man-who-conceived-ulster-solemn-league.html (Accessed 5 July 2014).
63 <http://clydesburn.blogspot.co.uk/2012/04/man-who-conceived-ulster-solemn-league.html> (Accessed 5 July 2014).
64 Forgotten Moore was one of the great Irish satirists <http://www.irishidentity.com/extras/famousgaels/stories/mooore.htm> (Accessed 3 January 2015).
65 Cambridge University Library <http://www.lib.cam.ac.uk/deptserv/rarebooks/200701.html> (Accessed 3 January 2015).
66 Lucy, Gordon, *The Ulster Covenant, An Illustrated History of the 1912 Home Rule Crises* (2012).
67 Ulster Volunteers, January 1913 – Ulster-Scots Community Network http://www.ulster-scots.com/uploads/901740969819.PDF – 5 August 2013.
68 Ingram, Rev Brett, *Covenant and Challenge* (1989).
69 Bowman, Timothy, *Carson's Army: Ulster Volunteer Force, 1910-22* (2007).

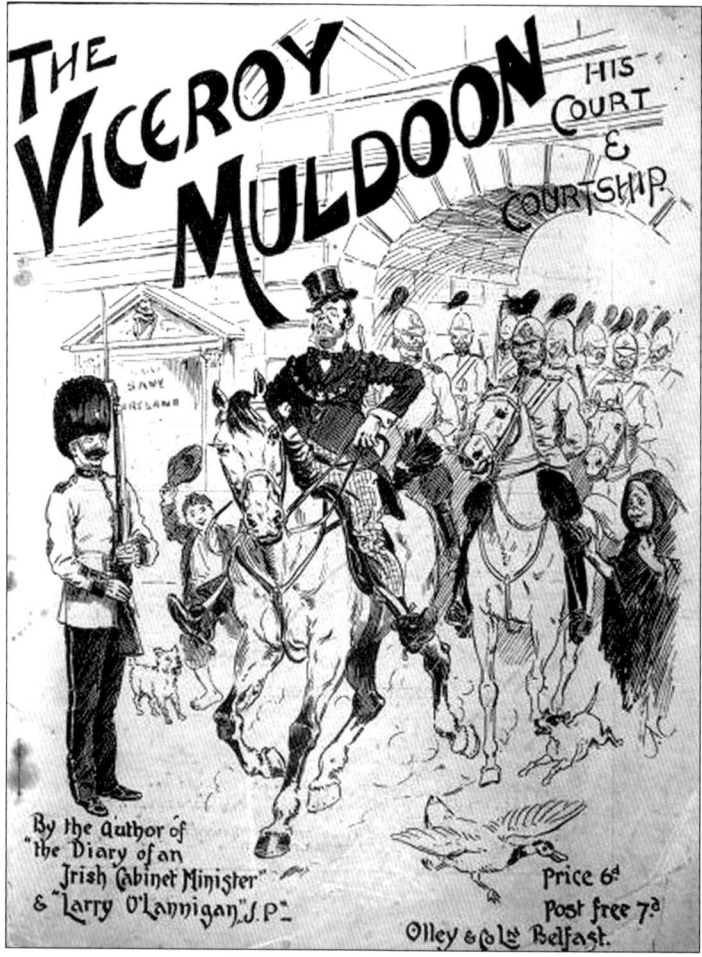

The cover of *The Viceroy of Muldoon*. (D.R. Orr)

A brass enamel buttonhole badge issued to members of the Unionist Clubs of Ireland (UCI), founded in 1893 by Viscount Templetown at Castle Upton, Templepatrick. Manufactured by Sharman D Neill Ltd, Belfast. (Somme Museum)

THE ORIGINS OF HOME RULE 23

Fred Crawford also claimed to have established a number of rifle clubs and revived the North of Ireland Rifle Club's range to allow practice shooting.[70]

A pamphlet appeared in 1893 entitled, *Why are the Methodists of Ireland opposed to Home Rule*, the answer to which was summed within it, "The Methodists of Ireland are opposed to Home Rule because they are sincere lovers of civil and religious liberty". It also warned of the influence which the Roman Catholic Church would have by its numerical superiority if Home Rule was enacted in Ireland.[71]

Again the Royal Irish Constabulary noted drilling activity of small groups of men.[72]

In 1894 Fred Crawford approached Lord Ranfurly with a plan to kidnap Gladstone. The plan was simple, if audacious; Gladstone had a habit of taking the air along Brighton seafront. He would be taken by fast steam yacht to a quiet Pacific island, given a copy of Homer, a Bible, paper for writing and an axe for felling palm trees[73] and be kept there in comfortable seclusion until a change of Government could be achieved thereby preventing Home Rule. Crawford was to be disappointed when Ranfurly refused to risk the 10,000 pounds necessary to fund the venture.[74]

The Conservative Party represented the most staunchly Protestant and Imperialistic sections of British society and was joined in 1886 by those Liberal Unionists who under Chamberlain had broken away from Gladstone because of Gladstone's first Home Rule Bill. By changing its name from the Tory Party to the Conservative and Unionist Party it established its position to oppose all and any attempts to threaten the Act of Union with Ireland of 1801 and the integrity of the British Empire.

With Randolph Churchill ill, support from London for the Ulstermen came in the guise of Arthur James Balfour, nephew of Lord Salisbury, leader of the Conservative Party. In early 1887, Sir Michael Hicks Beach resigned due to ill health as Chief Secretary for Ireland and Balfour was appointed his successor by Lord Salisbury. In Parliament he resisted any overtures to the Irish Parliamentary Party on Home Rule, and allied with Joseph Chamberlain's Liberal Unionists, strongly encouraged Unionist activism in Ireland. It was during this period of 1886–1892 that he sharpened his gift of oratory and gained a reputation as one of the most effective public speakers of the age.

When Balfour arrived in Belfast in April 1893 a copy of the Home Rule Bill was publicly burned and trampled in the streets of Belfast and he spoke from the same platform as Randolph Churchill had in the Ulster Hall, six years earlier.[75]

During his time as Chief Secretary of Ireland, Arthur Balfour dismantled what remained of the Protestant Ascendancy, by encouraging farmers to buy out their landlords with the aid of government loans. The landlords, who had lost real control over their estates, and the tenants, could not agree a price. The price wrangling dragged on until prompted by a bonus payment from Westminster the Irish Land Act of 1903 was drawn up. The result was literally a dramatic change in the landscape of Ireland; in 1903 there were over 500,000 tenant farmers whereas by 1909 270,000 had bought and 46,000 more were negotiating to buy their estates. Another ten years later the British were responsible for buying out the very landlords sent to settle Ireland 200 years previously. Through these steps the Conservative Party had attempted to 'kill' Home Rule with kindness and for a time it did placate Ireland and her Nationalists. Despite this many in Ireland

---

70 Bowman, Timothy, *Carson's Army: Ulster Volunteer Force, 1910-22* (2007).
71 Hume, David, *"For Ulster and Her Freedom": The story of the April 1914 gun-running* (1989).
72 Bowman, Timothy, *Carson's Army: Ulster Volunteer Force, 1910-22* (2007).
73 Hyde, H Montgomery, *Carson* (1953).
74 Shearman, Hugh, *Not an Inch: A Study of Northern Ireland and Lord Craigavon* (1942).
75 Ingram, Rev Brett, *Covenant and Challenge* (1989).

believed that having Irish MPs still sitting in Westminster as opposed to Dublin still did not meet their aspirations.

During this period the Permanent Under Secretary in Dublin Castle, Sir Anthony MacDonnell, wrote to George Wyndham, the Irish Secretary who was absent through illness, that he was along with Lord Dunraven a sympathetic Home Rule peer, drafting a scheme of 'devolution' of local legislation and decentralised financial arrangements, transferring a degree of control from Westminster to Dublin.

When details of the scheme were published not surprisingly Ulster members at Westminster were immediately up in arms. Edward Carson also threatened to resign his post as Solicitor–General if the Chief Secretary committed to such a scheme. Carson told Balfour, "You know it is only for the sake of the Union that I am in politics at all, and this idea is a particularly insidious attack upon the Union.[76]

Meanwhile others took their opposition to the heart of the Empire and hired the Royal Albert Hall, London, for an event on 22 April 1893 which attracted a gathering of VIPs from every walk of life. The 'star' speech was delivered by Bishop William Alexander from Londonderry (his wife wrote *Once in Royal David's City* and *All things bright and beautiful*').[77] He had been the last bishop of Ireland to sit in the Westminster House of Lords before the disestablishment of the Church of Ireland on 1 January 1871 by the Irish Church Act 1869. On 25 February 1896 he was promoted to become the Archbishop of Armagh and Primate of All Ireland.[78]

Within Ulster the situation had developed differently compared to the rest of Ireland. The historic plantation of Ulster had succeeded to the extent that the province had established a homogeneous community in addition to landed estates. Buying out landlords was one thing, but it would be very difficult to effectively buy out an entire planted nation.

The industrially prosperous Ulster, established over the nineteenth century, was in contrast with the rural poverty of the rest of Ireland. To many in Ulster the Union with Britain appeared to guarantee this prosperity whilst the fact that many Catholics were in favour of Home Rule meant, as summarised by a popular slogan of the time that, "Home Rule means Rome Rule."

During the debates surrounding the second Home Rule Bill the opposition did not reply to the Ulster argument that Ireland was in fact two nations and not one. Perhaps they refused to risk partition, an issue which Carson would later suggest in a memorandum he wrote for Bonar Law on November 1911; "During the opposition to the bill in 1893 we frequently discussed this question [separate treatment for Ulster] and Mr Chamberlain I think was always in favour of creating the difficulty for the government, but the Irish members never would agree to it and I don't think it was ever raised as a substantive amendment."; Carson was correct.[79]

Despite the weight of opposition, the Home Rule Bill passed its third reading being passed by the House of Commons with a small enough majority of 34 votes but was again successfully defeated by the House of Lords by 419 to 41 votes. This was a foregone conclusion. The members of the House of Lords turned out in unprecedented numbers to vote against the bill, rejecting it by 378 votes. However these successive actions of the Tory dominated House of Lords would cast the die for developments around the next attempt for Irish Home Rule.

The failure of the bill had other consequences. The Young Ulster movement operating under the guise of a gymnastic movement petered out with the defeat of the Home Rule Bill as Crawford became increasingly worried about the possibility of arrest.[80]

---

76 Hyde, H Montgomery, *Carson* (1953).
77 Ingram, Rev Brett, *Covenant and Challenge* (1989).
78 <http://en.wikipedia.org/wiki/William_Alexander_%28bishop%29> (Accessed 12 January 2014).
79 Lewis, Geoffrey, *Carson: The man who divided Ireland* (2006).
80 Bowman, Timothy, *Carson's Army: Ulster Volunteer Force, 1910-22* (2007).

THE ORIGINS OF HOME RULE   25

The defeat also ultimately led to Gladstone's retirement from politics a few months later. However the subject of the Union had again been questioned and would not be so easily put back to bed. The Conservative party would hold Ireland's future and fortune in their hands until losing the General Election in 1906.

During this period Carson found himself at an event where he was beside Sir William Harcourt, the Liberal Chancellor of the Exchequer who was shortly to become the Leader of the House of Commons. Harcourt asked Carson, "You're a young man, full of enthusiasm for your cause are you not?" Carson replied, "Yes." Harcourt continued, "And you put absolute trust in your party, I can see that." Carson again replied in the affirmative, "Yes." Harcourt almost prophetically continued "Well, sir, sooner or later there is going to be terrible disillusion for you. The Conservatives, mark my word, never yet took up a cause without betraying it in the end, and I don't think you'll betray it with them."[81]

After the failure of the second Home Rule Bill there was a gradual rise in revolutionary nationalism as opposed to more constitutional methods. The protagonists, although being an amalgamation of Gaelic and Anglo-Irish, saw themselves in a romantic vision of descendants of an ancient Gaelic tradition. In 1893 a cultural society was formed called The Gaelic League. It believed that all English influences had to be eradicated, such as "foreign and fantastic field sports such as lawn tennis, polo, croquet, cricket and the like." However by 1899 the rising cultural nationalism was expressed in a more political manner by Arthur Griffith, Dublin journalist and co-founder of the weekly newspaper *United Irishman*. Griffith was fiercely critical of the Irish Parliamentary Party's alliance with the British Liberals. Through *United Irishman* the concept of "Sinn Fein" (Ourselves Alone) emerged, a doctrine of self-help and passive resistance to British rule, however by 1905 Griffith's ideas had developed into a political party.

The General Election of July 1895 found the alliance of the Conservatives and Liberal Unionists, known as the Unionist Party sweeping to victory, effectively safeguarding the future of the Union, at least in the interim.[82]

The following year Edward Carson was briefed for the defence in a state trial, his principal client being Leander Starr Jameson or "Dr Jim" as the popular press named him.[83] The Jameson Raid was a botched raid with Cecil Rhodes's approval on Paul Kruger's Transvaal Republic by Jameson with his British South Africa Company 'police' and Bechuanaland policemen over the New Year

Edward Carson (Somme Museum: 1993-20)

---

81   Hyde, H Montgomery, *Carson* (1953).
82   Lewis, Geoffrey, *Carson: The man who divided Ireland* (2006).
83   Lewis, Geoffrey, *Carson: The man who divided Ireland* (2006).

weekend of 1895–96. The intention was to trigger an uprising by the primarily British expatriate workers in the Transvaal but it failed to do so. Instead the small force of over 500 mounted police were surrounded by Boer commandos and forced to surrender, being handed over to the British authorities. In England they faced charges under the Foreign Enlistment Act, which made it a criminal offence to fit out a military expedition against a friendly state.

Jameson and Carson, both Imperialists were to become close during the subsequent Ulster crises nearly 20 years later.[84]

The Irish Land bill of 1896 was intended to make it easier for tenant farmers to buy the land they were working and enable them to benefit from any improvements they themselves had made to the land, reducing the price they would have to pay. Carson made amendment after amendment in committee and argued in long speeches in the House against it. Balfour's opinion of Carson's stance was recorded in a letter to the Queen when he said, Carson, "has always taken a very exaggerated view of the possible injuries to Irish Landlords which the Irish bill may possibly produce." To Sir Joseph Ridgeway he was more forthright, "there never was a more remarkable instance of the power which one able man has of doing infinite mischief. I really believe that if Carson had not put his finger in the pie, we should not have had the slightest difficulty with the measure …"[85]

On 3 March 1905 the Ulster Unionist Council (UUC) was formed by a group of Ulster MPs, largely through the efforts of Mr William Moore, later Lord Chief Justice of Northern Ireland, who had succeeded Colonel Saunderson as MP for North Armagh.[86, 87] It was intended to represent all loyalist groups in the north of Ireland, banishing any remaining differences between Liberals and Conservatives in Ulster and encompassing many of the groups who had opposed the previous attempts at Home Rule; local Unionist Associations, Unionist Clubs and Orange Lodges in Ulster.[88] The original composition of the Ulster Unionist Council had a strong association with the Orange Order, a Protestant religious institution; represented by approximately 25 percent of delegates, however this reduced through the subsequent years. The UUC were at pains to emphasise their pan-unionist appeal, denying it was simply a vehicle for the Orange Order.[89]

Anti-Home Rule postcard depicting William Moore, KC, MP. (J Luke)

---

84 Lewis, Geoffrey, *Carson: The man who divided Ireland* (2006).
85 Lewis, Geoffrey, *Carson: The man who divided Ireland* (2006).
86 Hyde, H Montgomery, *Carson* (1953).
87 McNeill, Ronald, *Ulster's Stand for Union* (1922).
88 Ingram, Rev Brett, *Covenant and Challenge* (1989).
89 Parkinson, Alan F, *Friends in High Places: Ulster's Resistance to Irish Home Rule, 1912-14* (2012).

Prior to this the less formally organised Irish Unionist Party was sometimes, but not always, dominated by Unionists from Ulster.

In 1906 the Liberal Party swept to power with a large majority and formed a government. Before the election the Unionists had a majority of 68 in the House of Commons, after the election their opponents had a majority of 356. The issue of Home Rule had barely been mentioned during the election, instead public interest had being taken up with Tariff Reform and allegations of the misuse of Chinese labour in South Africa.[90]

Carson however realised that the bogeyman of Home Rule had not been exorcised and during his election speeches continued to challenge the Government to state if they had abandoned the idea of setting up a separate Parliament for Ireland. He believed that recent Conservative legislation extending local government in Ireland and providing £120 million to enable Irish tenants to purchase land should be "allowed to work itself out and bring about, as we desire, beneficial results" without further dismemberment of the Empire. In one of his speeches at the time he said "It should never be forgotten that we are a Unionist Party and it is our first duty to maintain the Union", also warning that "there are forces gathering which may necessitate our girding ourselves once more to go forth to do battle for the good cause."[91]

Despite his views against Home Rule Carson welcomed the Liberal government's announcement in 1908 to bring forward legislation to establish a Roman Catholic university. This was an issue he had supported ten years previously, arguing that he had no fear of his Catholic fellow countrymen but preferred them educated and highly educated to uneducated. However such a proposal awoke anti-Catholic prejudices amongst Protestant Unionists. Colonel Saunderson said it was "an infatuated blunder."[92]

With Irish Nationalists no longer holding the balance of power they found their cause very low down the Liberal agenda.[93] Ireland was quieter with less discontent that it had been in living memory. The reality was that the Irish had nothing materially to grumble about, in no small part to the passing of millions of acres of land into native ownership and the problems of absentee landlords with great estates vanishing augmented by the benefits of the social welfare provided by Chancellor Lloyd George at British expense, but they were indebted for the support of the Irish Nationalists.[94]

Amongst many new faces on the Westminster benches as a result of the election was Captain James Craig, the new Unionist MP for East Down who would soon supersede Colonel Saunderson on his death as principal spokesman for the Ulster Unionists at Westminster.[95]

Despite the Liberal majority in the House of Commons, the House of Lords remained largely under Conservative control.

Nationally money was needed for the Royal Navy to stay ahead of Imperial Germany in a naval arms race and for social welfare such as for old age pensions. This was to be achieved by increasing death duties and income tax, with a super tax of 20 percent on the value of land when it changed hands, essentially a direct attack on the rich and landowners. In 1909 the House of Lords repeatedly rejected Lloyd George's reforming "Peoples' Budget" despite being passed by large majorities in the Commons; breaking a 250 year convention that financial matters were the preserve of the House of Commons.[96]

---

90 Shearman, Hugh, *Not an Inch: A Study of Northern Ireland and Lord Craigavon* (1942).
91 Hyde, H Montgomery, *Carson* (1953).
92 Lewis, Geoffrey, *Carson: The man who divided Ireland* (2006).
93 Denman, Terence, *A Lonely Grave: The Life and Death of William Redmond* (1995).
94 Ryan, AP, *Mutiny at the Curragh* (1956).
95 Hyde, H Montgomery, *Carson* (1953).
96 Lewis, Geoffrey, *Carson: The man who divided Ireland* (2006).

Asquith called for a general election to be fought over the issue of stripping the power of veto from the unelected House of Lords. The subsequent election later found the Liberals and Unionists tied with 272 each; however the Unionists had received 300,000 more votes.[97] The Liberals combined with the Irish Nationalists and the Labour party to increase their majority over the Unionists from 124 to 126.[98]

On 21 February 1910, the day the new Parliament assembled to hear the King's Speech, Sir Edward Carson met with other members of the Irish Unionist Parliamentary Party and having been elected their Chairman, told them, "I dedicate myself to your service whatever may happen."[99]

With two general elections in 1910 and the King's agreement that if necessary he would create enough Liberal peers to ensure the budget's passage, the Lords were eventually forced to accede. The government now passed the Parliament Act, severely curbing the powers of the House of Lords, and seriously weakening the last defence against any future Home Rule legislation. In July 1911 the introduction of the Parliament bill produced fierce scenes in the Commons, such that elements of the Tory party refused to let the Prime Minister speak resulting in the house being cleared to restore order. Whilst leaving the Commons, the Nationalist MP, William Redmond approached James Craig and said "isn't a hard thing that you wouldn't let us speak?", to which Craig replied "not let you speak? My dear fellow, we'd listen to you for as long as you liked, it's only these accursed English Liberals." It was noted that the two men walked out into the lobby exchanging "expressions of mutual goodwill."[100] Under the Act, bills other than money bills, which were passed by the Commons in three successive sessions and which were rejected by the Lords, should automatically receive the Royal Assent and become law. The Lords could no longer be relied upon to block future attempts at Home Rule. Throughout this crisis the Irish Party had voted with the Liberal government. This was significant given that in the House of Commons since the 1910 elections the Liberal and Conservative parties had been equally matched and the votes of the Irish MPs under John Redmond were holding the balance of power. With the Irish Party again having a strong position of influence in Westminster the introduction of another Home Rule Bill was only a matter of time.

James Craig, later 1st Viscount Craigavon, leader of the Ulster Unionist Party and the first Prime Minister of Northern Ireland. He was created a baronet in 1918 and raised to the Peerage in 1927. (Somme Museum)

---

97 Beatty, Jack, *The Lost History of 1914: How the Great War was not inevitable* (2012).
98 Lewis, Geoffrey, *Carson: The man who divided Ireland* (2006).
99 Hyde, H Montgomery, *Carson* (1953).
100 Denman, Terence, *A Lonely Grave: The Life and Death of William Redmond* (1995).

Postcard depicting the Anti-Home Rule sentiment and the fears of how Belfast could be under Home Rule. (Somme Museum)

However this was not the only threat to the anti-Home Rule party unity. During the debate over the Parliament bill a strange phenomenon occurred, the Unionists began to tear themselves apart. They divided themselves along two distinct lines, those who were after a tactical retreat preventing the creation of the new peers, known as 'Hedgers', which included Balfour, Bonar Law, Walter Long and Lord Londonderry, and those who were prepared to resist at all costs, known as 'Ditchers', which included Carson, FE Smith and Austen Chamberlain. The rows between both sides intensified during the summer of 1911 coming to a conclusion on 10 August when the Government secured the vote of thirty-seven Conservative peers and thirteen bishops sealing the fate of the House of Lords. Lansdowne and the remaining Hedgers abstained. Carson did not hide his anger when he wrote to Lady Londonderry, "It will do a deep and lasting injury to the party …. as for the Judas Peers I hope they will be posted in every Unionist Club in the country until their names are a byword … and so ends the House of Lords!"[101]

Until this split over the House of Lords Carson had been able to work closely with the leadership, but this had indicated that he could not rely on them and it created a doubt as to how the leadership intended to fight Home Rule. Writing to Lady Londonderry on 28 August he said, "I will lead for myself this time."[102]

At this time in politics there were three distinct types of Unionism.

---

101 Lewis, Geoffrey, *Carson: The man who divided Ireland* (2006).
102 Lewis, Geoffrey, *Carson: The man who divided Ireland* (2006).

Ulster Unionism which was the determination of the Ulster Protestant community who wished to retain full rights and citizenship of the United Kingdom and represented by such men as Captain James Craig.

Irish Unionists who comprised the entire mass of Irish people who regarded the Union as valuable for the whole of Ireland, with the favourable benefits of social welfare and the ongoing elimination of old grievances about religion and land, and who saw home rule as real risk to these continued improvements. Such men saw the Union as a benefit to their country and included Sir Edward Carson.

These were not uniquely Protestant. There were a small number of Catholics who did not support Home Rule at all. Lord Middleton mentioned this group when he wrote to Balfour towards the end of 1911 when criticising Carson's speeches drawing up religious battle lines:

> I think you ought to know that the Unionists in the South are somewhat disturbed at the Carson campaign – or rather as to the speeches made.
>
> Much has been said of Home Rule on the Protestant versus Catholic lines, and this does harm in the South (as perhaps in England), for some of our staunchest Unionists are Catholics and they have a heavy fight already to maintain their business, if they declare themselves – to resist clerical influence.[103]

Thirdly there were the British Unionists, mainly comprising the Conservative Party and those individuals and groups with imperialist sympathies. Their key leader was Andrew Bonar Law.[104]

A 1907 Papal Decree, *Ne Temere* (literally meaning "not rashly" in Latin) would eventually lead to a bitter debate in the House of Commons; in a mixed marriage in Belfast, Mrs Agnes McCann, a Presbyterian, was said to have had her children removed at the instigation of her Catholic husband's priest.[105] The couple had married in a non-religious ceremony, however Alexander McCann was advised by a priest that in light of the decree the marriage could only be considered a proper one if they remarried in a Catholic church. His wife was reluctant to do so which resulted in Alexander leaving the marital home taking their two young children with him.[106]

Some used this as an example to those in England and Scotland as to what would happen if Home Rule in Ireland ever came into being.

Ironically this Papal Decree upset the regular custom in mixed marriages in Ireland whereby the sons were educated in the fathers' religion and the daughters in the mothers, a reasonable practice which had led to the growth of tolerance.[107]

---

103 Muenger, Elizabeth A, *The British Military Dilemma in Ireland: Occupation Politics 1886-1914* (1991).
104 Shearman, Hugh, *Not an Inch: A Study of Northern Ireland and Lord Craigavon* (1942).
105 Ryan, AP, *Mutiny at the Curragh* (1956).
106 Parkinson, Alan F, *Friends in High Places: Ulster's Resistance to Irish Home Rule, 1912-14* (2012).
107 Shearman, Hugh, *Not an Inch: A Study of Northern Ireland and Lord Craigavon* (1942).

2

Unionists Start to Prepare

In Ulster, Unionists were well aware of the likely political possibilities and started to make their own preparations. There also started to emerge a shift from the traditional Unionist leadership of the landed gentry to the self-made commercial classes of Belfast, often with military experience, though the influence of individual aristocrats was still immensely important.

In late 1910, Lord Templetown was invited by the Ulster Unionist Council to revive his Unionist Clubs, which had become dormant when the threat of Home Rule had receded after the defeat of the Second Home Rule Bill.[1]

In April 1911 the surviving members of the Council of Unionist Clubs of Ireland held a general meeting and whilst many of those present were to become prominent in the Ulster Volunteer Force not all were supportive of the move towards militancy.[2] By mid 1911 there were 164 clubs in existence[3] and by August 1912, 316; all but ten in the Province of Ulster. The membership was open to all Unionists over 16 years of age, whether electors or not. However the drive to mobilise the clubs may not have been widespread as recorded by the Royal Irish Constabulary County Inspector in County Tyrone, who noted in February 1911 that the, "movement to re-establish Unionists Clubs started but so far not much enthusiasm has been manifest in the matter."[4]

In spite of this view, a number of Unionist Clubs formed rifle clubs, affiliating to the National Rifle Association or the Society of Miniature Rifle Clubs, which gave the benefit of the members not requiring gun licenses providing the rifles were used on club premises

Anti-Home Rule postcard depicting The Right Hon. The Viscount Templetown. (J Luke)

---

1   Ulster Volunteers, January 1913 – Ulster-Scots Community Network http://www.ulster-scots.com/uploads/901740969819.PDF (Accessed 5 August 2013).
2   Bowman, Timothy, *Carson's Army: Ulster Volunteer Force, 1910-22* (2007).
3   Ulster Volunteers, January 1913 – Ulster-Scots Community Network http://www.ulster-scots.com/uploads/901740969819.PDF (Accessed 5 August 2013)
4   Bowman, Timothy, *Carson's Army: Ulster Volunteer Force, 1910-22* (2007).

and they were not carried to and from their club; miniature rifles being relatively cheap. However the government had concerns over this activity and in January 1913 introduced new regulations which required clubs in Ireland to re-affiliate to the Society of Miniature Rifle Clubs each year and provide a list of members to both the Society and the Irish Executive.[5]

In November 1910 the Grand Orange Lodge of Ireland sent a letter to every Orange Lodge in Ireland with forms to be completed by lodge members who were prepared to take "active steps" to resist the forced introduction of Home Rule in Ireland. This echoed a similar letter sent by the Grand Lodge during the First Home Rule Crisis in 1885.

The letter read:

> Brother Orangemen: we address you at a grave crisis in the history of Ireland. Mr Redmond the [Irish Nationalist leader] and the party servants of the American Fenians procured for their schemes the help of the socialist [the nascent Labour party] and the radicals [the Liberal Party] of England. Under cover of an attack upon the House of Lords they are striking a deadly blow at the Union. If they obtain a majority at the election, Home Rule may be carried over the veto of the second chamber in two years. In these circumstances you have two duties to perform; you must use every effort to defeat them at the polls, neglecting no opportunity of influencing votes in Great Britain. But you are equally bound to prepare for a struggle in this country if we should fail to carry the elections. Already steps are being taken to enrol men to meet any emergency. Orangemen must set the example to other Unionists by volunteering their service …[6]

By 22 December 1910, the County Grand Master of Belfast, Colonel Robert Wallace, who may have been responsible for the letter, reassured a Canadian sympathiser that they were "quietly organising" and that "the various lodges have received enrolment forms and will be taught simple movements."[7, 8]

Wallace was very influential in Orange circles, also holding the office of Provincial Grand Secretary of the Ulster area of the Orange Institution, which on 6 December 1911 became a temporary Grand Lodge. He was a 33 degree Mason, the highest degree in Irish Masonry and also held the position of Master of 'The County Down Masonic Lodge 86' and was an honorary member of 'Ark Lodge X'.[9] The original warrant for this lodge was issued to the Louth Regiment of Militia in 1809.[10]

In tandem with the arrangements being undertaken by the Grand Lodge, the Ulster Unionist Council (UUC) formed a secret committee to co-ordinate contacts with arms dealers to obtain arms and ammunition. In March 1911 the UUC approved the acquisition of the first weapons, approximately 2,000 guns being imported by early summer 1911.

Despite this, individual Orange Lodges were still taking matters into their own hands. The Orange Lodges in County Armagh area ordered rifles from the Midland Gun Company,

---

5   Bowman, Timothy, *Carson's Army: Ulster Volunteer Force, 1910-22* (2007).
6   An Army With Banners –South Belfast Friends of the Somme Association <http://www.belfastsomme.com/army_with_banners.htm> (Accessed 18 June 2009).
7   Steadfast for Faith and Freedom – Grand Orange Lodge of Ireland.
8   Ulster Volunteers, January 1913 – Ulster-Scots Community Network <http://www.ulster-scots.com/uploads/901740969819.PDF> (Accessed 5 August 2013).
9   Ulster Volunteers, January 1913 – Ulster-Scots Community Network <http://www.ulster-scots.com/uploads/901740969819.PDF> (Accessed 5 August 2013).
10 Grand Lodge News – March 2013 <http://www.irish-freemasons.org/GLN_pdf_Files/GLI_News_03_10.pdf> (Accessed 8 January 2014).

Edward Carson accompanied by Colonel Wallace on their way to an Ulster Covenant meeting in September 1912. (Somme Museum)

Birmingham with 24 Martini-Henry rifles and 1,000 rounds of ammunition arrived at Garvagh, 5 December 1911.[11]

This was made easier as one of the first acts of the Liberal Government on coming to power was to abolish the long standing prohibition of importing guns into Ireland.[12]

The law around the importation of arms into Ireland was shady at best. In April 1913 the Solicitor General noted, "Importation of Arms from abroad may be prohibited by Proclamation or Order in council under section 43 of Customs Laws Consolidation Act 1876 … Supplying of Arms for certain purposes might conceivably be dealt with under the old Riot Act of the Irish Parliament … [and] Prerogative Power of Lord Lieutenant. Only to be used in very extreme cases. Its limits have never been defined."[13]

Colonel Wallace took the preparations further by encouraging the Orangemen in Belfast to adopt some form of military discipline, learning basic drill movements and even marching on the Twelfth in fours as opposed to straggling along as had often become the custom.[14] He highlighted this in a letter in April 1911, to a fellow officer who had seen service in the Boer War; "I am trying to get my Districts in Belfast to take up a few simple movements – learning to form fours and reform two deep, and simple matters like that. I suggested some time ago the advisability for the men to march on the 12th in fours, and not to straggle along in the way that they have become accustomed to …"

---

11   Bowman, Timothy, *Carson's Army: Ulster Volunteer Force, 1910-22* (2007).
12   Ryan, AP, *Mutiny at the Curragh* (1956).
13   Bowman, Timothy, *Carson's Army: Ulster Volunteer Force, 1910-22* (2007).
14   Steadfast for Faith and Freedom – Grand Orange Lodge of Ireland.

A booklet on the Ulster Volunteers, January 1913, by the Ulster-Scots Community Network suggests correctly that at present it is impossible to state with any certainly when drilling first began. Reference is made to a book by Louis Treguiz, a French journalist, *L'Irlande dans la crise universelle* (Paris 1917), to drilling beginning in the Lecale district of East Down.[15] This view is considered 'eminently plausible' as Colonel Robert Hugh Wallace CB CBE PC(Ire),[16] lived at Myra Castle, near Strangford, Downpatrick, and James Craig, the area's MP, was a close friend of Wallace and had a home at Tyrella House, between Ardglass and Newcastle, also in the District.[17]

However other drilling was no doubt occurring but may not have been formally recorded, for example Sergeant Osbourne Young, a former member of the Imperial Yeomanry who had served in South Africa, was seen early in 1912 in Omagh drilling 52 men, and also on another occasion nine mounted men.[18] Whilst in Magherafelt the 'Catch my Pal' Temperance Society had been drilling twice weekly by May 1912.[19]

The same Ulster-Scots publication also highlights the County Tyrone claim, crediting the initial drilling to Captain Ambrose Ricardo of Sion Mills.[20]

Whilst James Craig qualified for a career as a stockbroker he also gained a commission in the 3rd Royal Irish Rifles (North Down Militia). He served in the South African War with the 46th (Belfast) Company, Imperial Yeomanry, until it was disbanded. After working briefly as Deputy Assistant Director of Remounts at Kroonstad, Orange River Colony, he was invalided home. As soon as he had recovered he received a commission from Lord Longford to raise a company of Irish Horse which enabled him to return to the South African War where he remained until it ended. After the war he returned to Ireland and turned to politics, first contesting North Fermanagh in 1903 and then wining the seat for East Down in 1906.[21]

Ambrose Ricardo from Sion Mills. (Somme Museum)

Wallace also had service in South Africa, having joined the Royal South Down Militia in 1879 he became its Lieutenant-Colonel in1898, seeing active service in South Africa in 1901-2

---

15   Ulster Volunteers, January 1913 – Ulster-Scots Community Network <http://www.ulster-scots.com/uploads/901740969819.PDF> (Accessed 5 August 2013).
16   <http://en.wikipedia.org/wiki/Robert_Wallace_%28British_Army_officer%29> (Accessed 15 September 2013).
17   Ulster Volunteers, January 1913 – Ulster-Scots Community Network <http://www.ulster-scots.com/uploads/901740969819.PDF> (Accessed 5 August 2013).
18   Bowman, Timothy, *Carson's Army: Ulster Volunteer Force, 1910-22* (2007).
19   History Ireland: Vol.10 No.1 Spring 2002 – The Ulster Volunteers 1913-14:Force or farce? – Timothy Bowman.
20   Ulster Volunteers, January 1913 – Ulster-Scots Community Network <http://www.ulster-scots.com/uploads/901740969819.PDF> (Accessed 5 August 2013).
21   Ulster Volunteers, January 1913 – Ulster-Scots Community Network <http://www.ulster-scots.com/uploads/901740969819.PDF> (Accessed 5 August 2013).

and commanded the 5th Royal Irish Rifles. He composed 'The South Downs', perhaps more commonly known as 'The South Down Militia' after its rousing chorus:

> You may talk about your King's Guards, Scots Greys and a'
> You may sing about your Kilties and your gallant Forty Twa
>
> Or any other regiment under the King's command
> But the South Down Militia is the terror of the land.

This increase in drilling by the Orange Lodges led to a Royal Irish Constabulary District Inspector in County Fermanagh to be somewhat dismissive and attributed it to 'bluster and bravado' and a calculated bid 'to get into the press of the United Kingdom to show what determined fellows the Orangemen are'.[22]

John McKenna who served in the Royal Irish Constabulary in Carnlough during the 'Ulster Crisis' claimed that he found himself under pressure "from Unionist minded superiors to find evidence of UVF drilling which was non-existent in the integrated village." He also asserted that this was intended in turn "to frighten Asquith with the size of the [Ulster] Volunteers' army and thus frustrate the hopes of nationalists like himself of Irish self-government under the Home Rule Bill.[23]

The sympathy of elements of the police and military is also evident from a recollection of Captain F Hall, military secretary to the UVF, in May 1914:

> At Lisburn, the signal to mobilise was given on the factory hooters, when they sounded a sergeant RIC (Roman Catholic) and four constables (Protestant) were just having their tea. The four constables dashed upstairs, put on plain clothes and were off. They went to the local Battalion Commander and asked if it was business or only a test mobilisation. He assured hem it was only a test. 'Oh well!' they said, 'then we needn't lose our jobs yet!' and went back and got into uniform.[24]

Edward Carson was born in Harcourt Street, Dublin where his father was a Dublin architect of lowland Scots descent. It is often cited that his grandfather was an artist of Italian origin called Carsoni.[25] However his ancestry was originally Scots Presbyterians who in a previous century had been Covenanters supporting Montrose, later fighting against Charles Edward Stuart, the Young Pretender. His grandfather William Carson had actually moved from Dumfries around 1815 to Dublin, establishing himself as a general merchant specialising in Leghorn and Tuscany hats. It seems likely that the manufacturers in Italy would address their communications to William as 'Signor Carsoni' possibly spawning the myth of Italian origins.[26] In 1892 Edward Carson was elected to parliament and made Solicitor General for Ireland.[27] He was appointed Solicitor General for England on 7 May 1900 receiving the usual ex officio knighthood.[28] As a London barrister he

---

22   Ulster Volunteers, January 1913 – Ulster-Scots Community Network <http://www.ulster-scots.com/uploads/901740969819.PDF> (Accessed 5 August 2013).
23   McKenna, John, *A Beleaguered Station: The Memoir of Head Constable John McKenna, 1891-1921* (2009).
24   Lawlor, Pearse, *The Outrages 1920-1922: The IRA and Ulster Special Constabulary in the Border Campaign* (2011).
25   Ingram, Rev Brett, *Covenant and Challenge* (1989).
26   Hyde, H Montgomery, *Carson* (1953).
27   Shearman, Hugh, *Not an Inch: A Study of Northern Ireland and Lord Craigavon* (1942).
28   Lewis, Geoffrey, *Carson: The man who divided Ireland* (2006).

had been earning four times as much as an MP for an Irish constituency and there was a possibility that he if he stayed in England he may have had a chance of becoming Prime Minister, however instead he took the financial losses and joined with the Irish Unionist cause as their leader, 21 February 1910.[29, 30]

Up until the beginning of 1910 the Ulster Unionists had been led in Parliament by Mr Walter Long who held the seat for South Dublin, but when he was returned instead at the start of the year for a London seat, the Ulster Unionists had to find a new leader.[31]

Carson presided at a meeting of the Ulster Unionist Council in January 1911 and was officially accepted by the Council as the 'Leader of Ulster' in July 1911.[32] During the same year membership of the Ulster Unionist Council rose to 370.[33]

After months of organisation[34] the third greatest Unionist rally was held on 23 September 1911 with 50,000 men from various Orange Lodges, all 139 Unionist Clubs[35] and other organisations such as the Women's Association[36] parading from Belfast City Centre and gathering in gardens of 'Craigavon', the East Belfast home of Captain James Craig.[37]

Sir Edward Carson. (Somme Museum: 1994-655)

The house which stood amongst lawns and meadows sloping down to the shores of Belfast Lough on the Circular Road in Belfast was formerly known as Seville House[38] and was built in 1870 for his father; also James Craig, a wealthy partner in Dunville's distilleries.

The purpose of the meeting was simple, to enable the rank and file to meet the new leader of the Irish Unionist Party and MP for Dublin University, Sir Edward Carson, who had arrived in on the Heysham boat at 1:30 p.m.[39]

Whilst Sir Edward Carson had served in a previous Conservative government and was one of the most brilliant barristers of his day, he is often remembered as the lawyer who had prosecuted Oscar Wilde.[40] Carson and Wilde knew each other through their time at Trinity College, Dublin,

---

29 Ingram, Rev Brett, *Covenant and Challenge* (1989).
30 Lewis, Geoffrey, *Carson: The man who divided Ireland* (2006).
31 Shearman, Hugh, *Not an Inch: A Study of Northern Ireland and Lord Craigavon* (1942).
32 Ingram, Rev Brett, *Covenant and Challenge* (1989).
33 Lewis, Geoffrey, *Carson: The man who divided Ireland* (2006).
34 Ingram, Rev Brett, *Covenant and Challenge* (1989).
35 Ulster Volunteers, January 1913 – Ulster-Scots Community Network <http://www.ulster-scots.com/uploads/901740969819.PDF> (Accessed 5 August 2013).
36 McNeill, Ronald, *Ulster's Stand for Union* (1922).
37 Ingram, Rev Brett, *Covenant and Challenge* (1989).
38 Eakins, Arthur, *The Somme – What Happened to the Casualties* (2008).
39 Ingram, Rev Brett, *Covenant and Challenge* (1989).
40 Hume, David, *"For Ulster and Her Freedom": The story of the April 1914 gun-running* (1989).

Members of the Orange Order and Unionist Clubs arrive at Craigavon House, September 1911.
(PRONI D961/3/001)

and whilst they were on speaking terms they were never friends. Carson disliked the long-haired genius and distrusted his flippant approach to life.[41]

Carson had also defended Land Leaguers against landlords and during his leisure time at Trinity College, Dublin, played the sport of hurling, or 'hurley'.[42]

Lady Londonderry recorded events surrounding the rally on the 23 September at Craigavon, "The morning was very wet and I was in despair, but it cleared up and the sun same out at the right moment." With the platform erected near the crest of the hill and with the slope of the lawn falling steeply to the shore road it ensured that everyone would have a view even if the absence of modern loudspeakers would mean that not everyone would hear first-hand what was said.

With the unavoidable absence of the Duke of Abercorn, the Earl of Erne presided over the event and quoting from a letter written by his ancestor Gustavus Hamilton, Governor of Enniskillen in 1689 warned, "We stand upon our guard, and do resolve by the blessing of God to meet our danger rather than to await it." Following a resolution from Mr Thomas Andrews, the veteran Liberal-Unionist and father of Thomas Andrews Jnr who designed the RMS Titanic, there were a number of resolutions welcoming Carson as their leader from the representatives of organisations present. Following singing and cheering an awed silence fell as Carson rose to speak.[43]

His first speech from a balcony to the assembled crowd, at what is often acknowledged as the start of the third Home Rule crises, was to indicate the path proposed by the Unionist leadership in opposition to Home Rule:

---

41 Hyde, H Montgomery, *Carson* (1953).
42 Hume, David, *"For Ulster and Her Freedom": The story of the April 1914 gun-running* (1989).
43 Hyde, H Montgomery, *Carson* (1953).

Lady Londonderry wearing the uniform of the Women's Legion, which she founded in 1915. (Somme Museum)

> I know the responsibility you are putting on me today. In your presence I cheerfully accept it, grave as it is, and I now enter into a compact with you, and every one of you, and with the help of God you and I joined together – I giving you the best I can, and you giving me all your strength behind me – we will yet defeat the most nefarious conspiracy that has ever been hatched against a free people.
>
> … We must be prepared, in the event of a Home Rule Bill passing, with such measures as will carry on for ourselves the government of those districts of which we have control. We must be prepared – and time is precious in these things – the morning Home Rule passes, ourselves to become responsible for the government of the Protestant Province of Ulster.

The speech inferred the possibility of forming a provisional government and clearly some means of enforcing it. The militant aspect was also inferred by imagery on the menu cards at Craig's luncheon party held at the event for invited guests; an illustration of crossed rifles and the motto, "The Arming of Ulster."

He also specifically referred to Asquith's plan for Home Rule which would lead to Ulster being expelled from the United Kingdom as "the most nefarious conspiracy."[44]

The bearing and precision of the marching displayed by a contingent of Orangemen from Sion Mills under the command of Captain Ambrose Ricardo impressed others at Craigavon that day and was often referred to.

Carson's image in public, through his height, solid frame and grim determination commanded respect, whilst in private he could be moody and uncertain. Despite this he acknowledged his role in Ulster Unionism by saying of his host on 23 June, "James Craig did all the work and I got all the credit." There was a certain reality to this statement as Craig's strengths were in the organising of the massive displays of loyalist solidarity, whilst Carson was the better orator. The aims of both men, whilst overlapping were slightly different. Carson was prepared to lead the Ulster Unionists,

---

44 Ingram, Rev Brett, *Covenant and Challenge* (1989).

as he wanted to maintain the Union for the whole of Ireland, whereas Craig was seeking to maintain the Union for the benefit of Ulster.

Edward Pearson of The Royal Irish Constabulary's Crime Special Branch reported on the day that:

> It was observed that by far the greater number of the men who marched in the procession carried themselves as men who had been drilled, particularly the members of the Unionist Clubs and the Orangemen from Counties Tyrone and Armagh. It has been ascertained that about 100 of the Armagh contingent, when going to and returning from the Railway Station at Armagh on this occasion 'fell in' in two ranks, numbered off, formed fours, and marched off at the word of Command of a retired Army Sergeant named Walker. These men were all young, and it is believed that they had previously learned drill in the Yeomanry, Militia or the Boys' Brigade.[45]

This is reinforced also in Pearson's report when he refers to many of "the Orangemen have served in the County Militia Regiments and that a young 22 year old former Boy's Brigade member had drilled 50 young men in Killylea Orange Hall with similar arrangements elsewhere with the aim of providing a 1,000 drilled men from County Armagh for the Easter Monday demonstration in Belfast." His report indicated that drilling was clearly fairly widespread by September 1911.[46]

Whilst the gathering at Craigavon was important and showed the world that Ulster was determined to stay within the United Kingdom, it was also significant in that it was the embryonic stage of the formation of the Ulster Volunteer Force. The Tyrone contingent in particular had impressed many by their bearing and the precision of their marching on the day.[47]

UVF Rally, Shaws Bridge, 1913. The passing of the third Home Rule Bill saw Protestant opposition channelled increasingly into the Ulster Volunteer Force, which was sworn to armed resistance. (Ulster Museum)

---

45 Bowman, Timothy, *Carson's Army: Ulster Volunteer Force, 1910-22* (2007).
46 Bowman, Timothy, *Carson's Army: Ulster Volunteer Force, 1910-22* (2007).
47 Ingram, Rev Brett, *Covenant and Challenge* (1989).

Two days later the Ulster Unionist Council under the chairmanship of Lord Londonderry assembled in the Rosemary Hall, Belfast and promised their unwavering support to their leaders in resisting the establishment of Home Rule in Ireland.[48] Under the direction of James Craig the Council appointed a commission to "frame and submit a constitution for a provisional Government of Ireland", comprising Captain James Craig, Colonel Sharman Crawford, both Ulster members of Parliament, Mr Thomas Sinclair, the Liberal Unionist, Colonel RH Wallace, a prominent member of the Orange Institution and Mr Edward Sclater, the secretary of the Unionist Clubs.[49] Despite the title, in reality it was focused on Ulster with little concern on the interests of the Loyalists in the other parts of Ireland.

This echoed the views of many Unionist leaders which focused on a belief of the distinctiveness of the Ulster-Scots which had been reinforced over the years through the publication of histories on Presbyterianism and books such as John Harrison's *The Scot in Ulster* (1888), JB Woodburn's *The Ulster Scot* (1914) and *The Scot in America and the Ulster-Scot* by Whitelaw Reid, the US Ambassador whose ancestors had come from County Tyrone. The latter was based on lectures which Whitelaw Reid had delivered in the Presbyterian Assembly Buildings in Belfast and also in Edinburgh.[50] Thomas Sinclair went further in arguing that "there is no homogeneous Irish nation" and that "Ireland today consists of two nations."[51]

Many Liberals thought the actions of Protestants in Ulster a bluff. The Irish question was just one issue concerning the British government of the day; the army were used against striking Welsh miners in 1910; a Liverpool railway strike, 1911; London dock strike and the rising Suffragette movement.

Reflecting the awaking of women's political awareness in Britain, an organisation, The Ulster Women's Unionist Council, was formed in early 1911[52] under the presidency of the Duchess of Abercorn whilst Lady Londonderry, a friend of Carson was the moving spirit behind it. However it was not confined to titled ladies and within twelve months of its creation over 40,000 women, many of them mill workers and shop girls joined; forming over eighty percent of the membership. Their resolution was simple and straightforward, to "stand by our husbands, our brothers and our sons on whatever steps they may be forced to take in defending our liberties against the tyrannies of Home Rule."[53, 54]

The day after the Ulster Unionist Council meeting Carson travelled throughout Ulster receiving messages of support for his Craigavon address. At a large meeting in Portrush and given the tone of his address in the grounds of Craigavon House, he was asked if Ulster would fight against the forces of the Crown.

> No, we are not going to fight the Army and the Navy, but if the Army and the Navy under a British Government come up to displace us, they will displace us at their peril. It is not that we mean to fight them. God forbid that any loyal Irishman should ever shoot or think of shooting the British soldier or sailor. But, believe you me, any Government will ponder long before it dares to shoot a loyal Ulster Protestant, devoted to his country and loyal to his King.[55]

---

48 Hyde, H Montgomery, *Carson* (1953).
49 Shearman, Hugh, *Not an Inch: A Study of Northern Ireland and Lord Craigavon* (1942).
50 Belfast Covenant Trail – Ulster Foundation.
51 Balfour, Chamberlain, Long, Wyndham, Beresford, Campbell, Sinclair et al., *Against Home Rule, The Case for Union* (1912).
52 McNeill, Ronald, *Ulster's Stand for Union* (1922).
53 Hyde, H Montgomery, *Carson* (1953).
54 McNeill, Ronald, *Ulster's Stand for Union* (1922).
55 Hyde, H Montgomery, *Carson* (1953).

UNIONISTS START TO PREPARE 41

A group of Royal Irish Constabulary escorting a group of women along the road. (Police Museum)

Edward Carson delivering one of his speeches at an outdoor rally.
(*Belfast Telegraph* & PRONI INF7A/2/84)

Whilst Bonar Law was concerned by the activities in Ulster he was reassured by Carson that he did not think there would be any rash moves. In the autumn of 1911 Violet Asquith received a letter from a friend, Hugh Godley in County Cavan, which gave an opinion of the people on the ground:

> All the people I have talked to of whatever station, from the Archbishop of Armagh to the boy who weeds the garden, are passionately anti-Home Rule. They *really* think that if it passes there will be a serious rising in Ulster and that all the Protestants in a little outpost like this will be set upon and murdered … It is very difficult till one gets among them to realise that all these deep feelings are not merely invented by politicians for party purposes.[56]

James Henry Mussen Campbell was born in Dublin and educated at Kingstown and Trinity College, Dublin. After being called to the Irish bar in 1878, Campbell was made an Irish Queen's Counsel in 1892 and six years later was elected Irish Unionist MP for the Dublin seat of St. Stephen's Green.[57] He became Solicitor-General for Ireland between 1901 and 1905 and briefly in 1905 Attorney General for Ireland, being appointed again to the post in April 1916, and was considered by many to be one of the finest Irish barristers of his time. In June 1918 he became the penultimate Lord Chancellor of Ireland. In 1911 he discovered a legal anomaly which assisted with the drilling of the Ulster Volunteers, however Unionists were less impressed when during a speech in Manchester on 4 December 1913 he revealed that a ban on the importation of arms would be proclaimed "within a day or two." Senior members of the UVF were furious that he had failed to give them advance notice which would have allowed them to bring in more arms before the ban came into effect.

The ban was effectively two separate prohibitions. The first forbade the importation of arms and ammunition, other than those intended for sporting, mining or other 'unwarlike' purposes and the second prohibited the carriage by sea of military arms and ammunition.[58]

He had also noted that as the Peace Preservation Act (Ireland) of 1881 had not been renewed in 1906 the only legislation in Ireland which impacted on the use or carrying of firearms was the Gun Licence Act of 1870, noting in August 1913 that it did not prohibit the possession or subject the possessor to licence duty, instead only prohibited the use and carrying of the gun. He highlighted that licencing was under the Revenue Act which was enforceable by the Excise authorities. This in turn led to a debate over the powers of the Royal Irish Constabulary in such issues.[59] The matter was finally settled by the English Attorney General, Sir John Simon, who stated clearly that the Royal Irish Constabulary, but not the Dublin Metropolitan Police, had the same powers as Customs Officers, noting, rather interestingly that the RIC were not slow to act in other excise matters, such as illegal distillation.[60]

Despite this Campbell was also a member of the Provisional Government of Ulster. On relinquishing his office as Lord Chancellor of Ireland in 1921 he was ennobled as Baron Glenavy, of Milltown, County Dublin. Following the partition of Ireland in 1922 he was nominated to the new Free State Seanad and then elected by almost all his fellow senators as the first Cathaoirleach (Chairman) on 12 December 1922.[61]

---

56 Lewis, Geoffrey, *Carson: The man who divided Ireland* (2006).
57 <http://en.wikipedia.org/wiki/James_Campbell,_1st_Baron_Glenavy> (Accessed 7 January 2014).
58 Bowman, Timothy, *Carson's Army: Ulster Volunteer Force, 1910-22* (2007).
59 Bowman, Timothy, *Carson's Army: Ulster Volunteer Force, 1910-22* (2007).
60 Bowman, Timothy, *Carson's Army: Ulster Volunteer Force, 1910-22* (2007).
61 <http://en.wikipedia.org/wiki/James_Campbell,_1st_Baron_Glenavy. (Accessed 7 January 2014).

The drill displayed openly by the Sion Mills men and others at Craigavon no doubt led to an increase in the amount of drill and practice of military skills being undertaken throughout the country. When Campbell confirmed that drilling was a legal activity, provided it was used by those training to make themselves more efficient citizens, for the purpose of maintaining the constitution of the United Kingdom and protecting their rights and liberties thereunder and provided it was authorised by two Justices of the Peace, then suddenly what had previously often been a form of underground military training was practiced openly. Colonel Wallace on behalf of the County Grand Lodge of Belfast applied for authorisation from two Belfast Magistrates on, 5 January 1912. The reason stated clearly echoed the advice from Campbell, that they desired "this authority as faithful subjects of His Majesty the King only to make them more efficient citizens for the purpose of maintaining the constitution of the United Kingdom as now established and protecting their rights and liberties thereunder."[62] This was the start of many more similar applications throughout the country.

Meanwhile the Grand Master of the Orange Order in County Londonderry, Captain Watt, proposed a resolution in Coleraine, 8 January 1912, which was passed by a Unionist meeting as opposed to only members of the Orange Order, calling on Unionists to resist Home Rule, if needs be by force of arms.[63]

Ingenuity emerged as the men continued to train and drill. During the winter nights the men marched with hurricane lamps at the fore and rear of the column whilst for those who didn't know their left from their right other measures had to be found. The story goes that they were told to put hay in one foot and straw in the other resulting in calling the step ringing to the words, 'Hayfoot! Strawfoot! Hayfoot! Strawfoot!'.[64]

A month later in February 1912, Augustine Birrell, the Chief Secretary for Ireland, circulated a report to the Cabinet which indicated that with the exception of Donegal and Monaghan, in the other counties of Ulster about 12,000 men were drilling but for the most part were unarmed.[65]

The embryonic Ulster Volunteer Force in 1912. (Somme Museum)

---

62 Ryan, AP, *Mutiny at the Curragh* (1956).
63 Bowman, Timothy, *Carson's Army: Ulster Volunteer Force, 1910-22* (2007).
64 Orr, Philip, *The Road to the Somme* (1987).
65 Ulster Volunteers, January 1913 – Ulster-Scots Community Network <http://www.ulster-scots.com/uploads/901740969819.PDF> (Accessed 5 August 2013).

This call to arms however was not restricted to the north of Ireland. Fowler Hall, Rutland Square, Dublin (now No.10 Parnell Square), named after Robert Fowler, the Archbishop of Dublin from 1779 until 1801, was one of Dublin's several Orange Halls; by 1914 there were still eleven lodges based in the building before being later forced out by the IRA. At an anti-Home Rule meeting in the Hall in February 1912, Mr HT Barrie, MP, informed a massive crowd of Dublin Orangemen that "the Loyalists of Ireland were going to stand or fall together."[66]

The Ulster Volunteer Force as its name suggested had been formed for those in Ulster to resist Home Rule reinforced by the initial prerequisite to sign the Ulster Covenant. However this meant that those Orange Lodges and other Protestant fraternities in Dublin City Centre, South County Dublin and North County Wicklow could not be members, forcing them to look to their own creation of anti-Home Rule organisations.[67] Within Dublin this led to the creation of the Loyal Dublin Volunteers (LDV) which at its peak had a membership of some 2,000 men. Whilst not members of the UVF they were instead affiliated to it, with the men largely uniformed in khaki with 'LDV' die-struck shoulder titles on their shoulder straps;[68] its commander was Colonel Henry McMaster, Dublin Grand Master of the Orange Order.[69]

In 1914 the LDV was organized into two battalions; 1st Battalion commanded by Colonel Henry Maxwell was for members of the Orange Order whilst the 2nd Battalion, commanded by Colonel Frederick Shaw (5th Royal Dublin Fusiliers) was for those who were not.[70] Whilst the majority of members were Dublin born and bred there were a number who were Ulster born; 768 men and women signed the Ulster Covenant and Declaration within the city. From mid 1913 right up until the outbreak of the First World War the Loyal Dublin Volunteers, like its northern sister organisation, drilled weekly.[71]

In 1913 *The Irish Times* published an article explaining the motivation of the new organisation:

Badge of the Loyal Dublin Volunteers. (T Wylie)

> While Ulster is preparing to resist Home Rule by force if necessary, and is busy building up a great citizen army, the spirit of militarism that has gripped that province and fired the enthusiasm of its young manhood is also at work in Dublin … Should a Home Rule Parliament be established in Dublin, this volunteer force is intended to be used in the preservation of

---

66 <http://www.newsletter.co.uk/features/the-loyal-dublin-volunteers-a-forgotten-organisation-1-3719467> (Accessed 5 February 2014).
67 'Duty Without Glory: The story of Ulster's Home Guard in the Second World War and the Cold War' – David R Orr, 2008.
68 Tom Wylie, 'Bulletin of the Military Historical Society', Vol 45, No.194.
69 <http://www.newsletter.co.uk/features/the-loyal-dublin-volunteers-a-forgotten-organisation-1-3719467> (Accessed 5 February 2014).
70 <http://1914-1918.invisionzone.com/forums/index.php?showtopic=182134&page=2 – Great War Forum – (Accessed 5 February 2014).
71 <http://www.newsletter.co.uk/features/the-loyal-dublin-volunteers-a-forgotten-organisation-1-3719467> (Accessed 5 February 2014).

UNIONISTS START TO PREPARE   45

This is a branch of the UVF formed in Toronto, Canada by Ulstermen. These men in the photograph are all originally from Tobermore, County Londonderry. (Belfast Telegraph)

the civil and religious liberties of Protestants in Dublin and the south … Should civil war break out in Ulster as a consequence of Home Rule, the leaders of the Dublin Volunteers have undertaken to hold in readiness a force of at least 2,000 men for service wherever required by the Commander-in-Chief of the Ulster Army.[72]

The LDV also attracted the interest of the authorities. Staff Sergeant Ensell, King's Own Yorkshire Light Infantry, was charged in July 1914 with stealing five rifles from his own battalion's armoury in Dublin with the intention of supplying them to the Loyal Dublin Volunteers.[73, 74]

There was at least two other units formed outside Ulster attracting those in opposition to Irish Home Rule; the Loyal Cork Volunteers and the Loyal Wicklow Volunteers, the latter becoming part of the Wicklow Battalion of the IAVTC during the Great War.[75]

Ulster Volunteers were not confined to the island of Ireland. The *Belfast Telegraph* reported in May 1914 that a group of men from County Londonderry had formed a branch of the UVF in Toronto and had promised to return to Ulster later when needed.[76]

The Nationalist press did not ignore the actions in Ulster. In September 1911 the *Irish News* attacked Carson's supporters and the threats of civil war as an "orgie of Ulsteria" (sic). It went further claiming that during Carson's "dull, monotonous" speech most of the audience were sitting on the grass, smoking and talking about football.[77]

At the same time intelligence gathered by the Dublin Castle administration and the Royal Irish Constabulary suggested that there was little evidence of a 'rush to the colours', one RIC County Inspector believing that in his view many Unionists

> … are confident that a Home Rule Bill will not become law for many years, if ever, and consequently they believe that it is not necessary to prepare for armed resistance, but that should

---

72 Richardson, Neil, *According to their lights: Stories of Irishmen in the British Army, Easter 1916* (2015).
73 Bowman, Timothy, *Carson's Army: Ulster Volunteer Force, 1910-22* (2007).
74 *Northern Whig* – 23/7/1914.
75 Richardson, Neil, *According to their lights: Stories of Irishmen in the British Army, Easter 1916* (2015).
76 Parkinson, Alan F, *Friends in High Places: Ulster's Resistance to Irish Home Rule, 1912-14* (2012).
77 *Irish News* – 25 September 1911.

such a measure become law they believe that by passive resistance to taxation, followed by active resistance if necessary, the operation of such a scheme would be rendered unworkable.[78]

Even by July 1912, the Deputy Inspector General of the RIC noted that the only positive information he had received regarding the illegal importation of weapons concerned 200 rifles from Hamburg to Belfast which had been interrupted with the weapons being returned to Germany due to police surveillance. However he also believed that his officers needed to take more positive action to ensure Unionist attempts to gather weapons were interrupted. In response, in September 1912 he sent County Inspector Holmes of the Crime Special Branch to Ulster to interview 34 officers, stressing to them that "There appears to be a general impression that rifles are being collected in large quantities in the North of Ireland, and that they are being hidden away so as to be ready for use if required." He also highlighted that they consider their position if such activities were occurring in their locales.[79]

On 1 February 1912 the Presbyterian Convention met in Belfast, organised by Thomas Sinclair amongst others, the purpose of which was to show to the people of England and Scotland and in particular the other Non-Conformists that the Presbyterians of Ireland were opposed to Home Rule. It was also intended to correct an impression being spread by Home Rule supporters that the opposition to Home Rule was really only from within the Anglican landlords. Due to the numbers expected to attend the convention it was impossible to host it in a single venue, instead it was spread over several locations in Belfast; reported applications numbered 47,000.[80]

Winston Churchill underestimated the sincerity of the feeling in Ulster, believing in October 1911 that "when the worst comes to the worst we shall find that civil war evaporates into uncivil words". The actions of the next years were to prove this belief to be seriously misplaced, in fact he witnessed an example of the strength of feeling himself when he visited Belfast, as the Liberal Government's Home Secretary in February 1912. It was at the invitation of the Ulster Liberal Association, which included Lord Pirrie, the Director of Harland and Wolff, the Rev. James Armour of Ballymoney and Captain White of Ballymena, the son of Sir George White VC.[81]

When word of the visit was made public passions were heightened. The Liberal *Daily News* informed its outraged readers that a leaflet had been circulated at an Orange meeting which called upon Germany, as the great Protestant power, to come and save Ulster from being ruled by the Pope.[82]

Such was the fear of disorder following his arrival in the city that four battalions of infantry and a squadron of cavalry at Victoria Barracks and three battalions of infantry at Holywood and extra police were brought into the city in case of riots.[83]

Lord Edward Gleichen, who commanded an infantry brigade in Belfast recorded that part of the force were stationed at Celtic Park with the rest "lying doggo at different points in the town."[84]

The novelist EM Forster, who was staying in the city at the time, wrote to a friend, "There are all sorts of rumours about the meeting. According to some, the employers have served out clubs and revolvers to the men and the tent will be set on fire in the best Durbar style."

Churchill was supposed to address an audience at the Ulster Hall, however, his views contrary to the conservative anti-home rule views of his father were met with strong disapproval.

---

78 PRONI D1568/6/10/14.
79 PRONI D1568/6/10/14.
80 Belfast Covenant Trail – Ulster Foundation.
81 Leslie and Quail, *Old Belfast* (2013).
82 Ryan, AP, *Mutiny at the Curragh* (1956).
83 Ryan, AP, *Mutiny at the Curragh* (1956).
84 Ryan, AP, *Mutiny at the Curragh* (1956).

A postcard depicting soldiers deployed along Donegall Road, Belfast near Celtic Park in advance of Winston Churchill's speech. (T Wylie)

This resulted in the refusal of the members of the Belfast Corporation who were against Home Rule to permit him to use the Ulster Hall. An act which was strengthened by the Ulster Unionists booking it for the day before,[85] and preparation being made to have members of the Ulster Volunteers move in and occupy the premises against all comers for the next 36 hours.[86] Attempts by Belfast Liberals with the support of the Government Patronage Secretary, to find a suitable alternative venue included offering Mr FW Warden, manager of the Grand Opera House, a knighthood and a large sum of money which he refused. As an alternative the Nationalists offered their largest building, St Mary's Hall, but the Liberals declined, not wanting to be under such an open debt to the Redmond supporters.[87] Instead Churchill was eventually forced to address approximately 7,000 Home Rule supporters[88] in a rain-sodden marquee lashed to the Grand Stand in Celtic Park,[89] a football ground in a Nationalist district of the city. He told the assembled crowd that Home Rule would, "meet the grievance, heal the quarrel, bury the hated, link the interests, conciliate, consolidate the Empire." He was followed by Redmond and Joseph Devlin, Nationalist MP for West Belfast, with Devlin trying to allay Unionist fears by saying "I will find myself in closer touch with Protestant artisans of Belfast and Ulster than I would with Catholic famers of Munster and Connaught." A direct reference to his past record of campaigning for better working conditions for Protestant factory workers.[90]

---

85 Ingram, Rev Brett, *Covenant and Challenge* (1989).
86 Hyde, H Montgomery, *Carson* (1953).
87 Hyde, H Montgomery, *Carson* (1953).
88 Grayson, Richard S, *Belfast Boys – How Unionists and Nationalists fought and died together in the First World War* (2009).
89 Grayson, Richard S, *Belfast Boys – How Unionists and Nationalists fought and died together in the First World War* (2009).
90 Grayson, Richard S, *Belfast Boys – How Unionists and Nationalists fought and died together in the First World War* (2009).

Platform Ticket for Ulster Liberal Association event addressed by Winston Churchill at Celtic Park, Belfast, 1912. (PRONI D2868/D/7/3)

A postcard depicting Winston Churchill addressing the crowd from the platform at Celtic Park, Belfast.

Following the success in denying the Ulster Hall for the address, the Standing Committee of the Ulster Unionist Council passed a resolution urging all Unionists, "to abstain from any interference with the meeting at the Celtic football ground, and to do everything in their power to avoid any action that might lead to any disturbance." It was passed to all Orange Lodges and Unionist Clubs in Belfast and neighbouring districts with urgent direction that it was brought to members' attentions and displayed in prominent locations; to avoid a repetition of the terrible Belfast city riots of 1886. In an effort to prevent widespread disorder, Carson and

A postcard depicting the Anti-Home Rulers' reception in Belfast City Centre for Winston Churchill's visit.

the other leaders made arrangements to ensure that they too would be at hand in Belfast whilst the meeting was taking place.[91]

EM Forster described the scene in Royal Avenue when Churchill emerged from the Grand Central Hotel, where he had stayed during his visit and prior to heading to Celtic Park, "He came forth between us in grand style, looking very pale – sea kale colour". The hostile crowds were jostling against his car, singing "God save the King," threatening to tip the vehicle over, but held back when they saw Mrs Churchill was there also. When he left the area, Edward Carson and Lord Londonderry appeared at the windows of the Reform Club to great cheers from the crowd.[92] A black effigy meant to represent Churchill was burnt by the crowd.[93]

Meanwhile in Nationalists' areas of the city, effigies of Carson and Lord Londonderry could be seen, in one instance in a cage representing a provisional government. People in those areas welcomed Churchill with cheers, hoping to shake his hand on route to the Celtic Park meeting whilst three battalions of soldiers and a number of police kept watch on the Falls Road with four other battalions deployed elsewhere in the city.[94]

Only one heckler was reported at the meeting in Celtic Park, a suffragette, who in a broad Ulster accent shouted out, "Will you give the suffrage to women?",[95] however it was also reported than the meeting was attended by many pickpockets as a pile of empty wallets were found later.

---

91 Hyde, H Montgomery, *Carson* (1953).
92 Leslie and Quail, *Old Belfast* (2013).
93 Ryan, AP, *Mutiny at the Curragh* (1956).
94 Leslie and Quail, *Old Belfast* (2013).
95 Ryan, AP, *Mutiny at the Curragh* (1956).

Three members of the Royal Irish Constabulary outside Celtic Park, Falls Road, Belfast, holding over 100 purses and wallets, the harvest of pickpockets after Winston Churchill's address in February 1912. (Police Museum)

After the meeting, instead of returning to his hotel, Churchill left soon afterwards and on the advice of the police via an indirect route using back streets[96] for the Midland railway station,[97] trying also in the process to avoid the thousands of shipyard workers from Queen's Island who had come out to greet him with "Queen's Island confetti"; their pockets full of rivet heads.[98] The last part of his journey to the docks at Larne was a slow train journey as it crawled along the line that was scrupulously searched for ambushes and explosives.[99]

As Churchill boarded his vessel in Larne a number of Unionist dockers on the quayside recognised him and hurled some rotten fruit at him.[100]

The city saw no rioting as a result of his visit and Sir Edward Carson made a speech in the centre of Belfast congratulating the people on their victory of duty, peace and common sense.[101]

Some Unionists were to claim that he left as a "thief in the night", a direct reference to his father's speech in the Ulster Hall 25 years earlier when he warned Ulstermen that Home Rule would come upon them as a "thief in the night".

---

96 Ryan, AP, *Mutiny at the Curragh* (1956).
97 McNeill, Ronald, *Ulster's Stand for Union* (1922).
98 Shearman, Hugh, *Not an Inch: A Study of Northern Ireland and Lord Craigavon* (1942).
99 Shearman, Hugh, *Not an Inch: A Study of Northern Ireland and Lord Craigavon* (1942).
100 Hyde, H Montgomery, *Carson* (1953).
101 Shearman, Hugh, *Not an Inch: A Study of Northern Ireland and Lord Craigavon* (1942).

Despite this Churchill was not alone in his disbelief of the sincerity of the Ulster Unionists, many Liberals and Irish Nationalists also believed that their rhetoric was a "gigantic game of bluff and blackmail."[102]

Writing to Lady Londonderry, 27 March 1912, Carson shared some of his views around what was developing:

> I dine tonight with Craig to meet Lord Roberts and I hope something may come of it. This is very private. I have made up my mind to recommend very drastic action in Ulster during this year and also in the House when the H[ome] R[ule] bill is on. There is a growing feeling that we do not mean business. I certainly think this is the critical year and am prepared for any risks.

He also acknowledged the support they were receiving from elsewhere, "I think the British League to help Ulster is a good move and will be a great success."[103]

The formation of the British League for the Support of Ulster and the Union was announced by a letter appearing in the London newspapers on 27 March 1913. It was signed by 100 Peers and 120 Unionist Members of the House of Commons. A small executive committee chaired by the Duke of Bedford had an office in London. Their manifesto emphasised the Imperial aspect of the current issues and stressed that it was "quite clear that the men of Ulster are not fighting only for their own liberties. Ulster will be the field on which the privileges of the whole nation will be lost or won."[104]

Field Marshal Lord Roberts VC. (Somme Museum)

In Ulster it was decided it was time to stage another meeting to clearly illustrate the opposition to the proposed Home Rule legislation. The organisers wanted a large spacious area for the event, initially identifying Ormeau Park in south Belfast as a suitable venue, however they eventually settled on Balmoral Showground with Fred Crawford on behalf of the Ulster Unionist Council securing it for the fee of £75 with agreement that they would also pay for any damage caused during the event.[105, 106] The growing support from Britain and the links with the Conservative Party were well illustrated when the Conservative Leader, Andrew Bonar Law arrived in Belfast on 8 April 1912. Bonar Law was the son of a Presbyterian minister of Ulster farming stock.[107] He was met by groups of eager supporters, such as the men of Workman Clark's North-East Unionist Clubs who marched to the Midland Railway Station in York Street. Workman and Clark's was

---

102 John Redmond, Leader of Irish Party.
103 Hyde, H Montgomery, *Carson* (1953).
104 McNeill, Ronald, *Ulster's Stand for Union* (1922).
105 Parkinson, Alan F, *Friends in High Places: Ulster's Resistance to Irish Home Rule, 1912-14* (2012).
106 Haines, Keith, *Fred Crawford: Carson's Gunrunner* (2009).
107 Ryan, AP, *Mutiny at the Curragh* (1956).

the smaller of the two Belfast shipyards and known as the 'Wee Yard'.[108]

On his route from Larne to the City he had noted the fervour of the crowd at the train's various stopping places which caused him to ask, "Are all these people landlords?"; a humorous retort to the Liberal suggestions that Ulster Unionism had been manufactured by a few aristocratic landlords. Instead he was being met by enthusiastic crowds of men and women who were clearly from the poorer classes of Ulster.[109]

He was in Belfast to attend a magnificent reception scheduled to be held the next day, Easter Tuesday, 9 April. Arrangements for the day included no alcohol being permitted to be sold in the grounds, and in order to emphasise the air of responsibility being sought "Morning dress and silk hats had to be worn" by the dignitaries.[110] Such was the expectation of the numbers likely to attend that 70 extra trains were laid on to transport people to the event.[111] At Balmoral, south Belfast, about 200,000 Unionists, including contingents from the Orange Order and Unionists Clubs which had now risen to number 232,[112] marched from the city centre[113] past his platform. Many of the marchers had gathered at Belfast Orange Halls and unionist club premises across the city from before 9:00 a.m. in the morning to march from the city centre an hour or so later. *The Times* correspondent noted that contingents were from all parts of Ireland, including, "even distant Kerry and rebellious Cork and Clare."[114]

Andrew Bonar Law depicted on the Canadian Conservative Candidate ticket in 1891.

At the showgrounds a resolution against Home Rule was passed and the largest ever woven Union flag was unfurled from a 90 foot flagpole; the flag measured 48 by 25 feet.

Bonar Law was joined on the platform by Carson, Lord Londonderry and Walter Long, the former leader of the Irish Unionist Party. Following a prayer from the Primate of All Ireland the assembled crowd sang the Ninetieth Psalm,[115] 'O God Our Help in Ages Past', considered the battle hymn of the Ulster Unionist movement. Sir Edward Carson, leader of the Irish Unionist Party, then started the speeches, quoting the last stanza of Rudyard Kipling's poem *Ulster 1912*,

---

108 Leslie and Quail, *Old Belfast* (2013).
109 McNeill, Ronald, *Ulster's Stand for Union* (1922).
110 Haines, Keith, *Fred Crawford: Carson's Gunrunner* (2009).
111 Leslie and Quail, *Old Belfast* (2013).
112 Ulster Volunteers, January 1913 – Ulster-Scots Community Network <http://www.ulster-scots.com/uploads/901740969819.PDF> (Accessed 5 August 2013).
113 <http://www.proni.gov.uk/index/search_the_archives/ulster_covenant/background_to_the_covenant.htm>
114 Parkinson, Alan F, *Friends in High Places: Ulster's Resistance to Irish Home Rule, 1912-14* (2012).
115 Ryan, AP, *Mutiny at the Curragh* (1956).

UNIONISTS START TO PREPARE 53

The Ulster Volunteer Force. Under the Old Flag

A postcard depicting the Ulster Volunteer Force on parade in front of a large Union flag. (J Luke)

which he had written especially for the occasion. Waving a Union flag on a blackthorn stick he called upon those assembled, "Raise your hands. Repeat after me: Never under any circumstances will we have Home Rule". The crowd responded with a thunderous response.[116] Following this the new leader of the Conservative Party, Andrew Bonar Law, supported by 70[117] English, Scottish and Welsh Conservative MPs, assured his listeners that they were not alone as their cause was also that of the Empire [118, 119] and declared that Conservatives would "do all that men could do to defeat a conspiracy as treacherous as had ever been formed against the life of a great nation."[120] Bonar Law told the crowd that if Scotland was treated as Protestant Ulster was, he believed that rather than submit to such a fate "the Scottish people would face a second Bannockburn or a second Flodden."[121] He also pledged to the vast crowd his party's support for the Unionists, comparing the Orange and Unionists volunteers to Cromwell's Ironsides.[122] He adapted Pitt the Younger's words when advocating Union in 1800, amending them to appeal to the audience before him:

> Once again you hold the pass for the empire. You are a besieged city. Does not the past, the glorious past, with which you are so familiar, rise again before your eyes? The timid have left you. Your Lundys have betrayed you but you have closed your gates. The Government have erected, by their Parliament Act, a boom to shut you off from the help of the British people. You will burst that boom. That help will come, and when the crisis is over, men will say to

---

116 Lewis, Geoffrey, *Carson: The man who divided Ireland* (2006).
117 Leslie and Quail, *Old Belfast* (2013).
118 <http://www.proni.gov.uk/index/search_the_archives/ulster_covenant/background_to_the_covenant.htm>.
119 Ryan, AP, *Mutiny at the Curragh* (1956).
120 Downing, Taylor (ed)., *The Troubles* (1990).
121 Ryan, AP, *Mutiny at the Curragh* (1956).
122 Orr, Philip, *The Road to the Somme* (1987).

you, in words not unlike those once used by Pitt – "You have saved yourselves by your exertions, and you will save the Empire by your example."[123]

One reporter noted that while the men marched in military formation past the saluting base that "throughout one saw mingled in the ranks patrician and plebeian, clergy and laity, masters and men – that effacement of class distinction this is significant of the movement in the truest sense national." He also noted that it was "a remarkably well dressed crowd, the Belfast shipwrights looking especially well turned out." Such was the atmosphere at the gathering that Lord Edward Gleichen's troops were not needed and hardly any police were visible;[124] a stark contrast to Churchill's visit to Belfast earlier in the year. Gleichen would later describe the occasion as "most impressive."[125]

Following the show of strength at Balmoral, the London press portrayed the two sides of the argument, the *Westminster Gazette*, close to Asquith's position, depicted a cartoon of a costermonger's donkey cart in which Carson, Londonderry and Bonar Law, refreshed by 'Orangeade' took an "Easter jaunt in Ulster", whilst the Tory *The Morning Post* printed a contribution by Rudyard Kipling which, as MacNeill stated, finely voiced, "the indignant sense of wrong that prevailed in Ulster."[126, 127]

PRAYER
To be said daily by each member of the Ulster Volunteer Force—Morning and Evening.

O HEAVENLY FATHER, hear we pray Thee, the prayer of Thy children who call upon Thee in their time of danger and difficulty. Forgive me, I pray Thee, for all my sins which I have so often committed against Thee in thought, word, and deed. Make me " ready to endure hardness, as a good soldier of Jesus Christ." Fill me with Thy Holy Spirit, that I may know Thee more clearly: love Thee more dearly: and follow Thee more nearly. Strengthen and uphold me in all difficulties and dangers, keep me faithful unto death, patient in suffering, calm in Thy service, and confident in the assurance that Thou Lord wilt direct all things to the glory of Thy name and the welfare of my church and country. Bless the King, whom we serve, and all the Royal Family. O Lord grant me Thy grace that no word or act of mine may be spoken or done rashly, hastily, or with anger towards those who differ from me. Bless all my comrades in the Ulster Volunteer Force; and make me loving and gentle: obedient to my leaders, and faithful to my promises: and in Thine own good time bring peace to Ireland. All this I beg for Jesus Christ's sake. AMEN.

M'Watters, Armagh.

A daily prayer for the members of the Ulster Volunteer Force. (Somme Museum)

---

123 Lewis, Geoffrey, *Carson: The man who divided Ireland* (2006).
124 Ryan, AP, *Mutiny at the Curragh* (1956).
125 Haines, Keith, *Fred Crawford: Carson's Gunrunner* (2009).
126 Ryan, AP, *Mutiny at the Curragh* (1956).
127 McNeill, Ronald, *Ulster's Stand for Union* (1922).

The dark eleventh hour
Draws on and sees us sold
To every evil power
We fought against of old.
Rebellion, rapine, hate,
Oppression, wrong and greed
Are loosed to rule our fate,
By England's act and deed.

The faith in which we stand
The laws we made and guard,
Our honour, lives and land
Are given for reward
To Murder done by night,
To Treason taught by day,
To folly, sloth and spite.
And we are thrust away.

The blood our fathers spilt,
Our love, our toils, our pains,
Are counted us for guilt,
And only bind our chains,
Before and empire's eyes,
The traitor claims his price.
What need of further lies?
We are the sacrifice.

We know the war prepared
On every peaceful home,
We know the hells declared
For such as serve not Rome –
The terror, threats, and dread
In market, hearth, and field –
We know, when all is said,
We perish if we yield.

Believe, we dare not boast,
Believe, we do not fear –
We stand to pay the cost
In all that men hold dear.
What answer from the North?
One Law, one Land, one Throne.
If England drive us forth
We shall not fall alone.

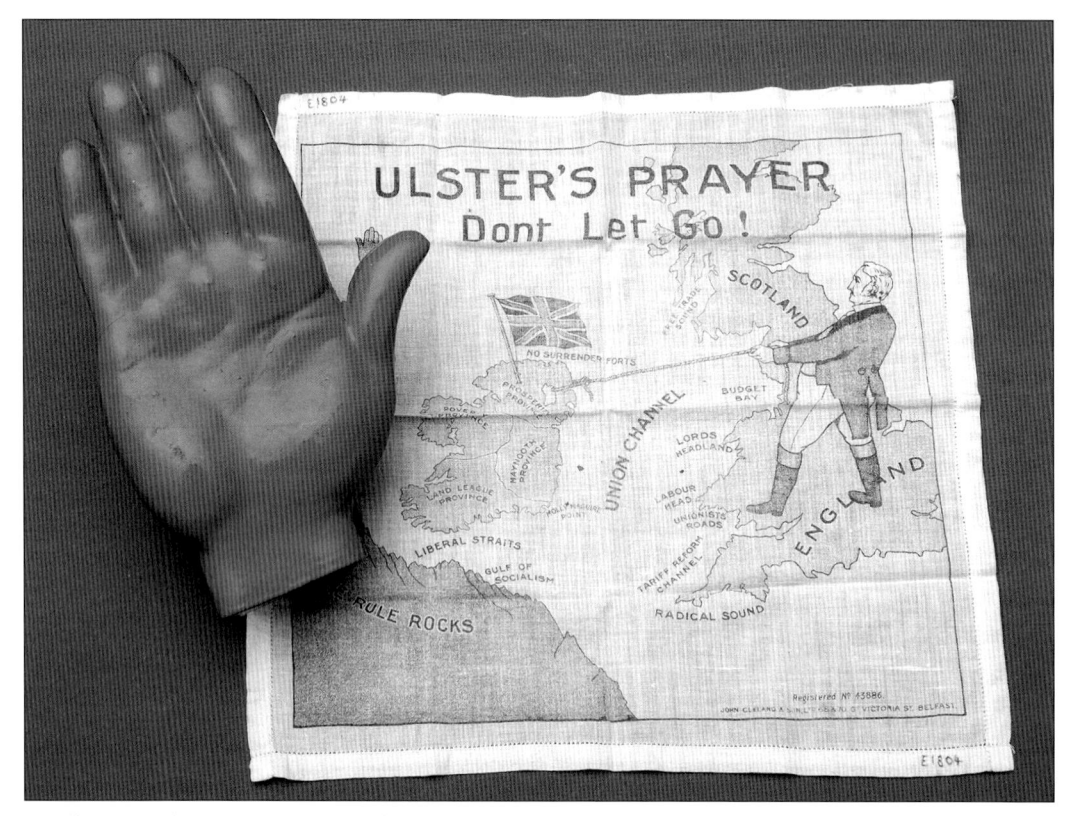

A silk square depicting a cartoon of John Bull standing on Great Britain with rope attached to Ulster with the motto 'Ulster's Prayer – Don't let go!'. Alongside is a red painted 'right' hand as used by the Ulster Volunteers. (Somme Museum)

An article in *The Star* on the day of the demonstration said, "It is, we know, a popular delusion that Ulster is a braggart whose words are empty bluff. We are convinced that Ulster means what she says, and that she will make good every one of her warnings." The newspaper also went on to implore to Liberals not to be driven "into an attitude of bitter hostility to the Ulster Protestants," with whom *The Star* declared they had much in common.[128]

Two days later on 11 April the Liberal Government under Asquith introduced the third Home Rule Bill in which the authority of the United Kingdom Government "over all persons, matters and things in Ireland" was clearly acknowledged[129] though granting a modest form of devolution; control of internal affairs, reduced Irish representation at Westminster (42 MPs), but with Westminster control over foreign policy, defence and revenue. Ironically close to the arrangements willingly adopted by the Act of Parliament in 1920 which established the Northern Ireland parliament.[130]

The Protestant churches in Ireland also publically proclaimed their opposition to Home Rule, the Presbyterians and Methodists through special Conventions whilst the General Synod of the Church of Ireland issued a resolution in April 1912 which summed up their views:

---

128 McNeill, Ronald, *Ulster's Stand for Union* (1922).
129 <http://www.proni.gov.uk/index/search_the_archives/ulster_covenant/background_to_the_covenant.htm>.
130 Ryan, AP, *Mutiny at the Curragh* (1956).

As Irish men who love their country and earnestly desire its welfare, we hereby record our devotion to the great Empire of which the United Kingdom is the centre and head. We recognise the advantage and honour we derive from our present Imperial position, and the conspicuous place which Irishmen have long held among those to whom the Empire owes its prosperity and its fame. We, therefore, protest, in the interests both of our country and of the empire, against any measure that could endanger the Legislative Union between Great Britain and Ireland. We appeal to our co-religionists in Great Britain not to desert their brethren in Ireland, nor to suffer them to be thrust out from their inheritance and citizenship.[131]

Carson wrote to Lady Londonderry on 14 April 1914 recalling his impression of the events, "The whole proceedings at Balmoral seem like a dream – it was the most thrilling experience I ever had or will have. But it has a demoralising effect in making me think of the criminal folly of decadent England in tampering with such a splendid people for the sake of throwing a sop to her implacable foes."[132]

Embroidered card with the motto "Ulster Forever" depicting the right hand of the Ulster Volunteers. (Somme Museum)

On 17 April 1912 as the *Belfast News Letter* informed its readers of the loss of the Titanic two days earlier, the first important vote on the third Irish Home Rule Bill was being taken amongst angry scenes in the House of Commons.

The House of Commons passed the bill by 10 votes but again the House of Lords voted against it by 26 to 69,[133] however the enactment of the Parliament Act of 1911 meant this was only a delaying action with the bill ultimately destined to receive Royal Assent.

The bill envisioned a parliament with the powers of a "glorified County Council" or as Redmond assured an English audience, "be solely to deal with those plain, common, hum-drum, everyday Irish affairs which you cannot understand as the people themselves do."[134]

On 19 May the second reading of the bill was carried by 101 votes; through a combination of Liberal, Labour and Nationalist MPs. The Committee stage opened on 11 June and on that date an amendment was put down for debate from a Liberal back-bencher, the Honourable TGR Agar-Robartes, MP for St Austell Division of Cornwall. The amendment proposed excluding four counties; Antrim, Armagh, Londonderry and Down from the jurisdiction of the Dublin Parliament,

---

131 Hume, David, *"For Ulster and Her Freedom": The story of the April 1914 gun-running* (1989).
132 Hyde, H Montgomery, *Carson* (1953).
133 Metcalfe, Nick, *Blacker's Boys* (2012).
134 Beatty, Jack, *The Lost History of 1914: How the Great War was not inevitable* (2012).

the rationale being the simple fundamental divisions between Protestants and Catholics or as Agar-Robartes put it, "Orange bitters and Irish Whisky will not mix."[135]

Ulster Unionists had to give this amendment careful consideration as any obvious support for it would encourage their enemies to claim that they had deserted the Irish Loyalists outside the four counties being considered for exclusion. However if they dismissed it and Home Rule was carried and forced through and they took over the government of those districts they could control, as declared in the statements at Craigavon, then they could be accused of fighting for something they had already been offered but ignored. For this reason Carson and the Ulster members decided to support the amendment, believing that if it came to the worst, that they would be more use outside of a Dublin Parliament than a hopeless minority within it.[136]

This concept was not simply an Ulster perspective as Southern Unionists understood and many shared the position. In the subsequent debate, Mr Walter Guinness, later Lord Moyne said:

An anti-Home Rule postcard. (J Luke)

> For Ulster to refuse this salvation could not be to help her friends, but would merely be taking up an attitude of mock heroics …. It would merely be a dog-in-a-manger policy for us who live outside Ulster to grudge relief to our co-religionists because we could not share it. Such self-denial on their part would in no way help our co-religionists in the North. We know perfectly well that Ulster fully shares our detestation of the bill from a wider point of view than her own interests.

Ironically the Government had as much intention of accepting this amendment as the Redmond supporters. Instead they tried to divide the two sections of Irish Unionists with claims of desertion.

---

135 Hyde, H Montgomery, *Carson* (1953).
136 Hyde, H Montgomery, *Carson* (1953).

UNIONISTS START TO PREPARE 59

After a three day debate the Agar-Robartes amendment was defeated by sixty-nine, an indication of a falling away of Government support.

Carson however was clear in how he saw the Government's action against the amendment. In the Albert Hall, 14 June, he said, "We will accept the declaration of war." He continued, "We are not altogether unprepared. I think it is time we should take a step forward in our campaign, and I will recommend that to be done."137

Support against Home Rule was also growing in Great Britain. This was demonstrated when a member of the Carlton Club in London, a Conservative gentleman's club, proposed that "the Union Jack should be kept flying on the roof until the Home Rule were defeated or withdrawn."138

In Edinburgh on 1 November 1911, the Liberal statesman Lord Rosebery, was reported the next day in *The Scotsman* newspaper as acknowledging the calibre of the people with whom Asquith risked conflict by telling his Scottish audience that, "he loved Highlanders and he loved Lowlanders, but when he came to the branch of their race

An anti-Home Rule postcard. (J Luke)

which had been grafted on to the Ulster stem he took his hat off with reverence and awe. They were without exception the toughest, the most dominate, the most irresistible race that existed in the universe."139

Church parades gave the opportunity to demonstrate the ecumenical nature of the Ulster Volunteers Force often illustrated by the clergy from Anglican, Presbyterian and Methodist churches officiating at the services. Whilst these services usually occurred in churches or cathedrals there were a few occasions when British Army drumhead style services were held; one such drumhead service was held at Forth River Football Grounds for over 3,000 members of Belfast UVF.140

---

137 Hyde, H Montgomery, *Carson* (1953).
138 Ryan, AP, *Mutiny at the Curragh* (1956).
139 McNeill, Ronald, *Ulster's Stand for Union* (1922).
140 Bowman, Timothy, *Carson's Army: Ulster Volunteer Force, 1910-22* (2007).

Sir Edward Carson inspecting the Ulster Volunteers c. 1913. (Somme Museum)

Conversely much smaller church services still attracted the same attention from the organisers; the Clough Company of the UVF having their parade services held in the local Presbyterian Church in March and April 1914 with printed orders of service in pamphlet form printed by the 'Down Recorder'.[141]

The manner of dress of the Volunteers came under scrutiny in Battalion Orders for 1st Battalion, North Antrim Regiment, when the volunteers were informed that on all church parades they were to wear, headdress, bandoliers, belts, frogs and puttees. In the orders it was noted that no man would be asked to, nor would be expected to put on puttees on top of his best trousers, instead he would be expected to change into a pair of trousers over which he would usually put on his puttees.[142]

At the end of January 1914, headquarters gave permission for colours to be carried at "Divine Service Parades" when they would require to be accompanied by an armed colour party. The only proviso stated was that arrangements must have been made beforehand with the respective clergy in order to place the colours in a proper position inside the church.[143]

---

141 Bowman, Timothy, *Carson's Army: Ulster Volunteer Force, 1910-22* (2007). & PRONI D.1263/6.
142 Orders – 1st Battalion, North Antrim Regiment – 3 June 1914 – Somme Heritage Centre.
143 UVF Order 06, 1914 – Somme Museum.

3

Tensions Mount

On 29 July 1912 a Presbyterian Sunday School outing of about 500 strong, mostly women and children from the Whitehouse area of North Belfast,[1] accompanied by a band, met four bands of the Ancient Order of Hibernians, some 300 strong, as they prepared to commence their return journey home from Castledawson. One of the Hibernians, who were on their way to a political demonstration in Maghera, dashed into the outing and disorder ensued. The outing party was reinforced by Protestants from the town and stones were thrown by both sides. When the police attempted to restore order, one of the constables was violently kicked in the stomach.[2] The following day, Sunday, the minister who had accompanied the children told his congregation not to talk about the incident in case it would stoke up tension against their Catholic neighbours.[3] When word of the attack however reached the Belfast shipyards the apprentices and riveters' assistants in the predominately Protestant workforce called for the expulsion of all 'Fenians' and 'Home Rulers' with Catholic workers subsequently pelted by Belfast confetti, the metal discs punched out by riveters. The sporadic violence which followed led to around 2,000 workers being forced from their jobs in the yards.[4] The Catholic clergy in the north of Ireland demanded a proactive response to the attacks on Catholic workers, preferably from the military, as they condemned what they perceived as "inactivity" by the Royal Irish Constabulary.[5]

Twenty-three of the Hibernians involved in the Casteldawson attack were prosecuted afterwards.[6]

As a result of his incident, when the Reverend John Donnelly, who was the leader of the Innisrush UVF, wanted to hold his usual Sunday School Sports which would involve the children marching through the Nationalist area of Claudy, he approached Harry Clarke, second in command of 2nd Battalion, South Londonderry Regiment, UVF, suggesting an escort from the Innisrush and Tamlaght companies. At this stage there had been little or no evidence of the UVF appearing in public under arms. A young 12 year old boy, Alex Crockett later recalled seeing the Tamlaght men march off, their long bayonets glinting in the sun, wearing Australian style slouch hats, pinned up at one side and their bandoliers across their chests; Harry Clarke following the column with reserve ammunition in his car. The Royal Irish Constabulary had obviously prior knowledge and were outside their barracks in some strength. The Ulster Volunteers halted opposite them, turned into line and fixed bayonets in front of the police; they had unfixed their bayonets before getting to Innisrush. The police didn't react, instead the children assembled beside the Volunteers and proceeded to march through Claudy with their escort of armed men in front and behind them. It was reported that despite some Nationalist women stoning the procession the day went off quietly.[7]

---

1   Parkinson, Alan F, *Friends in High Places: Ulster's Resistance to Irish Home Rule, 1912-14* (2012).
2   Ryan, AP, *Mutiny at the Curragh* (1956).
3   Lewis, Geoffrey, *Carson: The man who divided Ireland* (2006).
4   Orr, Philip, *The Road to the Somme* (1987).
5   Parkinson, Alan F, *Friends in High Places: Ulster's Resistance to Irish Home Rule, 1912-14* (2012).
6   Clark, Wallace, *Guns in Ulster* (1967).
7   Clark, Wallace, *Guns in Ulster* (1967).

A postcard from the Historic Event series (No.20 depicting the Ulster Volunteer Force protecting a Sunday School excursion. (J Luke)

During 1912 whilst the third Home Rule Bill was negotiating the parliamentary process Ulster Protestants took to the streets to demonstrate their opposition leaving silent the shipyards, mills and engineering works throughout Belfast. The ill feeling persisted all during the summer and led to a rise in sectarian tensions until it peaked in early September at a football match in Celtic Park where Churchill had spoken earlier in the year.[8] An enormous crowd of Protestant football supporters converged on Celtic Park in West Belfast for the Belfast Celtic v Linfield football match, waving Orange banners and chanting 'obscene versions' of Orange songs. This culminated in serious rioting with indiscriminate shooting which required the Royal Irish Constabulary to send reinforcements to restore order; the injured numbering 60 persons who required hospital treatment.[9]

Carson was becoming concerned that such disorder between the working classes on both sides of the political divide could derail what he was striving for. He realised that he needed some form of 'safety valve' which would prevent or at least provide some form of control on the Ulster Protestant community. This would involve solemnity, religion and military discipline.[10]

In July 1912 at Blenheim Palace, the largest private house in England, Bonar Law addressed the Conservative Party and committed himself and therefore indirectly his party to unprecedented support for Ulster Unionists when he said, "I can imagine no length of resistance to which Ulster can go in which I shall not be prepared to support them." This was not merely support for Ulster Unionists, as Conservatives saw Home Rule as a direct threat not only to the United Kingdom but also the Empire and to question this was to question British Imperialism and everything it stood for. This stance was reinforced by a series of public meetings undertaken by Carson which began in Enniskillen on 18 September and finished in Belfast, on the eve of Ulster Day, 28 September.

---

8   Lewis, Geoffrey, *Carson: The man who divided Ireland* (2006).
9   *Irish News* – 16 September 1913.
10 Lewis, Geoffrey, *Carson: The man who divided Ireland* (2006).

An anti-Home Rule postcard. (J Luke)

SURRENDER – NEVER!

During this speaking tour he was accompanied by several House of Commons colleagues, including Admiral Lord Charles Beresford, Lord Castlereagh, Lord Hugh Cecil, Mr Ronald McNeill and Mr FE Smith.[11]

At the Enniskillen rally on 18 September 40,000 members of the Unionist Clubs marched past Carson[12] who was escorted to Portora Hill by two mounted squadrons of volunteers.[13]

The mounted unit had been formed by William Copeland Trimble, the editor of *The Impartial Reporter* newspaper.[14] Earlier in the month on 3 September, Trimble called upon his fellow Unionists; "Other places may have their meetings. Enniskillen must have one great distinctive feature of its own ... This escort will be the greatest feature of the day." He went on to highlight that as the Enniskillen meeting was the first to addressed by Carson it would draw a significant interest from the newspapers and therefore it was, "more incumbent on us that our mounted escort be no childish affair with clumsy men and unmanageable horses, but a fine turn out of smart soldiery-looking men, well groomed horses, and all showing the effects of organisation and discipline."[15]

The Royal Irish Constabulary had a different view, reporting that when the unit was formed, "the prominent people disapproved of the thing altogether." The first hint that the RIC had received of the formation of such a force was from Sergeant Patrick Hughes in a report to District Inspector JW Mahon on 4 September 1912 when he reported that Trimble was forming a mounted unit for Carson's visit, expected to be 150 strong and that several men belonged to the armed

---

11   Hyde, H Montgomery, *Carson* (1953).
12   Metcalfe, Nick, *Blacker's Boys* (2012).
13   McNeill, Ronald, *Ulster's Stand for Union* (1922).
14   Ulster Volunteers, January 1913 – Ulster-Scots Community Network <http://www.ulster-scots.com/uploads/901740969819.PDF> (Accessed 5 August 2013).
15   Bowman, Timothy, *Carson's Army: Ulster Volunteer Force, 1910-22* (2007).

A postcard depicting Edward Carson traveling in a motor car whilst being escorted by a mounted unit of the Ulster Volunteer Force. (J Luke)

forces. He reported that two were ex-Sergeants from the Imperial Yeomanry along with two other ex-members. Mahon passed this report to the Crimes Special Branch along with two other circulars dated 30 August and 3 September, published by Trimble and obtained by Sergeant Henry Conway.[16]

On 25 September in Portadown, Carson was again met by a mounted escort, this time 50 men under the command of Mr Holt Waring, JP of Waringstown. Each man was wearing a grey slouch hat and carried a long bamboo cane topped by a Union Jack pennon in imitation of lances.[17] Unlike the previous venues Carson was met by a guard of honour who presented arms and paraded with dummy rifles. A group of women paraded as nurses accompanied by an ambulance and there was also the presence of two mock cannon or artillery pieces, made of wood and painted a steel grey lead. In response FE Smith, noted for his staunch opposition to nationalism and a prominent leader of the Unionist wing of the Conservative Party commented "The battle is already won". His wife however wrote to her sisters, "We all thought the dummy cannons were absurd. It was only at Portadown we had them. We none of us knew anything about them. We all said 'How the Radicals will laugh!'"

In a direct reference to the views of some of the Unionist detractors, Carson's Portadown speech asked the question "Was bragging a characteristic of the Ulster Scot? Was it by bragging that they won Derry, Aughrim and the Boyne?" This also hinted that the Ulster Unionist may be willing to engage in more active steps than mere speeches and rhetoric to defend his position.[18]

---

16   Grob-Fitzgibbon, *Turning Points of The Irish Revolution: The British Government, Intelligence and th Cost of Indifference, 1912-1921* (2007).
17   Ryan, AP, *Mutiny at the Curragh* (1956).
18   Belfast Covenant Trail – Ulster Historical Foundation.

Ulster Volunteers on parade with their wooden canon, Portadown. (PRONI D2638/E/16)

During this programme of meetings across Ulster Carson was preceded by men drilling with dummy rifles, sometimes by torchlight and often to the sound of martial tunes before addressing the assembled crowds.[19]

However the drilling with wooden dummy rifles could lead to scorn from their political opponents, causing the first committee meeting of the County Down UUC to question if and when the volunteers would be issued with arms, the matter being raised by Lord Bangor.[20]

By August 1913 one enterprising Belfast firm, Gregg and Company, had identified a marketing opportunity and were offering for sale dummy wooden rifles to UVF units at between one shilling and one shilling six pence; depending on the quality of the wood used.[21]

During September 1912 2,000 people established the non-sectarian and non-political Young Citizen Volunteers of Ireland (YCV) at the City Hall in Belfast. The concept behind this group was to apply the principles of the scout movement, introduced to Ireland in 1908 to middle class youths rather than boys; "to develop the spirit of responsible citizenship and municipal patriotism", and "to cultivate, by means of modified military and political drill, a manly physique, with habits of self-control, self-respect and chivalry."[22] It may also have been as a reaction to the Haldane Reforms of 1908 in the British Army, as the arrangements for a Territorial Force was not extended to Ireland and it is believed that a number of prominent Belfast citizens thought that if such a force existed the War Office may have recognised them.[23]

At a meeting in the Lord Mayor's Parlour on 6 June 1912, Fred T Geddes, one of the joint-secretaries of the Belfast Citizens Association for Clifton and Duncairn wards in north Belfast, outlined his idea for a scheme of a 'Young Citizen's Volunteer Corps'. It was reported by the *Belfast News Letter* that the desire to form such a corps was proposed by GW Ferguson, JP, and seconded by EM Reid. Also present at the meeting were Major Fred Crawford, Major Fred Cunningham, JP, Lieutenant Colonel WEC McCammond, JP, W Joseph Stokes, JE Dawson and JD Williamson, JP. Also proposed was to form a committee with the power to co-opt others.[24]

---

19 Orr, Philip, *The Road to the Somme* (1987).
20 Hume, David, *"For Ulster and Her Freedom": The story of the April 1914 gun-running* (1989).
21 Bowman Timothy, 'The Ulster Volunteers: Force or Farce?', *History of Ireland*, Vol. 10, No. 1, spring 2002.
22 Bartlett, Thomas and Jeffery, Keith (ed), *A Military History of Ireland* (1996).
23 Bowman, Timothy, *Carson's Army: Ulster Volunteer Force, 1910-22* (2007).
24 Ulster-Scots Community Network, *Young Citizen Volunteers: 10 September 1912*.

Ulster Volunteer Force nurses in front of the manor house at Cultra. (Somme Museum)

The subsequent committee met days later again in the Lord Mayor's Parlour, 12 June, when Geddes submitted a comprehensive set of rules which were approved unanimously with a few minor alternations.[25]

The inaugural meeting of the new Corps was held in the Great Hall of Belfast City Hall, 10 September. The Belfast Lord Mayor, RJ McMordie, MP, addressed the 2,000 men who turned up to enrol, "In times of difficulty men had to carry their guns while they followed the plough ... the nation or the people that had lost the fighting instinct was sure to be swamped by others who possessed that instinct." Membership was open to anyone aged between eighteen and thirty-five years of age who was over five feet in height and could present 'credentials of good character'.[26] Each member was to pay 2s 6d on joining and a further 6d each month. They

An enamelled lapel badge for the Young Citizen Volunteers. (Somme Museum)

---

25 Ulster-Scots Community Network, *Young Citizen Volunteers: 10 September 1912*.
26 Crawford, FH, *Guns for Ulster* (1947).

Members of the Young Citizen Volunteers, Irish Football Association, their football strip bearing the distinctive shamrock with the initials Y.C.V. The men at either end of the back row are wearing the grey uniform of the YCV. (Somme Museum: 1999-82)

were to attend weekly drills, to learn 'modified military and police drill, single stick, rifle and baton exercises, signalling, knot-tying and other such exercises.' Where possible they were also to learn some skill in 'life saving and ambulance work'.[27]

The first 'Volunteer Executive' was formed from 70 individuals, the President being, RJ McMordie, MP, with others including Major Fred Crawford, councillor Frank Workman, of the Workman Clark shipyard and James Mackie, of Mackie's Foundry. Despite the YCV's constitution stating that it was "strictly non-sectarian and non-political" there were no prominent Nationalists on the Committee.[28] This non-sectarian stance was further reinforced in the rules which stated that the battalion band should not play party tunes.[29]

On 11 September the *Belfast News Letter* reported enthusiastically of the launch; "The banqueting hall was well occupied by fine specimens of the young manhood of the city." Whilst the *Northern Whig* proclaimed, "We can picture it (the YCV) in the event of a threatened foreign invasion guarding the shores of Belfast Lough and bringing to that duty the discipline of *Landwehr* and the enthusiasm of sons of the empire."[30] (*Landwehr* were German militia units)

The constitution and by-laws of the YCV insisted that members should not take part in any political meeting or demonstration nor wear the uniform of the Corps if attending a political meeting, and explained that the organisation's objectives were stated as being non-sectarian and

27 Orr, Philip, *The Road to the Somme* (1987).
28 Bowman, Timothy, *Carson's Army: Ulster Volunteer Force, 1910-22* (2007).
29 Bowman, Timothy, *Carson's Army: Ulster Volunteer Force, 1910-22* (2007).
30 *Northern Whig* – 10/9/1912.

The brass letters YCV represented the Young Citizen Volunteers and were worn as shoulder titles. (Somme Museum)

non-political and were considered to be, "...to develop the spirit of responsible citizenship and municipal patriotism by means of lectures and discussion on civic matters ... to cultivate, by means of modified military and police drill, a manly physique, with habits of self-control, self–respect and chivalry ... to assist as an organisation, when called upon, the civil power in the maintenance of the peace." Despite the stated aim of being non-sectarian and although some Catholics did join the majority of recruitment was Protestant.

The Municipal Technical College in College Square East was used as a venue for some of the instruction given to members of the YCV.[31]

The Northern Whig noted that the YCV would be intended to act as special police assisting the Lord Mayor, taking the place of the regular army in the event of rioting or the breaches of the peace.[32] This was a theme the *Irish News* and *Belfast Morning News* picked up on suggesting that it could be used to suppress industrial strikes; memories of the bitter transport strike of 1907 in Belfast still lingered in some memories.[33] Whilst there may have been those who thought they may have been used against industrial strikes the Ulster Volunteer Force in Belfast comprised a significant number of men employed in trades in the shipyards and other industries and as such were members of trade unions. This strong connection was reinforced in April 1914 when a meeting was held in the Ulster Hall by trade unionists against Home Rule.[34]

William 'Billy' John Gibson, from Ainsworth Avenue, Shankill Road, worked for the Singer Sewing Machine Company, Queen Street, Belfast, when the joined the "YCV to try and keep peace in Belfast, a sort of second police force as there was trouble with riots between the Protestants and Catholics." He later served as a signaller in the 14th Battalion Royal Irish Rifles saying he "had joined the army to keep the Germans away."[35]

Billy McFadzean, later a Victoria Cross recipient with the 14th Battalion, Royal Irish Rifles, joined the YCV in 1912 at Newtownbreda Presbyterian Church along with many other boys. It is believed that he was influenced by a lecturer at the Belfast Technical College.[36]

Whilst the intent was to extend the YCV organisation outside of Belfast this did not materialise, possibly due to the costs of membership and the expensive uniform; the majority of members having a reasonable job or a comfortable background.

---

31 Belfast Covenant Trail – Ulster Historical Foundation.
32 *Northern Whig* – 11/9/1912.
33 *Irish News and Belfast Morning News* – 11/9/1912.
34 Bowman, Timothy, *Carson's Army: Ulster Volunteer Force, 1910-22* (2007).
35 Billy Gibson, 14th RIR, RIF, WW1 Interview 097 – Somme Museum.
36 Billy McFadzean, WW1 Interview 103 – Somme Museum.

TENSIONS MOUNT

The Senior Non-Commissioned Officers of the Young Citizen Volunteers. (Somme Museum)

The uniform was similar to some of the territorial regiments in England, the cloth was a light blue-grey with dark blue facings.

The Young Citizen Volunteers were to be formed in companies limited to 50 strong, each commanded by a captain and according to the local press it was hoped to form a number of battalions with one based in Londonderry. There was also to be a process for the appointment of officers though the process appeared to be a complicated arrangement through their superior officers, a battalion executive and the central volunteer executive.[37]

The fact that the concept did not evolve further and remained as one battalion based in Belfast City may be related to the costs associated with membership.[38] The Lord Mayor appealed for £1,500 in order that the corps' light grey uniforms could be purchased

Rifleman William Frederick McFadzean, VC. C Company, 14th Battalion, Royal Irish Rifles. Died 1 July 1916. (Somme Museum)

---

37 *Northern Whig* – 10/9/1912.
38 Bowman, Timothy, *Carson's Army: Ulster Volunteer Force, 1910-22* (2007).

and allow the members of pay of the total of £1 10s for their uniform in monthly instalments.³⁹

At the time the average weekly wage in west Ireland was 10s 9d⁴⁰ whilst the national average weekly wage was £2.⁴¹

Newspapers appear to suggest there was a permanent staff which attracted certain running costs; ex-Sergeant Bentley, as chief instructor (£1 per week, rising to £1 15s from January 1913, ex-Sergeant Elphick, as his assistant from December 1912 (£1 10s per week), Mr Stevenson, general secretary (apparently on a voluntary bases) and Miss Morrison, typist (9s per week).⁴²

From the outset the corps had financial difficulties and appears to have failed to attract the support from local business which they had hoped for. From those firms initially approached for support only York Street Flax Spinning Company (£25), Inglis's Bakery (£5) and William Ewart & Son Ltd (£100) contributed very modest sums whilst assuring the Lord Mayor the corps had "their sincere sympathy". By January 1914 the financial situation was critical; the current account was £11 in credit and the uniform account was £389 in debit.⁴³

Major Ferrar was initially approached to be their Commanding Officer, however he appears to have declined and Colonel R Spencer-Chichester was approached and agreed. He sought an expansion of the company size, the early purchase of rifles and additional instructors. He also allayed some of the financial difficulties by initially contributing £100 and paying for the

Tunic of the Young Citizen Volunteers. (Somme Museum)

A Young Citizen Volunteers officer's epaulette. (Somme Museum)

---

39 Bowman, Timothy, *Carson's Army: Ulster Volunteer Force, 1910-22* (2007).
40 <http://www.bbc.co.uk/news/uk-northern-ireland-17557619> (Accessed 25 May 2014).
41 <http://www.titanic-nautical.com/RMS-Titanic-Chronology.html> (Accessed 25 May 2014).
42 Bowman, Timothy, *Carson's Army: Ulster Volunteer Force, 1910-22* (2007).
43 Bowman, Timothy, *Carson's Army: Ulster Volunteer Force, 1910-22* (2007).

instruments for the corps band. By the end he had donated a total of £260 6s 8d to the Young Citizen Volunteers.[44]

Other suggested events for the corps such as an open air fete and a fancy dress ball were largely to raise much needed funds, but were not endorsed by the volunteer committee.[45] However the committee did support the proposal from the Lord Mayor that the corps should find "suitable employment" for its members by acting on the suggestion of Councillor Riddell that employers should be informed of the availability of eligible young men who would be recommended by their officers for potential vacancies. Another proposal from Captain May and a number of other officers was to mirror similar arrangements for members of exclusive London Territorial Force Units. This was that members in return for their subscriptions should have access to facilities; such as a central club room with billiards and refreshments.[46]

At their launch the secretary FT Geddis expressed his hope that the YCVs would be fostered by the government. Later in 1913 it became clear that many members were having difficulty in finding the money to pay for uniforms and were in fact paying off costs in monthly instalments. As a result an application was made to the government for financial assistance in return for placing the YCV at the government's disposal as a 'territorial' unit. This offer however was declined.

This refusal by Government resulted in a large body of the YCV advocating that they should throw their lot in with the UVF who by April 1914 had weapons; Colonel Chichester being inclined to the UVF. However as result of this debate there were a number of resignations from within the YCV.[47] At a volunteer council meeting on 2 April a resolution proposed by Mr Geddes and seconded by Captain Mitchell stated, "That the Office bearers and Council of the YCV of Ireland deeply regret that they were not consulted prior to the recent amalgamation of the 1st Battalion YCV with the Ulster Volunteer Force, and they take this opportunity of informing the public that it was done without their authority and consent." With no Annual General Meeting held the previous December, there were only two further committee meetings, the last in May. These heard concerns of members regarding the amalgamation with the UVF, given the original object of the corps as non-political and non-sectarian, and also considered taking legal action against Colonel Chichester. It was against this background that it appears that 400 or so Catholic members of the YCV left, unwilling to remain as a separate unit.[48] However by May 1914 the majority of the YCV had agreed to apply for membership of the UVF, becoming a battalion within the Belfast regiment.[49]

The first occasion when the YCV and UVF paraded together was a more sombre one. Shortly after returning from a holiday in the south of France, Belfast Lord Mayor, Robert Mordie consulted his doctor about influenza, however the following day his condition worsened and he was diagnosed with acute bronchitis and pneumonia. Later the same day he suffered a fatal heart attack. *The Belfast Telegraph* reported the presence of both the Ulster Volunteers and the YCV at his funeral;[50]

---

44 Bowman, Timothy, *Carson's Army: Ulster Volunteer Force, 1910-22* (2007).
45 Bowman, Timothy, *Carson's Army: Ulster Volunteer Force, 1910-22* (2007).
46 Bowman, Timothy, *Carson's Army: Ulster Volunteer Force, 1910-22* (2007).
47 PRONI D1568/6/10/14.
48 PRONI D1568/6/10/14.
49 PRONI D1568/6/10/14.
50 Moore, Steven, *The Chocolate Soldiers: The story of the Young Citizen Volunteers and 14th Royal Irish Rifles during the Great War* (2016).

Band members of the Young Citizen Volunteers. (Somme Museum)

Each of the city battalions sent 50 men, who marched behind the Young Citizen Volunteers. The YCV were in uniform, and the UVF in civilian attire. As the cortege passed out of the gates of Cabin Hill bearing its manly owner through familiar scenes for the last time, the Volunteers lined on either side of the Newtownards Road stood to attention.

This reluctance and lack of co-operation in expanding the UVF was not without issues from other areas. As late as August 1913 a number of Unionist Clubs were refusing to co-operate with the Ulster Volunteer Force, resulting in Captain Frank Hall, secretary of the Unionist Clubs of Ireland and a senior staff officer in the UVF to write in a circular letter:

> With reference to Sir Edward Carson's letter forwarded to you last week asking your club to assist in the immediate

Head dress badge of the Young Citizen Volunteers, later the 14th Royal Irish Rifles. (Somme Museum)

organisation of the UVF, the following points may be of value to your Committee in obtaining that end:

1. The existing Clubs' organisation, complete as it is, has not gone far enough in the actual formation of a purely military force, which will be absolutely essential when the crises comes.
2. To meet this difficulty the Ulster V.F. has been formed, and enrolment has already proceeded apace. All Unionists who are willing to assist in defending themselves, their homes, and their neighbours should enrol irrespective of whether they are already members of clubs, or Orange Lodges.
3. The details of organising this are in the hands of 'County Committees'…
4. You will understand that there is no idea or intention of breaking up the existing Clubs' Organisation, and where drill has been carried on systematically to the satisfaction of the County Committee, such drill will continue and be utilised to the full extent by the UVF.

   The Clubs will continue to exist and all such work as education on the Home Rule question, linking with Clubs across the water, speakers and canvassers classes, etc., must be kept going and encouraged by them in view of the possibility of a general election before the actual passage of the Home Rule Bill, and the consequent outbreak of hostilities.[51]

By May 1914 other emerging issues were becoming evident. The mixed arms and ammunition available to the UVF units through the various different approaches to arming the local units could have proved a logistical nightmare if conflict occurred. In an effort to address this issue, Colonel Hacket-Pain suggested that in the absence of agreement between the counties to redistribute the arms then only a couple of options remained. One was to through mutual inter-regimental agreement to collect into battalions of one regiment "the whole of one type" and secondly to arm the men of the marching battalion in the regiment with what was considered the most appropriate rifle leaving the remainder for those carrying out protection duties.[52] This suggestion linked to the orders of 7 May 1914 which required the formation in each Regiment of as many "marching battalions" (*battaillon de marche*) of suitably armed men who were prepared to move in any direction in service of the cause when the emergency arose.[53]

A description of the situation was expressed in verse by Sir William Watson in his poem *Ulster's Reward* which appeared in *The Times* a few days before the signing of the Covenant in Belfast:[54]

> What is the wage the faithful earn?
> What is a recompense fair and met?
> Trample their fealty under your feet –
> That is a fitting and just return.
> Flout them, buffet them, over them ride,
> Fling them aside!
>
> Ulster is ours to mock and spurn,
> Ours to spit upon, ours to deride
> And let it be known and blazoned wide

---

51 Bowman, Timothy, *Carson's Army: Ulster Volunteer Force, 1910-22* (2007).
52 Bowman, Timothy, *Carson's Army: Ulster Volunteer Force, 1910-22* (2007).
53 Circular Memorandum to Div, Regt and Batt Commanders – 7 May 1914.
54 McNeill, Ronald, *Ulster's Stand for Union* (1922).

ULSTER AT BAY
AS IN 1690 AND NOW.

MACAULAY, writing of the Siege of Derry, 1690, says—" There, at length on the verge of the ocean, hunted to the last asylum, and baited into a mood in which men may be destroyed, but will not easily be subjugated, the imperial race turned desperately to bay."

W & G BAIRD, L'T'D BELFAST.

An anti-Home Rule postcard. (J Luke)

> That this is the age the faithful earn:
> Did she uphold us when others defied?
> Then fling her aside.
>
> Where on the Earth was the like of it done
> In the gaze of the sun?
> She had pleaded and prayed to be counted still
> As one of our household through good and ill;
> And with scorn they replied,
> Jeered at her loyalty, trod on her pride,
> Spurned her, repulsed her,
> Great-hearted Ulster;
> Flung her aside.[55]

The point that the objections to Home Rule were not necessarily confined to religious backgrounds was reinforced by the *Bangor Spectator* in October 1912.

> … we are the champions of the great multitude of Irish people in the South and West, both Protestant and Catholic, who dread Home Rule, knowing well what its nature would be, but dare not take adequate steps to defend themselves. Our action is no selfish endeavour to keep privilege, or even security for ourselves. It is a noble struggle for the welfare of the whole land.[56]

The concept of tolerance was voiced later in 1914, at a church service for the UVF, when the Rev John Lyle Donaghy, First Larne Presbyterian Church, reminded the assembled men that they were not organising on military lines to gain ascendancy over Roman Catholics or because they were bigots, he stated "They should remember that their quarrel was not so much with their Roman Catholic fellow countrymen as with the treacherous British government … which had sold them to the avowed enemies of their country …". He also went on to say that Protestants bore no personal grudges against their Roman Catholic countrymen continuing:

> … with their Roman Catholic countrymen they had lived, done business, co-operated in the land courts and fought side by side on foreign battlefields where Irish pluck had again and again brought glory to the British armies. They were still willing to accord them the same civil privileges they themselves enjoyed, but they would never willingly allow them to occupy a position of supremacy which could be turned by their spiritual advisors into an engine for spiritual annihilation …[57]

Amongst those opposed to Home Rule the idea of a solemn oath or pledge against Home Rule had been discussed and it appears that James Craig was given the task of working on this. It is reported that whilst Craig was sitting in the Constitutional Club in London making drafts from pencil and paper he was joined by BWD Montgomery who on asking what he was doing was told, "Trying to draft an oath for our people at home and it's no easy matter to get what will suit." Montgomery is reported as replying, "You couldn't do better than take the old Scotch

---

55   Shearman, Hugh, *Not an Inch: A Study of Northern Ireland and Lord Craigavon* (1942).
56   *Bangor Spectator* – 11 October 1912.
57   Hume, David, *"For Ulster and Her Freedom": The story of the April 1914 gun-running* (1989).

An anti-Home Rule postcard.
(J Luke)

Covenant. It is a fine old document, full of grand phrases, and thoroughly characteristic of the Ulster tone of mind at this day."[58] With the help of the club librarian the two men found a History of Scotland which contained the full text of the old Scottish Covenanters' oath; which by strange coincidence was drawn up in 1581 by a John Craig.[59] However it wasn't long before it was realised that the language employed and the length of the old covenant, which was a religious declaration, could not be easily used for the political purposes which they intended. Despite this Thomas Sinclair took up the task and following widespread consultation the final version was agreed on 19 September 1912.[60]

---

58 McNeill, Ronald, *Ulster's Stand for Union* (1922).
59 Hyde, H Montgomery, *Carson* (1953).
60 Belfast Covenant Trail – Ulster Historical Foundation.

4

The Ulster Covenant

The Covenant was deliberately named after the document signed by Scottish Presbyterians in 1638, intended to stamp out Roman practices in the Church. The Ulster Covenant conceived with more than a passing nod to the popish conspiracies of the seventeenth century and the victories of William of Orange who delivered them "out of the hands of our enemies" was a declaration of faith based on 1600s principles. It also drew comparisons between the Ulster Covenant and the Old Testament Covenant of the Israelites.

The link to the Scottish Covenant was also significant as the Protestant population of Ulster was littered with old clan names which would have been equally recognisable to those associated with the Scottish Covenant. During the English Civil War Major General Monro's army was sent to Ireland by the King and seized Belfast in 1644. After the King negotiated a cessation of hostilities with the rebels in southern Ireland the Solemn League and Covenant was signed, in practice binding the Ulster community to the cause of the English parliament against the King; making the Ulstermen at war with both the Irish rebels they were sent to fight and the King who sent them.[1]

Despite these references to the various Covenants in Scottish history the final one drawn up in Ulster had no actual resemblance to any of the historical precedents.[2]

The final text read:[3]

> Being convinced in our consciences that Home Rule would be disastrous to the material well-being of Ulster as well as the whole of Ireland, subversive of our civil and religious freedom, destructive of our citizenship, and perilous to the unity of the Empire, we, whose names are underwritten, men of Ulster, loyal subjects of His Gracious Majesty King George V, humbly relying on the God whom our fathers in days of stress and trial confidently trusted, do hereby pledge ourselves in solemn Covenant throughout this time of threatened calamity to stand by one another in defending for ourselves and our children our cherished position of equal citizenship in the United Kingdom, and in using all means which may be found necessary to defeat the present conspiracy to set up a Home Rule Parliament in Ireland. And in the event of such a Parliament being forced upon us we further solemnly and mutually pledge ourselves to refuse to recognise its authority. In sure confidence that God will defend the right we hereto subscribe our names. And further, we individually declare that we have not already signed this Covenant. God save the King.

---

1 Shearman, Hugh, *Not an Inch: A Study of Northern Ireland and Lord Craigavon* (1942).
2 Shearman, Hugh, *Not an Inch: A Study of Northern Ireland and Lord Craigavon* (1942).
3 Ryan, AP, *Mutiny at the Curragh* (1956).

Edward Carson briefing news reporters at Craigavon House, September 1912. (Somme Museum)

The local press were informed of the Covenant campaign on 17 August 1912 leading to a public debate over the next month on its content.[4]

Writing to James Craig from Bad Homburg on 21 August 1912, Carson described his views on the Covenant, "I would not alter a word in the declaration which I consider excellent. I also agree with what the Council have resolved about Northern Ireland. I do not know whether it is feasible but I think if 'Ulster Day' could wind up with bonfires all through the country it would be impressive and create enthusiasm."[5]

The document stated that the signatories would use "all means" to defeat the Home Rule Bill and keep Ulster within the United Kingdom. Carson, bareheaded and smoking a cigarette, announced the terms of the Ulster Covenant from the steps of Craigavon House in September 1912.[6,7]

On 23 September 1912 the Ulster Unionist Council (UUC) passed a resolution pledging itself to the Covenant and set out a case for doing so. During its meeting one of the largest Union Flags ever made – measuring 48 by 25 feet – was hung as a backdrop.[8]

Carson was very aware of the significance of the wording in the Covenant advising delegates of the UUC, "responsible men from every district in Ulster, that it is your duty, when you go back to your various districts, to warn your people who trust you that, in entering into this

---
4   Parkinson, Alan F, *Friends in High Places: Ulster's Resistance to Irish Home Rule, 1912-14* (2012).
5   Hyde, H Montgomery, *Carson* (1953).
6   Leslie and Quail, *Old Belfast* (2013).
7   Ryan, AP, *Mutiny at the Curragh* (1956).
8   <http://www.proni.gov.uk/index/search_the_archives/ulster_covenant/preparations.htm>.

solemn obligation, that they are entering into a matter which whatever may happen in the future, is the most serious matter that has ever confronted them in the course of their lives."[9]

A central Ulster Day Committee was appointed to handle the preparations associated with obtaining as many signatures as possible at various centres throughout Ulster. Headed by Richard Dawson Bates, Secretary of the UUC, the Committee also included Col. TVP McCammon of the Orange Order and Captain Frank Hall representing the Unionist Clubs.[10]

As part of these arrangements over 500 halls and other suitable premises were to be made available in order that Unionists would have the opportunity to sign the Covenant in their own local districts.

A series of speeches throughout Ulster were designed to build the atmosphere, one Ulster King's Counsel asked his listeners, "What do you care about the criticisms of men who tricked their King and smashed the constitution as to whether your action is legal or whether it is illegal?"[11]

From Wednesday, 25 September 700 large cardboard boxes were sent out from the Old Town Hall, Belfast, for further distribution within the city and in the various rural areas, all being delivered by the Friday. Each box contained copies of the Covenant and the Declaration printed in large bold type on cardboard for display in the halls.

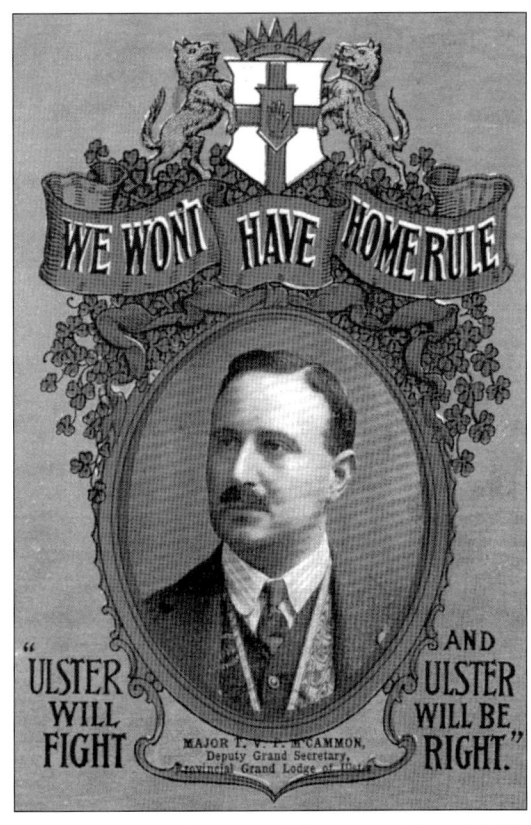

Anti-Home Rule postcard depicting Major TVP McCammon, (J Luke)

There were also the forms to be signed which were foolscap-sized sheets, each headed by the text of the Covenant together with the Parliamentary Division and District. The area for signing had lines ruled with spaces for ten signatures underneath names and addresses of each of the signatories. These were in turn made up into blocks of ten sheets per folder with the agent's name on the folder cover. In addition there were also an individual parchment copy of the Covenant in old English type and headed with the Red Hand of Ulster to be given to each signatory.

On Friday 27 September messages of support were received by the organisers; these included a pledge from a number of peers not to take a seat in either House of an Irish Legislature. Lord Roberts, the last Commander-in-Chief of the British Army; and Lord Curzon wished every success to the men and women of Ulster; Admiral the Hon. Sir ER Fremantle offered his sincere sympathy to Ulster in resisting by all means in her power; Admiral of the fleet Sir Edward Seymour prophesied that Home Rule would mean financial ruin; Lord Robert Cecil who said, "if the situation

---

9   McNeill, Ronald, *Ulster's Stand for Union* (1922).
10   <http://www.proni.gov.uk/index/search_the_archives/ulster_covenant/preparations.htm>.
11   Ryan, AP, *Mutiny at the Curragh* (1956).

Preparations for dispatching boxes of Covenant forms to be signed across the Province of Ulster. (PRONI D3275/2)

results in civil war – which may Heaven avert – the responsibility will rest not on Ulster but on the government."[12]

That evening Carson attended a meeting at the Ulster Hall where, although fatigued from the programme of speeches, said:

> We will take deliberately a step forward, not in defiance but in defence, and the Covenant which we will most willingly sign tomorrow will be a great step forward, in no spirit of aggression, in no spirit of ascendancy, but with a full knowledge that, if necessary, you and I – you trusting me, and I trusting you – will follow out everything that this Covenant means to the very end, whatever the consequences.[13]

Such was the crowd who attended the event that a specially erected platform was constructed from an upper window of the Ulster Hall, over the glass porch of the main entrance to allow Carson to address the crowds gathered outside in Bedford Street; it was estimated that 25,000 had gathered in the street.[14, 15]

Once outside and facing the gathered crowd of 25,000 people he was presented with a faded yellow silk flag, with a cross of St George in the corner[16] which Colonel Wallace, Grand Master of the Belfast Orangemen, explained had been carried at the Battle of the Boyne by an Ensign Watson, which had been retained by his descendants ever since. Carson responded in true style, "May this flag ever float over a people that can boast of civil and religious liberty."[17]

A sceptical Catholic Belfast newspaper questioned the authenticity of this claim suggesting that if it was true then, "the man who manufactured it deserves undying fame for strength and durability of material."[18]

---

12 Ryan, AP, *Mutiny at the Curragh* (1956).
13 Hyde, H Montgomery, *Carson* (1953).
14 Lucy, Gordon, *The Ulster Covenant, An Illustrated History of the 1912 Home Rule Crises* (2012).
15 Parkinson, Alan F, *Friends in High Places: Ulster's Resistance to Irish Home Rule, 1912-14* (2012).
16 Hyde, H Montgomery, *Carson* (1953).
17 Lucy, Gordon, *The Ulster Covenant, An Illustrated History of the 1912 Home Rule Crises* (2012).
18 Ryan, AP, *Mutiny at the Curragh* (1956).

The temporary stand erected over the canopy of the Ulster Hall for the night of 27 September 1912. (Somme Museum)

Lord Charles Beresford, FE Smith, Craig, Carson and other leaders arriving at Belfast City Hall for the signing of the Ulster Covenant, September 1912. They are following a flag which was claimed to have been carried at the Battle of the Boyne by an Ensign Watson. (PRONI INF/7A/2/36)

The crowd gathered at the City Hall, Belfast on Ulster Day for the signing of the Covenant, 28 September 1912. (Somme Museum)

'Ulster Day', on 28 September 1912, and the signing of the 'Solemn League and Covenant' was conducted in an atmosphere of near religious fervour. This was enhanced by more than 500[19] religious services held throughout Ulster in Protestant churches which were intended to invoke divine aid and to encourage more signatures. The services were often accompanied by the favoured hymn being 'O God, our help in ages past', lessons from Isaiah, the Psalms and Ephesians all concluded by the national anthem.[20] Charles Frederick D'Arcy, later Archbishop of Armagh, explained his Church's reason for supporting the Covenant: "We hold that no power, not even the British Parliament, has the right to deprive us of our heritage of British citizenship".[21]

Following the reading of the Covenant in most of the churches on Ulster Day those attending were invited to sign, the Rev ST Nesbitt at St John's Church, Ballyclare, ended his sermon with the words, "Let us sign the Solemn League and Covenant which will bind us together, as one man, not to acknowledge a parliament in Dublin, or obey its laws, being fully assured that if God be for us, he is greater than all that can be against us, and that He will defend the right."[22]

The Rev. Dr Henry Montgomery, moderator of the Presbyterian Church, in an address in the Assembly Hall reminded his audience of their background again linking into the inspiration of the Covenant they would be sign that day, "The large majority of us here today look back to a Scottish ancestry; we cherish the same faith and hold the same doctrine."[23]

Throughout the City of Belfast, factories and the shipyard fell silent as the workers were allowed the opportunity to attend the church services, ending around noon and then proceed to the City Hall. At the service attended by Edward Carson the Presbyterian minister declared, "The Irish question is at bottom a war against Protestantism. It is an attempt to establish a Roman Catholic ascendancy in Ireland to begin the disintegration of the Empire by securing a second Parliament in Dublin … We are plain blunt men. We will not have Home Rule."

The night before Craig had presented Carson with a silver key, symbolising Ulster as the key to the situation and a silver pen for him to sign the Covenant.[24, 25] When Carson arrived in Bedford Street his arrival was greeted with a respectful silence and an uncovering of heads instead of roaring cheers, a small but significant indication that the crowd realised the exceptional day that

---

19 Ryan, AP, *Mutiny at the Curragh* (1956).
20 Ryan, AP, *Mutiny at the Curragh* (1956).
21 <http://www.proni.gov.uk/index/search_the_archives/ulster_covenant/ulster_day.htm>.
22 Hume, David, *"For Ulster and Her Freedom": The story of the April 1914 gun-running* (1989).
23 Belfast Covenant Trail – Ulster Historical Foundation.
24 *From the shipyard to the Somme* – 36th Ulster Division Memorial Association – 2013.
25 McNeill, Ronald, *Ulster's Stand for Union* (1922).

Brassard worn by the City Hall Guard on Ulster Day, 28 September 1912. (Somme Museum)

they were part of.[26] An escort of men wearing bowler hats and carrying sticks preceded by the Boyne Standard displayed the night before at the Ulster Hall, preceded Edward Carson and other Unionist leaders as they walked the short distance along Bedford Street to the City Hall. The sticks or batons of the guard of honour were made of greenheart, a glossy reddish wood, one made by Major Fred Crawford, himself.[27] The wood was extremely hard and strong, so hard that it couldn't be worked with standard tools; durable in marine conditions it was used to build docks and other structures.[28] Hundreds of marshals guarded the perimeter of the City Hall.[29]

On reaching the entrance of the City Hall, Carson was welcomed by the Lord Mayor and Corporation, the Poor Law Guardians, the Water Board and the Harbour Commissioners. In the entrance hall a circular table had been draped with the Union Flag with a copy of the Covenant, a silver inkstand and Carson's silver pen. Edward Carson, flanked by Lord Londonderry and Admiral Beresford[30] appended the first signature to the Covenant at midday followed by Lord Londonderry, his son Lord Castlereagh[31] and the representatives of the Protestant Churches and finally James Craig; Craig's name does not appear on the first page.[32, 33]

The Northern Whig commented on the calibre and status of the men who signed along with Carson, "By 12.15 there was gathered round the flag-covered drumhead a body of men who represented a very large part of the capital, the talent, the genius, and the energy of the City of Belfast. If the Covenant is treason, nearly all that makes for progress in this city will have to be impeached."[34]

As soon as Carson had signed the Covenant a signaller perched on a parapet outside the dome of the City Hall immediately semaphored a message, "Carson has signed the Covenant" which

---

26 McNeill, Ronald, *Ulster's Stand for Union* (1922).
27 Ingram, Rev Brett, *Covenant and Challenge* (1989).
28 <http://en.wikipedia.org/wiki/Chlorocardium_rodiei – accessed 13 April 2014>.
29 Parkinson, Alan F, *Friends in High Places: Ulster's Resistance to Irish Home Rule, 1912-14* (2012).
30 Ingram, Rev Brett, *Covenant and Challenge* (1989).
31 Belfast Covenant Trail – Ulster Historical Foundation.
32 Belfast Covenant Trail – Ulster Historical Foundation.
33 McNeill, Ronald, *Ulster's Stand for Union* (1922).
34 Lucy, Gordon, *The Ulster Covenant, An Illustrated History of the 1912 Home Rule Crises* (2012).

At Belfast City Hall 2,500 members of Unionist Clubs of Ireland guarded the grounds. They were organised in sections of 500, all under the command of Major (later Colonel) Fred H Crawford, organiser of the 1914 gun-running. The photograph shows a section of these guards, with staves, taking up position. The inscription on the red, white and blue armbands is 'City Hall Guard'.
(PRONI INF/7A/2/32)

led to the message being passed by a chain of signals from Belfast to Belleck, Killybegs, across the Antrim hills to Portpatrick in Scotland.[35]

Ronald McNeill described the scene when Carson signed his name:

> The sunshine sending a beam through the stained glass window on the stairway threw warm tints of colour on the marbles of the column and the tessellated floor of the Hall, sparkled on the Lord Mayor's chain, lent a rich glow to the scarlet gowns of the city fathers and lit up the red and blue and white of the imperial flag, what was the symbol of so much that they revered to those who stood looking on … whilst behind them, through the open door could be seen a vast forest of human heads, endless as far as eye could reach, every one of whom was in eager accord with the work in hand and whose blended voices while they waited to perform their own part in the great transaction, were carried to the ears of those in the Hall, like the inarticulate noise of moving waters.[36]

---

35 Ingram, Rev Brett, *Covenant and Challenge* (1989).
36 Parkinson, Alan F, *Friends in High Places: Ulster's Resistance to Irish Home Rule, 1912-14* (2012).

Sir Edward Carson signing the Covenant on Ulster Day in Belfast City Hall. (Somme Museum: 1994-642)

After this the doors of the City Hall were opened to the crowds gathered in Donegall Square, Donegall Place and Royal Avenue. A body of 2,500 men drawn from Orange lodges and Unionist Clubs marshalled the crowds outside the City Hall throughout the day, admitting four or five hundred at a time into the City Hall where lines of specially made temporary desks were set out along the corridors, stretching approximately half a mile, allowing 540 signatures to be taken at a time. A parallel arrangement at the Ulster Hall was established to enable women to sign the Declaration.

Martin Ross (of Somerville & Ross fame) wrote:

> Four at a time the men stooped and fixed their signatures and were quickly replaced by the next batch. Down the street in a market house the women were signing, women who had come in flagged motors, and on bicycles and on foot ... In the City Hall of Belfast the people were signing at the rate of about a hundred and fifty a minute; here there was no hypnotic force of dense masses, no whirlwind of emotion, only the unadorned and individual action of those who had left their fields and taken their lives and liberties in their hands laying them forth in the open sunshine as the measure of their resolve.[37]

---

37 <http://www.proni.gov.uk/index/search_the_archives/ulster_covenant/ulster_day.htm>.

A postcard depicting the Ulster Clubs entering the Belfast City Hall to sign the Covenant on Ulster Day, 28 September 1912. (J Luke)

By the time the doors were shut at 11:00 p.m. approximately 35,000 men had filed into the City Hall to sign their support[38] with an average of about 160 signing every minute. No one under the age of 16 was allowed to sign and those who were illiterate or unable to sign their own name had their name written by a member of the local committee and initialled.[39]

Across Ulster there were similar scenes. The Duke of Abercorn who was in failing health, signed under an oak tree on his estate at Baronscourt whilst Lord Templetown signed at Castle Upton on an old drum of the Templepatrick Infantry.[40]

After a local religious services in Ballynure Presbyterian Church, over 300 local men signed the Covenant and almost 200 women the Declaration, and then a crowd of several hundred men, women and children processed in ranks of four from the village to the nearby town of Ballynure, led by a large crimson banner with the words "Ballynure will not have Home Rule". At the recreation grounds in the town, they joined in a large public demonstration with other Unionists from Straid and Ballyeaston. From the platform a number of speakers called on them to withstand Home Rule, the strength of feeling was summed up by the Belfast MP, Mr James Chambers, "when the last question of Home Rule was fought in Ireland their Unionist Club had only 300 members, while at present it boasted a membership of 1,500. That meant that Ballyclare was five times as determined as ever it had been to resist the establishment of parliament in Dublin."[41]

It was reported in Bangor that on Ulster Day, "from almost every house, business place or residence, the flag of the Union waved, and many houses were decorated with streaming lines of bunting."[42]

---

38   Belfast Covenant Trail – Ulster Historical Foundation.
39   Ryan, AP, *Mutiny at the Curragh* (1956).
40   <http://www.proni.gov.uk/index/search_the_archives/ulster_covenant/ulster_day.htm>.
41   Hume, David, *"For Ulster and Her Freedom": The story of the April 1914 gun-running* (1989).
42   Hume, David, *"For Ulster and Her Freedom": The story of the April 1914 gun-running* (1989).

The Rev. William Ramsay warned a large congregation in Carnalbanagh Presbyterian church of the possibility of civil war and went on to say that Home Rule would be conductive toward friction, disturbance and unrest and would not lead to harmony between the different religious and political sects.[43]

After highlighting that Unionist opposition to Home Rule transcended class barriers, the rector of St Nicholas Parish Church, Rev FJ McNeice, went on to point out the Non-Conformist nature of opposition to Home Rule:

> There was a large emigration from Ulster to America. Many of those who went, carrying with them bitter recollections of the wrong done to them were Ulster Presbyterians. In the American War of Independence many Ulster Presbyterians fought on the American side. Their brethren who remained in Ulster were then bitterly hostile to England – discontented and disloyal. The Ulster Presbyterians of our day are the descendants of men who suffered many a wrong, and who as a consequence were disaffected. But the Act of Union of 1800 (sic) had made a change. The Presbyterians of Ulster have experienced the benefits and blessings of the Union, and under it they have helped to build up great industries … When we think of the Presbyterians of a past time who were hostile and disloyal, and think of the Presbyterians of our own day, who under other circumstances are passionately loyal to the constitution of the United Kingdom, surely it is an argument for the belief that the policy that has affected such a change in them can effect a like change in others.[44]

The Duke of Abercorn, President of the Ulster Unionist Council, signing the Ulster Solemn League and Covenant at Baronscourt, County Tyrone, 1912. (Somme Museum: 1994-158)

He further highlighted the fears felt by many of being a religious minority under Home Rule, "… has any parliament predominantly Roman Catholic, ever done justice to a Protestant minority?" going on to cite examples, such as the Protestant minority presently in Quebec, which

---
43 Hume, David, *"For Ulster and Her Freedom": The story of the April 1914 gun-running* (1989).
44 Hume, David, *"For Ulster and Her Freedom": The story of the April 1914 gun-running* (1989).

The crowds outside the Belfast City Hall on Covenant Day, September 1912. (Somme Museum)

had dwindled from 17,000 to 4,500 and in the past in Italy, France and Spain, with governments which were predominately Roman Catholic.[45]

The Covenant was also signed outside the confines of Ulster. In Dublin it was signed by 2,000 men who could prove that they were born in Ulster. It was also signed in major cities in England and Scotland including London, Glasgow, Manchester, Liverpool, Bristol and York. In Edinburgh a number of Ulstermen signed the Covenant in the old Greyfriars Churchyard on the 'Covenanter's Stone', the memorial linked to the Scottish Covenant of the seventeenth century.[46]

It was also signed in places further afield including aboard the SS *Lake Champlain* which was carrying emigrants to Canada.[47] A letter was later received from this vessel which included the signatures of 12 second-class passengers, four men and eight women, whilst amongst the third-class passengers, 34 had also acquired the Covenant text, stuck it to a piece of paper and signed.[48]

Signatories were also added in the United States of America, Canada, Australia, South Africa and even Nanking in China, where six Belfast men signed whilst on board the cruiser HMS *Monmouth*.[49]

An RIC District Inspector reported that a large number of Sergeants and Privates of the Royal Inniskilling Fusiliers based at Omagh signed the Covenant, a number of them being in plain

---

45 Hume, David, *"For Ulster and Her Freedom": The story of the April 1914 gun-running* (1989).
46 McNeill, Ronald, *Ulster's Stand for Union* (1922).
47 Belfast Covenant Trail – Ulster Historical Foundation.
48 <http://www.proni.gov.uk/index/search_the_archives/ulster_covenant/ulster_day.htm>.
49 Belfast Covenant Trail – Ulster Historical Foundation.

Ulster's Solemn League and Covenant.

Being convinced in our consciences that Home Rule would be disastrous to the material well-being of Ulster as well as of the whole of Ireland, subversive of our civil and religious freedom, destructive of our citizenship and perilous to the unity of the Empire, we, whose names are underwritten, men of Ulster, loyal subjects of His Gracious Majesty King George V., humbly relying on the God whom our fathers in days of stress and trial confidently trusted, do hereby pledge ourselves in solemn Covenant throughout this our time of threatened calamity to stand by one another in defending for ourselves and our children our cherished position of equal citizenship in the United Kingdom and in using all means which may be found necessary to defeat the present conspiracy to set up a Home Rule Parliament in Ireland. And in the event of such a Parliament being forced upon us we further solemnly and mutually pledge ourselves to refuse to recognise its authority. In sure confidence that God will defend the right we hereto subscribe our names. And further, we individually declare that we have not already signed this Covenant.

The above was signed by me at THE CITY HALL, BELFAST. "Ulster Day," Saturday, 28th September, 1912.

James Craig.
Captain.

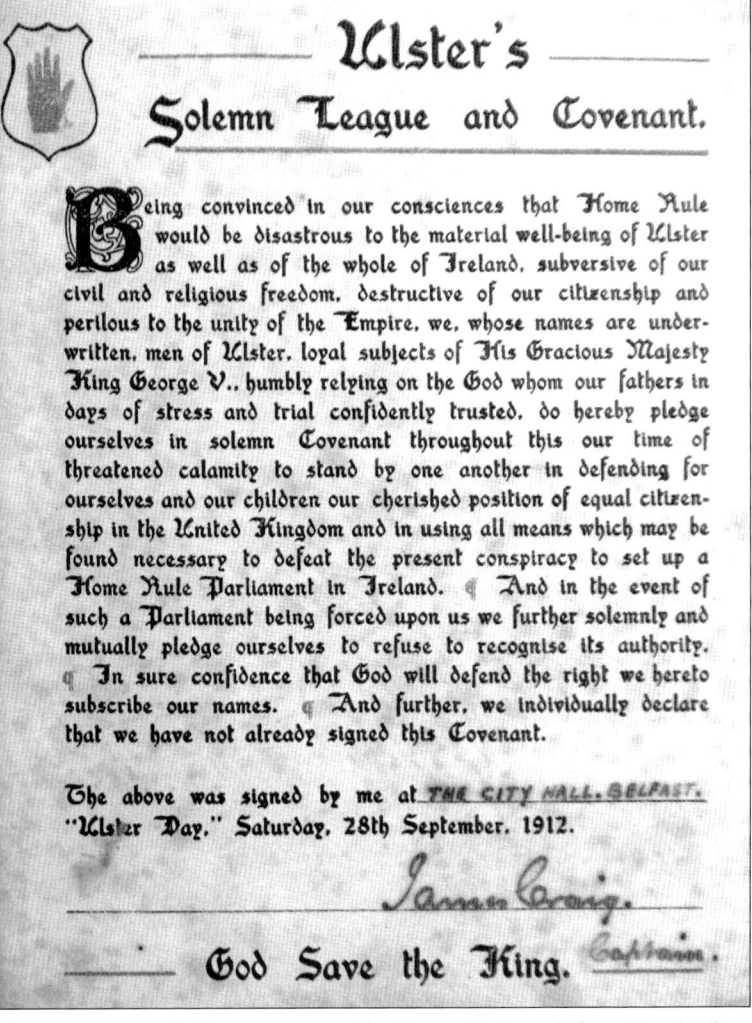

God Save the King.

The Ulster Solemn League and Covenant signed by James Craig on Ulster Day, 28 September 1912. (Somme Museum)

clothes as opposed to uniform; amongst those who signed were, Colour-Sergeant Young and Sergeants Hanna, Williamson, Eames and Homes.[50]

Participation in both the Covenant campaign and the actual signing was supported widely across all classes of Unionism; labourers, professionals, gentry, aristocracy and clergy.

It is often reported that some of those who signed the Covenant added to the mysticism of the event by signing in their own blood.[51] In Ryan's publication, 'Mutiny at the Curragh' he records that 20 men signed the Covenant in their blood which was a direct link to the tradition which had occurred at the signing of the Scottish Solemn League and Covenant.[52] Contrary to popular belief,

---

50 PRONI D1568/6/10/14.
51 Downing, Taylor. (ed), *The Troubles* (1990).
52 Ryan, AP, *Mutiny at the Curragh* (1956) and McNeill, Ronald, *Ulster's Stand for Union* (1922).

only one signature is believed to have been in blood, that of Frederick Hugh Crawford, who was to become the Ulster Volunteers' Director of Ordnance.[53] He claimed that he was following a family tradition; inasmuch as lineal ancestor had signed the Solemn League and Covenant in 1638.[54] However recent work undertaken by Public Records Office Northern Ireland (PRONI) via DNA testing has questioned this assertion. A scientific test carried out on the signature by Dr Alastair Ruffell, of Queen's University Belfast, has found no evidence to support the claim. "I'm 90% sure this isn't blood, but there is that margin of error, as this material has been uncontrolled for 100 years," said Dr Ruffell. The test involved a small quantity of a substance called Luminol which was injected into the signature. The substance is incredibly sensitive and can detect the tiniest traces, even in very old samples and is commonly used in forensic examinations and works by reacting with the iron in the blood's haemoglobin to produce a blue-white glow.[55]

As each person was given their own personal copy of the Covenant, it is possible that Fred Crawford later signed his own copy in his own blood, following a tradition started by one of his ancestors with the Scottish Covenant.[56]

One signature was signed in Irish, the script used being a stylised form and attributed to the address of 98 Fallswater Street, Belfast. The houses in Fallswater Street off the Falls Road, near Broadway were all odd numbers and only went up to 55.[57]

Fallswater Street
off Falls Road[58]
1. McMullen, Francis
3. Dickson, Wm. J., brick layer
5. Hegarty, Charles, clerk
7. McAlister, S., confectioner
9. Scott, Hugh, linen lapper
11. Buchanan, R., constable R.I.C.
13. Diamond, Mrs.
15. Lavery, Catherine
17. Lynch, J., litho-artist
19. Cunningham, Mary
21. Smylie, Jos., tile fitter
23. Diamond, R., brick layer
25. Ogilvie, Jas., motorman
27. Curran, James, joiner
29. Connell, C., constable R.I.C.
31. Russell, Ben., constable R.I.C.
33. Mull, Jos., sexton Broadway Presbyterian Church
35. Blood, Wm.
37. Sullivan, John
39. Duffy, Mrs.

---

53 <http://www.proni.gov.uk/index/search_the_archives/ulster_covenant/ulster_day.htm>.
54 McNeill, Ronald, *Ulster's Stand for Union* (1922).
55 'Signed in blood' claim challenged by scientific test <http://www.bbc.co.uk/news/uk-northern-ireland-politics-19747495> (Accessed 8 November 2014).
56 Ryan, AP, *Mutiny at the Curragh* (1956).
57 PRONI Family History Day – 4 August 2013.
58 1910 Belfast Street Directory – http://www.lennonwylie.co.uk/fcomplete1910.htm (Accessed 5 August 2013).

41. White, Mrs.
43. McDonnell, P., school officer
45. Toner, Richd., fitter
47. Gibson, Edw., finisher
49. Robinson, Samuel
51. Nesbitt, John, van driver
53. Ewins, Joseph, postman
55. Coulter, James, grocer

Fallswater Street
off Falls Road
St. Anne's Ward, South Par. Div.[59]
 1. McMullen, Francis
 3. Dickson, Wm. J., brick layer
 5, Hegarty, Charles, clerk
 7. McAlister, S., confectioner
 9. Scott, Hugh, linen lapper
11. Moles, Howard, tram conductor
13. Diamond, Geo., porter
15. Lavery, Mrs. Catherine
17. Lynch, J., litho artist
19. Cunningham, Mrs. Mary
21. Smylie, Jos., tile fitter
23. Liggett, T., mechanic
25. Ogilvie, Jas., motorman
27. Semple, W., constable R.I.C.
29. Derby, John, school teacher
31. McGahan, John, fitter
33. Taylor, David, signalman
35. Farrell, J., constable R.I.C.
37. Sullivan, John, painter
39. Fermin, Peter, R.I.C.
41. Beggins, M., constable R.I.C.
43. Tinsley, Mrs. Margaret
45. Toner, Richd., fitter
47. Gibson, Edw., finisher
49. Robinson, Saml., electrician
51. Nesbitt, John, van driver
53. Ewins, Joseph, postman
55. Meade, Mrs. Mary, grocer

It is also confirmed that a Catholic in County Fermanagh signed the Covenant.[60]
   To many, 28 September 1912 and the signing of the Covenant marked the start of the modern-day Ulster.

---

59 1918 Street Directory <http://www.lennonwylie.co.uk/fcomplete1918.htm> (Accessed 5 August 2013).
60 PRONI Family History Day – 4 August 2013.

Women's suffrage was also an increasing aspect of the political landscape in the United Kingdom with 1912 being a turning point for the Suffragettes movement. However at the last minute Asquith refused to sign a document which would have given women over 30 and either married to a property-owner or owning a property themselves the right to vote; afraid that women may vote against him in the next General Election.

This increase in political awareness was reflected in the turn out of Ulster women who signed their own Declaration in parallel to the Covenant; one such signatory was Jennie Rosenzweig, the daughter of Belfast's Rabbi.[61]

> Ulster Women's Declaration
> We whose names are underwritten, women of Ulster, and loyal subjects of our gracious King, being firmly persuaded that Home Rule would be disastrous to our country, desire to associate ourselves with the men of Ulster in their uncompromising opposition to the Home Rule Bill now before Parliament, whereby it is proposed to drive Ulster out of her cherished place in the Constitution of the United Kingdom and to place her under the domination and control of a Parliament in Ireland. Praying that from this calamity God will save Ireland, we hereto subscribe our names.[62]

Whilst the men made their way to the City Hall to sign, the women signed their Declaration at a number of venues around the city. One such location included Westbourne Presbyterian Church, where during the service 'an earnest appeal' was made to the women to sign with 1,000 women signing it at the close of the service.[63]

This was not limited to Ulster as the Ulster Women's Unionist Association opened offices in Westminster, Manchester, York, Liverpool, Edinburgh and Glasgow to facilitate their sisters in Great Britain who wished to sign the Declaration.[64]

Over the next two weeks further opportunities were provided for people to sign the Covenant and Declaration in Belfast and at almost 100 locations. On 4 October in the Old Town Hall, which was open each day from 9:00 a.m. to 8:00 p.m. until 14 October (except Sunday), it was reckoned that another 1,300 men had signed on that single day. By the end of the fortnight it was thought that around 130,000 men and women had signed their support in Belfast alone.

In total 471,414 signed; the Covenant by 237,368 men, and the Declaration by 234,046 women.

These figures indicate a high turn-out of women and are significant in light of the rising women's suffrage movement – 228,991 women signed in Ulster compared to 218,206 men, and 5,055 women signed elsewhere as against 19,162 men.[65, 66]

The Ulster Reform Club, originally the Reform Club, was opened on 1 January 1885, its membership largely drawn from the Presbyterian merchant class of Belfast which meant the ethos of the club reflected their Liberal Unionist outlook. One of the founders was Thomas Sinclair and Fred Crawford served as Club Secretary. Serving originally as the headquarters of the Liberal Party, members were required to hold liberal unionist views and most were opposed to Home Rule.[67] It

---

61 Belfast Covenant Trail – Ulster Historical Foundation.
62 Celebrating the Ulster Covenant – Bishop D Arcy of Down, Connor & Dromore.
63 Belfast Covenant Trail – Ulster Historical Foundation.
64 Ryan, AP, *Mutiny at the Curragh* (1956).
65 http://www.proni.gov.uk/index/search_the_archives/ulster_covenant/aftermath.htm.
66 Belfast Covenant Trail – Ulster Historical Foundation.
67 Leslie and Quail, *Old Belfast* (2013).

THE ULSTER COVENANT

Women signing the declaration at Raphoe. (PRONI D1422/B/13/32)

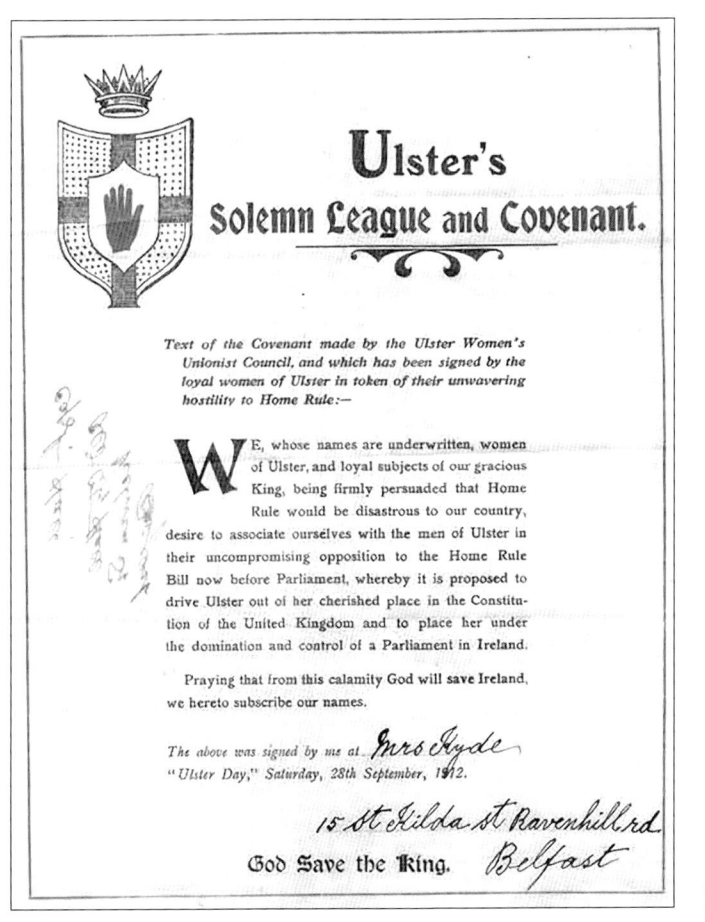

Ulster's Solemn League and Covenant.

Text of the Covenant made by the Ulster Women's Unionist Council, and which has been signed by the loyal women of Ulster in token of their unwavering hostility to Home Rule:—

WE, whose names are underwritten, women of Ulster, and loyal subjects of our gracious King, being firmly persuaded that Home Rule would be disastrous to our country, desire to associate ourselves with the men of Ulster in their uncompromising opposition to the Home Rule Bill now before Parliament, whereby it is proposed to drive Ulster out of her cherished place in the Constitution of the United Kingdom and to place her under the domination and control of a Parliament in Ireland.

Praying that from this calamity God will save Ireland, we hereto subscribe our names.

The above was signed by us at *Mrs Hyde*
"Ulster Day," Saturday, 28th September, 1912.

15 St Hilda St Ravenhill rd

God Save the King. *Belfast*

Ulster Covenant, Woman's Declaration. (Somme Museum)

The crowds of supporters gather outside the Ulster Club, Castle Junction, Belfast on the evening of Ulster Day to see Edward Carson on the balcony. (PRONI D961/3/003)

later merged with the Ulster Club in 1982 which had originally been founded in 1857 by landowning gentry desiring a place to meet, converse and dine when they were in Belfast.[68]

After signing the Covenant Edward Carson retired to the Reform Club from where he made his main speech from a first floor window of the Reform Club in Royal Avenue. Later in the afternoon he crossed to the Ulster Club, Castle Place, where he enjoyed dinner with the Lord Mayor and his lieutenants.

Following this he participated in more balcony speeches. Around 8:30 p.m. a band outside the Ulster Club struck up a number of patriotic tunes including "See the conquering hero come" as Carson left the Club and travelled the short distance to the docks by a man-drawn wagonette.[69] The journey to catch the steamer for Liverpool should have taken minutes, instead with crowds around 70,000 strong thronging Castle Place and calling on him not to leave, it took an hour.

---

68 The Ulster Reform Club <http://www.ulsterreformclub.com/our_club.html> (Accessed 28 January 2015).
69 Parkinson, Alan F, *Friends in High Places: Ulster's Resistance to Irish Home Rule, 1912-14* (2012).

As he crossed the gangway at Belfast under an immense Union flag there was a salute of revolver shots fired in his honour.[70] From the deck of the steamer he gave another speech illuminated by a spotlight[71] before the steamer *'Patriotic'* eventually set sail with Carson on board and the crowd stood singing 'Rule Britannia', 'Auld Lang Syne', and as it slowly made its way up Belfast Lough into the dark 'God Save the King'.[72, 73]

A bonfire built by Unionists on Whitehead promenade was lit as Carson sailed out of Belfast Lough as were other bonfires around Carrickfergus and along the County Down coast, such as the moat in Donaghadee, one of the Copeland islands and the beach at Holywood and Grey Point Fort. Rockets and fireworks were also discharged, including from Seacourt at Bangor and along with two huge tar barrels lit at Pickie Point and Luke's Point.[74]

When *'Patriotic'* came in sight, the local Orange band in Bangor struck up from the pier against a sky lit up from flares and rockets. In response the steamer sounded her siren as she moved up and out of the lough.[75]

The whole day in the city had passed off with one of the lowest instances of drunkenness and rowdiness for a Saturday, despite a few clashes between rival groups of supporters after a football match between Distillery and Belfast Celtic in West Belfast.[76]

On arriving in Liverpool and disembarking the next morning at the Prince's Landing Stage, Carson was greeted by a 150,000 strong crowd who sang 'O God our help in ages past'.[77] As he stepped ashore with FE Smith he said to Alderman Salvidge, "I shake hands with you across the sea." Carson continued; "I bring a message from the democracy of Belfast to the democracy of Liverpool. All that they ask is to be allowed to stay with you, and I do not think you will permit them to be driven out."[78]

The next night, Monday, Liverpool was host to a torchlight procession to Shiel Park, accompanied to bands and fireworks.[79] At the demonstration in the park, FE Smith who was on his home ground, publically assured Carson that if it came to a fight between Ulster and the Irish Nationalists that, "we will undertake to give you three ships that will take over 10,000 young men of Liverpool."[80]

From Liverpool Carson travelled to Glasgow to even more supporters, including one indoor meeting of over 6,000 before he headed home to Rottingdean where the whole village turned out to welcome him home.[81]

Despite the apparent universal support for Ulster Day not all sections of the Ulster population viewed the events with such excitement. *The Irish News* who described the Covenant as "a farce" organised by people "who insist upon referring to 'Ulster' as their own private cabbage garden,"[82] presented a contrary view:

---

70 Ryan, AP, *Mutiny at the Curragh* (1956).
71 Hyde, H Montgomery, *Carson* (1953).
72 <http://www.proni.gov.uk/index/search_the_archives/ulster_covenant/ulster_day.htm>.
73 Hyde, H Montgomery, *Carson* (1953).
74 Hume, David, *"For Ulster and Her Freedom": The story of the April 1914 gun-running* (1989).
75 Hume, David, *"For Ulster and Her Freedom": The story of the April 1914 gun-running* (1989).
76 Parkinson, Alan F, *Friends in High Places: Ulster's Resistance to Irish Home Rule, 1912-14* (2012).
77 <http://www.proni.gov.uk/index/search_the_archives/ulster_covenant/ulster_day.htm>
78 Hyde, H Montgomery, *Carson* (1953).
79 Hume, David, *"For Ulster and Her Freedom": The story of the April 1914 gun-running* (1989).
80 Hyde, H Montgomery, *Carson* (1953).
81 Ryan, AP, *Mutiny at the Curragh* (1956).
82 *Irish News* – 30 September 1912.

At last the curtain has been rung down on the Ulster Day farce, and we may hope for, at any rate, a temporary return to the civic pride on which Belfast prides itself so tremendously. The Carson circus having toured North East Ulster…gave its final and greatest performance entitled, 'Signing the Covenant', in Belfast on Saturday, and wound up its fantastic career in a paroxysm of flag waving and noise, emblematic of the meaningless nonsense of the whole grotesque scheme from start to finish …[83]

… The stage lost an actor manager when the law and politics claimed Sir Edward Carson. His unfailing instinct for theatrical effect was never better exemplified than on the Saturday in his 'state' progress from the Ulster Hall to the City Hall. Something was expected from him as the central figure in the 'historic' scene and he rose to the occasion splendidly. He evidently aimed at mimicking some great pose from history; he had set himself apart which was a mixture of Cromwell, King William III, with just a suggestion of King Charles I on the way to execution; but he rather spoiled the effect by introducing a swagger reminiscent of Sidney Carton's farewell. Bareheaded, slightly stooped, and with a well assumed expression of portentousness, he strode between the ranks of his bodyguard – partly Orangemen and Unionist Club members – past batteries of cameras and cinematograph machines, while behind him a standard bearer carried the suspiciously fresh looking orange flag, which is supposed to have waved above the battle smoke of the Boyne. In its present keeping it is not likely to be flourished in anything more exciting than a street riot or a shipyard pog …

Taking the day's proceedings altogether they were tame as a demonstration of enthusiasm and highly ludicrous as an indication of the 'grim and determined' spirit. The whole grotesque production has been a political failure, though a comic success, and now that it is past and gone, one wonders how many thousands the Ulster Unionists have spent on staging it …[84]

Whilst such opposition was to be expected from the more traditional Home Rule supporters, support against Home Rule from Ulster Protestants was not totally universal. Opposition could occasionally be found within the one family; in one family, some Presbyterians favoured Home Rule whilst Church of Ireland members were vehemently against it. Such was evident in the author's own family. Well known Ulster Protestants who continued to support Home Rule included the Rev JB Armour, Captain JR White, Sir Roger Casement, Alice Milligan, Lord Pirrie, Bulmer Hobson and Joseph Campbell.[85]

The direct impact of Covenant Day on the actual Home Rule campaign is unclear. Whilst it clearly galvanised and provided a visual show of the strength of opposition it also served to strengthen the determination to see it through and not give in to such overt shows of strength from Unionists. When the Westminster Parliament reconvened for its autumn session, Asquith tried to force the bill through the Commons but it was narrowly defeated on 11 November by 228 votes to 206. During the debate, Bonar Law again returned to his belief that Home Rule in its current guise had not been endorsed by the British electorate and that alone was justification for Ulster to resist it whilst Carson declared that the whole object of the bill was to get hold of Belfast and the northern counties to tax them.[86]

Lord Curzon used a complicated but effective metaphor to describe the situation:

---

83   <http://www.proni.gov.uk/index/search_the_archives/ulster_covenant/ulster_day.htm>.
84   <http://www.proni.gov.uk/index/search_the_archives/ulster_covenant/ulster_day.htm>.
85   Orr, Philip, *The Road to the Somme* (1987).
86   Hyde H Montgomery, *Carson* (1953).

You are compelling Ulster to divorce her present husband, to whom she is not unfaithful, and you compel her to marry someone else whom she cordially dislikes, with whom she does not want to live; and you do it because she happens to be rich, and because her new partner has a large and ravenous offspring to provide for. You are asking rather too much of human nature.[87]

In the House in December the debate rumbled on with Carson offering an olive branch by moving an amendment to the bill which would exclude "the province of Ulster" but assured the listeners that it would be opposed as much as ever. Bonar Law supported him suggesting the amendment would get rid of the resistance of Ulster but said that Ulster would prefer foreign to Nationalist rule. Churchill retorted, laughing at the "latest Tory threat – Ulster will secede to Germany."[88]

Redmond and his supporters however would not agree to it, claiming that "Ireland for us is one entity" and Asquith was equally clear in his rejection of Carson's motion.[89]

Ironically Sinn Fein, through their publication '*Irish Freedom*' appeared more far-sighted than the British Government, declaring that war between Germany and England was not only inevitable, but could be Ireland's opportunity. They also highlighted that Ulster's preparation for armed resistance was a glorious demonstration of Ireland's independent spirit and one worthy of imitation, hinting of what was to come not only in the immediate years but the following decades.[90]

When Carson again went to Homburg in August during the summer recess of the House of Commons, he was at a luncheon party along with Lord Acton and other English visitors. One of those present at the party was the German Emperor, Wilhelm II. The subsequent conversation between Carson and the Emperor caused speculation that the Ulster Volunteers were scheming

Carson's Orange Cat.

Sir Edward Carson has a Cat,
   It sits upon the fender
And every time a mouse it gets,
   It shouts out No Surrender.

He left it by the fireside,
   When'er he went away
On his return he always found,
   It singing "Dollys Brae."

The Traitors grew indignant,
   At hearing such a noise
But Carson made the Cat sit up,
   And sing the "Protestant Boys."

The Traitors then decided
   To hang it with a rope
But every time they tried the rope,
   It yelled H—ll Roast the Pope.

The people came from far and near,
   To hear the Pussy sing
Good old Britannia Rules the Waves,
   And may "God Save the King."

A few said what a pity,
   The Cat is such a fool
But Carson's Cat yelled out the more,
   We will not have Home Rule.

A postcard depicting the anti-Home Rule poem, "Carson's Orange Cat." (J Luke)

---

87 Shearman, Hugh, *Not an Inch: A Study of Northern Ireland and Lord Craigavon* (1942).
88 Ryan, AP, *Mutiny at the Curragh* (1956).
89 Hyde H Montgomery, *Carson* (1953).
90 Shearman, Hugh, *Not an Inch: A Study of Northern Ireland and Lord Craigavon* (1942).

A carved caricature of Kaiser Wilhelm II which originally hung in the bar of a public house in Belfast Docks. (Somme Museum)

A postcard depicting Kaiser Wilhelm II.

with Imperial Germany. The reality was that their conversation was purely social with Carson deftly keeping the subject away from political subjects, though the Emperor was particularly interested in gardens and specifically referred to a picture he had seen of Lady Londonderry's at Mount Stewart. The Emperor informed Carson that he would have liked to go to Ireland, but his grandmother, Queen Victoria would not let him, adding "Perhaps she thought I wanted to take the little place."[91]

This apparent admiration of the actions in Ulster was again evident from a southern Irish journalist after the inaugural meeting of the National Volunteers in November 1913:

> In present circumstances accursed be the soul of any Nationalist who would dream of firing a shot or drawing a sword against the Ulster Volunteers. We are willing to fight Ulster or to negotiate with her, but we will not fight her over the miserable shadow of autonomy, we will not fight her because she tells England to go to hell. The sheen of arms in Ulster was always the signal for the rest of Ireland … And Ireland in this generation has answered the call.[92]

With all classes prepared to unite behind the Orange banner and having the sympathy of elements of the British Army, the Tory party and the open support of prominent British public figures, this had all provided a sound basis for the mobilisation of Unionist opinion during Ulster Day and had also proven to observers that the Covenant organisers had the ability to mobilise huge numbers of people to support a popular cause. Whilst aristocrats were prominent, it was the Belfast businessmen and the Belfast Protestant workers who were the core and most devoted followers. This solidarity between the various classes and social strata of Ulster Protestantism against what was perceived as a common threat was the secret of its strength.

At the end of January 1913 a special Commission, which had been established in Ulster to prepare the necessary scheme to introduce a provisional government, presented its draft report. It provided for the business of government in Ulster to be carried out by a central authority if Home Rule ever became law. The list of men who were prepared to serve in this provisional government included; the Archbishop of Armagh, the Moderator of the General Assembly of the Presbyterian Church in Ireland, legal luminaries and high-ranking naval and military officers. The draft ordinance which was to bring this defiant parliament into force began, "It is Hereby enacted by the Central Authority in the name of the King's Most Excellent Majesty that …"[93]

The Ulster Provisional Government was to comprise a number of separate boards; Military Council, Supply Board, Transport Board, Railway Board, Medical Board, Volunteer Advisory Board and Personnel Board, which appear to have met irregularly.[94]

The Ulster Defence Fund was established in Sir Edward Carson's name with financial contributions being made from both across Ireland and from wealthy supporters and benefactors in England; because as the crisis deepened the appeal for subscriptions increased. Much of the money raised was used to subsidise political literature and underpin major events such as the Balmoral demonstration and the Covenant fortnight.[95]

Towards the end of 1912 the Standing Committee of the Ulster Unionist Council decided that the disparate volunteer groups which were often linked with Orange Lodges should be brought together under a coordinated command structure. In January 1913 this unified concept was announced at the annual meeting of the Ulster Unionist Council, to be one cohesive organisation

---

91 Hyde H Montgomery, *Carson* (1953).
92 Shearman, Hugh, *Not an Inch: A Study of Northern Ireland and Lord Craigavon* (1942).
93 Ryan, AP, *Mutiny at the Curragh* (1956).
94 *Northern Whig* – 25/9/1913.
95 Parkinson, Alan F, *Friends in High Places: Ulster's Resistance to Irish Home Rule, 1912-14* (2012).

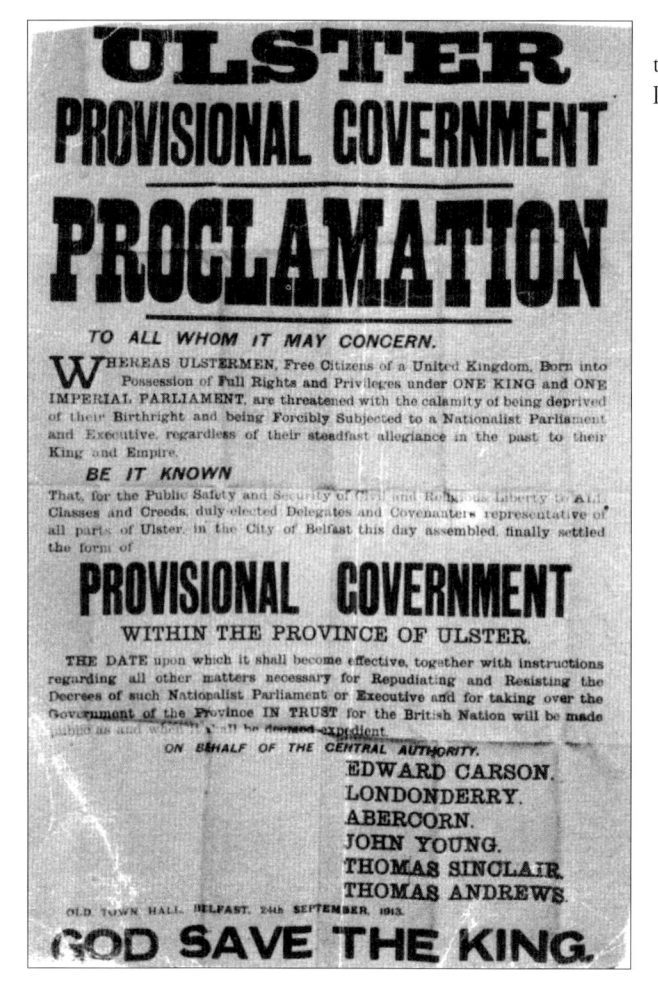

Proclamation declaring the creation of the Ulster Provisional Government. (Somme Museum)

under a unified command structure. The rationale behind the Ulster Unionist Council taking this step as opposed to the Grand Orange Lodge of Ireland was that whereas all Orangemen were Unionists, not all Unionists were Orangemen. The unified organisation was to be named the Ulster Volunteer Force and recruitment was opened to those aged between 17 and 65 who had signed the Covenant and was limited to 100,000 men.

As part of this process it appears that a number of local leaders were identified and approached by the Ulster Unionist Council asking them

To enrol a force of men for self-preservation and mutual protection of all Loyalists in and adjoining their own Districts and generally to preserve the Peace ... To only enrol persons who from personal knowledge, or after careful enquiry, are capable and willing to perform the duties above mentioned and:

1. are between the ages of 18 and 60.
2. have signed the Covenant.
3. will sign a Declaration upon volunteering.[96]

---

96 Bowman, Timothy, *Carson's Army: Ulster Volunteer Force, 1910-22* (2007).

Members of Ballynafeigh and Newtownbreda Unionist Club practising semaphore.
(PRONI INF7A/2/21)

This in turn led to local Ulster gentry often taking the lead in organising the Volunteers who, despite Westminster depriving them of many of their privileges in the nineteenth century, regarded the preservation of the Union as vital to protecting their remaining power and position.

Lord Castlereagh, a Member of Parliament and rarely in Ulster, was the commanding officer not only of the Mountstewart estate contingent of the UVF, but also the Newtownards Battalions and the entire North Belfast Regiment.[97]

James Colville from north Belfast joined the UVF when he was about 16 years old and learnt to drill at the old skating rink down off Legan Street, with their training in rifle drill being provided by Captain Phill and Jack Wright, a former 'Rifles' man who used to play for Cliftonville.[98]

Interestingly a reference to a special UVF Form, of which no complete copy still exists, was designed for those individuals 'not eligible' to sign the Covenant, opening the possibility for some Catholic membership in the force;[99] in Lisburn four Catholics from the same family joined the UVF with three subsequently converting to Anglicanism.[100]

The instructions from the UUC appear to have been interpreted depending on local circumstances. In County Down, with a large Unionist majority, it appears that the county committee felt that 'only those who had drilled or were willing to drill and to bear arms should be enrolled';

---

97 Bowman, Timothy, *Carson's Army: Ulster Volunteer Force, 1910-22* (2007).
98 James Colville, DOB 25/08/1897, 2010/113(e), DVD conversion from VHS tape 2011-07-13 – Somme Museum.
99 PRONI D1238/178 – UVF Order 74, 18/7/1914.
100 Bowman, Timothy, *Carson's Army: Ulster Volunteer Force, 1910-22* (2007).

UVF recruitment form in respect of William Alex Little, Ballagh, Newtwownbutler, County Fermanagh. (Somme Museum)

whereas in those parts of Ulster such as County Tyrone where Unionists were a minority all male Protestants over 14 years of age were actively conscripted.[101]

The estates of many of the landed gentry or the local 'big houses' were used as training locations; Baronscourt, the Duke of Abercorn's estate in County Tyrone, Shane's Castle, Lord O'Neill's estate in Country Antrim and Tobar Mhuire, the Cleland estate at Crossgar, County Down.[102]

On his Mountstewart estate, Lord Castlereagh, a former captain in the Horse Guards and MP for Maidstone, drilled his family's tenants and estate workers.[103]

---

101 Bowman, Timothy, *Carson's Army: Ulster Volunteer Force, 1910-22* (2007).
102 Orr, Philip, *The Road to the Somme* (1987).
103 Bowman, Timothy, *Carson's Army: Ulster Volunteer Force, 1910-22* (2007).

Other estates provided storage as well as training facilities. Castle Hume, County Fermanagh, on the shores of Lough Erne, stored arms for the Volunteers and witnessed not just the infantry drills of the volunteers but also of the cavalry in the guise of the 'Enniskillen Horse' raised by the newspaper owner WC Trimble.[104]

Other locations provided to the Volunteers included the courtyard of Killyleagh Castle and Donard Park, Newcastle both in County Down.

However in Belfast other solutions were found. In May 1913 in East Belfast Sir Edward Carson officially opened a drill hall especially built for the Ulster Volunteers. It was located behind the Willowfield Unionist Hall on the Woodstock Road. It incorporated a firing range and was later converted into a cinema.[105]

It cannot be assumed that all landowners or gentry either took the lead or indeed were actively involved with the volunteers. However where they were involved it helped in "allaying any misgivings" the Volunteers held in participating.[106] In Florencecourt, County Fermanagh, the local Unionist Club complained that Lord Cole did not take more interest in their drilling. The South Down Unionist Clubs in August 1913 held an inspection in a field near to Murlough House, home of the Marquess of Downshire, who spent most of the time in England and refused to become involved in the force.[107]

There were also examples of Ulster industrialists and businessmen effectively forming volunteer detachments from their own workers. For example Sion Mills, County Tyrone, owned by EC Herdman provided the employment for the majority in the locality and he formed the local Protestant population into his own UVF unit. A similar story was evident in Comber, County Down, where John M Andrews, owner of the local distillery and linen mill self-styled himself 'Captain', with no previous rank whatsoever in the British Army, and organised his volunteer company into four sections with a reserve of 64 men and 23 men on the 'night work section', again suggesting they were drawn from his workforce.

Andrews's son designed the RMS Titanic and died on her ill-fated maiden voyage.

Men of the 4th (Portadown) Battalion, Armagh Regiment, Ulster Volunteer Force. (H Laverty)

---

104 Orr, Philip, *The Road to the Somme* (1987).
105 From the shipyard to the Somme – 36th Ulster Division Memorial Association – 2013.
106 Parkinson, Alan F, *Friends in High Places: Ulster's Resistance to Irish Home Rule, 1912-14* (2012).
107 Bowman, Timothy, *Carson's Army: Ulster Volunteer Force, 1910-22* (2007).

Ulster Volunteers, County Down. (Somme Museum)

However this approach should also be viewed from the businessman's perspective. J Milne Barbour, owner of the linen firm at Hilden close to Lisburn realised that with a number of his workers enlisted and involved with the UVF, including departments such as the Boiler House and Engine Drivers, that if there was an extensive mobilisation of the force it could have a very significant impact on the industry, which he quite rightly noted "is just as important from a political standpoint as for any commercial reason."[108]

The age range of the volunteers enlisting was wide with the upper limited of 65 years often ignored or lied about. Hugh Stewart from Lisburn attempted to join the platoon which his father commanded, but aged 16 years he was refused, however he promptly went and joined another platoon, claiming he was aged 17.[109]

The men of villages and townlands banded together to form platoons or companies depending on the number of available volunteers. According to the scheme detailed on the papers of Frank Hall, Military Secretary of the UVF,[110] they were then organised on a county basis into Divisions with the four Belfast parliamentary constituencies and Londonderry City being treated the same as counties, providing fourteen Divisions. Each Division was sub-divided into Regiments which in turn were sub-divided into Battalions, the number of each determined by the strength of volunteers in each county area or equivalent.

---

108 Bowman, Timothy, *Carson's Army: Ulster Volunteer Force, 1910-22* (2007).
109 Orr, Philip, *The Road to the Somme* (1987).
110 Ulster Volunteers, January 1913 – Ulster-Scots Community Network <http://www.ulster-scots.com/uploads/901740969819.PDF> (Accessed 5 August 2013).

The following example illustrates the formation of the Fermanagh Regiment, Ulster Volunteers:

Fermanagh Regiment – Viscount Crighton DSO[111]
1st Batt Fermanagh Regt – Major CC D'Arcy Irvine
    Ballinamallard
    Irvinestown
    Kesh
    Pettigo
    Belleek

2nd Batt Fermanagh Regt – Earl of Lanesborough
    Maguiresbridge
    Lisnaskea
    Newtownbutler

3rd Batt Fermanagh Regt – Mr Charles F Falls
    Enniskillen
    Lisbellaw
    Tempo
    Brookeborough
    Derrygonnelly

A detachment of the Ulster Volunteer Force drilling outside, Necarne Castle, formerly known as Castle Irvine, in County Fermanagh, July 1913. (*Belfast Telegraph*)

---

111 Canning, WJ, *Ballyshannon, Belcoo, Bertincourt* (1996).

Cyril Falls, the later chronicler of the 36th (Ulster) Division on the Western Front, was the son of an Enniskillen Solicitor who was commander of the 3rd Battalion, Fermanagh Regiment, Ulster Volunteer Force, and was employed in the Foreign Office as a clerk during the Third Home Rule Crisis.[112]

The Fermanagh Regiment, 3rd Battalion, had rifle ranges at Topped Mountain and Florencecourt and each man had to pass his musketry test and proficiency test in drill before he could be issued with the bronze UVF badge with the motto "For God and Ulster" which was to be worn on their coat.[113] Other badges available to the Force included a large one which could be screwed onto the bonnet of a motor car.[114]

Those members of the Ulster Signalling & Despatch Riding Corps and the Motor Car Corps were issued with badges bearing the letters "SD" and "MC" respectively which were issued from the respective Corps, the individuals would not receive badges from their respective Counties; if they had already been issued other badges these were to be returned and they would be removed from the County Enrolment Books, with the Corps they belonged to being noted in the remarks column. This also reflected that fact the no-one in the greater Belfast area could have their motor car enrolled in both their local Battalion and County whilst being on the list for use within the Headquarters Motor Car Corps.[115]

Brass car badge for the UVF Motor Car Corps, 1912. (Royal Ulster Rifles Museum)

The Ulster Volunteer Force for uncertain reasons adopted their own rank structure as opposed to that used in the British Army; Divisional, Regimental, Battalion, Company, Half Company, Section Commanders, Squad Leaders, Second in Command, Adjutant, Quarter-Master, Sergeant-Major and Quarter-Master Sergeant.[116] However this deviation from 'the norm' may not have been universally popular as UVF Headquarters had to reprimand some units in February 1914, reminding them of the appropriate designations which should be adopted and used.[117]

Orders issued by Lieutenant-Colonel George CC Young on 30 September 1913 informed the volunteers in North Antrim of the decision of the County Antrim Committee that the County was now to be divided into Regimental areas.[118] The following shows how such arrangements were to happen in practice.

The area in which your locality is, is called:

---

112 Ulster Volunteer Force, January 1913 – Ulster-Scots Community Network – <http://www.ulster-scots.com/uploads/901740969819.PDF> (Accessed 5 August 2013).
113 Canning, WJ, *Ballyshannon, Belcoo, Bertincourt* (1996).
114 Ingram, Rev Brett, *Covenant and Challenge* (1989).
115 UVF Order 14, 1914 – Somme Museum.
116 PRONI D.1238/101 – UVF Order 10, 7/2/1914.
117 UVF Order 10, 1914 – Somme Museum.
118 Ulster Volunteer Force – Lieut-Col Young 30 September 1913.

THE FIRST BATTALION OF NORTH ANTRIM REGIMENT" (or The Ballymena Battalion), with its headquarters in Ballymena.

This Battalion, so far has been divided into the following Companies:-
A Company in Ballymena
B Company in Ballymena
C Company in Harryville (including localities of Ballymarlow, Slatt, Tullygarley, etc.)
D Company – The Braid (including Raceview, Buckna and Skerry)
E Company – Cullybackey. Formed of two District Half Companies:-
   1. Cullybackey
   2. Hilmount
F Company – Formed by two District Half Companies:-
   1. Glenwherry
   2. Craigwarren
G Company – Formed by the following Units:
   Ahogill and Portglenone; Galgorm and Gravehill

It is now necessary for each locality leader to get his men to elect their own Company Commander, or in the case of separate Half-companies, their Half Company Commanders (i.e. Sub-Commanders).

The Scheme is as under:

Each 12 men form a Squad, one to be Squad Leader. 2 squads form 1 Section – 24 men, with one Section Leader in addition to the 24 men. 2 Sections make a Half Company – 48 men + 2 Section Leaders – 50 men, with a Half Company Commander in command, called a Sub Commander. 2 Half Companies – Company.

Company will therefore consist of:

Commander	1	} Officers
Sub Commanders	2	
Section Leaders	4	NCOs
Men, including Squad Leaders	96	
Total	103	

But it is fully realised that this is impossible all at one, the main point is to get Company Commanders, Half Company Commanders (i.e. Sub Commanders), and Section Leaders chosen as quickly as possible; it is also realised that the size of Companies must of course vary according to numbers of serviceable men enrolled in each locality. Please have this carried out as quickly as possible, and let me know Names of Officers with their full addresses, and Regimental Numbers, as soon as appointed.

BY ORDER
GEORGE C C YOUNG
Lieutenant Colonel
Commanding 1st Battalion North Antrim Regiment
Ballymena
September 30 1913

Sir Edward Carson inspecting the Ulster Volunteers, 1913. (*Belfast Telegraph*)

The Belfast UVF District was commanded by a retired colonel, Colonel Couchman, who also received pay from UVF funds with a staff officer to assist him as well as a retired colour-sergeant for his office and four retired regular officers, one of who was FP Crozier.[119] Percy Crozier was described by Myles Dungan in his *Irish Voices from the Great War*, as "A small pudgy figure with a thin wispy moustache … in many respects, the epitome of the cartoon-British officer class."[120]

The membership of the Belfast regiments appears to have differed somewhat from regiment to regiment. *The Times'* military correspondent, Charles à Court Repington described the North Belfast Regiment as being recruited

Field telephones were part of the modern equipment utilised by the Ulster Volunteers. Captain Crozier using the field telephone at Craigavon House. (Somme Museum)

---

119 Crozier, Brig-Gen FP CB, CMG, DSO, *Ireland for Ever* (1932).
120 Dungan, Myles, *Irish Voices from the Great War* (1998).

from a district "mainly occupied by artisans of the skilled type – shipwrights, engineers, Queen's Island workers, the very strongest of Belfast Unionists. Other classes too must be represented in the regiment for a certain part of North Belfast is purely suburban."[121, 122] This compares to Lilian Spender's description of the West Belfast Regiment as:

> the poorest of all, I mean its men are of a lower class than the others, as they are all in Devlin's constituency, which is the slummiest in the city. Many of the men looked just the type you see loafing about public houses, and were no better dressed, but they marched every bit as well as the others, and looked just as keen and determined.[123]

The YCV which was tied to geographical parts of the city was however seen as "a body of young businessmen", which may have deprived a number of the other Belfast units of the middle-class membership which contributed to the officer shortage evident in parts of the city.[124]

Command of the West Belfast Regiment was given to Colonel JH Patterson, born in Forgney, County Longford, he had enlisted in the 3rd Dragoon Guards in 1885, leaving the army as a sergeant in 1897. He rejoined the army at the outbreak of the South African War, joining the 76th Company, Imperial Yeomanry, as a second Lieutenant. During the war he was awarded the DSO and by January 1902 had achieved the rank of Lieutenant-Colonel. He was famous at the time as the author of *Man-eaters of Tsavo* which recounted his stalking and killing two lions which were attacking the men building the Mombasa to Uganda railway line in 1898 when he was commissioned by the British East Africa Company to protect the undertaking.[125, 126]

Young Citizen Volunteers (YCV) Uniform Button. (Somme Museum)

From 1907 to 1909 he was Chief Game Warden in the East Africa Protectorate, however during this time he was forced to leave the army due to questions regarding the death of a fellow British Army officer on a hunting safari. The Honourable Audley Blyth, the son of Lord Blyth and one of the heirs to the Gilbey liquor fortune, had died as a result of a gunshot wound (possible suicide – exact circumstances unknown). Witnesses confirmed that Patterson was not in Blyth's tent at the time of the shot, and it was reported that Blyth's wife who was with him at the time was reported as running (screaming) from the tent immediately after the shooting. However Patterson had Blyth buried in the wilderness and then to the surprise of everyone, insisted on

---

121 Bowman, Timothy, *Carson's Army: Ulster Volunteer Force, 1910-22* (2007).
122 *The Times* – 16/4/1914.
123 Bowman, Timothy, *Carson's Army: Ulster Volunteer Force, 1910-22* (2007) and PRONI D1633/2/19 – Lilian Spender Diary – 6/5/1914.
124 Bowman, Timothy, *Carson's Army: Ulster Volunteer Force, 1910-22* (2007).
125 Bowman, Timothy, *Carson's Army: Ulster Volunteer Force, 1910-22* (2007).
126 <http://www.africahunting.com/threads/john-henry-patterson-1867-1947.2822/> Africa Hunting – (Accessed 26/5/2014).

continuing the expedition instead of returning to the nearest post to report the incident. Shortly afterward, Patterson returned to England with Mrs. Blyth amid rumours of murder and an affair, and although he was never officially charged or censured, this incident would follow him for years afterward, most notably in the film *The Macomber Affair* (1947) which was based on Ernest Hemingway's adaptation of the incident.[127]

He appears to have continued with African engineering projects and safaris until returning to Britain in 1913 to take up his command in the Ulster Volunteer Force. Although a Protestant, he would later become a Zionist and form the Zionist Mule Corps which he commanded at Gallipoli and later the Jewish Battalion of the Royal Fusiliers in the Middle East.[128]

With regards recruitment to the Ulster Volunteers, the eastern areas of Ulster witnessed improved recruitment compared to those in the west. The Donegal County Inspector of the Royal Irish Constabulary reported to Dublin Castle in July 1913 that, whilst the majority of Protestants in the county were very bitter against Home Rule, he doubted whether they would do much to prevent its introduction such was the genuine friendly feelings between the Roman Catholics and Protestants.[129]

This may have been influenced by the Presbyterians of the fertile farmland of the north-east of County Donegal resenting the prominent position of the Church of Ireland, clergy and landlords. This, combined with a reluctance of Protestant professional and business families to jeopardise their business through full support of the Ulster Volunteers, meant that by the summer of 1914 the Donegal UVF had only attracted a minority of the adult Protestant males.

Men of the 4th (Portadown) Battalion, Armagh Regiment, Ulster Volunteer Force on parade. Believed to be at Carrickblacker House prior to rifle practice at Tandragee in the summer of 1914, (H Laverty)

---

127 <http://www.africahunting.com/threads/john-henry-patterson-1867-1947.2822/> Africa Hunting – (Accessed 26/5/2014).
128 Bowman, Timothy, *Carson's Army: Ulster Volunteer Force, 1910-22* (2007).
129 PRONI D1327/4/3.

A Ulster Volunteer Force detachment believed to be parading at Walkers factory, Newtownards. (Somme Museum: 1994-282)

In July 1913, the Belfast Commissioner of the Royal Irish Constabulary reported to Dublin Castle that between the Orange Order and the Unionist Clubs approximately 20,000 men had been drilled in Belfast.

> To sum up the situation you have in Belfast some 300,000 Protestants and 100,000 Catholics – the latter mainly dependant on the former for livelihood – of the Protestant population all are bitterly opposed to Home Rule ... I am convinced that there will be serious loss of life and wholesale destruction of property in Belfast to the passing of the Home Rule Bill.

The County Inspector, Royal Irish Constabulary in Antrim was convinced of the seriousness of the Ulster Volunteers reporting, "There is no doubt that the cry of 'bluff' must be laid aside." The government however continued to be not so convinced.[130]

Recruitment into the Ulster Volunteers in the North Down area was such that in July 1913 Sir Edward Carson was able to review 2,000 volunteers from Bangor, Conlig, Carrowdore, Comber, Donaghadee and Newtownards, just outside Bangor at Six Roads Ends; at the house of Betsy Gray, of 1798 Rebellion fame.[131] A similar event for contingents from all around Ballymena was organised and inspected by Carson on Friday, 18 July 1913, at the Agricultural Show Grounds, Ballymena. The orders called for them to have formed up in the field in front of Ballymena Castle at 3:30 p.m. promptly from their previously assigned muster points. A mounted guard of honour was provided by the Ballymena horse under the command of Captain the Hon, A O'Neill, MP, having had their first drill for the event seven days earlier. From the Castle the Battalion was to

---

130 Lewis, Geoffrey, *Carson: The man who divided Ireland* (2006).
131 *Belfast Evening Telegraph* – 25/7/1913.

move off at 4:45 p.m. and march via Warden Street to the Show Grounds, accompanied by two flute bands; White's Conquerors Flute Band and Juvenile Band. The men were instructed that as far as possible all were to wear dark clothes and hard bowler hats.[132]

With regards the organisation of the Ulster Volunteers each County/Division was administered and overseen by a committee. The composition of the County Down Committee in December 1912 gives an illustration of the membership of the different county committees; the chairman was Lord Dunleath, five other individuals were landowners or 'gentlemen', a Presbyterian Minister, the secretary Charles Murland was a flax spinner, a manufacturer, a baker, a contractor and a medical practitioner. For an Edwardian 'Army' it was strangely democratic with gentry in the ranks willingly accepting orders from others considered of lower social standing such as tenants and employees. This concept was clearly articulated by Lord Dunseath when he wrote to Carson in March 1915 describing the UVF as 'a democratic army'. Others have described it as probably the only truly 'citizen' army in the British Isles up to that time.

This was clearly displayed in the Seaforde Company in County Down. Major William George Forde JP, DL, the local major landowner and his 16 year old son were within its ranks, whilst the Company was commanded by Alexander McMeekin, the family's coachman.[133] In fact McMeekin was one of the first to enrol in the Seaforde UVF on 20 January 1913, whilst Major Forde only enlisted 27 September 1913, after his coachman, butler and gamekeeper.[134]

The neighbouring village of Clough was one of first locations visited by Carson to inspect the local Ulster Volunteer Force detachment.[135]

This democratic concept permeated in theory at least down the ranks with squads of 12 men electing a squad leader, a section leader for each two squads and again electing a half company commander for each two sections.[136]

In reality the elections or nominations for command could depend on the location and personalities involved. In the Tyrone Regiment of the Ulster Volunteer Force they were informed that men with previous military experience who were instructors should not be elected as Section Commanders, but perhaps Company Commanders, though it was felt that they would be most valuable in the role of Colour Sergeants.[137, 138]

The continuing reluctance of some individuals to join the Ulster Volunteer Force or for other groups to give up their independence may have been reduced when both Carson and Colonel RW Wallace urged all Orange Lodges and Unionist Clubs to amalgamate into the UVF.[139]

At the peak of the anti-Home Rule campaign 1,438 Ulster Unionists from East Down had mobilised into the UVF compared to the total Unionist vote recorded in 1918, 6,007. Until the outbreak of the First World War there was evidence of Unionists, both men and women, being active anti-Home Rulers although by mid-1915 police intelligence noted a significant reduction of UVF exercises and by 1916 it was reported that they were inactive,[140] which was also a reflection of the creation of the Ulster Division and many others being recalled to the Colours.

---

132 UVF Orders – Somme Museum.
133 Ulster Volunteers, January 1913 – Ulster-Scots Community Network <http://www.ulster-scots.com/uploads/901740969819.PDF> (Accessed 5 August 2013).
134 Bowman, Timothy, *Carson's Army: Ulster Volunteer Force, 1910-22* (2007).
135 *Northern Whig* – 16/7/1913.
136 Bowman, Timothy, *Carson's Army: Ulster Volunteer Force, 1910-22* (2007).
137 Bowman, Timothy, *Carson's Army: Ulster Volunteer Force, 1910-22* (2007).
138 Ulster Volunteers, January 1913 – Ulster-Scots Community Network <http://www.ulster-scots.com/uploads/901740969819.PDF – 5 August 2013.
139 Bowman, Timothy, *Carson's Army: Ulster Volunteer Force, 1910-22* (2007).
140 Fitzpatrick, D (ed), *Ireland and the First World War* (1988).

Ulster Volunteers receive instruction in the use of firearms. (Somme Museum)

In Newtownbutler, County Fermanagh, Viscount Crichton, eldest son and heir of the Earl of Erne attended drilling in the village though not in a leadership position. Perhaps his lack of direct involvement was to protect his position as equerry to the King and his commission in the Royal Horse Guards.[141]

Despite reluctance in some quarters the figures from the Royal Irish Constabulary's monthly intelligence reports reported that recruitment was vigorous:

April 1913	41,000
September 1913	56,651
November 1913	76,757
January 1914	80,000

Against these figures the targets set by the Ulster Unionist Council were probably more or less achieved, with Belfast raising 30,000 volunteers, Antrim and Down, 11,000 each and Cavan and Monaghan raising 2,000 each.[142]

Chief Secretary Birrell noted on a written memorandum that statistics claiming that there were 100,000 Ulster Volunteers in April 1913 were exaggerated, which appears supported by Royal Irish

---

141 Ulster Volunteers, January 1913 – Ulster-Scots Community Network <http://www.ulster-scots.com/uploads/901740969819.PDF> (Accessed 5 August 2013).
142 Ulster Volunteers, January 1913 – Ulster-Scots Community Network <http://www.ulster-scots.com/uploads/901740969819.PDF> (Accessed 5 August 2013).

Members of the North Down Volunteers, Ulster Volunteer Force at camp in 1914. (Somme Museum)

Constabulary figures, however he also concluded his remarks with there is "little evidence to show that the movement has taken any real hold, except in Belfast itself, among the Presbyterians."[143]

The appeal of the UVF for many young men and some boys was no doubt the attraction of carrying rifles and performing military exercise which came as a thrill and a welcome distraction to the reality of their world, particularly for some of those in Belfast. In the city a 'half-time' system existed whereby boys from the age of 12 onwards went to work in the flax mills on alternative days, working from 6:00 a.m. to 6:00 p.m. and going to school on the other days.[144] For many others their family home life was not always stable or supportive so the camaraderie of the Force was again welcome. To those who had been involved in the Boys Brigade and the Church Lads Brigade with its emphasises on drill along with its uniform, flutes and drums, the Ulster Volunteer Force often appeared to be a logical progression.

Jack Christie later recalled that he was only 14 when he joined the UVF, drilling at the time as a member of the Church Lads Brigade belonging to St. Luke's Company in Northumberland Street. Whilst there he did courses in First Aid and became a First Aid man in the UVF, as he said, "because I could put on a bandage or make a sling and things like that." He also recalled that his detachment had a full uniform.[145]

To some families however the involvement of their young men was not always welcomed. Alexander Martin, a local blacksmith in Crossgar, County Down was supported in the family business by his eldest son, William. However his younger son, John, a bicycle mechanic, joined

---

143 Muenger, Elizabeth A, *The British Military Dilemma in Ireland: Occupation Politics 1886-1914* (1991).
144 Orr, Philip, *The Road to the Somme* (1987).
145 Jack Christie, WW1 Interview 096 – Somme Museum.

Ulster Volunteers undertaking training at Clandeboye. (Somme Museum)

the Volunteers along with his friend Hugh James Adams, keeping his membership secret from his mother who was worried at the prospect of her son carrying arms.[146]

Many of the Ulster Volunteers instructors were ex-British Army non-commissioned officers who had served during the South African War.[147] No doubt many of the military stories and experiences of these men would have appealed to the eager young recruits.

The funding to enable the raising of the Ulster Volunteer Force and to supply the necessary equipment came from a range of sources such as wealthy, sympathetic individuals like the gentry and businessmen, through to more ingenious systems such as a method used in Waringstown area whereby people would pay for poems to be written about themselves by local rhymesters. It was reported that one girl with two brothers in the UVF was reputed to have spent five shillings for one such poem, a considerable sum considering she only received £14 a year in wages.[148] Other methods to raise a few shillings included fund raising suppers and ceilidhs held either in local halls or neighbouring houses.

Funds also came in the form of generous donations from wealthy supporters in Britain including Waldorf Astor, Lord Rothschild, the Duke of Bedford and Rudyard Kipling; Astor and Kipling offered in the region of £30,000, a substantial sum in 1914, whilst Lords Rothschild and Iveagh offered £10,000. Kipling's support to the Ulster cause was linked to his strong advocacy of Imperialism, seeing the Ulster situation as an indication not only for Ireland, but for the United Kingdom and also the security of the British Empire.[149]

In March 1913, Charles Craig, MP for South Antrim, said publically that "ten thousand pounds spent on rifles would be a thousand times stronger than the same amount spent on meetings, speeches and pamphlets."; a sentiment which again suggested that Ulster should resist

---

146 Orr, Philip, *The Road to the Somme* (1987).
147 Metcalfe, Nick, *Blacker's Boys* (2012).
148 Orr, Philip, *The Road to the Somme* (1987).
149 Parkinson, Alan F, *Friends in High Places: Ulster's Resistance to Irish Home Rule, 1912-14* (2012).

the introduction of Home Rule by force of arms.¹⁵⁰

As recruitment increased and support for the Ulster Volunteers grew the Irish Nationalists were particularly irritated by one particular line of support from within the Conservative connection. The Duke of Norfolk, the leader of the British Roman Catholic nobility, associated himself with the Ulster cause.¹⁵¹

Whilst men came forward to join the ranks of the various regiments the Ulster Women's Unionist Council recruited 40,000 women for nursing and other duties. Simultaneously to William Lenox-Conyngham of Springhill House, near Moneymore, County Londonderry, raising two battalions of the UVFs South Derry Regiment, his wife who was involved with the UVF's Nursing Corps arranged for eleven hospitals in the area.¹⁵²

Between October 1913 and May 1914 the St John's Ambulance Association organised 141 first aid classes and the further 64 nursing classes, all of but six related to UVF activities, attended by just under 6,800 women.¹⁵³

Meanwhile in Westminster the Unionists from various strata continued to put up fierce opposition to each stage of the Home Rule Bill such that the third reading was not passed by the House of Commons until 16 January 1913 with a majority of 110 votes.¹⁵⁴

Anti-Home Rule postcard depicting Charles C Craig, MP. (J Luke)

In the streets outside there were no serious clashes between the jubilant Irish Nationalists and the protesting Ulster Unionists however scuffles were reported a couple of hundred yards away outside the Constitutional Club in Whitehall where hundreds of unionists had gathered. Meanwhile in Belfast, as word reached the streets, Nationalists paraded in the streets of Nationalist areas whilst unionist staged 'orderly' protests which included burning copies of the bill.¹⁵⁵

However, like its predecessor it was also rejected by the House of Lords by 326 votes to 69. Though on this occasion as a result of the terms of the 1911 Parliament Act the Lords only had a veto for two years before the bill would automatically become law, at the end of 1914. Time was now against the Unionists.

---

150 *Battle Lines: Journal of The Somme Association* – Capt. Charles Curtis Craig MP – Jackie McQuiston
151 Shearman, Hugh, *Not an Inch: A Study of Northern Ireland and Lord Craigavon* (1942).
152 Orr, Philip, *The Road to the Somme* (1987).
153 Ulster Volunteers, January 1913 – Ulster-Scots Community Network <http://www.ulster-scots.com/uploads/901740969819.PDF> (Accessed 5 August 2013).
154 Parkinson, Alan F, *Friends in High Places: Ulster's Resistance to Irish Home Rule, 1912-14* (2012).
155 Parkinson, Alan F, *Friends in High Places: Ulster's Resistance to Irish Home Rule, 1912-14* (2012).

Sir Edward Carson inspecting UVF nurses in full uniform in 1912. The medical corps was excellently provided for, with the latest equipment and ambulances. (Somme Museum)

Ulster under the leadership of Edward Carson and with the open support of the Tory party under Bonar Law made it very clear it would be opposing any attempt to set up a Home Rule parliament in Ireland.

Despite majority support in southern Ireland the delay in implementing Home Rule played into the hands of a small number of extremists. James Connolly, a revolutionary socialist, had already founded the Irish Citizen Army during the Dublin strike and lock-out in October 1913. The Irish Republican Brotherhood (the Fenians) sponsored the formation of the Irish Volunteers, directly in opposition to the Ulster Volunteers. Amongst the hundreds of recruits who came forward were poet Patrick Pearse and Eoin O'Neill, professor at University College, Dublin. They had been impressed by Carson's success in Ulster and the lack of action the Government had taken against them. The Irish Volunteers were formed to advance Home Rule, by force if necessary, being inaugurated 25 November 1913 in the Rotunda in Dublin when four thousand volunteers enrolled.[156]

By 1914 the Royal Irish Constabulary reported that the Irish (National) Volunteers were "recruited mainly from the working and artisan classes."[157]

Only a small number of Ulster Catholics supported the revolutionary Irish Republican Brotherhood as the majority of their support still lay with John Redmond and his Irish Parliamentary Party. His brother William Redmond, in an article written for the *Irish News*, on 10 February 1913 reminded Ulster Nationalists of their support throughout the Empire, "If Ireland's

---

156 Lewis, Geoffrey, *Carson: The man who divided Ireland* (2006).
157 Fitzpatrick (ed), *Ireland in the First World War* (1988).

Recruitment poster for the Irish Volunteers. (Somme Museum)

> **Oglaigh na hEireann.**
>
> **ENROL UNDER THE GREEN FLAG**
>
> Safeguard your rights and liberties (the few left you).
> Secure more.
> Help your Country to a place among the nations.
> Give her a National Army to keep her there.
> Get a gun and do your part.
>
> **JOIN THE IRISH VOLUNTEERS**
> (President: EOIN MAC NEILL).
>
> The local Company drills at _____
>
> Ireland shall no longer remain disarmed and impotent.

claim for justice came before a tribunal of the Empire. There is no doubt as to the verdict. If Home Rule for Ireland depended upon the approval of the British Empire, Ireland would be immediately emancipated."[158]

This view was somewhat vindicated when congratulations from the Dominions of Canada, South Africa and Australia were received by Redmond with the successful passage of the Third Home Rule Bill through the House of Commons, even though it conceded less than Dominion status on Ireland. Despite this the majority of Irishmen still supported it.

In a speech in April 1913, Carson reminded the Ulster Volunteer Force that they had, "… no quarrel with individuals. We welcome, aye, and we love, every individual Irishman, even those opposed to us. Our quarrel is with the government."[159]

Despite this tensions increased and were manifested as sectarian incidents on the streets. The Orange commemoration of the relief of the Siege of Derry in 1689, held in the city of Londonderry in August 1913, resulted in several days of serious rioting in the city. Windows of Catholic churches

---

158   Orr, Philip, *The Road to the Somme* (1987).
159   Hume, David, *"For Ulster and Her Freedom": The story of the April 1914 gun-running* (1989).

Members of the UVF at camp. (Somme Museum)

were smashed, Catholic business premises were attacked, Catholic homes were shot at and Catholic residents were intimidated going to and from their work. As part of the rise of violence a Protestant man was shot dead by the police in the Fountain Street area of the city.

In the same month, Colonel Wallace, Secretary of the Ulster Provincial Grand Lodge of the Orange Order wrote to the masters of the Orange Lodges to ask them to ensure that all members joined the UVF.[160]

At the start the Ulster Volunteer Force had no uniforms; instead they paraded and drilled in their ordinary clothes with the addition of belts, bandoliers and haversacks. Unit designations were indicated by the wearing of armlets or brassards made of khaki canvas, printed in black with the name of the Regiment and Battalion. Rank was also denoted by markings on the armlets, one thin black line, squad leader; two lines a section commander and three lines a sergeant-major whilst officers wore red or blue canvas armbands printed in black.[161]

Regimental Commander	Red, Hand and Two Rings
Battalion Commanders	Red, Hand and One Ring
Adjutants and 2nd in Command	Red, Hand
Company Commanders	Red, Two Rings

160 Bowman, Timothy, *Carson's Army: Ulster Volunteer Force, 1910-22* (2007).
161 Metcalfe, Nick, *Blacker's Boys* (2012).

Half Company Commanders	Red, One Ring
Sergeant-Majors	Drab, Three Lines
Section Commanders	Drab, Two Lines
Squad Commanders	Drab, One Line
Rank and File	Drab

By July 1914 considerable difficulties had arisen with the supply of the canvas armlets leading to Headquarters issuing directions that the manufacturers would no longer provide small supplementary requisitions. It was directed that all requests for additional armlets should be received by Headquarters no later than 1 August 1914 as they had given the manufacturer an undertaking that the next order would be the last; requests had to be on the specified form and not by letter or verbally delivered. All were informed that after this date any further requisitions for armlets would be the responsibility of each respective Battalion along with any costs incurred.[162]

In battalion orders for 1st Battalion, North Antrim Regiment, the officer commanding reminded those concerned that in each company there could be only four Section Leaders or two section Leaders to the Half Company.[163]

Some units such as the Special Service Sections appear to have taken matters into their own hands and sourced their own uniforms. Those who were not so fortunate still however maintained some form of uniform appearance.

No.5 (Avoneil) Battalion, East Belfast Regiment, Ulster Volunteer Force, Special Service Force. (Somme Museum)

---

162 UVF Order 79, 1914 – Somme Museum.
163 Orders – 1st Battalion, North Antrim Regiment – 3 June 1914 – Somme Museum.

CE Falls, Battalion Commander, 3rd Battalion, Fermanagh Regiment, in Battalion Orders for Easter Monday 1914 instructed the volunteers to be 'quietly and neatly dressed and to parade "without arms, but wearing bandoliers, haversacks, water bottles, armlets and belts, and if possible puttees or gaiters."[164] He also asked his men to wear a soft grey felt hat, to improve the overall appearance on parade, even going so far as to inform them that such hats could be obtained in the town of Enniskillen; one can only hope that the supplier in question had sufficient in stock.

The question of head-dress was also a matter for UVF Orders in November 1913 when headquarters acknowledged that numerous requests had been received regarding the purchase of head-dress. Those concerned were reminded that headquarters would not lay down any special pattern of head-dress but instead if any UVF Battalions wished to have head-dress then prior sanction had to be obtained from the regimental or division commander with the arrangements and costs borne by those concerned. In the absence of a regimental commander the matter was to lie with the battalion commander.[165]

The efficiency of the UVF was improved when in August 1913 on the recommendation of Lord Roberts of Kandahar, through Colonel Thomas Hickman, an English member of parliament and a man willing to serve in the Ulster Provisional Government, Lieutenant-General Sir George Richardson,[166] was appointed their commander; he had retired from the British Indian Army in 1909.

When Richardson went to Belfast to visit his new command he found it numbered between 50 and 60,000 with more joining every day.[167]

Lieutenant General Sir George Lloyd Reilly Richardson KCB.
(Somme Museum)

---

164 Ulster Volunteers, January 1913 – Ulster-Scots Community Network <http://www.ulster-scots.com/uploads/901740969819.PDF5> (Accessed 5 August 2013).
165 UVF Order 29, 1913 – Somme Museum.
166 Shearman, Hugh, *Not an Inch: A Study of Northern Ireland and Lord Craigavon* (1942).
167 McNeill, Ronald, *Ulster's Stand for Union* (1922).

While the UVF, at least in Belfast, had been initially formed in workplaces, notably in the case of the various shipyards in Belfast, on taking command Richardson appears to have insisted on the Ulster Volunteer Force units being enrolled by street, similar to the form adopted in Derry.[168] For example in Derry City when a volunteer moved to another part of the city he was transferred to the relevant company in the battalions or regimental area,[169] not being permitted to stay with his original unit.

Richardson had served in the 38th (1st Staffordshire) Regiment of Foot in 1866, transferring to the Indian Army in 1871. He had seen action in a wide variety of colonial campaigns, commanding the Zhob Valley Field Force and the Tirah expedition. He was a veteran of the Second Anglo-Afghan War and Boxer Rebellion having led the final assault on Peking. Before retiring from the Army he had commanded the Poona Division in the Indian Army.[170] This previous military experience was also reinforced when newly married Captain Wilfred Bliss Spender, who at the time was the youngest staff officer in the British Army, threw his lot in with the Ulster Volunteers in September 1913, being appointed as their Quartermaster General.

Spender chose a career in the Army as opposed to following the family tradition of journalism and politics. In 1897 he obtained a commission in the Royal Artillery, seeing service in various parts of the Empire, including Bermuda, Canada and Malta, though the greater time was spent with a mountain battery on the North West Frontier in India.[171]

In 1905 he passed out first in military subjects from Camberley Staff College, Surrey. In 1909 he was a member of the Home Defence Section of the Committee of Imperial Defence. It was during this time, when he was involved in drawing up defence plans for the United Kingdom that he became convinced of the strategic importance of Ireland and concluded that Home Rule posed a serious threat to the security of the Empire as a whole.[172]

Spender organized, and partly financed, a national petition against Home Rule, and helped establish the Junior Imperial League. In 1912 he accepted an invitation to stand for Parliament in Hull west, but withdrew when the rules were changed to place officers on half pay if they entered the House of Commons.

The War Office viewed his political activity with distaste, resulting in him being sent back to India having been informed that he could never hold a staff appointment again. Whilst his superiors wished him to resign, Sir John French, Chief of the Imperial General Staff, wished to have him cashiered. Spender believed that his resignation would imply a slur on his integrity; he wished to be able to retire and managed to push his case from his Commanding Officer to the King himself.[173, 174]

In 7 August 1913 he was allowed to resign from his £120 per annum army commission. A confidential inspection report of 1913 commented that Captain Spender had been led away by a "too active conscience" and had been very injudicious, risking his prospects in life.[175] His actions may

---

168 Bowman, Timothy, *Carson's Army: Ulster Volunteer Force, 1910-22* (2007).
169 Bowman, Timothy, *Carson's Army: Ulster Volunteer Force, 1910-22* (2007).
170 Ulster Volunteers, January 1913 – Ulster-Scots Community Network <http://www.ulster-scots.com/uploads/901740969819.PDF> (Accessed 5 August 2013).
171 Ulster Volunteers, January 1913 – Ulster-Scots Community Network <http://www.ulster-scots.com/uploads/901740969819.PDF> (Accessed 5 August 2013).
172 Ulster Volunteers, January 1913 – Ulster-Scots Community Network <http://www.ulster-scots.com/uploads/901740969819.PDF> (Accessed 5 August 2013).
173 Ulster Volunteers, January 1913 – Ulster-Scots Community Network <http://www.ulster-scots.com/uploads/901740969819.PDF> (Accessed 5 August 2013).
174 Baguley, Margaret (ed)., *The Spender Correspondence, World War I and the Question of Ulster, The correspondence of Lilian and Wilfred Spender* (2009).
175 <http://en.wikipedia.org/wiki/Wilfrid_Spender> (Accessed 17 September 2013).

Ulster Volunteers undertaking training. (Somme Museum)

have ultimately damaged his promotion prospects during the Great War as on three occasions he was recommended for promotion to Brigadier General, but instead ended the war as a Lieutenant Colonel.[176]

Richardson's Headquarters staff was presided over by Colonel GW Hacket Pain, CB, also a former Indian Army officer.[177] He joined the British Army in 1875, serving in the Sudan in 1888 during the Mahdist Wars as a Captain in the West Surreys. He also served with the Nile Frontier Force in 1889. On 15 May 1894 Hacket Pain became a Major to the Worcestershire Regiment and accompanied the expedition to Dongola in 1896. The same year he was promoted to Lieutenant Colonel. He served in South Africa throughout the South African War of 1899-1902, and on returning to Britain his promotion to full Colonel was confirmed on 23 February 1907.

Colonel TE Hickman, MP for Wolverhampton South and a key figure in the British League for the Support of Ulster and the Union was heavily involved in recruiting English officers for the UVF.[178] However the British military authorities were interested in discovering who amongst the retired and serving officers were involved in the Ulster Volunteer Force as they could be prosecuted under section 451 of King's Regulations for being involved in political matters; by which an officer or soldier is forbidden to institute or take part in any meetings, demonstration or procession for party or political purposes in barracks, quarters, camps or their vicinity.[179] This was highlighted

---

176 Ulster Volunteers, January 1913 – Ulster-Scots Community Network <http://www.ulster-scots.com/uploads/901740969819.PDF> (Accessed 5 August 2013).
177 Metcalfe, Nick, *Blacker's Boys* (2012).
178 Ulster Volunteers, January 1913 – Ulster-Scots Community Network <http://www.ulster-scots.com/uploads/901740969819.PDF> (Accessed 5 August 2013).
179 Bowman, Timothy, *Carson's Army: Ulster Volunteer Force, 1910-22* (2007).

when Lieutenant AM Alexander of the 2nd Royal Inniskilling Fusiliers was observed by Sergeant J English, Royal Irish Constabulary, addressing an Orange Lodge in Carrickmore, 23 December 1912. Alexander refused to complete a UVF membership form along with the others, stating that he could take no part in the proceedings whilst still serving in the Army, but added that as soon as Home Rule became law he would sever his connection with it.[180] On the same date Sergeant James English also submitted a report warning that he had received reliable information about the formation of "an organisation known as the 'Ulster Volunteer Movement'", echoing comments from Acting Sergeant Joseph Edwards from the Belfast Detective Branch in a five page report on a "strictly private" meeting held on 13 December between prominent members of the Ulster Unionist Council. Sergeant English went further, providing information as to how their squads and companies would be formed.[181]

Whilst no less than six reports had been submitted by Constables and Sergeants of the Royal Irish Constabulary by the end of January 1913 into the creation and formation of the Ulster Volunteer Force, by far the most important was that submitted by Sergeant William Hall. He had obtained from "a very confidential friend" a copy of the UVF's 'Little Book' and Hall made a copy of it before returning it and submitting his copy to the Crime Special Branch. This pamphlet contained full descriptions of the objectives of the force, duties of volunteers, qualifications to join and its organisational structure. According to the book and in the words of the UVF leadership it had been formed to act "for self-preservation and mutual protection of all Loyalists and generally to keep the peace."[182]

Two members of the Ulster Volunteer Force. (Somme Museum)

Another significant figure in the organisation was Major Frank Hall of Narrow Water Castle, who had before the formation of the UVF had played a crucial role in the revival of the Unionist Clubs 'to bring in the staunch Unionists who are not Orangemen' and also in the success of Ulster Day.[183] Having joined the Royal Artillery in 1895 he retired in 1911 with the brevet rank of Lieutenant Colonel.[184]

---

180 PRONI D1568/6/10/14.
181 Grob-Fitzgibbon, *Turning Points of The Irish Revolution: The British Government, Intelligence and th Cost of Indifference, 1912-1921* (2007).
182 Grob-Fitzgibbon, *Turning Points of The Irish Revolution: The British Government, Intelligence and th Cost of Indifference, 1912-1921* (2007).
183 Ulster Volunteers, January 1913 – Ulster-Scots Community Network <http://www.ulster-scots.com/uploads/901740969819.PDF5> (Accessed 5 August 2013).
184 Ulster Volunteers, January 1913 – Ulster-Scots Community Network <http://www.ulster-scots.com/

Ulster Volunteer Force marches into Narrow Water Castle, County Down, 1913. (*Belfast Telegraph*)

Timothy Bowman has identified seven serving regular officers in the British Army who risked court martial by assisting the UVF; examples included Major JB Scriven, 21st Empress of India's Lancers, who served as a member of UVF HQ's staff early in 1914, and Captain Basil Brooke, 4th Queen's Own Hussars, who drilled his family's estate workers in County Fermanagh whilst home on leave.[185]

This support from the military was summed up by Carson in a speech in September 1913 when he said, "I tell the government that we have pledges and promises from some of the greatest generals in the army, who have given their word that when the time comes, if it is necessary, they will come over and help us keep the old flag flying."[186]

Despite this, at the parade at the Balmoral Show Grounds 27 September 1913, of the 14 Belfast City UVF battalions on parade, only five were commanded by men with military rank. The Royal Irish Constabulary estimated that 10,390 paraded with up to 25,000 spectators.[187]

A week prior to the parade the Royal Irish Constabulary had received copies of the orders for the parade which stated that the parade would be made up of the four UVF Regiments from the Belfast Division, each numbering 800 men. The total parade with fourteen battalions would number 11,200 men. Each battalion would carry a coloured flag indicating its regimental designation and battalion number; the orders specified the colours and its assigned position in the parade.

---

uploads/901740969819.PDF> (Accessed 5 August 2013).
185 Bowman, Timothy, *Carson's Army: Ulster Volunteer Force, 1910-22* (2007).
186 Shearman, Hugh, *Not an Inch: A Study of Northern Ireland and Lord Craigavon* (1942).
187 Bowman, Timothy, *Carson's Army: Ulster Volunteer Force, 1910-22* (2007).

A postcard depicting the Belfast Volunteers at Balmoral on 27 September 1913. (J Luke)

A postcard depicting Edward Carson reviewing the parade of Belfast Volunteers at Balmoral on 27 September 1913. (J Luke)

This information along with attentive constables and sergeants along the route provided the RIC with all the information they required to gain a very accurate picture of the Belfast UVF. On the day before the parade the Crime Special Branch also obtained an official UVF pamphlet from an anonymous source which listed all those holding leadership positions on the Belfast UVF down to Battalion commander level; 12 were former officers in the British Army and one was a sitting Member of Parliament.[188]

---

188 Grob-Fitzgibbon, *Turning Points of The Irish Revolution: The British Government, Intelligence and the Cost of*

A postcard depicting the South Belfast Regiment, Ulster Volunteer Force, at Shaftesbury Square, Belfast enroute for Balmoral, 27 September 1913. (Somme Museum)

Clearly ignoring the earlier parade at Balmoral, the *Northern Whig* reported the parade as, "The inspiring spectacle at Balmoral was one that will never fade from the memory of those who were privileged to witness it. Nothing approaching it in character and significance had ever been seen before in the history of Ireland."[189]

After the parade Carson expressed his opinion on the gathering, "I desire to express to the Belfast Regiments of the Ulster Volunteer Force, who assembled on Saturday, at Balmoral, my grateful appreciation and admiration of the splendid turnout on that occasion. Any country may well be proud of such a body of men, who are prepared to make every sacrifice in defence of the elementary rights of citizenship."[190]

These positive comments were echoed by Colonel Hacket Pain who recorded his appreciation and thanks to the officers and men of the Belfast Division and highlighted in particular the Detachment of Military Police provided by the men from Dunmurry, Lisburn and Holywood for their tact and judgement in executing their duties. Likewise he mentioned the Ulster Volunteer Nursing Corps carrying out their medical duties and the Corps of Despatch Riders who carried out "their arduous duties with much zeal and intelligence."[191]

Perhaps this added impetus to the organisation of the UVF and encouraged WC Trimble to write to the War Office in August 1913 on behalf of his Enniskillen Horse, seeking free ammunition and referring to the decision not to extend the Territorials to Ireland, suggesting a "Third Irish Yeomanry here", as he went onto to say, "Here, in the Enniskillen Horse, you have a regiment readymade, with only a few appointments to add, with men having the finest physique, and seven-eighths of the horses suitable 'troopers.'"[192]

Indifference, 1912-1921 (2007).
189 *Northern Whig* – 29/9/1913.
190 UVF Orders 04, 1913 – Somme Museum.
191 UVF Orders 04, 1913 – Somme Museum.
192 Bowman, Timothy, *Carson's Army: Ulster Volunteer Force, 1910-22* (2007).

Enniskillen Horse on parade, 18 September 1912. (Somme Museum)

The view of District Inspector PA Marinan, Royal Irish Constabulary, on the parade involving the Enniskillen Horse gave a slightly different perspective, "In the few drill movements performed, however, I noticed great confusion and bad horsemanship; and although in general the troopers were of a good type physically and fairly well mounted, by no stretch of the imagination could the body be called an effective cavalry force."[193]

During September 1913, Lord Loreburn, a Liberal ex-Lord Chancellor, previously one of the strongest Home Rulers in the Cabinet, wrote a letter to *The Times* in which he pointed out that as a consequence of the Parliament Act, the Home Rule Bill would become law in June 1914, which if it did so in its current form would result in very serious riots in the north of Ireland if not civil war. He urged all Ministers "who assuredly have not taken leave of their senses…to consider proposals for accommodation." Carson welcomed the letter whilst it alarmed Redmond who saw it as a weakening of the Liberal position.[194]

King George V. (Private collection)

---

193 Bowman, Timothy, *Carson's Army: Ulster Volunteer Force, 1910-22* (2007).
194 Hyde H Montgomery, *Carson* (1953).

The King at Balmoral met with leading politicians in an attempt to bring the opposing parties together in a friendly atmosphere. Bonar Law warned the King that as soon as Home Rule was passed, not only would Carson establish the Provisional Government, but only the forces appointed by it would be allowed to operate. With support from the entire Unionist Party and that Ulster was right the question arose, what would happen if the entire Unionist Members were turned out of the House of Commons, did Mr Churchill believe that the Army would obey orders against Ulster? After the meeting Bonar Law wrote to Carson informing him of the conversation and reiterating that he believed the only option was to leave Ulster as it was with some form of Home Rule for the rest of Ireland. Carson replied to his letter of 23 September 1913:

> … As regards the position here I am of opinion that on the whole things are shaping towards a desire to settle on the terms of leaving 'Ulster' out. A difficulty arises as to defining Ulster. My own view is that the whole of Ulster should be excluded but the minimum would be the six plantation counties, and for that a good cause could be made.
>
> The South and West would present a difficulty, and it might be that I could not agree to their abandonment, though I feel certain it would be the best settlement if Home Rule is inevitable.[195]

Alexander Whitla from Newtownards in his Ulster Volunteer uniform. (D Truesdale)

On 24 September 1913 the Ulster Unionist Council met to put the final touches to their framework for a provisional government.[196] These arrangements included a military Council, an Indemnity Guarantee fund, which would compensate UVF members for losses suffered if they had to fight and a centre for operations in the Old Town Hall, Belfast. By the next day 25 September the Indemnity Fund had reached the quarter-million mark with Carson, Craig and Londonderry heading the subscription list, each having subscribed £10,000.[197] Sir Samuel McCaughey, reputed to be one of Australia's best known millionaires, having emigrated from County Antrim and having amassed vast flocks of sheep, telegraphed from Australia, inviting the Treasurer of the fund to call upon him "for any sum necessary".[198] A short time later the fund had reached over £800,000, with a £1,000,000 sterling being assured by members of the Executive of the Provisional Government.[199] This sum is unlikely to have been in hard cash but more likely sureties.[200] As part of these contingency arrangements, Spender was to organise food supplies for the civilian population of Ulster in the

---

195 Hyde H Montgomery, Carson (1953).
196 Ryan, AP, *Mutiny at the Curragh* (1956).
197 Hyde H Montgomery, Carson (1953).
198 Ryan, AP, *Mutiny at the Curragh* (1956).
199 Canning, WJ, *Ballyshannon, Belcoo, Bertincourt* (1996).
200 Bowman, Timothy, *Carson's Army: Ulster Volunteer Force, 1910-22* (2007).

event of armed conflict and the establishment of four committees to deal with the Volunteers, local subjects, education and customs, excise and postal services. Each committee was to include a member of the Ulster Women's Unionist Council,[201] another indication of the inclusion of women at a time of increasing suffrage demands. Special religious services to mark the formal organisation of the Provisional Government were held.[202]

The Old Town Hall building had originally provided municipal offices for Belfast when it was still a town. However after being given city status in 1888 and the construction and completion of the Belfast City Hall in Donegall Square it became the headquarters of the Unionist Clubs of Ireland, the network of groups created by Lord Templetown to promote a better understanding of Unionism in the years after the second Home Rule crisis in 1893. From 1911 it was rented for two years by the Ulster Volunteer Force.[203]

Although the UVF had been formed in January 1913, it was September before it had a named Commander in Chief or put a professional HQ staff in place. Once these were in place it resulted in local autonomy for the Force, each county being initially run by a committee who elected five representatives to HQs. In reality this effectively left some rural UVF detachments as Unionist Clubs.[204]

The HQ's staff of the Ulster Volunteer Force comprised ten former and serving soldiers and twelve civilians:[205]

> James Craig MP – Political Staff Officer, UVF
> Formerly Captain 133rd Company (29th Irish Horse), Imperial Yeomanry (South African War) and 3rd Royal Irish Rifles (1900-08)
> TVP McCammon – In Charge of Administration
> Major 5th Royal Irish Rifles, Deputy Grand Secretary of the Provincial Grand Lodge of Ulster.
> Colonel TE Hickman, MP – Inspector General
> Lieutenant-Colonel Robert Davis – Secretary, UVF Medical Board
> Retired officer, Indian Medical Service
> Major FH Crawford – Director of Ordnance
> Retired Officer, Royal Artillery
> Lieutenant-General GW Hacket Pain – Chief Staff officer
> Captain Wilfred Spender – Assistant Quartermaster General
> HO Davis – Senior Officer for Instructors
> Former Lieutenant in Army
> Lloyd Campbell – Director of Intelligence

With the threat of Volunteers, both Ulster and Nationalist, arming themselves, the Government re-imposed the ban it had lifted on the import of arms into Ireland, through two Royal Proclamations published 5 December which retrospectively prohibited the importation of arms and ammunition into Ireland and their carriage around the coast.[206]

---

201 Ryan, AP, *Mutiny at the Curragh* (1956).
202 Ryan, AP, *Mutiny at the Curragh* (1956).
203 Leslie and Quail, *Old Belfast* (2013).
204 Bowman, Timothy, *Carson's Army: Ulster Volunteer Force, 1910-22* (2007).
205 Bowman, Timothy, *Carson's Army: Ulster Volunteer Force, 1910-22* (2007).
206 Ryan, AP, *Mutiny at the Curragh* (1956).

The Old Town Hall, Belfast. Headquarters of the Ulster Anti-Home Rule and the Ulster Volunteer Force. (PRONI INF7A/2/2)

The same month the Government seized a shipment of arms which had been imported into Ulster from Europe with the seized weapons being held in the Customs House in Belfast. The owners of the weapons subsequently demanded their return, however the Attorney General consulted the Cabinet in February 1914 on the correct procedure to be adopted. The Government view was clear, they could not be returned as they had been imported "in furtherance of a seditious conspiracy." However this created a problem in that it was feared that the Ulster Volunteers would attempt to rescue the arms by force.[207]

The threat of action by supporters of Home Rule was also in the mind of the

Embossed UVF crest on letterheaded paper. (Somme Museum)

---

207 Muenger, Elizabeth A, *The British Military Dilemma in Ireland: Occupation Politics 1886-1914* (1991).

UVF administration. Orders were issued asking the local commanding officers of regiments "to report anything in the way of drilling or organising on the part of Home Rulers which may come to their notice." The orders went further requiring them to make themselves familiar with the local activities and organisation of the both the Royal Irish Constabulary within their Districts and the local Coastguard stations, with particular attention to places where the government may attempt to land troops or additional police. They were also to consider suitable schemes to resist such landings.[208]

At the end of 1913, the Attorney General, Sir John Simon, queried J.H. Campbell's interpretation of the law regarding the legality of drilling. He told the Cabinet that:

> 'drilling' without lawful authority was illegal under the Unlawful Drilling Act of 1819. He further stated that in his opinion, "even if those who are drilling Ulster Volunteers have secured documentary authority from two Justices of the Peace, I do not think this would amount to lawful authority in a case where the whole proceeding is a seditious conspiracy. Indeed I think the Justices of the Peace who gave such authority would be accessories to the crime."[209]

The Attorney General was not the only person to hold this view. At a speech at Ashgrove on the outskirts of Newry, September 1913, Carson said, "Drilling is illegal. Only recently I was reading the Act of Parliament forbidding it. The volunteers are illegal, and the government knows they are illegal, and the government dare not interfere with them."[210]

Despite this opinion clearly suggesting that the authorised drilling by the Ulster Volunteers was illegal there is little evidence that the government sought to actually prevent the drilling or prosecute those involved.

Whilst monthly intelligence reports of the Royal Irish Constabulary observed that several Unionists had been prosecuted for unlawful assembly and 'bound over' to 'keep the peace' it had not dissuaded those involved. To the contrary, it had only increased attendance at drill practice and led to a demand for small arms such that "local shopkeepers had to renew their stock of revolvers."[211]

Whilst illegal drilling was one illegal action identified by the Attorney General for the cabinet in December 1913, there were four other breaches of the law for which he believed a conviction could be brought against the UVF. The first was a charge of treason-felony which he explained; thus "The avowed objects of the Ulster Volunteer Force make those who are actively responsible for it liable to be prosecuted for treason-felony, for that crime consists in conspiring to make rebellion in order by force to compel the King to change his counsels, or in order to put constraint upon and intimidate either Houses of Parliament."

The next was the engaging in unlawful assemblies, defined by law as "meetings organised for the purpose of preparing or threatening armed resistance to lawful authority." Under the Coercion Act 1887 any person attending such a meeting could be imprisoned and prosecuted summarily before a court of summary jurisdiction without conviction by jury.

The final charge was that of illegal storing of ammunition which was prohibited by the Explosives Act of 1875 which limited the amount of ammunition which could be stored in any

---

208 Commanding Officer, County Antrim volunteers officers of Antrim Regiments 21 October 1913.
209 Ulster Volunteers, January 1913 – Ulster-Scots Community Network <http://www.ulster-scots.com/uploads/901740969819.PDF> (Accessed 5 August 2013).
210 Ulster Volunteers, January 1913 – Ulster-Scots Community Network <http://www.ulster-scots.com/uploads/901740969819.PDF> (Accessed 5 August 2013).
211 Muenger, Elizabeth A, *The British Military Dilemma in Ireland: Occupation Politics 1886-1914* (1991).

A squad of Ulster Volunteers at Craigavon House. (Somme Museum)

A battalion of the Ulster Volunteer Force at Killyleagh Castle, County Down. (Somme Museum)

one place. There was also the possibility of arms being seized and those involved in the smuggling arrested. The Attorney General also recommended that the cabinet consider "whether retired [military] officers and reservists should be permitted to draw pensions while assisting the Ulster movement."[212]

The decision of whether to act was left to the cabinet, however during the first months of 1914 the drilling continued uninterrupted. [213]

General Sir George Richardson inspected the Fermanagh Volunteers in December 1913 which stimulated further much needed recruitment in the county which had been behind its other sister counties in the Province. When he returned a few months later for a further inspection, he reviewed 30 officers and 1,827 other ranks.[214]

---

212 Grob-Fitzgibbon, *Turning Points of The Irish Revolution: The British Government, Intelligence and the Cost of Indifference, 1912-1921* (2007).
213 Grob-Fitzgibbon, *Turning Points of The Irish Revolution: The British Government, Intelligence and the Cost of Indifference, 1912-1921* (2007).
214 Canning, WJ, *Ballyshannon, Belcoo, Bertincourt* (1996).

5

Greater Organisation

From the outset the Volunteers had had little in the way of uniform and equipment, the most distinguishing feature of the formations being the provision of belts, bandoliers and haversacks. A new Volunteer would be given a small bronze badge with a red hand of Ulster on it bearing the motto "For God and Ulster". On the back of each bronze metal badge which was to be worn on coat buttonholes was stamped the County Letter and the Organisation Number. UVF Orders stressed that the number of the badge must correspond to the volunteer's number in the county enrolment book. Badges were only being issued to those men who were believed to be trustworthy and well drilled and the battalion commanders were empowered to withhold the badge from any volunteer who they considered did not merit it and this authority was extended to district committees where battalions had not yet been formed.[1] The impact of the threat of withholding the badge can only be speculated upon; did it encourage discipline and morale or perhaps the rules were relaxed depending on personalities? General Sir WT Adair, officer commanding Antrim UVF, authorised his officers to issue the bronze badge to men who had completed 10 drills.[2]

Permission was also granted to issue it to those enrolled as non-effectives, such as those enrolled to do special but non-military work.[3] In November 1913, UVF HQs further directed that "It has been decided that the Badge, in addition to being worn on Parade, should be worn on all occasions, it should therefore be thoroughly impressed on all members of the Volunteer Force, that are in a position to do so, that the badge should be worn always."[4]

When a man moved from one battalion area to another, providing that he remained within the County or City from which he received his organisation number and badge, his number and Badge were not affected. However if he moved from one county or city to another then his battalion was instructed to inform his own county secretary who would strike his name from the county enrolment book, and sending his enrolment form to the secretary of the county or city to which he was moving. His new county or city secretary would issue a new organisation number and his new battalion commander would then issue him a metal badge bearing his new organisation number on receipt of his original metal badge which was then returned to the Secretary of the original issuing county or city.[5]

In UVF Orders in May 1914 battalion commanders were informed that headquarters were aware of numerous cases of persons approaching Messrs. Sharman D Neill Limited (jewellers) for bronze metal cap badges. They were reminded of the direction in UVF Order No.26, 1914,[6] which required that orders for the badges were only to be submitted by a rank no lower than battalion commander and for quantities of no less than 300 badges; the cost of which was 1/3 per dozen.

---

1 UVF Order 07, 1913 – Somme Museum.
2 Handwritten note to UVF Orders 20 October 1913 by WT Adair – Somme Museum.
3 UVF Order 02,1914 – Somme Museum.
4 PRONI, D.1238/115 – UVF Order 20.
5 UVF Order 17, 1914 – Somme Museum.
6 UVF Order 59, 1914 – Somme Museum.

A selection of UVF bronze lapel badges showing clearly the 'right' hand of the UVF and fastener for a lapel button hole. The fastener also clearly shows the unique identifying number stamped onto each badge. (Somme Museum)

The issue of the special bronze cap badge was for use only in head-dress provided by the battalion, though headquarters remained of the opinion that no expenditure should be made on headdress until a battalion was fully equipped with the more essential articles.[7]

A Volunteers unit designation would be a canvas armband with the details of his regiment and battalion printed on it and secured with a strap and buckle attachment.[8] In an effort to standardise the image of the Force, UVF Headquarters during the winter of 1913 issued a detailed list of suppliers in Belfast where articles of equipment could be purchased; including puttees, gaiters, belts, water bottles, army boots, rifle slings, waterproof groundsheets and greatcoats.[9] Each member was also encouraged to gather a personal store of rations; "Every volunteer should be urged as strongly as possible to keep always in his possession some food, such as tinned meat, sardines, chocolate, or potted meat, tea … which in addition to bread and biscuits … he may be able to collect at his home in case of emergency."[10]

The UVF lapel badge was designed to be worn in the buttonhole on the lapel of a jacket. (Somme Museum)

Other individuals within each company were given responsibility for entrenching tools, maps and cooking utensils.

There were those who saw the creation of the Volunteers as an opportunity to capitalise which resulted in a directive being issued from Headquarters warning all members that it had come to their attention that certain traders were selling articles named as UVF pattern or some similar description, leading members to believe that they may have been officially endorsed. All members

---

7   UVF Orders 26, 1914 – Somme Museum.
8   UVF Order 08, 1913 – Somme Museum.
9   Orr, Philip, *The Road to the Somme* (1987).
10 UVF Directive – PRONI D1238/9/17.

were cautioned that no authority for such labelling existed and that such items could in some cases be of indifferent quality or excessively priced.[11]

The 1st Battalion, North Antrim Regiment, issued orders with regards to the issue and storage of equipment. Within the regiment those Volunteers considered "effective" were to be issued a pair of puttees, a belt and frog, a haversack and a leather bandolier. In order that no items would be lost it was suggested that this equipment should not be handed to the Volunteer to keep, but instead it should be kept in each drill centre or some other suitable house by the local officer in command, and handed out to each man when he came on parade and returned at the end of parade, mobilisation or field day. These orders also included how the items were to be worn; the haversack to be hung over the right shoulder, bag hanging to left side; put on the belt with the frog handing to the left side, with the belt over the bands of the haversack, frog hanging inside or behind the bag, not on the outside; the bandolier was to worn over the left shoulder, buckle on the top of the shoulder, little loop strap on the right side, to be attached to the belt.[12]

Cap badge of the 1st Battalion, South Antrim Regiment, Ulster Volunteer Force. (T Wylie)

Men of the 4th (Portadown) Battalion, Armagh Regiment, Ulster Volunteer Force on parade, believed to be at Carrickblacker House (H Laverty)

---

11 UVF Order 03,1914 – Somme Museum.
12 North Antrim Regiment UVF Orders – 23 March 1914.

An Ulster Volunteer Force motor cycle unit in 1913. (*Belfast Telegraph*)

Perhaps it was Spender's experience of being a member of the Home Defence Section of the Imperial Defence Committee in 1909, which was then involved with the general defence of the United Kingdom, which led to the Ulster Volunteer Force developing an impressive array of specialist units which would be the envy of many contemporary professional armies.

As the UVF expanded it developed this extensive array of specialist units which included special service sections, medical corps, motor car corps, signalling and despatch riders' corps.

Within the Signalling and Despatch Riding Corps was Godfrey Boyton from Convoy, County Donegal, the son of the Dean of Derry, who had been the winner of the Isle of Man TT race in 1913.

Whilst Fermanagh had a large number of despatch riders who carried orders and communications between the various battalions and the headquarters in Belfast,[13] the continued use of the horse for reconnaissance and mounted infantry was still acknowledged. As a result there were two mounted units; one was in Enniskillen whilst the other was situated in Ballymena.

With women playing a very active role against Home Rule, the UVF enlisted them in more active roles as well as the more typical roles, such as nurses. These more active roles included signallers, motorcycle despatch riders, ambulance drivers and in intelligence within UVF Headquarters deciphering intercepted police messages. It has been estimated that up to 5,000 women were involved in assisting the UVF.[14]

In County Tyrone up to 40 women were pictured receiving rifle training and were described as "all fine shots" and were believed to have participated in a training exercise. The *Belfast Telegraph* caption alongside the photographs read; "Their objective is to be able to defend their homes and parents if their brothers are called upon to service with the Ulster Volunteers."[15]

The Ulster Women's Unionist Council helped administer the activities of the women which extended to working with English ladies who were helping by preparing their homes to receive

---

13 Canning, WJ, *Ballyshannon, Belcoo, Bertincourt* (1996).
14 Parkinson, Alan F, *Friends in High Places: Ulster's Resistance to Irish Home Rule, 1912-14* (2012).
15 Parkinson, Alan F, *Friends in High Places: Ulster's Resistance to Irish Home Rule, 1912-14* (2012).

Madeline Lyttle served with the Ulster Volunteer Force Nursing Corps and the Voluntary Aid Detachment in hospitals throughout Ulster 1915-1918. (Somme Museum)

Large button of the UVF Nursing Corps. (Somme Museum)

'loyalist' refugees from Ulster – a useful dress rehearsal as it turned out for Belgians escaping the German occupation of Belgium in 1914.[16]

This network in England included the aristocracy, with the Duchess of Somerset informing the Irish Unionist Party leader that she had "undertaken to house 100 women and children from Ulster."[17]

Part of the women's role is illustrated by a diary entry by Lilian Spender, Wilfred Spender's wife, who recorded a visit to Craigavon House on 20 March 1914; "The drawing room is full of typewriters and women clerks and every other room teems with men in uniform. In essence James Craig's drawing room had become a Staff Room with 'an enormous map of Ulster showing every unit of the UVF.'"[18]

---

16 Ryan, AP, *Mutiny at the Curragh* (1956).
17 Parkinson, Alan F, *Friends in High Places: Ulster's Resistance to Irish Home Rule, 1912-14* (2012).
18 Ulster Volunteers, January 1913 – Ulster-Scots Community Network <http://www.ulster-scots.com/uploads/901740969819.PDF> (Accessed 5 August 2013).

Shortly after her arrival in Belfast Lilian Spender also secured the services of Jack Scriven, a regular cavalry officer attached to UVF Headquarters to drill her and a small number of female friends.[19]

Signals and Despatch Riders

The Ulster Signalling and Despatch Riding Corps was established to overcome the vulnerability of the postal and telephone systems, ensuring that the UVF had its own totally independent means of conveying secret information.[20] A number of women were involved in the Corps, out on hillsides at night signalling to distant locations.[21] The origins of the unit came from the plans for Covenant Day, September 1912, when a group of Belfast signallers arrived in Armagh to meet with the Armagh newspaper owner to plan the chain of signals from the Belfast City Hall right across Ulster to Bundoran to coincide with the moment Carson signed the Covenant. He asked the very pertinent question, "What happens to your semaphore if Ulster Day is foggy?" This led to the forming of a corps of despatch riders. The motorbikes of 1912 were still very expensive and only starting to appear in many Ulster towns, names such as Triumph, BSA, and Indian with the engine driving the rear wheel via a belt instead of a chain, yet capable of 50 mph, though very noisy.[22]

Despite the use of motorcycles, local signalling initiatives such as that adopted within the South Londonderry Regiment still proved effective for local communications. Flagpoles were erected on prominent hills the in the area, such as at Mayagoney and another at Drumoolish, hills on either side of Tamlaght. When a red flag was flown it meant "Report at once with your rifle."[23]

At a week-long camp at Tynan Abbey in the summer of 1913 motorcycle riders from all over Ulster converged to be taught the skills they would need to become the flying column of Carson's developing army. Along with carrying thousands of messages during the hours of darkness after their normal work and at their own expense, it was intended to demonstrate by way of the exercise the capabilities of the UVF if any were in doubt. The specifics and objective of the operation was to show the capability of the Ulster Volunteer Force of controlling a vital bridge if the British Army were ordered north from Dublin against Ulster. Carson saw off the squadron of despatch riders from Tynan who had orders to 'capture' the Boyne Bridge. When the detachment of riders reached Drogheda they erected a specially prepared notice on the bridge which said, "This bridge has been captured by the Ulster Volunteer Force," and after, 'holding' the bridge for three hours, a time considered adequate to demonstrate their power, they returned to base.[24]

All despatch riders wore the badge of two signalling flags inscribed, "U.S.D.R.C." – The Ulster Signalling and Despatch Riding Corps.[25]

An exercise on Saturday 13 September 1913 was intended to give an opportunity for both the signallers and despatch riders to test their skills in concert. The signallers successfully maintained a continuous service with all messages correctly sent and received between Belfast, Bangor and Blackhead, County Antrim also Belfast as far as Montober, County Tyrone, and then by despatch riders to Derry City. The success was highlighted in a UVF Order from Colonel Hacket Pain when

---

19   Bowman, Timothy, *Carson's Army: Ulster Volunteer Force, 1910-22* (2007).
20   PRONI – D1327/4/3.
21   Orr, Philip, *The Road to the Somme* (1987).
22   Ingram, Rev Brett, *Covenant and Challenge* (1989).
23   Clark, Wallace, *Guns in Ulster* (1967).
24   Ingram, Rev Brett, *Covenant and Challenge* (1989).
25   Ingram, Rev Brett, *Covenant and Challenge* (1989).

A postcard depicting the Ulster Volunteer Force flying squadron at the Balmoral Showground, 27 September 1913. (J Luke)

he complimented the efficient state of the force despite the extremely unfavourable weather and road conditions.[26]

In October 1913 units were given notice of the formation of a Despatch Riding Corps, and it was highlighted that those lads too young for the ranks would be useful as cyclists.[27]

By the end of 1913 a newspaper article had noted the activities of the 'Ulster Women Despatch Riders' operating in County Fermanagh.[28]

UVF Orders issued in November 1913 confirmed that the Despatch Riders Service was now running a regular service once a week between the following locations; Armagh, Ballyclare, Ballygawley, Banbridge, Belfast, Cookstown, Dungannon, Enniskillen, Larne, Lisburn, Londonderry, Newry, Omagh, Portadown and Strabane. The timetables were held at post-houses in each town.[29]

The command structure of the Ulster Signalling and Despatch Corps was modified in March 1914 to improve its effectiveness. Whilst all County and District Signalling Officers retained their ranks in the US & DRC and all Signallers were made members of the US & DRC this in turn brought all signalling arrangements under the control of the Officer Commanding US & DRC.

With the exception of Belfast all signallers in the county were attached to battalions and under the command of the respective battalion commander, unless required for special duties at which time the battalion commander would receive specific instructions from the officer commanding US & DRC, through the County Signalling Officer. As part of these changes, as far as possible, in cases of emergency two despatch riders were detailed to every battalion. The Belfast Signallers and

---

26 UVF Order 01/1913 – Somme Museum.
27 Commanding Officer, County Antrim volunteers officers of Antrim Regiments 21 October 1913.
28 *Belfast Evening Telegraph* – 20/12/1913.
29 UVF Order 10, 1913 – Somme Museum.

Ulster Volunteers laying a field telephone line at Craigavon House. (Somme Museum)

Despatch Riders remained unaffected by these arrangements and remained under the command of the US & DRC at headquarters.[30]

By May 1914 the interest in semaphore signalling was increasing with schoolboys and farmers alike practising either with or without flags or even improvising using branches from trees to communicate with neighbours and friends on neighbouring hills.[31]

A master-plumber in Belfast, Andy Sayers, was gifted at signalling and wrote an instruction manual which was used widely within the organisation. He also realised that teenagers were the future lifeblood of the Corps and he therefore organised them into a Cadet Corps who could act as emergency messengers on foot and by bicycle. On the reverse of their membership cards he printed, "Points Cadets should know." These included:

> Where are the nearest Railway Stations? Post Offices? Telegraph Offices? Telephone Callrooms, Garages for motor repairs? Farriers? Bakers? Grocers? Butchers? Police Stations? Fire Stations? Drinking places for horses … and what is the quickest way to get to them? Where is the nearest UVF post-house? Where can the following be got? Pick axes, shovels, crowbars, spades, barbed wire, ropes, sacks, bricks, petrol wagons, wheelbarrows. Where can you get the best view of the country around?[32]

---

30   UVF Order 24, 1914 – Somme Museum.
31   Ingram, Rev Brett, *Covenant and Challenge* (1989).
32   Ingram, Rev Brett, *Covenant and Challenge* (1989).

James Craig and Edward Carson with members of the Signalling and Despatch Riding Corps. (PRONI INF7A/3/43)

Another initiative was a signal light which was specially designed for the UVF by a Belfast student called Inglis which is reported to have amazed Royal Navy officers with its clarity and rapidity; there were three in the team, one who operated the lamp, another read the replies and the third wrote down the messages.[33]

In January 1914 Headquarters directed that battalion commanders should arrange if possible to have eight men per company trained in semaphore attaining the standard set by Headquarters; it was felt that insufficient time existed to ensure the men would achieve a reasonable standard in Morse signalling. However if battalion commanders wished to have the option of Morse signallers then they could, however they were left in no doubt that if they selected this option then they had to arrange the training and equipment privately as the Ulster Signalling and Despatch Riding Corps could not arrange such training.[34]

Also in January 1914, as part of the expansion of the Corps, the 1st North Antrim Regiment Commanding Officer George C Young called upon all motor cyclists who were willing to enrol or may be interested in the Ulster Volunteer Despatch Riding Corps to attend a meeting in the Protestant Hall, Ballymena to discuss the possibility of joining; everyone was reassured that their attendance would in no sense commit them to joining or enrolling, unless of their own free will.[35]

Mrs Ainsworth Barr was appointed Chief of the Post-House Staff in January 1914.[36]

---

33 Ingram, Rev Brett, *Covenant and Challenge* (1989).
34 UVF Order 01, 1914 – Somme Museum.
35 10 January 1914 – Letter from OC 1st North Antrim Regiment.
36 UVF Order 05, 1914 – Somme Museum.

A Board of Enquiry was set for Monday 20th July 1914 to enquire into the organisation and to report their opinion of the Signalling and Despatch Riding organisation. The President of the Board was Colonel G Hacket Pain, CB whilst the members were Lieutenant Colonel TVP McCammon and Captain WB Spender.[37]

Following this Board orders were issued in August 1914 re-organising a number of command structures. The office of Officer Commanding, US & DRC was abolished and the organisation of the Corps was placed directly under Headquarters. The following appointments were also made:[38]

  Director of Communications   Captain F Hall
  Assistant Director of Communications
  Officer Commanding Headquarters Signallers   Mr J Watters
  Officer Commanding Despatch Riders   Mr JA Thompson
  Special Service Force – Signallers and Despatch Riders

Mr A Sayers was appointed Communication Officer for the above under OC, Belfast Division UVF. The organisation and establishment of this section was taken up separately.

With regards county, divisional and regimental signallers and despatch riders, the officers commanding divisions and regiments were to appoint without further delay a County or Divisional Communication Officer; there was allowance made for several counties to be grouped under one Communications Officer. Battalion commanders were to appoint battalion signalling instructors.

The Ulster Volunteer Force changing of the guard at the gates of Craigavon House.
(Somme Museum)

---

37 UVF Order 77, 1914 – Somme Museum.
38 UVF Orders 88, 1914 – Somme Museum.

Towards the end of August 1914 a question was asked by Battalion Signalling Instructors in Ballymena regarding the status of "lady signallers" within the UVF. They wanted to know if female signallers were officially recognised by UVF Headquarters and if they were, who was responsible for them both as regards general discipline and instruction.

Were they to be treated as entirely separate regarding their own officers, instructors etc.? At the time both male and female were managed together and it was felt that it made it difficult to deal with both together.[39] The answer was a very succinct; "no." Whilst ladies may prove "of great utility" at wireless telegraph stations, and as telegraph and telephone officers, they had no place in the field with troops. The Battalions Signalling Instructor had no responsibilities for the ladies, however if he had spare time he could offer to teach them flag signals "for their amusement."[40]

However at the end of June 1914, women of the UVF's Signalling Corps underwent training at Magilligan Camp in County Londonderry where they were instructed on the sending of telegrams and 'passed examinations' in despatch riding.[41]

In November 1914 following the outbreak of hostilities against Germany orders were issued that all lamp and helio signalling was to be discontinued unless carried out within enclosed premises, whilst flag signalling was only permitted in those areas not visible from the sea.[42]

Special Service Sections

The Special Service Force was raised in January 1913 and was formed by each Belfast Battalion raising a Special Service Company, wherever possible from former army personnel and members of the Special Reserve.

The concept was that the Special Service units would provide mutual assistance to other UVF districts. However this depended on both sufficient Ulster Volunteers of a suitable calibre being available, and also being willing to serve away from their families and homes who may then be at the mercy of Irish Volunteers or government forces.

Despite attempts to raise a Special Service Force for the rural areas the concept failed to be effective as rural units were unable to spare sufficient numbers of men; experienced former soldiers were often essential to some units in instilling the military ethos and training required. This was linked to UVF recruiting being more effective in those areas of Ulster less likely to be calling upon them. For example Colonel Oliver Nugent who was involved in raising and training the Cavan UVF (CVF), supervising their manoeuvres on the estate of his neighbour and friend, Lord Farnham,[43] described County Cavan as "geographically and politically isolated from North East Ulster, with a small Unionist community scattered over an area of 460,000 acres in the midst of a Nationalist population." He went onto say, "It is clear that as far as this County is concerned there will be no men available for other work after the requirements of home defence have been provided for."

This also echoed Nugent's personal belief that whilst opposed to Home Rule, the role of the Cavan Volunteer Force, literally on the periphery of the main Ulster resistance movement, was to be defensive. His instructions to it were clear:

> It must not be forgotten that the CVF is formed for defence and not for aggression and that that is the main principal reason why its organisation has a civil and not a military basis. The CVF is formed for mutual support and for defence against unprovoked attack. It is not

---

39 Question regarding Status of Lady Signallers – 27 August 1914.
40 Answer regarding Status of Lady Signallers – 28 August 1914.
41 Parkinson, Alan F, *Friends in High Places: Ulster's Resistance to Irish Home Rule, 1912-14* (2012).
42 UVF Orders 134, 1914 – Somme Museum.
43 Perry, Nicholas (ed)., *Major General Oliver Nugent and the Ulster Division 1915-1918* (2007).

Member of the UVF Special Service (or front line) unit on parade. (Somme Museum)

intended that it should be used against any of the Armed Forces of the crown, but on the contrary, to assist them, should occasion arise, in the maintenance of peace and security on the County.[44]

This view was not restricted to the border counties of Ulster as Captain the Hon. Arthur O'Neill, MP, commanding officer of County Antrim made it clear that his men would not serve outside County Antrim.[45]

In a letter to his wife in February 1916 General Nugent stressed that the conditions in which he agreed to take part in the UVF was "not for the purpose of rebellion or civil war", stating that he had disagreed all along with the policy which had led to the creation of the Ulster Volunteer Force, but had joined believing that he could do more good in his "own country by organising a force for defence in case of attack" and that he would "never consent to leading them in an unprovoked attack on anyone."[46]

Ulster Special Service Force cap badge with the red hand painted to highlight it from the bronze badge. (Somme Museum)

---

44 Perry, Nicholas (ed)., *Major General Oliver Nugent and the Ulster Division 1915-1918* (2007).
45 *History of Ireland*: Vol.10 No.1 Spring 2002 –The Ulster Volunteers 1913-14:Force or farce? – Timothy Bowman.
46 Perry, Nicholas (ed), *Major General Oliver Nugent and the Ulster Division 1915-1918* (2007).

A British military intelligence report in March 1914 believed that from an estimated strength of 80,000 to 110,000 all ranks in the UVF "a striking force of 10-15,000 has been formed – promised £1 per week on embodiment".[47]

Mounted Infantry

Whilst a number of cavalry detachments were available in Aghadowey, Newtowncunningham, South Down and Ballymena, the Enniskillen Horse was the only full cavalry regiment raised.[48]

The Commanding Officer of the County Antrim Volunteers wrote to his officers of the Antrim Regiments on 21 October 1913, requesting that they compile a list of all the names of men suitable for a mounted Corps and to have their horses examined and registered if found fit.[49] The Ballymena unit was formed by The Hon. Arthur O'Neill, a Captain in the 2nd Life Guards and the MP for mid-Antrim. O'Neill was killed in action at Klein Zillebeke Ridge on 6 November 1914, aged 38, the first member of the House of Commons to die in the Great War.[50, 51]

At the opposite side of Ulster the Enniskillen Horse was brought under the UVF in October 1913 and was later addressed at one of its parades by Major Viscount Crichton, Royal Horse Guards, and grandson of the Earl of Erne,[52] who said of it, "if there were more bodies like the Enniskillen Horse throughout the Empire it would be a very good thing for it."[53]

The three officers secured by Trimble for his Enniskillen Horse held commissions in the Leicester, York and East Kent Yeomanry Regiments. The absence of their presence being mentioned in Royal Irish Constabulary reports regarding parades suggests, that whilst they may have been in command of elements of the Enniskillen Horse, they were not always present; questioning their effectiveness in the event of mobilisation.[54] However their absence may also have been to prevent their court martial, still being serving officers.

At field training at Castle Hume in June 1914 the UVF General Officer Commanding (GOC) inspected the Enniskillen Horse, which had turned out nearly at full strength, and observed them defending a position dismounted, which it was reported they did well, although it was acknowledged that the attacking force was far too weak.[55]

Reports indicated that the South Down units were present at parades in September 1913 at Kilkeel, Newry and Banbridge, when again the General Officer Commanding inspected local detachments of UVF, which were described in orders as "a well mounted handy looking lot of men". At the Dromore parade a mounted escort of UVF provided the Guard of Honour.[56]

Likewise in October 1913 in subsequent UVF Orders favourable comment was made of the "well-mounted detachment" which formed an escort for Sir Edward Carson when he visited Cookstown.[57]

Whilst the Ulster Volunteer Force had been raising their own units the GOC of British Troops in Belfast, Brigadier General Count Gleichen, believed that in the event of civil war, the North

---

47 Bowman Timothy, 'The Ulster Volunteers: Force or Farce?', *History of Ireland*, Vol. 10, No. 1, spring 2002.
48 Bowman, Timothy, *Carson's Army: Ulster Volunteer Force, 1910-22* (2007).
49 Commanding Officer, County Antrim volunteers officers of Antrim Regiments 21 October 1913
50 <http://en.wikipedia.org/wiki/Arthur_O%27Neill> (Accessed 17 September 2013).
51 UVF Order 139, 1914 – Somme Museum.
52 Bowman, Timothy, *Carson's Army: Ulster Volunteer Force, 1910-22* (2007).
53 Irish Times – 18/10/1913.
54 Bowman, Timothy, *Carson's Army: Ulster Volunteer Force, 1910-22* (2007).
55 UVF Orders 68, 1914 – Somme Museum.
56 UVF Order 02, 1913 – Somme Museum.
57 UVF Orders 05, 1913 – Somme Museum.

A section of the Enniskillen Horse who provided a cavalry element to the UVF in 1914. (Somme Museum)

Irish Horse, a supplementary reserve unit, would go over to the Ulster Volunteers, alleviating to some degree the UVF shortage of mounted units.

Nurses and Ambulance

In November 1913 the General Officer Commanding UVF gave the Volunteer Medical Board full responsibility for the Ulster Volunteer Medical and Nursing Corps.[58]

The male members of the Voluntary Aid Detachment (VAD) had their duties defined by the Secretary of the UVF Medical Board as follows:

> The duties of the VAD (male) with us will have to include Field Ambulance, and also we will have to arrange the carriage of the sick to the nearest hospitals. It is impossible for us in the short time at our disposal to organise any extensive Field Ambulance, so our VAD must be trained and organised that they will convey the sick from the place where they are injured to the nearest Dressing Station, from thence to whatever hospital is nearest, whether it is a Clearing Hospital or a Field Hospital. All we can hope for in our male VADs is that they should have fair knowledge of the stretcher drill and the handling of the sick. Amongst them should be a number who would be available as dressers in applying First Aid, Splints, etc.

Issues concerning field training were referred to the local battalion commander who had to ensure VADs were kept acquainted of the field movements of the battalion and its companies. This

---

58 UVF Order 10, 1913 – Somme Museum.

Inspection of the UVF nursing staff, 1914. (Somme Museum)

often involved a number of men posing as casualties and given tickets or cards which described their injuries which had to be dealt with by the Divisional Stretcher bearers and the VADs.[59]

It was intended that during active operations the VADs would operate as far as possible within their Regimental District under the orders of their Regimental Commander, receiving their direction from the County Commander. However in the event of having to operate outside their area or County they would come under the orders of the senior UVF officers in the district in which they were operating.[60]

The following for County Antrim provides an example of the identified structure for dressing stations, clearing hospitals and base hospitals:

Dressing Stations
North: Dunloy, Rasharkin, Loughgille, The Vow, Ballybogey, Ballintoy, Dunseverick, Moss Side, Armoy, Hill Mount, Clough, Galgorm Road, Ballee, Connor
Central: Carrickfergus, Greenisland, Larne, Greencastle, Glynn, Ballyclare
South: Randalstown

Clearing Hospitals
North: Ballymoney, Dunderave, Stranocum, Ballycastle, Clare Park, Gledheather, Cushendall
Central: Carrickfergus, Whitehouse, Whiteabbey, Kincraig, Thronemount, Balyclare
South: Antrim Castle, Shanes Castle, Crumlin, Glenavy, Dunmurry

Base Hospitals
Portrush, Ballymena, Larne, Lisburn, Holestone (Convalescent)

---

59 Letter from Div Com WT Adair on Voluntary Aid Detachments – 13 June 1914.
60 Letter from Div Com WT Adair on Voluntary Aid Detachments – 13 June 1914.

A recruitment poster for the Voluntary Aid Detachment. (Somme Museum)

The principle role intended for female VAD members was to take charge of the various dressing stations and hospitals. Whether dressing stations and hospitals were required to be opened in any district of the county was left to a decision made between the District Commanding Officer and the Medical Officer.

With regards identification of the designated hospitals, in County Antrim General Adair informed his commanders that Red Cross flags could be obtained by reference to him, they were 3½ feet by 2½ feet at a cost of 1/6d each and postage.[61]

The Ulster Volunteer Force was fortunate to secure the services of experienced skilled nurses to deliver the necessary training to the emerging corps. Lilian Spender commented very favourably on the training she received in practical nursing ; "Miss Ketch, an Army nurse, who has had five years Red Cross work in India, and is used to training ordinary Tommies for ambulance work at a moment's notice, so to speak, and so is exactly what we want."[62]

Lady Spender purchased Ambulance Uniform hats the day after the UVF landed their arms and ammunition in Ulster ports.[63]

Each battalion's First Aid Corps would include 72 stretcher bearers and 18 stretchers.[64] The doctor in charge of the North Down Regiment, 1st Battalion, issued a directive instructing that the battalion's First Aid Corps should be under the direct control of a 'Battalion Surgeon'. "The First Aid and Stretcher Corps will accompany the battalion in the field, marching in the rear, and will form a dressing camp. The wounded will be collected and carried back to the field dressing camp by the stretcher-bearers from whence they will be conveyed back to the nearest hospital."[65] His direction went on to explain how each Battalion's First Aid Corps would comply with the central direction and include 18 stretchers and 72 stretcher bearers.[66]

---

61 No134/1914 – North Antrim Regiment – 17 June 1914 – Somme Museum.
62 Bowman, Timothy, *Carson's Army: Ulster Volunteer Force, 1910-22* (2007).
63 Parkinson, Alan F, *Friends in High Places: Ulster's Resistance to Irish Home Rule, 1912-14* (2012).
64 Orr, Philip, *The Road to the Somme* (1987).
65 PRONI – D1540/60A-B.
66 Eakins, Arthur, *The Somme – What Happened to the Casualties* (2008).

Stretcher bearers of the Ulster Volunteer Force. (Somme Museum)

On 11 August 1914 the Women's Unionist Council offered the services of the UVF Nursing Corps and its dressing stations throughout Ulster to the war effort.[67]

Transport

Writing to the officers of the regiments under his command on 21 October 1913 the Commanding Officer, County Antrim Volunteers, gave them prior warning that in the near future directions would be issued from Headquarters requiring the registration of all motor and horse vehicles which their owners were prepared to place at the disposal of the UVF, free of charge. There was also to be the enrolment of chauffeurs and drivers, however it was highlighted that they would not be expected to attain efficiency for the ranks.[68]

The UVF Transport Board suggested that each UVF company should obtain two first-line transport carts, one to be used for ammunition whilst the second would carry tools. In addition two heavier wagons were to be obtained for second line transport.

Intelligence

The Intelligence Branch within Headquarters was involved in the deciphering of intercepted police messages.

---

67 Grayson, Richard S, *Belfast Boys – How Unionists and Nationalists fought and died together in the First World War* (2009).
68 Commanding Officer, County Antrim volunteers officers of Antrim Regiments 21 October 1913.

The code of the Government's intelligence department was known to the Unionist leaders and its wires were frequently tapped for information, particularly around the period of the Larne gun-running, giving the Ulster Volunteers a definite advantage[69] in their planning.

Motor Section

Whilst Wilfred Spender has recorded that the UVF Motor Corps was very well organised this may not always have been the case. General Adair wrote to one of his Regimental Commanders prior to the Larne gun-running about the need to have sufficient transport for 1,000 rifles, highlighting that "We are lamentable [sic] short in Co. Antrim + have not half the transport we want."[70]

The local Volunteers in around Waringstown, County Down, undertook route marches known locally as 'Sunday afternoon strolls' which despite what their name might suggest could be up to ten miles in length. However not all the locals were sympathetic with their activities such as Mr Richardson, a Quaker from Moyallen, who would inform them on occasions and in no uncertain terms that were breaking the Sabbath, even if it was for a "fight against popery".[71]

Four thousand Ulster Volunteers paraded through Armagh City on Saturday, 4 October 1913, a parade which included nurses, stretcher bearers and cavalry. Despite the Nationalist controlled Armagh Urban District Council refusing permission for displays of loyalist bunting, flags and posters, the day itself passed off quietly.[72]

The meeting ended with the singing of the National Anthem which included a specially written verse;[73]

> God bless our native land!
> May Heaven's protecting hand
> Still guard our shore
> May peace her power extend
> Foe be transformed to friend
> And Ulster's right depend,
> On War no more.

Despite often being derided by Nationalists and Liberals alike, the drilling and parading of the UVF attracted positive comments from others. After a large scale inspection of Volunteers in County Antrim the following appeared in the *Yorkshire Post* on 22 September 1913:

> As far as I could detect in very careful observation, there were not half a dozen of them unqualified by physique or age to play a manly part. They reminded me more than anything else – except that but a few of them were beyond the best fighting age – of the finest class of our National Reservists. There was certainly nothing of the mock soldier about them. Led by keen, smart-looking officers, they marched past in quarter column with fine, swinging steps, as if they had been in training for years … officers who have had the teaching of them tell me that the rapidity with which they have become efficient is greater than has ever come within their experience in training recruits for either the Territorials or the Regular Service.

---

69   Shearman, Hugh, *Not an Inch: A Study of Northern Ireland and Lord Craigavon* (1942).
70   Bowman, Timothy, *Carson's Army: Ulster Volunteer Force, 1910-22* (2007) and PRONI D.1238/72 – letter from Gen Adair to Capt Hon. A O'Neil – 21/04/1914.
71   Orr, Philip, *The Road to the Somme* (1987).
72   Orr, Philip, *The Road to the Somme* (1987).
73   Bowman, Timothy, *Carson's Army: Ulster Volunteer Force, 1910-22* (2007).

A group of Ulster Volunteer Force members. (Somme Museum)

In Armagh City in October 1913 over 4,000 Ulster Volunteers from the County Armagh Regiment turn out for Edward Carson's visit to the city. (T Wylie)

That is a tribute to the resolute and determined spirit which animates them. They are drawn from every section of the community. There were in the ranks landowners, businessmen, mill hands, farmers and their sons, country peasants, gardeners, fishermen, plasterers, and shopkeepers, and in one contingent even such indispensable members of the body politic as golf greenkeepers had taken the day off to attend the parade.

Ulster Volunteers under firearms instruction at one of the training camps. (Somme Museum)

By July 1914, Headquarters felt it necessary to issue a reminder to all that unless special circumstances demanded it no parade for inspections or ceremonies were to occur without prior application and approval from UVF Headquarters.[74]

In order to consolidate and improve the expanding Force a series of camps of instruction were established to standardise and embed military style training.

These would evolve into often elaborate training events, including in the autumn of 1913, camps of instruction for officers and NCOs.[75]

It is believed that the idea for a military style training camp was first mooted in August 1913 by Ambrose Ricardo who held the rank of Colonel in the UVF.

Ricardo, great-grandson of the famous eighteenth century economist David Ricardo, had served in the Royal Irish Fusiliers and saw service both on the North West Frontier in India and in the Boer War. During this military service he was awarded the Distinguished Service Order with three bars for gallantry. He met his future wife Ella Herdman whilst in India where she was visiting relatives and he returned with her to the Herdman family home in Sion Mills. On retiring from the Army in 1904 he became a director of the family flax mill, Herdmans Ltd, Sion Mills. They had married in 1893 and whilst they had no children of their own, they provided movie shows and concerts for the village children and led a very active life, being involved with many charitable activities.[76, 77]

---

74 UVF Orders 75, 1914 – Somme Museum.
75 Bowman, Timothy, *Carson's Army: Ulster Volunteer Force, 1910-22* (2007).
76 Orr, Philip, *The Road to the Somme* (1987).
77 Ulster Volunteers, January 1913 – Ulster-Scots Community Network <http://www.ulster-scots.com/uploads/901740969819.PDF> (Accessed 5 August 2013).

Edward Carson addressing the Ulster Volunteers at Clandeboye. General Sir George Richardson is mounted in the foreground. (Somme Museum: 1994-282)

The first such camp was held in October 1913 at the Duke of Abercorn's estate, Baronscourt. It was intended for officers and NCOs of the fifteen Battalions of the Tyrone Regiment, except for a few special cases. In order to accommodate those attending the camp, the stables and a few vacant cottages on the estate were turned over for billeting.

On Friday 10 October, the Ulster Menu Company arrived at Baronscourt to provide food for the camp and two marquees were erected a few yards from the stables, offering venues for lectures on 'military topics'. Despite the late harvest causing problems for the farmers who were to be involved, the men began to arrive on Saturday 11 October, handing over their £1 and admission ticket. The attendees were again a true cross-section of Edwardian society, including, an auctioneer, a barrister, a chauffeur, a cooper, a fishery inspector, a French polisher, a watchmaker and six clergymen.

The next morning reveille was sounded at 7:00 a.m. and following church and lunch there was a Sunday afternoon walk through the estate.

On Monday those attending the camp were divided into six companies for training purposes and were visited by Lieutenant-General Richardson in the afternoon.

On Tuesday there was musketry and infantry training, followed by a lecture on 'field defences' and a sing-song.

The next day the men were given a lantern lecture on the South African War and the lessons learned, whilst Thursday involved squad drill, musketry and battalion drill followed by a lecture on scouting. The benefit of some of the military lectures may have been questionable, delivered as they were by army officers who had served in the furthest outposts of empire to men with no military experience. For example the lecture on 'Scouting and Intelligence Duties in the Field' advised those listening that 'a low thick dust indicates infantry while a light, high cloud of dust is raised by cavalry', perhaps more relevant in South Africa rather that the fields and drumlins of Ulster.

The Young Citizen Volunteers at Ormiston House, Belfast. (*Belfast Telegraph*)

Friday involved more advanced work on targeting in rifle fire and an inspection of defence works, such as trenches, sandbags and high wire entanglements at a nearby fortified farm.

Their day on Saturday culminated with a march to Newtownstewart railway station from whence they departed. During their time there, they consumed over a ton of potatoes and 1,470 lb of beef. No one who attended was financially worse off as compensation for any loss of wages was provided, where necessary.[78]

Knowledge of the existence of the camp had obviously spread near and far as during the week a group of English suffragettes arrived with firearms apparently intent on receiving some military style training. However they were told they could not participate with Ricardo ultimately having to take their guns and march them out of the camp.[79]

The UVF Headquarters only made small grants towards the running of the camps, requiring the organisers to find the additional finance necessary. Attendance at the camps often resulted in men using their annual holiday time from their employment and also being out of pocket.[80] The catering at a number of the camps appears to have been supplied by commercial firms.[81]

As well as at camps, classes of instruction were held in other appropriate locations such as one held in 'Ormiston' for various leaders in November 1913 by Colonel R Spencer Chichester, Officer Commanding East Belfast Regiment.[82]

In June 1914 Colonel Hacket Pain issued instructions to divisional, regimental and battalion commanders to assist further with musketry training, the intention being to improve the men's familiarity with the sights on their rifles and in particular the sight window when on a target. The solution was simple, taking advantage of the bright summer evenings and setting a few men out a various known ranges, 600, 800, 1000 or 1200 yards as directed, standing, kneeling and lying down. The men under instruction would then align their sights from a tripod to the various

---

78   Orr, Philip, *The Road to the Somme* (1987).
79   Orr, Philip, *The Road to the Somme* (1987).
80   Bowman, Timothy, *Carson's Army: Ulster Volunteer Force, 1910-22* (2007).
81   Bowman, Timothy, *Carson's Army: Ulster Volunteer Force, 1910-22* (2007).
82   UVF Order 17, 1913 – Somme Museum.

Edward Carson on the platform watches the ranks of the Ulster Volunteers drawn up at 'The Great Review' at Balmoral, 27 September 1913. (Somme Museum)

targets the men presented. It was also suggested that the 'targets' could add variety by concealing themselves until a pre-agreed signal, then availing of the available cover, again re-appearing in a different position thus providing a more complex aiming exercise for the men under instruction.[83]

Ever conscious of British public opinion a vigorous campaign was instigated to ensure the regular reporting of UVF parades and demonstrations in British national and regional newspapers in an effort to maintain their support. However the result was mixed; condemnation from the *Daily News*, the *Manchester Guardian* and the *Daily Herald*. Whilst *The Times* had sympathy with the cause of the Ulster Protestants it was alarmed by the activities of the Ulster Volunteer Force. However, Tory newspapers such as the *Morning Post*, the *Yorkshire Post* and the *Liverpool Daily Courier* openly gave their support; the latter paper compared a review at Balmoral to being unequalled since the marshalling of Cromwell's Puritan Army. It also acknowledged the eclectic mix of the membership from shipyard and factory workers, through to clergy, doctors and professional men and clerks.[84]

During the Easter camps organised at the request of the Ulster Unionist Council in April 1914, UVF Headquarters arranged for a series of passes to be issued which enabled the admission of certain selected cinematograph operators and photographers to the camps and parades held between 8 and 18 April. To assist in their passage those concerned would also have in their possession a letter signed by the Officer i/c Administration, UVF Headquarters, and countersigned by Mr Dawson Bates, Secretary, Ulster Unionist Council.[85]

The British League for the Defence of Ulster and the Union, organised under Lord Willoughby de Broke was active in recruiting ex-officers to service in the UVF.[86]

---

83   Musketry Instructions – 30 June 1914.
84   Orr, Philip, *The Road to the Somme* (1987).
85   UVF Orders 36, 1914 – Somme Museum.
86   Bowman, Timothy, *Carson's Army: Ulster Volunteer Force, 1910-22* (2007).

Volunteers emptying their bandoliers at Craigavon House. (Somme Museum)

From May 1913 they were compiling lists of able-bodied men who would be willing and able to join the loyalists in Ulster. However there were those in UVF HQs who believed their priority was arms and ammunition and not additional untrained or semi-trained volunteers.[87]

Despite these views, by the spring of 1914 the British League claimed to have secured 5,000 volunteers in Liverpool. On 10 July 1914 the Ulster Volunteer Force paraded in Glasgow, being inspected by General Sir Reginald Pole-Carew. Their initial drilling was apparently carried out in the city as athletic clubs attached to Orange Lodges.[88]

During 1913 one of the new recruits to the British League was Captain Frank Percy Crozier.

Coming from an Anglo-Irish family he had wanted to follow the strong family tradition of joining the British Army, however his attempts were frustrated in 1896 because he was too short and too light. Instead he headed to Ceylon as a tea planter. The outbreak of the South African war in 1899 gave him the opportunity to enlist as standards were less tight abroad. Following fighting in the Boer War he joined the West African Frontier Force fighting the Hausa tribesmen in Nigeria. After treatment for a drink problem and malaria he moved to Canada where he helped raise a squadron of Saskatchewan Light Horse, met Shackleton of Antarctic exploration fame, helped lay a telephone line through Manitoba, and was also most killed in a hurricane until he finally became a teetotaller.[89]

---

87 Bowman, Timothy, *Carson's Army: Ulster Volunteer Force, 1910-22* (2007).
88 Bowman, Timothy, *Carson's Army: Ulster Volunteer Force, 1910-22* (2007).
89 Orr, Philip, *The Road to the Somme* (1987).

The Special Service men of the West Belfast Volunteers parade for a review by Sir Edward Carson at Glencairn, Belfast, 6 June 1914. (Somme Museum)

He had little experience of the issues of Ulster and her politics, with one exception; on one occasion as a result of his military duties he was involved in quelling riots on the Falls Road in Belfast during which he became impressed with both sides during the action.[90]

Once out of the army and on the reserve, Crozier became involved through the Conservative party in the British League for the Support of Ulster and the Union. On signing a form and joining the League he received in the post a few days later a package which resembled a wrapped umbrella, but when he opened the unmarked parcel he discovered a .303 calibre carbine with a falling block mechanism. Later he received an invitation to luncheon at the Hotel Cecil and a meeting presided over by Lord Londonderry which was in turn addressed by Sir Edward Carson and Captain James Craig.[91]

A few months later he arrived in Belfast and was handed 300 blank attestation forms, documents very like the army form, 300 names of men, clothing, arms and ammunition and a place to parade and told to get on with it.[92] The task he was given was the recruiting of 300 men as part of the Special Service Section from the West Belfast Regiment. The Special Service Section in the Belfast area was to be a force of approximately 3,000 men drawn from each of the four City Regiments, intended to be cream of the UVF, well trained, uniformed and ready for immediate action, described by Crozier as 'shock troops'.[93]

Whilst he had a respect for the men under his command, his reformed ways meant that his tolerance for alcohol abuse was non-existent. Any man in his Special Service unit who was caught indulging or under the influence received a personal dismissal from Crozier.[94]

In early 1914 attendance at drills by the West Belfast UVF often numbered no more than 50 men, however 'Divine Service Parades' could attract up to 350 men.[95] However by April 1914 the West Belfast UVF could muster 400 men for almost daily route marches under the command

---

90 Crozier, Brig-Gen FP Crozier, CB, CMG, DSO, *Ireland for Ever* (1932).
91 Crozier, Brig-Gen FP Crozier, CB, CMG, DSO, *Ireland for Ever* (1932).
92 Crozier, Brig-Gen FP Crozier, CB, CMG, DSO, *Ireland for Ever* (1932).
93 Crozier, Brig-Gen FP Crozier, CB, CMG, DSO, *Ireland for Ever* (1932).
94 Orr, Philip, *The Road to the Somme* (1987).
95 Grayson, Richard S, *Belfast Boys – How Unionists and Nationalists fought and died together in the First World War* (2009).

Ulster Volunteers on guard at the gates of Craigavon, the East Belfast home of Sir James Craig, MP. (Somme Museum)

of Matthew Glover, a former lance-sergeant in the King's Royal Rifle Corps. One company drilled under the instruction of two former members of the Royal Irish Rifles, Sergeant Major WJ Brannigan and Sergeant Samuel Roberts, in Stewart's Yard, Shankill Road, whilst another company was drilled by two former Royal Irish Fusiliers, Charles Bell and his brother Francis.[96]

By February 1914, Captain Spender had hoped that each county should have been able to supply several complete squadrons of vehicles to be co-ordinated eventually as a province-wide Motor Car Corps; FH Rogers was appointed as Commander of the Motor Car Corps in February 1914.[97] A UVF Circular from the Old Town Hall required that one squadron should be capable of conveying one company of the Ulster Volunteer Force or '100 refugees', with a removable UVF emblem being provided for each vehicle. A list was also to be prepared of garages owned by 'reliable Unionists',[98] which obviously inferred that there were others who may not have been relied on.

The corps was organised into sections of four cars and in squadrons of 17 cars each.[99]

---

96 Grayson, Richard S, *Belfast Boys – How Unionists and Nationalists fought and died together in the First World War* (2009).
97 UVF Order 13, 1914 – Somme Museum.
98 PRONI – D1540/36A-B.
99 McNeill, Ronald, *Ulster's Stand for Union* (1922).

The motor squadron, 2nd Battalion, 3rd County Down Regiment was capable of carrying a total of 212 people in its 31 vehicles which also included two charabancs. By May 1914 the commander of the squadron, RS Redmond, had given each member a series of careful instructions; each vehicle should carry ten yards of strong rope for breakdowns; when out driving, a companion should be taken and in case of accident there should be three short sharp blasts of a horn or whistle. Whilst all cars should carry arms it was also advised that passengers should carry a stout stick or baton.[100]

Discipline

In 1913 Lord Londonderry observed that "It is easy to baton an undisciplined mob into surrender, but it is a harder task to coerce a disciplined and organised community". The ability to instil this discipline was evident in Captain FP Crozier's men from the Shankill Road, as ATQ Stewart observed the only sanction Crozier had over them was threat of dismissal, "rather than face the disgrace of having his rifle and uniform taken from him, and having women and children call after him in the street, a special volunteer would make any sacrifice, even to giving up drink". A direct reference to occasions when on dismissing a man from his unit, he subsequently called at their house to retrieve their uniform, resulting in ridicule from wives and children.

In October 1913 Robert Nesbitt, adjutant commanding the 2nd Battalion, South Down Regiment, UVF, was accompanied by a local band on a route march from Newry to Bessbrook. A policeman asked Nesbitt not to march his men to the 'pump', an area recognised by both Unionists and Nationalists as neutral. Nesbitt agreed to the request ordering the battalion to 'about right wheel' and marched them back. The leader of the band refused to comply. Nesbitt later reported to the battalion's Commanding Officer, Captain Roger Hall, brother of the UVF's Military Secretary, that despite one of the UVF instructors falling out to follow the band the remainder of the battalion displayed splendid discipline by following their orders.[101]

Such discipline is to acknowledge that whilst it was a part-time, unpaid force, the usual military sanctions available to the regular army had little impact and if pushed too hard the individual under censure could simply tender his resignation. However there were options available to the Ulster Volunteer Force which the regular army had not. Where a volunteer was 'employed' by an officer there was always the option of some form of financial sanction, though there is no evidence of this being employed.

In Kilrea on 11 July 1914 local Unionist and Nationalist crowds found themselves in a stand-off following revolver shots and cries from Unionists of "Bring out the rifles"; the local Royal Irish Constabulary aided by local Unionists managed to diffuse the situation.[102]

To those who didn't attend drill the threat of dismissal could however be ineffective; Lord Northland's letter as Commanding Officer of 4th (Dungannon) Battalion, Tyrone Regiment, to those members who were not regularly attending meetings left those concerned in little doubt:

> On 31st March, 1914, any enrolled man who is not an efficient Volunteer in either the Active or Reserve Branches of the UVF will be struck off the strength of the Battalion.
> It must be borne in mind that, should times of hardship and distress arrive, those who do not take the trouble to make themselves efficient will be left to shift for themselves.

---

100 PRONI – D1540/23A.
101 Ulster Volunteers, January 1913 – Ulster-Scots Community Network <http://www.ulster-scots.com/uploads/901740969819.PDF> (Accessed 5 August 2013).
102 *Northern Whig* – 13/7/1914.

A Company, Ulster Volunteer Force, Dungannon. (T Wylie)

> Except under special circumstances there will be no Recruits' Classes after the month of January, 1914, so that those who do not start now will not have a chance of doing so again.[103]

The letter appears to have some effect when 14 of the 30 to whom it was addressed returned to drill whilst others claimed business, family or ill-health for their reasons of non-attendance.

The carrot and stick approach has often proven to be an effective method and this was also evident in the Ulster Volunteer Force with the use of certificates in drill, musketry and machine guns issued on a local basis to those competent in their use. The design of a Certificate of Proficiency was approved in September 1913, being obtained from the printers, Messrs W&G Baird, Belfast, with costs being borne by the respective County.[104]

Especially after the arrival of additional weapons one of the strongest sanctions available to a UVF officer was withholding or withdrawing a rifle from a Volunteer; they were seen as a prized possession. Officers were encouraged to issue them only to those who were "fitted in all ways to be entrusted with them."[105]

By the time enrolment to the UVF was closed on 28 February 1914[106] there was between 90,000 and 100,000 men on the lists.[107]

Regardless of the closure of recruitment into the UVF the young men of Ballydivity, near Dervock, County Antrim, approached their local clergyman to drill them. Having no previous experience he approached John Leslie Stewart-Moore who was home from Dublin for the Easter break from his studies at Trinity College where he had joined the Officer Training Corps. Drilling them in the local Orange Hall he took his men to a parade of the North Antrim Battalion on

---
103 PRONI, D/1132/6/17 – Letter from Lord Northland.
104 UVF Order 09, 1913 – Somme Museum.
105 Bowman, Timothy, *Carson's Army: Ulster Volunteer Force, 1910-22* (2007).
106 UVF Order 06, 1914 – Somme Museum.
107 Orr, Philip, *The Road to the Somme* (1987).

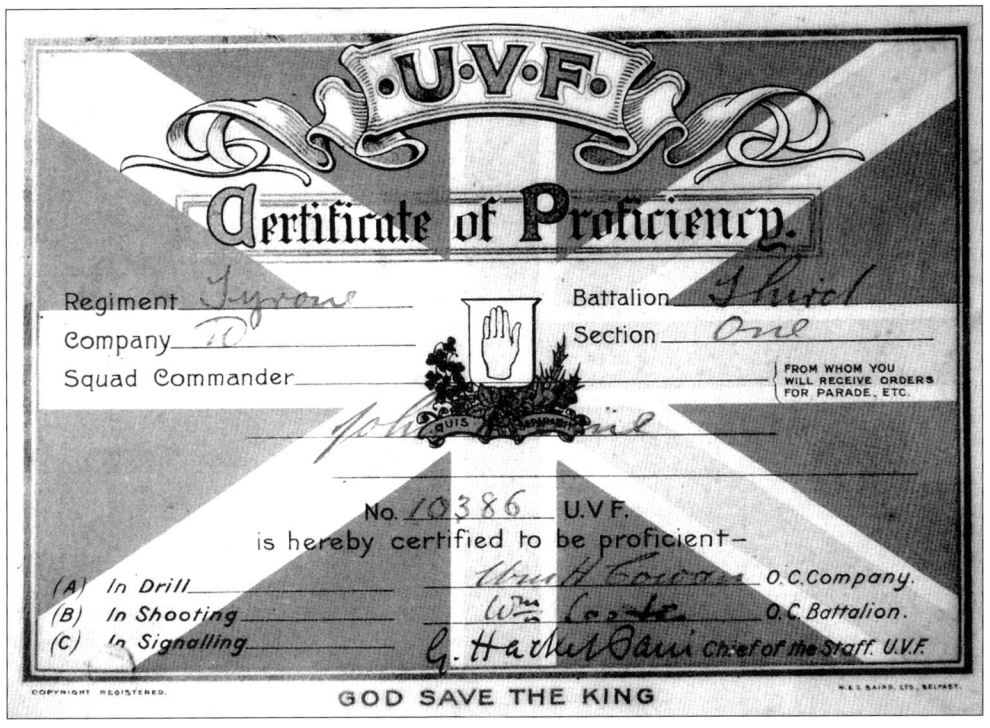

Ulster Volunteer Force Certificate of Proficiency. (I Kyle)

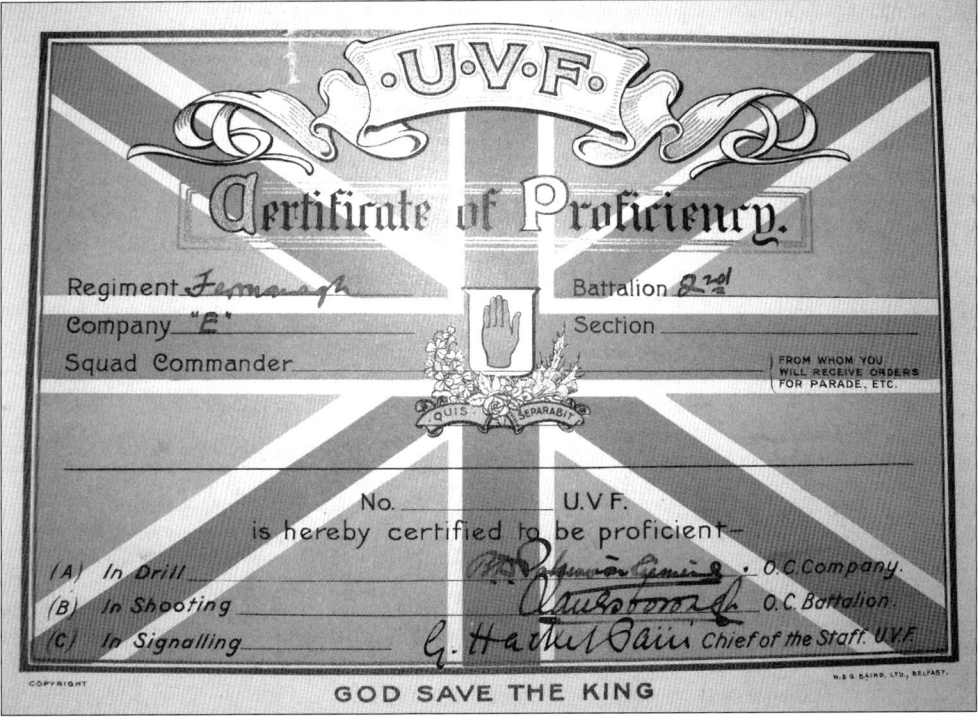

UVF Certificate of Proficiency in respect of 'E' Company, 2nd Battalion, Fermanagh Regiment. (Somme Museum)

A receipt from W.N. Ferguson and Sons to The Right Hon. Lord Creighton for four dozen wooden guns at the cost of £1 8 shillings in June 1914. (Somme Museum)

Easter Monday. Despite an outraged adjutant not being welcoming to the apparent ad hoc group they were eventually included into the Dervock Company of the local Battalion, proudly joining a parade service, complete with dummy rifles, in Amoy Presbyterian Meeting House the following Sunday.[108]

The demand for sufficient weapons was not only coming from the membership. It was also becoming more pressing from other quarters as the delaying action caused by the Parliament Act was due to run out in the summer of 1914 and with it the final introduction of Home Rule.

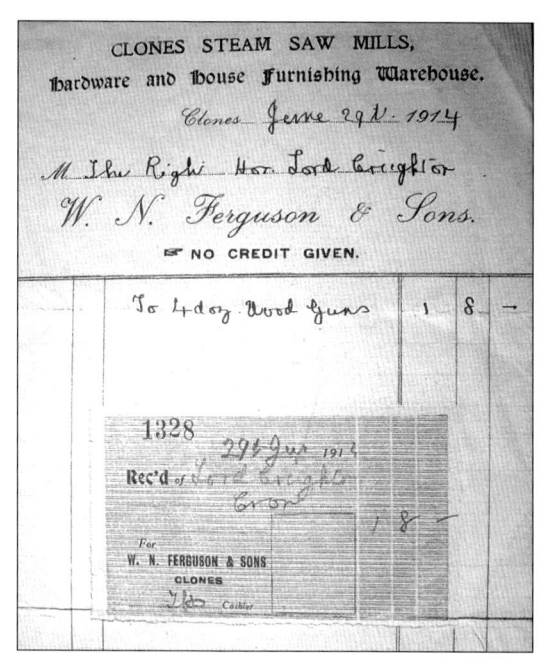

Early in 1913, Frank Hall and Fred Crawford imported six Vickers Maxim machine guns at the cost of £300 each from the Vickers Company in boxes; labelled 'Wireless apparatus'. Hall and his brother Roger test fired one of the weapons from the tennis court at the family home, Narrow Water Castle, bullets ricocheting of a bank and raining down on estate workers a 1,000 yards away, with thankfully no casualties recorded.[109]

Other attempts at importing weapons included the story of a case of arms being dropped into the sea with a float, off the coast of Ballycastle, whilst two Customs Officers were being seasick on another part of the vessel.

For a period of time an antique shop in Hammersmith, London, sent regular consignments to Ulster until the police in June 1913 intercepted a consignment which contained between 6,000 and 7,000 Italian rifles; a forgotten Act of Parliament being invoked, on the subject of testing gun barrels, to justify the seizure. The Gun Barrel Proof Act, 1868 had been introduced to protect British industry rather than to prevent illegal use. The guns were never 'claimed' as the penalty for this breach of statue would have attracted a fine of two pounds per barrel and the guns had cost considerably less than £2 each. Around the same time approximately 500,000 rounds of ammunition were also confiscated disguised in cement bags.[110, 111]

On another occasion Fred Crawford in the guise of Mr John Washington of the USA purchased machine guns from Vickers at Woolwich for use in the Revolutionary War in Mexico, resulting in a generous commission which ultimately found its way into the Ulster Unionist Council funds.[112]

Crawford, working initially along with Sir William Bull, MP, and Bull's brother in-law Captain H A Budden, led to Budden and Bull establishing a 'front' firm, John Ferguson and Company,

---

108 Orr, Philip, *The Road to the Somme* (1987).
109 Ulster Volunteers, January 1913 – Ulster-Scots Community Network <http://www.ulster-scots.com/uploads/901740969819.PDF> (Accessed 5 August 2013).
110 Shearman, Hugh, *Not an Inch: A Study of Northern Ireland and Lord Craigavon* (1942).
111 Bowman, Timothy, *Carson's Army: Ulster Volunteer Force, 1910-22* (2007).
112 Shearman, Hugh, *Not an Inch: A Study of Northern Ireland and Lord Craigavon* (1942).

based in stable yards adjoining the Windsor Hotel, Hammersmith. For their activities they also had available a legitimate firm of coach builders, FM Foyer & Co. Ltd, owned by Bull's former chauffeur and based also in Hammersmith. Crawford would later become convinced that police success against their Hammersmith operation was as a direct result of Budden, an alcoholic with financial troubles, informing to the police in return for a financial reward.[113]

In Belfast, Sergeant Joseph Edwards, Royal Irish Constabulary, Belfast Detective Branch, reported that the Orange Order in Belfast was making arrangements to arm its members and other Orangemen who were willing to pay 6d each per month towards the cost of their arms.[114] This contrasts with comments from Fred Crawford concerning promises of practical support from Ulster and, specifically referring to the Orange Order, he noted that the leaders of the Order would talk "glibly about fighting and resistance but when I offered them rifles they looked at me askance."[115]

On 6 June 1913 several hundred Italian rifles were seized in Dublin being transferred in a furniture van from Liverpool, the consignment addressed to Lord Farnham in County Cavan.[116] A second consignment was seized in Belfast, consisting of 12 cases of over a 1,000 rifles with bayonets attached being shipped from Manchester to Liverpool as 'electrical plant'.[117]

Three days later, 9 June Lord Roberts VC, the last Commander-in-Chief of the British Army, a position he held for three years until 1904,[118] wrote to another old soldier, Colonel TE Hickman, Conservative MP for Wolverhampton:

> Dear Hickman,
> I have been a long time finding a Senior Officer to help in the Ulster business, but I think I have got one now. His name is Lieut.-General Sir George Richardson, KCB, c/o Messrs, Henry S King & Co., Pall Mall, SW. He is a retired Indian officer, active and in good health. He is not an Irishman, but has settled in Ireland … Richardson will be in London for about a month, and is ready to meet you at any time.
> I'm sorry to read about the capture of rifles.
> Believe me,
> Yours sincerely,
> ROBERTS[119]

Born in India with both his parents Southern Irish Protestants Roberts had been approached to lead the Ulster Volunteer Force. However despite his strong sympathy with the Ulster cause he was preoccupied with recruiting for the British Army in light of developing world events.[120]

In the autumn of 1913 there was an active campaign of propaganda instigated in England and Scotland which was undertaken by Ulster speakers and supported by the Ulster Women's Unionist Association (UWUA). To help this campaign the UWUA employed 93 voluntary workers who visited 90 constituencies and addressed 230 meetings. By the conclusion it was reckoned that over 100,000 electors had heard the case for Ulster from the lips of Ulster women.[121]

---

113 Bowman, Timothy, *Carson's Army: Ulster Volunteer Force, 1910-22* (2007).
114 Bowman, Timothy, *Carson's Army: Ulster Volunteer Force, 1910-22* (2007).
115 Parkinson, Alan F, *Friends in High Places: Ulster's Resistance to Irish Home Rule, 1912-14* (2012).
116 Hume, David, *"For Ulster and Her Freedom": The story of the April 1914 gun-running* (1989).
117 Ryan, AP, *Mutiny at the Curragh* (1956).
118 <http://www.nam.ac.uk/exhibitions/online-exhibitions/dads-army/roberts-family/lord-roberts> (Accessed 11 March 2014).
119 Ryan, AP, *Mutiny at the Curragh* (1956).
120 Ingram, Rev Brett, *Covenant and Challenge* (1989).
121 McNeill, Ronald, *Ulster's Stand for Union* (1922).

Florence Kerley (left) in UVF uniform with Master and Mrs Belshaw of Melrose Street, Belfast. (Somme Museum)

Members of the Ulster Volunteer Force at camp. (Somme Museum)

Between September 1911 and July 1914 there were over 5,000 meetings relating to Home Rule organised by Ulster Unionists and the Conservatives throughout towns and cities in England.[122]

Whilst speaking in Dublin in November 1913 Bonar Law urged the army in Ireland not to fight if they were ordered to move against Ulster, highlighting that the civil war which was feared would be impossible if the army refused to fight. He was not alone in calling on the army to consider its position in the emerging situation. The Reverend RGS King, a rector in County Londonderry, published a pamphlet in an attempt to convince the military that there was no moral alternative except to refuse to bear arms against Ulster.[123]

In December 1913, amidst widespread suspicions that sympathy for the Ulster cause might make army officers reluctant to move against the Ulster Volunteers, the Chief of the Imperial Staff Sir John French, recommended that Spender be cashiered (stripped of his commission – a social disgrace which disqualified the victim from any further Crown employment) *"pour decourager le autres"*, but this did not happen.[124]

JEB Seely, Secretary of State for War, in a cabinet memorandum in early December 1913 considered the problem of the army and its behaviour from the point of view of both the War Office and the serving officer:

> The law clearly lays down that a soldier is entitled to obey an order to shoot only if that order is reasonable under the circumstances. No one, from General Officer to private, is entitled to use more force than is required to maintain order and the safety of life and property. No Soldier can shelter himself behind an order given by a superior, if in fact that order is unreasonable and outrageous.
>
> If, therefore, officers and men in the Army were led to believe that they might be called upon to take some outrageous action, for instance, to massacre a demonstration of Orangemen, who were causing no danger to the lives of their neighbours, bad as were the effects on discipline in the Army, nevertheless it was true that they were in fact and in law justified in contemplating refusal to obey.
>
> There never had been and was not now any intention of giving outrageous and illegal orders to the Troops to crush helpless Ulstermen. The law would be respected and must be obeyed.
>
> What had to be faced was the possibility of action being required … where the police were unable to hold their own … There had been attempts … to dissuade troops form obeying lawful orders given to them when supporting the civil power. This amounted to a suggestion that officers or men could pick and choose between lawful and reasonable orders, saying that in one case they would obey and not in another … Such a state of affairs would of course be impossible. The Army had been quite steady. During the past year, there had not been brought to the notice of the authorities one single case of lack of discipline in this respect.
>
> … I plan to inform the Commanders-in-Chief … that I would hold each of them individually responsible to see that there was no conduct in their commands subversive to discipline. They would let it be clearly understood that any such conduct will be dealt with forthwith under King's Regulations. If any officer should tender his resignation they would ask for his reasons, and if he indicated in his reply that he desired to choose which order he would obey I would at once submit to the King that the officer would be cashiered.[125]

---

122 Parkinson, Alan F, *Friends in High Places: Ulster's Resistance to Irish Home Rule, 1912-14* (2012).
123 Muenger, Elizabeth A, *The British Military Dilemma in Ireland: Occupation Politics 1886-1914* (1991).
124 Holmes, Richard, *The Little Field Marshal: A Life of Sir John French* (2004).
125 Muenger, Elizabeth A, *The British Military Dilemma in Ireland: Occupation Politics 1886-1914* (1991).

Sir George Richardson taking the salute beside Edward Carson at an Ulster Volunteer event. James Craig is in the centre of the photograph. (Somme Museum)

This highlights that the thought of the possibility of the army and indeed its officers disobeying orders was already being considered in Whitehall.[126]

With an emphasis on the need for caution the following advice delivered by Carson in a speech at Plymouth was circulated to all UVF detachments in December 1913 with orders for it to be read at three successive parades:[127]

> I am bound to give those who trust me in the North of Ireland this piece of advice – and I have tried always never to go beyond a single step that was necessary, because I want to hurt neither your Constitution nor ours any more than we can help. I feel bound to give them this advice: – Let there be more secrecy, and less confidential relations with the authorities. Let them tell the Press less, and let them keep their own counsels more. I don't do it out of any hostility to the Government of the United Kingdom; I do it for self-preservation and self-defence.

On 20 January 1914, a deputation from County Antrim led by General Sir William Adair, Divisional Commander, a retired Royal Marine, met with Carson and Craig expressing their 'very great dissatisfaction … at the inadequate supply of arms – even for instructional purposes.' For the County Antrim force of 10,700 men they informed the leadership that they had just 150 .303 carbines and 50 Vetterli riles, the latter with no ammunition.[128]

On the same date and three days after reviewing the weaponless East Belfast UVF, Carson met with Fred Crawford and James Craig. Whilst Crawford had been initially reluctant he agreed to the request from Carson and Craig to organise further gun-running, however his condition was that it should be for at least 20,000 rifles in one consignment as opposed to the previous piecemeal

---

126 Muenger, Elizabeth A, *The British Military Dilemma in Ireland: Occupation Politics 1886-1914* (1991).
127 UVF Order 30, 1913 – Somme Museum.
128 Bowman, Timothy, *Carson's Army: Ulster Volunteer Force, 1910-22* (2007).

approach.¹²⁹ At a further meeting at 5 Eaton Place, London, at the beginning of February¹³⁰ Crawford warned Carson that some members of the Unionist Military Committee had no conception of the seriousness of the enterprise being proposed and he fully believed that if the reality dawned on them they would want it stopped. He made it clear that, "Those who back me up must run the risk equally with me of imprisonment."¹³¹ Whilst Crawford made it clear he was prepared to undertake the mission regardless of the risk to himself he wanted a reassurance from Carson that he had his backing. Carson reportedly rose to his full height, his face stern and grim, advanced to Crawford's chair, stared down and shook his clenched fist in his face and speaking in a steady, determined voice said, "Crawford, I'll see you through this business if I should have to go to prison for it." Crawford rose from his chair, held out his hand and said, "Sir Edward, that is all I want. I leave tonight. Goodbye"¹³², ¹³³ The next day the lean, red-haired Crawford was in Hamburg. He was building on plans which he had instigated when the Liberals came to power and would later recall that as early as 1907 he used his position as the secretary of the Reform Club, Belfast, to use the address for advertisements from a 'Hugh Matthews' in French, Belgian, Italian, German and Austrian newspapers seeking 10,000 rifles and a 1,000,000 rounds of small-arm ammunition.¹³⁴ It is unlikely that Crawford expected much of a response, but surprisingly he received a number of replies, consequently purchasing a few rifles and obtaining samples of others. Most importantly though he obtained a working knowledge of the second-hand weapons trade in continental Europe.¹³⁵

In Keith Haines's life of Fred Crawford he put forwards an argument which may suggest that an error has been made with the date for this attempt to find arms suppliers. It is suggested that it relates to a request sent on 22 November 1910 to four arms manufacturers in England, Germany and Austria asking if they could supply for immediate delivery 20,000 military rifles with and without bayonets and 1,000,000 rounds of appropriate ammunition and the associated price. The four replies were received by Crawford as Honorary Secretary of the Ulster Reform Club.¹³⁶ In case none of these enquiries proved fruitful, he also placed advertisements in six European newspapers, *Le Temps* (Paris), *L'Etoile Belge* (Brussels), *Frankfurter Zeitung*, *Neueste Nachrichten* (Berlin), *Pester Lloyd* (Budapest) and *Der Zeit* (Vienna); "Wanted 20,000 good second hand small bore military rifles with one million rounds of ammunition for same".¹³⁷

Around the same time as Crawford was heading to secure arms for the Ulster Volunteers the King authorised his Private Secretary, Lord Stamfordham, to approach Carson at home and persuade him not to make a violent speech when the Home Rule Bill was next introduced in parliament. When the time came Carson reassured him that all he wished for was a "settlement which would satisfy the people of Ulster." Therefore he would be pressing the Prime Minister to say whether or not his government would favour an exclusion for Ulster.

When the bill was introduced for the third time into the House of Commons and the Prime Minister moved its second reading on 8 March it had a new feature. The government had included an aspect intended to conciliate Ulster. Any county in Ulster, including the county boroughs of Belfast and Londonderry, was to be able to vote itself out of the jurisdiction of the proposed

---

129 Hume, David, *"For Ulster and Her Freedom": The story of the April 1914 gun-running* (1989).
130 Shearman, Hugh, *Not an Inch: A Study of Northern Ireland and Lord Craigavon* (1942).
131 Ryan, AP, *Mutiny at the Curragh* (1956).
132 Hume, David, *"For Ulster and Her Freedom": The story of the April 1914 gun-running* (1989).
133 Hyde, H Montgomery, *Carson* (1987).
134 Shearman, Hugh, *Not an Inch: A Study of Northern Ireland and Lord Craigavon* (1942).
135 McNeill, Ronald, *Ulster's Stand for Union* (1922).
136 Haines, Keith, *Fred Crawford: Carson's Gunrunner* (2009).
137 Haines, Keith, *Fred Crawford: Carson's Gunrunner* (2009).

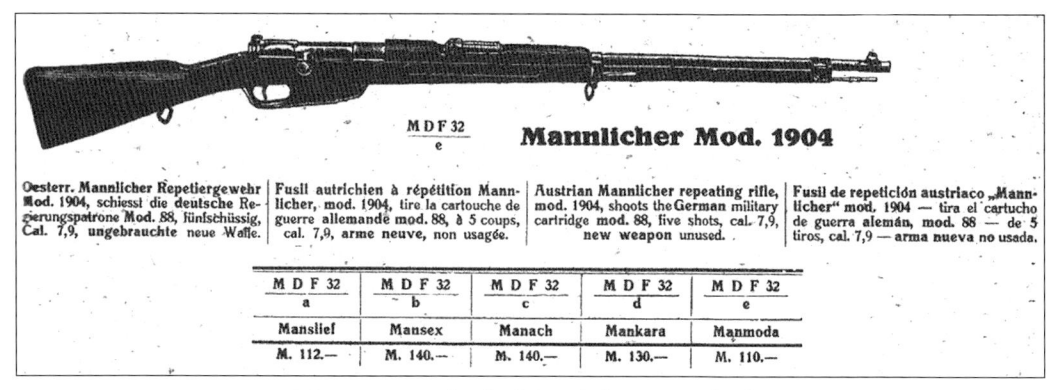

Advertisement for the Mannlicher M1904 rifle.

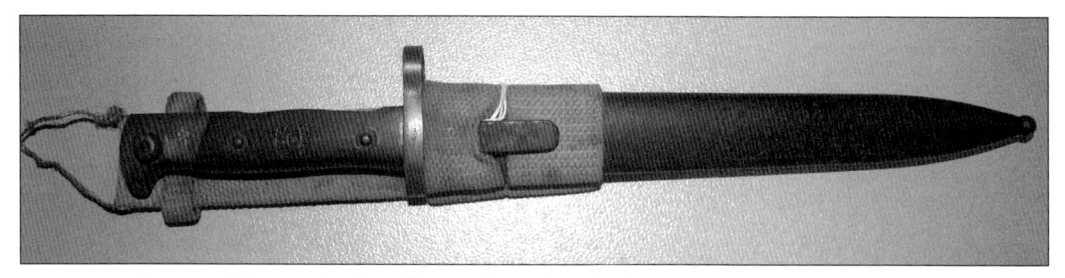

UVF Bayonet. The wooden handle is embossed with the UVF insignia. (Somme Museum)

Dublin government for a period of six years. After this time they must come under Home Rule unless the Imperial Government in London decided otherwise. This was still unacceptable to the Ulster Unionists as they would still be forced into Home Rule from Dublin. Carson made clear their position, "So far as Ulster is concerned, be exclusion good or bad, Ulster wants the question settled now and for ever. We do not want sentence of death with a stay of execution for six years." The main issue was the time limit. Carson offered to submit the amended bill to a convention in Belfast if the government would remove the limit; at the same time he ominously warned the government that Ulster was "ready for any exigency".[138]

There was an element in the country who posed a risk to a number of those involved in the Volunteers, an example being when Major Lord Farnham, commander of a County Cavan battalion, was on his way home in an open topped car in January 1914 and narrowly avoided being decapitated by a wire stretched across the road.[139] Further to this the local Dungannon press presumed that the assault of William McMenemy by two men in April 1914 was down to his being an instructor for the local UVF.[140]

Meanwhile preparations and training continued. In County Monaghan; the Northern Battalion held manoeuvres in the Leslie demesne and paraded through Glaslough in January 1914. The Southern Battalion gathered on the Murray-Ker demesne at Newbliss, and in February 1914 125 men from Monaghan were given a fortnight's intensive training on the Earl of Ernes's estate at Knockballymore.

---

138 Hyde H Montgomery, *Carson* (1953).
139 Bowman, Timothy, *Carson's Army: Ulster Volunteer Force, 1910-22* (2007).
140 Bowman, Timothy, *Carson's Army: Ulster Volunteer Force, 1910-22* (2007).

In Belfast training took place at Fernhill House close to the Shankill Road, the home of businessman James Cunningham, on Ballygomartin Road and at the soccer ground at Forth River and any other available space such as public parks and even outside a picture house in East Belfast.[141]

Knockballymore House, close to Clones in County Monaghan, just inside County Fermanagh's jurisdiction, was also the site of a large camp attended by men of the Fermanagh Volunteers in early 1914. The camp was confined to the battalion staffs, company commanders, section and squad leaders and drill instructors of the three Fermanagh and two Monaghan battalions of the UVF, numbering 250 men. The large vacant house with an extensive yard and offices provided the accommodation; the officers used the house whilst the men were accommodated in the large and airy offices surrounding the courtyard. Meals were provided in a marquee which was erected in the courtyard. Following the various exercises of the day, there were evening lectures delivered by Major Madden, formerly of the Irish Guards. Military disciple was in force during the camp with men being required to have a written permit before being allowed to leave the camp and camp police being posted on the perimeter and gates of the site during the day-time, replaced with armed guards at night.[142]

The local police were reported to be watching in the vicinity of the camp gathering information on the activities. This extended to two or three constables who appeared to be counting the number of men attending church on Sunday. Another incident was also noted involving the police when a sergeant and constable entered the camp and headed to the area where a squad of men were at musketry practice. When they asked the men for their names and addresses the men refused referring the two policemen to the officer in charge. After the sergeant was prevented from inspecting the rifles, they both left. Their visit prompted a question in parliament around their conduct during the visit.[143]

In February 1914 a confidential memo from UVF Headquarters directed that police were not to be allowed to enter any private demesnes where Ulster Volunteer Forces were assembled, with force to be used if necessary. Likewise "in the event of the police unduly interfering with any movements of the UVF, on duty, or going and coming from any such Camps or exercises, the police are to be warned that if they persist in such interference force will be used to prevent the same." These directions were to include all parades, musketry and training held anywhere and at any time when in connection with UVF activities.[144]

In March 1914, 431 members of the Armagh UVF held a field day at Loughgall where they carried out an exercise in which they reacted to a German invasion of Ireland, during which they had ample rifles and

Ulster Volunteers refusing the Royal Irish Constabulary admission to Craigavon House. (Somme Museum)

---

141 Parkinson, Alan F, *Friends in High Places: Ulster's Resistance to Irish Home Rule, 1912-14* (2012).
142 Canning, WJ, *Ballyshannon, Belcoo, Bertincourt* (1996).
143 Canning, WJ, *Ballyshannon, Belcoo, Bertincourt* (1996).
144 Memo from WT Adair – 14 March 1914.

Ulster Volunteers undertaking weapons training. (Somme Museum)

ammunition, and sympathetic farmers supplied horses, carts and drivers on a signed requisition agreement with the Volunteers.[145]

Early in 1914, Sir Hugh McCalmont permitted the Whiteabbey and Clougfern Division of the Carrickfergus command of the Ulster Volunteer Force the use of his demesne at Abbeylands, Whiteabbey. However the house which was lying empty since vacated by the late General Sir EP Leach, commander Northern Regimental District, was destroyed by fire in March 1914. The local UVF volunteers numbering 250 were called out, but both they and the Fire Brigade were unable to save the empty house. The UVF also sent patrols out around the area. Attempts by Sergeant McFarlane, RIC to investigate the incident were seriously hampered by the presence of so many civilians in the vicinity who had destroyed all the evidence such as footprints. However a broken window at the rear and the presence of fire lighters suggested arson. Later the same day some literature was found between the house and the shore suggesting to some that the fire may have been a malicious act on behalf of the suffragette movement. It was reported that a copy of 'The Suffragette' and three postcards addressed to Sir Edward Carson were pinned to the paper. The cards bore the following messages; "to betray women is to court disaster"; "The women's blaze will illuminate the world"; "We need to be provoked – goaded like oxen as we are – into a trot."[146]

Eight Companies of a Regiment of the Derry City Regiment paraded for a drill Inspection on 7 February 1914. Colonel Hacket Pain commented on the great improvement which had been made since he last inspected them in various drill halls the previous December when their work was very elementary. However, now a battalion representative had successfully taken the battalion 'steadily and efficiently' through a ceremonial parade, marching past in column and quarter column, advancing in line and all the usual battalion formations. Following the parade Colonel Hacket

---

145 Cousins, Colin, *Armagh and the Great War* (2011).
146 *Belfast News Letter* – March 1914.

Ulster Volunteer Force. (Somme Museum)

Pain highlighted the need to progress now on field work, which must entail the sacrifice of the mid-week half day holiday. He emphasises that particularly at the current time such a sacrifice was worth it to achieve the efficiency required in the field.[147]

Reports from Royal Irish Constabulary Special Branch officers in Belfast noted that "all principal football clubs in the city have voted to suspend practice until the end of the season to give the men time to drill with the UVF."[148]

Despite the extensive drilling undertaken by many of the Ulster Volunteer formations headquarters issued a directive in May 1914 which questioned the end product of the drilling. It stated that it had been noticed that when changing direction or forming that there was a great tendency to make more or less a wheel instead of individual movement. It was stressed that on every possible occasion, that in order to be able to rapidly get into extended formation, i.e. battle order, the 'five drill exercises' must be absolutely and thoroughly mastered. Headquarters made it clear that no men could be considered properly drilled or instructed until they can move into a new direction at once. Headquarters believed that the problem may have arisen from being drilled in drill halls, however it was suggested that if a 'Model Squad' of a dozen men was first carefully drilled then they could later give displays of the five drill exercises allowing the other men to pick up the movement quicker.[149]

An influential member of the Ulster Unionists, Thomas Sinclair, died on 14 February 1914. His funeral cortege to the Belfast City Cemetery on the Falls Road included an escort of 1,000 Belfast UVF; he is buried in Section D-9.[150, 151]

On 26 February 1914 the Ulster Women's Unionist Council met in the Assembly Rooms, Monaghan town, to discuss the arrangements for setting up a field hospital should civil war break out.[152]

---

147 UVF Orders 15, 1914 – Somme Museum.
148 Gregory, Adrian and Paseta, Senia Ed, *Ireland and the Great War 'A War to Unite Us All'?* (2002).
149 UVF Orders 47,1914 – Somme Museum.
150 Belfast Covenant Trail – Ulster Historical Foundation.
151 Celebrating the Ulster Covenant – Bishop D Arcy of Down, Connor & Dromore.
152 Orr, Philip, *The Road to the Somme* (1987).

The cook section of an UVF emergency hospital established in the Orange Hall, Clifton Street, Belfast circa 1913. (A Hogg - Ulster Museum)

The Unionist leadership saw the Ulster Volunteer Force as fundamental in convincing the government of their determination against Home Rule, this stance was vocalised by Michael Elliott Knight, Clones solicitor, member of the Standing Committee of the Ulster Unionist Council, County Grand Master of Monaghan and Adjutant of the Monaghan Regiment, when he made a speech at Wattsbridge in February 1914; "the formation of the UVF had brought home in a very striking way the determination of Ulster."[153]

Whilst he had been thinking about it for a year, on 1 January 1913 Carson formally proposed his amendment to the Home Rule Bill that all nine counties of the entire province of Ulster be excluded from any deal. He had already raised the matter with the Ulster Unionist Council in Belfast the previous December. Whilst it was not warmly welcomed, leaving as it did the Southern Unionists at the mercy of Home Rule it was eventually agreed unanimously.

In the House of Commons, Carson told the House that he was convinced that without the use of force the Ulster Protestants could not be compelled to submit to Home Rule. He used the example of the signing of the Covenant as an indicator of the sincerity with which the Ulster Protestants believed in their cause.[154]

---

153 Ulster Volunteers, January 1913 – Ulster-Scots Community Network <http://www.ulster-scots.com/uploads/901740969819.PDF> (Accessed 5 August 2013).
154 Lewis, Geoffrey, *Carson: The man who divided Ireland* (2006).

However in south Tyrone local Nationalists staged a mass meeting at Donaghmore, Sunday 9 November 1913, where the first speaker, JP Convery, United Irish League, denounced the partition proposals by warning that under no circumstance would they allow "Ulster or any portion of it to be taken from the map of Ireland." The next speaker, J Skeffington, was reported in the *Irish News* of 12 November 1913 as saying that if "a vote of Nationalist Ulster was taken, they would fight on sooner than accept any form of Home Rule which would make the government of Ulster different in any respect from which would obtain the rest of Ireland." Such calls were sure to inflame the situation.

On 25 November 1913 at a meeting in the Rotunda, Dublin, the Irish Volunteers (*Oglaigh na hEireann*) were formed under Eoin MacNeill with the purpose of ensuring the implementation of Home Rule. The resulting recruitment was particularly encouraging from amongst Ulster Nationalists, again adding to the rising tension in the Province.[155]

In January 1914 a County Committee was established in County Fermanagh with arrangements made to establish eight battalions. The Enniskillen battalion contained 300 men, drilling once a week, storing their few weapons at Joe Gillen's furniture store. When permission was received from the Nationalist-dominated Fermanagh County Council they moved their drill to the old gaol.[156]

In February 1914, Patrick Pearse, a member of the Irish Volunteers National Executive, established the first County Donegal unit in Dungloe. Within weeks there were units in all parts of the county.[157]

The most militant Irish Volunteers in Ulster appear to have been in east Tyrone, supported by the Catholic clergy and under the influence of the new Sinn Fein under a medical student from Carrickmore, Patrick McCartan.[158]

With both groups of volunteers recruiting, drilling and preparing the risk of conflict and bloodshed increased. Asquith's government was desperate to find a compromise. Early the following year as a result of the increased pressure from Asquith, John Redmond reluctantly agreed that individual counties would be allowed to opt out of any Home Rule proposals for six years. His supporters in Ulster were not feeling as conciliatory, even for six years. However a permanent rift in the Nationalist camp was averted by Carson's response on 9 March 1914 which left no doubt that such as "stay of execution" was unacceptable. He demanded nothing less than the permanent partition of the nine counties of Ulster, knowing that the government would refuse this.

On 7 February 1914 the Irish Volunteer movement published their official newspaper paper entitled, '*The Irish Volunteer*'.[159] The issue dated 4 July 1914 carried an advertisement addressed to 'Comrades!', in which were offered: Mauser automatic pistols, sighted 1,000 yards, 4 pounds ten shillings; a .22 German target rifle at twenty-five shillings; or a Bull Dog revolver at seven shillings and six pence.

Bandoliers, belts and haversacks were also on offer.[160] Shortly after the newspaper was censored for the first time by the British authorities, on 5 December 1914 Eoin MacNeill wrote, "Ireland needs armed Irishmen, not disarmed Irishmen. When the present confusion passes away, as it is

---

155 Orr, Philip, *The Road to the Somme* (1987).
156 Orr, Philip, *The Road to the Somme* (1987).
157 Orr, Philip, *The Road to the Somme* (1987).
158 Orr, Philip, *The Road to the Somme* (1987).
159 Irish Volunteers launch their own newspaper <<http://www.rte.ie/centuryireland/articles/irish-volunteers-launch-their-own-newspaper> (Accessed 11 January 2015).
160 A Most Seditious Lot: The Militant-Separatist Press 1896-1916 <<http://theirishrepublic.wordpress.com/tag/the-irish-volunteer/> (Accessed 1 January 2015).

The first edition of *The Irish Volunteer* newspaper. Saturday 7th February 1914.

rapidly passing, the more armed Irishmen we have, no matter what shade of national politics may be theirs, the better for Ireland."[161]

Whilst MacNeill saw the formation of the Irish Volunteers to counter the threat posed by the Ulster Volunteers, protecting against any betrayal of the Irish Parliamentary Party, he did not see it acting as an insurrectionary force. He had declared that he did not contemplate any conflict with the Ulster Volunteers, in fact he saw them as an empowering model for Irish Nationalism, "The action of the Ulster Volunteers, interpret it as you will, is the very essence of nationalism. They show that, whatever English parties may say, they are going to have their own way in their own country … The North began, the North held on, God bless the Northern land."[162]

---

161 Gregory, Adrian and Paseta, Senia (ed)., *Ireland and the Great War 'A War to Unite Us All'?* (2002).
162 McGarry, Ferghal, *The Rising – Ireland: Easter 1916* (2010).

A tunic of the Irish National Volunteers, each button depicts a harp. (Somme Museum)

The media in the guise of the newspapers were reporting on the developments and activities of the Ulster Volunteer Force. *The Times* publishing a map of the UVF centres of organisation showing 65 Battalions which it indicated were each over a 1,000 men strong. In early 1914 one article in *The Times* highlighted the ability of the UVF with regards mobilisations:

> For example, a mobilisation was ordered at 6:00 a.m. one morning lately to the Third Battalion of the Tyrone Regiment. A despatch rider left Ballygawley at the hour named and delivered Orders to the Drill Instructors at nine different centres for the Companies to mobilise at five and six hours' notice for the urban and rural districts respectively. From 90 to 100% of the enrolled men came up within the time appointed, each with a dummy rifle and two days' rations.

Recruitment in County Fermanagh for the UVF had been slow until the future of the county became a hot matter during the compromise debate.[163]

In the extreme western county of Donegal three Battalions were raised in the Donegal Regiment, Ulster Volunteer Force. The 1st Battalion had 750 men, mostly farmers' sons with a sprinkling of shopkeepers, business and professional men, enrolled by March 1914. On 4 March 600 officers and men paraded on the Rossnowlagh strand and were inspected by General Sir George Richardson accompanied by the regiment's commanding officer, the Earl of Leitrim. Equipped with their bandoliers, belts and haversacks they represented a serviceable and workmanlike turn-out. Despite this impressive show of strength there was noted a shortfall in their field work, which was attributed to the dearth of instructors, yet Headquarters commended the officers and staff for the good work given the circumstances.[164, 165]

That same day the 3rd Battalion, Donegal Regiment, were inspected at Newtowncunnigham which despite very inclement weather provided an excellent parade and it was reported that they demonstrated an attack on a position "well and intelligently."[166] The cavalry detachment present at Newtowncunnigham was also highlighted for their good work under the command of Mr Cooke.[167]

---

163 Orr, Philip, *The Road to the Somme* (1987).
164 Canning, WJ, *Ballyshannon, Belcoo, Bertincourt* (1996).
165 UVF Orders 21, 1914 – Somme Museum.
166 UVF Orders 22, 1914 – Somme Museum.
167 UVF Orders 23, 1914 – Somme Museum.

An inspection of the Donegal Regiment, Ulster Volunteers at Raphoe, 2 October 1913 by Sir Edward Carson. (Somme Museum)

Early in 1914 Seely asked Churchill for a Royal Naval vessel to help protect Carrickfergus Castle, as he had received rumours that it might be attacked by the Ulster Volunteers seeking the 85 tons of army ammunition which was held in storage there. The request was refused; it would be another two months before this was finally approved.[168] Gleichen cast doubt on such rumours asserting that neither he nor the police had any evidence to support this stating that "our intelligence was rather good.", but he balanced it with "we are after all not omniscient."[169] A sensible precautionary observation.

Gleichen also believed that in the event of civil war, the Ulster Volunteer Force would have access to a few aeroplanes which would assist them with reconnaissance and also that whilst the UVF had no organised field artillery he believed there were "a few isolated field guns" at their disposal.[170]

In an attempt to assert its authority against an increasingly militant Ulster the Liberal Government moved troops north and the Royal Navy were tasked to carry further reinforcements across the Irish Sea.

The UVF response was to prepare for mobilisation with the entire staff HQ taking up residence at Craigavon, guarded by Crozier's Special Service men.

Carson received a letter from a spy in the government camp which gave him an indication as to the tactics Asquith might employ regarding the resistance to Home Rule in Ulster and the apparent delay in the Cabinet in seeking compromise; "The plan is to procrastinate until the patience of the hooligan element in Belfast is exhausted and they begin to riot. That is the moment when the troops will step in and crush the riot … They have agents in Belfast … who … are to say when it is the right moment to stir up a riot."[171]

On 9 March 1914, Asquith announced the compromise that any of the six counties in Ulster could vote themselves out of Home Rule for six years, or two general elections, long enough for them to judge the competence of a Dublin Government. After this Asquith assumed those counties opting out would wish to opt in; regardless of this however after the six years then they would automatically come under Home Rule. Unionists, not unreasonably, asked the question why have an automatic inclusion if they would come in willingly. Redmond viewed the six year opt out as "the extremist limit of concession", whilst Carson rejected the whole scheme.[172]

The Government was receiving reports from sources in Ulster which further warned of the seriousness of the developing situation. The Royal Irish Constabulary in County Down had sourced a UVF confidential circular which requested volunteers to gather information on the strength and

---

168 Ryan, AP, *Mutiny at the Curragh* (1956).
169 Ryan, AP, *Mutiny at the Curragh* (1956).
170 Bowman, Timothy, *Carson's Army: Ulster Volunteer Force, 1910-22* (2007).
171 Beatty, Jack, *The Lost History of 1914: How the Great War was not inevitable* (2012).
172 Beatty, Jack, *The Lost History of 1914: How the Great War was not inevitable* (2012).

James Craig siting with a detachment of Ulster Special Service Volunteers outside Craigavon House. (Somme Museum)

A group of Royal Irish Constabulary outside a rural barracks. (Police Museum)

disposition of government forces, such as those defending police barracks and coastguard stations. Meanwhile in County Tyrone the police had obtained a UVF document outlining the seizure of "all arms at military barracks ... and it is said that wax impressions of keys of military stores and magazines are in the possession of the Volunteers." However it went further and also included the number of troops at each military depot willing to assist the Volunteers.[173]

Further rumours and intelligence reports, though not from the military in Ulster, came to the attention of the Government, suggesting that raids were being planned on the stores of arms and ammunition held at Armagh, Omagh, Enniskillen and again at Carrickfergus Castle.[174]

The military authorities at Armagh Barracks were concerned enough to post armed sentries day and night in March 1914 to protect the 1,000 rifles and two Maxim machine guns stored in the armoury against the threat of them falling into the hands of the Ulster Volunteers.[175]

Another document simply titled, "The Coup" outlined with tactical knowhow the steps the Volunteers were to take to deliver a "sudden, complete, and paralyzing blow." The following steps were to be taken simultaneously:

1. Cut rail lines so that no police or army could be sent to Ulster;
2. Cut telegraph and cable lines;
3. Seize all depots containing arms, ammunition, etc;
4. All avenues of approach by road for troops or police into Ulster should be closed by isolated detachments;
5. Guns of field artillery (calibre) should be captured either by direct attack – or else by previous arrangement with the gunners;
6. All depots for supply of troops or police should be captured.

The Ulster Volunteers, Dartrey, County Monaghan, 26 December 1913. (Somme Museum)

---

173 Beatty, Jack, *The Lost History of 1914: How the Great War was not inevitable* (2012).
174 Ryan, AP, *Mutiny at the Curragh* (1956).
175 Cousins, Colin, *Armagh and the Great War* (2011).

The Prime Minister's reaction to this information was to appoint a five-man committee to explore the government's response to the growing crises. The members were Attorney General John Simon, Secretary[176] of War John Seely, First Sea Lord of the Admiralty Winston Churchill, Crewe and Birrell.[177]

Fearing that Ulster was about to overturn democratic governance, Churchill as First Sea Lord ordered eight battleships based in Gibraltar and eight destroyers of the Fourth Flotilla in England to sail to the Irish Sea and North Channel, "where they would be in close proximity to the coasts of Ireland in case of serious disorders occurring." Perhaps more significantly and likely to be driven by the intelligence gathered around Volunteer actions to secure arms and ammunition, Churchill sent HMS *Pathfinder* and HMS *Attentive* to Belfast Lough with orders to defend "by every means" the eighty-five tons of ammunition at Carrickfergus Castle that was guarded by only twenty soldiers.[178]

Brigadier General Edward Gleichen, commander of the 15th Infantry Brigade with headquarters at Belfast but stationed throughout Ireland, received a telegram on 18 March from John Seely, Secretary of state for War, informing him that the Carrickfergus garrison was to be strengthened and that the gates of all barracks throughout Ireland were to be sealed with the guard doubled. Whilst he received no explanation for the order, he obeyed it. The next day 19 March he was further ordered to send two infantry companies to Enniskillen, one to Omagh and one to Armagh. An infantry company already stationed at Enniskillen was to move to Londonderry and the battalion stationed at Victoria Barracks were to move to the barracks at Holywood, again no explanation was given.[179]

Meanwhile at 10:00 p.m. on a March night in Belfast whilst FP Crozier was explaining the difference between 'fixed sights' and 'fixed bayonets' to a squad of the Special Service Section in a yard which during daytime was used as a stable, he received an emergency call. Their orders were to parade early in the morning 'opposite the Liverpool boat' fully armed, but they were not told the reason. The second part of Crozier's orders were to register that night at a certain commercial hotel under an assumed name and to keep in contact with another representative from UVF Headquarters who was staying in a different hotel under a' nom de guerre'. The attested men of the Special Service Sections were mostly drawn from the shipyards, mills or heavy industries and whilst they were entitled to the pay of their jobs when they were called up, arrangements had been made to keep their jobs open in such eventualities. As Crozier marched to the quay at the head of his men the gathering crowd and the number of police on duty started to indicate that something unusual was occurring; Colonel Couchman whispered a last minute instruction to him, 'Stick to him through thick and thin and damn the consequences'. The detail of the event and who Couchman was referring to soon became clear when Sir Edward Carson and Captain James Craig walked down the gangway of the Liverpool boat and climbed into the waiting car which would take them both to Craigavon where they were both to stay.[180]

The reason for the call out of the UVF Special Service Section became clear later. The previous day Carson had left the House of Commons suddenly at a quarter past five in the afternoon after a noisy debate on a motion of censure,[181] catching the train to Liverpool, borrowing a five pound note from Ronald McNeill to pay for his ticket.

---

176 Beatty, Jack, *The Lost History of 1914: How the Great War was not inevitable* (2012).
177 Ryan, AP, *Mutiny at the Curragh* (1956).
178 Beatty, Jack, *The Lost History of 1914: How the Great War was not inevitable* (2012).
179 Grob-Fitzgibbon, *Turning Points of The Irish Revolution: The British Government, Intelligence and the Cost of Indifference, 1912-1921* (2007).
180 Crozier, Brig-Gen FP Crozier, CB, CMG, DSO, *Ireland for Ever* (1932).
181 Shearman, Hugh, *Not an Inch: A Study of Northern Ireland and Lord Craigavon* (1942).

Slouch hat and cap badge UVF Special Service Section. (Somme Museum)

During the debate, Carson declared:

> I hate all this talk about the Army being sent to Ulster. Ulster people have always been, and are to the present moment, on the best of terms with your Army, and it is the only part of Ireland where that can be said. Your Army is welcome there as is your Fleet … as much as in any part of the United Kingdom, so much so that you think, before you commence your operations, of removing the regiments which are there at the present moment.[182]

In London whilst Carson was travelling orders were sent by Churchill, First Sea Lord, to the Vice Admiral commanding the Third Battle Squadron to mobilise elements of his forces, whilst Sir Arthur Paget was travelling west to Dublin with special instructions in his pocket.[183] It appeared that the Government had agreed to the issue of warrants for the arrest of Carson and a number of his associates, hence the registrations in the hotel under assumed names.[184]

Crozier recorded that the tension was relieved in silence, "by a broad wink delivered to me by a burly police sergeant from Derry, which told me that all was well." They escorted Carson's car at walking pace until they were clear of the densely packed streets when Craig indicated to Crozier to mount the running board where he told him they would proceed to Craigavon unguarded but that they were to follow on behind. The orders were to guard the gates and see that no one entered without a pass, and each Unionist and UVF leader was guarded though the night against any possible government action. Crozier was there for two weeks.[185]

In a field by the house a huge mess tent and a small hospital tent had been erected with a huge Union flag flying from a flagpole.[186]

---

182 Hyde, H Montgomery, *Carson* (1953).
183 Shearman, Hugh, *Not an Inch: A Study of Northern Ireland and Lord Craigavon* (1942).
184 Crozier, Brig-Gen FP Crozier, CB, CMG, DSO, *Ireland for Ever* (1932).
185 Crozier, Brig-Gen FP Crozier, CB, CMG, DSO, *Ireland for Ever* (1932).
186 Lewis, Geoffrey, *Carson: The man who divided Ireland* (2006).

A postcard depicting Sir Edward Carson in the motor vehicle being escorted by men of the Ulster Volunteer Force marching past the Belvoir Bar. (Somme Museum)

At the same time that the UVF Headquarters staff was sheltering from the developing political storm in Craigavon, guarded by two hundred men,[187] they were joined by certain political leaders such as Lords Londonderry and Castlereagh, Charles Craig, MP, (brother of James Craig)[188] and for a brief period, FE Smith. However they were not totally isolated from developments elsewhere. They were kept up to date with the events developing at the Curragh by certain individuals at the Sandes soldiers' home and Major-General Nevil Macready.[189]

Carson wrote to Bonar Law, 10 March, describing Craigavon House as an "armed camp" and informing him of the wider situation in Ulster, "The Government have been moving troops and police all day through the province and from the south. Imagine it is a scare on their part and that they were under the impression our people were going to take action – or it may be they desire to provoke an outbreak…"[190]

Whilst the Volunteers patrolled the shores of Belfast Lough and protected Craigavon House the police also patrolled the locale with both sides eyeing each other warily but not in an unfriendly manner. This unusual relationship is illustrated by an encounter, sometime after midnight, between the Assistant Commissioner of Police who was inspecting the police in the area and Colonel Spencer Chichester, commander of the local Volunteers. The Assistant Commissioner Belfast asked, "Don't you think that we might all go to bed?"

"No, I don't think we can," replied Chichester, "because we happen to know that you have a certain telegram, and it is upon that information we are out."

Chichester had obtained a copy of a coded telegram addressed to the Belfast Police from the Commandant in Dublin Castle as a result of friends of the Volunteers working in the Belfast GPO. The Assistant Commissioner didn't realise that the Volunteers hadn't been able to decode it and replied, "Oh, if it's only that, you need not be taking all this trouble. Read it yourself. There's nothing in it," he said, handing a copy of the decoded version to Chichester.

---

187 Shearman, Hugh, *Not an Inch: A Study of Northern Ireland and Lord Craigavon* (1942).
188 *Battle Lines; Journal of The Somme Association* – Capt.Charles Curtis Craig MP – Jackie McQuiston.
189 Crozier, Brig-Gen FP Crozier, CB, CMG, DSO, *Ireland for Ever* (1932).
190 Hyde H Montgomery, *Carson* (1953).

Bedsteads and chairs unloaded at Craigavon House for the use of the Ulster Volunteer Force garrisoning Craigavon House during the stay of Sir Edward Carson. (Somme Museum)

Chichester read it, "Expect important document tomorrow morning." This innocent message and encounter had a much greater significance though. With both a coded and decoded message in their possession the Volunteers were now able to decode all the secret messages which passed between Dublin, Belfast and London.[191]

The arrival of the two Royal Navy cruisers in the Lough was reported to Carson by UVF despatch riders.[192]

Carson also maintained good relations with the police, trying to minimise the risk of any provocations against him or the UVF. Likewise he wished to ensure peaceful relations between Protestant and Catholic neighbours. This is illustrated in a document issued to the Ulster Volunteers in Fermanagh which came into the possession of the local police:

REMEMBER YOUR RESPONSIBILTY, RESTRAIN THE HOTHEADS. Remember we have no quarrel with our Nationalist neighbours. Do not molest them or be offensive to them in any way ... If the Nationalists take aggressive action against us restrain your men to your utmost and at once report to Company or Battalion Commander. Send a quiet man to interview an influential Nationalist, who will show him these instructions ... Go on training your men quietly. Don't stand still but progress, and prepare for the worst and hope for the best. For God and Ulster! God Save the King![193]

---

191 Hyde H Montgomery, *Carson* (1953).
192 Hyde H Montgomery, *Carson* (1953).
193 Lewis, Geoffrey, *Carson: The man who divided Ireland* (2006).

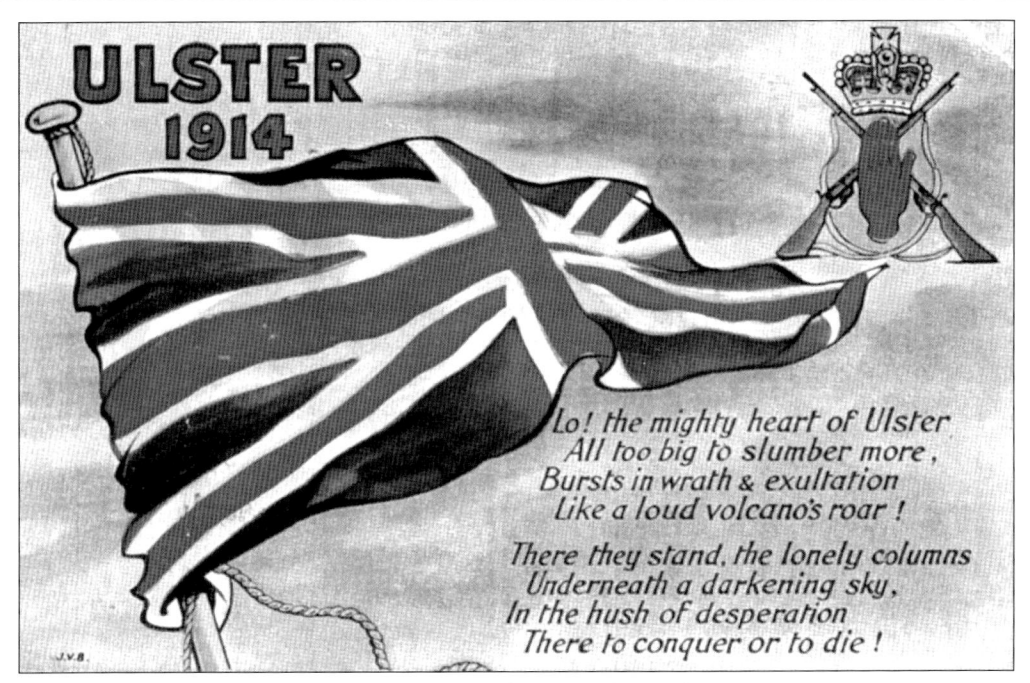

> Lo! the mighty heart of Ulster
> All too big to slumber more,
> Bursts in wrath & exultation
> Like a loud volcano's roar!
>
> There they stand, the lonely columns
> Underneath a darkening sky,
> In the hush of desperation
> There to conquer or to die!

An anti-Home Rule postcard. (J Luke)

After the Curragh incident, Macready was made General Officer Commanding Belfast District and was designated as military governor-designate of Belfast in the event of civil war breaking out. He was given the unusual powers of a Resident Magistrate, ensuring that he had control of the local police within his command area; with the Royal Irish Constabulary being an armed force it gave him valuable additional resources.[194]

As tensions increased an order was issued by commanding officer 1st North Antrim Regiment to his commanders that on the 20th of each month a return was to completed of the total number of men "who can reasonably considered 'effective', (i.e., who can be relied upon in case of need)" that were attached to their respective units. This was replicated across the UVF organisation.[195]

14 March 1914, Winston Churchill, spoke at Bradford:

> First, I have greatly desired that we should not do the unliberal or hard thing to the Ulster community, mistaken though I think they are, and secondly, and not less strongly, I have felt that we cannot let ourselves be bullied." (Cheers) "We cannot let ourselves be prevented by threats of force, or, let me add, by force itself from doing justice to the rest of Ireland and from making good arrangements for the future of the whole of Ireland and from maintaining the authority of the State.[196]

The final sentence of his speech left those 3-4,000 Liberals listening little doubt that he was delivering a call to arms:

---

194 Hyde H Montgomery, *Carson* (1953).
195 UVF Orders – Monthly returns of 'effectiveness' – 1st North Antrim Regiment.
196 *The Times* – 16 March 1914.

If Ulstermen extend the hand of friendship, it will be clasped by Liberals and by their Nationalist countrymen in all good faith and in all good will; but if there is no wish for peace; if every concession that is made is spurned and exploited; if every effort to meet their views is only to be used as means of breaking down Home rule and of barring the way to the rest of Ireland; if the Government and Parliament of this great country and greater empire are to be exposed to menace and brutality; if all the loose, wanton, and reckless chatter we have been forced to listen to these many months is in the end to disclose a sinister and revolutionary purpose; then I can only say to you, "Let us go forward together and put these grave matters to the proof.[197]

The following day also at Bradford, Joseph Devlin, MP for West Belfast, made a speech reinforcing Churchill's position of no further concessions; "The Nationalists had gone to the utmost limits to conciliate them. They would not go one single inch further. They had strained the feelings of the people in Ireland, and particularly in Ulster, almost to the breaking point."[198]

At a Unionist rally in Hyde Park, Carson branded Churchill as "Lord Randolph's renegade son who wanted to be handed down to posterity as the Belfast butcher who threatened to shoot down those who took his father's advice."[199]

By Saturday 21 March the situation had changed again.

On Monday 16 March in the House of Commons Asquith attempted the compromise of a temporary exclusion for Ulster from Home Rule. On Thursday 19 March, the opposition responded, Bonar Law asked Asquith if the Government would agree to hold a referendum on Home Rule. The response from Asquith was to ask if Unionists would agree that the government "would be justified in coercing Ulster" if Home Rule was passed? Law nodded a response, resulting in Asquith looking across the despatch box at Carson asking if Ulster would agree. Carson's answer was simple, "Let the Prime Minister give me a fair offer and then I will answer him."[200]

Also on the 19 March UVF Headquarters warned all units that the current position was "extremely grave" and everyone was warned

A postcard of Joseph Devlin, Ulster Nationalist leader depicting a sentiment held by many in favour of Home Rule for Ireland.

---

197 *The Times* – 16 March 1914 Beatty, Jack, *The Lost History of 1914: How the Great War was not inevitable* (2012).
198 *The Times* – 16 Mach 1914.
199 Beatty, Jack, *The Lost History of 1914: How the Great War was not inevitable* (2012).
200 Beatty, Jack, *The Lost History of 1914: How the Great War was not inevitable* (2012).

to prepare to mobilise at a moment's notice.²⁰¹ The Royal Irish Constabulary reports for March later showed the extent of Ulster Volunteer preparations on the 19 March. It was believed that the Government were intending to despatch a large military force to Ulster to arrest leaders of the Volunteer movement. As a consequence, "bundles of books and documents were sent over to London; and orders were issued for the immediate mobilisation of the Volunteer Force at Belfast and in some other places … Other parties were in readiness at the City drill halls during the night of the 19th ult."²⁰²

Specifically referring to Churchill's threat in Bradford Carson dramatically announced to the House that he would be leaving to catch the night boat to Belfast from where he would lead his forces against Churchill's battleships, referencing the despatch of Royal Naval vessels to the Ulster coast. As if mocking him a heckler in the House shouted, "With your sword drawn?" Carson slammed the despatch boxes and echoed Churchill's last line; "Let the Government come and try conclusions with them in Ulster." On his leaving the Commons, the opposition rose and cheered.

In an effort to undermine the use of force against Ulster Bonar Law had planned to instruct his fellow Tories in the House of Lords to attach an amendment to the Army Annual Act which would forbid the army from being used to suppress any resistance in Ulster other than acting against a foreign power.²⁰³, ²⁰⁴

This raised the question that, if the amendment was successful, would the Government concentrate the Royal Irish Constabulary in Ulster instead. When asked by Austen Chamberlain, Carson replied that firstly there were not enough of them, secondly they wouldn't do it, and thirdly that the Ulstermen would love to fight them for they were all Catholics!²⁰⁵

However Law was advised by Sir Henry Wilson, Director of Military Operations in the War Office, that he believed that if the army were ordered to coerce Ulster that there would be wholesale defections and as such the politically risky amendment would be unnecessary²⁰⁶, ²⁰⁷ (Wilson's family had arrived with the forces of William III in Ireland in the late seventeenth century, acquiring land in Antrim).²⁰⁸

During correspondence between Asquith and the King following further disruption in Ulster, the King responded, clearly concerned:

> Do you propose to employ the Army to suppress such disorders? This is, to my mind, one of the most serious questions which the Government will have to decide, In doing so you will, I am sure, bear in mind that ours is a volunteer Army; and Soldiers are none the less Citizens; by birth, religion and environment they may have strong feelings on the Irish question … Will it be wise, will it be fair to the Sovereign as head of the Army, to subject the discipline, and indeed the loyalty of his troops, to such a strain?²⁰⁹

---

201 Precautionary Period – Lt Col McCammon 19 March 1914.
202 Muenger, Elizabeth A, *The British Military Dilemma in Ireland: Occupation Politics 1886-1914* (1991).
203 Beatty, Jack, *The Lost History of 1914: How the Great War was not inevitable* (2012).
204 Ryan, AP, *Mutiny at the Curragh* (1956).
205 Hyde H Montgomery, *Carson* (1953).
206 Beatty, Jack, *The Lost History of 1914: How the Great War was not inevitable* (2012).
207 Ryan, AP, *Mutiny at the Curragh* (1956).
208 Ryan, AP, *Mutiny at the Curragh* (1956).
209 Muenger, Elizabeth A, *The British Military Dilemma in Ireland: Occupation Politics 1886-1914* (1991).

King George V.
(Somme Museum)

In the House of Commons, Bonar Law pressed Asquith further on how the government intended to impose its will on Ulster:

> What about the Army? If it is only a question of dealing with civil disorder, the Army, I'm sure, will obey you. But if it is really a question of civil war, soldiers are citizens like the rest of us. The Army will be divided and you will have destroyed the force ... upon which we depend for the defence of this country.

Asquith retorted, "Who is to judge whether a particular contest in which the armed forces of the Crown are called upon to intervene does or does not fall into the category of civil war?" He believed that to leave the decisions to the judgement of individual officers would be "to make the Government subject to the Army."

Ironically his stance would result two days later in a number of high ranking army officers, for the first time in over 200 years, making their opinion clear to their government.[210]

---

210 Beatty, Jack, *The Lost History of 1914: How the Great War was not inevitable* (2012).

6

Curragh Incident

It has been generally claimed that British Army officers are non-political, though this is not always the case. During the previous Irish Home Rule controversies in the 1880s and 1890s many officers only regarded the Irish superficially and any change of status to Ireland as troublesome if not dangerous. However those officers from Ulster were more directly affected by the issue and were more likely to feel the need to preserve the Union. As one officer put it, "Like most officers in the army I favoured Unionism as likely to avoid complications, but I was not so hot about it as many of my contemporaries – especially those who actually came from the north of Ireland, to whom Home Rule seemed a very conception of the Devil."[1]

The outlook and training of regular officers is traditionally conservative and in 1914 nearly all cavalry and infantry officers came from that social class which traditionally supported the Conservative Party.[2]

In 1913 Birrell wrote to Asquith on the impact of the Home Rule controversy on the Royal Irish Constabulary, "The state of the RIC is very serious. There are practically no recruits and the resignations are pouring in. They are undoubtedly worse paid than any other police force in the three kingdoms and we simply must … increase their pay."[3] Whilst the reports received from District and County Inspectors in the Crime Department Special Branch of the RIC tended to reflect their sympathy with the Anglo-Irish establishment, there was apprehension as to the political inclinations of the lower ranks, and the ability of the police to handle disorder either in the south of Ireland or in Ulster. A report believed to be written in early 1914 and sent to General Sir Arthur Paget, referring to County Clare noted, "the police are trusted to do their duty in local work, but many would not go to Ulster to quell riots. Police officers say that the force is insufficient to deal with serious outbreak, and would require troops to deal with them." With regards Limerick the report said that the police were not to be trusted and were "said to be much in sympathy with the Hibernians". The writer of the report "urged the necessity of a strong force of troops" and concluded, "The greatest danger to the peace of the country is the demoralisation and discontent of the police."[4]

An article in the *Irish Times* in February 1914 also highlighted problems within the Constabulary, low morale, resignations and that it was anticipated by the men within the Constabulary:

> that should a serious outbreak of disorder occur in the North, and if the Ulster Volunteer Force, armed and trained men be mobilised, the first thing which Dublin Castle will do will be to collect an immense force of Constabulary in the disturbed area for what will be military duty pure and simple. It will result in wholesale resignations from the Force in every province

---
1 Muenger, Elizabeth A, *The British Military Dilemma in Ireland: Occupation Politics 1886-1914* (1991).
2 Harris, HED, *The Irish Regiments in the First World War* (1968).
3 Muenger, Elizabeth A, *The British Military Dilemma in Ireland: Occupation Politics 1886-1914* (1991).
4 Muenger, Elizabeth A, *The British Military Dilemma in Ireland: Occupation Politics 1886-1914* (1991).

The local station party of Royal Irish Constabulary parading at the opening of the Winter Assizes along the Ulster border. (Police Museum)

of Ireland, and in particular Ulster. The conditions of service for the rank and file at present are so deplorable that all who can do so, without serious monetary loss, will at once comply with the rule on leaving the service and give one month's notice.[5]

To prevent the Ulster Volunteer Force from obtaining weapons from army stores, Seely, the Secretary of State for War, sent Sir Arthur Paget, Commander-in-Chief in Ireland a list of four depots requiring additional protection. Initially he refused as such a move would cause "intense excitement in Ulster". However he was summoned to London to meet Seely, Churchill and Birrell at the War Office.

On Wednesday morning, 18 March he was briefed by Sir John French, Chief of the Imperial General Staff and ministers on six possible situations which may arise and as a consequence he may have to respond to.[6]

1. There might be armed opposition to small bodies of troops moving to reinforce depots.
2. There may be attacks on the depots or on the artillery at Dundalk.
3. The blowing up or destruction of the railway lines.
4. Serous conflict between Protestants and Catholics in Belfast following the announcement of the provisional Government or simply as part of other developments.
5. He must not turn a blind eye to any sporadic disorder as reprisals against scattered Protestants in the south or west Ireland by Catholics which would call for the large scale use of troops.

---

5   Muenger, Elizabeth A, The British Military Dilemma in Ireland: Occupation Politics 1886-1914 (1991).
6   Ryan, AP, *Mutiny at the Curragh* (1956).

6. If there was "an organised, warlike movement of Ulster Volunteers under their responsible leaders" then it would have to be met by concentrated military force; if necessary reinforcements would be sent from England.[7]

The last option was considered the worst and he was reassured that it would most likely not come to that. Likewise no one in Government believed that precautionary troop movements would lead to bloodshed. Paget was not comforted that day or the next, Thursday though he did get the concession that those officers domiciled in Ulster would be exempted from taking part in any operations. As the War Office described it, they could "disappear," and when it was all over resume their places without their careers being affected.[8]

French briefed Sir Henry Wilson, the Director of Military Operations about the plan immediately after. That night, 18 March, Wilson met Carson, Lord Milner and Sir Leander Jameson at dinner and informed the politicians of the plan to disperse troops all over Ulster, the rationale being that the political situation necessitated the dispersal which was at odds to all true military strategy.[9]

Simultaneously, Asquith agreed at a meeting in Downing Street, Wednesday 18 March, that on Friday 20 March troops should be moved to reinforce Omagh, Armagh, Dundalk, Enniskillen and Carrickfergus. Also that troops in Belfast should be moved out and that Royal Navy ships should be sent to effect a combined operation, "to be complete by dawn, Saturday the 21st, with all secrecy." With the urgency of the order, Major-General Friend who was still in Belfast was ordered to move a battalion of the Dorset Regiment and their stores and ammunition, amounting to some thirty tons,[10] from Victoria Barracks, Belfast, "with all ammunition and bolts of rifles, if unable to move rifles themselves."[11] It was also understood that hasty troop movements from the south were planned, in essence to ring Belfast.[12]

Whilst Paget was still in London orders were received on Thursday afternoon by troops in the Curragh military camp that all guards should be issued with ball (live) ammunition. An hour later this was widened to include all men in barracks.[13]

The Navy also received orders on Thursday from the Admiralty. The 3rd battle squadron in Arosa Bay off Portugal were ordered to sail to Lamlash on the Firth of Clyde, ninety miles from Belfast. The senior naval officer at Bantry, County Cork, was to send HMS *Attentive* and HMS *Pathfinder* to Kingstown, Dublin by noon, 20 March. On arrival one company of the Bedfordshire Regiment was to embark on HMS *Attentive* and proceed to Belfast Lough. The Commander of HMS *Attentive* was to go with his ship to Bangor and make contact with the General at Holywood barracks to discuss, "as to co-operation with military in certain eventualities."[14] The Captain of HMS *Pathfinder* was to liaise with the senior military officer in Carrickfergus Castle, especially its defence against attack "by every means"; if necessary guns and searchlights of the warship were to be used. The Commander-in-Chief, Portsmouth was to send one destroyer from the 4th Flotilla to reach Kingstown the next evening. HMS *Gibraltar* was order to sail to Kingstown with HMS

---

7   Ryan, AP, *Mutiny at the Curragh* (1956).
8   Ryan, AP, *Mutiny at the Curragh* (1956).
9   Hyde H Montgomery, *Carson* (1953).
10 McNeill, Ronald, *Ulster's Stand for Union* (1922).
11 Ryan, AP, *Mutiny at the Curragh* (1956).
12 Shearman, Hugh, *Not an Inch: A Study of Northern Ireland and Lord Craigavon* (1942).
13 Ryan, AP, *Mutiny at the Curragh* (1956).
14 Shearman, Hugh, *Not an Inch: A Study of Northern Ireland and Lord Craigavon* (1942).

The East Wing of the Curragh Camp. (Somme Museum)

Royal Arthur and be prepared to embark 275 infantry in each ship for transportation to Dundalk where they were to disembark early on the morning 20 March.[15]

On returning to Dublin, Paget informed Seely that all movements had started successfully, he then convened a meeting of his senior officers (Friday morning). As discussed with the Army Council he gave those officers, what is now considered to be a garbled version of the instructions he had received from the War Office.[16] Those with homes in Ulster had the option to "disappear for the period",[17] however the others had the option to obey orders or resign their commissions as "very likely being involved in operations in Ulster."[18] They had two hours to make up their minds as troops had to move that night.[19]

Hubert Gough, General Officer Commanding 3rd Cavalry Brigade, conferred with his officers and sent a memo to Command HQ seeking a clearer definition of the likely duties; if they were the maintenance of order and preservation of property nature, all were required to carry them out; but if they were expected to initiate active operations against Ulster then he and 64 other officers would "respectfully and under protest prefer to be dismissed."

Paget's first telegraph to Seely informed him that the commanding officer of the 5th Lancers reported that all his officers except two and one doubtful were resigning their commissions and he feared the same situation existed in the 16th Lancers and he also feared that the men themselves may refuse to move.

On Friday afternoon Paget sent a second telegram to Seely, "Regret to report Brigadier and 57 officers, 3rd Cavalry Brigade, prefer to accept dismissal if ordered north."[20]

---

15   Ryan, AP, *Mutiny at the Curragh* (1956).
16   Harris, HED, *The Irish Regiments in the First World War* (1968).
17   Harris, HED, *The Irish Regiments in the First World War* (1968).
18   Harris, HED, *The Irish Regiments in the First World War* (1968).
19   Beatty, Jack, *The Lost History of 1914: How the Great War was not inevitable* (2012).
20   Beatty, Jack, *The Lost History of 1914: How the Great War was not inevitable* (2012).

Collecting the cartridges of Ulster Volunteers going off duty at Craigavon House. (Somme Museum)

Suddenly the support from the British Army for the Ulster cause became much more visible. The 57 cavalry officers of the 70 stationed in the Curragh, the Irish military headquarters in Dublin, declaring that they would resign and face dismissal rather than fight or obey an order against 'loyal Ulster' was just the beginning.[21] Gough contacted his brother, a highly decorated colonel stationed at Aldershot and so the news spread throughout the army with officers affirming they would follow lawful orders although it appeared more were siding with Gough's position. Nor was this limited to the army, Churchill's navy contained a significant number of high ranking officers with strong Ulster connections, including the Commanders in Chief of the Home Fleet and the Second Battle Squadron who both threatened to resign if ordered "to go against Ulster".[22]

Ironically the ship sent by Churchill to deny the Ulster Volunteer Force the weapons held in Carrickfergus Castle became embroiled in the incident. The Captain of HMS *Pathfinder,* Francis Martin-Leake, sent the admiral in charge of his Division, Rear-Admiral J. M. de Robeck, on 24 March the following communiqué:

> It seems to me only fair to you as my Admiral to let you know that I have no intention of going against Ulster should the occasion arise. During my stay here I have done my best to ascertain the situation on shore and find that everything is being done to keep things quiet, but undoubtedly in spite of this there exists an opinion on the part of responsible people that an outbreak might be precipitated by irresponsible people.[23]

---

21   Bartlett, Thomas and Jeffery, Keith (ed), *A Military History of Ireland* (1996).
22   Beatty, Jack, *The Lost History of 1914: How the Great War was not inevitable* (2012).
23   <http://www.dnw.co.uk/auction-archive/catalogue-archive/lot.php?auction_id=265&lot_id=88075> – Dix Noonan Webb – Vice-Admiral F. Martin-Leake (Accessed 23 February 1914).

A postcard of HMS *Pathfinder*, which was the lead ship of the Pathfinder class of scout cruisers, launched in July 1904. (T Wylie)

In fact he met socially with the UVF Commander and allowed his sailors to be "entertained" by Sir Edward Carson and the Volunteers also engaged in signal practice with them.[24] When word reached Churchill he was not unexpectedly angry[25] and when word leaked to the British press Churchill's annoyance is evident in the message sent on 31 March:

> Please call upon the Captain of the Pathfinder for his explanation in writing of the signals which passed between him and the shore during his stay at Carrickfergus, which were published in yesterday's newspapers. He should be asked whether he had received instructions from General Macready to make such communications. Instructions should also be given to the commanding officers of the two Scouts now on duty in Belfast Lough that they are not to hold unnecessary communication with the shore, nor to accept from or to offer hospitality to civilians; nor to allow their men to go into Belfast unless there is a special reason for it. The discussion of political questions is not allowed on board ships, nor are the officers to enter into the discussion of such questions with civilians.[26]

When Sir Nevil Macready, GOC visited Carson in his stronghold at Craigavon he was welcomed by the guard who turned out to salute him at the entrance. Macready questioned Carson why the Ulstermen should object to His Majesty's troops in the principal city. Carson replied; "So far from objecting, we are delighted to see His Majesty's uniform at all times. There is nowhere in the King's dominions where the British soldier is assured of a more cordial welcome than in Belfast."[27]

The GOC 5th Division called in a mediator, General Fergusson, a Scotsman who asked them all to forget all about the incident and to return to their duties. Gough asked for an assurance and

---

24 Hyde H Montgomery, *Carson* (1953).
25 Beatty, Jack, *The Lost History of 1914: How the Great War was not inevitable* (2012).
26 <http://www.dnw.co.uk/auction-archive/catalogue-archive/lot.php?auction_id=265&lot_id=88075> Dix Noonan Webb – Vice-Admiral F. Martin-Leake – (Accessed 23 February 1914).
27 Hyde H Montgomery, *Carson* (1953).

they were provided with a written one which reminded them of the duty of officers to obey lawful orders of His Majesty's Government right up to the use of the military to aid the civil power to maintain law and order. It also said there was "no intention of using this right to crush opposition to the policy or principles of the Home Rule Bill."[28] Gough demanded concessions which would exclude him and others from being employed in any operations in Ulster. He eventually left London with a letter, initialled by the Chief of the Imperial General Staff, Field Marshal Sir John French, promising that the army would not be used to "enforce present Home Rule on Ulster".[29, 30]

Asquith immediately disowned the agreement as it placed "the Government and the country at the mercy of the Army."[31]

The Press broke the story on Saturday 21 March. French and Seely both resigned.[32] Asquith became his own War Minister and a Special Army Order re-stated the Army position in such circumstances. The Tories demanded Churchill to follow, but he rode out the storm, summing up the situation, "The Army have done what the Opposition failed to do." As the *Daily Express* headline reported; "HOME RULE IS DEAD", it might make the statute books but it was unenforceable in Ulster.[33]

There were those who accused them of being arrogant, aristocratic playboys who behaved like Conservative politicians rather than disciplined holders of the King's Commission, however many in and out of parliament and not just those of strong political convictions supported them.[34]

The actions of the officers attracted considerable criticism in Liberal, nationalist and overseas newspapers, The *Manchester Guardian* asking if the British Army was "a national army or the private army of a class and party", whilst a French journalist described it as "anarchy and disorder within the British Army."[35]

Despite frantic messages within Whitehall the King first heard of what had developed when he opened his newspaper. He wrote to Asquith that he was "grieved beyond words at this disastrous and irreparable catastrophe which has befallen my army."[36, 37] However his indignation was increased when he discovered how freely his name had been used to try and persuade officers to comply.[38] Over the preceding months the King had treaded a fine line in attempting to help resolve a number of the issues whilst not overstepping the bounds of constitutional propriety.[39] The King took the unusual step of calling all interested parties to Buckingham Palace in an attempt to reach a constitutional settlement, however these attempts were still ongoing when war broke out in August 1914.[40]

There is a belief amongst some that had the war not broken out when it did then the government could not have avoided a general election either before or immediately after the placing of Home Rule on the statute book. If this was the case then the Unionists had little doubt of the result, and

---

28 Harris, HED, *The Irish Regiments in the First World War* (1968).
29 Beatty, Jack, *The Lost History of 1914: How the Great War was not inevitable* (2012).
30 Harris, HED, *The Irish Regiments in the First World War* (1968).
31 Harris, HED, *The Irish Regiments in the First World War* (1968).
32 Harris, HED, *The Irish Regiments in the First World War* (1968).
33 Beatty, Jack, *The Lost History of 1914: How the Great War was not inevitable* (2012).
34 Ryan, AP, *Mutiny at the Curragh* (1956).
35 Parkinson, Alan F, *Friends in High Places: Ulster's Resistance to Irish Home Rule, 1912-14* (2012).
36 Beatty, Jack, *The Lost History of 1914: How the Great War was not inevitable* (2012).
37 Ryan, AP, *Mutiny at the Curragh* (1956).
38 Ryan, AP, *Mutiny at the Curragh* (1956).
39 Ryan, AP, *Mutiny at the Curragh* (1956).
40 Harris, HED, *The Irish Regiments in the First World War* (1968).

A sketch from the *Illustrated London News* depicting 30 March as Mr Asquith, Prime Minister, retired from the House of Commons, having felt it necessary, for the time at any rate, to assume the office of Secretary of State for War following the issue of the British Army and the Ulster difficulties. (Somme Museum)

Members of the Ulster Volunteer Force in the courtyard of Craigavon House. (Somme Museum)

even if the government chose to disregard the expected view of the electorate, the plans for Ulster refusing to become subject to a Dublin Parliament were already in place.[41]

Despite the Government denying there was any 'plot' to coerce the Northern Unionists into action, backed by Asquith's biographers, and Churchill claiming the movements of the Royal Navy were thought to produce a peaceable solution, other evidence suggests the contrary. Unionists both in parliament and in Ulster were convinced that a plan existed to attack Ulster on Saturday 21 March but it was, in the words of Sir Henry Wilson, "frustrated by our action in the army". The full scope of the government's plan was revealed through confidential documents which fell into the hands of Carson and the Ulster Unionist Council; a blockade of Ulster provoking the Ulstermen into making the first strike.[42]

Colonel Repington, military correspondent for *The Times* summarised aspects of Paget's plan of invading and disarming Ulster before the Volunteers could react in a letter he wrote at the time to James Craig:

> The plan was for Paget to sweep north with all the troops at his disposal, and for ships at Lamlash to sweep down the coast from the north ... a coup against Craigavon from Holywood may have formed part of the plan. The General Staff at the War Office are contemptuous of the plan, declaring that Paget would now be languishing in a Belfast gaol had he set out. It reads more like fiction concocted in a madhouse than fact, but Winston is capable of anything. Seely is a perfect ass, Birrell only a makeweight, and French a mere tool. A pretty junta for making war on peaceable inhabitants of the still United Kingdom! Paget accidently let the cat out of the bag ... and then providence sent us Hubert Gough.[43]

Despite Carson and his Parliamentary colleagues calling for a judicial enquiry on 28 April into the whole issue of the army and naval movements, the Government refused to allow one. Churchill described the tactic as a vote of censure by the criminal classes on the police.[44]

During a visit to Ulster during 1914 an Austro-Hungarian diplomat commented on what he perceived as the strange situation which was developing; "Ulster's grim determination to offer armed resistance was brought home to me in Belfast, where I saw Protestant clergy in full canonicals bless the colours of the volunteers ... The extraordinary character which marked this whole crisis was especially emphasised on this occasion by the loud cheers for the king, against whose government the men of Ulster were arming."[45]

On 22 March the officer commanding the County Antrim UVF noted verbal instructions from Sir Edward Carson regarding the Royal Irish Constabulary. When mobilisation was ordered the local RIC were to be arrested and their weapons seized whilst they were patrolling. Under no circumstances would the Volunteers use their own firearms until they had been fired on. If any UVF Commander was arrested his next in command was to take "the best action" that he could regarding mobilisation. In the case of an attempted arrest or attempted seizure of arms, if the senior Ulster Volunteer was present and with sufficient force, then the arrest was to be prevented, again taking care that the UVF were not the first to fire. If sufficient force was not available then as much resistance as possible was to be made "without needless sacrifice of life."[46]

---

41 McNeill, Ronald, *Ulster's Stand for Union* (1922).
42 Hyde H Montgomery, *Carson* (1953).
43 Hyde H Montgomery, *Carson* (1953).
44 Lewis, Geoffrey, *Carson: The man who divided Ireland* (2006).
45 Parkinson, Alan F, Friends in High Places: Ulster's Resistance to Irish Home Rule, 1912-14 (2012).
46 Notes by General Adair of verbal directions of Sir Edward Carson – 22 March 1914.

On Monday 23 March, Carson issued a statement from Craigavon which said, "The conclusion I draw from the acts of the government is that in a fit of panic they have made up their mind to attempt two things – one to intimidate and the other to provoke. They will fail in both."[47] However across the Continent the events were being viewed with a different perspective; by Berlin with eager interest and opportunity and in Paris with grave anxiety at the government's handling of the events.

It has been suggested that the Curragh incident in March, combined with the Unionist and Nationalist gun-runnings in April and July, convinced German military strategists that Britain would be preoccupied with potential civil war in Ireland, distracting her from possible involvement should a European conflict break out.[48]

The Curragh incident was a very significant event, for although this is often described as a mutiny, none of the officers were court-martialled, essentially because no order had been issued which they refused. They had instead stated their position and, more importantly, signalled to the British government the real possibility that if the Ulster Volunteer Force were to resist Home Rule by force the British Army might not be available to confront them. These options both Winston Churchill, the First Lord of the Admiralty and Colonel JEB Seely, the Secretary of State for War, appear to have been both seriously contemplating.[49]

Badge of the Royal Naval Air Service armoured car squadron. By the end of 1915, trench warfare meant there was no scope for armoured cars on the Western Front and most of the RNAS's armoured car squadrons were disbanded by the Admiralty. However, three squadrons of RNAS armoured cars were assembled and sent by ship to Murmansk, Russia as the Armoured Car Expeditionary Force (ACEF). The ACEF was commanded by Oliver Locker-Lampson who opposed Irish Home Rule and raised funds for Edward Carson. This unit had a number of volunteers in its ranks drawn from the Ulster Volunteer Force. (Somme Museum)

As a consequence, directives for military action were withdrawn and the tension eased.

In mid-March warnings were sent to UVF divisional, regimental and battalion commanders warning them of the possible arrest of leaders and the steps they were required to take to mitigate the impact of such actions. They were to immediately warn their second in command, adjutant or other officer whom they wished to act on their behalf in the event of their arrest to hold themselves in readiness and also to arrange a suitable means whereby communications from headquarters delivered to their address were immediately passed on.[50]

---

47 Shearman, Hugh, *Not an Inch: A Study of Northern Ireland and Lord Craigavon* (1942).
48 The Curragh Crises – RTE <http://www.rte.ie/centuryireland/articles/the-curragh-crisis-march-1914> (Accessed 16 March 2014).
49 Ulster Volunteers, January 1913 – Ulster-Scots Community Network <http://www.ulster-scots.com/uploads/901740969819.PDF> (Accessed 5 August 2013).
50 Letter from Lt Col McCammon to Divisional, Regimental and Battalion Commanders – 18 March 1914

The Ulster Unionist Council issued a long document on 17 April 1914 which purported to contain the 'actual facts' of the plan Paget had been ordered to put into effect. These 'facts' included the mobilisation of 10,000 troops from Lichfield and Aldershot who were to march into Ulster with naval support. It also explained how the Belfast police were to take forcible possession of the Old Town Hall, action which would no doubt have placed them into direct conflict with the Volunteers and possible bloodshed.[51]

Against this Colonel Repington, the military correspondent of *The Times* reported in two articles following a ten-day visit to Ulster that the UVF was capable of mobilising a large force rapidly, that it would fight and that it would resist desperately.[52]

On Saturday 4 April Hyde Park, London, became the scene of a rally which would not have looked out of place in Belfast. A procession of people, ranging from members of the Carlton Club, Members of Parliament, Ladies Imperial Club, Stock Exchange and working men and women, departing from 22 different assembly points, converged on the park where 14 speakers' platforms had been erected. The purpose of the demonstration was to gain assent to the resolution; "we protest against the use of the army and the navy to drive out by force of arms our fellow subjects in Ireland from their full heritage in the Parliament of the United Kingdom. And we demand that the government shall immediately submit this grave issue to the people."[53] The speakers on the platforms included, Austen Chamberlain, Robert Cecil, Balfour, Lord Charles Beresford, Milner, Walter Long and FE Smith, Lord Londonderry and Carson.[54]

The Times published a letter from two German professors, Kuno Meyer and Theodor Schiemann, on Good Friday which attacked the "hope and belief" expressed by the Ulster Covenanters that "in the case of Home Rule becoming law, Germany might be induced to interfere in the cause of Protestantism in Ulster". They referred specifically to the Ulster Unionist leaflet and specifically the paragraph, "if the Home Rule Bill is passed, we shall consider ourselves absolutely justified in asking and rendering every assistance at the first opportunity to the greatest Protestant nation on earth, Germany, to come over and help us." The response of the two professors was simple:

> The amazing delusion that such an appeal would find sympathy and perhaps response is another proof of the fact that the Covenanters live wholly in the idea and sentiments of a bygone age. We fear Ulster will wait in vain for another William to come to her defence … Today it is no longer a question of Protestantism versus Catholicism or vice versa. The great modern principle of religious equality has in every civilised nation superseded those antiquated and bigoted ideas of hostility and exclusion. No civilised country, least of all Germany, could look favourably on any policy which would run counter to the spirit of religious comprehension.[55]

However the real possibility of the Army being used against Ulster caused the Unionist leadership to consider the need to ensure the Ulster Volunteer Force was adequately equipped with arms and ammunition.

This would bolster the weapons already in Unionist hands; some of these gathered in rural areas in direct response to Home Rule threats in previous decades.

---

51   Ryan, AP, *Mutiny at the Curragh* (1956).
52   Ulster Volunteers, January 1913 – Ulster-Scots Community Network <http://www.ulster-scots.com/uploads/901740969819.PDF> (Accessed 5 August 2013).
53   Ryan, AP, *Mutiny at the Curragh* (1956).
54   Ryan, AP, *Mutiny at the Curragh* (1956).
55   Ryan, AP, *Mutiny at the Curragh* (1956).

1st and 2nd Companies of the Ulster Volunteer Force outside Killyleagh Castle. (Somme Museum)

Early training in the use of firearms was provided under the auspices of 'sporting gun clubs' in the Lurgan and Portadown area, where local farmers already in the Volunteer movement were able to provide basic shooting practice to local townspeople on Sunday afternoons.[56]

In the beginning the weapons available to the UVF ranged through mid-nineteenth-century muzzle-loading rifles with gunpowder and ball, antique shotguns and Webley revolvers issued to officers in the Boer War.[57] This was complemented by small-scale smuggling of guns brought in, sometimes in boxes of herring on fishing boats through ports such as Kilkeel.[58] The Waringstown Volunteers received guns landed from fishing boats or colliers which were then transported by train to Lurgan where a carriage would be diverted down by Brownlow Terrace where a local driver could unload the weapons to deliver them around the local countryside.[59]

The Donegal Volunteers were well armed thanks in no small part to Lord Leitrim's chauffeur, Stephen Bullock, a tall Cockney,[60] who was eventually sent to Birmingham to live. Bullock drove Lord Leitrim all over the

Kaiser Wilhelm II. (Somme Museum)

---

56 Orr, Philip, *The Road to the Somme* (1987).
57 Orr, Philip, *The Road to the Somme* (1987).
58 Stewart, ATQ, *The Ulster Crises* (1967).
59 Orr, Philip, *The Road to the Somme* (1987).
60 Ingram, Rev Brett, *Covenant and Challenge* (1989).

A Ulster Volunteer, smuggling guns from Birmingham to Ulster in the spring of 1913, stops briefly for a photograph. (Somme Museum)

county in a Clément-Talbot motor car night after night inspecting the units until one morning he was summoned to the Castle to see his Lordship.

He found Leitrim sitting in front of a large map of west Britain and was greeted with; "I have a dangerous job for you, you don't have to do it if you don't wish, but you have the ability and I hope you will."[61]

He then proceeded to explain to Bullock how he intended to purchase arms in Birmingham and bring them to Donegal for the Volunteers. He owned a small packet steamer, the SS *Graniamore*, which sailed weekly between Glasgow, Portrush, Derry and Mulroy. The *Graniamore* was normally used to take migrant workers to Glasgow.[62] He told Bullock it would be his job to get the consignments of arms every week, moving them by lorry from Birmingham where he would pick up a prearranged consignment and drive it to Glasgow, 300 miles away, which was quite a journey for a 1913 motor vehicle.[63] If any hint of their activities reached the authorities it could

---

61 Ingram, Rev Brett, *Covenant and Challenge* (1989).
62 Captain Henry Gallaugher DSO – Donegal Annual – *Journal of the County Donegal History Society* – No.59, 2007.
63 Canning, WJ, *Ballyshannon, Belcoo, Bertincourt* (1996).

have resulted in police, coastguard or Customs pouncing and Bullock being arrested and jailed.[64] Despite the risk Bullock agreed and went by train to Belfast where he bought a four-ton Dennis lorry, eventually driving it into a grease works in Birmingham where two days later he was met by John Manning, the manager of the Rosapenna Hotel. The hotel was owned and built by Lord Leitrim near his home in Carrigart in North Donegal. The barrels of grease were to be for the Donegal fishermen.[65]

Manning had arrangements in place and Bullock left the next morning with his first consignment. The initial loading place was the remote seaport of Workington, Cumberland where boats of a Belfast coal firm were also loaded. However within a month this location had to be abandoned when Bullock was recognised by a crane driver who had been previously employed on the SS *Graniamore* and then informed the police. The alternative site was a rented timber yard in Renfrew which was staffed by sympathetic Scots who repacked the 'grease' and arranged the shipping. All was going accordingly to plan until one night a driver misjudged the narrow ramp and the lorry slipped off. A crate was punctured by railing spikes revealing 'something odd' to a resident overlooking the location. Suspicious that it was a rifle the police were informed. Luckily, within the hour a friendly Glasgow policeman informed Bullock that there was to be a full scale police raid the following night. Bullock and his staff feverishly transferred their large stock of Birmingham rifles across by ferry to an engineering works in Clydebank where they were hidden amongst ships' boilers.[66] Many different ruses were used to disguise the frequent journeys north with the clandestine cargo; grease barrels half full of .303 ammunition and half full of cotton waste with a little tar poured inside the bung, labelled "Specially prepared pitch"; furniture crates addressed to a reputable Londonderry firm which had cheap roomy dressers with space for 'extras'; cases of petrol tins with every fourth tin containing an extra and wooden barrels used for carbide enclosing a tin container with the pretext it was for lamps in Donegal; amongst poles and finally a specially designed steel cylinder manufactured by a Coleraine firm. This four feet high tube with a flat top was billed as containing 'filters' and on either side was stencilled the words, 'inlet' and 'outlet'.[67, 68] Those barrels searched by Customs men always contained grease![69]

With only one load left at Clydebank to move, one of the shipments of 'furniture' was seized in Londonderry and the authorities in Scotland alerted. Rather than abandon the remaining load, Bullock loaded the lorry and headed up towards Loch Lomond, from there he headed north towards Inverary but the lorry came to a halt on the steep gradient, 'Rest and be Thankful', resulting in Bullock and his accomplice carrying the load to the summit by hand before bringing up the lorry, repacking and driving on to Inverary, south into Kintyre and into the Mull of Saddell, knowing that the Laird of Saddell was a close friend of Lord Leitrim. It was from here that the last load would be loaded onto the SS *Graniamore*, bringing to an end the arming of the Donegal Volunteers.[70]

This piecemeal approach to arming the volunteers was complicated by the authorities keeping a close watch on the British ports to stop the Ulster Volunteers from landing guns on Irish shores.

---

64 Ingram, Rev Brett, *Covenant and Challenge* (1989).
65 Ingram, Rev Brett, *Covenant and Challenge* (1989).
66 Ingram, Rev Brett, *Covenant and Challenge* (1989).
67 Hume, David, *"For Ulster and Her Freedom": The story of the April 1914 gun-running* (1989).
68 Ingram, Rev Brett, *Covenant and Challenge* (1989).
69 Ingram, Rev Brett, *Covenant and Challenge* (1989).
70 Ingram, Rev Brett, *Covenant and Challenge* (1989).

Such steps did not prevent the Earl of Lanesborough simply purchasing 175 Martini-Enfield .303 rifles from Harrods department store in London, which appear to have been delivered to the Earl of Erne in Enniskillen.[71]

By March 1914, frustration in the UVF leadership was beginning to show. At a meeting at Craigavon House Major Robert McCalmont, Central Antrim Regiment, voiced the concerns of other regimental commanders and adjutants who were present. Unionist leaders were claiming the UVF would "fight to the bitter end" yet they didn't have sufficient arms and ammunition to do so if it came to it. This frustration was also against the tension created by the belief that the government was working on a plan to arrest up to 200 unionist leaders and break the opposition to Home Rule by force. McCalmont received applause for stating what others felt, however Carson who was present could not inform the UVF commanders that secret plans were already underway to resolve their shortage of weapons.[72]

Meanwhile the various units of the Ulster Volunteers continued to drill and exercise. Cyril F Falls, commanding officer, 3rd Battalion, Fermanagh Regiment, UVF, issued battalion orders for Easter Monday, 13 April 1914. The Battalion was to assemble at 11:00 a.m. and form up in Quarter Column on the Cricket Ground, Broad Meadow, Enniskillen. Company commanders were told that every effort would be made to secure sufficient train accommodation and reduced fares with the battalion instructed to proceed to Derrygore where they would undertake company, battalion and extended order drill, marching back to Enniskillen in sufficient time for those travelling by rail to catch the train at 4:40 p.m. Each Volunteer was to parade without arms but wearing bandoliers, haversacks containing their own rations, water bottles, armlets and belts and if possible puttees or gaiters. Order of dress was to be neat and it was desirable that they would wear a grey soft felt hat which they were told could be obtained in Enniskillen.

The discipline expected on the day was obvious from a note appended to the order which reminded each man that no one would be allowed to leave the ranks without the leave of the company commander which had to be obtained through his squad leader. Each man was also reminded that they would be under Military discipline until they were finally dismissed at their drill centres and that if any man disobeyed this order or conducted himself in a manner which may bring discredit on the Force he would be struck off the roll of the UVF.[73]

The order even went as far as reminding each Volunteer to carefully and thoroughly cleanse his water bottle with boiling water before using it.

On 15 April 1914, Captain FP Crozier issued the following special order to the men under his command:

Special Service Section
(West Belfast Regiment)
UVF

The mere title of this Section denotes that special efforts are required of its members. It is impossible for those who do not attend parades, etc., regularly to be efficient for war. This is obviously unfair on those who are, by their united efforts, making themselves efficient; and will be a real source of danger in the unfortunate event of service in the field.

---

71 Bowman, Timothy, *Carson's Army: Ulster Volunteer Force, 1910-22* (2007).
72 Hume, David, *"For Ulster and Her Freedom": The story of the April 1914 gun-running* (1989).
73 Canning, WJ, *Ballyshannon, Belcoo, Bertincourt* (1996).

D Company, 1st Battalion, North Down Regiment, Ulster Volunteer Force, 1914 at Bangor Castle. (Somme Museum)

A representation of the appearance of the Ulster Volunteer Force Special Service Section. A civilian jacket, shirt and tie along with a UVF lapel badge, belt with bayonet and frog and ammunition bandolier. The headgear is the slouch hat with the UVF Special Service badge with the arm brassard giving the unit designation. (Somme Museum)

At a future date, therefore, any man who has not shown by his attendance, that he intends to do his best to fit himself for active service, will be struck off the strength (1.i. not finally approved), and revert to the original company; handing in his clothing and equipment.

Many men desire to join S.S.S.

Parades in future will be at Forth River Football Ground, on Mondays, Tuesdays and Wednesdays, at eight p.m. and as notified.
F.P. Crozier, Captain.
Commanding S.S.S., W.B.R., U.V.F.
222 Shankill Road,
Belfast. 15-4-14

Crozier later claimed that this order produced 'panic' in certain Unionist circles in the House of Commons and deep resentment and anger among Nationalists and the government with elements wanting him arrested and for him to state who he intended to fight. Crozier's approach was simple, he was being "paid by the Ulstermen to train men to fight, hence the document."[74]

---

74 Crozier, Brig-Gen FP, CB, CMG, DSO, *Ireland for Ever* (1932).

7

Unionist Gun-running

The man given the task of arming the Volunteers en-masse was an influential member of the Belfast Volunteer hierarchy. Fred Crawford, from one of the oldest Presbyterian families in Ulster,[1] had been with the Volunteer movement since 1911 and had previously served as an artillery officer in the British Army. He had already established a good personal and professional relationship with a Jewish German national, Bruno Spiro, grandson of the founder of the company Waffen, Munition and Militar-Effekten, with offices in both Hamburg and Berlin. It is possible Spiro had responded to one of Crawford's earlier newspaper advertisements. Crawford had been importing thousands of rifles, primarily Vetterlis from Hamburg under the nom-de-guerre of WH Jones and the business alias of John Ferguson & Co, Shipping Agents, to his Wilson Street premises. These rifles were then repackaged, taken down to a yard behind the offices in Mill Street from where they were loaded into cars at night, and as Crawford noted, "the first few thousand rifles were all sent to the districts where the Nationalists were strong and the Unionists weak."[2]

In order to fulfil the demand for a greater number of weapons Crawford used his contact with Spiro and developed a plan to purchase rifles and ammunition in Hamburg and ship them on a suitable steamer with possibly a mid-voyage transfer to another vessel and then land them in Ulster. The UVF 'business committee' approved the proposed plan and Crawford put the scheme into operation.

Codenamed Operation 'Lion' it was planned in complete secrecy and in meticulous detail.

On arriving in Hamburg Spiro gave him three options for the supply of weapons:

a) Twenty thousand Vetteli rifles, with bayonets (ammunition would have to be specially manufactured).
b) Thirty thousand Russian rifles with bayonets (lacking scabbards) and ammunition.
c) Fifteen thousand new Austrian and 5,000 German army rifles with bayonets, both to take standard Mannlicher cartridges.

The third option was the most expensive, being twice the cost of the first and nearly treble that of the second. However it had the advantages that the Austrian and German patterns were first-rate and used up-to-date clip loaders with ammunition easily obtainable from the United Kingdom, America or Germany. Conversely the ammunition for the Italian weapons was only manufactured in Italy and would have to be obtained from there, while the Russian weapons although new and unused were of an obsolete pattern.[3]

Due to the costs involved Crawford had to return to Belfast via London to seek approval from Carson and Craig for the purchase.

---

1 Ryan, AP, *Mutiny at the Curragh* (1956).
2 Haines, Keith, *Fred Crawford: Carson's Gunrunner* (2009).
3 McNeill, Ronald, *Ulster's Stand for Union* (1922).

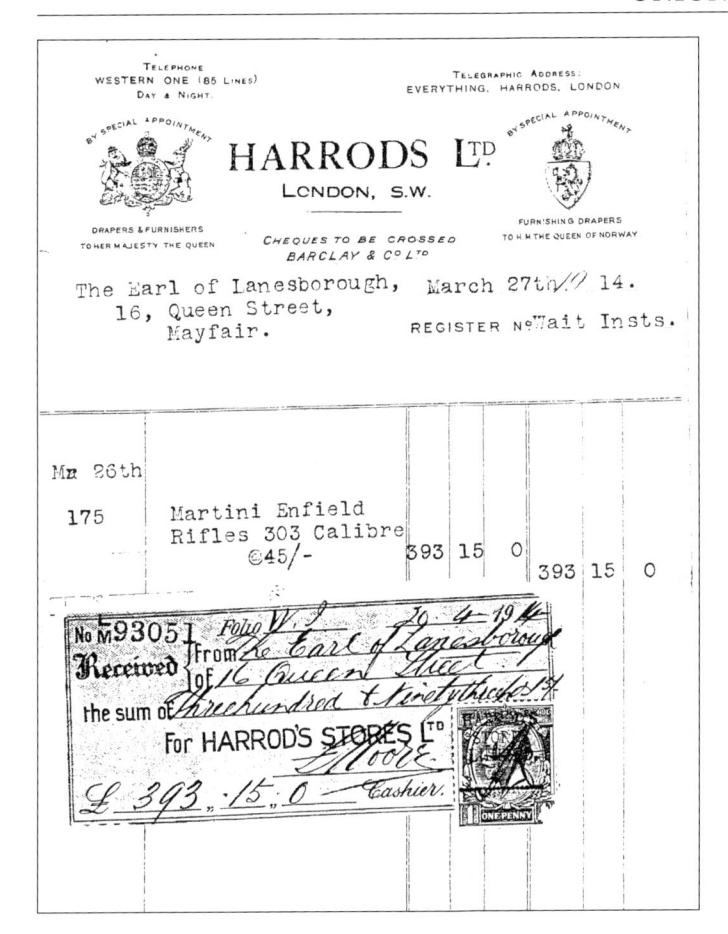

A receipt from Harrods Ltd, London to The Earl of Lanesborough, 27 March 1914 for 175 Martini Henry rifles. Their destination was the Ulster Volunteer Force. (Somme Museum)

The consignment was to include 15,000 new Austrian rifles which still had to be bought from the factory, 5,000 German rifles with bayonets, all to take standard cartridges, 10,000 Italian rifles, previously purchased and stored and 3,000,000 rounds of small arms ammunition.[4] The cost of the cargo was £70,000.[5]

Crawford's attention to detail meant that one rifle and 100 rounds of ammunition were packed together and then five rifles were wrapped together with straw packing, each package weighing about 75 pounds.[6] This rearrangement cost £2,000 and took a month's work.[7] However it meant that they were ready for instant use and were easily unloaded, a sensible precaution given that if the anticipated police and army attempts to stop the cargo being landed were realised then as he stated "our men would run any risk rather than lose their rifles."[8]

In order to cover the activities of the gun-runners it was announced that on the night of the 24 April 1914 there was to be a test mobilisation of the UVF.[9]

---

4   Shearman, Hugh, *Not an Inch: A Study of Northern Ireland and Lord Craigavon* (1942).
5   Shearman, Hugh, *Not an Inch: A Study of Northern Ireland and Lord Craigavon* (1942).
6   Shearman, Hugh, *Not an Inch: A Study of Northern Ireland and Lord Craigavon* (1942).
7   Shearman, Hugh, *Not an Inch: A Study of Northern Ireland and Lord Craigavon* (1942).
8   Ryan, AP, *Mutiny at the Curragh* (1956).
9   Orr, Philip, *The Road to the Somme* (1987).

A postcard depicting *The Fanny*. (T Wylie)

To further confuse the authorities as to what was happening at Larne the Belfast Volunteers were to march a contingent of men to the Belfast docks where the SS *Balmerino* would dock as a decoy. A large wagon was also sent to the dock as if awaiting a load to be disembarked. When the customs officers attempted to search the vessel, the activities of the volunteers to frustrate their activities would help to encourage the belief that the *Balmerino* contained weapons for the UVF.[10] In the dark the vessel came up the Musgrave Channel in a furtive and suspicious manner drawing the attention of the authorities. When she finally docked after blundering at her moorings every hindrance was put up against the authorities who began to investigate. The skipper asked if they could not wait until daylight, then questioned their authority, claiming to have misplaced his keys for the ship's papers until the hatches were finally opened to reveal a load of coal.[11]

The plan began to be implemented when Crawford, accompanied by Andrew Agnew, a sea captain, went to seek out suitable vessels.[12] Agnew was the skipper of one of the Antrim Iron Ore Company's coasting steamers and had already been a great assistance to Crawford.[13] He also brought with him his mate, chief and second engineers.[14] Posing as John Washington, an American from New York, Crawford purchased the SS *Fanny*, a steamer from Bergen in Norway, for £2,000,[15] after she had arrived there from Newcastle carrying a cargo of coal.[16] In order to ensure that her ownership could not result in her confiscation by the British government, arrangements were put in place to ensure she sailed under the Norwegian flag. The Norwegian captain sailed it as his own vessel and gave Crawford a mortgage on her for 60,000 marks.[17, 18]

---

10   Orr, Philip, *The Road to the Somme* (1987).
11   McNeill, Ronald, *Ulster's Stand for Union* (1922).
12   Ryan, AP, *Mutiny at the Curragh* (1956).
13   Shearman, Hugh, *Not an Inch: A Study of Northern Ireland and Lord Craigavon* (1942).
14   McNeill, Ronald, *Ulster's Stand for Union* (1922).
15   Ryan, AP, *Mutiny at the Curragh* (1956).
16   Hume, David, *"For Ulster and Her Freedom": The story of the April 1914 gun-running* (1989).
17   Ryan, AP, *Mutiny at the Curragh* (1956).
18   Shearman, Hugh, *Not an Inch: A Study of Northern Ireland and Lord Craigavon* (1942).

Whilst Agnew prepared the vessel, Crawford returned to Belfast and made arrangements to keep in communication with Spender. The agreed rendezvous was at Lough Laxford on the west coast of Sutherlandshire, Scotland.[19]

The next problem was how to get the weapons into the hold of the *Fanny*, a dilemma which Crawford and his associates, Spiro and Schneider, worked on until one night Spiro and Crawford were talking over matters in a restaurant. Crawford later claimed he heard a voice say, "Go with the guns tonight and don't loose sight of them until you have handed them over in Ulster". With a start he questioned Spiro if he had spoken, Spiro denied it but the voice repeated it four times. Crawford took this as an omen and set off down the River Elbe.[20]

His tug flew a black flag, which he was advised would indicate to all pilots that he had right of way, however at Kiel the master told him three men had boarded to try and find out where they were going and what their cargo was. The men were assumed to be Mexicans as some rebels from that country were also in the market for arms and ammunition, perhaps linked to Crawford's previous activities in this regard. This was a minor incident compared to when a German official who boarded stated that they could sail no further because their papers were not in order as he believed they had rifles in the lighters. Despite attempts at reassuring and negotiating with the official, Schneider informed Crawford, "This man is going to cause trouble." Crawford could not speak German but told Schneider, "Give him some money". Schneider put a 100-mark note in the officials' hand who looked at it, smiled, slipped it into his pocket and said "I see that your papers are in order and shall detain you no longer. Good night."

The two vessels rendezvoused as arranged in the Kattegat between the Danish islands of Langeland and Funen[21] where the cargo for the UVF was transferred to the *Fanny* whilst still in Danish territorial waters. However the plan was jeopardised when the Danish authorities boarded the *Fanny* and demanded to see the ship's papers. They spent half an hour examining the bales but did not open any of them, eventually seizing her papers and that of the tug, saying they would be forwarded to the Danish authorities in Copenhagen to be dealt with but they would be returned the next morning.[22] They may have believed that her cargo had been en route from Bergen to Iceland where there was another Home Rule crises developing between Iceland and Denmark.[23] This Danish official was not prepared to accept the bribe like the German.[24] Crawford would later explain how he felt like a rat caught in a trap because if he made a run for it, he would have to sail within half a mile of a torpedo station in the channel. He was also concerned about letting down the Ulster Volunteers after all the promises which had been made to them time and time again at various demonstrations and from speakers' platforms and also the possibility that the failure would result in the leaders being made a laughing stock in the eyes of the world. In his own book, *Guns for Ulster*, he said:

> I went into my cabin and threw myself on my knees, and in simple language told God all about it, what this meant to Ulster, that there was nothing sordid in what we desired, and that we wanted nothing selfishly. I pointed out all this to God and thought of the old psalm. 'O God our help in ages past, our hope for years to come.'[25]

---

19 Shearman, Hugh, *Not an Inch: A Study of Northern Ireland and Lord Craigavon* (1942).
20 Ryan, AP, *Mutiny at the Curragh* (1956).
21 Hyde H Montgomery, *Carson* (1953).
22 McNeill, Ronald, *Ulster's Stand for Union* (1922).
23 Hume, David, *"For Ulster and Her Freedom": The story of the April 1914 gun-running* (1989).
24 Ryan, AP, *Mutiny at the Curragh* (1956).
25 Crawford, FH, *Guns for Ulster* (1947).

The gunrunners onboard the *Fanny* in the Kiel Canal. Back row: Fred Crawford, Captain Andrew Agnew, Bruno Spiro. Front row: Captain Marthin Falck and Helen Crawford. (PRONI D961/3/002)

Emerging on deck he discovered from Schneider that the men wanted to cease loading, but after an offer of doubling their wages, the men set about the task with renewed vigour.[26, 27] The next morning, as if his prayers had been answered, he awoke to find mist hanging over the water and a gale blowing, visibility down to some 3 or 400 yards.[28] He waited until 8:00 a.m., the time the Danish customs officials were meant to return. When they did not appear he ordered the captain, Captain Marthin Faick, to weigh anchor and sail out into the mists of the Baltic.[29] Now without papers the *Fanny* was legally a pirate ship.

As soon as they were into the open sea all hands began cutting the iron letters, 'Fanny' off the funnel, changing the colour and painting the name 'Bethia' onto the bows and stern of the vessel; named for Crawford's youngest daughter.[30]

On 31 March Sir Henry Moore Lowther, the British Ambassador in Denmark, sent a telegram from Copenhagen to Sir Edward Grey, the British Foreign Secretary, which informed him that he had received information from a vice consul at Svendborg that a Norwegian steamer named the *Fanny* was heading to Ireland laden with arms and ammunition for the UVF. After a follow-up

---

26 Ryan, AP, *Mutiny at the Curragh* (1956).
27 Shearman, Hugh, *Not an Inch: A Study of Northern Ireland and Lord Craigavon* (1942).
28 Ryan, AP, *Mutiny at the Curragh* (1956).
29 Hume, David, *"For Ulster and Her Freedom": The story of the April 1914 gun-running* (1989).
30 Ryan, AP, *Mutiny at the Curragh* (1956).

letter from Lowther dated, 1 April and another from Water Hearn, the British Consul General in Hamburg, dated 3 April the British government heard nothing more of the vessel for three weeks.[31]

On the 1 April news broke that the *Fanny* was en-route with a cargo of arms and ammunition for the UVF with one customs official speculating that there were 30,000 guns on board, but the unanswered question on everyone's lips was where would she land them.[32] One English newspaper ran the headline, "Guns Transhipped in the Baltic, Carson or Castro?"[33]

Calling at Trelleborg in Sweden they saw a newspaper which carried a report of the *Fanny* and her cargo. Crawford whilst crossing the North Sea had the crew paint 'Anvers' on the stern instead of 'Bergen', then came down with an attack of malaria. While he was indisposed they were hit by a gale which shattered one of the lamp glasses, leaving them only showing a port light. After a few close encounters with other vessels they realised that they would have to put into the nearest port to get a new glass. Late on the evening 7 April, they put into Great Yarmouth, Agnew going ashore to buy the new starboard light. He was also given orders, given the events to date, to go to Belfast and get another steamer and bring it to the rendezvous to meet the *Bethia* at Lundy Island in the Bristol Channel and to transfer the cargo to another vessel. Before heading for the English Channel they changed the name of the *Fanny* again, this time to *Doreen*, Crawford's second daughter.

However things were still not running smoothly with Crawford again coming down with a bout of malaria, leaving him unable to eat anything. They proceeded down the English Channel in a fierce gale, keeping close to the French coast and only maintaining a speed of four knots.[34]

Just off the coast of Dunkirk, Captain Falke went into Crawford's cabin and had a fierce argument with him. Falke believed that Crawford's illness was so severe that he would be dead within two days. Crawford was having none of it and after holding a .38 Colt automatic pistol to Falke's head he agreed to follow Crawford's orders.[35]

As a result of high seas and gales the *Doreen* was late at Lundy Island and had to wait in the area of the Bristol Channel from 11 to 13 April[36] whilst they were observed by fishermen, steamship crews and were constantly approached by a number of pilot boats offering their services, however they were able to avoid them.

Views differed amongst those planning the operation with regards to the landing site, some favoured Belfast whilst others favoured Larne. However the intelligence report of the chairman of the Larne Harbour Board, William Chaine, was no doubt of interest to the military committee. Chaine's detailed report included a survey of the religion and in some cases the politics of the post office and railway workers, local coastguards, the Royal Irish Constabulary and even to the extent that the station master at Larne was a Presbyterian, although his politics were "very doubtful" whilst the porters were considered "mixed" and the cleaners were all unionist with some of them in the UVF. Others were identified as being suspect, the Chief Clerk at Larne Harbour Station was the President of the Ancient Order of Hibernians in the town, the Glynn station master and the Kilwaughter postmaster's politics were believed to be "Unitarian". Whilst mainly focused

---

31 Grob-Fitzgibbon, *Turning Points of The Irish Revolution: The British Government, Intelligence and the Cost of Indifference, 1912-1921* (2007).
32 Hume, David, *"For Ulster and Her Freedom": The story of the April 1914 gun-running* (1989).
33 Hyde H Montgomery, *Carson* (1953).
34 Shearman, Hugh, *Not an Inch: A Study of Northern Ireland and Lord Craigavon* (1942).
35 Ryan, AP, *Mutiny at the Curragh* (1956).
36 Before heading for the English Channel they changed the name of the 'Fanny' again, this time to 'Doreen', Crawford's second daughter. However things were still not running smoothly with Crawford again coming down with a bout of malaria leaving him unable to eat anything.

An Acting-Sergeant from the Royal Ulster Constabulary and two Constables outside their barracks. (Police Museum)

on Larne, the report also listed the numbers of RIC and their religion in Larne, Glenarm and Carnough and also that of the coastguards in Glenarm.[37]

Whilst the shipment was heading for Ireland there were reports in Dublin newspapers that a mysterious vessel – called the *Fanny* and rumoured to be carrying arms for Ulster – had been captured by Danish authorities. Spender who had been in Dublin hoping to telegraph Crawford before he left Kiel, left the post office and noticed a news report which read "Ulster's Mystery Arms-Ship Captured".[38] Disheartened at the apparent situation and the loss of the £70,000 invested in the plan[39] he returned to Craigavon to update Craig, Carson and Richardson on developments. On entering Craigavon one of the committee said to him, "See what your mad plans have brought us to," but was taken by the arm by Craig with the words, "come and have a meal."[40]

Carson was more practical as they sat down to dinner, "Now we must begin all over again like a general after a defeat. We must have a new plan."[41]

After several days with no update, a coded message was received at Craigavon indicating that Crawford was in London. Spender headed to meet him with all haste, however on arrival it was not Crawford, but the Hamburg packer of arms who informed him that Crawford and the vessel had escaped, but they had lost their papers and were probably somewhere in the North Sea.[42] Wilfred Spender immediately headed to Loch Laxford in Sutherland in the Scottish Highlands to try and make contact with the steamer.[43] He waited here for a week, but the ship never appeared.

---

37 Hume, David, *"For Ulster and Her Freedom": The story of the April 1914 gun-running* (1989).
38 Hyde H Montgomery, *Carson* (1953).
39 Hyde H Montgomery, *Carson* (1953).
40 Shearman, Hugh, *Not an Inch: A Study of Northern Ireland and Lord Craigavon* (1942).
41 Hyde H Montgomery, *Carson* (1953).
42 Shearman, Hugh, *Not an Inch: A Study of Northern Ireland and Lord Craigavon* (1942).
43 Hume, David, *"For Ulster and Her Freedom": The story of the April 1914 gun-running* (1989).

Coded UVF message.
(Somme Museum)

> MEMO No 157/14.
>
> Aug 3rd/1914
>
> 1. At a conference of Commanders held in Belfast on 31.7.14. representations were made as to the difficulty at present attending the preparation of any scheme for general operations in consequence of the increasing activity of the Nationalists and the arms they are distributing.
>
> HOBSF ZTHMH BDYOY FYDLI
> SIHKD QOTLC OFTPQ COCSI FZWRT PIFVD
> PGIOT PTGZW YOMH.
>
> 2. The delay caused by the present political truce will make matters more difficult.
>
> SIIZF KDVDB XPIZD WSIKU PGPHO STKOF
> YODBO QPWZH YGKAM NZLGK DQPIS TNKPG
> and commanders must watch importation
> IOEAG EZXOQ CLZDK NLBOC GPRNX PRYDQ
> of arms very closely.
> HNGOT KSPDQ OTOKL FWRQX GPXDM KPHOV.
>
> 3. Battalion Commanders must now be most
> CBPDQ DOFKO DNKBO BCLZI STKWT POKBG or as so
> energetic about obtaining correct information
> GKNTP IKHWM IPHDB CKYYT DRDEO HMHDN
> on these points, and prepare a scheme for
> PBPGD SHOIL WRDQO TOKOS IFPHT KHOPT
> disarming them immediately on mobilisation
> CLZTP GQZPG CQHNG KFGMT IOQCW RHOIR
> But no action is to be taken without orders from
> IFOGK BKGIO DQFKD TONMD FOHTD QOTMC
> Headquarters or from me.

However in Ulster members of the military committee had taken 'cold feet' as a result of the Royal Naval activity in Belfast Lough and military troop movements in Ulster, and sent a message to Crawford. Whilst Crawford was sitting off Lundy on board the *Doreen*, the little steamer *Balmarino* owned by Lord Leitrim came alongside. Andy Agnew, who was on board the *Balmarino*, informed Crawford that he had been in London and seen both Carson and Craig, and that the situation was becoming more desperate with the threat of a division of troops being sent to Ulster from Aldershot and Belfast being bombarded by the Royal Navy, but that a group of army officers had refused to fight against Ulster.[44] Captain Morrison, the skipper of the *Balmarino* gave a letter to Crawford which instructed him to return to the Baltic and not land his cargo. He was told to cruise there for three months or return the guns for storage in Hamburg until the excitement at home had died down, "keeping in touch with the Committee during that time."[45]

---

44 Ryan, AP, *Mutiny at the Curragh* (1956).
45 Ryan, AP, *Mutiny at the Curragh* (1956).

Needless to say, Crawford was not impressed with the sudden reluctance to see the task through, especially given the tribulations he had encountered so far. He told Captain Morrison:

> I do not know who gave you this document, but take it to the person or persons who gave it to you and had not the courage to put their names to it, and tell them to go to hell … If I do not receive an official document with instructions for landing my cargo within the next six days, I shall run the ship aground in Ballyholme Bay at high water, and rouse the County Down Volunteers to come and take her cargo off.[46, 47, 48]

Crawford realised the *Fanny*, no matter what name she bore, would not be able to land the weapons in an Irish port, so another vessel; a harmless coal boat, would be needed.

He sent Agnew with the *Doreen* to the rendezvous point of Wexford whilst he boarded the *Balmerino* and headed for South Wales.[49] He went ashore at Tenby, being interrogated by the customs officer, and went to catch the Irish mail train to Rosslare where he was again questioned by another customs officer who seized his Colt automatic,[50] before he managed to catch the mail boat to Dublin, travelling on to Belfast by train. On arriving in the city he headed to Craigavon to confront the senior unionists and again reiterated that he would run the vessel and her cargo aground before he would sail them away. He arrived at Craigavon as the committee were sitting down to dinner, Crawford stormed, "You promised our fellows not wooden guns but real guns!"[51] Refusing to shake the hand of James Craig, who put his arm around him saying "Come on Fred; everything will be all right."[52] The matter was resolved when he was told by Carson, "Well done Crawford; I'm proud of you", echoing the sentiment between the two men at their earlier London meeting when the scheme was discussed.[53, 54] Crawford would later write, "I knew my man and never mistrusted him. He and James Craig would back me against the whole committee if necessary."[55]

In the courtyard of Craigavon House, (left to right), Lord Londonderry, Sir Edward Carson and Captain James Craig. (Somme Museum)

---

46 Crawford, FH, *Guns for Ulster* (1947).
47 Hume, David, *"For Ulster and Her Freedom": The story of the April 1914 gun-running* (1989).
48 Ryan, AP, *Mutiny at the Curragh* (1956).
49 Shearman, Hugh, *Not an Inch: A Study of Northern Ireland and Lord Craigavon* (1942).
50 Ryan, AP, *Mutiny at the Curragh* (1956).
51 Shearman, Hugh, *Not an Inch: A Study of Northern Ireland and Lord Craigavon* (1942).
52 Shearman, Hugh, *Not an Inch: A Study of Northern Ireland and Lord Craigavon* (1942).
53 Crawford, FH, *Guns for Ulster* (1947).
54 Hume, David, *"For Ulster and Her Freedom": The story of the April 1914 gun-running* (1989).
55 Shearman, Hugh, *Not an Inch: A Study of Northern Ireland and Lord Craigavon* (1942).

During the rest of the day the meeting started to develop a plan for the landing of the guns into the hands of the Volunteers. The next part of the scheme would be to purchase another vessel to transfer the guns from the *Fanny*. On the advice of Sam Kelly of Kelly's Coal, Crawford went to Glasgow and purchased a small vessel which was up for sale and had previously been carrying coal from Scotland to Belfast for some months previously, thereby providing the perfect cover. The name of the boat was the 'SS *Clyde Valley*.[56, 57]

Before leaving Craigavon, Crawford made it clear he would expect no further change of orders from the committee "unless they were signed by Sir Edward Carson personally."[58] Whilst the plan was that the *Clyde Valley* would land her cargo right up Belfast Lough at the docks, Crawford and Spender both agreed that Larne was a better location with the radiating roads for dispersal of the cargo.[59]

Crawford bought the vessel in Glasgow and made arrangements for the *Clyde Valley* to rendezvous at Llandudno Bay. He set off of to join Agnew and the *Doreen* off Wexford on 18 April, a day later than planned.[60] However a more pressing issue was the exact location of the *Doreen* and her precious cargo as she was nowhere to be seen. Crawford again crossed the Irish Sea and was put ashore at Fishguard, and headed to Great Yarmouth through London, but there was no sign of the vessel. When he finally received a telegram from Agnew, it was good news, all was going according to plan, but he had to get to Holyhead. eading back to London he caught the Irish night mail train from Euston to Holyhead and successfully rendezvoused with the *Clyde Valley*.[61, 62]

During the night of 19-20 April the *Clyde Valley* successfully rendezvoused with the *Doreen* in a Welsh bay, the two ships were lashed together with one showing a port light and the other a starboard light. With the help of 16 transport labourers from Belfast, Agnew arranged the transfer of the cargo in less than half the time taken by the Germans when loading the *Fanny*.[63, 64]

By the time Crawford arrived a good part of the cargo had already been transhipped.[65] To provide more political significance and a perceived good omen to the events Crawford arranged for the *Clyde Valley* to be briefly renamed *Mountjoy II*, after the *Mountjoy* which broke the boom across the Foyle in 1689 to relieve the besieged Protestants in the City of Derry. The temporary renaming was achieved by using strips of canvas six feet long and twelve inches broad which were cut and painted with white letters on a black background, and affixed to her bows and stern; this was done mainly so the men waiting at Copeland would know the identity of the approaching vessel.[66]

Whilst Crawford's initial orders were to sail the *Clyde Valley* and its cargo to Belfast, thankfully these were countermanded by orders signed by Carson which ordered him to go to Larne first, then land guns on the North Down coast, more in keeping with Crawford's and Spender's original idea.[67] These orders were received off the Copeland Islands, near the mouth of Belfast Lough, when they encountered a tender belonging to Messrs. Workman Clark, on which were Mr Couser, a friend of Crawford's, and Mr Dawson Bates, secretary to the Ulster Unionist Council and later

---

56 Hume, David, *"For Ulster and Her Freedom": The story of the April 1914 gun-running* (1989).
57 Kilmarnock Somme Association.
58 Ryan, AP, *Mutiny at the Curragh* (1956).
59 Shearman, Hugh, *Not an Inch: A Study of Northern Ireland and Lord Craigavon* (1942).
60 Shearman, Hugh, *Not an Inch: A Study of Northern Ireland and Lord Craigavon* (1942).
61 Ryan, AP, *Mutiny at the Curragh* (1956).
62 Shearman, Hugh, *Not an Inch: A Study of Northern Ireland and Lord Craigavon* (1942).
63 Kilmarnock Somme Association.
64 Ryan, AP, *Mutiny at the Curragh* (1956).
65 Shearman, Hugh, *Not an Inch: A Study of Northern Ireland and Lord Craigavon* (1942).
66 Kilmarnock Somme Association.
67 Hume, David, *"For Ulster and Her Freedom": The story of the April 1914 gun-running* (1989).

Two coal shovels off the *Clyde Valley*. (Somme Museum)

The back of the top of the handles are embossed with the letters 'NDR-UVF' – The North Down Regiment – Ulster Volunteer Force. (Somme Museum)

the Minister of Home Affairs of the Northern Ireland Government.[68] Crawford, expecting orders to retreat, initially ignored them and ordered Agnew to hold his course, and continued to ignore them until he recognised them when they shouted they had important instructions. They then confirmed that they had orders signed personally by Carson.[69]

Meanwhile Colonel Couchman kept the police busy in Belfast harbour arguing over the opening of the hatches of a mysterious collier in the harbour which was thought to contain rifles, but in fact had only a cargo of coal.[70]

At the same time as the weapons were being transferred the County Antrim divisional commander, General Sir William Adair, on 20 April issued a call to members of the Motor Corps which said, "In accordance with your kind agreement to place a motor car at the disposal of the Provisional Government in case of necessity it is absolutely necessary that your car should arrive at Larne on the night of Friday-Saturday 24th-25th instant at 1:00 a.m. punctually but not before

---

68 Shearman, Hugh, *Not an Inch: A Study of Northern Ireland and Lord Craigavon* (1942).
69 McNeill, Ronald, *Ulster's Stand for Union* (1922).
70 Crozier, Brig-Gen FP Crozier, CB, CMG, DSO, *Ireland for Ever* (1932).

that hour, for a very secret and important duty."[71] Secrecy was the watchword for the events which were about to unfold.

John Watters had been acting as adjutant to the Ulster Signalling and Despatch Riding Corps and regularly called in to the Old Town Hall to carry out any necessary administration and to report to his OC. On one occasion he was asked by his OC if he would be prepared to do something for the Ulster Volunteer Force. He would not disclose the nature of the work but advised there was a certain amount of risk involved. Watters decided that if something momentous was going to happen he wanted to be involved so responded "right, I'll do it." After a renewed promise to maintain absolutely secrecy his OC advised him of the intention to land arms for the volunteers.

He was asked to go to Larne via the boat train on the night of 24/25 April to take charge of the signal communications between Larne and Belfast. He was handed the code for the night, told to study it and destroy it in the event of trouble. Having discussed and agreed the system of sending messages, the signalling stations to be used and the men to be employed, it was decided to use the cover story of warning the officers and men that an all-night signalling scheme was to be held on the night in question.[72]

In Larne itself a meeting between the County Antrim Divisional Commander, Sir William Adair, Major McCalmont, William Chaine and Lord Massereene finalised the arrangements for the forthcoming Friday evening. Three local UVF nurses were told to provide food and white armlets for 300 men, resulting in them carefully buying bread and sandwiches and ham and eggs from nearby farms,[73] so as not to arouse suspicion.

In order to ensure as smooth an operation as possible planning was meticulous. Larne was taken over by the County Antrim Regiment of the UVF under the cover of darkness, whilst other men from local Battalions were posted at key points on the routes approaching the port to ensure that those drivers who were unfamiliar with the route were directed to their destination. In support of these arrangements reserve supplies of petrol and tools to enable repairs to vehicles which might suffer a breakdown were also strategically located.

The order to the members of Larne UVF issued on 24 April from Squad Leader S Fullerton said, "Mobilise tonight at market yard at 7:30 p.m. sharp bringing overcoat, food for a few hours and stout stick. No Firearms."[74]

Earlier on the Friday John Watters told his family that he might not be back until the next morning as there was an all-night signalling exercise. Whilst he was en route though the city to the boat train for Larne he called at the Old Town Hall to pick up final instructions. Later on the train he observed several prominent UVF members and overheard a young lady remark to her friend that there were more people travelling than was usual.[75]

On reaching Larne, Watters reported to General Adair and was issued a white armband which would ensure his admittance to the quay. He reconnoitred the area, deciding where would be the best location for the despatch riders giving them a clear run to and from the quay yet ensuring their motorcycles were convenient and able to get away promptly. General Adair asked him to stop some of the engines of the motorcycles as he did not want to attract too much attention, as despite the quay and its vicinity being crowded with men there was practically no noise.[76]

---

71 Hume, David, *"For Ulster and Her Freedom": The story of the April 1914 gun-running* (1989).
72 The Ulster Volunteer Force Gun-running at Larne, April 1914. By JWT Watters http://www.orangenet.org/gunrun.htm (Accessed 30 November 2011).
73 Hume, David, *"For Ulster and Her Freedom": The story of the April 1914 gun-running* (1989).
74 Hume, David, *"For Ulster and Her Freedom": The story of the April 1914 gun-running* (1989).
75 The Ulster Volunteer Force Gun-running at Larne, April 1914. By JWT Watters http://www.orangenet.org/gunrun.htm (Accessed 30 November 2011).
76 The Ulster Volunteer Force Gun-running at Larne, April 1914. By JWT Watters <http://www.orangenet.org/

A sketch from the *Illustrated London News* by a Belfast artist of the scene at Larne while the guns and ammunition were being unloaded from the *Mountjoy* and cars for carrying them were arriving by the score. In the foreground, Island Magee. (Somme Museum)

Customs Officer George Goodman was patrolling along the coast towards Glenarm at 7:40 p.m. when he saw two lorries and several motor-cars facing out to sea with their headlights turned off along with members of the UVF. As be approached them the vehicles began to flash their lights out to sea. He then noticed a ship showing no lights or distinguishing marks moving into the harbour. As he hurried along the road in the same direction he was stopped by members of the UVF who refused to allow him to pass despite his demanding to be let through. The reply from the UVF members was simple, "No, not even the King should pass nor the police." When he again attempted to pass he was forcibly stopped. Being alone and unable to proceed he headed back to the RIC Barracks in Larne. When he arrived there he informed Head Constable James McHugh that the UVF had a mobilisation along the coast road and were not letting anyone of authority pass through the cordon. McHugh along with Constable Charles Roberts and Goodman headed back towards the harbour. They were stopped at the junction between the Bay Road and Curran Road and McHugh was approached by the man who McHugh knew to be Thomas Robinson and who was swinging a baton larger than those carried by the police. Robinson told McHugh bluntly, "We have orders not to let anyone past, and we have better batons that you have." Realising that this was no bluff, McHugh set off to find the District Inspector.[77] Acting Sergeant Robert Gordon and Constable Quinland had already told District Inspector William Moore than something was afoot and he was already en route to the harbour. Observing several lights along the coast road he sent Gordon to investigate whilst he continued with Quinlan towards the harbour. They were stopped by 40 or 50 Ulster Volunteers with the distinctive arm armbands worn on the night. Moore could see two ships moored off Barr Point but the Ulster Volunteers would not let either of them pass. Instead the two policemen cut across a field to Bay Road. Whilst they were crossing the field Sergeant Gordon caught up with them and informed Moore that the lights on the coast road had come from 11 motor cars signalling out to sea guarded by twenty Ulster Volunteers who threatened him as he approached. On reaching Bay Road the three policemen met with McHugh and Roberts who asked for their assistance at the corner of Bay and Curran Roads.

Moore approached the roadblock but was prevented from proceeding; he demanded to speak to Robinson who had threatened McHugh. Robinson arrived and told Moore that he had been ordered by Major McCalmont, a Member of Parliament, not to allow anyone in authority to pass, but if he wished to wait he could speak to McCalmont himself. Meanwhile Moore sent Head Constable McHugh back to the barracks to request help from Belfast, however when McHugh

---

gunrun.htm> (Accessed 30 November 2011).
77 Grob-Fitzgibbon, *Turning Points of The Irish Revolution: The British Government, Intelligence and the Cost of Indifference, 1912-1921* (2007).

Those Ulster Volunteers who escorted Edward Carson to Craigavon House unloading their rifles and revolvers. (Somme Museum)

reached the barracks and went to telephone the city he discovered the line had been cut and likewise, when he tried to send a telegram, the telegraph line was also inoperative. Meanwhile McCalmont arrived to speak with District Inspector Moore. Moore demanded an explanation for the cordons, to which McCalmont said he had orders "from Sir William Adair to block the roads leading to the harbour against everyone and particularly the police and customs officers." When questioned if he would use force to achieve this, McCalmont said he would block the roads at all cost and was supported by 700 men. Against these numbers there was clearly little than District Inspector Moore could do with only one Head Constable, one Sergeant and two constables.[78]

By 8:00 p.m. the town was sealed off from the rest of the Province. The Royal Irish Constabulary were well used to the UVF test mobilisations so that by the time the police realised exactly what was going on, on this occasion, it was too late.

One group of UVF controlled the harbour, whilst others kept guard on the main street and other key points in the town. The cordon of checkpoints, on all the roads leading into Larne were manned by Lord Massereene's South Antrim Regiment whilst the roads to Glenarm, Ballymena and Ballyclare along with the Shore Road to Carrickfergus were also sealed off.[79]

According to the plan the local police barracks was surrounded and the telephone wires were cut.[80] Captain F. Hall, the military secretary to the UVF, recorded details of these plans in a memo-

---

[78] Grob-Fitzgibbon, *Turning Points of The Irish Revolution: The British Government, Intelligence and the Cost of Indifference, 1912-1921* (2007).
[79] Hume, David, *"For Ulster and Her Freedom": The story of the April 1914 gun-running* (1989).
[80] Hume, David, *"For Ulster and Her Freedom": The story of the April 1914 gun-running* (1989).

randum. It included details of the tapping of the private telephone line connecting Hollywood Barracks to Exchange, as well as the short-circuiting of phone and telegraph wires into Larne after the last train, and the 'shorting' of the main rail lines.

From the afternoon some (such as those Ulster Volunteers from County Tyrone) began their journey to Larne; the road network and the capability of motor vehicles in 1914 not being the same as those today. One participant later recorded that as he travelled northwards out of Belfast, UVF Signallers in UVF uniform were visible along the Shore Road and through Carrickfergus. Just outside Larne at Glyn village the vehicles were stopped and checked and again on the outskirts of Larne itself by a line of men across the road. Crossing the railway line and heading for the Curran Road they joined a long line of cars waiting to reach the harbour. Another individual reported how that as darkness fell he saw a "snake of bright lights appear on the hills – a great cavalcade of motor cars with brilliant headlights." Lily McKee of Larne later recalled how as a young woman she saw the long line of car headlights heading for the town while her mother took tea out to the Volunteers gathering at the harbour.[81] A reporter for the Larne Times later wrote that the procession of cars leading into the town was over three miles in length.[82]

Elsewhere across Ulster, volunteers had received orders to assemble in their drill halls, including those areas not directly connected with the landing. Many of them had no idea the purpose of the exercise until the end of their vigil the next morning.

The 24 April was a cold, wet night and many of those present in the port, wearing their white armlets, had already carried out a full day's work.

At 10:30 p.m. the *Clyde Valley* steamed into Larne and started to dock though as a result of difficulty with mooring it was 11:00 p.m. before she was fully docked and her cargo began to be unloaded.[83]

A postcard depicting the unloading the weapons for the Ulster Volunteers with the cation "Bravo, Ulster Volunteers! The *Mountjoy* unloading 'the stuff' at Larne Harbour." The *Clyde Valley* had been temporarily renamed in order to land the Volunteers arms and ammunition on 24 April 1914.
(Somme Museum)

---

81   Hume, David, *"For Ulster and Her Freedom": The story of the April 1914 gun-running* (1989).
82   Hume, David, *"For Ulster and Her Freedom": The story of the April 1914 gun-running* (1989).
83   Hume, David, *"For Ulster and Her Freedom": The story of the April 1914 gun-running* (1989).

John Watton sent his first message of the night to the GOC in Belfast by sending off the first motorcyclist with an update. The despatch rider rode the seven miles from the quay to the tunnel at Whitehead, from where the message was signalled the eight miles across Belfast Lough to Orlock, and then the six miles from Orlock to Helen's Tower. From here it was signalled to a hill at Lisnabreeney, another nine miles, and then another three miles to a corner of Malone Golf Links and from there by despatch rider to the GOC at his house. The lamps used were electric with a parabolic lens enclosed in a round cylinder case about one foot long and eight inches wide with a focussing arrangement at the bottom for throwing a parallel ray.[84]

The unloading of the weapons was illuminated by the headlights of 500 motor vehicles. The various units of the UVF motor corps then transported parcels of weapons to secret locations in their home locales.

The first cars to be loaded were those from County Tyrone with the last of those leaving Larne at midnight, finally making it home at around 11:00 a.m. the next morning.[85]

The weapons to supply the Volunteers waiting at Belfast and Donaghadee were loaded into two other smaller local ships. The *Roma* was loaded by crane with 70 bundles of rifles for Belfast which were later landed at the wharf of Workman, Clark & Co,[86] however the *Innismurray*, which was bound for Donaghadee, was discovered to have a Nationalist crew which had to be replaced with a more sympathetic UVF crew.[87] During the operation a group of ladies dispensed tea and sandwiches from a hut on the quay.[88]

According to contemporary newspaper reports the last rifle left the harbour at 4:00 a.m.[89] With everyone seemingly gone, John Watton realised he had not made arrangements to get back home, but spied William Bob Lyttle, a despatch rider, with his motorcycle and side car heading home to Whitehead who offered him a lift, their contribution to the night's success complete.[90]

At 5:00 a.m. the *Clyde Valley* set sail for Bangor where her remaining weapons were to be offloaded by the local volunteers. As she left the harbour still masquerading as the *Mountjoy II*, her skipper and crew stood to attention and gave three cheers for "The King" and three for "The Volunteers", which were responded to by those on the shore.[91]

Responsibility for securing Bangor was given to Colonel McCammon who moved the 1st Battalion, North Down Regiment, into the town just after 9:00 p.m. The *Bangor Spectator* noted that most of the men believed they were to attend a benefit performance for the UVF at the local picture house.[92]

At 2:30 a.m. cars from as far as Banbridge and Donacloney arrived in the town and it was not long before approximately 100 cars were lined up along the Esplanade. In anticipation of the

---

84 The Ulster Volunteer Force Gun-running at Larne, April 1914. By JWT Watters <http://www.orangenet.org/gunrun.htm> (Accessed 30 November 2011).
85 Hume, David, *"For Ulster and Her Freedom": The story of the April 1914 gun-running* (1989).
86 Parkinson, Alan F, *Friends in High Places: Ulster's Resistance to Irish Home Rule, 1912-14* (2012).
87 Hume, David, *"For Ulster and Her Freedom": The story of the April 1914 gun-running* (1989).
88 Hume, David, *"For Ulster and Her Freedom": The story of the April 1914 gun-running* (1989).The Ulster Volunteer Force Gun-running at Larne, April 1914. By JWT Watters http://www.orangenet.org/gunrun.htm (Accessed 30 November 2011).
89 Hume, David, *"For Ulster and Her Freedom": The story of the April 1914 gun-running* (1989).
90 Hume, David, *"For Ulster and Her Freedom": The story of the April 1914 gun-running* (1989). The Ulster Volunteer Force Gun-running at Larne, April 1914. By JWT Watters http://www.orangenet.org/gunrun.htm (Accessed 30 November 2011).
91 Hume, David, *"For Ulster and Her Freedom": The story of the April 1914 gun-running* (1989).
92 Hume, David, *"For Ulster and Her Freedom": The story of the April 1914 gun-running* (1989).

THE ILLUSTRATED LONDON NEWS

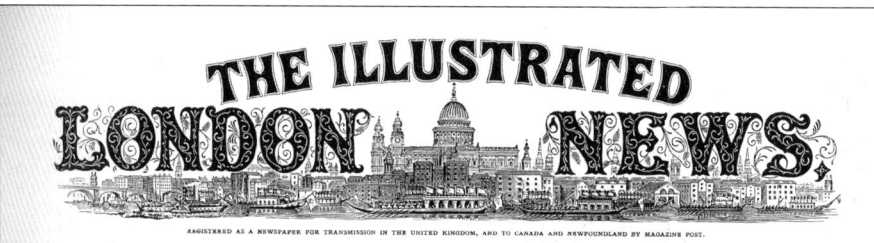

No. 3915.—VOL. CXLIV.   SATURDAY, MAY 2, 1914.   With Literary Supplement, SIXPENCE.

THE GUN-RUNNING BY THE ULSTER VOLUNTEER FORCE: LOADING ARMS INTO A MOTOR TOURIST-CAR AT DONAGHADEE.

During the night of Friday, April 24, and the early hours of the Saturday morning, the Ulster Volunteer Force landed some 35,000 rifles and 1,000,000 rounds of ammunition from a steamer disguised as the "Mountjoy," said to have been the "Fanny." The weapons were taken ashore at Larne, Bangor, and Donaghadee, and from thence distributed in various parts of Ulster. Referring to the matter in the House, Mr. Asquith said: "In view of this grave and unprecedented outrage, the House may be assured that his Majesty's Government will take without delay appropriate steps to vindicate the authority of the law and to protect officers and servants of the King and his Majesty's subjects in the exercise of their duties and in the enjoyment of their legal rights." It may be noted that the motor-car used at the moment illustrated is run between Donaghadee and Bangor in the summer time for the benefit of tourists. Donaghadee is five miles east-south-east of Bangor, and is the terminus of a branch from the Belfast and County Down Railway. Bangor is on the south shore of Belfast Lough. Larne is on Lough Larne, a few miles north of Belfast Lough.

DRAWN BY FRÉDÉRIC DE HAENEN FROM A SKETCH SUPPLIED BY COURTESY OF THE "BELFAST NEWS LETTER."

This is how the *London Illustrated News* reported the UVF gunrunning on Saturday, 2 May 1914 and in particular the landing of the weapons in Donaghadee. (Somme Museum)

A postcard depicting the landing of the UVF guns and ammunition in Bangor, April 1914.
(Somme Museum)

A sketch from the *Illustrated London News* based on a sketch by a Belfast artist showing how the rifles and ammunition were conveyed from the ship to the interior of Ulster. The view from the end of the Main Street depicts the cars with bales of the arms are leaving Bangor Harbour.
(Somme Museum)

arrival of the *Clyde Valley*, Samuel Kelly had been requested to have 30 tons of coal on the quay in order that it could be refuelled.[93]

As she was running behind schedule, dawn was breaking as the *Clyde Valley* appeared at Bangor at 4:25 a.m. One hour and thirteen minutes later, 40 tons of rifles had been unloaded and were being transported out along the County Down roads.[94]

As the town started to stir at 7:30 a.m. the last of the clandestine cargo was being driven away from the harbour, mirroring the successful unloading at Belfast and Larne.

On leaving Bangor she set a course for the river Clyde in Scotland, discarding the canvas name and once again becoming the familiar coal ship. Crawford refused to leave the ship in either Larne or Bangor, preferring to stay aboard until he was sure the crew were safe from arrest by the naval authorities. Just as Agnew was casting off from Bangor they received a message from UVF headquarters that a 30-knot cruiser was out looking for the *Fanny*.[95] As luck would have it, fog again came to their rescue and came down as she changed course, heading south and landing Crawford at Rosslare. Agnew then proceeded along the French and Danish coasts to the Baltic and the rendezvous with the *Fanny* to bring back the Ulstermen of her crew, after which the 'mystery ship' was disposed of in Hamburg.[96, 97]

At around 6:00 a.m. the *Innismurray* and her replacement crew arrived in Donaghadee to be met by James Craig and the men from Comber and Newtownards areas, who formed the 2nd Battalion, North Down Volunteers. Although the unloading was carried out in broad daylight, the local coastguards, police and customs did not interfere.

Postcard from the Historic Event series depicting the unloading of the UVF Guns at Donaghadee. (Somme Museum)

---

93 Hume, David, *"For Ulster and Her Freedom": The story of the April 1914 gun-running* (1989).
94 Hume, David, *"For Ulster and Her Freedom": The story of the April 1914 gun-running* (1989).
95 McNeill, Ronald, *Ulster's Stand for Union* (1922).
96 Kilmarnock Somme Association.
97 McNeill, Ronald, *Ulster's Stand for Union* (1922).

Robert Smith, a Customs and Excise officer stationed at Donaghadee, later reported that on 24 April he was sent to the harbour where he was informed by the local RIC District Inspector that a landing of weapons was expected. Arriving at the quay they found six motors already there with more arriving. Smith reported that when the vessel arrived he saw packages unloaded, about four foot six inches long, and he "counted as many as 60 packages on a lorry." When he attempted to approach the vessel as it was being unloaded he reported that he was surrounded by volunteers and "was told to move further along the quay." By 9:00 a.m. everything was unloaded.[98]

RIC District Inspector Shankey, along with Sergeant Orr, reported that they were watching the developments from the cover of the shadow of some coal wagons, when Lord Dunleath arrived with several hundred Volunteers around 2:00 a.m., and directed his men to search the pier and discovered them, holding them captive until all the weapons were unloaded. Shankey estimated that 500 vehicles were present.[99, 100]

However it was considered too risky to move the weapons in daylight so they were hidden in various sites in the locale and moved under cover of darkness the next night to their final destinations.[101]

The commander of one of the destroyers sent by Churchill to deny the Volunteers weapons later said that he "turned a blind eye."[102] The cost of the naval action against the gun-running was estimated at approximately £3,500 a day.[103]

At his London home, on 25 April Sir Edward Carson received a telegram which contained one word, "Lion." It was the code word of the gun-running operation which signalled that the operation had been successfully completed.[104]

During the operation 'Gough' was used as a password in honour of the stance taken by Hubert Gough during the earlier Curragh incident.[105]

The 500 motor vehicles the UVF were able to assemble at Larne on the night the *Clyde Valley* landed her cargo compared very favourably with the 827 motor-cars and 15 motorcycles which the British Expeditionary Force possessed at the outbreak of the Great War later in the year.[106]

Whilst the motor cars provided much needed transport, more traditional methods were still employed with the Magheramorne men bringing their guns back in horse-drawn carts, the local women coming out to make sure they had arrived home safely before the weapons were hidden under the floorboards of the nearby Presbyterian Church.[107]

Monica Massy-Beresford, of St Huberts, County Fermanagh, helped her father drive to Larne to collect weapons from the *Clyde Valley*. On occasions she hid guns in her skirts when the car she was travelling in was encountered by the police.[108]

The caches of weapons were soon located all over Ulster, some in distribution points whilst others were taken directly to Volunteer units with the necessary precautions and steps taken to ensure the authorities could not recover them. Stranocum village was guarded by Volunteers with orders to prevent the police from entering, however no RIC appeared and by 4:30 a.m. the tired

---

98 *Newtownards Chronicle & Co Down Observer* – 1 May 2014.
99 *Newtownards Chronicle & Co Down Observer* – 1 May 2014.
100 Grob-Fitzgibbon, *Turning Points of The Irish Revolution: The British Government, Intelligence and the Cost of Indifference, 1912-1921* (2007).
101 Hume, David, *"For Ulster and Her Freedom": The story of the April 1914 gun-running* (1989).
102 Beatty, Jack, *The Lost History of 1914: How the Great War was not inevitable* (2012).
103 Parkinson, Alan F, *Friends in High Places: Ulster's Resistance to Irish Home Rule, 1912-14* (2012).
104 Hume, David, *"For Ulster and Her Freedom": The story of the April 1914 gun-running* (1989).
105 Parkinson, Alan F, *Friends in High Places: Ulster's Resistance to Irish Home Rule, 1912-14* (2012).
106 Orr, Philip, *The Road to the Somme* (1987).
107 Hume, David, *"For Ulster and Her Freedom": The story of the April 1914 gun-running* (1989).
108 Orr, Philip, *The Road to the Somme* (1987).

A sketch from the *Illustrated London News* by a Belfast artist of the gun-runners on the road with the motors employed in the carrying of the arms and ammunition for the Ulster Volunteer Force. In the scene they are passing a UVF 'Picket' and are being escorted by a motor-cyclist of the Despatch Riding Corps. (Somme Museum)

men were ordered home. Stewart-Moore arrived at Stranocum House to find his uncle, revolver in hand, organising the loading of a car with wrapped bundles of rifles. The weapons had been delivered at 7:00 a.m., but word was received of a RIC fishing trip on the nearby river, with five policemen and one fishing rod, resulting in the need to quickly distribute the weapons to other locations. Stewart-Moore himself took a bundle of rifles and hid them on the floor of his cart, stopping briefly at a neighbour's house for afternoon tea before he returned home and, after nightfall, with the help of his sister hid them in an unused loft above the scullery.[109]

In Crossgar rifles were hidden under floorboards in houses around the village whilst in Lisburn they were stored in various buildings around the town.

The Lenox-Conynghams in Springhill, County Londonderry, were key players in supplying the weapons to the local Volunteers. In the days before Operation Lion Sir Edward Carson had visited the family for a dinner party, and whilst in public Carson was always defiant in his views, in private he often expressed his concerns and doubts of the path on which he was engaged. Later at Springhill as Mina Lenox-Conyngham walked with Sir Edward Carson in the gardens, she recalled that Carson said "I see terrible times ahead – bitter fighting – rivers of blood!"[110]

The guns, approximately 35,000, were mainly German Mauser and Austrian Mannlicher rifles, the majority of which went to Belfast, Antrim and Down with some to Londonderry and Tyrone. There were also several thousand veteran Italian Vetterli rifles which went to Armagh, Fermanagh,

---

109 Orr, Philip, *The Road to the Somme* (1987).
110 ATQ Stewart, *Edward Carson* (Gill & Macmillan). pp83, 92.

A sketch from the *Illustrated London News* based on a sketch from the *Belfast Telegraph*. In the sketch the cars proceeding from the foreground are on their way to be loaded whilst the cars coming in from the other direction are returning loaded. In the foreground are an officer and men of the UVF cordon across the road leading to the quay. A guard of Volunteers is in front of the sheds whilst on the quay to the right are Volunteers ready to relieve those unloading the *Mountjoy*. (Somme Museum)

Monaghan and Londonderry. However the Italians weapons gained a certain notoriety as they were stamped with "annunciata" which was interpreted as meaning, 'blessed by the Pope'.[111]

A certain irony exists regarding the origin of some of the guns and the approximately 2,000,000 rounds of ammunition, given the country a number of these men would be facing in battle in the subsequent years.

To some in the future a number of the rifles would become know as Mountjoy Specials after the temporary renaming of the SS *Clyde Valley* to the *Mountjoy II* used to smuggle them.[112]

Whilst much was and has been made of the landing of these weapons in equipping the UVF it was only sufficient to equip approximately a third of the 100,000 strong force. The weapons were mostly single shot weapons and did not include any field artillery.[113] It was however a greater number than had been smuggled in before and the positive moral impact on the Ulster Volunteers and their supporters far outweighed the logistical benefits.

Some of the weapons would lie undisturbed until recovered for use during the Second World War by the Local Defence Volunteers and the Ulster Home Guard, such as those hidden under the floorboards of Seymour Hill House. When lifted to supply the LDV in Dunmurry, they revealed approximately 200 old UVF rifles including a number of Lee-Metfords and a few old Austrian rifles.[114, 115] It is also believed that some rifles are still lying hidden in small arms dumps in the Ulster countryside.[116]

---

111 Orr, Philip, *The Road to the Somme* (1987).
112 Metcalfe, Nick, *Blacker's Boys* (2012).
113 Parkinson, Alan F, *Friends in High Places: Ulster's Resistance to Irish Home Rule, 1912-14* (2012).
114 Interview with Robin Charley – 19th January 2005.
115 Orr, David, *Duty Without Glory* (2008).
116 Hume, David, *"For Ulster and Her Freedom": The story of the April 1914 gun-running* (1989).

It is reported that there were only three casualties associated with the night of the gun-running. One was a coastguard who suffered a fatal heart attack in Donaghadee; HE Painter, who had been cycling furiously to wake his commanding officer.[117] Carson would later open a fund for his widow, another was a driver whose car hit the rear of another near Carrickfergus, and the third one the crew of the SS *Clyde Valley*, who fell in the hold of the ship and was injured.[118]

The Royal Irish Constabulary compiled detailed reports of the night's activities, including who was involved and where the weapons were being stored. These were forwarded to the Crime Special Branch who forwarded them to the Chief Secretary. The Government within days had the details of the night including the intimidating behaviour towards the police and disregard for the Royal proclamation forbidding arms importations.[119]

The British press had a mixed response to the events with even the right-wing papers harbouring some concerns about the 'illegal' actions. *The Daily Express* had a reporter who travelled to Larne with a UVF Motor Transport unit and later published a cartoon showing both Asquith and Churchill as sleeping coastguards whilst the gunrunning vessel steamed away on the horizon.[120]

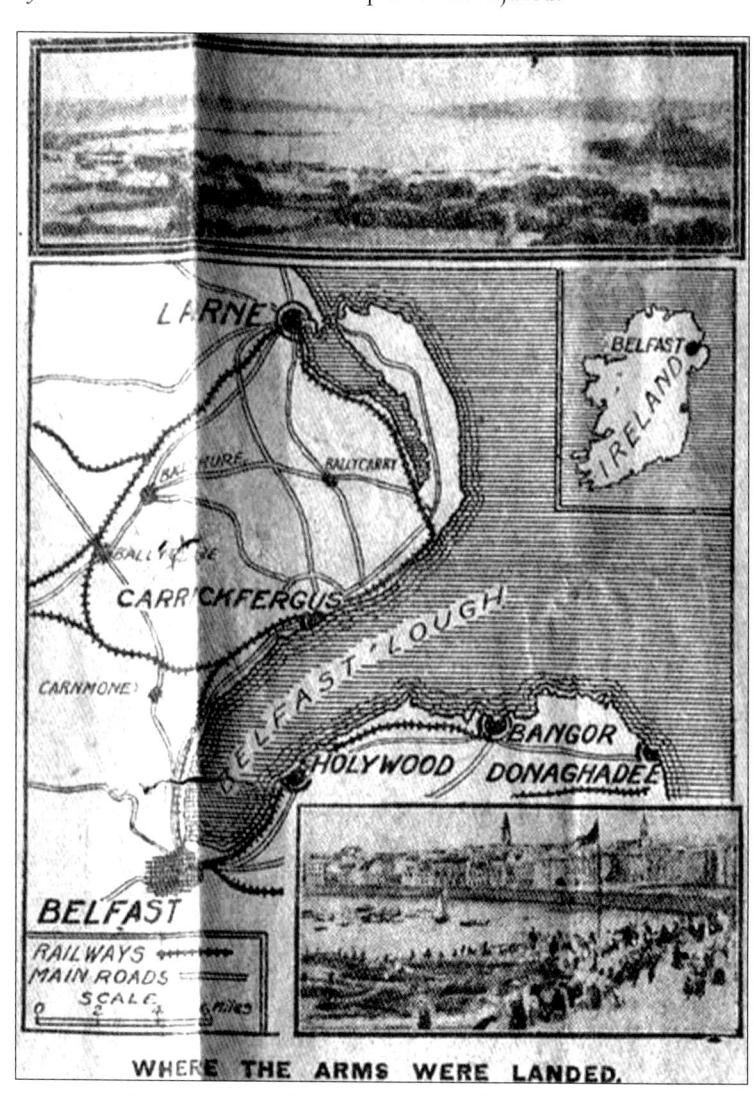

An image from the *Daily Express* newspaper illustrating to their readers where the UVF landed their weapons. (*Daily Express* 1914 & PRONI D1239/38)

---

117 Bowman, Timothy, *Carson's Army: Ulster Volunteer Force, 1910-22* (2007).
118 Hume, David, *"For Ulster and Her Freedom": The story of the April 1914 gun-running* (1989).
119 Grob-Fitzgibbon, *Turning Points of The Irish Revolution: The British Government, Intelligence and the Cost of Indifference, 1912-1921* (2007).
120 Parkinson, Alan F, *Friends in High Places: Ulster's Resistance to Irish Home Rule, 1912-14* (2012).

Training with the new weapons started almost immediately utilising any suitable space which could be found. One press photographer photographed a company of Ulster Volunteers drilling on a seafront on the Isle of Man.[121]

Other methods of obtaining arms were through the simple ingenuity of the individuals involved. Robert Adgey had started as a milkman's boy before starting to work for a pawnbroker and being 'educated' at night in a working man's institute. At the time of the Ulster crises he was a pawnbroker in Peter's Hill, Shankill, Belfast, and had gained a reputation within the UVF for clandestine gun-running.

Colonel TVP McCammon told Adgey he urgently wanted 100 Webley Service revolvers for the UVF despatch riders. That night Adgey withdrew £200 in sovereigns from the Ulster Bank and with a friend took the Liverpool boat from Belfast with two large suitcases. The next day at Webley and Scott, in Birmingham, they collected a consignment of revolvers, catching the night ferry back from Liverpool. When challenged by a railway porter at New Street station as to the weight of their bags they replied that they were brass plumbing fittings. Adgey's network of 'contacts' proved invaluable, with a friend on the ferry who locked them along with their suitcases in a single berth, another at the Belfast dockside who ensured they got through untroubled. Less than 48 hours from McCammon's request the guns were presented in the Old Town Hall building to the UVF.

---

121 Parkinson, Alan F, *Friends in High Places: Ulster's Resistance to Irish Home Rule, 1912-14* (2012).

8

Volunteers Prepare

During April 1914 the whole Donegal Regiment carried out a practice mobilisation. Following mobilisation orders issued at midday and despite the size of the county all company commanders received their orders within two hours, which were to be at their drill centres at eight that evening. Despite most people working a six-day week and training two evenings a week many of the companies had a full turn out by the time required; by the end of the exercise when they were dismissed the strength of the regiment was ninety-five percent.[1]

A short time after this Lord Leitrim acted as camp commandant of a large training camp hosted by the Duke of Abercorn at Baronscourt, the Donegal Regiment being joined by Derry City men for a total of 900 men. As well as the usual range of training activities a field hospital was organised and supervised by Dr Crosbie.[2]

At a subsequent camp of instruction for the Tyrone Regiment at Baronscourt between Saturday 30 May and Saturday 6 June the UVF GOC had the opportunity to witness the battalions working together in the field. As a result of the effective presence of the Bicycle Corps it was suggested that it might be extended in size as the opportunity arose.[3]

It was believed in some quarters that the Ulster Provisional Council was in possession of all the confidential instructions issued to the Royal Irish Constabulary, before they reached the police on the ground, which indicated a willingness of some within Dublin Castle to abuse their trust in the handling of confidential information.[4] The gun-running therefore either took the government by surprise or if it did not they issued no orders to the police to deal with it.

There are those who see the arming of the UVF as the beginning of the arming of the Irish people, leading to the Irish Volunteers, the Irish Republican Army, the conflict with England, the establishment of the Irish Free State and the start of the dissolution of the British Empire.[5]

Despite claims that the gun-running was a model of organisation and secrecy, with the police unaware of the untoward happenings in the respective areas, this is not completely true. For example in the Lisnaskea District of the RIC the local District Inspector had received word that the arms had been landed and were en route to the house of Mr J Porter-Porter of Belleisle in his District. Having sought direction and received none as to what action he should take from his authorities, the District Inspector set off for Belleisle with a few men to note what would occur. On arriving at the Demesne the District Inspector found Mr and Mrs Porter-Porter at the front gate. The District Inspector sat on the other side of the road and exchanged remarks with them from time to time until a number of cars appeared with bundles on the back seats. The police officer recognised a number of drivers and noticed that some of the number plates had been changed. He did not think it would have taken a large number of police to seize the weapons, however it

---

1 Canning, WJ, *Ballyshannon, Belcoo, Bertincourt* (1996).
2 Canning, WJ, *Ballyshannon, Belcoo, Bertincourt* (1996).
3 UVF Order 61, 1914 – Somme Museum.
4 Augusteijn, J, Ed, *The Memoirs of John M Regan* (2007).
5 Augusteijn, J, Ed, *The Memoirs of John M Regan* (2007).

Ulster Volunteers at Baronscourt. (Somme Museum)

would likely have been a different matter to prevent them being re-taken when the local Volunteers were fully mustered. As all was peaceful the police returned to their barracks and no orders were received from Headquarters pertaining to further action on the matter.[6]

Other local police officers were subject to ruses to remove them from the area of operations; one such ruse was an invite to a fishing expedition, but when the officer arrived at the house, the owner was unable to go, leaving the police officer to carry on fishing on his own. Such deception pushed personal friendships to the limit as it could have had a very negative effect on police careers.[7]

After the gun-running, news leaked out that a representative from Buckingham Place had been with the GOC UVF on the night of the operation. Whilst this was true he had been acting on his own authority and without the King's knowledge or permission.[8]

The reaction to the gun-running brought different responses from different quarters. The Union Defence League and others promoting the British Covenant were impressed.

The British Covenant which coincided with the Larne gun-running largely mirrored the Ulster Covenant in 1912. It was announced on 4 April 1914 at a massive rally in Hyde Park where hundreds of thousands assembled to hear Lord Milner, Long and Carson speak. Lord Milner who had returned to politics to support the Unionists asked Leo S Amery, a Liberal Unionist Member of Parliament (MP) for Birmingham South, to write a British Covenant. This said that the signatories would, if the Home Rule was passed, "feel justified in taking or supporting any action that may be effective to prevent it being put into operation, and more particularly to prevent the armed forces of the Crown being used to deprive the people of Ulster of their rights as citizens of the United Kingdom".[9] Those signing were pledging to "resist a government dominated by men disloyal to the Empire …to whom our faith and tradition are hateful."[10]

---

6   Augusteijn, J, Ed, *The Memoirs of John M Regan* (2007).
7   Augusteijn, J, Ed, *The Memoirs of John M Regan* (2007).
8   Crozier, Brig-Gen FP Crozier, CB, CMG, DSO, *Ireland for Ever* (1932).
9   Adams, R.J.Q., *Bonar Law* (1999).
10 Beatty, Jack, *The Lost History of 1914: How the Great War was not inevitable* (2012).

Ulster Volunteers on parade. (Somme Museum)

The signature campaign was largely organised through the Primrose League, an organisation founded in 1883 to spread Conservative principles in Great Britain, and also Walter Long's Union Defence League. By the middle of the summer, 2,000,000 signatures were obtained,[11] together with £12,000 and a pledge to house 5-6,000 women and children.[12] Signatures included Field-Marshal Lord Roberts, Admiral of the Fleet Sir Edward Seymour, Rudyard Kipling, Captain Wilfred Spender[13] and Sir William Ramsay FRS.[14] Key people in England such as Sir Edward Elgar also openly supported the Unionist cause and contributed thousands of pounds to the gun fund.[15]

The Daily Herald however condemned the campaign, "… the fact that Lords Selbourne and Curzon, to say nothing of Lord Milner, are all members of that treasonous and seditious conspiracy known as the 'British Covenant' in support of armed revolution in Ulster."[16]

During the first four days of the following week after the gun-running, the Westminster Government held four cabinet meetings to discuss what they described as the "criminal" and "treacherous" acts in Ulster.[17] Despite these threats from the government to prosecute those involved in the gun-running John Redmond advised the Prime Minister not to proceed with such an action, and at the same time urged the Government to withdraw the proclamation against importing arms.[18]

Lord Roberts, the Ulsterman who had fought during the Afghan War of 1878-1880 and had been in command during the Boer War, had been Carson's choice to lead the UVF but had declined on the grounds of old age. When he was told of the landing of the weapons in Ulster he is

---

11 Adams, R.J.Q., *Bonar Law*. John Murray (1999).
12 Diana Elaine Sheets, *British Conservatism and the Primrose League: the changing character of popular politics*, quoting from Minutes of the Grand Council of the Primrose League.
13 Ulster Volunteers, January 1913 – Ulster-Scots Community Network <http://www.ulster-scots.com/uploads/901740969819.PDF> (Accessed 5 August 2013).
14 McNeill, Ronald, *Ulster's Stand for Union* (1922).
15 Beatty, Jack, *The Lost History of 1914: How the Great War was not inevitable* (2012).
16 *New York Tribune*, June 07, 1914.
17 Parkinson, Alan F, *Friends in High Places: Ulster's Resistance to Irish Home Rule, 1912-14* (2012).
18 Gwynn, Stephen Lucius, *John Redmond's Last Years* (1919).

reputed to have said to Carson, "Magnificent! Magnificent! Nothing could have been better done; it was a piece of organisation that any army in Europe might be proud of."[19]

The success of the gun-running was seen by many as a sign of God's hand guiding the Ulster Protestants, endorsing the rightness of their cause.

However not all attempts at landing arms and ammunition for the Ulster Volunteer Force had been so successful. In December 1913 the Royal Irish Constabulary had seized 40,000 rounds of ammunition in Limerick. Following the declaration of war in August 1914 this ammunition was given to the army for military use. Early in 1914 nine tonnes of ammunition was also seized en route from Yorkshire to Belfast at Belfast docks, Customs and Special Branch officers having been tipped off by an informer. The ammunition had been sealed in cement trucks for its carriage across the Irish Sea, as "pure cement ballast".[20]

Having returned from another trip to Belfast, General Macready informed Asquith, on 19 May, of the fears of the Lord Mayor of Belfast "for the safety of his city". The Prime Minster informed Macready that "in case of serious faction fighting between Orangemen and Nationalists, troops should not intervene and run the risk of having to be extricated, but should isolate the area of the fighting until reinforcements arrived. If Carson proclaimed his provisional government the only course of action was to remain on the defensive and do nothing." This lack of action was also extended to the UVF moving units to smaller towns and villages. Thoroughly discouraged Macready returned to Belfast the same night noting sarcastically in his memoirs, with "these heroic instructions in my pocket."[21]

The Young Citizen Volunteers marched to the Balmoral Showground, on Saturday 6 June 1914, with their new comrades in the Ulster Volunteer Force to be reviewed by Sir Edward Carson. The crowd of 25,000 roared when the YCV marched past at 4:45 p.m.[22]

The YCV formed up on the right of the line, with the Special units of East, South and North Belfast lined up next to them, in that order.[23]

The *Belfast News Letter* reported;[24]

> This was the first occasion upon which the Young Citizen Volunteers had paraded before Sir Edward Carson since they became attached to the East Belfast regiment of the Ulster Volunteer Force, and their conduct on parade bore striking testimony to the efficient training they have received under the experienced direction of their commanding officer, who devotes a good deal of time and energy to the improvement of the corps, with a view to making them one of the most effective units of Ulster's army.

The Northern Whig, *Belfast Evening Telegraph* and the *Belfast News Letter*, three local Belfast newspapers, all gave their support to the move of the YCV to join the UVF. However the *Irish News*, the city's Nationalist newspaper, took a different perspective in its Monday morning editorial; reminding the YCV of their original claims to be 'non-political' and non-sectarian'.[25]

---

19 McNeill, Ronald, *Ulster's Stand for Union* (1922).
20 Gregory, Adrian and Paseta, Senia (ed), *Ireland and the Great War 'A War to Unite Us All'?* (2002).
21 Grob-Fitzgibbon, *Turning Points of The Irish Revolution: The British Government, Intelligence and the Cost of Indifference, 1912-1921* (2007).
22 *Belfast News Letter* – 8 June 1914.
23 Moore, Steven, *The Chocolate Soldiers: The story of the Young Citizen Volunteers and 14th Royal Irish Rifles during the Great War* (2016).
24 Moore, Steven, *The Chocolate Soldiers: The story of the Young Citizen Volunteers and 14th Royal Irish Rifles during the Great War* (2016).
25 *Irish News* – 8 June 1914.

A postcard depicting an armed battalion of the Young Citizen Volunteers marching up High Street, Belfast. (J Luke)

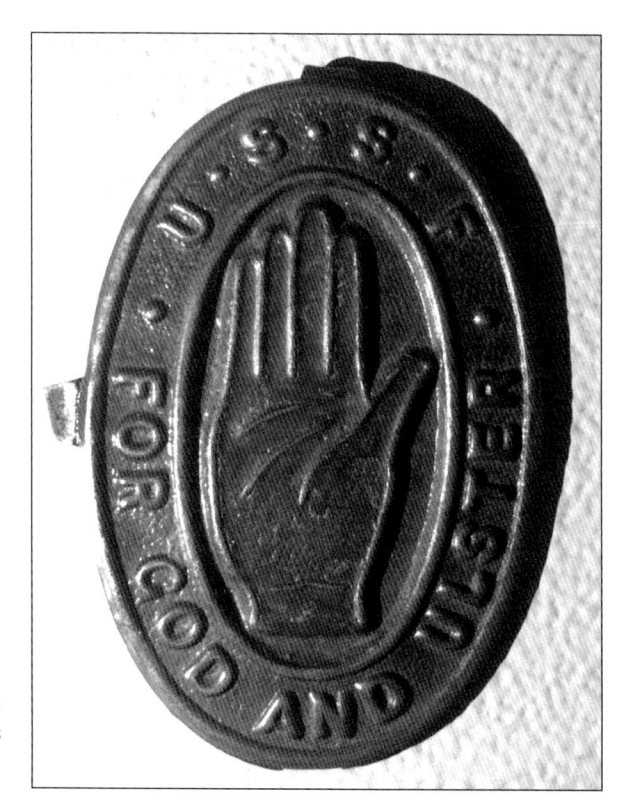

Cap badge for the USSF – Ulster Special Service Force. The hand in the centre has been painted red. (Somme Museum)

At the Whitsun camp (8 June) a number of men of the Special Service Section broke camp and retired to the local taverns in the town for a drink, whilst still in their uniforms. This occasionally resulted in the Royal Irish Constabulary having to lift those who were drunk, throw them in the police cells and send for Captain Crozier to come and fetch them.[26] Crozier had an uncompromising view of men caught in such a situation particularly whilst in uniform.

On the Enniskillen Horse drill fields at Castle Hume, near Enniskillen, the 3rd Battalion, Fermanagh Regiment, numbering over 1,000, 200 officers and other ranks, including 71 nurses with their full complement of transport, were inspected by Major General Sir George Richardson, accompanied by Colonel Hacket-Pain.[27]

The *Down Recorder* reported an incident in June 1914 when "files of motors conveying rifles (presumably UVF) through Castlewellan on Monday night were hooted at by a hostile Nationalist crowd. Later, around 11:00 p.m., a number of revolver shots were fired in the square."[28]

In June 1914, Augustine Birrell, the Chief Secretary for Ireland, believed that there would be widespread civil unrest if the discipline of the UVF was to break down, however the leaders across the organisation ensured that discipline was maintained and Birrell's fears never materialised.[29]

---

26 Crozier, Brig-Gen FP Crozier, CB, CMG, DSO, *Ireland for Ever* (1932).
27 Ballyshannon, Belcoo, Bertincourt – WJ Canning, 1996.
28 *Down Recorder* – 20 June 1914: Ireland and the First World War – edited D Fitzparick, 1988.
29 Ulster Volunteers, January 1913 – Ulster-Scots Community Network <http://www.ulster-scots.com/uploads/901740969819.PDF> (Accessed 5 August 2013).

9

National Volunteers begin to arm

With the continued organising of the UVF in the North articles started to appear in the Nationalist press such as *An Claidheamh Soluis*, a Gaelic League paper, and in Sinn Fein's newspaper acknowledging that Ulster was turning to physical force and setting the model for the rest of Ireland. Patrick Pearse said that he was "… glad that the Orangemen have armed for it was a goodly thing to see arms in Irish hands." He believed that guns would deliver Ireland.[1]

What the North had begun the South was inevitably to follow. The *Roscommon Herald* echoed what some Nationalists were starting to believe, "If Nationalist Ireland means to hold its own it must cease talking and dreaming; it must get down to real practical work, and that work is to get in the guns and get the men to use them."[2]

However, aware that the UVF had smuggled in as many as thirty times the number of weapons the National Volunteers were planning there was a belief that a shipment should be made in "a sufficiently spectacular manner" to encourage more financial donations, enabling more weapons to be bought. It was therefore decided to land the rifles in broad daylight.[3]

On 26 July 1914 the Irish Volunteers mirrored the actions of the UVF by landing their own arms and ammunition, 1,500 Mauser rifles and 45,000 rounds of ammunition[4] at Howth, though in broad daylight as opposed to the cover of darkness. The Dublin Regiment of the National Volunteers marched to Howth arriving at 1:00 p.m., the same time as a yacht owned by Erskine Childers loaded with arms and ammunition.[5] These supplies from Germany had been arranged by Sir Roger Casement, Bulmer Hobson and Erskine Childers. Casement was the Dublin-born son and a captain of the Light Dragoons from an Ulster Protestant father and a Catholic mother. Erskine Childers, author of *The Riddle of the Sands*, family were English squires and officers in the Royal Navy and Army, though his mother was Irish.[6] With the yacht's cargo safely unloaded within half an hour and loaded into motor cars, except 2,000 rounds held back by the guards,[7] the National Volunteers started to march back at 2:00 p.m.[8] Members of the Dublin Metropolitan Police along the route notified their superiors.[9] The Assistant Commissioner of the Dublin Metropolitan Police, Mr David Harrell, having insufficient police at his disposal, called on the

---

1 Beatty, Jack, *The Lost History of 1914: How the Great War was not inevitable* (2012).
2 Beatty, Jack, *The Lost History of 1914: How the Great War was not inevitable* (2012).
3 Grob-Fitzgibbon, *Turning Points of The Irish Revolution: The British Government, Intelligence and the Cost of Indifference, 1912-1921* (2007).
4 Downing, Taylor. (ed), *The Troubles* (1990).
5 Shearman, Hugh, *Not an Inch: A Study of Northern Ireland and Lord Craigavon* (1942).
6 Ryan, AP, *Mutiny at the Curragh* (1956).
7 Grob-Fitzgibbon, *Turning Points of The Irish Revolution: The British Government, Intelligence and the Cost of Indifference, 1912-1921* (2007).
8 Shearman, Hugh, *Not an Inch: A Study of Northern Ireland and Lord Craigavon* (1942).
9 Grob-Fitzgibbon, *Turning Points of The Irish Revolution: The British Government, Intelligence and the Cost of Indifference, 1912-1921* (2007).

Irish Volunteers landing weapons and ammunition at Howth. (Somme Museum)

local military commander for assistance[10, 11] through setting up a series of cordons to intercept the arms. Near Clontarf the two forces met a company of British soldiers who blocked the road two deep armed with rifles and bayonets. Eighty policemen from the Dublin Metropolitan Police stood along each side of the road at right angles to the lines.[12] Following a short parley between the two sides Harrell informed Hobson that the Volunteers were "an illegal body, illegally importing arms". He ordered his officers to seize the weapons leading to a short scuffle during which the Irish Volunteers scattered with most of their rifles and successfully evaded the official forces.[13] Harrell realised he had failed to prevent the arms reaching Dublin; the police only seized 19 rifles. He dismissed the soldiers, telling them they were no longer needed and called his own men away.[14] Tired and frustrated from standing around all day in the heat the King's Own Scottish Borderers marched back to their barracks followed by a hostile crowd. Some of the crowd started to throw stones at the soldiers. On the Quays at Bachelor's Walk the company commander ordered his men to disperse the crowd and in the ensuing commotion a number of soldiers shot into the crowd killing four civilians and wounding 38.[15, 16] The British Government was embarrassed and infu-

10 Harris, HED, *The Irish Regiments in the First World War* (1968).
11 Ryan, AP, *Mutiny at the Curragh* (1956).
12 Grob-Fitzgibbon, *Turning Points of The Irish Revolution: The British Government, Intelligence and the Cost of Indifference, 1912-1921* (2007).
13 Shearman, Hugh, *Not an Inch: A Study of Northern Ireland and Lord Craigavon* (1942).
14 Grob-Fitzgibbon, *Turning Points of The Irish Revolution: The British Government, Intelligence and the Cost of Indifference, 1912-1921* (2007).
15 Beatty, Jack, *The Lost History of 1914: How the Great War was not inevitable* (2012).
16 Harris, HED, *The Irish Regiments in the First World War* (1968).

riated and the Cabinet immediately appointed a Commission to look into the shootings.¹⁷ The activities of the soldiers were condemned by the Royal Commission which investigated it, but by the time it was published many of the young men involved in both sides were fighting alongside each other on the western front.¹⁸ Known as the "Bachelors' Walk Massacre" this inflamed many of the local population and led to a surge of popular public support for the Irish Volunteers. Assistant Commissioner Harrell was declared the guilty party for calling out the military which was deemed to have been wrong, however this act of making him the scapegoat had a very negative impact on the morale and initiative of the constabulary at the time.¹⁹ General Macready later recorded in his memoirs that it would be hard in history to find a "more disgraceful exhibition of weakness on the part of a Government", the result of which was that the "already shaken morale of the Irish Police, became "broken for all time." He also believed that Harrell's dismissal had significant long term consequences; "Years afterwards I saw evidence of this, the Harrell case being pointed to as the reward of an official who endeavoured to carry out an obvious duty."²⁰

The landing of guns by the Irish Volunteers at Howth. (PRONI T2125/3/27)

Birrell's private secretary, Andrew Magill also noted:²¹

> I could never understand why a circular sent to every junior district inspector of constabulary throughout Ireland, instructing him in the event of anyone attempting to land arms, to do exactly as Mr Harrel [sic] did – viz., to call out the military and stop the landing by force if necessary – was not referred to in the report of the Commission, as I believe the Commissioners had a copy before them ... In my opinion the dismissal of Mr Harrel [sic] was a crucial factor in disheartening the police throughout the whole of Ireland. They saw that if they did their duty they would not be supported and being human beings and not being angels, they took the safest course from that date, and refused to do anything without an order from their superior officers.

---

17 Grob-Fitzgibbon, *Turning Points of The Irish Revolution: The British Government, Intelligence and the Cost of Indifference, 1912-1921* (2007).
18 Harris, HED, *The Irish Regiments in the First World War* (1968).
19 Shearman, Hugh, *Not an Inch: A Study of Northern Ireland and Lord Craigavon* (1942).
20 Grob-Fitzgibbon, *Turning Points of The Irish Revolution: The British Government, Intelligence and the Cost of Indifference, 1912-1921* (2007).
21 Grob-Fitzgibbon, *Turning Points of The Irish Revolution: The British Government, Intelligence and the Cost of Indifference, 1912-1921* (2007).

NATIONAL VOLUNTEERS BEGIN TO ARM

On the same day the weapons were landed at Howth, Asquith informed The House of Commons of the Austrian ultimatum to Serbia.[22] Meanwhile in Ulster two six-pounder field guns were witnessed being taken into the main yard of Craigavon House and being placed beside a large existing quantity of arms and ammunition. In Londonderry, Sir Henry Hill spent the day commanding a contingent of UVF in building a barricade around his house from 1,000 sandbags while watched by the police.[23]

In the wake of the Bachelors' Walk shooting, John Redmond left the House of Commons in no doubt of the depth of feeling in the majority of Ireland, "Let the house clearly understand that four-fifths of the Irish people will not submit any longer to be bullied, or punished, or shot, for conduct which is permitted to go scot-free in the open light of day in every county in Ulster by other sections of their fellow countrymen."[24]

In Sligo a gathering of 300 Irish Volunteers heard a speaker who after referring to the shooting by the army said, "… if a shot is fired at our people in the North we are prepared to meet them …I say here publically, in the presence of the press, that Ireland is out for blood and murder."[25] In order to prevent bloodshed and secure public support John Redmond reluctantly demanded and with difficulty obtained Irish Party control over the Irish Volunteers though the real leadership lay with the secret directorate of the Republican Brotherhood, which included James Connolly, Arthur Griffith, James Clarke and Patrick Pearse, which with the outbreak of war revived an old adage, "England's difficulty, Ireland's opportunity."

The Irish Volunteers used the cover of darkness to land the remainder of the weapons from Germany, approximately 600 Mauser rifles and 20,000 rounds of ammunition on 2 August at Kilcoole, County Wicklow.[26, 27]

Ironically, following the outbreak of war the King's Own Scottish Borders were given a "rousing send-off" by Dubliners as they marched to the docks to embark for France.[28]

Within the Irish Volunteers recruitment was brisk, exceeding 180,000 and all committed to defending Home Rule from the menace of the UVF. The combined effect of the Curragh incident and the landing of the arms for the Ulster Volunteer Force at Larne provided the Irish Volunteers with a great recruiting boost.

Kevin O'Shiel a student in Dublin at the time, described the prevailing mood:

> It seemed then to us young nationalists, as our pristine childlike faith in Liberal promises began to weaken and dissolve, that, after all, it was but the old, old game all over again … the effect of the Curragh mutiny on Irish nationalism was terrific … but it was mild compared with that of the Larne gun-running; and particularly so, on young nationalists. It created in us a deep mental and psychological reaction, and violently shook our faith in constitutionalism.[29]

---

22   Denman, Terence, *Ireland's Unknown Soldiers: The 16th (Irish) Division in the Great War* (1992).
23   Grob-Fitzgibbon, *Turning Points of The Irish Revolution: The British Government, Intelligence and the Cost of Indifference, 1912-1921* (2007).
24   Denman, Terence, *Ireland's Unknown Soldiers: The 16th (Irish). Division in the Great War* (1992).
25   Beatty, Jack, *The Lost History of 1914: How the Great War was not inevitable* (2012).
26   26—27 July 2014: Heritage weekend to mark centenary of Kilcoole gun-running, Kilcoole, Co. Wicklow <http://www.decadeofcentenaries.com/26-27-july-heritage-weekend-to-mark-centenary-of-kilcoole-gun-running-kilcoole-co-wicklow/> (Accessed 7 January 2015).
27   Equally audacious: the Kilcoole gun-running <http://www.irishtimes.com/culture/heritage/equally-audacious-the-kilcoole-gun-running-1.1869586> (Accessed 7 January 2015).
28   Horne, John (ed)., *Our War: Ireland and the Great War* (2008).
29   McGarry, Ferghal, *The Rising – Ireland: Easter 1916* (2010).

The home of Captain James Craig, Craigavon House, Belfast. (Somme Museum)

It was believed their numbers on 15 June was in region of 80,000 but was increasing at the rate of 15,000 a week, so that by 9 July, based on police information they had reached 132,000 of whom nearly 40,000 were Army reservists.[30] The Irish Volunteers were renamed the National Volunteers in May 1914.

Despite obvious claims of collusion between the Ulster Volunteers and the authorities over the Larne gun-running, in contrast to the reaction to the Irish Volunteers who were intercepted by the police and army, the manner adopted by the two respective organisations gives the lie to collusion claims. The Ulster Volunteers' plans were organised as a secret operation whereas Bulmer Hobson of the Irish Volunteers sought to create a propaganda coup.[31] The Ulster Volunteers split their weapons into three different caches, used a decoy vessel to distract the authorities, and landed their arms under the cover of darkness whilst the Irish Volunteers landed theirs in the middle of the day, under a "blaze of publicity" and as close to the capital, Dublin, as possible.

The next day following the landing of weapons in Howth by the Irish National Volunteers General Hacket Pain wrote a confidential letter to all UVF Divisional, Regimental, Battalion and Headquarters Corps Commanders, advising them that following discussions with Sir Edward Carson the time had come, at each of their own discretions, that the members of the Ulster Volunteer Force could carry their arms openly, whether they possessed a gun licence or not. They were advised that any attempts by individuals or the police to seize the weapons were to be resisted in accordance with previous directions contained in Circular Memorandum dated 14 May 1914. The ammunition was to remain stored by responsible individuals and only issued to the men in cases of emergency or for practice purposes. The guns would only be given to men who could be trusted to look after them, including cleaning. As there was still a few instances of weapon shortages consideration was to be given where considered necessary to establishing armouries where arms could be deposited and shared. However he warned of the risk of Nationalists or government authorities raiding those armouries to seize the weapons. To that end they were only to be established in localities which were favourable for their protection. He signed off by reminding all the commanders that this was not a mandatory order, but instead was designed to allow them latitude to make the necessary decisions at a local level.[32]

---

30   Gwynn, Stephen Lucius, *John Redmond's Last Years* (1919).
31   Jackson, Alvin, *Home Rule – An Irish History 1800-2000* (2003).
32   Letter from General Hacket Pain on the carrying of arms openly – 27 June 1914.

An anti-Home Rule postcard. (J Luke)

However the day before the landing of weapons at Howth, General Adair had sent orders to his commanders of North and South Antrim Regiments for defence schemes to prevent the passage eastward of small numbers of opponents across the following bridges over the River Bann; the railway bridge, five miles above Coleraine, and the road bridges over Agivey, Kilrea, Portgelnone and Toome. This involved securing all boats which could be used and liaising as necessary with the UVF Commander for County Derry.[33]

In August 1914 at a meeting in Ballymena of the County Antrim Executive of the Irish National Volunteers representing 5,000 National Volunteers, the following statement was recorded, "That we protest in the strongest possible manner against the brutal conduct of the military in shooting down defenceless women and children in the streets of Dublin on Sunday last, and demand that the perpetrators of this outrage be dealt with as ordinary criminals." At the same meeting they also recorded their confidence in the Irish Parliamentary Party under the leadership of Mr John Redmond.[34]

The threat of conflict had now moved from the UVF against the army to the Ulster Volunteer Force against the Irish Volunteers. Whether Home Rule was or was not introduced there appeared to be a real risk of conflict. This was summed up by one Nationalist MP who stated, "It was now abundantly clear that if passing Home Rule meant civil war, so also would abandonment of Home Rule."[35]

A memorandum circular under Lieutenant-Colonel TVP McCammon's name as Chief Staff officer was issued by UVF Headquarters which reflected this increasing tension, albeit issued

---

33 Scheme Defence of River Bann – General Adair, 25 July 1914.
34 Unknown newspaper clipping, 8 August 1914.
35 Gwynn, Stephen Lucius, *John Redmond's Last Years* (1919).

some months previously. Acknowledging the possibility of the passing of the Home Rule Bill and what was referred to as "Nationalist rowdyism" all divisional commanders or the regimental commanders in their absence were authorised to take whatever steps they deemed necessary "to maintain the peace and to prevent disloyal processions, burnings, bonfires, or other provocative actions or displays taking place in Unionist territory throughout their command." This order was later cancelled 5 June 1914.[36]

Further correspondence within the UVF reflected other uncertainties over the quickly developing situation. The County Antrim divisional commander sought clarity from Colonel Hacket Pain on a number of issues. He asked if the General Officer Commanding wished the UVF to occupy vacated Coastguard stations and if UVF signallers should watch the coast at such places as Portrush and Ballycastle. The response from headquarters was a short and direct "no." He also asked what action was now to be taken by the UVF with regards to the Nationalists and their volunteers. The response was that the approach to be taken was one of tolerance. Finally he asked if he should proceed with the present arrangements for disarming the Nationalists on the first occasion of their giving the UVF any trouble. The response from Headquarters was very specific, "if it was absolutely necessary in case of violence, threatenings, or outrages" then they should be disarmed. In the light of this response Adair advised the Commander of 1st North Antrim Regiment that whilst uncertainty existed as to what was to be done about the Home Rule Bill it would be better to advise the men to withdraw from the National Rifle Association if Nationalists joined the same club.[37]

On 23 May 1914, UVF Headquarters issued five separate written orders, one of which informed all concerned that magazines issued by Headquarters were only to be used as single loaders[38] whilst Order number 54 provided a methodology to mobilise only a certain number of men as opposed to the entire Battalion in an area. It was designated as 'Assembly for Particular Service' and required that where it was necessary to assemble men for 'Particular Service' in any part of Ulster then the instructions would be issued on a canary yellow coloured card in the same coloured envelope and sent by Despatch Rider direct from UVF Headquarters to the commanders concerned.[39] One of the orders though, was simply to inform members of the availability of the UVF Headquarters staff between the hours of 11:00 a.m. and 1:00 p.m.[40, 41]

Ulster Volunteers guarding the armoury at Craigavon House. (Somme Museum)

---

36 UVF Circular Memorandum, 18 May 1914 – Somme Museum.
37 Correspondence between Adair and Hackett Pain – 9 August 1914.
38 UVF Order 51, 1914 – Somme Museum.
39 UVF Order 54, 1914 – Somme Museum.
40 Bowman, Timothy, *Carson's Army: Ulster Volunteer Force, 1910-22* (2007).
41 UVF Order 55, 1914 – Somme Museum.

A circular of memorandum on the same day directed that when selecting the number of Volunteers to be assembled for particular duties which may extend into the following day, and therefore prevent them from attending their normal employment in mills or factories where large numbers of women worked, then they should have been "warned" for those duties. The rationale was that if the men were unavailable for work then a large number of women may be temporarily stopped from working and as a result may then congregate on the streets; it was felt that in certain conditions this might lead to disturbances. It was stressed that every possible step should be taken to ensure that women were able to work as usual.[42]

Whilst such orders and directives from headquarters were issued to commanders, many had to be translated into something which could be disseminated amongst the officers and volunteers at battalion level. These in turn also often contained issues specific to local command. George Young, Officer Commanding 1st Battalion, North Antrim Regiment, issued his own orders on 3 June 1914. These included the instruction on the use of rifles as single loaders with additional information on the need to ensure volunteers were fully instructed in their use and the need to ensure that there was no risk of the weapons being seized or their hiding places discovered by the police.[43]

General Sir WT Adair, the County Antrim Commander, had sought the advice of the County Inspector, Royal Irish Constabulary, with regards the increasing tensions. He was advised by County Inspector Morrison, Lisburn, that "the best assistance which party leaders can this moment render is to restrain their followers and advise all who look to them for guidance to avoid giving or taking offence." He went on to say that "the assembling of bodies of men in localities where the peace seems likely to be disturbed is not calculated to be a preventative" and that in accordance with their public duty the police were making the best arrangements they could to preserve the peace."[44]

On 25 May 1914 the Home Rule Bill was passed[45] for the last time without incident through the Westminster House of Commons before moving up to the House of Lords.

Whilst the UVF had been warned to hold themselves in readiness for any emergency, it was acknowledged by the UVF GOC that the Force had displayed discipline, common sense and discretion, and he thanked the officers and men for carrying out his orders. He particularly highlighted how Derry was a location, "requiring special tact and discretion" and sent his appreciation to all those concerned in Derry City for their splendid discipline.[46]

Whilst a last resort, the partition of Ireland was a serious consideration though ironically neither Carson nor Redmond wanted that option.

However with both sides prepared to resist with force and the likelihood that the British Army was unlikely to take action against the Ulster Volunteer Force there was no alternative but to try and find a compromise solution.

Asquith wanted to find some form of agreement between the Irish parties and prevent the impending threat of conflict. In an effort to assist the King called a conference at Buckingham Palace for those concerned.

Meanwhile UVF plans were afoot to evacuate 'refugees' to England and Scotland.[47] In June 1914 General WT Adair confirmed to his officers that Mr WHM Lyons, Strandtown, Belfast, had agreed to act as agent for the sending of any women or children from County Antrim who had

---

42 UVF Circular Memorandum 23 May 1914 – Somme Museum.
43 Orders – 1st Battalion, North Antrim Regiment – 3 June 1914 – Somme Museum.
44 Letter from County Inspector Morrison, 23 May 1914 – Somme Museum.
45 Metcalfe, Nick, *Blacker's Boys* (2012).
46 UVF Order 57, 1914 – Somme Museum.
47 Stewart, ATQ, *The Ulster Crises* (1967).

Edward Carson attending a Ulster Volunteer drumhead service on the slopes of the Cavehill, Belfast.
(Somme Museum)

to be evacuated to Great Britain in the event of hostilities. In the same communication he asked all his battalion commanders to forward a statement of the total amount of funds held for their battalion, in order that the Secretary of the Carson Fund could be updated, and also an estimation as to how long the funds could support their battalions in the event of mobilisation without support from headquarters.[48]

Hacket Pain sent a memorandum dated 10 July 1914, the same day as the Ulster Unionist Council met for the first time as the provisional government under Carson,[49] to divisional, regimental and battalion Commanders asking them to co-operate with the committee responsible for the evacuation of refugees from Ulster. The plan identified the following categories to be dealt with first:[50]

a) Wives and families of the U[lster] V[olunteer] Fighting Force, whose protection would set free the men to fight where required.
b) Women and children in exposed and outlying districts where they cannot be easily safeguarded.

Officers were to obtain information through company commanders as follows:

Category A – men employed to Marching Battalions and men who would most likely move from their homes for particular service. Those who did not have a system for the protection of their families, such as moving to and staying with relatives in a place of safety then names would be taken for the possible evacuation of their dependants to England or Scotland.

---

48 Letter from Gen WT Adair – 13 June 1914 – Somme Museum.
49 Lewis, Geoffrey, *Carson: The man who divided Ireland* (2006).
50 Memorandum – Refugees – 10 July 1914.

Category B – Company Commanders were to supply names of unprotected women and children in the area of their command.

It was also suggested that it may be necessary to evacuate a proportion of the total number of refugees before actual hostilities would break out, again names should be gathered where a Volunteer was willing to send his family away in advance.

The venue for the King's conference was Buckingham Palace from 21-24 July 1914, held in a large room on the ground floor overlooking the garden and easily accessible from the King's private apartments.[51]

Membership comprised, Asquith, Lloyd George, Redmond and his deputy John Dillon, and Bonar Law, Lord Lansdowne, Carson and his deputy James Craig.

The King greeted them with:

> Gentlemen, it is with feelings of satisfaction and hopefulness that I receive you here today and I thank you for the manner in which you have responded to my summons. My intervention at this moment may be regarded as a new departure but the exceptional circumstances under which you are brought together justify my actions. For months we have watched with deep misgivings the course of events in Ireland. The trend has been surely and steadily towards an appeal for force and today the cry of civil war is on the lips of the most responsible and sober minded of my people. We have, in the past, endeavoured to act as a civilised example to the world, and to me it is unthinkable, as it must be to you, that we should be brought to he brink of fratricidal strife upon issues apparently so capable of adjustment as these you are now asked to consider, if handled in a spirit of generous compromise. My apprehension in contemplating such a dire calamity is intensified by my feelings of attachment to Ireland and of sympathy with her people, who have always welcomed me with warm-hearted affection. Gentlemen, you represent in one form or another the vast majority of my subjects at home. You also have a deep interest in my Dominions overseas who are scarcely less concerned in a prompt and friendly settlement of this question. I regard you then in this matter as trustees for the honour and peace of all. Your responsibilities are indeed great. The time is short … I pray that God, in His infinite wisdom, may guide your deliberations.

The King then left the room and the Speaker took the chair.[52]

Redmond reportedly told associates after the first day, "as an Irishman you could not help being proud to see how (Sir Edward Carson) towered above the others."[53]

Carson proposed that the whole of Ulster be excluded from Home rule. Bonar Law recorded that it was Carson's opinion that if this was done "generously" then it would be likely that Ulster would later come willingly into a united Ireland, "whereas if any attempt to coerce any part of Ulster were made, a united Ireland within the lifetime of any one now living would be out of the question." This proposal again showed Carson's strong desire to retain a united Ireland. With a Catholic minority in the whole of Ulster yet a majority in some counties it was not an unreasonable assumption but it was too far-sighted; Redmond and Dillon whilst in favour of it privately could not support it publically.[54]

---

51 Ryan, AP, *Mutiny at the Curragh* (1956).
52 Ryan, AP, *Mutiny at the Curragh* (1956).
53 Beatty, Jack, *The Lost History of 1914: How the Great War was not inevitable* (2012).
54 Lewis, Geoffrey, *Carson: The man who divided Ireland* (2006).

For three days they argued and debated but compromise was to prove very elusive, however it did establish that some form of exclusion for the Province of Ulster would have to be considered; Asquith later noting that they always returned to "that most damnable creation of the perverted ingenuity of man, the county of Tyrone."⁵⁵ Options discussed the day before the Buckingham Palace conference included ignoring county boundaries and trying to create a solid block along a religious divide. To achieve this the Prime Minister was willing to consider paying for migration to smooth the rough edges, but Carson and his friends were not ready to deal on this basis.⁵⁶

The conference collapsed, the dilemma was the exact area to be excluded and whether the exclusion would be temporary or permanent. Asquith had persuaded Redmond to accept the concept of Ulster being excluded from Home Rule for a specified period of time, however Redmond wanted the majority Catholic counties under Home Rule from the outset, including Fermanagh and Tyrone.⁵⁷

John Edward Redmond, leader of the Irish Parliamentary Party from 1900 to 1918. (Somme Museum)

Before the conference broke up, the King met with each of those who attended in private audience. When the King spoke with Craig he expressed his concern that the provisional government might be established in Belfast at any moment. Whilst Carson told him that when Home Rule became law Ulster would see it as a betrayal and rise up, Craig told the King that he and Carson did not "see eye to eye on that". Craig informed his Majesty that he believed that a General Election could still save the situation. He advised the King to sign the Home Rule Bill if he was given it by his constitutional advisers but to call an election immediately after. If the election gave the Unionists an overwhelming majority it would provide the mandate to repeal Home Rule whereas, if it were a small majority then it would justify the exclusion of Ulster. If on the other hand the Unionists were defeated, then Craig believed that Ulster could still secure as good as terms as being currently offered. Craig believed that north-east Ulster could go its own way whilst Carson still hoped to save the Union.⁵⁸

Whilst waiting their audience the Speaker, Lansdowne and Bonar Law read in the press of Austria-Hungary's ultimatum to Serbia.⁵⁹

Three days after the failed Buckingham Palace conference, Macready was ordered to Belfast on a permanent basis by Asquith, despite his warning to the Prime Minister that if "the Home Rule Bill became law, disturbances, if they occur, would be more in the nature of civil war than of faction fights." His orders from Asquith were clear, there was "no change from the former policy, troops

---

55 Downing, Taylor. ed., *The Troubles* (1990).
56 Lewis, Geoffrey, *Carson: The man who divided Ireland* (2006).
57 Beatty, Jack, *The Lost History of 1914: How the Great War was not inevitable* (2012).
58 Lewis, Geoffrey, *Carson: The man who divided Ireland* (2006).
59 Ryan, AP, *Mutiny at the Curragh* (1956).

Kaiser Wilhelm and Paul von Hindenburg at Spa. (Somme Museum)

were to 'sit tight' and make no moves of any kind." A position which Macready later recorded as "[a] more unsatisfactory position for any soldier it is hard to imagine."[60]

The idea of some form of partition had already been muted as early as the summer of 1912 when it was suggested by a Liberal MP during Parliamentary debates on Home Rule. The proposal suggested that the Protestant-dominated counties of Londonderry, Antrim, Armagh and Down be excluded from any Home Rule arrangement.

However the die was cast. The Ulster Unionists supported by most peers of the realm and the Conservative and Unionist Party were committed to establishing an illegal provisional government in Ulster and preventing the will of the Westminster Liberal Government and the majority of Westminster MPs and of the Irish people by force if necessary. This would be achieved by their military wing, the Ulster Volunteer Force, armed with weapons smuggled from Imperial Germany with the tacit approval of the Kaiser.

Alfred Harmsworth, Lord Northcliffe, the owner of the *Daily Mail* and *The Times*, later described by Lord Beaverbrook as "the greatest figure who ever strode down Fleet Street", independent from the control of any political party, articulated his personal views through his papers. In July 1914 he agreed to write an article for the *New York Times* to "educate" American readers on the Irish question. In his article he contended that there was "room for two happy prosperous states in Ireland", the "shrewd and industrious Northern Irish", who were, "by nature better equipped for work than for talk" and the "charming and poetical, but 'unpractical' southern Irish neighbours." He also described the Ulster Volunteer Force as being "the last word in military organisation" and

---

60   Grob-Fitzgibbon, *Turning Points of The Irish Revolution: The British Government, Intelligence and the Cost of Indifference, 1912-1921* (2007).

a force, "already larger than that which the South African Boers put into the field in 1899." Having visited Ulster just before the outbreak of war he further described the UVF;[61] "Apart from their vast stores of ammunition, their night and day signalling system, their automobile transport and great stocks of gasoline, they are equipped with hospitals far ahead of those used by the Japanese in their [recent] war with Russia and their nursing and ambulance arrangements have met with the approval of interested experts from all over the world."

It was becoming clear that Ulster would be excluded in some form from the impending Home Rule, however it was still unclear if this would be a temporary arrangement favoured by Nationalists or permanent, favoured by Unionists. Also to be agreed were the arrangements with regards the extent of the area to be excluded, Nationalists reluctantly contemplated a four-county exclusion, whilst Unionists maintained that it should be the full nine counties of Ulster.

Despite those involved in the political discussions other UVF members had been watching developments over the years with interest. These included Colonel Oliver Nugent who stressed that County Cavan was "geographically and politically isolated from North East Ulster", and others who feared the Unionist leadership would accept a compromise at the cost of others. Gerald Madden from County Monaghan and a prominent Unionist wrote in October 1913, "I hope there is no talk in Belfast of accepting Churchill's hint of withdrawing only the 4 N.[orth] E.[eastern] Counties, that would be betraying the rest of Ulster, who are Covenanters like themselves, and any separation should be resisted at all costs."[62]

Lloyd George met each of the parties separately; Carson and Craig for the Ulster Unionists; Redmond, Dillon, Joseph Devlin, the Ulster Nationalist Leader and TP O'Connor for the Nationalists.

No Unionists from the south and west were consulted. Agreement in principle was quickly achieved, subject to those they represented agreeing to the detail. The offer was that Home Rule would be implemented immediately in the 26 counties in the south and west. The remaining six counties of Antrim, Armagh, Down, Fermanagh, Londonderry and Tyrone along with the parliamentary boundaries of Belfast, Londonderry and Newry were to be excluded and remain part of the United Kingdom.

Carson knew he had to gain support for these proposals as the alternative was likely to be another weak executive in Dublin, putting off Home Rule until the end of the war with highly likely hostilities from Ulster and the prospect of not getting any more than was currently on offer.

The key for Carson was that the division would be permanent, not temporary or provisional. Lloyd George agreed, writing to Carson 29 May, "We must make it clear that

Sir Edward Carson. (Somme Museum)

---

61 Parkinson, Alan F, *Friends in High Places: Ulster's Resistance to Irish Home Rule, 1912-14* (2012).
62 Bowman, Timothy, *Carson's Army: Ulster Volunteer Force, 1910-22* (2007).

at the end of the provisional period Ulster does not, whether she wills it or not, merge in the rest of Ireland." It seemed plain enough that the six counties were to be excluded, however it would emerge later that Redmond had been given the impression that the arrangements were provisional only, he never considered the question closed.[63]

Carson travelled from London to Belfast on 5 June along with the Londonderrys, Mr and Mrs Ronald McNeill, the Duke of Abercorn and Lord Farnham who had come home from France to take part in the meeting with the Ulster Unionist Council which was held on 6 June. The meeting was held in private, but McNeill reported that Carson spoke for almost two hours. They adjourned for a week so that the delegates could consult their constituents. On 12 June the Ulster Unionist Council gave Carson consent to continue with the negotiations with Lloyd George on the basis that the six Ulster counties would be excluded.[64]

Following this decision Carson wrote to Bonar Law, "For my own part I have had a very painful and difficult task in trying to induce the Six Counties to accept the terms the Government have offered … I feel very lonely in the whole matter, but I have found confidence reposed in me in the North of Ireland which was, to say the least of it, refreshing."[65]

Major Somerset Saunderson, son of the first leader of the Ulster Unionist and one of the county Cavan delegates, wrote to Carson making very clear his feelings and that of many of his compatriots, "we have been sold and betrayed by our leaders in the Coalition by reopening the Home Rule question."[66]

The diehard element within Ulster Unionists saw Home Rule during the war as a reward for the lawless violence of the Easter Rebellion and betrayal of the Unionists. This opposition would lead to the proposal stalling; it would not be implemented during the war.[67]

The Ulster Unionist Council ultimately accepted Lloyd George's proposals in the aftermath of the Easter rebellion, for the immediate implementation of Home Rule in return for six-county exclusion and again in March 1920 when they 'accepted' the Government of Ireland bill on the basis of a six-county exclusion as opposed to the nine counties. Whilst the Ulster Unionist Council decision in June 1916 caused great pain and anguish to the Unionists of Cavan, Donegal and Monaghan, this would be nothing to the feelings of the Ulster Unionist Council delegates from Cavan, Donegal and Monaghan in May 1920 when they were unsuccessful in overturning the decision reached by the Council earlier in March 1920 which defined the future of Ulster. The delegates of the three border counties were supported in their cause by Ambrose Ricardo.[68] This feeling of almost betrayal of their fellow Ulstermen was displayed in homes in Cavan, Donegal and Monaghan as their copies of the Ulster Covenant which they had signed only a couple of years earlier now appeared worthless and meaningless.

Others hold the view that there was no betrayal. Their argument was that there is no mention of the number of the counties included in the Covenant, however it is the 'Ulster' Covenant suggesting at least that it was intended to be the nine counties. Reference is also made to a speech made by Carson in September 1911, a year before the Covenant when he said, "on the morning of Home Rule … we must be prepared to govern … those districts of which we have control." For

---

63 Lewis, Geoffrey, *Carson: The man who divided Ireland* (2006).
64 Lewis, Geoffrey, *Carson: The man who divided Ireland* (2006).
65 Lewis, Geoffrey, *Carson: The man who divided Ireland* (2006).
66 Lewis, Geoffrey, *Carson: The man who divided Ireland* (2006).
67 Lewis, Geoffrey, *Carson: The man who divided Ireland* (2006).
68 Ulster Volunteers, January 1913 – Ulster-Scots Community Network <http://www.ulster-scots.com/uploads/901740969819.PDF> (Accessed 5 August 2013).

"There is in Ulster the prospect of acute dissension and even civil strife." A sketch from the *Illustrated London News* depicting Asquith moving the second reading of the Home rule bill and dealing with those changes the Government believed inevitable in the government of Ireland. (Somme Museum)

example, was Cavan in the Unionists control, where only 18 people out of every 100 wished to stay in the United Kingdom?[69]

Despite these views in some of the border counties opposition in Dublin against Home Rule remained every bit as staunch as in Ulster. At a meeting in the Metropolitan Hall in July 1914 resolutions were heard from the city's Orangemen to "risk all in defence of their rights" and calling on their leaders to take whatever steps they considered necessary. At the same meeting those assembled heard how Dublin had a large body of "disciplined and armed" Orangemen, full of "grim determination", leaving those present in no doubt that the Loyal Dublin Volunteers would back up the Orange resolutions.[70]

However this was not the first indications of feelings in Ireland's capital. As early as September 1913, Army Command in Ireland had information which suggested that the Ulster Volunteer Force had formed two battalions, over 2,000 strong in Dublin with arrangements in the event of civil war to send their families to England, enabling them to act as a reserve for the UVF in Ulster.[71]

This would supplement the concept of reserve units which were set up early in the UVF organisation. Within the 1st (North) Tyrone Regiment there was to be a Reserve Force which would comprise those who could not join the regular force as a result of age or similar disability. This effectively provided three tiers; Special Service Force units capable of being mobilised rapidly, original battalions for mobilisation in the event of trouble in their own districts or further afield and the reserve force used only for home area defence.[72]

---

69 Ingram, Rev Brett, *Covenant and Challenge* (1989).
70 <http://www.newsletter.co.uk/features/the-loyal-dublin-volunteers-a-forgotten-organisation-1-3719467> (Accessed 5 February 2014).
71 Bowman, Timothy, *Carson's Army: Ulster Volunteer Force, 1910-22* (2007).
72 Bowman, Timothy, *Carson's Army: Ulster Volunteer Force, 1910-22* (2007).

The 3rd Battalion, North Belfast Ulster Volunteer Force parading in the grounds of Belfast Castle, 1913. (A Hogg, Ulster Museum)

In the same edition of *The Times* newspaper published on 29 June 1914 which reported the assassination of the Austrian Archduke Franz Ferdinand in Sarajvo, the editorial declared, "Complete disaster is now but a few weeks – it may be only a few days – away."[73]

Whilst weapons had been landed and distributed to the Ulster Volunteer Force it was the start of July 1914 before the UVF Headquarters finally authorised the issue and carrying of weapons. The order stated, "It has been decided that, at the discretion of the COs, the time has come when arms may be carried openly by members of the Ulster Volunteer Force, and that any attempt to seize arms from individuals who may be carrying them in accordance with these instructions is to be resisted, in accordance with former instructions issued on this subject."[74, 75]

On 14 July orders were issued that not more than five percent of service ammunition was to be used for target practice pending further orders. The reserve stock of .303 ammunition was also issued to regiments.[76]

When Carson visited Ulster again in July 1914 he addressed a huge crowd of Orangemen in a field near Drumbeg outside Belfast. Acknowledging the presence of the additional weapons which were proudly displayed by the parading regiments and battalions of Ulster Volunteers he pleaded with them to "take care to understand what the rifle means". He went on to urge them to use the weapons in "such a way as may be necessary for the maintenance of our rights", pleading with them to remain resolute and non-provocative.[77]

Fred Crawford wrote to his fellow gun-runner, Andy Agnew, on 12 July 1914 of how he was watching the 12th parade pass 'Cloreen', his house on the Malone Road, when his daughter made reference to the gun-running for the UVF.

---

73 Beatty, Jack, *The Lost History of 1914: How the Great War was not inevitable* (2012).
74 *Northern Whig* – 2/7/1914.
75 Bowman, Timothy, *Carson's Army: Ulster Volunteer Force, 1910-22* (2007).
76 Ammunition – 16 July 1914.
77 Parkinson, Alan F, *Friends in High Places: Ulster's Resistance to Irish Home Rule, 1912-14* (2012).

Edward Carson inspecting a detachment of the Ulster Volunteer Force outside the Ulster Hall, Belfast, July 1914. (*Belfast Telegraph*)

The 'Boys' are just passing my house here as I write … My eldest girl [Naomi] is full of mischief and she made a black banner and put a skull and crossbones upon it under, in large letters, *Hello Fanny*. They placed this over our gate and Bob Wallace (the Colonel) took off his hat to it. He was sitting beside the Chief [Sir Edward Carson]. When he saw me he shook me by the hand as the carriage passed.

The British Cabinet were reminded by the military members of the Army Council on 4 July 1914 that there were 200,000 armed men in Ireland from opposing forces, and as a consequence, if civil war broke out it was projected that it might be necessary to commit the entire British Expeditionary Force, the Special Reserve and the Territorial Army to restore order which as a consequence they concluded "we shall be unable to give any assistance to either Egypt or India if required, be unable to meet our obligations abroad." This was a direct reference to the Anglo-French military talks which had been on-going against a possible attack by Germany.[78, 79]

The memo from the Chief of the Imperial Staff concluded with the apologetic assurance that the War Council did not mean "to intervene in a political question" but felt obliged to point out the seriousness of the situation.[80]

---

78   Beatty, Jack, *The Lost History of 1914: How the Great War was not inevitable* (2012).
79   Muenger, Elizabeth A, *The British Military Dilemma in Ireland: Occupation Politics 1886-1914* (1991).
80   Muenger, Elizabeth A, *The British Military Dilemma in Ireland: Occupation Politics 1886-1914* (1991).

On the same date, 4 July, a major review of Ulster Volunteers occurred in the centre of Belfast with a significant number from the north-Belfast detachments whilst an estimated 4,000 fully armed Volunteers paraded in central Belfast on 25 July, the same day as the Howth gun-running.[81]

Against this background, during June 1914 UVF Headquarters became aware that large scale enrolments were being contemplated in some parts of Ulster and that large numbers of men who had been engaging in drill were anxious to join the Ulster Volunteers. The officers in the areas concerned were reminded of previous UVF Orders on the subject, namely Order No.49 of 1914, and that all men who wished to enrol themselves as Volunteers would be required to "put in" 15 drills in order to show their intentions were bona fide However, as Order No.49 allowed, the officers could use their discretion with regard to enrolling men with special qualifications.[82]

When Sir Edward Carson made his first formal visit on 11 July 1914 to Larne, following the clandestine landing of arms and ammunition, he inspected around 2,000 UVF from Larne, Carrickfergus and Ballyclare at Drumalis to which he had been a frequent visitor.[83] The elegant house, which still stands on the site, was built by Hugh Smiley in 1872. Smiley was the main owner of the *Northern Whig* and after her husband's death in 1909 Lady Elizabeth Smiley carried on the political connection. A record still exists of the ladies of the East Antrim Nursing Corps of Ulster Volunteers assembling in the front of Drumalis, Lady Smiley having put Drumalis at their disposal.[84]

Drumalis was sold by Lady Smiley in 1927 and was bought by the Sisters of the Cross and Passion in 1930. Since that date it has been home to the community of Sisters and a Retreat House.[85]

Addressing the Volunteers assembled at Drumalis Carson informed them:

> I am very proud to be in Larne today and to see such a magnificent turnout. Larne will for ever hold a place in the history of this great movement (Cheers). The exploits of the gun-running night will lie in history long after we have passed away. I am grateful, men, to you for the part – the worthy and noble part – you played that night, and your country is grateful to you, and will continue to be grateful to you, and will continue to be grateful to you to the end. (Cheers)

As he addressed them he unfurled one of the canvas strips used to rename the *Clyde Valley* on her last leg of her journey. Describing it to the assembled crowd as "a valued trophy of Ulster", the crowd burst into cheering on seeing the word "Mountjoy"[86]

During the summer of 1914 training continued with practice turnouts and mobilisation exercises at Company level.

Whilst the Ulster Volunteer Force rarely took part in Orange Order parades one exception was during the Derry Twelfth of July parades in 1914, when UVF members, armed with sticks, acted as stewards assisting in preventing a repeat of the rioting which had occurred in the previous year.[87]

When the Right Honourable Walter Long, MP, (1st Viscount Long) passed through Ballymena on 11 July 1914, the 1st Battalion, (Ballymena) North Antrim Regiment, were requested to turn out in full equipment with as many as they could for an inspection by Long to be held in the

---

81　Parkinson, Alan F, *Friends in High Places: Ulster's Resistance to Irish Home Rule, 1912-14* (2012).
82　UVF Order 60, 1914 – Somme Museum.
83　Hume, David, *"For Ulster and Her Freedom": The story of the April 1914 gun-running* (1989).
84　<http://www.drumalis.co.uk/Background_and_History.aspx – Drumalis> (Accessed 17 February 2014).
85　<http://www.drumalis.co.uk/Background_and_History.aspx – Drumalis> (Accessed 17 February 2014).
86　Hume, David, *"For Ulster and Her Freedom": The story of the April 1914 gun-running* (1989).
87　Bowman, Timothy, *Carson's Army: Ulster Volunteer Force, 1910-22* (2007).

A period postcard depicting a detachment of the Ulster Volunteer Force drawn up for parade at Fortwilliam in North Belfast, September 1913.

William 'Bill' Hunter McDowall, born Paisley, Scotland later moved to Larne, County Antrim working as groom and chauffeur to Lord Hugh Houston Smiley, proprietor of the *Northern Whig* newspaper. As a signatory of the Ulster Covenant, by family tradition it is probable that Bill (the family chauffeur) was involved in the Larne Gun Running and although there are no records of it, he was doubtless a member of the Ulster Volunteers who paraded in the grounds of the Drumalis estate. He later served as a Sergeant, 12th Bn Royal Irish Rifles. He was killed in action in France, 26 March 1918, age 36. (Laura Spence)

Left – King's Colour, 2nd Battalion, South Belfast Regiment, Ulster Volunteer Force. Right – Yellow Regimental Colour, 2nd Battalion, Ulster Volunteer Force. (Somme Museum)

grounds of Ballymena Castle.[88] Having been Chief Secretary for Ireland he had also served as Leader of the Irish Unionist Party in the House of Commons from 1905 to 1910. In the opposition he was one of the leading voices against the Liberals' plans for Home Rule in Ireland, helping to found the Ulster Defence League in 1907. He was also Sir Edward Carson's predecessor as leader of the Irish Unionist Parliamentary Party.

The idea for the presenting of colours to various units appears to have originated with the promise of a King's Colour to the Queen's Island Ulster Volunteer Force by the Countess of Bective, daughter of the 4th Marquess of Downshire, in August 1913, however it appears that as a result of Richardson's reorganising of the UVF by place of residence it was never presented.[89] Colours were certainly presented to the following units; 1st South Antrim Regiment; 1st North Belfast Regiment; 1st and 2nd North Down Regiment; 2nd East Down Regiment; 1st South Belfast Regiment; 1st and 2nd West Belfast Regiment; 5th East Belfast Regiment and 6th North Belfast Regiment.[90]

As a result of enquires to UVF Headquarters regarding the issuing of colours, guidance was issued to those donating, though it was stressed that it was not intended to interfere with any Colours already presented or being made for presentation. Colours should not exceed the size of three feet by three feet nine inches and in all cases Colour belts should be provided to ensure they may be properly carried at the Carry. Whilst it was not considered essential that a Battalion must have both the King's Colour and a Regimental Colour, in those cases where a Battalion only has a Regimental colour, it should have a small Union Jack in the top corner next to the Colour-pike. The guidance further suggested that where possible the Regimental Colour of each Battalion in a Regiment should be the same with Regimental Colours, in all cases having upon them the name of the regiment and the number of the battalion in additional to any other devices.

The following firms were provided as suggested makers; Messrs S Wilson & Co, 1 Clarence Street, Belfast, Messrs. Thos. Pratt & Son, Tavistock St, Strand, London and Messrs. Hamburger, Rogers & Co, 30 King St. Covenant Garden, London.

---

88 Urgent and Special Order for 1st Batt, North Antrim Regiment UVF – 7 July 1914.
89 Bowman, Timothy, *Carson's Army: Ulster Volunteer Force, 1910-22* (2007).
90 Bowman, Timothy, *Carson's Army: Ulster Volunteer Force, 1910-22* (2007).

Suggested costs were also provided as a guide; Regimental Colour embroidered on best silk with cords, £30 to £35, Regimental Colour painted on best silk, £10 to £15, King's Colour, £6 to £15 and colour-pole costs from £1 5s to £3 17s 6d.[91]

The 4th Battalion, North Belfast Regiment received theirs on 25 June 1914.[92]

On 21 July 1914, Hobson's of London received an order for a pair of colours which on one included the device and inscription "The Donegal Regiment." Whilst there is no record of who placed the order or how they were paid for, Hobson's still have the original tracing for the design of the Colours.[93]

1st and 2nd Battalions of the West Down Regiment were presented with their Colours by Mrs Holt Waring and the women of West Down on Saturday 23 May 1914 at Lenaderg. It was reported in UVF orders that the two battalions formed an impressive parade with credit given to Captain Waring and the officers and men under his command. Also on parade was the detachment of the Ulster Volunteer Medical and Nursing Corps and the Despatch Riders.[94] The 1st Battalion South Down Regiment had already received their colours at an Inspection of the Battalion at Donard Lodge, Newcastle, Saturday 16 May 1914.[95]

Ulster Volunteer Colour Party on parade. (Somme Museum)

---

91 UVF Orders 115 – Somme Museum.
92 UVF Orders 72, 1914 – Somme Museum.
93 Canning, WJ, *Ballyshanon, Belcoo, Bertincourt* (1996).
94 UVF Orders 56, 1914 – Somme Museum.
95 UVF Orders 53, 1914 – Somme Museum.

The 3rd Battalion, East Down regiment, received their colours at Hillsborough on Saturday 28 February 1914 where, despite very inclement weather, it was commented that Battalions capable of maintaining their discipline in such conditions should have no difficulty in picking up field work.1st Battalion (Lisburn) South Antrim Regiment, under the command of Mr AP Jenkins formed the detachment representing the Regiment at the ceremony.[96]

The 1st Battalion, North Antrim Regiment, were presented their Colours in the big field in front of Ballymena Castle, 6 May 1914 at 6:30 p.m.[97] Officers were to wear their uniform hat with officer's plume, haversack over the left shoulder and officer's belt over right shoulder over the haversack.[98] Mr JH Wright, A Company, was to carry the King's Colour and Mr John Nelson, C Company, the Regimental Colour. Detailed directions were issued with regards the nature and formation of the parade for the ten companies concerned and the colour party. Directions were given specific instructions regarding the carrying of the colours; never to be sloped at the halt and to be carried at the slope when marching home after the parade.[99]

The Colour Presentation of the East Down Regiment was held at Drum, whilst the 1st, 2nd and 3rd Battalions of the Central Antrim Regiment received theirs at Larne, all on Saturday 11 July 1914.[100, 101]

The 1st and 2nd Battalions, Monaghan Regiment, were presented with their colours at Glaslough, Tuesday 28 July 1914,[102] and the 2nd, 3rd, 4th, 5th and 6th Battalions of the South Belfast Regiment being presented theirs, with the Special Service Force and the Ulster Volunteer Medical and Nursing Corps also turning out.[103]

The 5th Battalion, Tyrone Regiment were presented their colours at Cookstown 10 September 1914.

UVF Colours were dedicated in the grounds of Belfast Castle, the ceremony performed by the Presbyterian Moderators for 1914 and by D'Arcy, Bishop of Down, with Carson standing between them with his blackthorn stick.[104]

Meanwhile, with increasing European tensions, on the world stage the posturing and actions of the Ulster Volunteer Force received mixed reactions. The American Ambassador in Berlin had reported to his government that Sir Edward Carson's threats were "the biggest bluff in history" whilst Baron von Kulhmann, a German agent staying in Belfast and watching the unfolding events, had reported to his government that England would not be able to enter a European war due to her Irish trouble.[105]

---

96 UVF Order 19, 1914 – Somme Museum.
97 Orders from OC 1st Batt North Antrim Regiment – 29 April 1914.
98 Orders from OC 1st Batt, North Antrim Regiment – 5 May 1914.
99 Presentation of Colours to 1st Batt, North Antrim Regiment.
100 UVF Orders 77, 1914 – Somme Museum.
101 UVF Orders 78, 1914 – Somme Museum.
102 UVF Orders 89, 1914 – Somme Museum.
103 UVF Orders 90, 1914 – Somme Museum.
104 Ingram, Rev Brett, *Covenant and Challenge* (1989).
105 Crozier, Brig-Gen FP, CB, CMG, DSO, *Ireland for Ever* (1932).

10

Ulster stands at the Brink

Despite the escalation of events in Ireland with the landing of the Irish Volunteer weapons at Howth, one week after the Buckingham Palace Conference attention was to focus again in mainland Europe as governments were enveloped in war. On 26 July the Austro-Hungarian Empire declared war on Serbia and on 30 July Imperial Russia mobilised her army in support. Germany demanded that the Russians demobilise and when they failed to do so declared war first on Russia and two days later on France. Germany asked Belgium on Sunday 2 August for permission to move through her borders, which was refused. The Belgians appealed to the other signatories of the 1839 treaty guaranteeing her neutral borders, of which somewhat ironically, Prussia was one.[1]

On 30 July 1914 *The Times* newspaper reported that "Over the last forty-eight hours (there) has been a sudden and complete change in the Irish attitude. On Wednesday night Ulstermen and Nationalists were … going on deliberately with their preparations for combat. Then came the grave words … in the House of Commons on Thursday … Now Irishmen of all complexions have suddenly become Britons."[2]

Carson met with some opposition Members of Parliament on Sunday 30 July in the home of Sir Edward Goulding. Amongst them, at the request of members from the Committee of Imperial Defence, was Captain Wilfred Spender to establish the intention of the Ulster Volunteer Force.

Carson's response was simple "a large body of Ulster Volunteers will be willing and ready to give their services to Home Defence and many will be willing and ready to serve anywhere they are required."[3]

During the weekend as the world slid into conflict a number of UVF parades and demonstrations were held.[4] These were in direct response to a UVF Circular Memorandum headed "Very Urgent and Most Important", which requested that as many men as possible (equipment was not necessary) should be mustered, and in view of the current Imperial crises, each volunteer asked if they were prepared to volunteer to serve under the Imperial Government under the following conditions:

1. Anywhere in the United Kingdom
2. Foreign Service
3. In Ulster only[5]

The specifics in the orders to the UVF Company commanders asked them to ascertain how many men in their company or unit would be prepared to volunteer their service for Home Defence, which was defined as "not to leave the British Isles, on the understanding that they

---

1   Harris, HED, *The Irish Regiments in the First World War* (1968).
2   *The Times* – 30 July 1914.
3   *The Times* – 1 August 1914.
4   *Belfast News Letter* – 3 August 1914.
5   Circular Memorandum – OC 1st Batt, North Antrim Regiment – 7 August 1914.

The Ulster Volunteer Force in 1913. (Somme Museum)

would be armed and paid and equipped (clothed) by the Imperial Government." It was expected that these men would serve together and would not be distributed or mixed with other men and as far as possible officered by their own officers.[6]

Further UVF Orders dated 1 August directed that all persons in charge of ammunition were to ensure that it was packed in boxes or tins to enable its ease and suitability for transport in the field. Specific instructions were also issued as to how to identify the different types of ammunition. Each tin or box was to be distinctly marked with a painted band about two inches in width as follows:

German or Austrian Pattern Rifle	7.9mm	Black Band
British Rifles	.303	White Band
Vetterli-Vitali Rifles	10.4mm	Yellow Band[7]

Whilst Redmond realised the importance of British opinion in achieving Home Rule there were limits to how far he would go in support of the war. The same day as Carson's article in *The Times* offering the services of the Ulster Volunteer Force, Asquith's wife Margot wrote to Redmond asking him to set "an unforgettable example to the Carsonites" by going to the Commons and "in a great speech offer all his soldiers to the government."

The next day Redmond told the House of Commons that the British Government, "may tomorrow withdraw every one of their troops from Ireland." The rationale being that the role of home defence would be undertaken by the Irish Volunteers, though he went further; "For that purpose the armed Catholics of the south will be only too glad to join with the armed Protestant Ulstermen." He voiced what he appeared to consider as an opportune aspiration; "Is it too much to hope that out of this situation a result may spring which will be good, not merely for the Empire but for the future welfare and integrity of the Irish nation?" Whilst he stopped short of offering the Irish Volunteers for overseas service like Carson, when he finished speaking the Conservatives rose and cheered. One Nationalist MP reported that many from the Unionist ranks approached him in the lobby expressing their gratitude.[8]

---

6   Circular Memorandum – OC 1st North Antrim Regiment, 3 August 1914.
7   UVF Orders 82, 1914 –Somme Museum.
8   Denman, Terence, *Ireland's Unknown Soldiers: The 16th (Irish) Division in the Great War* (1992).

Asquith had prepared an amending bill to the intended Home Rule legislation, permitting any Ulster county to vote itself permanently out of the Home Rule scheme. This appeasement of the Unionists was risky as Redmond's Nationalists could bring down his Liberal Government, however Redmond knew that replacing it with a Unionist Government would doom his cause of Home Rule, so he reluctantly agreed. Despite this, at the last moment when the House met to take up the Amending Bill, Asquith announced that as a result of the events unfolding in Europe it was important "to present a united front" and he postponed the bill indefinitely.[9]

The background to the change of position was simple; whilst Asquith was still preparing his speech for the last reading of the Amending bill he received a telephone call from Bonar Law asking him to come and see both Law and Carson at his Kensington residence, even sending a motor car for him. Asquith later recorded, "It was quite an adventure, for I might easily have been kidnapped by a section of Ulster Volunteers."[10] Instead Law proposed that the whole issue of Home Rule should be suspended, given the developing international situation.

Herbert Henry Asquith, 1st Earl of Oxford and Asquith KG PC KC, served as the Liberal Prime Minister of the United Kingdom from 1908 to 1916. (Somme Museum)

On Tuesday 4 August 1914 Britain showed her hand and declared war against Germany when she refused to comply with the 12 hour deadline to withdraw its forces from Belgium. The Irish Home Rule Act 1914 was placed on the statute books with a caveat that it would pass into law accompanied by a suspending Act, effectively postponing Home Rule until peacetime.[11] This resulted in the introduction of Home Rule being delayed for the duration of the war and averted the inevitable civil war.

The Ulster question had been apparently resolved, however whilst Carson had hoped to have the whole of Ulster excluded, he felt a good case could be made for the "six plantation counties" at least to be excluded.

In Belfast however some did not appreciate the King giving his Royal assent to the legislation. Pictures of King George V were booed and in some Protestant churches members of the congregations walked out when the National Anthem was played.[12]

How close was it to a different outcome?

Up to the last minute Craig had been arranging the delivery of mass quantities of flour, tea and other staples from Glasgow, on behalf of the Ulster Provisional Government who expected Churchill to use the Royal Navy to blockade Ulster once the establishment of the Provisional

---

9   Beatty, Jack, *The Lost History of 1914: How the Great War was not inevitable* (2012).
10 Beatty, Jack, *The Lost History of 1914: How the Great War was not inevitable* (2012).
11 <http://www.proni.gov.uk/index/search_the_archives/ulster_covenant/aftermath.htm>.
12 Lewis, Geoffrey, *Carson: The man who divided Ireland* (2006).

Ulstermen on the way to the recruitment station at the outbreak of war. (Somme Museum)

Government was proclaimed. During the time when Austrian guns were shelling Belgrade in Serbia, Craig wired Carson in London, telling him that once he was advised by a pre-arranged code-word all their preparations would be executed, reassuring Carson that "All difficulties have been overcome and we are in a very strong position."[13] Carson received Craig's telegram a few hours before the meeting with Bonar Law and Asquith. We will never know the true implications or impact if he had wired back the pre-arranged code to instigate the Provisional Government and all which accompanied it.[14]

Crozier had been told, whilst the GOC UVF, that this position would be a member of the Provisional Government responsible for the police and the maintenance of law and order as well as the army, he would be a chief executive officer for this purpose. As part of this role Crozier was ordered to prepare a plan, akin to martial law, whereby he would have control of the a police function and the defence of Belfast without regard to creed or politics, which would be put into force with the proclamation.[15]

Other arrangements included that all men not bearing arms who were in support of the Provisional Government and those supportive women would wear orange rosettes so that all others could be easily identified.[16]

Lord Milner had even been working on designs for a currency for the Provisional Government when Russia mobilised against Austria-Hungary.[17]

A strange situation had emerged. The UVF had sought aid and assistance in the form of arms from Imperial Germany, who looked upon the deal as advantageous to its European plans, as civil war in Ireland would likely draw British military forces away from possible action in Europe, yet the Ulster Volunteer Force declared unstinting loyalty to King and Empire.

---

13 Beatty, Jack, *The Lost History of 1914: How the Great War was not inevitable* (2012).
14 Beatty, Jack, *The Lost History of 1914: How the Great War was not inevitable* (2012).
15 Crozier, Brig-Gen FP Crozier, CB, CMG, DSO, *Ireland for Ever* (1932).
16 Crozier, Brig-Gen FP Crozier, CB, CMG, DSO, *Ireland for Ever* (1932).
17 Beatty, Jack, *The Lost History of 1914: How the Great War was not inevitable* (2012).

On 3 August 1914, Asquith, the British Prime Minister, told JA Pease, the Liberal Party Whip, that it was providential that the one bright spot in this hateful war was the settlement of the Irish civil strife and added, nearly breaking down, "Jack, God moves in a mysterious way, his wonders to perform." The next day Britain was at war and ironically brought the risk of "Revolt in Ulster" to an end.[18]

These events may have turned out differently; if the Austrian Chief of Staff, Conrad von Hotzendorff, had succeeded in urging Count Berchtold the Foreign Minister to postpone Austria's ultimatum to Serbia until mid-August, the situation in Ireland may have played out differently.[19]

Within days of the declaration of war the small British Expeditionary Force had set sail for France, many Irishmen of both traditions amongst them. However even supplemented by the Territorial forces they encountered problems against the power of Imperial Germany. Parliament passed a bill permitting the raising of 500,000 men for Kitchener's New Army. At the same time a wave of patriotism swept across Britain resulting in 2,000,000 volunteers flocking to the colours, before the horrors of the war were fully appreciated, and the resultant conscription which was introduced in early 1916.[20]

Appointed to the vacant post of Secretary of State for War, 6 August 1914, Kerry born Lord Kitchener was to raise a series of New Armies, each 100,000 strong in six Divisions (K1-6), to meet the increasing demands on the British Army. Unlike some of his cabinet colleagues who believed it would be a short war, or at best "over by Christmas", he believed that it could last at least three years, or even result in a stalemate between Britain and Germany, an opinion he only shared in private, while insisting he would need 1,000,000 men to win the war.[21]

K1 was raised in response to Army Order 324, dated 21 August 1914, and comprised six Divisions numbered 9-14, which included the 10th (Irish) Division.[22] This Division would include a large

UVF badge of a brass oval depicting a bleeding right hand. It is held in place by a split pin. (Somme Museum)

Lord Kitchener.
(Somme Museum: 1998-64)

---

18 Beatty, Jack, *The Lost History of 1914: How the Great War was not inevitable* (2012).
19 Beatty, Jack, *The Lost History of 1914: How the Great War was not inevitable* (2012).
20 Orr, Philip, *The Road to the Somme* (1987).
21 Moore, Steven, *The Irish on the Somme* (2005).
22 Metcalfe, Nick, *Blacker's Boys* (2012).

number of Ulster Volunteer Force members who were impatient to do their bit. However, other members of the Ulster Volunteers were reservists and were already being recalled to the colours, and as a result were sent to various units across the Army, making them unavailable for the new Irish Division.

One such individual was Major SWW Blacker, commissioned into the Royal Artillery in 1885 he had served on the Northwest Frontier and the South African War before retiring in 1903. He was a major influence in the Ulster Volunteers, commanding the Armagh Regiment and raised and commanded the 4th (Portadown) Battalion. He was recalled to the colours in early August 1914, his orders directing him to Piershill Barracks, Edinburgh.[23]

The following list is a nominal roll of officers already recalled to the colours whose services were later applied for service in the eventual Ulster Volunteer Division:

Army Rank	Name	Late Regt.	Present Appt.
Lt Col	Chichester RDPG	Guards Brigade	Guards Reserve
Lt Col	Mayhew, RS	Border Regt	
Lt Col	Lewis	Worcester Regt	
Major	Stone, LGT	Royal Fusiliers	Embn. Staff, S'hampton
Major	Blacker, WS	RFA	RFA Reserve, Edinburgh
Major	Farnham, Lord	–	North Irish Horse
Major	Head, RN	Rifle Brigade	RSO, Euston, London
Major	Bangor, Viscount	RGA	
Captain	Spender, WB	RGA	A/AGMG, Chatham
Captain	Malone, LE	Royal Fusiliers	7th Fusiliers, Falmouth
Captain	Penny, AF	Royal Fusiliers	
Captain	Chichester, Hon ACS	Royal Fusiliers	7th Fusiliers, Falmouth
Captain	Dobbs, AF	Antrim RGA	
Captain	Clanwilliam, Earl of	Household Cav	
Captain	Ricardo, A	R. I. Fusiliers	Depot, Omagh
Captain	Gaussen, HA	4th R. Irish Regt	
Captain	Egerton, AF	Cameron Highlanders?[24]	

The following men were Reserve Officers who were liable for service with the colours, whose services were later applied for duty with the Ulster Volunteer Division:

Colonel	Hacket-Pain, G	Worcester Regt
Colonel	Couchman, G	Somerset, L.I.
Major	McCalmont, RCJ	Irish Guards
Captain	Hall, F	RGA

Such was the success of recruiting for K1 that the process for K2 and K3, and another 12 Divisions started in early September. This included the 16th (Irish) Division which due to recruiting difficulties included men from the Channel Islands. This Division would have a predominately Catholic membership with many men coming from Redmond's National Volunteers, yet there was still a significant number of Irish Protestants in its ranks.[25] Both the 10th and 16th Divisions had two

---

23 Metcalfe, Nick, *Blacker's Boys* (2012).
24 UVF Orders – Somme Museum.
25 Metcalfe, Nick, *Blacker's Boys* (2012).

British Army recruiting poster depicting John Redmond. (Somme Museum)

brigades raised largely in the southern counties and one brigade raised largely from the north. K4 New Army followed in the autumn but was largely used for reserve battalions to provide drafts for existing battalions. K5 and K6 followed, however they were renamed K4 and K5.

The impact on the local effectiveness of the Ulster Volunteer Force was easy to see, many officers were being recalled to their regiments for military service whilst on the 8 August forms were distributed to the various UVF units to enable individuals to sign up for military service. It was against this atmosphere that Carson and Craig claimed that many of the 100,000 men were ready for some kind of service at home or abroad.[26] However, many of the Ulster Volunteer Force leaders saw their role in some form of home defence as opposed to service overseas, whilst other Ulstermen were reluctant to give any help to the war effort while the spectre of Home Rule hung over their heads. Spender suggested to the Committee for Imperial Defence that if the UVF was given the role of home defence then two British Army Divisions could be freed to join the British Expeditionary Force in France.

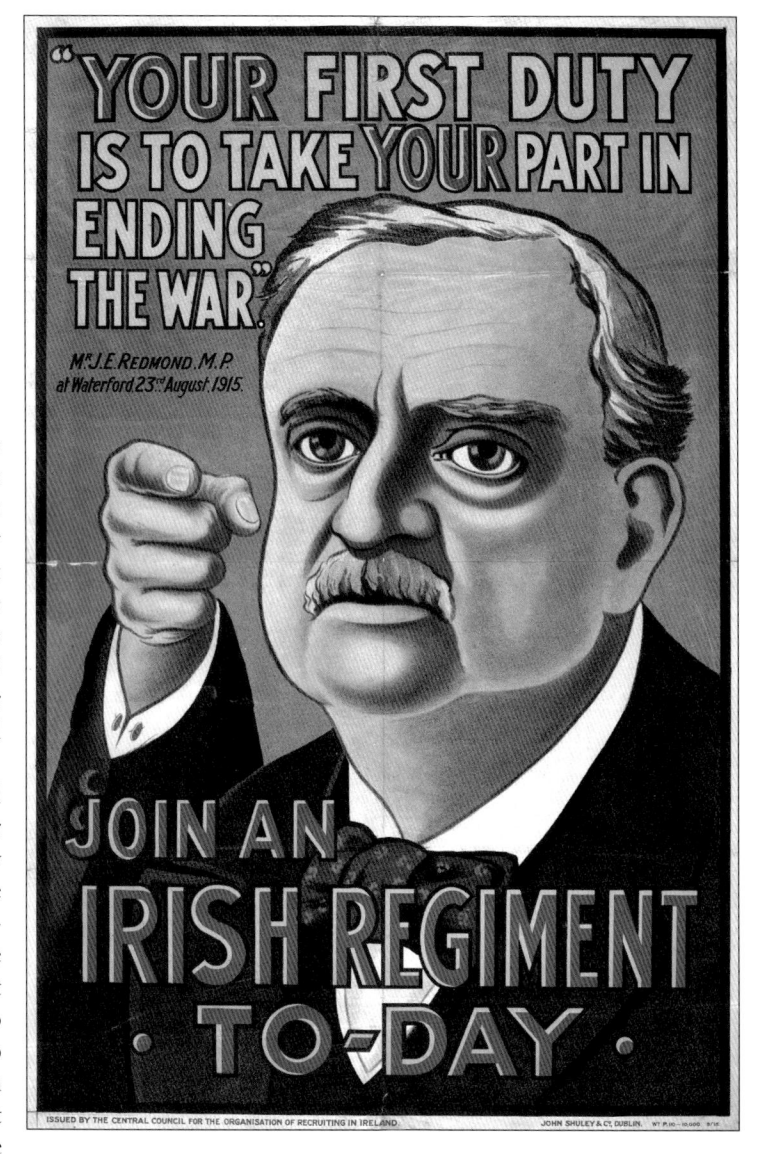

Redmond made a similar suggestion on behalf of the National Volunteers, echoing Spender's words in the House of Commons.

---

26 Stewart, ATQ, *The Ulster Crises* (1967).

Aged 20 years, Robert C. (Roy) Simpson, then residing at Coltrim Farm, Moneymore enlisted in the UVF later joining the Royal Garrison Artillery. He had compassion for the horses drawing the heavy guns to the frontline. His devotion to one animal was immortalised in the poem: 'A Battery Horse'. During the Second World War he was appointed a Sub-District Commandant in the Ulster Special Constabulary responsible for training platoons of Ulster Home Guard volunteers in Moneymore and District. (N Simpson)

By the middle of October 1914, Belfast would be shown to have the highest proportionate recruiting figures of all towns and cities in the United Kingdom, with men filling various sections of the army and the other services.[27]

It was not uncommon for both Ulster Volunteers and National Volunteers to join together in giving rousing send-offs to departing troops which also included some from within their own ranks. The *Irish News* reported on 6 August 1914:

> About six hundred men attached to the Irish Volunteers in Belfast were called up, and there was a great gathering to wish them God-speed and a safe return, when they departed yesterday evening for the regimental centres, quite a large demonstration attending the departure of one body, while at the same time a quota of the Ulster Volunteers were being 'seen off' by a cheering crowd with a band of pipers.[28]

This was not an isolated occurrence with the *Irish News* again reporting on 10 August of Ulster Volunteers and Irish Volunteers joining together in Omagh, on the night of Friday 7 August, to give the final draft of the Army Reserve of the Royal Inniskillings what was described as "a most hearty send-off" when "both bodies of Volunteers and military marched through the town together" and, perhaps more significantly, "as both bodies of Volunteers paraded the town, they met one another and respectfully saluted."[29]

Despite the patriotic surge in the country some believed that it could result in difficulties for Ulster after the war was over. One elderly Volunteer wrote to the *Belfast News Letter* warning that many of the "young and most efficient men" from the UVF may be tempted to join up, however,

---

27 Shearman, Hugh, *Not an Inch: A Study of Northern Ireland and Lord Craigavon* (1942).
28 *Irish News* – 6 August 1914.
29 *Irish News* – 10 August 1914.

Ulster Volunteers enlisting at the Town Hall, Belfast 1914.

after the war was concluded and the Home Rule question again had to be addressed the Volunteers would be a less formidable force. Such were his concerns that he questioned if it was desirable that any Volunteer should offer themselves for overseas service. Another letter writer also warned against Ulster Volunteers joining up as the Nationalist Volunteers in his district were simply waiting their opportunity to rise against England. However there were also those who saw practical benefits from joining up, in that they would receive thorough training would make them more efficient if the need arose to fight for their liberties in the future,[30] always assuming they would return.

Other men appeared impatient to discover exactly what the Ulster Volunteers would do with the nation going to war. The following report in the *Lisburn Standard* on the 18 September 1914 illustrated this:

> Lisburn was lethargic enough at the first, chiefly on account of the position of the Home Rule Bill; but once the path of duty stood out in clear relief … the men could not be enrolled soon enough. … Saturday last [the 12 September 1914] between the hours of 12:00 and 5:00 p.m. was fixed for recruiting, the Assembly Rooms being secured for the occasion. … So constant, however, was the stream that … it was nearer 9:00 p.m. when … the last man was taken on. … The number of rejects was small, the majority being boys whose chest measurement has not yet developed to the required military proportions; while a good few were men well over the standard age. … At the end of the day 327 had [enlisted] … the [event] was a great success [especially] when one considered how many … had been called up with the reserves and the very considerable number who in their eagerness could not wait to see what the UVF were going to do, and had [already] joined.[31]

---

30 Orr, Philip, *The Road to the Somme* (1987).
31 Friends School Lisburn – *World War One Archive* <http://www.friendsschoollisburn.org.uk/ww1/sources.asp?pagehead=tasks#E> (Accessed 2 July 2007).

ULSTER STANDS AT THE BRINK 267

Two days after Kitchener was appointed by Asquith as the new Secretary of State for War he sent for Colonel TE Hickman, MP, president of the British League for the Defence of Ulster, to tell him "I want the Ulster Volunteers."[32] He was well aware that the UVF were the best prepared civilians in Britain to go into the army, however Hickman suggested that Kitchener meet with Carson and Craig.[33] Kitchener disliked all politicians and regarded the Unionist and National leaders as fractious children who needed a stern talking to.[34] The subsequent meeting on 7 August 1914[35] did not proceed smoothly as Carson was keen to hold out for some form of political deal about the Home Rule issue before fully committing to and supporting the war effort. They argued about the Home Rule issue and Carson also insisted that any use of the UVF would have them retained as a distinctive force with its own identity which would include the prefix 'Ulster' against any proposed brigade or division. Kitchener was opposed to the creation of army divisions with political overtones and made his feelings known, echoing some of the Home Rule debates when he responded, "Surely you're not going to hold out for Tyrone and Fermanagh?" to which Carson retorted, "You're a damned clever fellow telling me what I ought to be doing." Kitchener wasn't finished, "If I'd been on the platform with you and Redmond, I should have knocked your heads together!" Carson in his richest brogue answered wryly, "Oi'd loike (sic) to see ye try", bringing the meeting to an abrupt end.[36] The negotiations continued for most of the month of August before Carson achieved a deal which he could accept.

A packet of Kitchener Cigarettes depicting the image of Lord Kitchener along with a lighter. (Somme Museum)

---

32 Falls, Cyril, *History of the 36th (Ulster) Division* (1922).
33 Canning, WJ, *Ballyshannon, Belcoo, Bertincourt* (1996).
34 Denman, Terence, *Ireland's Unknown Soldiers: The 16th (Irish). Division in the Great War* (1992).
35 Causeway; *Cultural Traditions Journal*, Spring 1995 – The Myth of the 36th (Ulster). Division – T Bowman.
36 Causeway; *Cultural Traditions Journal*, Spring 1995 – The Myth of the 36th (Ulster). Division – T Bowman.

This included the guarantee that although the Home Rule Bill would pass on 18 September it would not be enacted during the war. The Amending bill introduced in the next parliamentary session would give parliament the chance to alter its provisions to accommodate some of the Ulster needs.[37]

On the day it received Royal Assent, 18 September, Carson was absent from the House, he had been married for the second time the day before at a quiet service in Somerset.[38]

Carson had no choice but to declare in Belfast to the Ulster Unionist Council, 3 September 1914, that "England's difficulty is not Ulster's opportunity …" In his speech he appealed to the Ulster Volunteers to "Go help to save your country and to save your Empire; go and win honour for Ulster and for Ireland."[39] By offering 35,000 UVF members to the Imperial war effort, he went on to say "If we get enough men to go from the Ulster Volunteer Force they will go under the War Office as a Division of their own." In this he was announcing the formation of what was to become the 36th (Ulster) Division. Recruitment was to begin immediately at the Old Town Hall and other buildings across Ulster. The UVF Special Order for enlistment for the Imperial Forces is in Appendix V.

The *Belfast News Letter* reported that, "The first man to pass the medical examination and to reach the attestation room was William Hanna, aged 44 years, of 42 Brussels Street, a member of the Special Service Battalion, North Belfast Regiment." The paper went on to report that "Hanna, who served in the South African War with the Royal Irish Rifles, wore the ribbons of the Queen's and King's medals for that campaign, and he smiled cheerfully as his papers were completed, securing for him the distinction of being the first member of the Ulster Volunteer Force to be accepted as such by the military authorities."[40]

The War Office had authorised the Ulster Volunteer Force to operate a semi-independent chain of recruiting offices and also the freedom to choose its own officers and to recall former officers of the UVF who had been posted to other units on mobilisation.[41]

36th (Ulster) Divisional Flash. (Somme Museum)

The intention was that the men would be enrolled in territorial units formed out of local UVF regiments and trained, at least initially, in camps in Ireland. Large camps were envisaged at Ballykinlar, Clandeboye and Newtownards, County Down, and at Finner, County Donegal. As part of this initial wave, Craig arranged for 10,000 uniforms to be supplied by Moss Bros., London, to be financed from UVF funds and paid for by some of Ulster's 'rich English friends'.[42,43]

---

37 Orr, Philip, *The Road to the Somme* (1987).
38 Ryan, AP, *Mutiny at the Curragh* (1956).
39 Metcalfe, Nick, *Blacker's Boys* (2012).
40 Moore, Steven, *The Irish on the Somme* (2005).
41 Denman, Terence, *Ireland's Unknown Soldiers: The 16th (Irish) Division in the Great War* (1992).
42 Falls, Cyril, *History of the 36th (Ulster) Division* (1922).
43 Downing, Taylor. (ed), *The Troubles* (1990).

The camp at Finner, Ballyshannon. In the foreground are the bell tents with in the background a number of the wooden huts used to house the Ulster Volunteers after enlisting. (Somme Museum)

Belfast businessmen may not have financially supported the UVF to the level often assumed as Sir Edward Carson berated the local businessmen for their lack of support. The main use of the UVF funds was the purchase of the weapons and the salary of Lieutenant-General Sir George Richardson at £1,500 per annum.[44]

It seems unlikely that their funds were more than £150,000, placing a greater burden on those local initiatives to fund activities which had the obvious impact of creating local variations.[45]

Not everyone who enlisted in the army did so for 'King and Country' or even political motives. One UVF member from the Shankill, Jack Christie, later recalled that "when the war came it wasn't a challenge or anything to do with patriotism, it was simple; here's an escape route to get out of the mill, for surely life holds more than what this mill can offer?"[46]

Those who didn't join the new British Army formation were intended to be kept organised and ready at home; in the words of Carson, "I and those who remain behind will take care that Ulster is no invaded Province".[47]

Carson and other unionist leaders were also aware that by keeping the UVF together as a unit it would help in the redeployment of suitable forces to Ulster if the need arose in the future.[48]

A letter from Carson at 5 Eaton Place, London, to Lieutenant-General Richardson at the Town Hall, Belfast. dated 9 September 1914, sounded a cautionary note regarding enlistment at the cost of the efficiency of the remaining UVF, though perhaps also to ensure everyone regardless of ability would still be making a valuable contribution.

> Knowing as I do the loyalty and devotion of my friends in the Ulster Volunteer Force and on the Ulster Unionist Council, I am sure that many of them, whom age or physical causes debar

---

44 Bowman, Timothy, *Carson's Army: Ulster Volunteer Force, 1910-22* (2007).
45 Bowman, Timothy, *Carson's Army: Ulster Volunteer Force, 1910-22* (2007).
46 Grayson, Richard S, *Belfast Boys – How Unionists and Nationalists fought and died together in the First World War* (2009).
47 Orr, Philip, *The Road to the Somme* (1987).
48 Parkinson, Alan F, *Friends in High Places: Ulster's Resistance to Irish Home Rule, 1912-14* (2012).

Ulster Volunteers believed to be at Clandeboye. (Somme Museum: 1994-282)

from an arduous campaign, will Ulster pluck and regardless of personal consequences consider it their duty to tender their services to the new Ulster Division of Lord Kitchener's Army.

I earnestly beg of you as GOC, UVF, to make it known to all such Applicants or commissions of enlistment that it is my strongly expressed desire that such should remain with their several units of the UVF in Ulster and devote themselves to further recruiting and increasing the efficiency of the Force which remains.

I can assure them that the efficiency of the UVF for the defence of our shores and the training of the Drafts for the supply of men to the new Division now being formed is as patriots and as needful for the preservation of our great Empire as service with the colours.[49]

No-one who enlisted in the new Division was struck off the UVF lists; instead they were bound to return to the UVF when discharged from Imperial Service if the Home Rule crisis was not over.[50]

A year before war was declared, in May 1913, *The Morning Post* had described the Ulster Volunteer Force and hinted almost prophetically at the role which they were to play during the war:

> What these men have been preparing for in Ulster may be of value as a military asset in time of national emergency. I have seen the men at drill, I have seen them on parade, and experts assure me that in the matter of discipline, physique, and all things which go to the making of a military force they are worthy to rank with our regular soldiers. It is an open secret that, once assured of the maintenance unimpaired of the Union between Great Britain and Ireland under the Imperial Parliament alone, a vast proportion of the citizen army of Ulster would cheerfully hold itself at the disposal of the Imperial Government and volunteer for service either at home or abroad![51]

---

49 Letter from Sir Edward Carson to Lieutenant-General Richardson – 9 September 1914.
50 Memo No. 160 – Men Enlisting for Imperial Service – 12 September 1914.
51 McNeill, Ronald, *Ulster's Stand for Union* (1922).

In early September 1914 regimental and battalion commanders were informed that great care was to be taken in the cases of married men with dependant relatives; names of wives or relatives and the number of children were to be sent to the local sub-committee for the prevention and relief of distress caused by the war.[52]

The Commander of the Antrim Division, UVF, proposed to his Company Commanders that a "Roll of Honour" should be posted in a conspicuous place at each drill centre. This would contain "praiseworthy deeds" of any from the area who had distinguished themselves whilst on active service. It was hoped that this in turn would encourage further enlistments from within the ranks of the UVF.[53]

On the outbreak of war, 2,000,000 rounds of UVF ammunition were sold to the British Government at the cost of ninety shillings per 1,000 rounds, which Adgey claimed was cost price. An approach from Belgium for the UVF weapons was declined by Craig when the British Government refused to repeal the Home Rule Bill; it is likely the weapons would have been a free gift.[54]

Ambrose Ricardo, anticipating the formation of the 36th (Ulster) Division, raised two companies of the UVF in the late summer of 1914 which would become the nucleus of the 9th Battalion, The Royal Inniskilling Fusiliers, and was given the acting rank of Lieutenant Colonel. He would end the war with the rank of Brigadier General.[55]

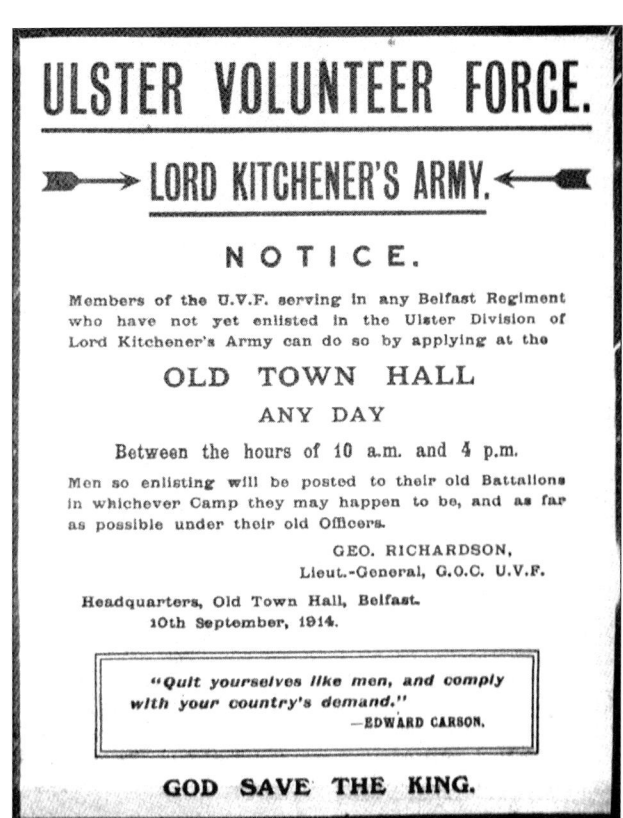

36th (Ulster) Division recruiting poster targeting at members of the Ulster Volunteer Force. (Somme Museum)

---

52 Memo – 3 September 1914.
53 Memo No. 162 – Antrim Division UVF – 21 September 1914.
54 Bowman, Timothy, *Carson's Army: Ulster Volunteer Force, 1910-22* (2007).
55 Ulster Volunteers, January 1913 – Ulster-Scots Community Network <http://www.ulster-scots.com/uploads/901740969819.PDF> (Accessed 5 August 2013).

Ulster Volunteers on parade, believed to be at Clandeboye. (Somme Museum: 1994-282)

In July 1914, Spender was instructed to hold himself in readiness to take up an appointment with the eastern command in Chatham despite Carson extracting a promise that regular officers involved with UVF would be posted to the 36th Division. On returning to England he was offered a position in his old department in the War Office. In October 1915 Spender, along with General Powell, General Nugent's predecessor to the Division, managed to have the decision reversed.[56] He ultimately joined the 36th (Ulster) Division as a General Staff Officer (GSO2) shortly before the Division embarked to France in October 1915.[57]

James Stronge, officer commanding the Tynan Company, 1st Armagh Battalion, Ulster Volunteer Force, and son and heir to the 5th Baronet, Sir James Stronge of Tynan Abbey, County Armagh, wrote a public letter to his men which was published 12 September 1914 in the *Portadown News*. His views were simple, that support of the Crown during this time of need would help in the long term to defeat the plans for Home Rule:

> … you have been given an opportunity, such as we scare dared hope for, of fighting, not amongst strangers, but side by side with your kindred, your friends and neighbours, for the honour of our country and the safety of our homes against a brutal enemy, as well as for the maintenance of the Union that we all hold so dear.
>
> The country looks to its sons to win for it a glorious place in the Army that Ulster is privileged to put at the orders of our beloved Sovereign. Do not let it look to you in vain, and rest assured that we shall not be allowed to suffer politically for doing our highest duty."[58]

At meetings in Upperlands, Innishrush and Maghera, County Londonderry, the Battalion second-in-command, H.J. Clark, explained to the Ulster Volunteers that they had received a call

---

56 Baguley, Margaret (ed)., *The Spender Correspondence, World War I and the Question of Ulster, The correspondence of Lilian and Wilfred Spender* (2009).
57 Ulster Volunteers, January 1913 – Ulster-Scots Community Network <http://www.ulster-scots.com/uploads/901740969819.PDF> (Accessed 5 August 2013).
58 Metcalfe, Nick, *Blacker's Boys* (2012).

Player's Cigarettes card depicting the insignia of the 36th (Ulster) Division. (Somme Museum: 1997-156)

to duty and a call to arms. Men volunteered at each meeting, while in Tobermore alone on one night thirty volunteered for army service.[59]

Unfortunately this call to serve with family, friends and neighbours would have grave implications for towns and villages across Ulster in the coming years.

The largest of Kitchener's New Armies was K5, comprising 142 locally raised battalions organised into twelve Divisions, numbered 30-41. The timing of the raising of the Ulster Division secured it the 36th designation. It was ultimately to comprise thirteen battalions formed from the larger UVF regimental areas; companies from the smaller areas in these and the platoons from local districts. There were also recruits from across Great Britain and Ireland with the level of Ulster Volunteer Force membership varying from unit to unit. Some men also transferred from the 10th (Irish) Division.[60]

The identification badge adopted by 36th Division was a red hand, the heraldic symbol for the Irish province of Ulster.

The 36th (Ulster) Division set up Headquarters in 29 Wellington Place, Belfast, and began the job of creating the Division. Three infantry brigades of 12 battalions in total along with three field companies of Royal Engineers, a signal company and Royal Army Medical Corps personnel were all to be recruited.

1 Brigade was from the City of Belfast, the 2nd from the counties of Antrim, Down, Armagh, Cavan and Monaghan and the 3rd from Tyrone, Londonderry, Donegal and Fermanagh with one battalion from Belfast.[61]

---

59 South Derry Volunteers: men 'of good courage' <http://www.newsletter.co.uk/news/features/south-derry-volunteers-men-of-good-courage-1-4888311> (Accessed 1 January 2015).
60 Metcalfe, Nick, *Blacker's Boys* (2012).
61 Metcalfe, Nick, *Blacker's Boys* (2012).

The regimental infantry badges of those regiments which the UVF members joined in the 36th (Ulster) Division. Left to right: Royal Irish Rifles; Royal Irish Fusiliers; Royal Inniskilling Fusiliers. (Somme Museum)

The engineers and Divisional signals were recruited in Belfast, the pioneer battalion was raised in County Down, although it had many men from County Armagh particularly from Lurgan.[62]

Within the Division there was also to be Royal Army Service Corps, raised mainly from men from rural areas with experience of horses, the cavalry was based on the Enniskillen Horse who had joined the Volunteers in 1913, and cyclist sections all formed primarily from men of the Ulster Volunteer Force. However as the UVF had no artillery the Divisional artillery was to be recruited in England from London; 153 and 154 Brigades, Royal Field Artillery, were to be recruited from Croydon, Norbury and Sydenham and the 172 and 173 Brigades from East and West Ham. They were planned to join the Division the following year. Therefore with no artillery being initially formed within the Division those men who had an interest on serving on horseback tended to join the mounted section of the Field Ambulance.[63]

James Craig, now Lieutenant-Colonel, and Captain Spender were given the task of building the Ulster Division. Spender became a General Staff Officer and Craig the Assistance Adjutant and Quartermaster General, whilst Sir George Richardson was unable to command the Division because of his seniority of rank, so that duty passed to Major General CH Powell, a former Indian Army officer.

Each of the three infantry regiments based in Ulster, the Royal Irish Rifles, the Royal Irish Fusilier and the Royal Inniskilling Fusiliers was licensed to create numerous supplementary battalions for Lord Kitchener's Army in addition to their regular and Territorial Army battalions. These Regiments would form the basis for the creation of the 36th Division infantry battalions.

---

62 Metcalfe, Nick, *Blacker's Boys* (2012).
63 Orr, Philip, *The Road to the Somme* (1987).

The order of battle was drawn up as follows:

107 Brigade
8th Bn, the Royal Irish Rifles (East Belfast Volunteers)
9th Bn, the Royal Irish Rifles (West Belfast Volunteers)
10th Bn, the Royal Irish Rifles (South Belfast Volunteers)
15th Bn, the Royal Irish Rifles (North Belfast Volunteers)

108 Brigade
11th Bn, the Royal Irish Rifles (South Antrim Volunteers)
12th Bn, the Royal Irish Rifles (Mid Antrim Volunteers)
13th Bn, the Royal Irish Rifles (1st County Down Volunteers)
9th Bn, the Royal Irish Fusiliers (Armagh, Monaghan and Cavan Volunteers)

109 Brigade
9th Bn, the Royal Inniskilling Fusiliers (Tyrone Volunteers)
10th Bn, the Royal Inniskilling Fusiliers (Derry Volunteers)
11th Bn, the Royal Inniskilling Fusiliers (Donegal and Fermanagh Volunteers)
14th Bn, the Royal Irish Rifles (Young Citizen Volunteers)

Pioneer Battalion
16th Bn, the Royal Irish Rifles (2nd County Down Volunteers)

Divisional Artillery
153rd Royal Field Artillery
154th Royal Field Artillery
172nd Royal Field Artillery
173rd Royal Field Artillery

Royal Engineers
121st Field Company, Royal Engineers
122nd Field Company, Royal Engineers
150th Field Company, Royal Engineers

Divisional Mounted Troops
1st Service Sqn, the 6th Inniskilling Dragoons
36th Divisional Signal Company, Royal Engineers
36th Divisional Cyclist Company

Royal Army Medical Corps
108th Field Ambulance
109th Field Ambulance
110th Field Ambulance
76th Sanitary Section

Other Divisional Troops
36th Divisional Train, Army Service Corps
48th Mobile Veterinary Section, Army Veterinary Corps

A postcard of the review of the cyclists of the 36th (Ulster) Division marching down Chichester Street, Belfast having passed the front of the City Hall before heading to England to complete their training. (J Luke)

Men of the Royal Army Medical Corps, 36th (Ulster) Division at Clandeboye Camp. (Somme Museum)

Men of D Company, 9th Service Battalion Royal Irish Fusiliers (Co Armagh, Monaghan and Cavan Volunteers) undergoing training at Clandeboye Camp. (Somme Museum)

Six reserve battalions were also formed to provide a draft for the Division as the ranks would be depleted during active service.

A number of Ulster Unionists in early September believed that so many UVF members would come forward, enabling two Divisions to be formed instead of one. The reality was somewhat different, with strong regional variations resulting in problems in many rural areas in achieving the number necessary for one Division.[64]

This reluctance of a force raised for home defence to enlist for overseas service is not dissimilar to similar problems experienced in Great Britain with the Territorial Force units who had been established in 1908 as purely a home defence force, yet with the deteriorating military situation were asked to take the Imperial Service Obligation and agreeing to serve overseas; some were highly willing with others less so at the turn of events.[65]

The 107 (Belfast Brigade) was commenced before recruiting for the rural battalions and by 10 September 1914, Lieutenant General Sir George Richardson reported the recruiting "practically complete" perhaps creating false expectations of how easy recruitment would be, perhaps again leading to the suggestion of a second Division. However this initial surge was both in the easier industrial part of Ulster and coinciding with the period of highest enlistment recorded in Britain.[66]

In reality, by December 1914 the Division was still stated to be 1,995 under strength, leading to recruiting notices being sent out to all UVF units to be read out during parades, calling on men to come forward to complete the Division.[67]

---

64   Bowman, Timothy, *Carson's Army: Ulster Volunteer Force, 1910-22* (2007).
65   Bowman, Timothy, *Carson's Army: Ulster Volunteer Force, 1910-22* (2007).
66   Bowman, Timothy, *Carson's Army: Ulster Volunteer Force, 1910-22* (2007).
67   Bowman, Timothy, *Carson's Army: Ulster Volunteer Force, 1910-22* (2007).

ULSTER VOLUNTEER FORCE ORDERS.

U.V.F. O. 148.
1914.

ULSTER DIVISION—ENLISTMENT. This order to be read out on three consecutive Parades. For the information of all concerned the undermentioned statement is published, showing the numbers still required by Trades, etc., in the Ulster Division, and the G.O.C. hopes that Regimental and Battalion Commanders will take every opportunity to point out to the men the necessity of responding to this appeal so as to complete the Division. Railway Warrants will be granted free, to join any units selected, and arrangements are complete whereby every man enlisting is immediately provided with full uniform, including great coat, and the difficulties regarding separation allowances have now been overcome.

	ESTABLISHMENT. MEN	STRENGTH. MEN.	STILL WANTED. MEN.
INFANTRY	13,911	12,854	1,057
CYCLIST COMPANY	290	—	290
CAVALRY	165	200	—
R.A.M.C.	706	609	97
R.E.	—	—	—
R.E.—Bricklayers	48	27	21
Carpenters & Joiners	80	37	43
Clerks	10	10	—
Harness Makers	7	—	7
Coopers	4	2	2
Masons	24	10	14
Draughtsmen	4	4	—
Electricians	4	4	—
Engine Drivers	8	8	—
Fitters & Turners	16	39	—
Blacksmiths, etc.	30	18	12
Surveyors	4	—	4
Tailors	8	6	2
Wheelwrights	10	2	8
Labourers	20	8	12
Shoeing and Carriage Smiths	4	2	2
Harness Makers	1	—	1
Telegraphist, Line	26	—	26
Telegraphist, Office	18	4	14
Blacksmiths, etc.	3	2	1
Signallers	50	37	22
Shoeing and Carriage Smiths	2	—	2
Drivers, Field	114	39	75
Drivers, Signal	44	—	44
A.S.C.—			
Wheelers	19	5	14
Saddlers	14	3	11
Farriers	15	1	14
Motor Drivers	4	—	4
Drivers (horse)	370	140	230
Clerks	20	—	20
General Duties	100	57	43
Trumpeters	5	2	3
	16,258	14,320	1,995

UVF Order No. 148 – 1914. (Somme Museum)

Captain Robert Orr, 3rd Battalion, Somerset Light Infantry, formerly adjutant and second in command, 1st Battalion, North Antrim Regiment, UVF, was killed in action on 19 December 1914. His last message to his comrades in the Ulster Volunteer Force, written two days previously, 17 December, was read to the members of his former Battalion on three successive drill nights in January 1915 and reinforced the belief that the UVF at home still needed to prepare:[68]

> I wish to impress on the Volunteers of the 1st North Antrim Regiment that it is of the *utmost* importance for every man serving in the UVF to turn regularly out to their drills and endeavour to become efficient in drill and musketry. As Adjutant I expect to find, if I am spared to return home again, that my regiment has gained ground in efficiency and discipline, and, at the same time, has responded to Sir Edward Carson's command "to hold Ulster intact" during their brother Volunteers' absence at the front. For my part, I shall sincerely rely on my regiment doing their duty, and I can't say more.

Whilst membership of the units was not always solely from the Ulster Volunteer Force most of its members though were from Ulster. However the list of the 14th Royal Irish Rifles (Young Citizen Volunteers) shows a slightly different make-up. Whilst undated it does not list deaths, suggesting it was compiled prior to overseas service and indicates that a number of members came from outside the Belfast recruiting area of the YCV; 20 percent came from elsewhere in Ireland, 29 percent came from Great Britain and 1 percent came from overseas, principally the USA.[69]

The 11th Royal Inniskilling Fusiliers was unusual for a rural battalion in that it relied on other recruits to fill its ranks; C Company being formed by the British League for the Support of Ulster and the Union, those Ulster Unionist sympathisers in Great Britain, whilst another full company was raised in Glasgow.[70]

Young Citizen Volunteers on parade in front of Sir Edward Carson at Balmoral, 6 June 1914. (Somme Museum)

---

68 Battalion Orders, 1st Batt North Antrim Regiment – 4 January 1915.
69 Bowman, Timothy, *Carson's Army: Ulster Volunteer Force, 1910-22* (2007).
70 Bowman, Timothy, *Carson's Army: Ulster Volunteer Force, 1910-22* (2007).

This shift of emphasis towards the war effort was reflected in the monthly reports from the Royal Irish Constabulary's Inspector General. Beginning with his September 1914 monthly report, he ceased to include a special section on the Ulster and Irish Volunteers, as he had since early 1913, instead including a section on "the State of public feeling in Ireland in connection with the War."[71]

Ireland's relationship with Germany prior to the outbreak of hostilities and even during the war reflected the complexity of the Home Rule issue.

In January 1911 James Craig had said that the Kaiser would be preferable to John Redmond.[72]

Less than a year later Fred Crawford said "if they were to be put out of the Union … he would infinitely prefer to change his allegiance right over to the Emperor of Germany";[73] Germany was a protestant country.

Prior to the outbreak of war and the reports of German actions in the overrun areas of Belgium and France, many Ulstermen looked upon Germany favourably with regard to their cause even though they now found themselves facing Germany as the enemy on the battlefield.

Those organising the Easter Rebellion in Dublin had hoped for German aid, largely based on the support they had already received in arms and ammunition. A rather vague arrangement existed with German contacts who had undertaken to send arms (20,000 rifles and then machine guns) to County Kerry 'by' Easter Sunday. The SS *Libau* had originally been the British ship the SS *Castro*, but had been captured by the German Navy in the Kiel Canal in August 1914. For the purposes of landing arms in support of the Easter Rebellion she masqueraded as the Norwegian vessel SS *Aud* with the camouflage of a cargo of timber.[74] Due to a combination of factors, which included the ship having no radio and leaked information, the armaments were not offloaded and the rendezvous with the German submarine carrying Roger Casement never occurred; Casement being arrested shortly after his landing. The *Aud* and her German crew tried to escape to the open sea again but instead she was cornered by British ships, including destroyers. The *Aud*'s Captain Spindler allowed himself to be escorted towards Cork harbour by HMS *Bluebell*[75] but scuttled his vessel en route before being then interned with his crew for the duration of the war.[76]

Communications with Germany, although a little difficult was still possible, with many messages being passed through Count Bernstorff, the German Ambassador in the United States of America.[77]

During the Easter Rebellion it was reported that two Austro-Hungarian officers were captured in Balbrigan, County Dublin, making bombs.

On Monday, 7 September the Belfast newspapers reported the departure of the first men of the Ulster Division to their camp at Ballykinlar. The following week they were reporting the arrival of men from Lisburn, Bangor and Holywood to encamp at Clandeboye.

Even with the departure of the first men, Belfast recruitment continued. William Williamson, aged 17 years and originally from off Donegall Pass joined up on 7 September at the Old Town Hall, having previously being in the Sandy Row UVF. William and his colleagues were marched to the County Down Railway before travelling to Newcastle at Slieve Donard where they built a

---

71   Grob-Fitzgibbon, *Turning Points of The Irish Revolution: The British Government, Intelligence and the Cost of Indifference, 1912-1921* (2007).
72   Stewart, ATQ, *The Ulster Crises* (1967).
73   Stewart, ATQ, *The Ulster Crises* (1967).
74   Shearman, Hugh, *Not an Inch: A Study of Northern Ireland and Lord Craigavon* (1942).
75   Shearman, Hugh, *Not an Inch: A Study of Northern Ireland and Lord Craigavon* (1942).
76   <http://en.wikipedia.org/wiki/SS_Libau> accessed> (Accessed 5 May 2014).
77   Shearman, Hugh, *Not an Inch: A Study of Northern Ireland and Lord Craigavon* (1942).

Men of D Company, 9th Service Battalion Royal Irish Fusiliers (Co Armagh, Monaghan and Cavan Volunteers) at Clandeboye Camp. (Somme Museum)

Postcard depicting the interior of a tent used by the 36th (Ulster) Division at Donard Camp, Newcastle. (Somme Museum: 1996-280)

camp which they stayed in for three months, sleeping on the ground on rubber with two blankets, one below and one on top.[78]

The camp at Ballykinlar had been re-opened initially for the UVF men drafted into the 7th Service Battalion, The Royal Irish Rifles (North Belfast Regiment), with other battalions being formed as soon as the men could be attested. The men of East, West and South Belfast Regiments UVF were marched down to the Old Town Hall, Belfast for medical examination and attestation. Major Hall, late of the Royal Welsh Fusiliers was appointed as Camp Commandant and Captain Page appointed as Adjutant and Quartermaster. When the first detail were medically examined and attested they paraded on Saturday 5 September and left Belfast at 8.30am on a special train for Ballykinlar Camp.[79]

It wasn't long before Ballykinlar was temporarily full, resulting in the 360 men from West Belfast UVF who had assembled at Stewart's Yard, being presented with a box of cigarettes, marched to and enlisted at the Old Town Hall and put aboard trains for a new camp at Donard Lodge in Newcastle.[80]

Permission was also granted to open a 'Halt' at Ballykinlar, between Tullymurry and Dundrum stations to better facilitate the movement of soldiers. The work was undertaken by the Belfast and County Down Railway with the halt opening in March 1915.[81]

The camp at Clandeboye was opened from Monday, 14 September 1914.[82]

In order "to give the volunteers who had enlisted a couple of hours'" enjoyment before they headed for their camp, the people of Portadown organised a concert in the town hall on 19 September 1914 for those members of the UVF. Organised by W Watt, the manager of the Portadown Spinning Company, there was a selection of variety acts, sketches and songs. One song was reported as being particularly well received, being what was perceived as a new version of a 'rebel' song. The refrain was "Gough Save Ireland" and it was reported that "the words seemed well known, as the Volunteers joined in heartily in the singing."[83]

Christmas card for 1914 from the 15th Service Battalion Royal Irish Riles (North Belfast Volunteers) being trained in Ballykinlar Camp illustrating their previous links with the Ulster Volunteer Force. (Somme Museum)

---

78 William Williamson, WW1 Interview 108, DOB 1897 – Somme Museum.
79 UVF Orders 106, 1914 – Somme Museum.
80 Grayson, Richard S, *Belfast Boys – How Unionists and Nationalists fought and died together in the First World War* (2009).
81 UVF Order 111,1914 – Somme Museum.
82 UVF Orders 110, 1914 – Somme Museum.
83 Cousins, Colin, *Armagh and the Great War* (2011).

Donard Camp, 22 September 1914. (Somme Museum)

Whilst the Ulster Volunteer Force were enlisting and training for service in the Imperial Army, Carson had a visit on 13 March 1915 from Alfred Graves, a Redmond supporter, with a proposal for a Home Rule Government in Ulster. Carson was interested in the suggestion of proportional representation which would protect the Catholic minority. Graves informed Redmond that Carson thought that if Catholics assisted in the Ulster government it could lead to either a fusion of the two Home Rule Governments, Dublin and Belfast, or if finance broke the Home Rule system then a return to the Union. Either way Carson was trying to retain the Union or at least a united Ireland.[84]

In Dublin massive numbers of the Loyal Dublin Volunteers enlisted with up to 80 members joining the Dublin 'Pals' Battalion' almost immediately on the outbreak of war. Perhaps more significantly, whilst not able to be members of the Ulster Volunteer Force, many travelled north to join their fellow 'volunteers' within the ranks of the 36th (Ulster) Division; a considerable number joined the 9th Battalion Royal Inniskilling Fusiliers (County Tyrone Volunteers), it having one entire platoon consisting of Dublin men. One individual, William Crozier from St Stephen's Green in Dublin applied for a commission to the 9th Battalion on the basis that he had drilled for 11 months with the Loyal Dublin Volunteers. Brigadier General Hickman endorsed the application, stating that; "This gentleman is quite the right stamp. If appointed he will be serving with and commanding some of the men he has trained during the last year."[85]

It is recorded that in September 1914 alone, 60 men left Fowler Hall for Ballykinlar Camp to join the 'Tyrones'.[86]

---

84 Lewis, Geoffrey, *Carson: The man who divided Ireland* (2006).
85 <http://www.newsletter.co.uk/features/the-loyal-dublin-volunteers-a-forgotten-organisation-1-3719467> (Accessed 5 February 2014).
86 <http://www.newsletter.co.uk/features/the-loyal-dublin-volunteers-a-forgotten-organisation-1-3719467> (Accessed 5 February 2014).

In preparation for overseas service those Ulster Volunteers who enlisted into the new 'Ulster' Division were divided into the following training camps:[87]

FIRST BRIGADE
Station – Ballykinlar Camp, Co. Down
15th Service Battalion Royal Irish Riles (North Belfast Volunteers)
8th Service Battalion Royal Irish Rifles (East Belfast Volunteers)
Station – Donard Lodge Camp, Newcastle
9th Service Battalion Royal Irish Rifles (West Belfast Volunteers)
10th Service Battalion Royal Irish Rifles (South Belfast Volunteers)

SECOND BRIGADE
Station – Clandeboye Camp, Co. Down
11th Service Battalion Royal Irish Rifles (South Antrim Volunteers)
12th Service Battalion Royal Irish Rifles (Mid Antrim Volunteers)
13th Service Battalion Royal Irish Rifles (Co. Down Volunteers)
9th Service Battalion Royal Irish Fusiliers (Co Armagh, Monaghan and Cavan Volunteers)

ATTACHED TO BRIGADE
Details – Field Companies, Royal Engineers
Details – Signal Companies, Royal Engineers

THIRD BRIGADE
Station – Finner Camp, Ballyshannon, Co. Donegal
9th Service Battalion Royal Inniskilling Fusiliers (Tyrone Volunteers)
10th Service Battalion Royal Inniskilling Fusiliers (Derry Volunteers)
11th Service Battalion Royal Inniskilling Fusiliers (Donegal & Fermanagh Volunteers)
14th Service Battalion Royal Irish Rifles (Young Citizen Volunteers)

By the end of October 1914, under instructions from Major-General Powell, CB, GOC the Ulster Division, the Ulster Volunteer Force, command decided to enlist another Battalion, the 16th Royal Irish Rifles, which was known as the 2nd Battalion County Down Volunteers; it was enlisted and located at Brownlow House, Lurgan,[88] becoming the Pioneer Battalion to the Division.

As part of the arrangements for the new battalions engaging in active service, FP Crozier was asked to arrange the ceremony for the handing over of the Colours of the 'Holy Boys', into the safe custody of Belfast St Anne's Cathedral.

The casual observer may have missed the subtly of elements of this event. A detachment of the 1st Norfolk Regiment was present with colours and colour party alongside the guard of honour from the UVF West Belfast Regiment, who along with their colours presented arms with the German Mauser rifles smuggled past the British fleet which helped in causing the disruption in the Curragh and Whitehall.[89] The UVF also later provided a guard of honour for the 1st Norfolk regiment when they embarked from Belfast to the war.[90]

---

87 UVF HQ's note.
88 UVF Orders 128, 1914 – Somme Museum.
89 Brig-Gen FP Crozier, CB, CMG, DSO, *A Brass Hat in No Man's Land* (1930).
90 Grayson, Richard S, *Belfast Boys – How Unionists and Nationalists fought and died together in the First World War* (2009).

10th Battalion, the Royal Irish Rifles at Brownlow House, Lurgan.
(The Royal Ulster Rifles Museum)

A presentation box from Stewart Blacker Quin, Stewarts Yard, Shankill Road, Belfast to the Ulster Volunteers from West Belfast who enlisted in 9th Battalion, The Royal Irish Rifles in camp at Donard Camp. September 1914. (Somme Museum)

Rifleman Duncan Davidson, 14th Battalion (Young Citizen Volunteers) The Royal Irish Rifles. (R Black)

The Colonel, Adjutant and Sergeants of the 14th Battalion, (Young Citizen Volunteers) Royal Irish Rifles at Randallstown Camp, 28 January 1915. (Somme Museum)

The Ulster Volunteers in East Belfast joined the division in large numbers, becoming the 8th Battalion the Royal Irish Rifles also known as "Ballymacarrett's Own".[91] Whilst in the west of the city the men of the Shankill were also joining there was some initial reluctance due to their fear of impending Home Rule. In order to encourage the men to join up and overcome what Percy Crozier referred to as "political paralysis of the top storey", he inflated the enlistment figures.[92] Crozier had been appointed Major and second-in-command of the 9th Battalion, The Royal Irish Rifles (West Belfast Volunteers), and had refused his recall to the colours in Dublin at the outbreak of war to form a company of Royal Irish Fusiliers. After speaking with James Craig he decided to stay in Belfast with the Ulster Volunteer Force.[93]

The Young Citizen Volunteers of Belfast enlisted into the 14th Battalion, The Royal Irish Rifles, along with many men who had not been in the YCVs. One such individual was American citizen, Jim Maultsaid, who had attempted to join the Inniskillings in Clifton Street on 5 August but was refused, but instead went with some friends who were YCVs and joined the 14th Rifles.[94]

One young man who enlisted into the 14th Battalion on 14 September recorded in his diary how, after his enlistment in the Old Town Hall, that later in the evening following tea, the magistrates appeared and took large groups at once for the swearing in, each man signing on for three years or the duration of the war. Whilst the YCV had been formed on eight companies, on joining the 14th Battalion each man chose his own company, many sticking with friends where possible. At their first muster the whole event was well organised under the leadership and direction of the men who had been NCOs in the YCVs.[95] These Belfast men were destined for Finner Camp in County Donegal to begin their army training.

---

91 Orr, Philip, *The Road to the Somme* (1987).
92 Orr, Philip, *The Road to the Somme* (1987).
93 Causeway; Cultural Traditions Journal, Spring 1995 – The Myth of the 36th (Ulster). Division – T Bowman.
94 Orr, Philip, *The Road to the Somme* (1987).
95 GHM 'Service with the 14th Battalion RIR in the 1914-18 war – RURRM – unpublished.

11

The UVF at Home and at War

Despite the recruitment of many Ulster Volunteers into the new division and the hold on Home Rule, Carson expressed a strong desire that special divine services be held across Ulster to commemorate the signing of Ulster's Solemn League and Covenant. The necessary arrangements were made with the heads of the Protestant churches with the proposal that the services would be held on Sunday, 27 September.

The respective battalion commanders were ordered to make arrangements for the whole battalion to parade for divine service, if convenient at one selected place, or where the battalions were scattered over a wider area then at a number of selected places. Within Belfast arrangements were held for the special services to be held in the Ulster Hall, St Anne's Cathedral and the Assembly Hall.[1]

In October the creation of the Ulster Division necessitated a restructuring of the various Ulster Volunteer Force battalions and companies across the country following the vacancies which enlistment had caused. All UVF Battalions were to continue on the eight (or more) company organisation with the battalions of the regiments of the Belfast, Antrim and Down Divisions to be drilled as 'Rifles' whilst the Battalions of the other Regiments were to be drilled as 'Infantry of the Line';[2] this was amended a month later such that the Belfast, Antrim and Down Divisions were also to be drilled as 'Infantry of the line'.[3]

Likewise a reorganisation was necessary and evident at headquarters with details of a headquarters council being circulated to the various units and detachments. The Headquarters Council comprised the following ten members:

```
GOC
CSO and Officer i/c/ Administration
Mr Lloyd Campbell, AQMG
Mr BWD Montgomery, DAAG
Mr George Clarke    }
Mr GP Morrish       } Members
Mr Edward Sclater   }
Mr Ed Archdale      }
Col. RG Sharman-Crawford, Finance
Mr R Dawson Bates, Secretary, UVF[4]
```

---

1 UVF Orders 114, 1914 – Somme Museum.
2 UVF Orders 123, 1914 – Somme Museum.
3 UVF Orders 133.1914 – Somme Museum.
4 UVF Orders 121, 1914 – Somme Museum.

KITCHENER'S ARMY in the Making at NEWCASTLE (South, West, and North Regiments, U.V.F.).

Postcard depicting the camp built at the foot of Slieve Donard, Newcastle for those men of the South, West and North Belfast UVF who enlisted in the 36th (Ulster) Division.
(Somme Museum)

With the reduction in membership due to enlistment into the Imperial Services, in the autumn of 1914 the Ulster Volunteer Force units undertook some of their last major parades in Ulster to assist recruiting to the British Army.[5]

Recruitment to the 36th Division was slower in the rural areas and Carson and John Stewart-Moore had difficulty in persuading the local UVF men to enrol for service overseas, only two or three came forward to join the division. Some had the belief that only the work-shy or worthless enlisted whilst others had memories of stories of soldiers returning from military service to find no jobs or prospects. Ironically Stewart-Moore himself had difficulty in enlisting. When he applied for a commission in the 12th Royal Irish Rifles (Mid-Antrim Volunteers) his parents objected that he hadn't the health for the job. A local doctor, possibly under the influence of his parents refused to pass him fit, however not to be deterred, Stewart-Moore travelled to Dublin where a doctor gave him a clean bill of health and he returned to Ballymoney Town Hall and enlisted in the 12th Rifles.

Hugh James Adams later estimated that perhaps only seven or eight out of every hundred young men in the Crossgar neighbourhood joined the 36th Division. However in the Lisburn area the response was much better with Albert Bruce of Lambeg being one of 250 who marched to Lisburn and joined the 11th Rifles (South Antrim Volunteers) as a group.

In County Armagh recruiting was slower, perhaps reflected by the comments of a Volunteer in later years, "You cannot get up and leave a farm the way you can walk away from a loom in a factory."[6]

---

5   Bowman, Timothy, *Carson's Army: Ulster Volunteer Force, 1910-22* (2007).
6   Orr, Philip, *The Road to the Somme* (1987).

Men of A and B Company of the Central Antrim Volunteers, 36th (Ulster) Division at Clandeboye Camp. (Somme Museum)

In Hamiltonsbawn outside Armagh, the officer commanding the local Volunteers, the Reverend Mr McLaughlin, attempted to encourage his men by informing them that their comrades in Tyrone and Belfast had enlisted. However, instead of enlisting the men wrote to their regimental commander Major Stewart Blacker, stating that "We signed the covenant to defend Ulster against a Dublin parliament and any of our commanders who asks [sic] us to leave Ulster or to fight for this notorious government now in office is betraying Ulster men and women worse than Lundy in Derry".[7]

In an effort to boost recruitment Carson began a series of recruiting speeches across the country.[8]

Royal Irish Constabulary reports on recruitment between 15 December 1914 and 15 December 1915 indicate that a total of 51,000 Irishmen had enlisted. Of these 10,794 were National Volunteers, 8,203 were Ulster Volunteers and 32,144 belonged to neither group.[9]

Tommy Jordan had tried previously to join the UVF but they told him "they wanted men not boys", however he recalled that:

> a few months later a man took us to an old dance hall opposite the Albert Clock where there were a lot of men. We were sworn in and given a shilling. I was 17. I was given boots, socks riding britches and a tunic and put them into a white kit bag. We were then given two days' pay and felt wealthy.

He then went to the Northern Railway were he caught the train which took him to the Depot in Omagh where he was put into the Cycle Corp, recalling "there were 6 platoons, it was lovely and we used to ride out to the Sligo road, great memories."[10]

---

7   Cousins, Colin, *Armagh and the Great War* (2011).
8   Orr, Philip, *The Road to the Somme* (1987).
9   Cousins, Colin, *Armagh and the Great War* (2011).
10 Tommy Jordan, VHS Tape – Somme Museum.

Postcard depicting the camp at Clandeboye occupied by the Ulster Volunteers who enlisted in the 36th (Ulster) Division. (Somme Museum)

In one speech, 8 January 1915, Carson reflected on the Government's passing of the Home Rule Act:

> ... it is true that the Government has broken a solemn truce with us and that it has endeavoured to betray us to our inveterate foes, but these disagreeable facts cannot be allowed to hinder us from doing our duty to the Empire. The Government is a transitory thing, the Empire abides. We cannot penalise the British people because a Government which does not represent the majority of the nation, is seeking to do us a grave wrong.[11]

Despite this Carson would claim that recruiting figures were evidence of Ulster's loyalty with the *Belfast News Letter* claiming in April 1915 that 35,000 recruits had joined the army from Ulster and only 15,000 from the other Irish provinces.

Other sources, based on figures from the Annual Register for 1914 suggested that recruiting in Belfast was better than other cities in the United Kingdom, with 305 soldiers recruited per 10,000 of the population.[12] The Division was also to have others join their ranks with FP Crozier relating how he collected about 100 recruits from London and another 800 from Glasgow,[13] whilst General Mackinnon, GOC Western Command, received reports that a Ulster Division officer was trying to enlist men from Liverpool.[14] In TJ Campbell's *Fifty Years of Ulster 1890-1940*, he stated that just as many National Volunteers enlisted in the New Army by the end of 1915 as had Ulster Volunteers. He went further, stating that of the 49,400 Irishmen who actually died in the war, 39,400 were from the south and 10,000 were from the six Ulster counties which were to be subject to partition. He also stated that as early as 1 November 1914 more than 16,000 National Volunteers had already enlisted.[15]

More recent research however suggests the total figure of Irish troops for the duration of the war was 206-210,000 of which 140,460 were volunteers. Approximately 65,000 were Catholic which means the majority of those who enlisted were Protestant, or at least non-Catholic; approximately 60 percent from the Province of Ulster. Likewise the total number of war dead is now estimated to be much lower; some 30-35,000.[16]

---

11   *The Northern Whig* – 8 January 1915.
12   McNeill, Ronald, *Ulster's Stand for Union* (2010).
13   Brig-Gen FP Crozier, CB, CMG, DSO, *A Brass Hat in No Man's Land* (1930).
14   Causeway; Cultural Traditions Journal, Spring 1995 – The Myth of the 36th (Ulster) Division – T Bowman.
15   Campbell, TJ, *Fifty Years of Ulster 1890-1940* (1941).
16   Hughes, Dr Gavin, *The Hounds of Ulster* (2012).

The Ulster Volunteers on parade at Clandeboye being watched by interested members of the public.
(Somme Museum)

Despite the call to serve with the 36th Division others chose not to. Frank Hall was offered the post of Assistant Paymaster of the Ulster Division at Newtownards, however he declined the post and instead travelled to England, enlisted and was offered a post in Military Intelligence. He became MI5's fifth most senior official, forming a section with responsibility for the Dominions, Colonies and Ireland.

With the codename 'Q' he was Belfast's MI5 chief and was responsible for scrutinising the activities of Sir Roger Casement and other Irish 'disloyals'. Hall was also one of the three men who interrogated Casement in London after his arrest in County Kerry.[17]

The *Lurgan Mail* reminded their readership in September 1914 that as a result of the enlistment of Volunteers the production in the local factories had halved and that "shoemakers, painters, plumbers, saddlers, carpenters and masons and printers too, all are feeling the effects of volunteering."[18]

Although many officers from the Ulster Volunteer Force had left to join the British Army the Unionist leadership still wanted to preserve the Ulster Volunteers as a viable force, very aware that the issue of Home Rule and partition would again be revisited when the war ended. There were also some fears, real or merely perceived, of a German naval raid on Ulster, and so the leadership recast the role of the Ulster Volunteers as a home defence force to ensure its continued existence until the end of the war and the introduction of Home Rule.

There were others at home who also wished to make a contribution to the defence of their homeland. At Ye Olde Castle Restaurant, Belfast, on 4 February 1915, a meeting was held to

---

17   Ulster Volunteers, January 1913 – Ulster-Scots Community Network <http://www.ulster-scots.com/uploads/901740969819.PDF> (Accessed 5 August 2013).
18   Cousins, Colin, *Armagh and the Great War* (2011).

inaugurate a defence corps. At the meeting it was agreed that membership would be open to all men between 18 and 60 year of age and it would be non-sectarian and non-political. Membership would be for the duration of the war, and clearly in attempt to support the recruitment into the Army, anyone eligible for service in the regular army would not be permitted to join.[19]

At a subsequent meeting on 27 April in St. George's Market, 500 men were enrolled in the Irish Home Defence Corps; membership costing one shilling per month.

The Belfast group, now called the Belfast Volunteer Defence Corps, comprised 500 members, a band, and an ambulance corps. Local military tailors also advertised Volunteer Defence Corps (VDC) uniforms for sale. By February 1916, the umbrella Volunteer Training Corps in Ireland was 2,434 strong with the Belfast Defence Corps being the single largest unit with 917 members.[20]

The Belfast Volunteer Training Corps (VTC) was given permission by Belfast Corporation Markets Committee to use the Long Market (St George's Market) as a rifle range, two days a week. This would involve bringing in targets, sandbags, etc., each day it was to be used. The purpose of the VTC was to protect the docks, shipyards and other vital points.[21] They also helped the Harbour Police at the sheds of outgoing passenger steamers.[22]

The organisation was to spread outside Belfast, to Newtownards on 23 August, where in the Town Hall a meeting passed a resolution to form a local corps.

Mr FT Geddes, Company Commander, Belfast Volunteer Defence Corps. (T Wylie)

Likewise at a meeting in the Assembly Rooms in Lisburn, following a vigorous speech from Mr John Bristow, the commandant of the Belfast Volunteer Home Defence Corps, those present agreed unanimously to form a Lisburn Branch of the Corps.[23]

By the 8 December 1915 the VDC mounted guards at Belfast docks (County Down side). Such was their success that the Belfast Harbour Commissioners via the Superintendent of Harbour

---

19 *Northern Whig* – 14 June 1915.
20 Bowman, Timothy, *Carson's Army: Ulster Volunteer Force, 1910-22* (2007).
21 Tom Wylie.
22 *Belfast News Letter* – 10th January 1916.
23 *Belfast News Letter* – 5 August 1915.

Police reported 5 January 1916 that the VDC had done an excellent job watching the docks.

There were a number of attempts to incorporate the Ulster Volunteer Force into the Volunteer Training Corps but these were opposed by the Ulster Unionist and UVF leadership, probably as a result of a fear of losing control and also that Ulster Volunteer Force and Irish National Volunteer members may have ended up serving in the same units.[24]

Throughout the year they held various route marches, rifle practices and drills.[25]

It appears that during the war some members of the Lisburn and Dublin UVF left and joined the VTC which they claimed was a more effective organisation.[26]

The Volunteer Training Corps remains today in the guise of a Masonic Lodge which was formed as lodge No.439 on 19 April 1918 by members of the Belfast Volunteers.[27]

By June 1915 the UVF Antrim Divisional Commander addressed the desire of some Volunteers in wanting to join the Irish Home Defence Corps. He informed his men that the matter had been referred to the GOC UVF and he "has decided that it must be left to the good sense of the men as to which organisation they will belong." Whilst not wanting to deter Volunteers from joining an organisation which appears to offer a more active form of duty to the State, he reminded them that if an actual danger threatened Ulster the UVF would in all probability be organised as a military Force equal to any of the Irish Home Defence Corps. The Divisional Commander also issued a warning that under no circumstances were any arms, ammunition or accoutrements which had been wholly or partially paid for by UVF funds to be used for any purpose not connected to UVF service.[28]

Whilst elements of the Volunteers were undertaking training within the new Ulster Division the remaining members of the Ulster Volunteers continued their training within the old structures. The Ulster Volunteer Force GOC watched field operations of the Left Half, 1st Battalion, North Down Regiment, Wednesday 3 March 1915, under the Command of Colonel Sharman Crawford. The exercise was a night operation during which the communications between various companies proved effective and the scheme well planned and executed; particular reference being given to the efficient ambulance arrangements.

When the date for the 36th Division to leave Ulster approached local Ulster Volunteer Force Companies held meetings in Orange Halls and presented gifts to their former comrades who had

Bronzed die-struck cap badge of The Belfast Volunteer Defence Corps. (T Wylie)

---

24 Bowman, Timothy, *Carson's Army: Ulster Volunteer Force, 1910-22* (2007).
25 Tom Wylie – *Bulletin of the Military Historical Society* – Vol.45, No.194.
26 Bowman, Timothy, *Carson's Army: Ulster Volunteer Force, 1910-22* (2007).
27 Tom Wylie – *Bulletin of the Military Historical Society* – Vol.45, No.194.
28 Memo 184 – Enlistment in Irish Defence Corps – Antrim Division UVF – 27 June 1915.

"Tandragee Orange Heroes", B Company, Royal Irish Fusiliers at Clandeboye Camp. (Somme Museum)

joined the British Army. Local women in Ulster's towns and villages formed 'comfort committees' organising collections of socks, mittens, mufflers and helmets for their 'lads'.[29]

Saturday, 8 May 1915, marked the day when Ulster officially said farewell to the 36th (Ulster) Division, and the former members of the Ulster Volunteers in its ranks bade farewell to those who remained in the Ulster Volunteer Force at home. The event was marked by a review of the 36th Division at Malone, Belfast where Major-General Sir Hugh McCalmont, KCB, CVO, former MP for North Antrim, took the salute. Many shops and works closed for the day as did schools, to enable the population to watch the 17,000 men of the Division march to the City Hall where the salute was taken by Major-General McCalmont and the Lord Mayor, taking an hour and a half to pass the dais.[30] After it passed the crowd sang 'God Save the King' before dispersing.

The Division, less the 9th Royal Inniskilling Fusiliers, quarantined by an outbreak of measles, finally left Belfast on 1 and 2 July by train to Dublin where they embarked from Kingstown (now Dun Laoghaire) for Holyhead, Wales, to complete their training at Seaforde on the Sussex coast.[31]

The loss of experienced officers both to the Ulster Division and, in the case of the Earl of Clanwilliam and Lord Castlereagh, to their respective former regiments, the Household Cavalry and the Royal Horse Guards had a significant impact on the remaining Ulster Volunteer Force. UVF Headquarters for example suggested that as the 3rd South Down Regiment had no Commanding Officer remaining, that the battalion could be run by a committee. This suggestion was not well received by elements within the Battalion, such that it appears that the unit folded soon after this as the UVF Headquarters washed their hands of resolving the situation. This decline was not by any means unique and by the autumn of 1914 a number of units had effectively ceased to exist.[32]

---

29 Orr, Philip, *The Road to the Somme* (1987).
30 Metcalfe, Nick, *Blacker's Boys* (2012).
31 Metcalfe, Nick, *Blacker's Boys* (2012).
32 Bowman, Timothy, *Carson's Army: Ulster Volunteer Force, 1910-22* (2007).

A review of the 36th (Ulster) Division, part of Kitchener's Army, marching down Chichester Street, Belfast having passed the front of the City Hall. (J Luke)

Inspection of the 36th (Ulster) Division passing in front of Belfast City Hall prior to leaving Belfast for further training in Seaforde, England. (Somme Museum)

In May 1915, due to the number of volunteers joining the Ulster Division, the Headquarters Council of the Ulster Volunteer Force decided to amalgamate the remaining elements of West Belfast Regiment, UVF into one Battalion.[33]

Carson however was keen that despite the creation of the Ulster Division that the Ulster Volunteer Force should remain, if only for political reasons. Shortly after the outbreak of war he wrote to Lieutenant General Richardson, highlighting that those remaining:

---

33 UVF Orders 22, 1915 – Somme Museum.

Major-General Sir Hugh McCalmont takes the salute with Major-General CH Powell commanding the Division at the review of the 36th Division at Malone, Belfast, 8 May 1915. (Somme Museum)

… should remain with their several units of the UVF in Ulster and devote themselves to further recruiting and increasing the efficiency of the Force which remains. I can assure them that the efficiency of the UVF for the defence of our shores, and the training of Drafts for the supply of men to the new Division now being formed is as patriotic and as needful for the preservation of our great Empire as service with the colours.[34]

The UVF Headquarters attempted to re-energize units during January 1915 by outlining a defence scheme for Belfast and the shores of Antrim and Down from a feared German naval raid, with the plan later expanded to encompass the whole of Ulster. As a consequence some units did formulate invasion planning as part of an Ulster Defence Scheme. To further instill more enthusiasm into those remaining within the Ulster Volunteer Force, the UVF Headquarters made available ammunition and finance in a hope that local units would organise shooting competitions.[35]

Steps were also taken to ensure those motor vehicles which had been previously registered with the UVF for their use would still be made available by their owners for the UVF against any mobilisation required to frustrate or prevent a German raid or invasion.[36]

This theme was reinforced in a speech by Sir Edward Carson in Belfast, 9 January 1915, when he suggested that drawing up defence plans could bring greater efficiency to the Volunteers and maintain their discipline. In the same speech he took the political opportunity to warn against newspaper articles in the Nationalist press and speeches by individuals such as Mr Dillon, exhorting

---

34 Bowman, Timothy, *Carson's Army: Ulster Volunteer Force, 1910-22* (2007).
35 Bowman, Timothy, *Carson's Army: Ulster Volunteer Force, 1910-22* (2007).
36 Memo No. 174 – Registration Motor Cars Foreign Invasion – 2 January 1915.

the Nationalist volunteers to go on and increase with avowed purpose. He warned; "I say to you, do not think for a moment that the danger is passed."

Extracts from the speech were issued to UVF Battalions; WT Adair circulating it to the County Antrim UVF, warning them that "If a man does not obey Sir Edward he is a danger to the Force, also he is failing to comply with the spirit of his COVENANT, and is a traitor to Ulster."[37]

One of the suggested shooting competitions emerged in the guise of a rifle competition held at Loughanmore, Monday 19 July 1915 at 7:30 p.m. Each competitor was to fall in at the "the order" with full accoutrements, service rifle and bayonet, when he would be given ten rounds of miniature rifle ammunition. On the order of "Go" each Volunteer in turn would run approximately 100 yards to the 50-yards firing point, where there was a miniature rifle waiting. With this rifle he was to fire five rounds at a figure target. He was then to take up his service rifle and run a similar course over an obstacle to a 25-yards range where he was to fire five rounds with a miniature rifle. Finally then with his service rifle he was to charge a dummy figure and stab at the heart. Points were awarded as follows; Bull's eye – five points, Inner – three points, Outer – one point and Stab in the heart – ten points. As penalties, two points was deducted for every five seconds or part of five seconds, over four minutes from the order "Go" to the point with the bayonet. As an extra general incentive five points was added if the competitor had attended 5 or more drills or practices between 1 January and 31 May 1915.[38]

With an estimated 600 of the 2000 members of the Loyal Dublin Volunteers enlisting in the Imperial Services and an emerging 'Ulster' solution to the Home Rule crisis becoming apparent, the focus of the 'fight' against Home Rule in Dublin undertook a change of emphasis. At a general meeting of the organisation in August 1915, it was proposed that they affiliate themselves with the Irish Association of Voluntary Training Corps (IAVTC). To this end, 200 immediately signed up, effectively making the men a reserve army unit.[39]

The IAVTC was formed in Dublin in May 1915 from various Home Defence Units. With the authority of the War Office on 11 May the Irish government granted it official recognition and to all the corps and rifle clubs affiliated to it. In mid-1916 after pressure from the Central Committee of the Volunteer Training Corps the Westminster government accepted the VTC as an auxiliary arm of the

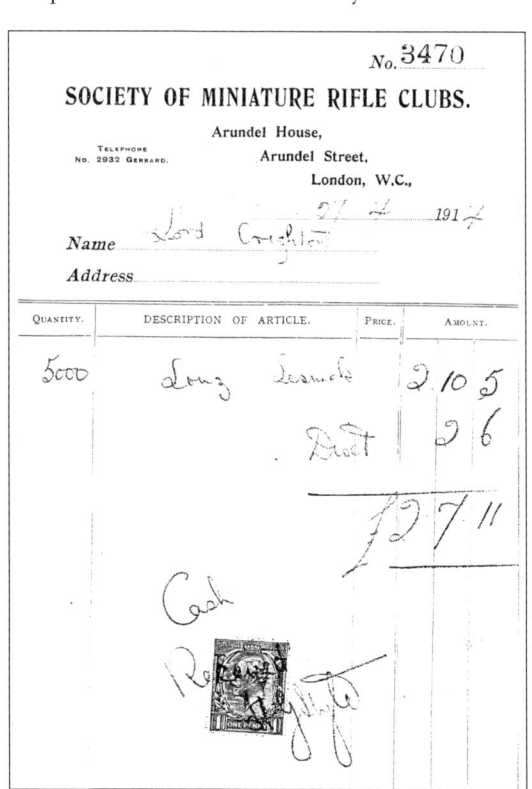

Receipt from the Society of Miniature Rifle Clubs to Lord Crighton, County Fermanagh, 27 April 1914. (Somme Museum)

37　Memo No.173 – County Antrim UVF – 12 January 1915.
38　Rifle Competition at Loughanmore – paper dated 28 June 1915.
39　<http://www.newsletter.co.uk/features/the-loyal-dublin-volunteers-a-forgotten-organisation-1-3719467> (Accessed 5 February 2014).

Royal Irish Constabulary at Coleraine, County Londonderry, circa 1910/11. (Police Museum)

Army. However this recognition was not extended to Ireland and the IAVTC,[40] an act which appeared deliberate.[41] As result, at a meeting of the IAVTC in Dublin on Saturday, 10 November 1916, Lord Justice Maloney presided over the final meeting of the IAVTC, which resolved to disband all its corps.

As part of the recruiting campaign on the outbreak of war all men in the Royal Irish Constabulary were called upon to volunteer to join the army, however, following an initial flurry of applications the number was quickly capped to prevent a drain on the Constabulary Force. By October 1915 the Inspector General stated that only 500 men could be spared from the force, however in the end approximately 52 out of its approximate strength of 10,000 were allowed to join the colours.[42]

Lance-Corporal Michael O'Leary, 1st Battalion, Irish Guards, son of a fervent Irish Nationalist, was awarded a Victoria Cross for conspicuous bravery at Cuinchy on the 1st February, 1915. He was further rewarded for his service, being advanced to a commissioned rank as a second lieutenant with the Connaught Rangers and was also awarded with a Russian decoration, the Cross of St. George (third class).Despite his popularity with the crowds in London and Macroom, he was jeered by Ulster Volunteers at a recruitment drive in Ballaghaderrin during the autumn of 1915. This treatment caused such a scandal that it was raised in the Houses of Parliament in December.[43] O'Leary was also given a gift of £25 from UVF funds.[44]

---

40   Tom Wylie, *Bulletin of the Military Historical Society*, Vol 45, No.194.
41   *Northern Whig* & *Belfast Post*, 13 November 1916.
42   Augusteijn, J, Ed, *The Memoirs of John M Regan* (2007).
43   Batchelor P and Matson C, *VC's of the First World War – The Western Front 1915* (1998).
44   Bowman, Timothy, *Carson's Army: Ulster Volunteer Force, 1910-22* (2007).

Irish demonstration Trafalgar Square, London,1915 for Sgt O'Leary, VC. Despite his popularity with the crowds in London, he was jeered by Ulster Volunteers at a recruitment drive in Ballaghaderrin during the autumn of 1915. This treatment caused such a scandal that it was raised in the Houses of Parliament in December.

Given the demands on labour as a result of the war effort the Headquarters Council of the Ulster Volunteer Force issued instructions that military instruction and drills for companies and other UVF units should not be too demanding when men were expected to also carry on war work in their civilian employments. Whilst training needs were left to the discretion of divisional, regimental and battalions commanders, in assessing their local needs the Council suggested that where possible one drill per week would be sufficient to keep men in a ready state with rifle drill and miniature range practice given the priority.[45]

In August 1915 the remaining Volunteers in Ulster were informed that it was proposed to present the Ulster Division with 16,000 sandbags. The cost of these was expected to be in the region of £366 and was to be met by voluntary subscription. All divisional, regimental and battalion Commanders were asked to appeal to the officers and men of the UVF to support this; the remittances were to be sent to the UVF Headquarters, Town Hall, Belfast at the earliest opportunity.[46] Before the end of October the GOC UVF sent the Ulster Division 20,000 sandbags in the name of the Ulster Volunteer Force. An extract from the letter of thanks sent from General Nugent stated that "When they arrive I promise that they shall be built into the first line of whatever trenches the Division may be holding at the time." He also took the opportunity to encourage

---

45   Circular Memorandum from GOC UVF – 13 May 1915.
46   Appeal for sandbags for Ulster Division – 26 August 1915.

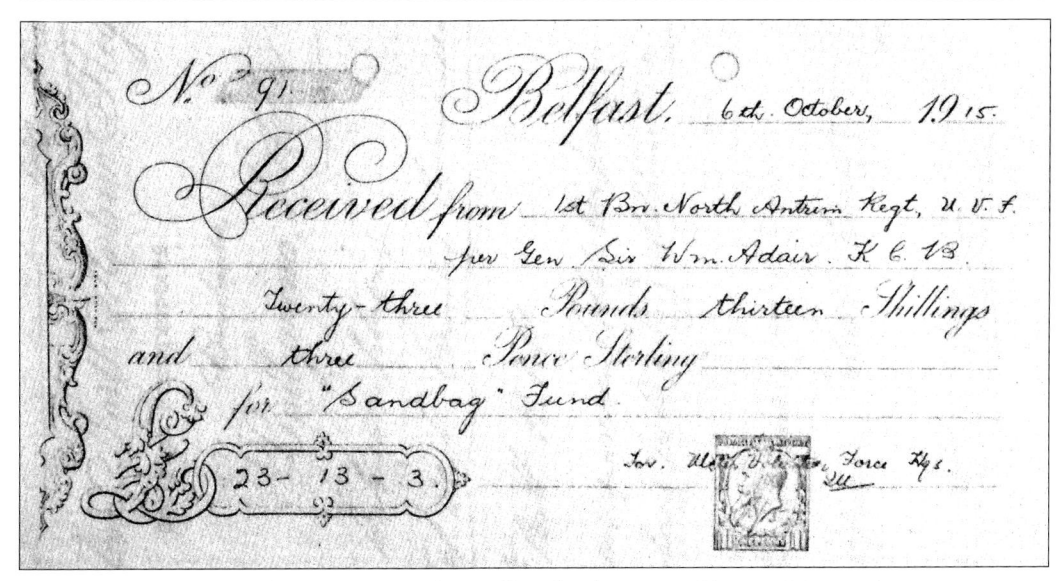

Receipt for payment to the sandbag fund in 1915. (Somme Museum)

more practical support, "On behalf of Ulstermen in the Field I beg you will tell our Ulstermen at home that we are counting on them to keep us up to our numbers in trained men."[47]

The local County Antrim Ulster Volunteers also raised funds to supply milk to the 12th Battalion, Royal Irish Rifles. By the middle of November 1915 the fund had reached £428 from 1132 subscribers. This included those who had subscribed through various UVF units and other organisations that had fund raised.[48]

Ulster Prisoner of War and Comforts Fund

During the autumn of 1914 the Ulster Prisoner of War and Comforts Fund was established. The organising committee was given a suite of rooms within the old Town Hall, the Headquarters of the Ulster Volunteer Force, from where a large number of ladies voluntarily undertook the work of packing and dispatching fortnightly parcels to every Ulster prisoner of war. The work was hard and monotonous and as the number of prisoners increased, especially after the last great German offensive in the summer of 1918, it became ever more strenuous. The staff of volunteers involved ultimately rose to almost 200, with work often continuing until at least 10:00 p.m. each night, and the rooms in the Town Hall could have been mistaken for the packing and dispatching department of a huge grocery and provision business. To facilitate this work contracts for all the necessary supplies and articles were entered into with many of the large manufacturing houses, many giving the materials at cost price or even less. From the inception of the Fund until the end of 1918 a sum of at least £150,000 was spent on supplying the parcels. Those involved were heartened by letters of thanks and occasional visits by repatriated prisoners who voiced their appreciation on the importance of the parcels for those in captivity.[49]

---

47 UVF Orders 35, 1915 – Somme Museum.
48 Fund for Supply of Milk to the 12th Batt Royal Ulster Rifles – 10 November 1915.
49 The History of Ulster – Ulster in the War <http://www.electricscotland.com/history/ulster/vol4chap28.htm> (Accessed 4 Dec 2011).

The Londonderry Supply Depot. The Irish War Hospital Supply Depot was a major charitable initiative. Thousands of women worked for the IWHS providing hospitals with surgical and other supplies. In Ireland a central depot was set up in Dublin, with 8 sub depots. In Ulster the main depot was in the Old Town Hall, Belfast. One important aspect of the IWHS was the production of sphagnum moss dressings as a substitute for cotton wool. (Somme Museum)

In a letter to the Lord Mayor of Belfast they also offered "practical citizenship" throughout Ulster.[50] In 1916 the UWUC also established a Sphagnum Moss Association with large depots at Belfast and Londonderry and with smaller ones in other locations across Ulster; they exported 5,000 dressings per month.[51] The sphagnum moss, which was naturally occurring in abundance in Ireland, was deemed to be a satisfactory substitute for cotton wool which was one of the first medical commodities to become expensive and scarce on the outbreak of war.[52] By 1918 it had collected £119,481.[53]

UVF Hospitals

After the Boer War, the War Office had concerns that in the event of another war the medical and nursing services would not be able to cope sufficiently. The medical needs and demands of the standing army in peace-time were very small compared to the demands during a war and the ability to find and train sufficient personnel at short notice was a problem which had to be overcome. Haldane's new Territorial scheme of 1907 introduced the possibility of co-operation between voluntary agencies and the Army. On 16th August 1909 the War Office issued its

---

50 Gregory, Adrian and Paseta, Senia (ed), *Ireland and the Great War 'A War to Unite Us All'?* (2002).
51 Ireland and the First World War – Edited D Fitzpatrick (1988), Minutes of UWUC 1911-70 (PRONI D1327/6).
52 Cousins, Colin, *Armagh and the Great War* (2011).
53 Fitzpatrick, D (ed)., *Ireland and the First World War* (1988).

A Red Cross contingent of the Ulster Volunteer Force. (J Luke)

'Scheme for the Organisation of Voluntary Aid in England and Wales,' which set up both male and female Voluntary Aid Detachments to fill certain gaps in the Territorial medical services. A similar scheme for Scotland was introduced in December the same year.[54]

Under the scheme the British Red Cross Society and the Order of St John of Jerusalem linked up and were given the role of providing supplementary aid to the Territorial Forces Medical Service in the event of war.

By early 1914, 1757 female detachments and 519 male detachments had been registered with the War Office.[55]

In July 1914 the *Northern Whig* reported that the Ulster Volunteer Force had 220 hospitals, 138 doctors and 410 nurses at its disposal and could also call upon the assistance of 3,520 nurses enrolled in the Voluntary Aid Detachment (VAD).[56]

In Ulster the VAD took their instructions from the Belfast Branch of the British Red Cross; in August 1916 the Ulster Joint VAD Committee was formed to control the British Red Cross in Ulster, comprising ten county directors and representatives from British Red Cross and Saint John's Ambulance Association.[57]

The Ulster Women's Unionist Council (UWUC) provided an ambulance for the 36th (Ulster) Division and funded a hospital in Pau established by the Tyrone Nursing Corps under its commandant Rosabelle Sinclair and the Duchess of Abercorn.[58] Ulster provided a total of 24 field ambulances for use at the front.[59]

As part of the medical plan for British casualties during the war, beds were set aside in many major hospitals for the treatment of sick and injured. In Belfast the main hospitals; The Royal Victoria, The Union (Belfast City Hospital) and the Mater Infirmorum were tasked to set beds

---

54   Scarlet Finders <http://www.scarletfinders.co.uk/181.html>.
55   Scarlet Finders <http://www.scarletfinders.co.uk/181.html>.
56   Ulster Volunteer Force, January 1913 – Ulster-Scots Scots Community Network <http://www.ulster-scots.com/uploads/901740969819.PDF>.
57   Cousins, Colin, *Armagh and the Great War* (2011).
58   Bowman, Timothy, *Carson's Army: Ulster Volunteer Force, 1910-22* (2007).
59   Cousins, Colin, *Armagh and the Great War* (2011).

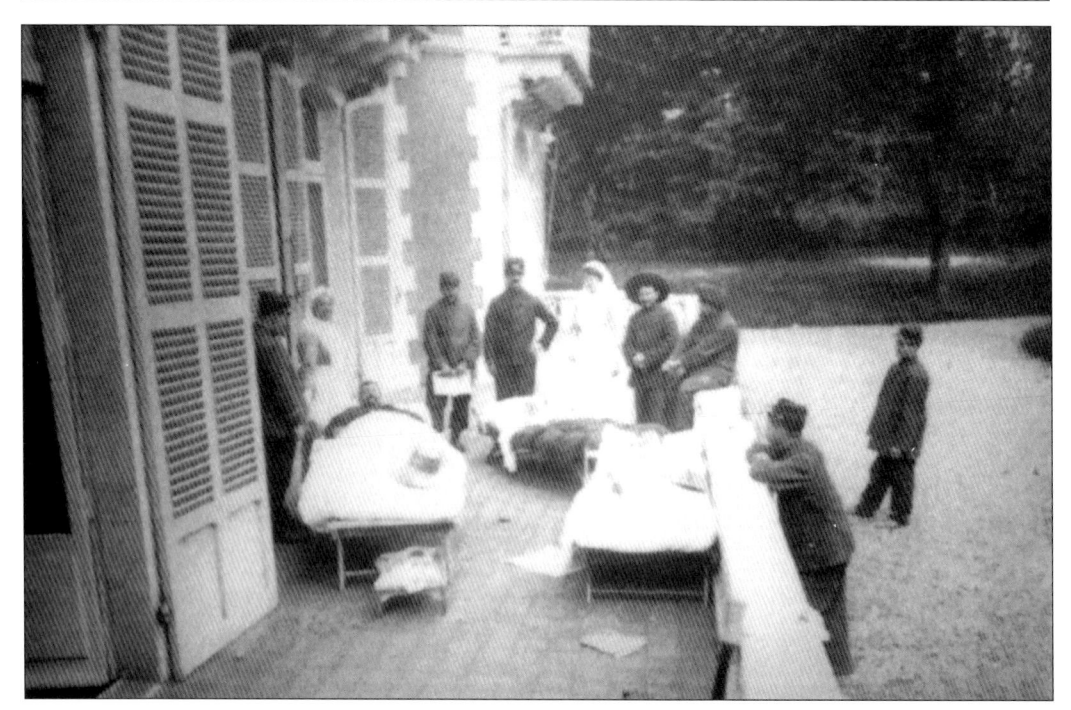

UVF Hospital in Pau, France. In 1914 the UVF hospital in Strabane was offered to the French Army. It reopened in Villa Beapre in Pau in November 1914. Until August 1917 it was effectively financed by the Ulster Women's Unionist Council and was staffed by many nurses and staff from Ulster. (Somme Museum)

Some of the ambulances presented by the people of Ulster to the UVF . The flags of the Allied nations in the war are draped to the right-hand side of the photograph. (Somme Museum)

Sir Edward and Lady Carson depicted inside the back of a Christmas card for 1914 from the 15th Service Battalion Royal Irish Riles (North Belfast Volunteers) being trained in Ballykinlar Camp. The link to the UVF is illustrated by the red 'right' hand of the Volunteers as opposed to the 'left' hand of the 36th (Ulster) Division. (Somme Museum)

aside to receive casualties. However both the Royal Victorian and the Mater were run voluntarily for the citizens of Belfast which left little spare capacity.[60]

To assist with this dilemma, in the autumn and with the number of war casualties increasing, an offer was made to the War Office that the Ulster Volunteers would equip and maintain, as long as necessary, a hospital of 100 beds.

The offer was accepted and a large glass building, the Exhibition Hall, the property of Belfast Corporation, was acquired rent-free, with the proviso that it would be returned when no longer needed; and was ultimately used until 1926. The location was ideal, in the Botanic Gardens with the building bounded on one side by a public park and on the other by the grounds of Queen's University, Belfast.[61] It was capable of housing 80 beds whilst the small and recently built Maternity and Gynaecological Hospital, the Samaritan, 22-24 Lisburn Road, could also take another 20 beds. The main hospital building adjoining the University, known as the Exhibition Hall, was opened 9 January 1915 by Lady Carson, accompanied by her husband Lord Carson.[62,63]

Lord Carson's speech outlined all that had been achieved with regards the hospital:

> The establishment of the new Hospital has been due to the instrumentality of the HQ Council of the UVF. On the outbreak of the war it was felt by those who control the affairs of the UVF that, in addition to raising the Ulster Division, the HQ Council should place their Hospital equipment at the disposal of the War Office. The Corporation were approached and granted the use of the Exhibition Hall for the purpose of the Hospital. As a result of the movement, 100 beds will be available for the purpose intended – 80 in the Exhibition Hall and 20 in the Samaritan Hospital. Duties of the Matron will be in the capable hands of Miss Bruce, and the nursing staff will consist of six staff nurses and eight assistant staff nurses, while probationers will aid UVF nurses. The six staff sisters are to be accommodated in the spacious and well-furnished residence at No.1 College Park East, which has been kindly provided by Mr and Mrs JC White, and assistant staff nurses will have apartments at Samaritan Hospital.[64]

---

60   Eakins, Arthur, *The Somme – What Happened to the Casualties* (2008).
61   Accessed 4 Dec 2011 – The History of Ulster – Ulster in the War <http://www.electricscotland.com/history/ulster/vol4chap28.htm>.
62   Orr, Philip, *The Road to the Somme* (1987).
63   Eakins, Arthur, *The Somme – What Happened to the Casualties* (2008).
64   *Northern Whig* – 9 January 1915.

X-Ray Room, UVF Hospital. (Somme Museum)

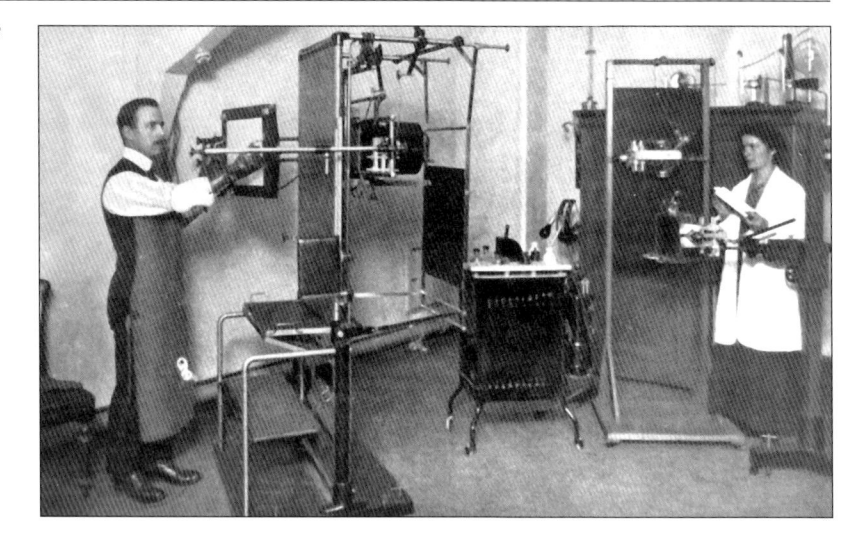

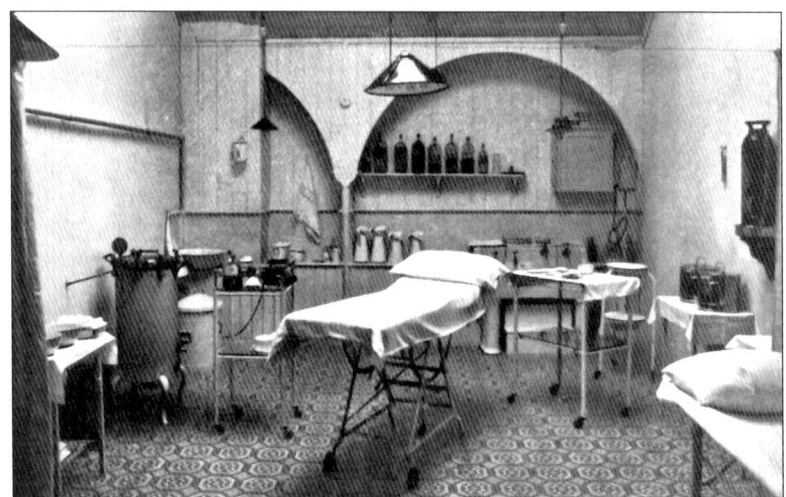

The Sinclair Operating Room, UVF Hospital. (Somme Museum)

Laboratory, UVF Hospital. (Somme Museum)

UVF Nurses outside the Galwally House. (Somme Museum: 1994-515)

Miss Bruce, a native of Tipperary, had received high testimonials from the Egyptian Government for her work in Kasr-el-Aini Hospital in Cairo.[65] Carson also thanked the University for the use of their pathology laboratories and their new x-ray equipment.

Within months the hospital was ready, with the leading Belfast Surgeon Professor Thomas Sinclair, providing the operating theatre at his own expense, causing one of his colleagues, TS Kirk, to comment that "As far as that went the equipment would be very good even for a permanent hospital whilst for a temporary hospital it was most excellent."[66]

Within the broader national medical system during the war the hospital was to provide an 'acute convalescent' function. It was intended for those servicemen who had been injured, given first aid and more definitive treatment in a military hospital before being evacuated to the United Kingdom; it was expected that further surgery would be required for some, hence the arrangements for surgeons, theatre nurses and physicians volunteering to act as the staff, including a number of them for the Royal Victoria Hospital.

The first patients arrived on 18 February 1915, having travelled by ambulance from forward hospitals behind the front lines, then by train to the Channel ports, then ferry to southern England before train to Liverpool and on to Belfast. Many of the first patients were from English and Scottish Regiments which had formed the British Expeditionary Force fighting in France and Belgium.

Such was the success of the hospital and with increasing casualty numbers the War Office asked if the accommodation could be increased. With the main hospital to the southern edge of Queen's University grounds it appeared logical that any expansion should be into these grounds.

---

[65] The Nursing Record and Hospital World, 24 February 1900 <http://rcnarchive.rcn.org.uk/data/VOLUME024-1900/page160-volume24-24thfebruary1900.pdf> (Accessed 3 September 2014).
[66] Eakins, Arthur, *The Somme – What Happened to the Casualties* (2008).

The University authorities, through their governing body, the Senate, gave the Vice-Chancellor, Rev Dr Thomas Hamilton, authority to grant a considerable strip of ground beside their own buildings to the UVF which enabled additional wards to be erected. The initial extension of 200 beds was opened by the Marquis of Londonderry, 1 October 1915, and named after him.[67] The hospital eventually expanded to such an extent that over 600 patients were able to be accommodated. The additional wards were in temporary wooden buildings which filled most the space on the southern side of the University.[68]

The War Office contributed three shillings capitation allowance per day per patient who was treated in the UVF facilities, with all other monies to provide the services required needing to be found elsewhere.[69]

Funding for the hospital was entrusted to Robert Liddell J.P., a highly respected industrialist with a linen factory at Donacloney and offices in Belfast. As Honorary Treasurer and supported by R Dawson Bates, a solicitor, as Honorary Secretary, they administered a funding committee which would become the UVF Patriotic Fund with a launch target of £100,000; an ambitious target with the average working man earning approximately £3 per week.[70]

The Londonderry Wing of the UVF Hospital. (Somme Museum)

---

67   Eakins, Arthur, *The Somme – What Happened to the Casualties* (2008).
68   Eakins, Arthur, *The Somme – What Happened to the Casualties* (2008).
69   Eakins, Arthur, *The Somme – What Happened to the Casualties* (2008).
70   Eakins, Arthur, *The Somme – What Happened to the Casualties* (2008).

The nursing staff of the UVF Hospital, Belfast at the side of Queen's University Belfast. (Somme Museum)

Union Jack Committee Ward, in the Londonderry Wing, UVF Hospital. (Somme Museum)

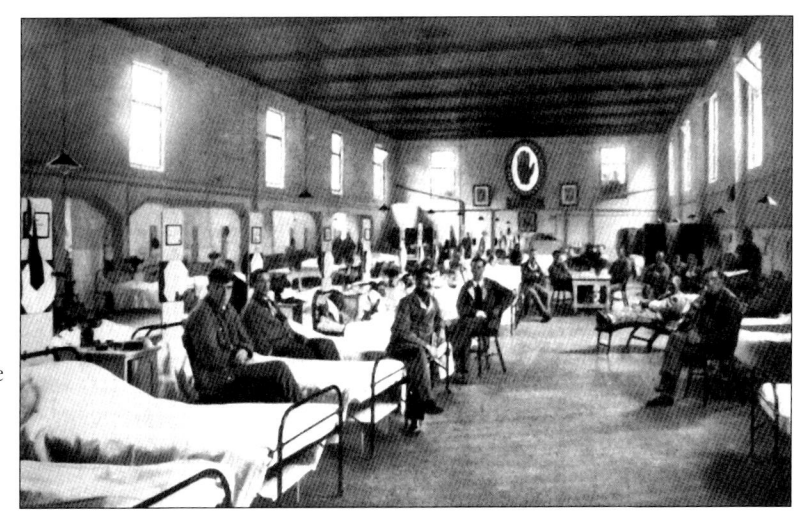

The Carson wing of the Ulster Volunteer Force Hosptal at Queen's University, Belfast. (Somme Museum)

In October 1916 the War Office asked for more beds to be made available. The UVF Hospital Board responded by proposing to the War Office that they provide 50 beds and appliances for the special treatment of limbless soldiers. This met a need identified by the Ulster Council, as those limbless soldiers from Ulster had to travel to England or Dublin to receive prosthetic limbs, and which was manifest in the building of another extension to the hospital. This was an orthopaedic and limbless unit that cost £12,000. It would consist of four wards, named Liddell, Roberts, Gough and Musgrave; Roberts ward named after Field Marshal Lord Roberts, Gough ward after General Gough, Royal Irish Fusiliers, and Musgrave ward from the family of Belfast industrialists. Each ward was arranged in the 'Nightingale' layout; two long rows of beds perfectly aligned with a ward office at one end which would bring all such injured people into one unit.[71] The new unit was opened by the Duchess of Abercorn, 3 February 1917.[72] Mr AG Campbell made artificial limbs or prostheses for the limbless soldiers, paying the UVF to carry out the service but in return he was paid by the War Office.[73, 74]

By the end of October 1916 the total number of casualties which had passed through the UVF hospital were; 1241 from the BEF in Belgium/France; 966 from Scottish Command; 57 from the BEF Mediterranean; in all over 500 operations were performed with no deaths.[75]

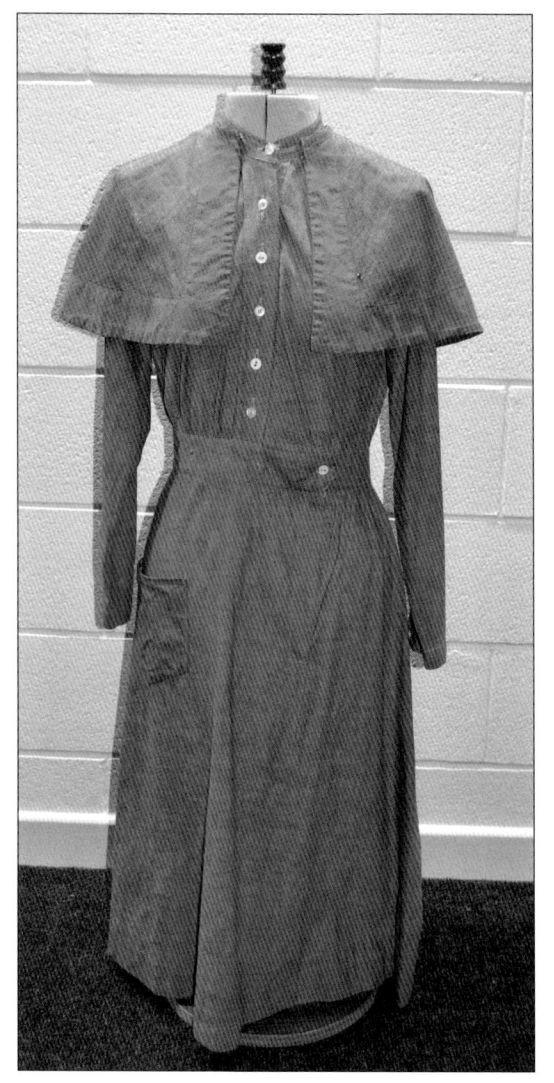

Nurse's uniform of the Ulster Volunteer Force. (Somme Museum)

Further support for the hospital and its work came from various quarters. Belfast City Corporation provided further assistance by allowing the necessary structural alterations to be made in the buildings and the University Senate also gave up some classrooms.[76] The Lord Mayor of Belfast, J. C. White, gave a house as a residence for the matron and nursing staff. Meanwhile the students of the university gave up their union club as a recreation and reading room for the men to relax away from the wards; the theological students of the nearby Presbyterian College voluntarily evacuated their range of residential chambers

---

71 Eakins, Arthur, *The Somme – What Happened to the Casualties* (2008).
72 *Belfast News Letter* – 3 February 1917.
73 Eakins, Arthur, *The Somme – What Happened to the Casualties* (2008).
74 *Belfast News Letter* – 3 February 1917.
75 Eakins, Arthur, *The Somme – What Happened to the Casualties* (2008).
76 Eakins, Arthur, *The Somme – What Happened to the Casualties* (2008).

"The charge of the Ulster Division at Thiepval, 1st July 1916" by William Connor. (Somme Museum: 1996-88)

which were converted into a home for the Voluntary Aid Detachments and nurses.

In response the UVF Hospital Council funded temporary accommodation for a student dining hall in Rosemary Hall, Elmwood Avenue.[77]

The VAD Glencairn group in Belfast comprised 111 women and girls from all classes and backgrounds training as nurses and supporting two surgeons.[78]

The artist William Conor, later famous for his images of tinkers and shipyard workers, produced images of the home front or soldiers under training showing Ulster as a 'nation' under arms. His images included women during the conflict such as the female munitions working at Mackie's engineering works, and more significantly for this history, of a nurse supporting a wounded soldier which was subsequently used on the front of an Ulster Volunteer Force Hospital fund raising brochure.[79, 80]

Conor's image of the charge of the Ulster Division at Thiepval, 1 July, was used as part of a series of paintings printed on Christmas postcards and sold in Ulster for a penny each in aid of the UVF hospitals treating the wounded.[81]

The following list is of War Hospital Supply Depots organised by private individuals throughout Ireland and is based on the document, "Reports by the Joint War Committee of the British Red Cross Society and the Order of St. John of Jerusalem in England on Voluntary Aid Rendered to the Sick and Wounded at Home and Abroad and to British Prisoners of War, 1914-1919"[82]

---

77 Eakins, Arthur, *The Somme – What Happened to the Casualties* (2008).
78 Ingram, Rev Brett, *Covenant and Challenge* (1989).
79 Jeffrey, Keith, 'Irish Artists in the First World War', *History of Ireland*, Vol. 1, No. 2, summer 1993.
80 'The Great War and Irish Memory' in Fraser, T.D. & Jeffrey, K. (eds), *Men, Women and War: Studies in War, Politics and Society* (1993).
81 Orr, Philip, *The Road to the Somme* (1987).
82 Scarlet Finders <http://www.scarletfinders.co.uk/178.html> (Accessed 5 August 2013).

IRELAND

1072 **CASHEL** MRS GRUBB, ARDMAYLE, CO. TIPPERARY
1119 **BELFAST** MRS MACKENZIE, CHETWOOD, NOTTING HILL, MALONE ROAD
1104 **BELFAST** MRS BALLARD, THE RED HOUSE CLUB, 100 HIGH STREET
1371 **CASTLEPOLLARD** MRS DROUGHT, RATHGRAFFE RECTORY
1401 **BELFAST** MRS C. A. WILKINS, 34 GLANTANE STREET, ANTRIM ROAD
1405 **BIRR** MRS BREDIN, 7 OXMANTOWN MALL
1409 **BELFAST** MRS C. A. WILKINS, 34 GLANTANE STREET, ANTRIM ROAD
1565 **KILLARNEY** MRS CROWIN, COLTSMANN GLENFLESK CASTLE
1591 **DUBLIN** D. R. PACK, BERESFORD, ESQ. 51 DAWSON STREET
1608 **DUBLIN** MRS DALLAS PRATT, 40 MERRION SQUARE
1609 **TULLAMORE** MRS MOORHEAD
1617 **NEWTOWNARDS** MRS A. S. BLOW, COMMANDANT DOWN, 60 THE CROFT
1678 **BANBRIDGE** MRS N. G. FERGUSON, CLONASLIE
1704 **KILKENNY** MRS JAMES, BUTLER HOUSE
1733 **ARMAGH** MRS CROZIER, THE PLACE
1778 **BELFAST** MRS R. J. MCCORDIE, CABIN HILL, KNOCK
1812 **STRABANE** MISS B. A. CLARKE, MAGHEREAGH
1816 **BALLINROBE** MRS BLOSSE LYNCH, PARTRY
1822 **CLONMEL** MAJOR W. W. DOBBIN, GOVERNOR, H.M. BORSTAL
1846 **GLANMIRE** MRS HARTOPP GUBBINS, LOTA PARK
1849 **LARNE** MRS COUSINS, LARK HILL
1882 **YOUGHAL** MRS R. H. WOOD, THE COTTAGE
4064 **MARKETHILL** MRS AUCHMUTY, THE RECTORY
4065 **NEWTOWN HAMILTON** MRS MCFERRAN
4066 **JERRETTSPASS** LADY MURIEL CLOSE, DRUMBANAGHER
4095 **FETHARD** MRS KELLETT, CLONACODY
4096 **CASTLEBAR** MRS LENDRUM, THE RECTORY
4069 **LARNE HARBOUR** MRS MCCANN, 1 GOLF VIEW, BAY ROAD
4172 **TANDRAGEE** MRS WHITE, ORANGE HILL
4203 **TYNAN** MISS ROSE STRONGE, TYNAN ABBEY
4214 **LURGAN** MISS E. GREER, 20 CHURCH PLACE
5518 **LURGAN** MISS E. GREER, 20 CHURCH PLACE
4213 **COOTEHILL** MISS CLEMENTS, ASHFIELD LODGE
4239 **CORK** MRS STARKIE 11 KING STREET
4282 **BALLYMENA** MRS MORTON, TOWN HALL
4426 **NEWTOWNARDS** MISS IVESTON, 10 FRANCIS STREET
4470 **RICHHILL** MRS WILSON, HOCKLEY LODGE
4323 **KILKENNY** MRS POWER, BELLEVUE HOUSE
4825 **LONDONDERRY** MRS HAYES, THE DEANERY
4364 **BALLYMONEY** MRS HAMILTON, ASHLEIGH
4376 **CRUMLIN** MRS C. E. MCCLINTOCK, GLENDARAGH
4373 **LIMAVADY** MRS MCCAUSLAND, DRENAGH
4419 **LISBURN** MRS G. R. BELL, ST. JOHN'S AMBULANCE
4487 **RICHHILL** MRS MAYSE, THE RECTORY, KILMORE
4526 **BALLYCASTLE** MISS GLOVER
4627 **DUNGANNON** MRS DARRAGH, THE VILLA
4729 **BANNOCKSTOWN** MRS HONNER, ARDENODI
4744 **NENAGH** THE LADY DUNALLEY, KILBEY

4798 **BIRDHILL** MISS GOING, CRAGG
4805 **CLOUGHJORDON** MISS MARY M. BARR
4819 **CARNDONAGH** MRS DUNCAN, THE RECTORY
4880 **TRALEE** MRS R. FITZGERALD, BALLYARD HOUSE
4926 **DONEGAL** MISS N. B. NEILSON, THE MANSE
4971 **DONEGAL** MRS SIMS WILLIAMS, BALLINTRA
4936 **DONEGAL** MISS J. POMEROY, SALT HILL, MOUNTCHARLES
5012 **DONEGAL** MRS MUNRO, THE RECTORY, GLENCOLUMBKILLE
5020 **DUNKINEELY** MRS H. S. G. MCCLENAGHAN, THE RECTORY
4934 **WHITEABBEY** MRS BRADLEY, JORDANSTOWN RECTORY
5051 **BANBRIDGE** MRS J. D. SMYTHE, MILLTOWN HOUSE
5045 **LOUGH ESKE** MRS RYAN, THE RECTORY
5066 **DUBLIN** MISS L. THOMPSON, 29 LOWER FITZWILLIAM STREET
5015 **LONDONDERRY** MRS STEVENSON, KNOCKAN
5074 **WARRENPOINT** MRS HALL, NARROW WATER
5090 **YOUGHAL** MRS WOOD, THE COLLEGE
5124 **FLINTONA** MRS WALKER
5129 **THURLES** MRS CLARKE, GRAIGUENOE PARK
5138 **KILKEEL** MRS FLOYD, BORCHA
5129 **KILKEEL** MISS G. WARING, LIONACRES HOUSE
5159 **BUNCRANS** MISS COLHOUN, ARDCASIN
5177 **PETTIGOE** MRS DICKSON, RIVERBANK
5221 **MILFORD** MRS OSBORNE, KNOCKNAGEANE
5333 **ROSSNOWLAGH** MRS TRINDER, ROSSNOWLAGH RECTORY
5224 **LIMERICK** MISS E. A. HANNA, INTERNATIONAL HOTEL
5229 **LOUGHGALL** MISS BATES, BEECHVILLE
5233 **CULDAFF** MRS R. C. YOUNG, CULDAFF HOUSE
5234 **MALIN** MRS HARVEY, MALIN HALL
5245 **BELFAST** MISS A. JOHNSTONE, MUNICIPAL T. INSTITUTE
5298 **CAVAN** MRS JACKSON, BANK OF IRELAND
5317 **OMAGH** MRS MACAFEE, THE MANSE
5351 **CASTLEBLAYNEY** MISS IRWIN, CARNAGH HOUSE, CARNAGH
5352 **DUNFANAGHY** MRS STEWART, HORN HEAD
5354 **PORTADOWN** MRS S. W. BLACKER, CARRICK BLACKER
5383 **TEMPLEPATRICK** MRS WALLACE, LYE HILL MANSE
5384 **STRABANE** MISS MCCREA, DERRY ROAD
5389 **BALLYMENA** MRS WILSON, GRACEHILL
5403 **STRABANE** MRS JAMES HILL, HAZELWOOD
5417 **LURGAN** MRS A. W. MANN, WINDSOR BUILDINGS
5455 **PORTRUSH** MISS H. COX, ARDEEVIN
5467 **ROSTREVER** MRS R. SINTON
5482 **TEMPLEMORE** MRS MADDEN, BARNANE RECTORY
5491 **DARTREY** THE COUNTESS OF DARTREY
5550 **LONDONDERRY** MRS WATT, THORN HILL
5592 **MOY** LADY W. MACGEOUGH BOND
5619 **KILMALLOCK** MRS FILDES, RIVERSFIELD
5635 **FRESHFORD** MRS C. S. PURDON, LODGE PARK
5643 **GRANGECON** MISS G. MITCHELL, BALLYNURE
5648 **MOVILLE** MRS MONTGOMERY, ST. COLUMBS

5715 **ARMAGH** T. G. F. PATERSON, 4 MALL VIEW
5717 **LONDONDERRY** MRS COCHRANE, SPRING HILL, QUIGLEY'S POINT
5725 **LONDONDERRY** REV. ROBERT DUGGAN, B.A., THE RECTORY, CULMORE
5732 **MAGUIRESBRIDGE** MRS ARMSTRONG, TODD HOLLY MOUNT

As the war progressed further accommodation and smaller branch hospitals were established elsewhere in the province. The UVF Hospital at Dunbarton House, near Gilford, County Down,[83] and later Bannvale House, together provided convalescent accommodation for 80 officers.[84] In 1926 a hospital was opened at Galwally; it later closed briefly, re-opening in 1941.[85]

In south Londonderry, 11 nursing centres had been prepared, one of them at Alex Clarke's house, Ampertaine, in Upperlands.[86]

In 1915 Sir James Craig allowed his home Craigavon, in the Belfast suburbs to become a convalescent home. This location was used for numbers of men labelled as NYD (Not Yet Diagnosed) or 'nervous' to await a more specialist opinion. In reality they were often suffering from shell-shock, known today as post-traumatic stress disorder, which could range from anxiety, overt psychiatric symptoms, vivid flashbacks to traumatic events to confusional states and hysteria. This location was intended to provide a relaxing peaceful place to recover,[87] as opposed to treating them alongside patients in the other hospitals. This was the first home for shell-shock cases established in the United Kingdom outside of London.[88]

Gilford Branch of the UVF Hospital in County Down. Nurses are standing on the veranda whilst patients wearing their hospital uniforms are lying on the lawn. (Somme Museum)

---

83 Leslie and Quail, *Old Belfast* (2013).
84 Eakins, Arthur, *The Somme – What Happened to the Casualties* (2008).
85 Leslie and Quail, *Old Belfast* (2013).
86 Clark, Wallace, *Guns in Ulster* (1967).
87 Eakins, Arthur, *The Somme – What Happened to the Casualties* (2008).
88 Accessed 4 Dec 2011 – The History of Ulster – Ulster in the War <http://www.electricscotland.com/history/ulster/vol4chap28.htm>.

Nursing and medical staff of the West Down (Gilford) Branch of the UVF hospital, Craigavon. (Somme Museum)

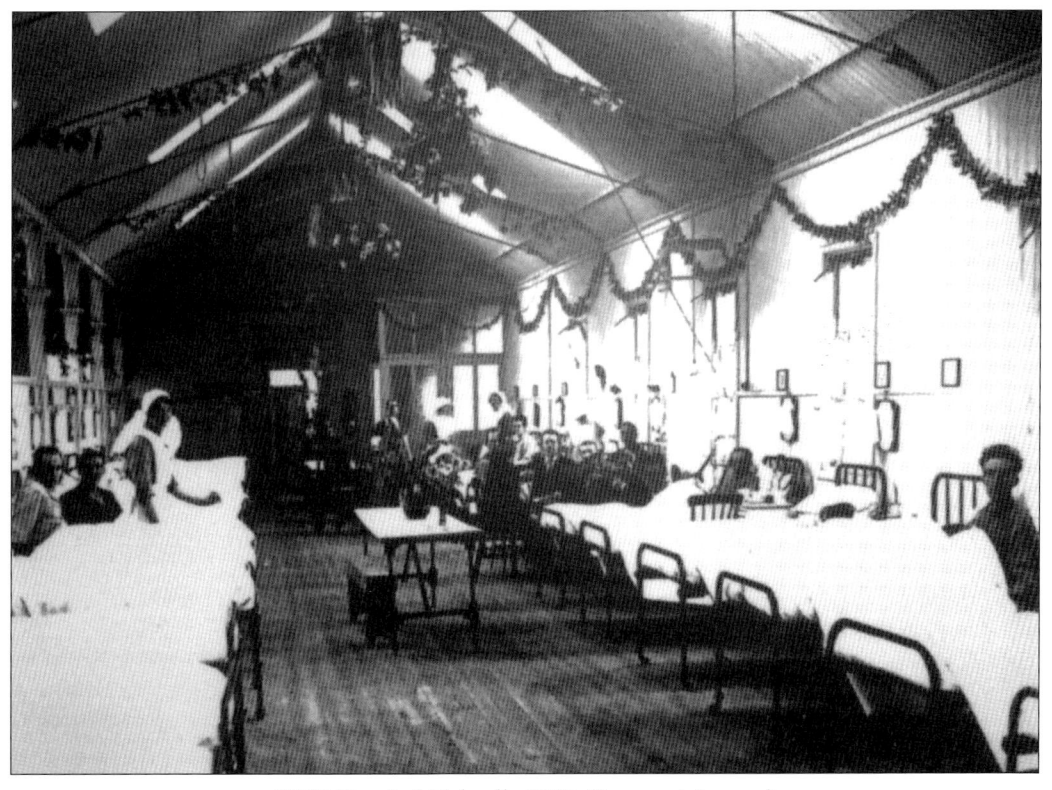

UVF Hospital Galwally 1919. (Somme Museum)

The Richardson Ward in the Ulster Volunteer Force hospital. (Somme Museum)

Under the control of a medical committee chaired by Dr McKissick it was called "UVF Hospitals – Craigavon Branch for Neurasthenia and Shell Shock." It provided 70 beds arranged in 11 single rooms and four rooms with three beds each, two rooms of seven beds each and three large wards containing an aggregate of 33 beds; two of the rooms were soundproofed. This reflected correspondence from a hospital operated in London by the War Office for convalescent and rehabilitation which emphasised the need for some small rooms.[89]

The Richardson ward, possibly in Craigavon House, was named after Lieutenant George Richardson, who was appointed GOC of the Ulster Volunteer Force in 1913.[90]

The committee considered work options for the patients which would provide both therapy and skills which may have assisted the patient on earning a living on their discharge. The range of activities considered included, gardening, motoring, carpentry, metal work, fretwork, turning, basket weaving, mat making, poultry farming, rabbit breeding, toy making, brush making, tailoring and cabinet making; subjects which reflected the socio-economic issues of the time. A number of these had the advantage of reducing costs to the hospital through the growing of vegetables for the hospital and producing items for sale. So enthusiastic were the visiting medical staff on the prospects of this approach that they gave an initial £150 to start a "Craigavon Industries and Recreation Fund" which would enable them to buy in part-time instructors to assist. The eventual setup costs for the different activities were £322 with annual running costs of £300.[91]

During 1917 there were some 640 hospital beds in use in Ulster.[92] Motor ambulances were provided for transporting the patients to and from the different hospitals.

---

89   Eakins, Arthur, *The Somme – What Happened to the Casualties* (2008).
90   Leslie and Quail, *Old Belfast* (2013).
91   Eakins, Arthur, *The Somme – What Happened to the Casualties* (2008).
92   Eakins, Arthur, *The Somme – What Happened to the Casualties* (2008).

This motor ambulance was subscribed for by the readers of the *Telegraph*. It made its first appearance in the streets the day before this photograph accompanied by a staff of nurses, who collected for Flag Day. (*Belfast Telegraph*)

With the beds operating at full occupancy an external treatment facility was set up which allowed some convalescents to be discharged as 'in-patients' yet still continue with their treatment.[93]

Known as 'M' and 'E' external these were for mechanical and electrical treatments. This was provided by adding masseuses to the staff and electrical treatments which were mainly low current shocks in an effort to start driving injured muscles into re-functioning and also to test conduction along damaged nerves. The necessary electrical equipment was bought from Lizar's in Belfast.[94]

By the end of the war the different branches of the hospital system established by the Ulster Volunteers had treated approximately 8,000 patients, not confined to Ulstermen, but wounded soldiers from all over the United Kingdom. As demand changed by the end of 1918 some branches had been given up, meanwhile others such as the limbless, orthopaedic and massage departments were still in full operation until the end of 1919 as was the neurasthenic hospital at 'Craigavon'.

Whilst Queen's University had magnanimously given ground and facilities for the creation of the UVF hospital facilities, with the end of the war student numbers had started to rise but the University did not have the finances to build new accommodation. In response the UVF Hospital Committee agreed to the University using the temporary hospital buildings as they became available with the closure of the various branches. It was anticipated that the hospital would close by 1919 however it remained open with the War Office requesting an extension of one year which was granted by the University, enabling two units to be made available to the University for the Departments of Geology and Engineering.[95]

Leading physicians and surgeons in Belfast gave their services free, many taking it in turn to visit the wards, prescribe for the patients and perform all necessary operations. Along with the financial support from the public, with upwards of £100,000 subscribed, there was also significant practical public support.

---

93 Eakins, Arthur, *The Somme – What Happened to the Casualties* (2008).
94 Eakins, Arthur, *The Somme – What Happened to the Casualties* (2008).
95 Eakins, Arthur, *The Somme – What Happened to the Casualties* (2008).

The cooks of the UVF hospital at the side of Queen's University Belfast. (Somme Museum)

The master-butchers of Belfast supplied a large quantity of free meat on a weekly basis. The master-bakers and their men made an arrangement whereby the masters supplied the materials while the men gave an hour or two of overtime on several days a week, as a result supplying nearly all the bread free of charge. Also as part of this arrangement the City Corporation gave permission for the use of the bakery attached to the Belfast Technical Institute to make the bread.

Other businesses sent weekly or monthly contributions of food and clothes, whilst fruit, flowers, and vegetables were regularly supplied from all over the country.

The committees of the Royal Victoria Hospital and the Mater Hospital supported the work of the Ulster Volunteers with both of the hospitals setting wings apart for the reception of wounded soldiers.

A former asylum was established as another hospital devoted to men suffering from mental breakdown and other nervous disorders. Both the Red Cross and St. John's Associations established and maintained for a considerable time a convalescent hospital for those men not requiring regular medical or surgical treatment, but not yet fit to report for duty. A prominent Belfast family also loaned a large mansion house to the committee for so long as it should be required, and a very considerable number of patients were treated there.[96]

Fund-raising for the various medical services also included a specific UVF Hospital's Fund (Belfast, Craigavon and Gilford) raising £100,000, whilst during the war years the joint Red Cross-St John Fund collected £146,579. Other Funds such as the Ulster Motor Ambulance Fund raised £12,000 whilst the Ulster Memorial Fund achieved £5,000.[97]

With funds accumulating, Robert Liddell had a Charitable Trust Deed drawn up in 1914 for an unincorporated charitable institution to be known as the Ulster Volunteer Force Hospitals, by which the charity would provide medical, hospital and convalescent treatment for the sick,

---

96 Accessed 4 Dec 2011 – The History of Ulster – Ulster in the War <http://www.electricscotland.com/history/ulster/vol4chap28.htm> (Accessed 4 December 2011).
97 Eakins, Arthur, *The Somme – What Happened to the Casualties* (2008).

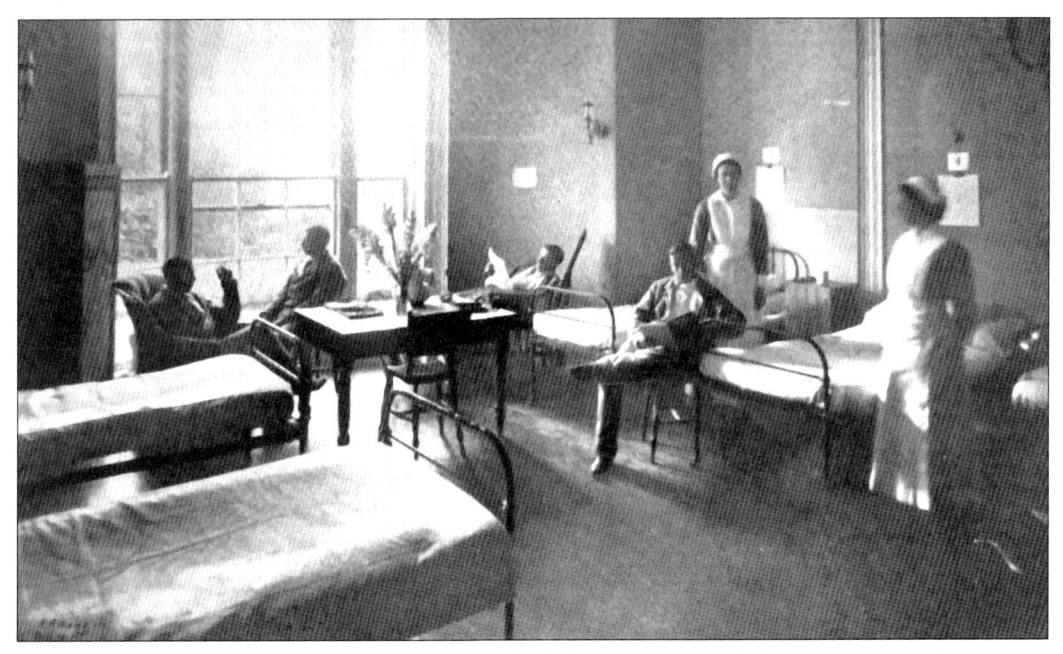

The Carson Wing of the Gilford Branch of the UVF Hospital. (Somme Museum)

wounded and disabled British Servicemen and ex-Servicemen. The Management Board, which included Robert Liddell, R Dawson Bates, Frederick Rogers and James Wilson as Trustees, along with others was to manage the hospitals and the property and funds which could be passed on.[98] The property they had initial responsibility for was that at Queen's University and Craigavon House, estimated at 27 acres. The Trust was replaced with a second in 1944 which gave authority to the trustees to use capital or interest in the furtherance of the objectives or to sell land if considered expedient.[99]

After the Armistice in 1918 the Ministry of War Pensions continued to send ex-service patients for treatment.

The UVF Council in July 1921 reviewed the current position and future operations of the Hospital. The UVF Hospital Board Minutes of 28 July 1921 show the relevant points;[100]

1. The numbers of Patients to be accommodated, and the duration of accommodation required are problematic.
2. The political situation is so uncertain that we have no guarantee whatever as to the forecast made by the Ministry of Pensions, who state they will require about 250 beds for four years.
3. We have at present a large number of patients who are practically convalescent, and therefore could quite well be transferred elsewhere. We have also a number of intern[al] patients who could get all the treatment they require at extern[al] department daily.
4. Having consulted the Commissioner of Medical Service (Ministry of Pensions) as to the above points we are satisfied that he has sufficient beds in the region under his charge, to justify us in closing down a larger number of beds than we previously thought possible. Whilst he would

---

98 Eakins, Arthur, *The Somme – What Happened to the Casualties* (2008).
99 Eakins, Arthur, *The Somme – What Happened to the Casualties* (2008).
100 Eakins, Arthur, *The Somme – What Happened to the Casualties* (2008).

Patients in their uniforms from the UVF hospital being inspected in the grounds of Belfast City Hall. (Somme Museum)

prefer to have 250 beds at his disposal he practically admits that by eliminating all but such patients as require strictly hospital treatment, whether Surgical or Medical and transferring convalescents elsewhere, he could do very well with about 160/180 beds.

With the end of the war Robert Liddell and the Board had to consider the uncertain political future of Ulster and what impact any partition of Ireland might have on the current Government funding and the necessity to conserve the publically subscribed funds for the continued support and treatment of the servicemen.[101]

The financial issue of maintaining 180 beds fully occupied as opposed to 250, with the associated overhead cost of maintenance and staff, pushed the average cost per bed above that being received as the daily grant per patient, and resulted in the Londonderry and Carson units being closed, leaving the 180 beds in the Abercorn unit for strictly surgical and medical cases. As part of the rationalisation Queen's University was offered the Londonderry Unit for £1,000 and it was proposed to buy Somerset House (119 University Street) as the accommodation for the 18 nursing staff considered necessary by the Matron, Miss Burnside, at a cost of £1,650. Whilst the Senate of the University accepted the offer of the Londonderry unit they were not in a position to purchase so instead it was handed over on loan for "educational purposes only".[102]

---

101 Eakins, Arthur, *The Somme – What Happened to the Casualties* (2008).
102 Eakins, Arthur, *The Somme – What Happened to the Casualties* (2008).

The veranda of the Londonderry wing of the Ulster Volunteer Force hospital. (Somme Museum)

In 1922 the newly-formed Royal Ulster Constabulary's Commissioner of Medical Services, Colonel Forrest, approached the Board of the Hospital for hospital accommodation. Thirty beds were offered to the RUC at the rate of 7s 6d per day, with beds reserved but not used being charged at 4s per day. Up to 2008 a total of 374 members of the RUC had received treatment at the hospital.[103]

The UVF Hospitals purchased Hilden House, Galwally, 18 March 1925, for £8,000. This site of 10 acres was acquired from the Joint British Red Cross/St John Ambulance War Committee who had used it during the war as a convalescent site. Utilising the large Victorian rooms of the house built in the 1880s and wooden hutted wards, it was capable of housing 80 patients, opening as a hospital in 1926.[104] It was closed four years later, being reopened in 1940 until finally closing in 1969, having cared for Ulstermen involved in all conflicts since and including the Great War.

The Abercorn wing was vacated in February 1926 and given to Queen's University for educational purposes with the only proviso that when it was no longer required it would be demolished and the materials sold for UVF Board funds.[105]

With the opening of Galwally the hospital at Craigavon was able to be closed and refurbished with two large wards named Craig and Abercorn and a surgical theater. The re-opening of Craigavon with beds for 86 patients coincided the same day with the closure of the main hospital at Queen's University, on 16 March 1926.[106]

The hospital at Galwally was closed in September 1930 and offered for sale. Despite interest from Foster Green Hospital and Princess Gardens Girls' School it could not be sold and was

---

103 Eakins, Arthur, *The Somme – What Happened to the Casualties* (2008).
104 Eakins, Arthur, *The Somme – What Happened to the Casualties* (2008).
105 Eakins, Arthur, *The Somme – What Happened to the Casualties* (2008).
106 Eakins, Arthur, *The Somme – What Happened to the Casualties* (2008).

Veterans at Craigavon House, Belfast. (Somme Museum)

instead leased to the Royal Ulster Constabulary who used it for parking police vehicles and police training.[107]

In the 1960s the UVF hospitals in Ulster were amalgamated and moved to an extended 'Craigavon' where a 30-bed 'Somme Wing' extension was built.

During the Second World War the hospital again found a role supporting wounded servicemen. In 1949, following complex negotiations between the Stormont and Westminster Governments, the UVF hospital came under the National Health Service.

By the late 1980s the UVF Hospital was in need of modernisation, resulting in the Trustees closing the hospital and opening a registered nursing home in the Somme Wing, which was extended and upgraded in September 1992. It was renamed the "Somme Nursing Home" in March 1995.

With numbers dropping and families wanting single rooms for their relatives the Trustees responded in 1998 by selling the Nightingale wards of the old UVF Hospital and the attached walled garden. The money went towards a major building and renovation programme, the renovated building being registered in August 1999 as a general category nursing home with the Registration and Inspection Unit of the Eastern Health and Social Services Board.[108]

The UVF hospitals have, in total cared for over 28,000 soldiers from the Great War.[109]

---

107 Eakins, Arthur, *The Somme – What Happened to the Casualties* (2008).
108 <http://www.belfastsomme.com/hospital.html> (Accessed 24 December 2012).
109 Orr, Philip, *The Road to the Somme* (1987).

Ulster Patriotic Fund

The concept of a patriotic fund was not a new idea. The Royal Patriotic Fund Corporation was a charitable body set up by Royal Warrant during the Crimean War to provide assistance to the widows, orphans and other dependants of members of the armed forces.[110]

During 1915 a number of leading businessmen connected with the Ulster Volunteers realised that a large number of demobilised soldiers might be unable to take up their former work after the war due to wounds or sickness, and as the pension allowed by the government would not be equal to their former wages, might have difficulty in supporting their families.

The fundraising was carried out through concerts, ballots, bowling club events and various other activities. The donations were recorded in a series of lists published monthly in the press, not only as a form of record keeping but as a form of social pressure encouraging others to give compared to their neighbours; donations ranged from several thousand pounds to three pence.[111]

Following the mass casualties in the Ulster Division on 1 July 1916, five days later a circular memorandum was sent out by UVF Headquarters inviting divisional and regimental commanders, officers and men of the UVF to draw their attention "to the urgency of ensuring to the 'UVF Patriotic Fund', "the success it deserves". In order to aid this it was suggested that divisional and regimental commanders should invite their battalion commanders to a meeting to ensure that the objective of the fund was brought to the attention of each man in the Ulster Volunteer Force. Receipt books and collecting cards were able to be supplied by the Town Hall, Belfast[112] to aid in the administration of the fundraising.

By the 20 July the Fund amounted to £30,000, but Headquarters expected that more than double this amount would be necessary to meet the heavy demands expected of it. To that end Lieutenant-General Richardson, GOC UVF, held a personal meeting with all regimental and battalion commanders at the Town Hall in an effort to boost contributions.[113]

Friday, 29 June 1917 was declared 'Forget-me-not Day', when flowers were sold in memory of the fallen and the money raised donated to the UVF Patriotic Fund.[114]

The fund, which amounted to over £100,000 within a year, was provided under the auspices of the Ulster Volunteers Headquarters and administrated by a committee which included many of the leading professional and businessmen in the province. The money was lodged in a bank in the names of several trustees to await the end of the war. Following the Armistice each county formed a committee to undertake the distribution of the fund to supplement the government pension. It was also intended to assist those men unable to take up their former employment with learning new trades, paying apprenticeship fees, and educating their families and helping in any other ways in which the respective committees felt appropriate.[115]

Whilst arrangements were being put into place for the future of those men who had answered the call and fought in the Imperial Force overseas, matters within Ireland also were on the minds of the UVF leadership. An urgent memo dated 23 December 1915 from Lieutenant General Richardson warned that he had obtained information from reliable sources that there were plans of an attack by Sinn Feiners within the next ten days on UVF armouries. As a consequence he

---

110 Rootsweb <http://archiver.rootsweb.ancestry.com/th/read/FERMANAGH-GOLD/2011-08/1314575885> (Accessed 4 Dec 2011).
111 Eakins, Arthur, *The Somme – What Happened to the Casualties* (2008).
112 Circular Memorandum – UVF Patriotic Fund – 6 July 1916.
113 Circular Memorandum – UVF Patriotic Fund from Lieut-Gen Richardson – 20 July 1916.
114 Grayson, Richard S, *Belfast Boys – How Unionists and Nationalists fought and died together in the First World War* (2009).
115 The History of Ulster – Ulster in the War <http://www.electricscotland.com/history/ulster/vol4chap28.htm> (Accessed 4 Dec 2011).

May 1916, details of the winners of a raffle to raise funds to purchase a x-ray machine for the Ulster Volunteer Hospital, Allee du Sacre Coeur, Lyon, France. (Somme Museum: 1-3-1996)

> ### The Ulster Volunteer Hospital in France.
>
> I wish to tell all who helped the Raffle to buy an X-Ray Machine for U.V.F. Hospital in France, that the ten winning numbers were—
>
> 137—JOHN ROBINSON, Pettigo.   363—EARL OF BELMORE, Enniskillen
> 503—MRS. ARCHDALE, Castle-Archdale   2702—MISS THOMPSON, Belfast.
> 1248—M. SIEVER, Liverpool.   2473—LADY DIXON, Co. Antrim.
> 1419—D. M'CAULEY, L'kenny   2649—PADDY BONAR, Dungloe.
> 1166—MRS. NEELY, Sion Mills   2079—ANDREW ADAMS, Beragh.
>
> The following copy of a Letter from France may interest all who so kindly helped the work.
>
> M. E. SINCLAIR, Holyhill, Strabane.
> 25th May, 1916.
>
> #### Ulster Volunteer Hospital,
> ALLEE DU SACRE COEUR, LYON,
> May 16th, 1916.
>
> We left the Pension yesterday and slept last night here in our new home; it was real camping. The house is unfurnished; all the electric light fittings are missing; the gas is not working, nor is the water; the cess-pool is overflowing. We are sleeping on hospital beds and my dressing table is the top of my suit case. We have six jugs and basins amongst us.
>
> The landlady was to have had all ready for us, but she lives at a distance, and is not a hustler, so no one took any notice of her various notes telling them to go on with the work. Our own infirmiers cleaned (?) the house. Before meals we wash under the pump in the yard. It is great fun and in a few days we shall be quite comfortable. A little restaurant next door sends us in delicious meals and has lent us tables and benches and supplies the crockery, &c., for the table. Downer is invaluable. The Mayoress is going to try and get us the loan of furniture for the home, so we do not like to buy anything "en attendant." Yesterday Skipper and I were tearing our hair over the number of small things that had to be bought, such as linoleum for the theatre and sterlizing room, etc, and wondering where the money was to come from. (At Pau we used to pay for that sort of thing out of the money the mayor used to give us from time to time.) While we were lamenting one of our V.A.D's., a Yorkshire girl called Lupton, came in and calmly

warned that extra precautions must be taken in order to safeguard the weapons and ammunition. In the first instance if trouble was expected the nearest police were to be informed, as he put it, "whose business it is to deal with disturbances." Interestingly, compared to the UVF attitude to the police on previous occasions, he stated that if the police demanded assistance then the nearest UVF officer was to ensure that suitable reinforcements were supplied.

If the UVF were called out, the piquet was to parade and protect the arms and in the event of any trouble Richardson stated that he was to be informed at once, supplying addresses and telephone contact details in order that he could be notified.[116]

A raid on the Randallstown armoury on the night of Friday 28 January 1916 was unsuccessful when the arms were not found.[117]

---

116 Possible attack on armouries by Sinn Feinners – 23 December 1915.
117 Memo from Adair to Young – Antrim UVF – 31 January 1915.

Ulster Volunteer Nurses parading down Market Square North, Lisburn past the Market House. (Somme Museum)

12

Easter Rebellion and the Somme

The Easter Rebellion in April 1916, launched by a section of the Irish Volunteers took the Irish Parliamentary Party by surprise, the Volunteers declaring an Irish Republic and taking over much of the centre of Dublin. The Volunteers had been infiltrated to a large degree by the separatist Irish Republican Brotherhood.

The Irish Volunteers had been planning to hold peaceful manoeuvres on Easter Sunday 1916. However, Professor Eoin MacNeill, Chief of Staff of the Irish Volunteers, found out that a group led by Patrick Pearse had made secret plans for an armed rising against British rule. MacNeill and other moderate Volunteers opposed the idea of an unprovoked rebellion because they felt it had no realistic prospect of success, he had previously argued that they should wait until a more opportune time, such as when Britain might introduce conscription or attempted to suppress the Volunteers. From that basis he believed they could fight in self-defence and gain mass support.

He therefore tried to countermand the order for the armed rebellion which led to chaos and confusion within the Volunteers, especially in areas remote from Dublin, where local commanders could not establish what was going on; consequently, there was no rising in Cork or Limerick.

Meanwhile in Dublin, the group led by Pearse, James Connolly and Tom Clarke, held a parade with whatever forces they could muster. The rebels occupied a circle of prominent buildings around the city centre of Dublin. Their headquarters was established in the General Post Office (GPO) on Sackville Street which appeared to have no strategic, administrative or symbolic value, whilst Dublin Castle, the seat of British power in Ireland, which was poorly defended was not significantly threatened. At 12:30 p.m. Pearse, a teacher and barrister, emerged from the GPO and read aloud to, described by historian Jeff Kildea as "a small and bemused crowd" the proclamation for the Irish Republic.[1]

They barricaded themselves into the occupied buildings with orders given to those outside Dublin equally vague with intent. Those Volunteers in the west were ordered "to hold the line of the Shannon" whilst Belfast's republicans were instructed to march across Ulster to join the fight in the west of the country.[2,3]

The believed impact of loss of the German munitions on the SS *Aud* and the capture of Roger Casement was highlighted in an intelligence summary issued by General Headquarters Egyptian Expeditionary Force on 28 April 1916; "The capture of the notorious SIR ROGER CASEMENT and two German officers (on the same very day when the disturbances broke out) whilst being landed off the Irish Coast from a disguised German Axillary cruiser has probably robbed the rebellion of all direction." The summary also referred to articles in Dutch and Italian newspapers

---

1 *Journal of the Australian War Memorial* – Kildea, Jeff, Called to arms: Australian soldiers in the Easter Rising 1916 <http://www.awm.gov.au/journal/j39/kildea/> (Accessed 3 January 2015).
2 The Easter Rising of 1916 <http://www.bbc.co.uk/history/british/britain_wwone/easter_rising_01.shtml#five> (Accessed 3 October 2014).
3 Eoin MacNeill Stop Order <http://www.bbc.co.uk/news/uk-northern-ireland-26418138> (Accessed 3 March 2014).

Irish Citizen Army Jacket. This jacket was worn by Captain Sean O'Neil who was one of the participants in the Easter Rising and fought in the College of Surgeons in Dublin. O'Neil was imprisoned after the Rising. He died during the Irish Civil War 1922-23 when he fought for the anti-Treaty forces. (Somme Museum)

Sir Roger Casement's Irish Brigade Jacket. He tried to form an Irish Brigade from Irish prisoners of war in Limburg POW Camp in 1915-16. The proposed Brigade would fight with the Central Powers against Britain. The uniforms were adapted from German army styles with the addition of dark green facings and shamrock insignia. (Somme Museum)

which it said "clearly stated that this rebellion had been organised in Germany to coincide with the approach of the spring when an Allied offensive was to be expected, and also relied [sic] to find in Ireland (excused from the Military Service Act) many men of military age who could be used to further the designs of the enemy."[4]

The reality was that Casement had in fact been arrested the previous Friday when he landed with two Irishmen with the mission to persuade Pearse and Connolly to call off the rebellion due to the lack of German support.[5]

On 28 April 1916 Richardson issued a Special Order to the UVF which highlighted that in the wake of the events of the past few days in Dublin it was necessary for all divisional, regimental and battalion Commanders to ensure the safety of the UVF arms. All guards were to be doubled and mounted on the armouries between 8:00 p.m. and 8:00 a.m. Piquets were to be readied so

---

4   Journal of the Australian War Memorial – Kildea, Jeff, Called to arms: Australian soldiers in the Easter Rising 1916 <http://www.awm.gov.au/journal/j39/kildea/> (Accessed 3 January 2015).
5   Journal of the Australian War Memorial – Kildea, Jeff, Called to arms: Australian soldiers in the Easter Rising 1916 <http://www.awm.gov.au/journal/j39/kildea/> (Accessed 3 January 2015).

Buglers of the newly-formed 36th (Ulster) Division at Clandeboye Camp. (Somme Museum)

that they could turn out in the event of an alarm and the nearest police informed if trouble arose. Again it was reiterated that the Ulster Volunteer Force was co-operating with both the military and the police.[6] This order was further clarified a few days later by way of a circular memorandum from Richardson which stated that armed assistance would be provided to military or police on a requisition signed by a military officer or a County or District Inspector of police, whilst unarmed guards could be provided on the request of any military officer or police.[7]

Richardson went further and offered the services of the Ulster Volunteer Force to the British Authorities. In real terms this appears to have consisted of 1,148 members of the UVF being sworn in as special constables in Belfast, members of the UVF providing guards on vulnerable armouries, the protection of the wireless station at Ballycastle and the loan of a number of UVF rifles to a Royal Army Medical Corps detachment located at Dundalk.[8]

Some local UVF Commanders also placed their men on standby, such as the Monaghan Regiment, John Leslie informing one of his battalion commanders, "Do not use arms unless the other side have already begun firing which I do not expect of them. Let the police know you are ready to help them."[9]

Whilst neither the Ulster Volunteer Force nor 36th (Ulster) Division as distinct entities saw service in Dublin during the Easter Rebellion, those 200 of the affiliated Loyal Dublin Volunteers who had became members of the Irish Association of Volunteer Training Corps did see active

---

6   UVF Orders 01, 1916 – Somme Heritage Centre.
7   Circular Memorandum – 1 May 1916.
8   Bowman, Timothy, *Carson's Army: Ulster Volunteer Force, 1910-22* (2007).
9   Bowman, Timothy, *Carson's Army: Ulster Volunteer Force, 1910-22* (2007).

service assisting troops from the Curragh in suppressing the violence. On the first day of the rising several Loyal Dublin Volunteers lost their lives.[10]

British reinforcements did not arrive until midweek. Amongst these reinforcements were the hastily formed Ulster Composite Battalion, a thousand men comprising many soldiers from the Ulster-based reserve battalions of the Royal Irish Rifles (4th based in Carrickfergus, 5th based in Holywood, 17th based in Ballykinler, 18th based in Clandeboye, 19th based in Newcastle, 20th based in Newtownards), Royal Irish Fusiliers (3rd based in Buncrana, 4th based in Carrickfergus, 10th based in Newtownards) and Royal Inniskilling Fusiliers (3rd based in Derry, 4th based in Buncrana, 12th based in either Enniskillen or Finner Camp). As a result of their recruiting area and as reserves for the 36th (Ulster) Division a number of its soldiers had also been signatories of the Ulster Covenant and members of the Ulster Volunteer Force.[11] On Easter Monday, the Assistant Adjutant General, Colonel H.V. Cowan, in the absence of both the General Officer Commanding in Chief and his Brigadier General, requested immediate assistance from Brigadier General Hacket-Pain, the General Officer Commanding the 15 Ulster Reserve Infantry Brigade, which arrived in Dublin at 2:00 p.m. on the next day.[12] Along with the 4th Royal Dublin Fusiliers and four 18-pounders from 5 (A) Reserve Artillery Brigade, they set up outposts on the north side of the city and began to harass the rebels in the Four Courts and the GPO.[13] The rebels defended their well-fortified positions in the centre of Dublin for six days, until British artillery forced the surrender of the GPO garrison the following Saturday. The rebellion which was put down in a week of fighting left large parts of Dublin city centre devastated by artillery bombardment and fire.

There were approximately 500 killed and 2,500 wounded.[14] Amongst the casualties were dead approximately 134 members of the British forces and Royal Irish Constabulary and Dublin Metropolitan Police, with approximately 387 more wounded; a number of the dead and wounded included soldiers from the Ulster Composite Battalion.[15] General Maxwell's actions against its leaders won sympathy for their cause when a total of 16 were shot within weeks of the Rebellion and another hanged several weeks later.

The Rebellion in Dublin and elsewhere in the south of Ireland resulted in 170 houses being burnt, £2,000,000 worth of property destroyed or damaged and 1,315 casualties, of which 304 were fatal.[16]

Lieutenant Colonel J.K. McClintock from Seskinore, Tyrone, the Commanding Officer of the 3rd Reserve Battalion of The Royal Inniskilling Fusiliers based in Londonderry, who was part of the Ulster Composite Battalion, was Mentioned in Despatches "for distinguished conduct in Dublin during the rebellion",[17] as was Brigadier General Hacket Pain for his actions in Dublin.[18]

The Easter Rebellion began the decline of constitutional Nationalism as represented by the Irish Parliamentary Party and the ascent of a more radical separatist form of Irish nationalism. John Redmond, protesting at the severity of the state's response to the Rebellion, wrote to Asquith;

---

10 http://www.newsletter.co.uk/features/the-loyal-dublin-volunteers-a-forgotten-organisation-1-3719467 (Accessed 5 February 2014).
11 Richardson, Neil, *According to their lights: Stories of Irishmen in the British Army, Easter 1916* (2015).
12 'Inniskillings' in Dublin, 1916 <http://www.inniskillingsmuseum.com/inniskillings-in-dublin-1916/> (Accessed 25 January 2016).
13 Richardson, Neil, *According to their lights: Stories of Irishmen in the British Army, Easter 1916* (2015).
14 Jeffery, K, *Ireland and the Great War* (2000).
15 Richardson, Neil, *According to their lights: Stories of Irishmen in the British Army, Easter 1916* (2015).
16 McNeill, Ronald, *Ulster's Stand for Union* (1922).
17 'Inniskillings' in Dublin, 1916 <http://www.inniskillingsmuseum.com/inniskillings-in-dublin-1916/> (Accessed 25 January 2016).
18 Richardson, Neil, *According to their lights: Stories of Irishmen in the British Army, Easter 1916* (2015).

Cumann na mBan tunic. Formed in April 1914, Cumann na mBan was the women's auxiliary group to the Irish Volunteers. This tunic was worn by Miss Rose MacNamara, during Easter week 1916, and in Kilmainham jail after the surrender. Members of Cumann na mBan played a significant role in the Easter Rising. (Somme Museum)

"if any more executions take place, Ireland will become impossible for any Constitutional Party or leader."

However the actions of the Government, with Asquith visiting Dublin after the event, speaking with Sinn Fein prisoners and saying that something had to be done for Ireland, and that plans being discussed for a new Home Rule Bill for Ireland all indicated a certain sense of uncertainty and panic, which had the effect of giving the depressed spirits of the prisoners a new lease of life and a cry of victory for their actions.[19]

It also had the unnecessary and unwelcome impact of re-awaking the Home Rule question across the whole island, especially during wartime,[20] and convincing many Ulster Protestants of the continued necessity of the Ulster Volunteer Force to 'hold the fort' at home against Nationalist moves towards Home Rule or worse.

In the wake of the Easter Rebellion, Asquith realised that the only way to prevent Sinn Fein from gaining all the popular support from Redmond was to concede to some form of Home Rule. Lloyd George was tasked with the mission to find a workable solution with the parties.[21]

By the end of May 1916 all UVF drills, instruction, machine gun and other classes were discontinued until further notice.[22]

Meanwhile, having been reportedly seized in Hamburg in August 1914,[23] by 1916 the *Clyde Valley* which had supplied the Ulster Volunteer Force with arms and ammunition was operating as a German Army Transport, but in January 1919 she was repatriated by Richard Cowser of Glasgow.[24]

---

19   Shearman, Hugh, *Not an Inch: A Study of Northern Ireland and Lord Craigavon* (1942).
20   Shearman, Hugh, *Not an Inch: A Study of Northern Ireland and Lord Craigavon* (1942).
21   Lewis, Geoffrey, *Carson: The man who divided Ireland* (2006).
22   Circular Memorandum – 29 May 1916.
23   <http://www.shipsnostalgia.com/showpost.php?p=92891&postcount> Ships Nostalgia – John Kelly (Belfast). Now Kelly Fuels (Accessed 20 February 2014).
24   Hume, David, *"For Ulster and Her Freedom": The story of the April 1914 gun-running* (1989).

Cap badge on cap belonging to the 2nd Battalion, North Down Regiment. (Somme Museum)

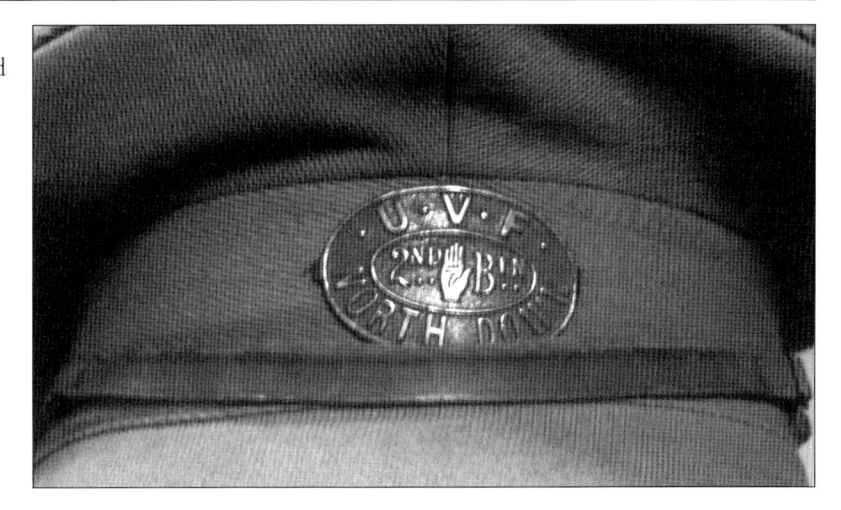

Somme

Saturday, 1 July 1916 in Ireland, was much like any other day during the war, and the population was oblivious to the events in France other than the *Belfast Telegraph* informing its readers that the 'long awaited Franco-British offensive' had begun. Major-General Nugent's special order to the 36th Division was published on Thursday with the paper reporting the following day the crucial role the Division had played in the opening of the offensive; there was also the first list of casualties. This was the prelude to small buff coloured envelopes arriving in increasing numbers at homes all over Ulster.

The newspapers started to print long lists of the casualties, letters from wounded men recovering in hospitals in England, and also tributes from political figures referring to the sacrifice of the Ulster Volunteers and their loyalty to King and country. It was often hoped that the sacrifice on the 1 July would tie Ulster more closely to Britain, the thoughts of Home Rule still in many minds. The *Belfast News Letter* reported "Ulster Protestants took their stand where their fathers stood … [in] costly self-sacrifice to our Empire."[25]

Major-General Sir Oliver Stewart Wood Nugent KCB DSO commanded the 36th (Ulster) Division during the First World War. (Somme Museum)

The losses were felt particularly by the Orange Order whose members had provided a significant number of those in the Ulster Volunteers who had then joined the 36th Division. As a direct consequence of the war, since 1915 the 12th July Commemorations had been muted however, with detailed lists of officer casualties appearing in the local papers, followed from 10 July by the longest lists of rank-and-file casualty lists which the Belfast papers would print in the entire war.[26] For the first time in its history the Orange Order

---

25 *Belfast News Letter* – 11 July 1916.
26 Grayson, Richard S, *Belfast Boys – How Unionists and Nationalists fought and died together in the First World War* (2009).

LES VAINQUEURS DE LA SOMME!
THE CONQUERORS OF THE SOMME!

A postcard depicting the "Conquerors of the Somme". On the left is a French soldier in uniform and on the right is a British soldier, his forage cap is sporting the cap badge of the Ulster Volunteers, the red hand in the oval. (Aribert Elpelt)

abandoned its traditional commemorative processions on 12 July and, at the suggestion of the Lord Mayor, five minutes silence was observed instead at noon that day.[27] During 1918 and 1919 the commemoration of the sacrifice at the Somme was tied up with the 12 July commemorations[28] and is still linked with and often commemorated on Lodge Banners today.

Captain Wilfrid Spender's account of the battle reinforced the link between the Division and the UVF:

> The Ulster Division has lost more than half the men who attached and in doing so, has sacrificed itself for the Empire which has treated them none too well. The much derided Ulster Volunteer Force has won a name which equals any in history. Their devotion, which no doubt has helped the advance elsewhere, deserves the gratitude of the British Empire. It is due to the memory of these brave fellows that their beloved province shall be fairly treated.

However, the introduction to his account was to strike a chord for many; "I am not an Ulsterman, but yesterday, the 1 July 1916, as I followed their amazing attack I felt that I would rather be an Ulsterman than anything else in the world."

As serving soldiers were not supposed to write for the press, Spender's account appeared in *The Times* and *Morning Post* as simply attributed to 'an eye-witness account' and 'a correspondent' respectively.

---

27 Jeffery, Keith, *Ireland and the Great War* (2000).
28 Grayson, Richard S, *Belfast Boys – How Unionists and Nationalists fought and died together in the First World War* (2009).

Sir Edward Carson expressed the views of many in his message which was circulated to all members of the UVF;[29]

> I desire to express, on my own behalf and that of my colleagues from Ulster the pride and admiration with which we have learnt of the unparalleled acts of heroism and bravery which were carried out by the Ulster Division in the great offensive movement of the 1st July.
>
> From all accounts that we have received, they have made the supreme sacrifice for the Empire of which they were so proud with a courage, coolness, and determination, in the face of the most trying difficulties, which have upheld the greatest traditions of the British Army.
>
> Our feelings are, of course, mingled with sorrow and sadness at the loss of so many men who were to us personal friends and comrades, but we believe that the spirit of their race will at a time of such grief and anxiety sustain those who mourn their loss, and set an example to others to follow in their footsteps.

In the accompanying orders, the GOC UVF also expressed his deepest sympathy and acknowledged the gallantry of the officers and men of the Ulster Division. He also went on to state that "Every effort must be made to fill up the casualties in the Division, and maintain the glorious lead given by the brave men of Ulster."[30]

The next week UVF Headquarters encouraged the men of the Ulster Volunteer Force to contribute to the UVF Patriotic Fund. However, in County Antrim, General Adair, following the initial request, informed his

Newspaper clipping from the *Northern Whig*, Saturday 15 July 1916, informing the Ulster readers of the actions of the 36th (Ulster) Division on the 1st of July 1916. (Somme Museum: 1997-250)

---

29   Ulster Volunteer Force Orders – Message to the Ulster People – 1916.
30   Ulster Volunteer Force Orders – Message to the Ulster People – 1916.

commanders that the accounts being read in newspapers seemed to point to the probability that a large number of County Antrim men had been taken prisoner and it was concluded that they could run the risk of being starved. Therefore he thought that in the first instance they ought to raise money for them by sending it to The Ulster Women's Gift Aid which was responsible for sending regular parcels to all prisoners they knew of. He also asked that they should notify immediately of any of their men being killed or taken prisoner, furnishing his regimental number, full name, address, battalion, name and address of next of kin and also his UVF organisation number.[31]

In Corrigan's history, *'Mud, Blood and Poppycock'*, he compares against other British cities how Belfast was impacted by the arrival of the black telegrams informing family of those who had died on the 1 July or from wounds on the two days after; Leeds 493, Barnsley 213 and Belfast 839.[32]

Perhaps not surprisingly the aftermath of the Somme led to a drop in enlistment to the Ulster Division. Recruitment problems had already been encountered in the Division as it had been elsewhere in the United Kingdom, however this was overcome somewhat in Great Britain through the introduction of conscription which was an element missing in Ireland.

An editorial in the *Armagh Guardian* in August 1916 openly criticised those members of the Ulster Volunteer Force still at home for failing to enlist saying that Unionists, "knew quite well that the ranks require filling up – but THEY WON'T GO. In Killylea, Tynan, Kilmore, Keady and the other districts there are families where there are two, three and even four or more brothers, and not one has joined to fight for Ulster."[33]

Women supporting a recruitment drive in Armagh 1916 after the Battle of the Somme.
(Somme Museum)

---

31 Memo from General WT Adair – 7 July 1916.
32 Corrigan, Gordon, *Mud, Blood and Poppycock* (2003).
33 Cousins, Colin, *Armagh and the Great War* (2011).

In the short term the vacancies in the Divisions' ranks were able to be filled from the existing reserve battalions of the 36th Division, however it was not long before English, Scots, Welsh and Catholic Irish were drafted into the 'Ulster Division', reducing the Volunteer spirit which was more evident when it was first formed. The link was further severed, perhaps significantly, when in May 1918 Major-General Nugent was replaced by an Englishman, Major-General Clifford Coffin, VC. Despite these changes in character there were of course men who had joined from the ranks from the Ulster Volunteers in 1914 who stayed and fought with the Division right through to the Armistice of 1918.

During July 1916 whilst Ulster came to terms with both the Easter events in Dublin and the first day of the Somme offensive, Asquith tried to negotiate a deal between Irish Nationalists and Unionists over the introduction of the suspended Home Rule Act 1914. This caused further problems for the Irish Parliamentary Party and failed due to the threat of partition. When Lloyd George became Prime Minister he again tried to resolve the Home Rule issue, being keen to appease Britain's ally, the United States of America, who was urging Britain to solve the Irish question quickly.[34]

The United States of America eventually entered the war against Germany as a result of the unrestricted German U-boat campaign. However President Woodrow Wilson, a Presbyterian, was not in sympathy with his co-religionists in Ulster and believed that Britain's failure to give self-government in Ireland was standing in the way of perfect co-operation during the war. This echoed the strong Home Rule lobby in America where Irish Catholics were providing funds and fomenting rebellion in Ireland.[35]

One act, made in the spirit of reconciliation, resulted in the release of all remaining republican prisoners and led to them calling on the President and Congress of the United States of America to assist with the Provisional Government's call for self-determination.

Lloyd George approached Redmond with the proposal of an Irish Convention. Redmond called a Convention in June 1917 comprising national celebrities, bishops, businessmen, university dons, revolutionaries, poets, landowners, aristocrats and others, all of who met for the first time 25 July 1917 at Trinity College, Dublin.[36]

The Convention was intended to submit to the British Government a constitution for the future government of Ireland with representation from local government, trade unions, and churches. However it was doomed from the start as Sinn Fein boycotted it and the Ulster Unionists refused to budge from the six-county exclusion.[37]

Redmond attempted to form an agreement with the Southern Unionists for Home Rule for Ireland which if agreed by 'substantial' agreement by the convention; with only Ulster disagreeing, then the Prime Minster would use his personal influence to bring it into law; this was contrary to the previous agreement that there would be no substantial agreement with the concurrence of Ulster.

In Dublin on 12 July 1917 Sinn Fein's new leader, Éamon de Valera, called upon Irish people to make English law impossible and combine under the Republican flag, and if Ulster stood in the way of Irish freedom, Ulster must be coerced.[38]

Carson therefore disagreed in principle with the proposals and again resigned on 21 January 1918. He gave up his seat at the University of Dublin in the 1918 General Election and was instead

---

34 Shearman, Hugh, *Not an Inch: A Study of Northern Ireland and Lord Craigavon* (1942).
35 Lewis, Geoffrey, *Carson: The man who divided Ireland* (2006).
36 Shearman, Hugh, *Not an Inch: A Study of Northern Ireland and Lord Craigavon* (1942).
37 Lewis, Geoffrey, *Carson: The man who divided Ireland* (2006).
38 Shearman, Hugh, *Not an Inch: A Study of Northern Ireland and Lord Craigavon* (1942).

The Craig Ward, Christmas 1916.
(Somme Museum)

Department of Recruiting, Ireland.

October 28th, 1915.

Sir,

Lord Kitchener sends me the attached message for YOU.

He wants 50,000 Irishmen at once for the period of the War. You will be equipped and will start your training in Ireland, and complete it in different parts of the world. Wherever you go you will be serving with Irishmen.

The relatives whom you look after will be looked after for you while you are away. Your Wives, your Children, or those dependent on you will receive an allowance every week.

Every great Irishman urges the appeal. The safety of your homes and your possessions depends on your answer.

Sons of Farmers—whose lands are passing into your own possession—You must come out and defend this heritage.

Townsmen, your interests are threatened too. You must equally respond to the call.

It is your privilege as an Irishman to come forward voluntarily. Will you come now? Fill in this form and post it to-day.

Yours faithfully,

Wimborne

Lord Lieutenant of Ireland and
Director-General for Recruiting.

[P.T.O.]

Letter from the Department of Recruiting dated 28 October 1915 seeking 50,000 Irishmen to enlist in the army for the duration of the war.
(Somme Museum: 1999-49-1)

Men of A and B Company of the Central Antrim Volunteers, 36th (Ulster) Division at Clandeboye Camp. (Somme Museum)

elected for Belfast Duncairn. The General Election also saw Unionists advance from 18 seats to 26 and Sinn Fein secure 73 seats with a mere half dozen Nationalists surviving.[39]

Ireland in 1918 saw an increase of illegal drilling, attacks on police barracks, disarming of isolated policemen, cutting of telegraph wires and blocking roads in parts of the south and west of the country. It was in the middle of this growing chaos that Redmond died in March 1918, with the Irish Parliamentary Party leadership being taken over by John Dillon.

The successes of the German Spring Offensive in April 1918 caused severe manpower shortages, resulting in a clumsy cabinet decision by Lloyd George in linking the implementation of Irish Home Rule to an extension of conscription to Ireland through a Manpower Bill which was passed at the beginning of April.

Carson wrote to Bonar Law on 8 April warning that the Nationalists would simply increase their demands and highlighted that it would be impossible to enforce conscription in Ireland. He also warned that any thought that the Irish would fight for a free country but not a subject nation was misplaced as Sinn Fein had no intention of joining the war against Germany.[40]

On the question of conscription, the Royal Irish Constabulary Inspector General, General Byrne, had already informed the Prime Minister that, "by passing and enforcing such a measure: both the whole of the Catholics and Nationalists in Ireland would be united against the British Empire." Also warning about riots, the difficulty of enlisting men and the doubtful worth of any potential recruits achieved this way.[41]

---

39 Shearman, Hugh, *Not an Inch: A Study of Northern Ireland and Lord Craigavon* (1942).
40 Lewis, Geoffrey, *Carson: The man who divided Ireland* (2006).
41 Gregory, Adrian and Paseta, Senia (ed)., *Ireland and the Great War 'A War to Unite Us All'?* (2002).

Ulster's Solemn Covenant Postcard: Heroes of the Union depicting Sir Edward Carson. c 1912 (Somme Museum)

ULSTER'S SOLEMN COVENANT

SIR EDWARD CARSON.

HEROES OF THE UNION

Behind this gallant Statesman are men who lead the cause,
The glorious cause of Union. Men of Ulster! do not pause.
We have signed the Solemn Covencnt, which binds us to defend
Our faith, our flag, our loyalty unflinching to the end.

During a debate in the Westminster House of Commons in April 1918 Lloyd George highlighted that it would be impossible to leave the reservoir of manpower in Ireland untouched when men aged 50, whose sons were already with the Colours, were to be called up in Great Britain. However such a suggestion led to a bitter attack from Nationalists in the House. Mr Byrne said "You will have another battle front in Ireland." They maintained that only an Irish Parliament had the right to introduce conscription and as since the beginning of the war they had accepted the provision that it should run its course before Home Rule came into operation, hence there could be no conscription. Mr William O'Brien, T.M Healy and Mr Dillon used all their skill and voting power to oppose the extension of conscription to Ireland. Healy had been an authority on the Irish land question which made him popular throughout Nationalist Ireland and also won his cause seats in Protestant Ulster. He had broken with Parnell in 1886 and although a strong supporter of Home Rule he generally remained at odds with subsequent leaders of the Irish Parliamentary Party. Called to the Irish bar in 1884 he became a Queen's Counsel in 1899. Dissatisfied with both the Liberals and the Irish Nationalists, after the Easter Rebellion in 1916 he supported Sinn Fein after 1917.

Healy and Carson, despite their political sympathies, were warm friends from the beginning of their acquaintance. Healy had great admiration for Carson's character, describing him as "a man whose word you could rely on." He went further, "When he said 'Yes' it was 'Yes', if it was 'No' with him, it meant 'No'. He said 'No' all his life to a United Ireland, more's the pity. But I would trust my soul to Carson."[42]

He was regarded as an elder statesman by the British and Irish governments, being proposed by both sides in 1922 as Governor-General of the new Irish Free State, a post that he held until his resignation and retirement in 1928. The debate also gave Healy the opportunity to refer to the Curragh Incident and to have a jibe at General Gough who had just been driven back by the overwhelming superiority of a German attack, and was reforming his 5th Army, and also at "Carson's Army." Choosing a more gentle style of tone for his response, Carson answered:

> My honourable friend talked of Carson's Army. You may, if you like, call it with contempt Carson's Army. But it has just gone into action for the fourth time, and many of them have paid the supreme sacrifice. They have covered themselves with glory, and, what is more, they have covered Ireland with glory, and they have left behind sad homes throughout the small hamlets of Ulster, as I well know, losing three or four sons in many a home.

On the question in hand Carson gave the full support of Ulster to the government's stance, having voted along with his colleagues against the exemption of Ireland from the Military Service Acts.

The Irish Parliamentary Party ultimately withdrew from Westminster in protest and joined forces with other Irish National organisations in massed anti-conscription demonstrations in Dublin.

Whilst the bill was carried through by 16 April despite Nationalist objections it would be still in drafting stages when on 18 May the Lord-Lieutenant made a proclamation that the Government had information "that certain of the King's subjects in Ireland had entered into a treasonable communication with the German enemy, and strict measures must be taken to put down this German plot." As a result 150 Sinn Feiners were arrested, including de Valera and Arthur Griffith, whilst on the 25 May a further statement was issued indicating a connection with Casement's activities in 1916. On 12 April a German agent had been captured in Ireland with papers showing de Valera had worked out a detailed organisation of the rebel army and an expectation to muster 500,000 trained men. On this basis Mr Bonar Law said it would be impossible for the government to proceed with their arrangements for a new Home Rule Bill.

The entry of America into the war removed the immediate need for Irish conscription however the threat of its introduction had radicalised further Irish politics. Sinn Fein, the political arm of the Volunteer insurgents had public opinion believe that they alone had prevented conscription.

---

42 Hyde, H Montgomery, *Carson* (1953).

13

Post-war

The war ended with the Armistice, 11 November 1918. The men arriving home were faced by a different political situation to the one which they left. The General Election of December 1918 resulted in Sinn Fein being elected in 73 constituencies (although four candidates were elected for two constituencies, resulting in the total number of Sinn Fein MPs being 69) out of a possible 105 MPs in 103 constituencies. In comparison the Irish Unionist Party secured 22 seats, largely limited to Ulster, with southern Unionists securing the constituencies of the University of Dublin and Rathmines. Three Labour Unionist and one Independent Unionist MP were also elected along with six Irish Parliamentary Party MPs.[1]

In January 1919 Sinn Fein boycotted the Westminster Parliament and formed Dail Éireann. On the same day the Irish Volunteers ambushed and killed two members of the Royal Irish Constabulary guarding quarry explosives at Soloheadbeg, County Tipperary.

The Dail recognised the Irish Volunteers as the Army of the Irish Republic, thus signalling the start of the Irish War of Independence between the Irish Republican Army (IRA) of the self-declared Irish Republic, and the forces of the United Kingdom in Ireland, the British Army and the Royal Irish Constabulary, supported by the 'Black and Tans' and the Auxiliary Division.

As 1919 continued the situation in Ireland became a surreal reality with an 'illegal' parliament, *Dail* Éireann, siting in Dublin, waging war against the Westminster Government, the British administration in Dublin and any of their agents or anyone who appeared loyal to it.[2]

The 'war' was largely a series of attacks against the police, soldiers, magistrates and anyone representing British rule, which included attacks on police barracks, police and soldiers being ambushed and murdered,

Wanted poster issued after the fatal attack on police at Soloheadbeg, County Tipperary on 21 January 1919. (Police Museum)

---

1 Metcalfe, Nick, *Blacker's Boys* (2012).
2 Kennedy, Dennis, *The Widening Gulf: Northern attitudes to the independent Irish State 1919-49* (1988).

raids for arms, railways blown up, trains derailed, bridges mined and blocked, cars commandeered and enemies of the republic shot in their beds, their houses burnt down, stores looted and boycotts enforced by death sentences.

The republicans believed they were at war whilst the British administration considered republican activities to be crimes and as such executed those they caught as common murderers. However this resulted in radicalising Irish opinion and often resulted in sums of money being placed on the heads of police and soldiers.

Despite the political differences in Ireland the former Ulster Volunteers returning home from service with the 36th (Ulster) Division and other Imperial Forces had one primary concern, full time employment. However many of their previous positions in Belfast factories and shipyards were now filled by migrant Catholic workers from across Ireland and this, combined with the inevitable economic depression and political tension following the end of the war, ultimately led to sectarian disturbances the following year.[3]

On 1 November 1919 Hacket Pain retired from the army again with the rank of Brigadier-General, and received the award of Knight Commander of the Order of the British Empire. He was immediately appointed as Belfast Commissioner of the Royal Irish Constabulary.

Joseph Devlin complained that this meant the former Chief of Staff in Carson's army was responsible for protecting Roman Catholics. After riots and the murder of a Royal Irish Constabulary District Inspector in Lisburn, Hacket Pain placed the town under military control in August 1920.

On Sunday August 22, 1920, District Inspector Oswald Ross Swanzy, who was living at 31, Railway Street, Lisburn, attended Morning Service at Christ Church Cathedral.

As he was walking home past the entrance to the Northern Bank he was shot by a team of five IRA men running in pairs on either side of the street with a fifth a little way behind in the center of the road.

A 39 year old single man from County Monaghan, but with a long family connection to Lisburn, he had been a member of the constabulary for 15 years.

Michael Collins was responsible for directing his murder, believing the officer had been the leader of the party of unidentified men who killed Tomas McCurtain, the Lord Mayor of Cork and Commandant of Cork Number One Brigade of the IRA.[4]

Swanzy had also been responsible for the seizure of Irish Nationalist Volunteer weapons in Cork.[5] As a consequence he was transferred to Lisburn, nearly the opposite end of the country but his location was traced by Collins with the help of RIC Sergeant Matt McCarthy who had provided Collins with information in the past.

Sean Culhane, the Intelligence Officer of B Company of the IRA's First Cork Battalion, was sent to Belfast to link up with local IRA activists.

Swanzy died at the scene as his attackers continued to fire as they ran along Castle Street to a waiting taxi.

As the IRA attackers passed the archway into the Cathedral on Castle Street they were attacked by a former army officer, who was also the local UVF commander, brandishing a stick. They fled the scene in the same taxi they arrived in, the registration number of the vehicle being noted by a person in the town. The driver was arrested at 4:00 p.m.; a total of six men were arrested for the murder.

---

3   Parkinson, Alan F, *Friends in High Places: Ulster's Resistance to Irish Home Rule, 1912-14* (2012).
4   Abbott, Richard, *'Police Casualties in Ireland 1919 to 1922'* (2000).
5   Lecture by Richard Abbott – October 2014.

The homecoming parade of the 36th (Ulster) Division marching up Chichester Street towards the front of the Belfast City Hall, 1919. (Somme Museum: 1994:517)

Soldiers and police patrolling Belfast during 1919 and the War of Independence. (*Belfast Telegraph*)

Commemorative medal issued by Belfast City commemorating the conclusion of the Great War 1914-1919. (Somme Museum)

Following Swanzy's death, rioting broke out in both Lisburn and Belfast with 22 people being killed in Belfast in one week. In Lisburn most of the Catholic business community's premises were burnt.[6]

In April 1920 the Royal Irish Constabulary Barracks in Leckey Road, in the city of Londonderry, came under attack by nationalists following the arrest of republican prisoners captured in an earlier skirmish who had been taken to Bishop Street jail; at least six of the attackers were wounded by gunshots. In the following days members of the Ulster Volunteer Force were involved in disturbances which also involved the British Army. The nationalists reacted by attacking two soldiers on 15 May 1920 which led to full scale riots culminating in Bridge Street being occupied by armed UVF men. As the police attempted to restore order during a four-hour gun battle between the rioting factions, Detective Sergeant Denis Moroney from the RIC Special Branch,[7] who was in plain clothes, was killed. He was with a small group of detectives who were following a group of protesters up the Quays when he was hit by revolver shots fired at police as along with a larger group of police he charged a large group of Sinn Fein supporters. He was the first policeman to be killed in Ulster since the beginning of the War of Independence.[8]

On the same day armed and masked UVF members also took control of Carlisle Bridge over the River Foyle, stopping and questioning vehicles and pedestrians; the military and police took no action.[9]

Further rioting took place in the city during June with the UVF taking control of the Diamond and Guildhall Squares on Saturday 19 June and opening fire from the city walls into the nationalist Bogside. The nationalists were unable to equal the UVF firepower and the RIC called for

---

6   Abbott, Richard, *Police Casualties in Ireland 1919-1922* (2000).
7   Lawlor, Pearse, *The Outrages 1920-1922: The IRA and Ulster Special Constabulary in the Border Campaign* (2011).
8   Irish Medals – War of Independence <http://irishmedals.org/r-i-c-d-m-p-k-i-a-.html> (Accessed 4 February 2015).
9   Lawlor, Pearse, *The Outrages 1920-1922: The IRA and Ulster Special Constabulary in the Border Campaign* (2011).

reinforcements from Ebrington Barracks in the form of the Dorset Regiment. The UVF re-established their checkpoint on Carlisle Bridge and attacked houses in Bridge Street. The IRA resources could not compete with that of the UVF, RIC and military, and called in reinforcements from Donegal which resulted in taking some ground held by the UVF; it is estimated that 20 members of the UVF men were casualties. The arrival of an additional 1,500 British soldiers on 23 June finally brought the violence to an end with unionist and nationalist deaths reaching forty.[10]

In early 1920 Lieutenant Colonel George Liddle was already in command of a reorganized UVF unit in the Lisbellaw area. When the home of an ex-army sergeant was attacked on 22 May, the factory hooters and sirens from Liddle's linen factory sounded the muster and 300 UVF men, many from Liddle's own factory, assembled for duty within 30 minutes.[11]

The efficiency of this UVF unit was again evident the following month on the night 8 June when the telegraph wires to the railway station went dead; it was a common IRA tactic to cut telegraph wires prior to an attack. The men took up their positions to guard potential targets, the railway station, the courthouse and the abandoned RIC barracks. They waited and watched as the republican volunteers approached their target, the courthouse and set fire to it, unaware of the UVF already in position. The church bell rang out the alert and the UVF opened fire, the IRA were taken by surprise, returned fire and withdrew towards Tempo and Enniskillen. When the army eventually arrived the IRA had left and only the armed UVF remained. They attempted to disarm the UVF who claimed they were fighting under the same flag and after an argument the army moved on.[12]

On 1 May 1919 the Ulster Volunteer Force had been 'demobilised' when Richardson resigned as its General Officer Commanding.[13] In Richardson's last orders to the UVF, he stated: "Existing conditions call for the demobilisation of the Ulster Volunteers. The Force was organised to protect the interests of the Province of Ulster, at a time when trouble threatened. The success of the organisation speaks for itself, as a page of history, in the records of Ulster that will never fade."

However, Royal Irish Constabulary County Inspectors continued to gather information on UVF strengths in their respective areas and those UVF members who retained their rifles and made no moves to surrender them to police or military authorities.[14]

As a response to IRA attacks within Ulster, local militias appeared loosely formed on the pre-war UVF.

Sir Ernest Clarke, appointed from 1920 to Northern Ireland as assistant under-secretary,[15] noted that these were mostly vigilance forces which simply patrolled with the intention of reporting anything suspicious to the local RIC.[16]

In order to protect the Belfast City Hall from a feared IRA raid in June 1920 the Lord Mayor enrolled a guard of twenty ex-UVF to protect the City Hall.[17]

It appears that initially a number of these units, whilst equipped with stored UVF rifles and using the UVF style of electing officers, avoided using the term UVF in their titles; Captain Sir

---

10 Lawlor, Pearse, *The Outrages 1920-1922: The IRA and Ulster Special Constabulary in the Border Campaign* (2011).
11 Lawlor, Pearse, *The Outrages 1920-1922: The IRA and Ulster Special Constabulary in the Border Campaign* (2011).
12 Lawlor, Pearse, *The Outrages 1920-1922: The IRA and Ulster Special Constabulary in the Border Campaign* (2011).
13 Bowman, Timothy, *Carson's Army: Ulster Volunteer Force, 1910-22* (2007).
14 Bowman, Timothy, *Carson's Army: Ulster Volunteer Force, 1910-22* (2007).
15 <http://en.wikipedia.org/wiki/Ernest_Clark_%28governor%29> (Accessed 23 June 2014).
16 Bowman, Timothy, *Carson's Army: Ulster Volunteer Force, 1910-22* (2007).
17 Bowman, Timothy, *Carson's Army: Ulster Volunteer Force, 1910-22* (2007).

Early Ulster Special Constabulary in their platoon vehicle. (D.R. Orr)

Basil Brooke formed his "Fermanagh Vigilance" in June 1920, perhaps to encourage Catholic involvement.

Brooke related the reasons for its formation:

1. I felt that the hotheads on the Ulstermen's side might take the matter into their own hands, if not organised.
2. The threat of raids was increasing.
3. There appeared to be a possibility that those of the Ulstermen who wished for a quiet life and finding no support elsewhere might turn to Sinn Fein.[18]

Brooke also travelled to Dublin and requested that Dublin Castle form a Special Constabulary in the six counties of the north-east, worried that the violence in the south would spread there. His request was refused, however he was informed that his unofficial force would be allowed to wear arm bands and carry whistles but that they were not to be armed.[19]

Colonel Fred Crawford, linked back to the Tiger's Bay area of Belfast where he formed his small oath-bound group named "Crawford's Tigers".

In the city of Armagh, John Webster, a local shopkeeper, in April 1920 established Webster's 'Protective Patrol' of just ten men who patrolled the city one night in every two armed with whatever UVF rifles, shotguns or even sticks were available. On the formation of a local committee an approach was made to Ulster Unionist Council for support and 174 UVF rifles were given to arm the expanding force. They would be the nucleus of the revived UVF in County Armagh.[20]

---

18 Bowman, Timothy, *Carson's Army: Ulster Volunteer Force, 1910-22* (2007).
19 Abbott, Richard, *Police Casualties in Ireland 1919-1922* (2000).
20 Bowman, Timothy, *Carson's Army: Ulster Volunteer Force, 1910-22* (2007).

In Lisburn a Loyalist Association was formed which created three 'Loyalist Battalions' under the command of Major Wilson, one the battalions being commanded by Captain Ensor, formerly of the 36th (Ulster) Division.[21]

Whilst most of these groups would patrol with the intention of reporting anything untoward to the Royal Irish Constabulary, some of them however were armed with UVF rifles from 1914. There were also a number of small loyalist paramilitaries whose membership also included ex-military, the most notable being the Ulster Imperial Guards, who may have overreached the UVF in terms of membership. Historian Peter Hart wrote the following of these groups:

> Also occasionally targeted [by the IRA] were Ulster Protestants who saw the republican guerrilla campaign as an invasion of their territory, where they formed the majority. Loyalist activists responded by forming vigilante groups, which soon acquired official status as part of the Ulster Special Constabulary. These men spearheaded the wave of anti-Catholic violence that began in July 1920 and continued for two years. This onslaught was part of an Ulster Unionist counter-revolution, whose gunmen operated almost exclusively as ethnic cleansers and avengers.

Meanwhile a group formed in the shipyard was named the "Ulster Imperial Guards."[22] However this latter group was believed to have socialist leanings[23] which may have eventually led to the Ulster Unionist Council officially reviving the Ulster Volunteer Force on 25 June 1920[24] in an effort to gain some control over these disparate groups just as they had in 1913.

November saw the first major demonstration of the Ulster Imperial Guards through their attendance at Armistice Services at a number of Anglican, Methodist and Presbyterian Churches, along with the 'People's Hall' gospel hall in Belfast, and it was claimed that the organisation comprised 14,000 members, organised in nine battalions. The *Northern Whig* reported that when equipped and organised it would be offered to the Premier of Northern Ireland to safeguard the interests of his parliament and that a very large percentage of the members were ex-servicemen who before the war had belonged to the Ulster Volunteer Force.[25, 26]

In early July 1920 Lieutenant Colonel Wilfred Spender was approached by Sir Edward Carson who urged him to return to Belfast to reorganise the Ulster Volunteer Force. The Ulster Unionist Council appointed Spender as the UVF's Commanding Officer. Also in July 1920, Crozier offered his services to the revived UVF, however this was turned down. He later wrote that perhaps "Spender had concerns about working with me who had outranked him the army."[27]

After the war Spender had briefly joined the Ministry of Pensions in London to assist demobilised soldiers and their families, but with the tacit agreement of the British government was given leave of absence from his post. It appears that Fred Crawford, then a Lieutenant Colonel in the Royal Army Service Corps was offered the post first, but had declined, perhaps hoping to remain in the post war-army. At the same time announcements were printed in Unionist newspapers calling on all former UVF members to report for duty.[28]

---

21 Bowman, Timothy, *Carson's Army: Ulster Volunteer Force, 1910-22* (2007).
22 Bowman, Timothy, *Carson's Army: Ulster Volunteer Force, 1910-22* (2007).
23 Bowman, Timothy, *Carson's Army: Ulster Volunteer Force, 1910-22* (2007).
24 Bowman, Timothy, *Carson's Army: Ulster Volunteer Force, 1910-22* (2007).
25 Bowman, Timothy, *Carson's Army: Ulster Volunteer Force, 1910-22* (2007).
26 *Northern Whig* – 14/11/1921.
27 Bowman, Timothy, *Carson's Army: Ulster Volunteer Force, 1910-22* (2007).
28 Bowman, Timothy, *Carson's Army: Ulster Volunteer Force, 1910-22* (2007).

However this call met with limited success; for example, whilst the original 20 Belfast battalions were revived, each battalion had little more than 100 men and they were left mostly unarmed. The UVF's revival also met with little backing from unionists in Great Britain.[29]

This poor recruitment into the revived UVF may have been as a result of a number of issues. Those men who had served in the Great War may not have been willing to return to a military lifestyle, even if only on a part-time basis. Many workers had the option of working overtime as direct result of the short-lived post war economic boom, meaning that volunteering for unpaid evening and weekends in the Ulster Volunteer Force had little appeal, added to the lack of an indemnity scheme being organised as there had been before. The threat from the IRA was viewed by moderate Unionists to be the responsibility of the military and police to control.

Unlike the general pro-UVF view of the military in 1914, the revival of the UVF in 1920 was viewed with mixed emotions. Leading officers such as General Sir Nevil Macready and Field Marshal Lord French believed that loyalist forces should be brought under military control, such as Special Reserve Battalions under clear military authority and discipline.

Owing to the sluggish recruitment into the revived Ulster Volunteer Force and its failure to forestall IRA activities in Ulster, James Craig called for the formation of a new Special Constabulary.[30]

Sir John Anderson and Macready both warned the government in the strongest possible terms about the establishment of a Special Constabulary, Macready stressing:

> It is well to analyse the expression 'Loyalist' as applied to Ulster. The force it is now proposed to mobilise is the same force who, for their own opinions, armed against the government of the day in the early part of 1914, and I am fairly convinced that they would take up arms again tomorrow if they thought that they could gain their own ends, even against the Constitution of the Empire, by doing so.[31]

The original reason for the consideration of a Special Constabulary was the shortage of troops and regular police coupled with the demand in the north eastern counties for greater protection. The IRA tactic of intimidation and boycotting of Royal Irish Constabulary men and their families had brought recruiting into the RIC to a near standstill with many men resigning rather than subject their families to the terror and threat they were subjected to. An extra eight Army Battalions were sent to Ireland in May

Lieutenant Colonel James Craig, MP.
(Somme Museum)

---

29   Bowman, Timothy, *Carson's Army: Ulster Volunteer Force, 1910-22* (2007).
30   Bowman, Timothy, *Carson's Army: Ulster Volunteer Force, 1910-22* (2007).
31   Augustein, Joost (ed)., *The Irish Revolution, 1913-1923* (2002).

THE NEW R.I.C.

'The New RIC'- Royal Irish Constabulary Christmas card depicting the RIC, Black and Tans, Auxiliaries and Station Defence. (Police Museum)

1920, with greater use of vehicles to make them more mobile and also to provide protection to outlying police stations.

However soldiers just out of the trenches were not particularly suitable for the mobile nature of the duties required. Consideration was therefore given to the raising of Special Emergency Gendarmerie, however instead recruiting began for Temporary Constables for the Royal Irish Constabulary in England on 1 January 1920, and a shortage of uniforms led to these officers wearing a mix of army and police uniforms, first witnessed 25 March 1920 and attracting the nickname 'Black and Tans'.

As part of the expansion in the support being given to the RIC it was decided in June 1920 to form the Auxiliary Division; the first recruits arriving in Ireland 27 July 1920.

Command of the new Auxiliary Division RIC was given to Brigadier-General Frank P Crozier, formerly of the UVF Special Service Section and the Ulster Division who after the war continued to hunger for active service, working as an officer in the newly-formed Lithuanian army before returning to Ireland. His military career ended with his resignation on 19 February 1921 amid a blaze of headlines and questions in the House, on the grounds that his dismissal of some of his men who had looted a licensed grocery store near Trim, County Meath had been countermanded by General Tudor pending an official enquiry.[32]

---

32 <http://www.spartacus.schoolnet.co.uk/FWWcrozierF.htm>.

This increase of support took the RIC back up to strength by September 1920 with Major General Henry Hugh Tudor being appointed as Police Adviser to the Viceroy, on both the Royal Irish Constabulary and Dublin Metropolitan Police.[33] When Deputy Inspector General Smith later resigned from his position in December 1920, Tudor was appointed 'Chief of Police' of both RIC and DMP.[34]

The Ulster ex-servicemen's association approached the King on 1 June 1920 offering the support of 3,000 trained ex-servicemen to restore law and order. On 23rd of the month in London the Prime Minister, David Lloyd George, held a conference which included most of his Cabinet and ministers of the Irish Administration, including Generals Macready, Tudor and Sir James Craig. At the meeting Winston Churchill, then Secretary of State for War, asked about the arming of the Unionists in the six counties in order to keep law and order and relieve seven Army Battalions and several thousand police which could be sent to the south and west of Ireland where they were needed. The response was emphatically negative from certain quarters; Mr Wylie the Assistant Attorney-General said it would be disastrous and lead to civil war, Sir John Anderson said it would set the south ablaze and could lead to the massacre of Protestants in south and west Ireland. Tudor was determined that the pre-war UVF should not be used and was against an irregular force being used to maintain law and order. James Craig however stated that he believed the proposal, providing it was official and legal with the men being properly sworn in and taking an oath of allegiance with their own officers, was quite practicable.[35]

With a deteriorating situation and sectarian rioting spreading for the first time since the start of the IRA campaign in 1919 the authorities were forced to swear in a number of special constables on 24 August 1920 in an effort to regain control. The following advertisement appeared in the *Belfast Telegraph* on 26 August 1920:[36]

> **Special Constables**
> Special Constables will be enrolled for the preservation of the peace and the protection of property in the City of Belfast. Such Special Constables will have all the powers of Special Constables under 2 and 3 William IV Chap. 108 and will be entitled to compensation if injured. Details as to enrolment will appear later.
> (Signed) EGT Bainbridge
> Major General
> Commanding First Division

Elements of the press targeted Carson and the Ulster Volunteers, the *Daily Herald* of 31 August 1920 reported:

> The bloody harvest of Carsonism is being reaped in Belfast. Race hatred, religious hatred, militarism, rebellion have been preached there year after year, and now we see the result … The gangs who have organised the reign of terror are the very people who protest *they* are afraid that they would, under even partial Home Rule, be persecuted and denied religious liberty.[37]

---

33 Abbott, Richard, *Police Casualties in Ireland 1919-1922* (2000).
34 Grob-Fitzgibbon, *Turning Points of The Irish Revolution: The British Government, Intelligence and the Cost of Indifference, 1912-1921* (2007).
35 Abbott, Richard, *Police Casualties in Ireland 1919-1922* (2000).
36 Abbott, Richard, *Police Casualties in Ireland 1919-1922* (2000).
37 Lewis, Geoffrey, *Carson: The man who divided Ireland* (2006).

Members of the Ulster Special Constabulary, 1920. (Police Museum)

At a subsequent conference on 2 September, Craig proposed the formation of 2,000 fulltime Special Constables to assist the RIC. He argued that the law-abiding people in the six counties were losing faith in the government's ability to protect them and were threatening recourse to arms, which Craig believed could lead to civil war. It was also proposed, as a last resort, to rearm and mobilise the UVF if there was a general rising by Sinn Fein in the six counties and the government was unable to deal with it.

On 3 September the Ulster Unionist Council called upon the Government to take immediate action to protect lives and property. This was reinforced on 7 September by a deputation of Unionists which included members of the Unionist Labour Association, who met members of the Westminster Cabinet. As a consequence there was a ministerial meeting the following day. General Macready echoed the views previously expressed by Tudor, disapproving of the arming of an irregular force which could lead to civil war, instead proposing that eight Army Battalions be specially raised in Britain for use in Ireland. The outcome of the meeting was that Hamar Greenwood, the Chief Secretary for Ireland, was to take the necessary steps to raise a Special Constabulary.[38, 39]

By 1 November 1920 the Government introduced Special Constables on a formal basis to Northern Ireland.

---

38 Abbott, Richard, *Police Casualties in Ireland 1919-1922* (2000).
39 Hezlet, Sir Arthur, *The 'B' Specials* (1972).

Members of the 'A' Category of the Ulster Special Constabulary at Ballymena Workhouse circa 1920/21. (J Luke)

The British Government passed a Home Rule Bill in 1920, all parties keen to resolve the Irish question. By the end of 1920 they had got an Act through establishing two governments in Ireland, one for the six north-eastern counties and the other for the remainder of Ireland; although Ulster Unionists accepted the solution with regret.

The Royal Irish Constabulary suffered boycott, ambush and death with little real government support. They were not supplied with armoured cars or any cars for transport purposes. It was the summer of 1920 before the Government took any action to assist in establishing order in Ireland with the introduction of the Black and Tans, a force of Temporary Constables recruited to assist the Royal Irish Constabulary.

On the night of 26 August 1920 serious rioting and firebombing broke out in Belfast with a number of the wounded being taken to local hospitals. Earlier in the day Sinn Feiners in the Ballymacarret area sniped at the military who returned fire, killing Fraser McCann and wounding another. Rioting later started in the Falls district of West Belfast with revolver shots near Kashmir Road, however the centre of the disturbances soon became Albert Street. An armoured car fired on the rioters with those wounded from the machine gun fire being treated in local hospitals. Crowds of shipyard workers waving Union flags appeared and cheered the actions of the soldiers as were members of the Fire Brigade fighting incendiary fires. The riots extended to the Grosvenor Road before being finally dispersed by the military.[40]

---

40 *The New York Times* – 27 August 1920.

A copy of Form SC10, the oath taken by Special Constables. (J Luke)

> **Form S.C. 10.**
>
> ## Oath to be taken by Special Constables
>
> 2 and 3 William IV., Cap. 108
> 31 and 32 Victoria, Cap. 72
>
> I..do solemnly and sincerely declare and affirm that I will well and truly serve our Sovereign Lady the Queen in the Office of Special Constable without favour or affection, malice or ill-will, and that I will to the best of my power cause the peace to be kept and preserved, and to prevent all offences against the persons and properties of Her Majesty's subjects: and that while I continue to hold the said office I will to the best of my skill and knowledge discharge all the duties thereof faithfully according to law. So help me God.
>
> Signed................................
>
> Taken before me this............day of............................19.......
>
> Signature................................
> (Justice of the Peace)
>
> W345.4m.7/57.D.gp.127.
> W1412.5m.10/57.

Rioting also occurred at the city end of Ballymacarrett around Vulcan Street. The disturbances later extended to the town of Newtownards, again involving shipyard workers.

A senior police officer reported that "Belfast could be no worse." In East Belfast there was also fierce rioting earlier in the day in Clonallon Street with the military firing a number of volleys and hitting a number of rioters. Further disturbances in Wolff and Foundry Streets were successfully dealt with by the police.

Following the disturbances one rioter was reported killed and 20 injured whilst the Fire Brigade reported 28 incendiary fires. Thirty-nine persons were arrested for rioting and other offences.

It was later reported that the rioting originated when a report was received that Nationalists had stoned children leaving the Comber Street National School at Ballymacarret. The Principal of the School, Robert Caldwell denied that the pupils were attacked, however the initial report was believed by both sides and in turn fuelled the tension in the city.[41]

On 22 October 1920 Dublin Castle announced its raising of a Special Constabulary for the six counties. The Ulster Special Constabulary (USC) was set up under the Special Constables (Ireland) Act, 1832, recruitment commencing 1 November 1920. This was an armed reserve police force whose main role, during 1920–1922, was to bolster the Royal Irish Constabulary and fight the IRA. Spender was responsible for its formation[42] and encouraged UVF members to join, and although many did so, the USC did not engulf the UVF (and other loyalist paramilitaries) until early 1922.[43]

---

41 *The New York Times* – 27 August 1920.
42 Ingram, Rev Brett, *Covenant and Challenge* (1989).
43 Bowman, Timothy, *Carson's Army: Ulster Volunteer Force, 1910-22* (2007).

Members of the 'A' Category, Ulster Special Constabulary on mobile patrol, circa 1921. (J Luke)

The oath taken by Special Constables before a Justice of Peace was as follows:

> I do swear that I will well and truly serve our Sovereign Lord the king in the office of Special Constable without favour or affection, malice or ill-will, and that I will to the best of my power cause the peace to be kept and preserved, and prevent all offences against the persons and properties of his Majesty's subjects; and that while I continue to hold the said office I will to the best of my skill and knowledge discharge all the duties thereof faithfully accordingly to law. So help me GOD.[44]

In November 1920 the Ulster Special Constabulary (USC) was proposed to consist of 910 'A' category and 12,000 'B' category. By February the establishment was fixed at 1,490 'A' Category and 19,500 'B' Category, although only 15,000 'B' Category had been recruited. The 'C' Category was 'indefinite', but 4,000 had been recruited.[45]

Craig hoped to "neutralise" the sundry loyalist paramilitaries by enrolling them in the C Division of the USC; a move that was backed by the British government.

Historian Michael Hopkinson wrote that the USC "amounted to an officially approved UVF."[46]

In October 1920, Brevet Lieutenant-Colonel WB Spender sent a memorandum to the Officers Commanding the Belfast Regiment of the UVF. It acknowledged the government's raising of

---

44 Hezlet, Sir Arthur, *The 'B' Specials* (1972).
45 Bowman, Timothy, *Carson's Army: Ulster Volunteer Force, 1910-22* (2007).
46 Bowman, Timothy, *Carson's Army: Ulster Volunteer Force, 1910-22* (2007).

the Special Constabulary in the six counties of Ulster and said that Sir Edward Carson and "our Leaders" were anxious to help the Government in maintaining order in the Province. Spender was confident that the UVF would do all they could to assist in making the new Constabulary Force a success, which in turn would make it possible for the government to do more in other parts of Ireland where "rebel forces predominate and our comrades are now being subjected to measures of terrorism." He went on state that he felt certain that all members of the UVF who joined the Special Constabulary would perform their duties conscientiously and impartially, under discipline and with restraint towards those who disagree with them, a position he said which had always marked the attitude of their organisation. Whilst Forms of Enrolment would be available at each police station they could be filled in individually or collected at any suitable centre and he suggested battalion headquarters to be processed in bulk. Following submission the names would be considered by a selection committee consisting of Magistrates specially appointed to the role along with other assistants. Whilst he acknowledged that the initial contract was for six months he was confident that those men who gave good service and wished to remain would have the chance of making it a career, clearly indicating that he did not see this as a short-term measure. Importantly, Spender stressed that whilst service would be restricted to the "Six Counties" any men who joined the new Constabulary Force would for all intents and purposes be part of the Royal Irish Constabulary, "serving under RIC officers and Sergeants of all religious creeds." He further highlighted that whilst they would probably be formed into companies serving under military officers and their own NCOs, there was no guarantee that anyone who joined would be selected for one of these companies and therefore anyone who was not prepared to serve loyally with the RIC should be urged not to join.[47]

An early Ulster Special Constabulary patrol at Rasharkin, circa 1921. (J Luke)

---

47 UVF Memorandum to OC Battalions Belfast Regiment UVF – 29 Oct 1920.

Members of the 'A' Category, Ulster Special Constabulary on mobile patrol circa 1921. (J Luke)

The USC was organised into a number of categories; 'A' Category was a uniformed regular cadre receiving £3 17s 6d per week with an extra sum of nearly 10s a week as a Bounty at the end of approved service in lieu of pension, married men also received additional allowances;[48] 'B' category was the largest and part-time, who served in their home districts and received an allowance of £10 per annum for performing one night's duty per week; 'C' category served only occasionally in static guard duties, near their homes with the 'C1' category forming the strategic reserve. The USC would also receive the same indemnity payments as those received by the Royal Irish Constabulary. About half of the 'A' Specials provided additional police for RIC barracks, while the remaining half were formed as motorised platoons carrying out a military role. 'B' Special Constables in Belfast were trained as police reservists whilst those in rural areas served as territorial defence troops.

In Spender's Memorandum to the Belfast regiment commanders he stated that it was not the intention of the authorities to employ any UVF members who joined the 'B' Category for duty in Nationalist areas. He also went on to explain that as far as he was aware patrols were likely to consist of three or more members of the Special Constabulary with one Royal Irish Constable. He again stressed that there were great advantages in this system and that any man who joined had to be prepared to work with the RIC. As 4,000 'B' Category were required for Belfast, he explained that this would be approximately 200 or 300 men from each Belfast UVF Battalion, a figure which he was confident would be forthcoming. Those with bicycles which were used on patrol would receive an allowance of one shilling for each night duty.[49]

---

48   UVF Memorandum to OC Battalions Belfast Regiment UVF – 29 Oct 1920.
49   UVF Memorandum to OC Battalions Belfast Regiment UVF – 29 Oct 1920.

Rasharkin, 'B' Specials outside the Royal Irish Constabulary Barracks in 1921. (J Luke)

Many men who had served in the Irish and Ulster Divisions during the war, particularly those who had been members of the UVF prior to war, would swell the USC ranks which reached over 40,000 by 1922/23. However along with these ex-veterans, Timothy Bowman believes that a major element of the USC was those 19-20 year-olds who had missed out on military service during the Great War, whilst a number of recruits into the 'A' Category were from outside Northern Ireland.[50]

The USC was almost wholly Protestant and was greatly mistrusted by Irish Catholics and Irish nationalists. Following IRA attacks its members were accused of sometimes carrying out revenge killings and reprisals against Catholic civilians during the 1920–22 conflict.[51]

During the treaty negotiations after the publication of the Government of Ireland bill in early 1920 it appears that Sir James Craig and other senior military figures were planning to call upon the various loyalist forces for aid if the negotiations broke down. Whilst Craig was planning to expand the Ulster Special Constabulary, Macready seems to have thought the best solution was re-raising the 36th (Ulster) Division with 12 battalions, each 1,000 strong. Craig opposed this, thinking the move would be unpopular and his solution would be cheaper. His option of including the UVF and the various other loyalist organisations in the 'C' Category was also supported by the British government and Lieutenant Colonel Fred Crawford who had succeeded Spender as Commander of the UVF by 1921.[52]

Whilst the Irish delegation wanted a republic for all of Ireland, the British were offering dominion status to Ireland with the exclusion of the six counties. One of the proposals put to Craig in London was that Northern Ireland would keep its powers, but would return representatives to the Dail as opposed to Westminster. Craig was stunned and turned to Bonar Law instead of Carson for help. Lloyd George threatened to withdraw the tax concessions being granted to Ulster under the 1920 Act, but Craig stood firm and was fully supported by the Conservatives.[53]

---

50   Bowman, Timothy, *Carson's Army: Ulster Volunteer Force, 1910-22* (2007).
51   Peter Hart in, Joost Augusteijn (ed), *The Irish Revolution* 1913-23 (2002).
52   Bowman, Timothy, *Carson's Army: Ulster Volunteer Force, 1910-22* (2007).
53   Lewis, Geoffrey, *Carson: The man who divided Ireland* (2006).

The Government of Ireland Act 1920, passed on 23 December 1920, provided Home Rule for Northern Ireland and Southern Ireland, giving Northern Ireland the option of Irish unity or Irish partition. The exemption of six Ulster counties from Home Rule by Dublin was the best compromise and this proposal was passed. Unionists prepared to put its provisions in place through the May General Election in the six Ulster counties excluded from Dublin Home Rule for the new local Belfast based Home Rule government. The Unionists gained 40 of the 52 seats, Sir James Craig was appointed Prime Minister and King George V under heavy security officially opened the new Northern Ireland Parliament in Belfast in the City Hall in June 1921.

In his address he said:

> I speak from a full heart when I pray that my coming to Ireland today may prove to be the first step towards an end of strife amongst her people, whatever their race or creed. I appeal to all Irishmen to pause, to stretch out the hand of forbearance and conciliation, to forgive and forget and to join in making for the land they love a new era of peace, contentment and goodwill.[54]

Whilst there had been a lull in the fighting at this time, after the King's visit events became more violent and confused.

The Government of Ireland Act also provided for a reduction in the number of Members of Parliament in Westminster who would represent both the North and South of Ireland, and under a single Viceroy there was to be a Council of Ireland which was to co-ordinate matters of common concern to the two parliaments, which it was hoped could ultimately evolve into a single Irish Parliament.

The King had asked his ministers to ensure that his speech for the opening of the first Northern Ireland Parliament, "would appeal to all his Irish subjects, appeal not only to the North but to the South."[55]

By this time the IRA, the armed wing of the illegal Government in the rest of Ireland, had also been engaged in violence within what was to become Northern Ireland.[56]

Carson and his fellow Ulster Unionists would have preferred the six counties to remain completely integrated in Great Britain but accepted the creation of a separate Northern Ireland Parliament within the United Kingdom as a compromise; ironically a form of Home Rule. Whilst the issue was being debated in parliament he wrote; "Ulster wants peace, and above all to be removed from the arena of party politics in the Imperial Parliament and we have therefore made up our minds that in the interests of Ireland, Great Britain, and the Empire, the best and only solution of the question is to accept the present bill and endeavour to work it loyally."[57]

A week after the Treaty was signed Carson gave his maiden speech in the House of Lords.

> What a fool I was. I was only a puppet, and so was Ulster, and so was Ireland, in the political game that was to get the Conservative Party into power. And of all the men in my experience that I think are the most loathsome it is those who will sell their friends for the purpose of conciliating their enemies.[58]

---

54 Shearman, Hugh, *Not an Inch: A Study of Northern Ireland and Lord Craigavon* (1942).
55 Churchill, Winston S, *Great Contemporaries* (1941).
56 Kennedy, Dennis, *The Widening Gulf: Northern attitudes to the independent Irish State 1919-49* (1988).
57 Hyde, H Montgomery, *Carson* (1953).
58 Lewis, Geoffrey, *Carson: The man who divided Ireland* (2006).

A bronze medallion commemorating the opening of the Northern Ireland Parliament, 22 June 1921 in the City Hall, Belfast, Sir James Craig, Bart, MBE, Prime Minister. (D.R. Orr)

In January 1921 he met in London over three days with Father O'Flanagan and Sir James O'Connor to try to find a mutual agreement that would end the Anglo-Irish war, but without result.[59]

An indication of the severity of the disorder is seen in the following figures. During 1920, 75 courthouses were destroyed, 26 RIC barracks were captured and destroyed and 518 others burned after being vacated, 193 policemen and 52 soldiers were killed and girls seen 'walking out' with a policeman were beaten and had their hair shorn.[60]

When the Civil War between pro-treaty and anti-treaty elements of the IRA erupted in 1921, the Orange Order was forced out of Fowler Hall, Dublin. The anti-treaty IRA seized the building as their headquarters, in the process destroying many important documents relating to both the Order and the Loyal Dublin Volunteers. Later in June 1935 when the Dublin Board of Works was removing presses from the cellar of the GPO Customs Parcels Section, located at 10 Parnell Square, formerly Fowler Hall, they exposed a large cavity several feet long. Within it in perfectly dry conditions lay a massive arms cache of over 90 rifles and over 2000 rounds of ammunition. Instead of the weapons belonging to the anti-treaty faction of the IRA who occupied the building in 1921 they were found to be those issued to the Ulster Volunteer Force, the Lee-Enfields and Martini-Henry's, and were accompanied by packages of Bible tracts and cap badges; they had belonged to the men of Dublin's 'Ulster Volunteer Force', the Loyal Dublin Volunteers.[61]

As the situation developed, the Chief of the Imperial General Staff, Field Marshal Sir Henry Wilson declared in March 1921, "It we lose Ireland we have lost the Empire."[62] This holds a certain irony, as well as being a 'colony' at the heart of the empire the Irish helped conquer, populate and govern many colonies overseas. The changes in Ireland would be the first of many changes in many parts of the Empire over the following decades; where Ireland led others followed.

---

59 "Memorandum by James O'Connor of an interview with Edward Carson"; RIA, Dublin, 1993 National Archives of Ireland file UCDA P150/1902.
60 Clark, Wallace, *Guns in Ulster* (1967).
61 <http://www.newsletter.co.uk/features/the-loyal-dublin-volunteers-a-forgotten-organisation-1-3719467> (Accessed 5 February 2014).
62 Kenny, Kevin (ed), *Ireland and the British Empire* (2004).

In mid-1921 the British Government signed a ceasefire with those fighting against the Government of Ireland Act.[63] The Anglo Irish Treaty was signed in London on the 6th of December 1921 and brought the Irish War of Independence to an end. It was more favourable to Ulster Unionists than some had believed and led to the gradual disintegration of the various Loyalist organisations.[64]

In 1921 Wilfrid Spender was reluctantly prevailed upon by Craig to become Cabinet Secretary to the new Northern Ireland Government and in 1925 he became Permanent Secretary at the Ministry of Finance, helping to lay the foundations of the Northern Ireland Civil Service.[65]

On 18 January 1922, Hacket Pain was returned unopposed as Member of Parliament at Westminster for South Londonderry.

After the partition of Ireland, Carson repeatedly warned Ulster Unionist leaders not to alienate northern Catholics, as he foresaw this would make Northern Ireland unstable. In 1921 he stated:

> We used to say that we could not trust an Irish parliament in Dublin to do justice to the Protestant minority. Let us take care that that reproach can no longer be made against your Parliament, and from the outset let them see that the Catholic minority have nothing to fear from a Protestant majority. Let us take care to win all that is best among those who have been opposed to us in the past. Whilst maintaining intact our own religion let us give the same rights to the religion of our neighbours.

His warnings were largely in vain.[66, 67] With this statesmanlike piece of advice he relinquished his political leadership.[68]

A truce was arranged and on 11 June 1922 Sinn Fein and Unionist leaders were invited to a Conference in London to explore the options; Britain offered dominion status similar to Canada or New Zealand to either Southern Ireland or the whole island of Ireland if the north would join the scheme. The resulting treaty allowed Northern Ireland the right to stay out of the Free State but a commission was to settle the frontier, which ultimately remained unchanged.[69] The treaty received a mixed reception in Ireland.

Following the Treaty there were four armed forces left in Ireland, the treaty section of the Irish Republican Army, the anti-treaty section of the Irish Republican Army, the British Army in Northern Ireland and the Northern Ireland Special Constabulary.[70]

Rioting and bombing started in Belfast on an extensive scale with raids over the frontier into Northern Ireland with large houses burnt down and those in uniform attacked and shot.[71]

On 5 December 1922 the British Government and the King approved the Constitution of the Irish Free State, the King signing the approval on the morning of 6 December. On 7 December the Northern Ireland Parliament voted itself out of the Irish Free State.[72, 73] As a result of the subsequent Irish Free State (Consequential Provisions) Act 1922 the office of Lord Lieutenant was abolished, being replaced by the new office of Governor of Northern Ireland.

---

63 Kennedy, Dennis, *The Widening Gulf: Northern attitudes to the independent Irish State 1919-49* (1988).
64 Bowman, Timothy, *Carson's Army: Ulster Volunteer Force, 1910-22* (2007).
65 Ulster Volunteers, January 1913 – Ulster-Scots Community Network <http://www.ulster-scots.com/uploads/901740969819.PDF> (Accessed 5 August 2013).
66 Dudley Edwards, Ruth (2005-05-29), Biography: Carson by Geoffrey Lewis, *The Times* (Retrieved 9-07-13).
67 Hyde, H Montgomery, *Carson* (1953).
68 Hyde, H Montgomery, *Carson* (1953).
69 Shearman, Hugh, *Not an Inch: A Study of Northern Ireland and Lord Craigavon* (1942).
70 Shearman, Hugh, *Not an Inch: A Study of Northern Ireland and Lord Craigavon* (1942).
71 Shearman, Hugh, *Not an Inch: A Study of Northern Ireland and Lord Craigavon* (1942).
72 Augustein, Joost (ed), *The Irish Revolution, 1913-1923* (2002).
73 Shearman, Hugh, *Not an Inch: A Study of Northern Ireland and Lord Craigavon* (1942).

RIGHT HON. SIR EDWARD CARSON.   LADY CARSON.

Sir Edward and Lady Carson. (Somme Museum)

Northern Ireland opting out of the Irish Free State ensured that WT Cosgrove and his supporters who broke with Éamon de Valera over the issue of the 1921 Anglo-Irish Treaty, any hopes of some form of a united Ireland was not to be, but at least he had hoped for the Boundary Commission's recommendations to be fully implemented without the coercion of Ulster, but likewise he believed that Ulster should not coerce others. Both Lloyd George and Cosgrove had the counties of Tyrone and Fermanagh in mind; the recent elections showed the great constituency of Tyrone-Fermanagh to have a 6,000 majority for remaining in the Irish Free State. The Boundary Commission ignored this, acting on the assumption that "the wishes of the inhabitants are made the primary but not the paramount consideration." Their report was leaked in November 1925 and the subsequent Boundary Agreement of December 1925 effectively marked the culmination of the Home Rule Crises which had begun in 1911.[74]

In March 1924 when John Dillon was paying tribute to John Redmond he summarised the situation; "Mr Redmond never agreed to the principle of partition. It is now a well-known fact that if he and I had agreed to give up Tyrone, Fermanagh and Derry City at the Buckingham Palace Conference, we could there and then, in June 1914, have steeled the question with goodwill of Ulster. We refused."[75]

At the unveiling of the Coleraine War Memorial in November 1922, Sir James Craig referred to what was considered by many Unionists in Northern Ireland as Ulster's blood sacrifice during

---

74 Augustein, Joost (ed), *The Irish Revolution, 1913-1923* (2002).
75 Peter Hart in, Joost Augusteijn (ed). *The Irish Revolution 1913-23* (2002).

the war, cementing the Union with Great Britain; "those who passed away have left behind a great message to all of them to stand firm, and to give away none of Ulster's soil."[76]

In his book *Carson's Army: the Ulster Volunteer Force 1910–22*, Timothy Bowman gave the following as his last thought on the UVF during this period:

> It is questionable the extent to which the UVF did actually reform in 1920. Possibly the UVF proper amounted to little more than 3,000 men in this period and it is noticeable that the UVF never had a formal disbandment … possibly so that attention would not be drawn to the extent to which the formation of 1920–22 was such a pale shadow of that of 1913–14.[77]

---

76 *Belfast Telegraph* – 11 November 1922.
77 Bowman, Timothy. *Carson's Army: The Ulster Volunteer Force 1910-22* (2007).

14

Not Forgotten

On 2 March 1921, the silk Union flag belonging to 11th Battalion, Royal Inniskilling Fusiliers, formed originally from the Donegal and Fermanagh Ulster Volunteer Force, along with men from the British League who had supported Ulster, was brought from Omagh to Enniskillen by a small Colour escort. Following a church service and the laying up of the Colours over 160 officers and men of the 11th Battalion, the Colour escort from the depot and the band were entertained by the Fermanagh UVF in the Protestant Hall where a luncheon was provided.[1]

In December 1957 the colours of the Donegal Regiment, UVF, held by Captain Curley MC, were handed over to St McCartan's Cathedral by a group of veterans, the Colour party commanded by Mr Stephen Bullock, former driver of Lord Leitrim and key player in some of the gun-running for the UVF. During this address Canon Clements said:

> We have just now received the Colours of the Donegal Regiment of the Ulster Volunteer Force into the Cathedral. We have accepted them and have dedicated them for safe keeping on the walls of the Cathedral here, where they will always remind us of things which happened before many of use were born. They will remind us of the watchfulness of men who were alert to the challenge of their age. They will remind us of men who act decisively when the need arose.[2]

Thiepval Tower

The most striking memorial to the Ulster Volunteers is the Ulster Tower at Thiepval, which is located on the site of the advance of the 36th (Ulster) Division on 1 July 1916, and was designed in the style of St. Helen's Tower, at Clandeboye, County Down, where many of the men had trained during 1914 and 1915. It was proposed by Sir James Craig in November 1919 and designed by Bowden and Abbott Ltd of London and built by Fenning & Co Ltd, specialists in granite memorials and the *Societe de Construction et Travaux Publics d'Arras*.[3,4] It was funded by public subscription and was erected in 1921 in memory of those men of the 36th (Ulster) Division and other Ulstermen in other forces who laid down their lives in the Great War. The avenue leading up to the tower is flanked by 42 trees.

The memorial was unveiled on 18 November 1921.[5] The original plan was for the Prime Minister of Northern Ireland, Sir James Craig, to welcome the visitors to the memorial and Lord Carson to unveil the commemorative tablet, however both were ill and unable to attend, though Carson's name still adorns the memorial tablet. Major J Boyle, standing in for Sir James Craig, formally

---

1 Canning, WJ, *Ballyshannon, Belcoo, Bertincourt* (1996).
2 Canning, WJ, *Ballyshannon, Belcoo, Bertincourt* (1996).
3 Metcalfe, Nick, *Blacker's Boys* (2012).
4 Jeffery, Keith, *Ireland and the Great War* (2000).
5 Cousins, Colin, *Armagh and the Great War* (2011).

Helen's Tower, Clandeboye, County Down. (Somme Museum: 1994-662)

asked Field Marshal Sir Henry Wilson to open the tower with a silver key and after addressing the crowd entered the memorial chamber where General Weygand, former Chief of Staff to Marshal Foch unveiled the commemorative tablet.[6]

In a letter to the editor of the *Lisburn Standard* in October 1921 from the former members of the Royal Ulster Rifles Battalion, an appeal was made for subscriptions to enable representatives from each of the Battalions of the Ulster Division to attend the forthcoming dedication ceremony of the memorial at Thiepval. It was estimated the cost of sending out a representative would be £25.[7]

One of the representatives at the unveiling of the Ulster Tower was local man, Sergeant Thomas Ward who had served in 11th Royal Irish Rifles. He had benefited from the appeal for contributions. He was the son of Matthew Ward, a baker from the Longstone Street area of Lisburn, and the Ward family suffered the loss of a son, Samuel, in 1916 after he had been gassed in Belgium.

It was reported that Thomas himself had been wounded in July 1916. Another brother, James, was also known to have served. The Lisburn Standard later reported that Thomas had remarked on his return from the unveiling ceremony that it had been "a very touching and unforgettable ceremony."

Those present at the ceremony took part in a tour of the battlefield. Local press reports stated that "scores of rifles rendered useless by exposure to the weather are still lying about, and there are pieces of shell, spades, picks, steel helmets, bayonets and even articles of clothing"; a stark reminder of the realities of war.

---

6   Metcalfe, Nick, *Blacker's Boys* (2012).
7   <http://www.lisburn.com/history/digger/Digger-2010/digger-05-11-2010.html> Early days of the Ulster Tower at Thiepval and Lisburn (Accessed 4 December 2014).

The Ulster Memorial Tower. (Somme Museum)

This is the first Royal British Legion visit to the Ulster Memorial Tower in the 1920's. (Somme Museum)

Following the unveiling the trust of the Memorial was handed over to the Ulster Patriotic Fund. A representative of the fund, Sir Robert Liddell, who was present at the ceremony stated "Our duty as Ulstermen is to see that the glorious traditions which were established by those who have gone before are handed down by us to future generations untarnished so that those who come after us will say 'This is our heritage'" The Marquis of Dufferin, in a speech to those present stated "To those who were alive they said thank-you … and to those who were dead they said – we may never see you again but we will ever remember you. We will tell our children how you died, and they will repeat it to their children, and thus your memory will remain green through countless generations …"

The recruitment and sacrifice for King and Country of the Ulster Volunteers through their raising and fighting in the ranks of the 36th (Ulster) Division would be perceived by Ulster Unionists as evidence that they were the dependable loyal citizens of Ireland upon who England could rely and would hopefully remember.

A description of the tower in 1921 included the following. "In the upper portion of the tower there is accommodation for a caretaker, who will act as a guide to the battlefield; and from the roof, which is reached by a circular turret staircase, a commanding view of the surrounding country is obtained."

Several sources make reference to the early caretakers at the Ulster Tower. In Major & Mrs Holte's *Battlefield Guide to the Somme* there is a reference to a "Sergeant-Major William MacMaster" and his wife who were residing in the tower and were acting as guardians; Gerald Gliddon in his book titled *A Battlefield Companion: Somme 1916*, also refers to William McMaster who he confirms was caretaker of the tower in August 1928. Other sources state that a Sergeant Savage was the original caretaker, and William McMaster arrived to take over the post in March 1922.

In 1964 to commemorate the 50th anniversary of the Larne gun-running the Northern Ireland Prime Minister, Terence O'Neill, unveiled a plague in memory of the event and the men who participated. It was located at Chaine Memorial Road, Larne, and was mounted on a large plinth

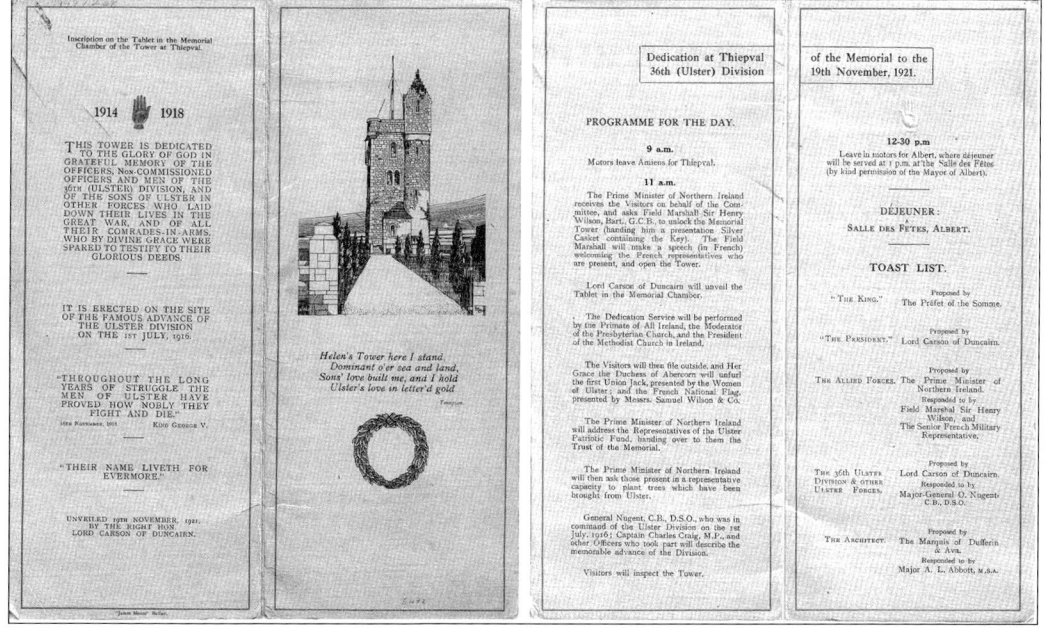

Programme for the dedication of the memorial to the 36th (Ulster) Division at Thiepval on 19th November 1921. (Somme Museum)

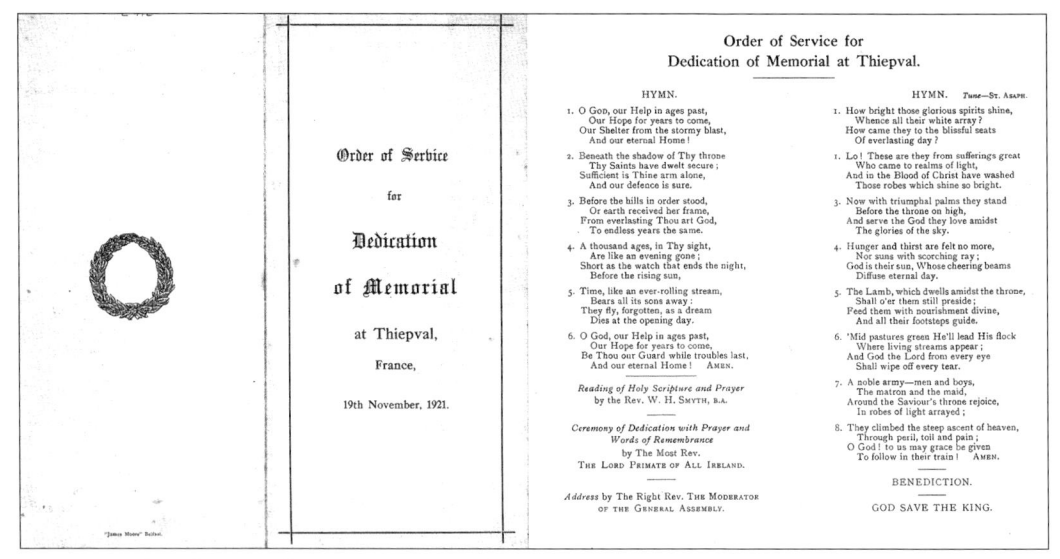

Order of Service for the dedication of the memorial at Thiepval, 19 November 1921. (Somme Museum: 1997-248)

which was topped by the old lamp which guided the *Clyde Valley* into the harbour, whilst inside was cemented one of the original rifles landed for the UVF, donated by Shaw Miliken of Islandmagee, along with copies of the *Belfast Telegraph* and *East Antrim Times*. To those gathered, which included former Ulster Volunteers, O'Neill paid tribute to the UVF movement for "putting teeth into all the efforts then to prevent the British government of the day imposing Home Rule upon us against our will." He went onto to say that thanks to their effort five decades previously they had assured the position of the Province within the United Kingdom. The event had been organised by the chairman of Larne Divisional Unionist Association, who had received a telegram from a Captain Mathison, Pennsylvania, who had sailed on board *Clyde Valley* which said, "I will remember to drink a toast on the 24th to the men, and particularly to Colonel Fred Crawford and Captain Andy Agnew."[8]

Mr McMaster of Lambeg, the first curator of the Ulster Memorial Tower. (Somme Museum)

---

8   Hume, David, *"For Ulster and Her Freedom": The story of the April 1914 gun-running* (1989).

Fred Crawford, who had received a CBE in the Royal Honours list, 1921, was not present at the commemorations. He had died 12 years earlier on 5 November 1952, and was buried in the City Cemetery, Falls Road, Belfast, at Section K-73/4. Upon news of his death he was described by the then Prime Minister of Northern Ireland, Sir Basil Brooke, as being "as a fearless fighter in the historic fight to keep Ulster British."

In 1966 1,200 men returned to the venue of many Ulster Volunteer demonstrations when the threat of Home Rule was foremost in many of their minds. This time thoughts were often of friends and comrades they had lost as they paraded in front of Queen Elizabeth II at the Balmoral Show Grounds to commemorate the 50th anniversary of the events of 1 July 1916.

One veteran, Malcolm McKee, was interviewed in an article in the *Belfast Telegraph* where he was scathing in his views of those who held the battle up as some mythical religious symbol:[9]

> What nonsense is struck onto the story … Certainly Major Gaffikin waved an orange handkerchief, but orange was the colour of our battalion … If he had said (and if anybody could have heard him) 'Come on, boys, this is the First of July!' – how many would have known the Boyne was fought on the First of July? I don't know what they plaster such incidents on our battle. Nothing was further from my mind than the Battle of the Boyne.

There is a certain irony in these comments of a veteran of the UVF and of the 1 July, given how their activities would be remembered by some in subsequent years.

In the mid-1960s the old six counties of Ulster which formed Northern Ireland were again threatened by those who wished to see a united Ireland, and therefore in effect Home Rule from Dublin. Determined to prevent any attempt at a united Ireland through the physical force of the IRA, in 1966 a group of approximately ten Loyalists formed a militant group, led by Gusty Spence,[10] taking their name from Carson's 1912 Ulster Volunteer Force. As part of their declared aim this loyalist militant group in Belfast began a hunt for IRA leaders and warned that all IRA men would be "executed mercilessly and without hesitation." In their quest for a leading IRA man, an elderly Protestant woman, Matilda Gould, died of burns received during a petrol bomb attack on a Catholic public house next door to her own and John Scullion, a Catholic, was shot while walking down Clonard Street off the Falls Road. Three Catholic barmen were shot when mistakenly identified as IRA leaders when leaving a pub in Malvern Street near the Shankill Road, one later died.[11] The Northern Ireland Prime Minister, Captain O'Neill, cut short a visit to Paris, returning home. He surprised Stormont by announcing a ban on the UVF and[12] declared them an illegal organisation under the Special Powers Act and the murderers, one of them Gusty Spence, was caught.

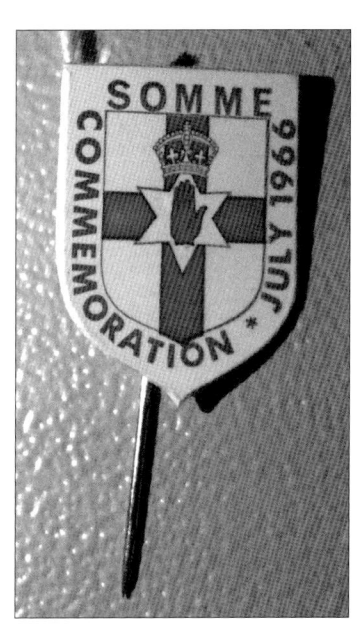

A lapel pin badge from 1966 commemorating the anniversary of the Battle of the Somme. (Somme Museum)

---

9   *Belfast Telegraph* – 30 June 1966.
10 Taylor, Peter, *Provos* (1997).
11 Downing, Taylor. (ed), *The Troubles* (1990).
12 Mercer, Derrik, *Chronicle of the 20th Century* (Longman, 1988).

The situation in Northern Ireland had taken a worrying and ominous turn for the worst and the name of the UVF would be inexplicably linked to the activities of a Loyalist terrorist organisation over the next 30 years.

Harry Currie who was in Carson's UVF later recalled that he joined "because all my gang joined and we followed the bands… Our Company was No.10 and our parade ground was at the North of Ireland Cricket Ground and the headquarters was the Brewery at Sandy Row… The UVF were the loyalists and the Nationalists were the opposition but when war broke out we both united and went to fight together." He stressed that "My friends in the football and billiard teams all went down together. I did not know what I was doing. I was just following the crowd." Although a member of the original UVF he had a clear opinion on more recent developments, "I have no interest in the present day UVF as I gave up on all that and carried on the other work."[13]

The story of the UVF and in particular the gun-running which supplied them with the necessary arms and ammunition would again come to the fore when a newspaper article reported that the *Clyde Valley* was still afloat and was in Canada. This sparked the imagination of Sam Campbell from Whitehead who became the driving force behind attempts to return the vessel to Ulster. A fund raising committee was established with a leaflet printed to help raise the funds necessary to bring her back across the Atlantic Ocean. The leaflet, written by the Reverend Brett Ingram, headed, "SOS" stated the task would cost £10,000 with time of the essence as she had to leave Canadian water that summer, reinforced with the phrase, "Don't delay. Crawford didn't!"[14]

The importance of the *Clyde Valley* was more than her role in Unionist resistance to Home Rule, by 1968 she was reported as the oldest iron-built ship still afloat.[15] She was built by MacIlwaine, Lewis and Company Ltd in Belfast, and launched in 1886 as the SS *Balniel* for the Wigan Coal and Iron Company. In 1909 she was sold to the Clydeside Steamship Company in Glasgow and in 1910 renamed SS *Londoner*, and in 1912 renamed again as SS *Clyde Valley*.[16]

The voyage to bring the *Clyde Valley* 'home' was not uneventful. Captain William Agnew, a retired master mariner from Kilkeel, sailed the vessel from Newfoundland on 5 October 1968 with a crew of ex-Merchant Navy men.[17] However on 11 October engine trouble forced her to

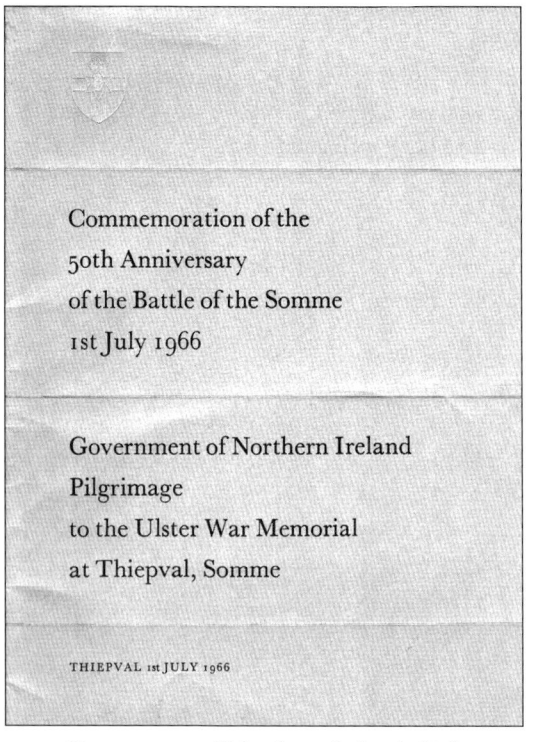

Government of Northern Ireland, 50th Anniversary Somme Pilgrimage. (Somme Museum 1996-437)

---

13 Harry Currie, WW1 Interview – Somme Museum.
14 Hume, David, *"For Ulster and Her Freedom": The story of the April 1914 gun-running* (1989).
15 Hume, David, *"For Ulster and Her Freedom": The story of the April 1914 gun-running* (1989).
16 <http://en.wikipedia.org/wiki/SS_Clyde_Valley_%281886%29> (Accessed 20 February 2014).
17 <http://www.shipsnostalgia.com/showpost.php?p=92891&postcount> Ships Nostalgia – John Kelly (Belfast). now Kelly Fuels (Accessed 20 February 2014).

return to Canada for extensive repairs. Two weeks later, after developing a list, she needed more repairs, ultimately resulting in costs of £16,000. Eventually the *Clyde Valley* was again within sight of the Ulster coastline and sailed into Larne harbour in December 1968. With her flags signalling the message "No Surrender" she was met by between 4,000 and 10,000 spectators which included Orangemen, bands and Lambeg drums.[18]

In 1968 against the backdrop of increasing civil disorder on the streets of Northern Ireland, to some it must have seemed like an omen when the SS *Clyde Valley*, the 82 year old UVF gun-running vessel from 1914 returned back to Larne from Canada. It was against this background that she was accompanied onboard for the last leg of the journey by the Reverend Ian Paisley and members of the Ulster Constitution Defence Committee.[19]

Following her welcome at Larne her next stop was Carrickfergus, partially following her route in 1914 when she headed for Bangor, however her arrival was delayed as she needed more repairs.[20]

She finally tied up in Carrickfergus, looking to some onlookers as not dissimilar in appearance to the coal boats seen in Carrickfergus. Despite attempts to raise sufficient funds to refurbish the vessel, she proved too old and expensive to maintain and after languishing in the harbour she was sold in 1974 and towed away to Lancaster being broken up for scrap.[21]

The *Clyde Valley* moored in Carrickfergus circa 1969. (D.R. Orr)

18   Hume, David, *"For Ulster and Her Freedom": The story of the April 1914 gun-running* (1989).
19   *Belfast Telegraph* – 28 December 1968.
20   Hume, David, *"For Ulster and Her Freedom": The story of the April 1914 gun-running* (1989).
21   Hume, David, *"For Ulster and Her Freedom": The story of the April 1914 gun-running* (1989).

Fred Crawford would in later years be presented with a solid silver casket as a gratitude for his part in the events of the period of 1912-14. His name and an inscription on the front has been done with coloured inlays on either side of the inscription. One of these depicted the Covenant signing, the other a UVF review. The reverse had a picture of Larne as seen from the sea by night and a reminder if any was needed of the landing of the guns on the night of 24 April 1914. At each end of the casket were pictures of Bangor and Donaghadee with the whole piece surmounted by a model of the SS *Fanny*, again direct references to his role in the arming of the UVF.[22]

In some ways he was the reluctant hero of the time, as he suggested to James Craig around 1912 that the Unionist Council should pay someone else "£1200 or £1500 per annum" to smuggle the weapons because as he told Craig, "I have five children and an aged mother to look after, and the business is all that stands between me and the Workhouse. You must let me off this work [i.e. importing arms] …I can't do it, James; my business, through neglect, is leaving me and I am making nothing."[23]

The Troubles which would afflict Northern Ireland in the subsequent decades was to claim one of the Ulster Division's officers. Sir Norman Stronge joined the Derry Volunteers (10th Battalion Royal Inniskilling Fusiliers) in September 1914, participated in the Battle of the Somme and was the first soldier after the start of the battle to be mentioned in despatches by General Haig. He survived the Great War and was decorated with the Military Cross and the Belgian *Croix de Guerre*. As part of the Irish Republican terrorist campaign on the evening 21 January 1981 the IRA murdered Sir Norman, aged 86, alongside his son James whilst watching television in the library of their home, Tynan Abbey, County Armagh.

A postage cover postmarked Hillsborough, 15 November 1985 where the Anglo-Irish Agreement was signed on the same date at Hillsborough Castle, by the British Prime Minister, Margaret Thatcher, and the Irish Taoiseach, Garret FitzGerald. It was a treaty between the United Kingdom and Ireland which aimed to help bring an end to the Troubles in Northern Ireland. The treaty gave the Irish government an advisory role in Northern Ireland's government while confirming that there would be no change in the constitutional position of Northern Ireland unless a majority of its people agreed to join the Republic. It also set out conditions for the establishment of a devolved consensus government in the region. The postage cover evokes previous opposition in the guise of the image of Sir Edward Carson and the legend, "We will not have Home Rule". (D.R. Orr)

---

22   Ingram, Rev Brett, *Covenant and Challenge* (1989).
23   Haines, Keith, *Fred Crawford: Carson's Gunrunner* (2009).

Epilogue

One hundred years after the events surrounding the third Home Rule Bill Ireland enters a decade of anniversaries. Amongst and of significance for Northern Ireland in particular are the signing of the Covenant, the forming of the Ulster Volunteer Force, landing of the weapons and the sacrifice of the 36th (Ulster) Division. Whilst these continue to be commemorated on some gable walls in Belfast in the form of murals there have also been a number of events to mark these occasions.

The centenary also resulted in attention from the arts. The Lyric Theatre, Belfast, hosted a theatrical production entitled *Lord Carson Signs Off*, which focused on Carson's early days as a student at Trinity College, Dublin, through to the signing of the Ulster Covenant and the founding of the Northern Ireland state.

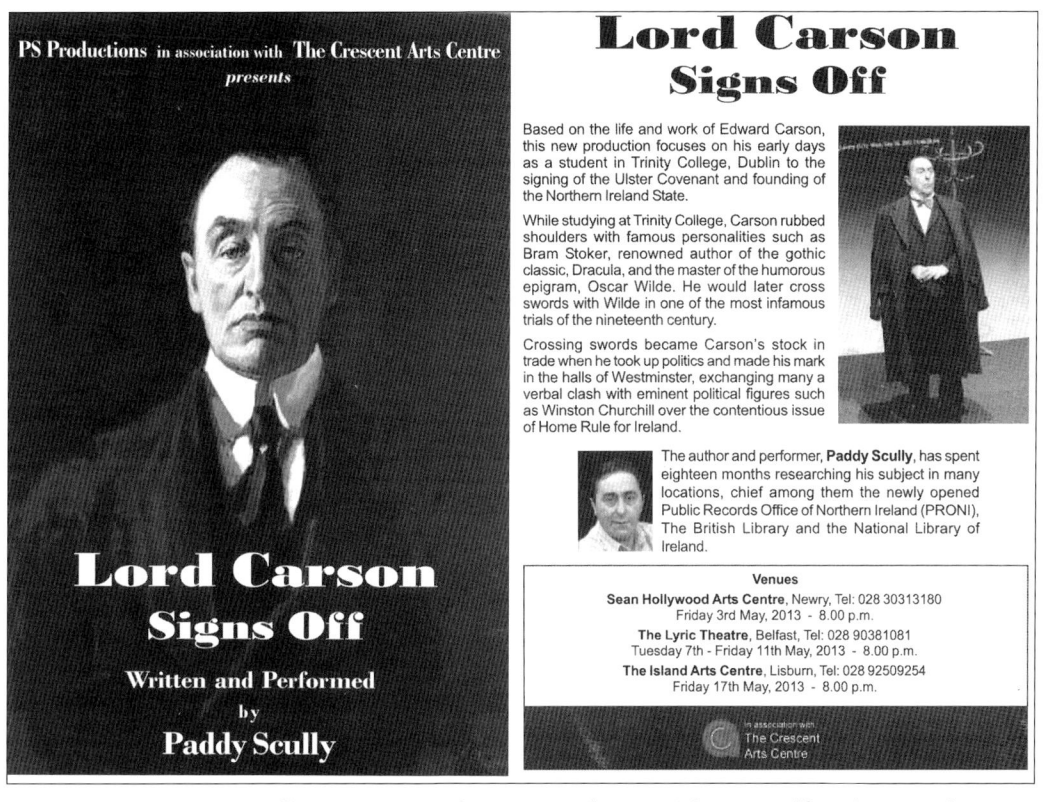

"Carson Signing off", a one man performance at the Lyric Theatre, Belfast. (D.R. Orr)

Signing of the Covenant

St Anne's Cathedral hosted a Service of Choral Evensong on Sunday September 23 to mark the centenary of the signing of the Ulster Covenant. Clergy who took part in the service, led by the Dean of Belfast, the Very Rev John Mann, included the Moderator of the General Assembly of the Presbyterian Church in Ireland, the Rt Rev Dr Roy Patton, and the Rev Donald Ker, representing the President of the Methodist Church. Dean Mann concluded his sermon with:

> We have a chance to celebrate and remember a crucial moment in the history of this place that showed the determination of a generation of the Protestant people of this island to shape their own destiny. Now, in a different age, we may do the same, but today we do it with everyone,

to seek to be two traditions in one community, not limping with one leg stronger than the other, but walking together, not just the length of ourselves, but to the top of the mountain that we need to move.[24]

On 29 September 2012 up to 30,000 people from eight loyal orders took part in the events, including a religious service and celebration at Stormont. Early in the day thousands paraded through Sandy Row in south Belfast, many wearing traditional dress and carrying dummy rifles reminiscent of 1912, before the 30,000 marchers completed the six-mile march from central Belfast to Stormont marking the 100th anniversary of the Ulster Covenant, to oppose Home Rule for Ireland in 1912.

Northern Ireland's First Minister, Peter Robinson, said; "Just as back in 1912, people set aside any differences that they might have within the unionist community, today we're not here as Ulster Unionists or TUV or DUP, we're here simply as unionists."

He also said "You can get a sense of what it must have been like 100 years ago", adding "It's good to get a sense of the occasion that there must have been 100 years ago, and we have a real expectation that this will be an enjoyable day for all who are taking part in it."[25, 26]

Marchers dressed as period members of the UVF march down High Street, Belfast on 28 July 2012 commemorating the centenary of Ulster Day and the signing of the Ulster Covenant. (D.R. Orr)

---

24 <http://www.belfastcathedral.org/news/item/460/service-marks-centenary-of-covenant-signing/> (Accessed 6 January 2015).
25 Ulster Covenant: Thousands on centenary parade <http://www.bbc.co.uk/news/uk-northern-ireland-19769191> (Accessed 6 January 2015).
26 Unionist parade to mark Ulster Covenant centenary begins peacefully in Belfast <<http://www.telegraph.co.uk/news/uknews/northernireland/9575713/Unionist-parade-to-mark-Ulster-Covenant-centenary-begins-peacefully-in-Belfast.html> (Accessed 6 January 2015).

Ulster Volunteer Force

20 April 2013 thousands of people took part in a parade through Belfast from Park Parade to Craigavon House in the east of the city to commemorate the formation of the Ulster Volunteer Force. The parade included bands and men dressed as Ulster Volunteers and women, many dressed at UVF nurses[27] with organisers estimating that between 8,000 to 10,000 participated in the parade. The culmination of the parade was a rally held in the grounds of Craigavon House. The BBC and other television crews reported that they were prevented from filming in Craigavon House grounds and from recording speeches.[28] The great granddaughter of Sir James Craig addressed the crowd and a minute's silence was held for volunteers who had died over the last century.[29, 30]

On Saturday 28 September 2013 more than 10,000 people, many dressed in period costume, took part in a parade to commemorate the centenary of the formation of the Ulster Volunteer Force in West Belfast. It was a re-enactment of a key event of the Home Rule crises when Sir Edward Carson inspected members of the West Belfast Ulster Volunteer Force at Fernhill House in the Glencairn area of Belfast. The event included artefacts involved in the original inspection, including drums. As part of the event the leader of the Progressive Unionist Party, Mr Billy Hutchinson, donned a top hat and tails to play the part of Lord Carson at the Saturday's event and used extracts from Sir Edward Carson's address 100 years previously in his speech on the day.[31, 32]

Gun-running

The application to the Northern Ireland Parades Commission estimated up to 80 bands and 12,000 marchers would be participating. On the day many were wearing period costumes and had travelled from across Northern Ireland with a few from Scotland, and paraded through the town of Larne to commemorate the landing of the arms and ammunition for the Ulster Volunteer Force in 1914.[33]

In Donaghadee on the night of Friday 25 April 2014 hundreds of people dressed as 1912 Ulster Volunteers, some with vintage bicycles, paraded into the town and then re-enacted the unloading of weapons onto the harbour. Despite the heavy rain a crowd spectated on the events being relived included the vintage vehicles. Prior to the event there had been an exhibition of memorabilia from the events 100 years ago, including UVF arm bands, commemorative pottery, authentic firearms and anti-Home Rule ephemera.[34]

---

27 In pictures: Parade marks UVF centenary <http://www.newsletter.co.uk/news/regional/in-pictures-parade-marks-uvf-centenary-1-5021355> (Accessed 7 January 2015).
28 Thousands on parade to mark centenary of UVF's founding <http://www.belfasttelegraph.co.uk/news/local-national/northern-ireland/thousands-on-parade-to-mark-centenary-of-uvfs-founding-29212027.html> (Accessed 7 January 2015).
29 10,000 loyalists march in Belfast parade to mark centenary of the Ulster Volunteer Force <http://www.irishcentral.com/news/10000-loyalists-march-in-belfast-parade-to-mark-centenary-of-the-ulster-volunteer-force-204070191-237583821.html> (Accessed 7 January 2015).
30 Thousands at UVF march in Belfast <http://www.u.tv/News/Thousands-at-UVF-march-in-Belfast/909d2c98-38ca-412d-8ead-441f22096b99> (Accessed 7 January 2015).
31 Massive Ulster Volunteer Force re-enactment marks centenary in West Belfast <http://www.belfasttelegraph.co.uk/news/local-national/northern-ireland/massive-ulster-volunteer-force-reenactment-marks-centenary-in-west-belfast-29619972.html> (Accessed 7 January 2015).
32 Thousands take part in UVF parade <http://www.u.tv/News/Thousands-take-part-in-UVF-parade/6efcb111-802b-49a6-b879-fdea1f306181> (Accessed 7 January 2015).
33 Thousands mark Larne gun-running centenary <http://www.bbc.co.uk/news/uk-northern-ireland-27175185> (Accessed 7 January 2015).
34 *Newtownards Chronicle & Co Down Observer* – 1 May 2014.

Wall mural in the Willowfield area of East Belfast, April 2012 commemorating the contribution of the 3,242 men and women of Willowfield who signed the Ulster Covenant and those who went on to form the 2nd Willowfield Battalion, East Belfast Regiment UVF under the command of Dr William Gibson. (D.R. Orr)

Wall mural in the Willowfield area of East Belfast, April 2012 commemorating the men of the 2nd Willowfield Battalion, East Belfast Regiment, UVF who went on to join 8th Battalion (East Belfast), Royal Irish Rifles, 36th (Ulster) Division, many of whom never returned. (D.R. Orr)

UVF re-enactors parading into Donaghadee from the harbour as part of commemorations of landing UVF guns. (*The Newtownards Chronicle* – J33-1/5/14)

UVF re-enactors unloading the guns from the boat at Donaghadee harbour, Friday, 25 April 2015. (*The Newtownards Chronicle* – J30-1/5/14)

The 36th (Ulster) Division

The name of the Somme and the losses of the 36th (Ulster) Division on 1 July 1916 have over the years become enshrined with Ulster Loyalism. One of the ironies being that the Division never actually fought near to the River Somme, instead being allocated a sector of the front which was bisected by the River Ancre and by marshy ground on either side.[35]

The 36th Ulster Division Memorial Association organised a parade in Belfast city centre on Saturday, 9 May 2015, to commemorate the centenary of the final Belfast parade of the Ulster Division, Saturday, 8 May 1915, the day Ulster officially said farewell before it headed off to England to finalise its training prior to leaving for the Western Front. The date chosen in 2015 coincided with many VE Day commemorations across the United Kingdom, marking the end of Second World War.

Thousands of people paraded and watched as a number of bands led the procession of old vehicles, some mounted with replica machine guns, men and women, many dressed in vintage military and nurses uniforms and carrying replica weapons.

As part of the commemoration there was a wreath-laying ceremony at the cenotaph Belfast City Hall.[36, 37]

The commemoration parade for the 36th (Ulster) Division in Belfast, June 2015. (*East Belfast Extra*)

---

35 Dungan, Myles, *Irish Voices from the Great War* (1998).
36 Belfast parade for 100 years since WW1 march <http://www.bbc.co.uk/news/uk-northern-ireland-32675752> (Accessed 10 May 2015).
37 WWI commemorative parade in Belfast <http://www.u.tv/News/2015/05/09/WWI-commemorative-parade-in-Belfast-36938> (Accessed 10 May 2015).

Appendix I

Order of Battle

(A guide based on available information at time of writing)

Ulster Volunteer Force
Officer Commanding – General Sir George Richardson
Adjutant – Colonel Hacket-Pain

Belfast UVF District
Commanding Officer – Colonel Couchman
Staff Officer –
Colour Sergeant –

North Belfast Regiment
6 x battalions

South Belfast Regiment

6th South Belfast Regiment (University)

3rd East Belfast Regiment – Dr William Gibson

West Belfast Regiment – Col JH Patterson
Special Service Section – FP Crozier

County Antrim – Divisional Commander – Major-General Sir William Adair

Derry City Regiment – Thomas Ernest Hastings
Batt
Batt
Batt

North Derry Regiment –
1st (Faughan Valley) Battalion – Major Ross Smith
2nd (Roe Valley) Battalion – JCB Proctor
3rd (Bann) Battalion – Captain Gausson

South Derry regiment –
1st (Aghadowey, Garvagh and Kilrea) Battalion – CE Stronge DL
2nd (Moneymore, Magherafelt, Maghera and Bellaghy) – Major Lennox Cuningham

County Down – Divisional Commander – Major-General C.H. Powell
1st South Down Regiment
H Company (Seaforde)
2nd Battalion South Down Regiment
4th (Mourne) Battalion South Down Regiment
Grey Abbey Company

Tyrone Regiment
4th (Dungannon) Battalion – Lord Northland

Fermanagh Regiment – Viscount Crighton DSO[1]
1st Batt Fermanagh Regt – Major CC D'Arcy Irvine
    Ballinamallard
    Irvinestown
    Kesh
    Pettigo
    Belleek

2nd Batt Fermanagh Regt – Earl of Lanesborough
    Maguiresbridge
    Lisnaskea
    Newtownbutler

3rd Batt Fermanagh Regt
OIC – Charles F Falls
2IC – Captain Arthur Egerton, DSO
Adjutant – SC Clark
QM – Cyril Falls
Transport Officer – Herbert C Gordon

A Coy (Lisbellaw)	Robert Devers
B Coy (Lsbellaw)	John Dunlop
C Coy (Tempo)	Rev JO Wilson
D Coy (Cooneen)	James Wilson
E Coy (Brookeborough)	Lieut. Col. Doran
F Coy (Enniskillen)	Charles Pierce
G Coy (Enniskillen)	George Evans
H Coy (Florencecourt)	Rev JF Hewitt
I Coy (Letterbreen)	Robert McCourt
K Coy (Beechmount)	John Crawford

Donegal Regiment – Earl of Leitrim
1st Batt Donegal Regt
OIC – Mr J Sproule Myles, JP of Ballyshannon[2]

A Coy (Ballshannon, Rosnowlagh, Ballymagroarty)	Charles Ross, JP
B Coy (Ballintra, Hilltown)	John Crawford

---

1   Canning, WJ, *Ballyshannon, Belcoo, Bertincourt* (1996).
2   Canning WJ, *Ballyshannon, Belcoo, Bertincourt* (1996).

C Coy (Ballynakillen, Bigpark)   James Johnston
D Coy (Laghey, Moyne, Cully)   James Wray
E Coy (Donegal, Clara)   Thomas Ervine
F Coy (Killynard)   Thomas Ervine
G Coy (Inver)   Joseph Kirk
H Coy (Killatee)   George Henry

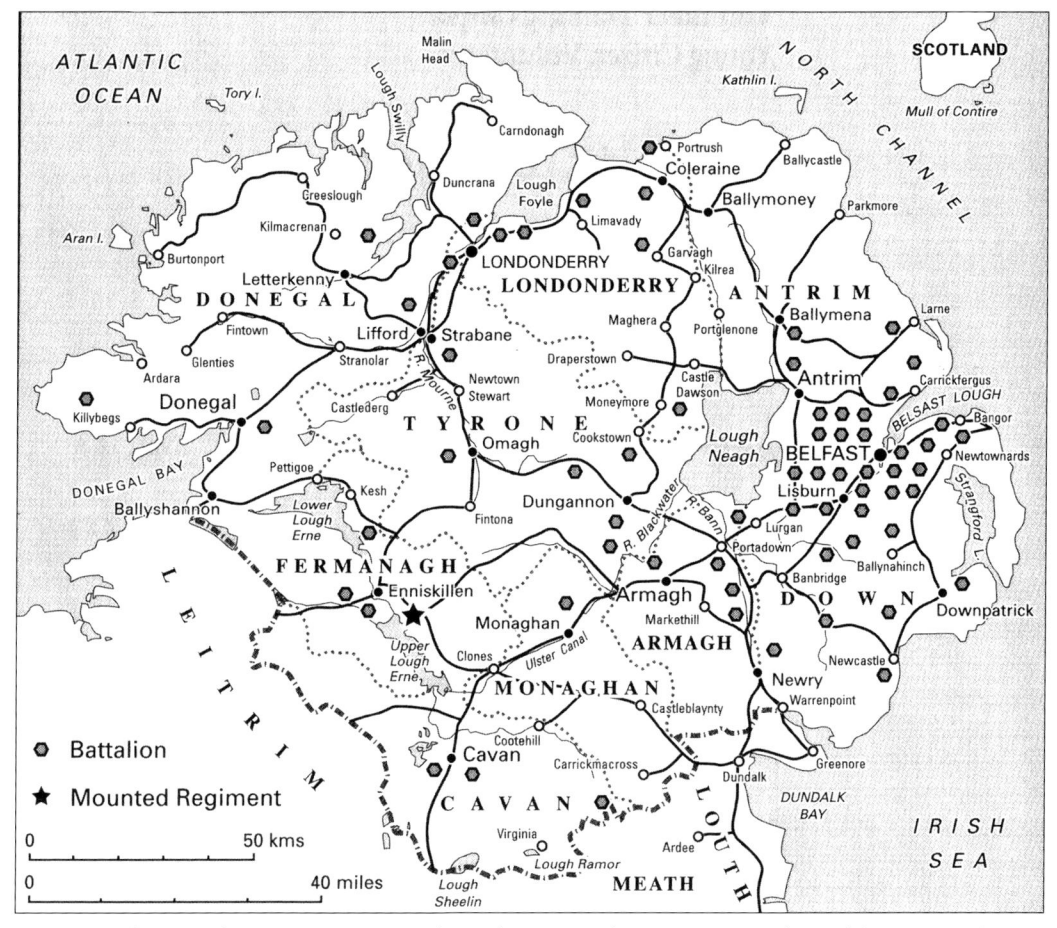

Distribution of UVF Units in March 1914. Source *The Times* 18 March 1914 (T Bowman)

UVF County Organisation Letter and Names of County Secretaries – June 1914[3]

Antrim	A	Gen Sir Wm Adair, Loughanmore, Dunadry
Armagh	B	Geo Crozier, Esq, Victoria House, Armagh
Belfast North	Cn	John Wilson, Esq, 60 Donegall Street, Belfast
Belfast South	Cs	JA Culbert, Esq, 11 Chichester Street, Belfast

---

3   UVF Orders 64, 1914 – Somme Museum.

Belfast East	Ce	A Greeg, Esq, Exchange Street, Belfast
Belfast West	Cw	TC Brown, Esq, Pinner, Malone Road, Belfast
Cavan	D	Wm Matthews, Esq, Church Street, Cavan
Derry County	E	JCB Proctor, Esq, Mai Street, Limavady
Donegal	F	WR Williamson, Esq, Brae Head House, L'derry
Down	G	CH Murland, Esq, Annsborough, Co Down
Fermanagh	H	Rev WB Stack, The Rectory, Aghadrumsee, Clones
L'derry City	I	JM Wilton, Esq, 24 Hawkins Street, Derry
Monaghan	K	Gen Rogers, Esq, The Hill, Monaghan
Tyrone	L	Philip Cruickshank, Esq, 17 Campsie Road, Omagh
US&DRC	SD	A Sayers, Esq, Old Town Hall, Belfast
MT Corps	MC	FH Rogers, Esq, 22 Derryvolgie Avenue, Belfast
HQ Staff	Z	Old Town Hall, Belfast
Engineer Corps	NG[4]	
Artillery Corps	AR	

Temporary Commands – August 1914

The following were the temporary changes to UVF Commands as a consequence of the Reserve Officers being called up for Army Service with the outbreak of war.

3rd Battalion Central Antrim Regiment	JK Sparrow, Esq, Greenisland Vice – Captain A Dobbs.
3rd Battalion South Antrim Regiment	WH Webb, Esq, Randalstown Vice – Lord Massereene
County Cavan Regiment	Col OS Nugent and Major HN Head have left. No new appointments reported.
City of Derry Regiment	Captain HA Guassen left No new appointment
1st Battalion North Derry Regiment	Major Quinn, Campsie House, Londonderry Vice – Major Ross Smythe
1st Battalion West Down Regiment	SG Fenton, Esq, Seapatrick, Banbridge Vice – Capt. Holt Waring
2nd Battalion West Down Regiment	HA Uprichard, Esq, Gilford, Co Down
1st Battalion East Down Regiment	J Alex McConnell, Esq, Assembly Hall, Downpatrick Vice-Viscount Bangor (this was later changed to Adjutant)
2nd Battalion East Down Regiment	Major G Moore Irvine, Thornhill, Knock Vice Capt. SH Hall-Thompson
3rd Battalion East Down Regiment	Edward Slater, Esq, Kilwarlin, Hillsborough Vice – The Earl of Clanwilliam
1st Battalion South Down Regiment	Chas. H Murland, esq, Annsborough Vice – R Magill, esq, Jun, MD
2nd Battalion South Down Regiment	The Earl of Kilmorey, KP, (left half) Mourne Park, Kilkeel Vice – The Viscount Newry
3rd Battalion Donegal Regiment	Capt. RL Moore left. No new appointment

---

4   UVF Order 70, 1914 – Somme Museum.

APPENDIX I

2nd Battalion Monaghan Regiment	ME Knight, Esq, Solicitor, Clones Vice – Col J Madden
Tyrone Regiment	Philip Cruikshank, Esq, 17 Campsie Road, Omagh Vice The Duke of Abercorn & Capt. Ricardo
1st Battalion Tyrone Regiment	Capt. JC Herdman, Sion Mills, Co Tyrone Vice – EC Herdman
4th Battalion Tyrone Regiment	R Stevenson, Esq, Northland Row, Dungannon Vice – The Viscount Northland

Further amendments were issued:

Derry County Division	RE Toker, Esq, Temperance Hotel, Limavady, to be Staff Officer, Vice – Capt Gaussen.
4th Battalion Armagh Regiment	TJ Atkinson, Esq, Eden Villa, Portadown, to Command. Vice – Major Stewart Blacker
1st Battalion Cavan Regiment	FL Clememnt Scott, Esq, The Rocks Castledoney to Command. Vice – Lord Farnham
3rd Battalion Cavan Regiment	TY Chambers, Esq, The Laurels, Bailieborough to Command. Vice – Capt. M Pratt
North Londonderry Regiment	Capt. HR Bruce, Clothworker's Arms, Coleraine to Command. Vice – Major Ross Smyth
3rd Battalion Donegal Regiment	WR Williamson, Esq, Brae Head House, Londonderry, Acting Adjutant
2nd Battalion Fermanagh Regiment	G Massey Beresford, Esq, St. Herbert's, Belturbet to Command. Vice – Earl of Lanesborough
2nd Battalion Monaghan Regiment	ME Knight, Esq, Solicitor, Clones to Command. Vice – Col. Madden
County Cavan Regiment	Capt. Somerset Saunderson, Castle Saunderson, Belturbet to Command. Vice – Col OS Nugent

Again further changes were notified:

North Antrim Regiment	Col Hugh Lyle, DSO Knocktarna, Coleraine. Vice – Capt. The Hon. A O'Neill, MP
Tyrone Regiment	Thos. MacGregor Greer, Esq, Tullylagan, Tullyhogue. Vice – Philip Cruickshank, Esq
2nd Battalion Tyrone Regiment	RW Bingham, Esq, Royal School Dungannon. Vice – R Stevenson, Esq

Further appointments included:

Belfast Division	Capt. WI Downe, late RN, will assume Command from this date during absence of Col. Couchman
South Londonderry Regiment	CE Stronge, Esq, Lizard Manor, Aghadower, to be Regimental Commander during absence of Major Lennox-Conyngham
2nd Bn. South Londonderry Regiment	H Clark, Esq, Ardtara, Up'lands, will assume Command from this date during absence of Major Lennox-Conyngham

2nd Bn. West Down Regiment	WF Uprichard, Esq, Elmfield, Gilford, Co Down to be in Command in the absence HA Uprichard, Esq
2nd Battalion East Down Regiment	J Hill-Dickson, Esq, Ardmore, Ballygowan
East Belfast Regiment	HV Coates, Esq, Clonalton, Strandtown to be second in command
East Belfast Regiment	J McConnell, Esq, Glendhu, Strandtown to be Adjutant
6th Bn. East Belfast Regiment	CWS Dream, Esq, Graylawn, Kensington Road, Knock, to Command
3rd Bn. City of Derry Regiment	W Pollock, Esq, Queen Street, Londonderry to Command
Down Division	Brig-General EH Molesworth, CB is appointed to the Command of the Down Division., Vice – Major-General Powell, vacated
2nd Bn. Fermanagh Regiment	WM Knight, Esq, Lisnaskea to be Adjutant
Tyrone Regiment	FJ Johnston, Esq, High Street, Omagh to be Adjutant
2nd Bn, Tyrone Regiment	FJ Johnston, Esq, High Street, Omagh to be Adjutant.
1st Bn. Fermanagh Regiment	SJ McCutcheon, Esq, Kiltieney, Kesh, to be Adjutant
2nd Bn. Fermanagh Regiment	Geoffrey RJ Corbett, Esq, Crom, Newtownbutler to be Adjutant
3rd Bn. Fermanagh Regiment	SC Clarke, Esq, Enniskillen to Command and be Adjutant
Belfast Division	Owing to the departure of Brig-General EH Molesworth, CB, Colonel JCF Gordon CIE, Chief Staff Officer assumes Command of the Belfast Division, in addition to his other duties, as temporary measure and pending permanent arrangements.
1st Bn. South Antrim Regiment	Alexander Woods, Esq, Seymour Street, Lisburn, to Command
5th Bn. Armagh Regiment	George Fleming, Union Street, Armagh to Command
1st Bn. South Antrim Regiment	EA Sinton, Esq, Ravarnette, Lisburn to be Second in Command
Derry Division	Rev BL Smith, Eastleigh, Coleraine to be Staff Officer
Young Citizen Volunteers	Mr Harold M Moore, Balmoral Avenue, Belfast, vice Colonel Chichester, vacated

Appendix II

Principal War Time Philanthropies and Amounts Raised[1]

Ulster Our Day Collection: British Red Cross Society, Order of St John of Jerusalem.
1916   £27,735   1s 8d
1917   £48,707   7s 8d
1918   £70,137   2s 2d
Total   £146,579 11s 6d

Ulster Women's Gift Fund for Prisoners of War etc.	£120,000
Ulster Patriotic Fund	£100,000
Ulster Volunteer Force Hospitals, Belfast, Craigavon and Gilford	£100,000
Prince of Wales Fund	£50,000
The Service Club, Belfast	£20,000
Ulster Motor Ambulance Fund	£12,000
Ulster Division Memorial Fund	£5,000

---

[1] Citizens' Committee, *The Great War 1914-1918: Ulster Greets her Brave and Faithful Sons and Remembers her Glorious Dead* (1919).

Gifts collected by the Dublin Women's Unionist Club. One of the largest of such organisations collecting comforts to send to soldiers was the Unionist Women's Gift Fund organised by the UWUC. By November 1918 it had raised almost £120,000 (nearly £1m today). (Somme Museum)

Appendix III

Weapons

Exact figures of the weapons held by the UVF at any time are impossible to ascertain as UVF Headquarters appears to have had no clear control over their supply.

By 31 March 1914, the RIC believed they had 24,879 whilst by 31 May 1914 the Administration in Dublin Castle believed they had 51,595, whilst around the same time, Count Gleichen, army GOC, thought that estimates of 80,000 had some credibility.

In October 1914, possibly as a result of a number of rifles going missing, an order was issued that all rifles of all patterns which were the property of the Ulster Volunteer Force were to be stamped on the right hand side of the butt, midway between the toe and heel and about two inches from the butt plate with an official cutting die which was supplied by headquarters to the Officers Commanding Regiments.[1] The instructions included for the stamping stated that a heavy hammer was required, but no heat was to be applied in any way.[2]

These arrangements also extended to those rifles which had been privately purchased but for which a grant had been paid.[3]

By 1917 the UVF were co-operating with the RIC to ensure that no Ulster Volunteer arms fell into the hands of the Irish Volunteers though probably not all Ulster Volunteers would be willing to hand their weapons into central armouries. The RIC suggested in a report of February 1917 that 53,130 rifles were with the Ulster Volunteers, though it was thought likely to be an under-estimation.[4]

This co-operation stemmed from measures in order to allay the fears and concerns of Lieutenant-General Sir BT Mahon, Commander-in-Chief, Irish Command, regarding the security of UVF weapons. UVF Headquarters considered that steps would have to be taken or else Mahon would have to consider other alternatives to ensure the weapons were safe and secure from falling into the wrong hands. One proposal in September 1917 was the removal of the bolts from rifles to

An example of the stamp mark of the UVF which was made on the woodwork of the organisation's rifles and bayonets.
(Somme Museum)

---

1 UVF Orders 124, 1914 – Somme Museum.
2 Memo No.170 – Antrim Division, UVF.
3 Memo No.167 – C/O Antrim Division UVF – 2 November 1914.
4 Bowman, Timothy, *Carson's Army: Ulster Volunteer Force, 1910-22* (2007).

be kept carefully in separate locations. It was noted that those rifles in the possession of individuals in outlying areas would require special attention whilst those collected in armouries or private quarters would need extra precautions and increased vigilance; the concentration being a greater target. The implementation of these proposals were left to the discretion of regimental commanders as was the matter of explaining the rationale for actions to the men so not to create unrest amongst the rank and file.[5]

In August 1918 it was believed a proclamation would be issued whereby all arms and ammunition belonging to the Ulster Volunteer Force would have to be surrendered when called for. In response arrangements were made whereby the UVF Authorities would collect arms and ammunition into certain centres where they would be safe from surrender. Any member of the Ulster Volunteers who would retain any arms or ammunition would do so at their own risk and would not receive any support from the UVF Authorities should they refuse to surrender them to the police or military on demand.[6]

In order to address sensitivities in some areas with regards to the seizures or ownership of the Ulster Volunteer weapons, yet ensure there were adequate measures to protect them, arrangements were agreed whereby a UVF officer could deposit his unit's weapons in armouries which would be protected by British troops. By October 1918 the Chief Secretary was able to report that 50,000 rifles and 11 machine guns, mostly UVF, had been handed over to the military authorities for safe keeping.[7]

The distribution of rifles and machine guns per county 1917[8]

Area	Lee Enfield (magazine)	Martini Enfield (single loader)	German & Austrian	Italian	Other Makes	Machine Guns	Total
Co. Antrim	2152	896	6606	55	101	0	9810
Co. Armagh	397	416	447	2920	0	0	4180
Belfast	6030	3353	1657	700	630	11	12381
Co. Cavan	188	746	31	41	88	0	1374
Co. Donegal	193	1578	5	8	0	0	1784
Co. Down	1002	1493	5043	130	859	0	8527
Co. Fermanagh	134	186	118	1830	50	0	2318
Londonderry (City)	805	205	800	0	60	0	1870
Londonderry (County)	366	575	860	1362	20	0	3183
Co. Monaghan	21	0	720	712	255	0	1678
Co. Tyrone	705	3471	1844	5	0	0	6025

At the end of the Ulster Volunteer Force and the creation of the Northern Ireland Government, those weapons held in storage found themselves being transferred from the responsibility of the War Department to the Ministry of Home Affairs in Belfast.

There are accounts that most of the rifles were used to equip the British-officered Ethiopian levies who helped to restore Emperor Haile Selassie to his throne in 1941. The reality is that a significant number ended up in the RUC stores at Sprucefield. Whilst a number of obsolete rounds of ammunition, rifles and bayonets were sold after the British Expeditionary Force evacuation

---

5 Removing Bolts of Rifles – 28 September 1917.
6 Rifles – Gen Sir WT Adair – 15 August 1918.
7 Bowman, Timothy, *Carson's Army: Ulster Volunteer Force, 1910-22* (2007).
8 Bowman, Timothy, *Carson's Army: Ulster Volunteer Force, 1910-22* (2007).

from Dunkirk during the Second World War, others were used to equip the newly-formed Ulster Defence Volunteers, Northern Ireland's sister organisation to the Local Defence Volunteers in Great Britain intended to counter potential German invasion. Small numbers were held in other local police stores in RUC barracks, finally being scrapped during 'The Troubles' post 1969. Even today others occasionally appear for sale between militaria collectors and enthusiasts.

Webley
Webley Mk IV Revolver

Length (gun):	11in
Barrel:	3in, 4in, 5in and 6in variants
Weight:	36oz
Calibre	:0.455in
Rifling:	7 grooves, R/H
Capacity:	6
Muzzle Velocity:	ca 650 ft/sec

The Webley Revolver (also known as the Webley Break-Top Revolver or Webley Self-Extracting Revolver) was, in various marks, the standard issue service pistol for the armed forces of the United Kingdom, the British Empire, and the Commonwealth from 1887 until 1963.

The Webley is a top-break revolver with automatic extraction. That is, breaking the revolver open for reloading also operates the extractor. This removes the spent cartridges from the cylinder. The Webley Mk I service revolver was adopted by the British Army in 1887 followed by minor amendments in Mk II and Mk III. The later version, the Mk IV which represented a marked improvement was officially adopted by the British Army in 1899[9] and rose to prominence during the Boer War of 1899–1902. As a consequence it was often known as the 'Boer War Model', being carried by all officers, non-commissioned officers, trumpeters of cavalry regiments and certain categories of artillery drivers. Many infantry officers also obtained private purchase models.[10]

The Mk V was introduced in December 1913, though only 20,000 were made.[11] However, the Mk VI, introduced in 1915 during the First World War, is perhaps the best-known model.

Webley Mk VI revolver.
(Somme Museum)

---

9   Millar, David, *The Illustrated Book of Guns* (2000).
10 Millar, David, *The Illustrated Book of Guns* (2000).
11 Millar, David, *The Illustrated Book of Guns* (2000).

Firing the large .455 Webley cartridge, Webley service revolvers are among the most powerful top-break revolvers ever produced. The 1932 Mk VI .455 calibre was officially abandoned in favour of a similar arm in .38in calibre, however many reserve officers continued to carry it after they were recalled in 1939.[12, 13]

Lee-Metford

Length (gun):	4ft 1.5in
Barrel:	30.2in
Weight:	9lb 4oz
Calibre	:0.303in
Rifling:	7 grooves, L/H (each 0.004in) (Later became Enfield rifling, 5 grooves L/H, 0.005in deep)
Magazine:	10 rounds

The Lee-Metford was introduced in 1888 to replace the Martini-Henry; technically[14] it was designated the Martini-Henry Mk 5, yet its official name was 'Magazine Rifle Mk I',[15] and it comprised vital components later incorporated in the 1895 Lee-Metford rifle. The most important aspect of this weapon was the box magazine. The
bolt action and a metal box magazine (reserve supply ammo) was designed by Scottish-born American James Paris Lee of Connecticut, who worked for the Remington Arms Company, while British ballistician William Ellis Metford designed the barrel, to tolerate the excessive fouling from the gunpowder used in early .303 cartridges. The charge was initially smokeless compressed black powder, but this was gradually replaced at the turn of the century by the Lee-Enfield. The old Lee-Metford barrels were then redesigned at Enfield, with more efficient rifling for the smokeless powder cartridges being introduced.[16]

Lee's bolt action mechanism was also a great improvement over other designs of the day. The rear-mounted lugs placed the operating handle much closer to the rifleman, over the trigger. This made it much quicker to operate than other, forward-mounted lug designs which forced the rifleman to move his hand forward to operate the bolt; also, the bolt's distance of travel was identical with the length of the cartridge, and its rotation was only 60 degrees compared to the 90 degree rotation of some French and Mauser-style actions.[17]

The Lee detachable box magazine was an improvement over the integral magazines in use with most repeaters, and this particular magazine offered greater capacity than the competing Mannlicher design.[18] In December 1890 the rifle underwent a number of minor modifications and was reintroduced as the Mk I*.[19]

The introduction of smaller, lighter cartridges increased the velocity of the shot and flattened its trajectory. Improved research introduced a cartridge with better combustion and less prone to deterioration during storage. This resulted in a bullet being introduced in 1892 with a nitro-glycerine compound called cordite, and this

---

12 Millar, David, *The Illustrated Book of Guns* (2000).
13 Webley Revolver <http://en.wikipedia.org/wiki/Webley_Revolver> (Accessed 3 October 2014).
14 Millar, David, *The Illustrated Book of Guns* (2000).
15 Skennerton, Ian, *The Lee Enfield Story* (1993).
16 Du Quesne-Bird, Nicholas, *The Observer's Book of Firearms* (1978).
17 <Lee-Metford <http://en.wikipedia.org/wiki/Lee-Metford> (Accessed 2 October 2014).
18 Lee-Metford <http://en.wikipedia.org/wiki/Lee-Metford> (Accessed 2 October 2014).
19 Skennerton, Ian, *The Lee Enfield Story* (1993).

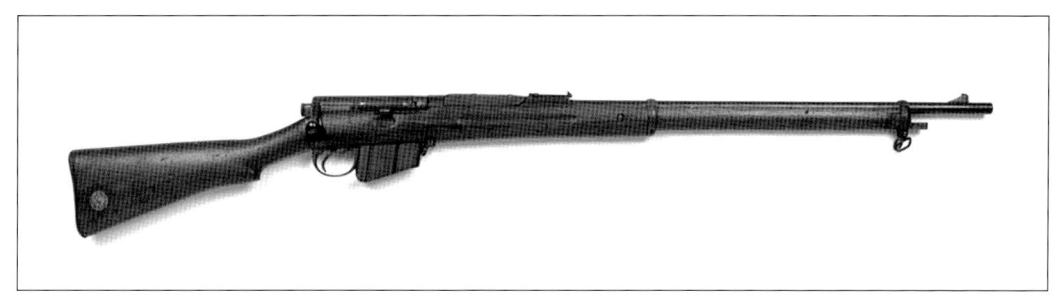

Lee-Metford. (Somme Museum)

would be used thereafter in the .303 round.[20] The one drawback with this improved propellant was greater heat, which reduced the barrel life.[21] The new Lee magazine held eight rounds, pushed down individually, and a metal plate on a strong spring forced the column of cartridges upwards. Loading the magazine could be done when it was either attached or detached from the rifle. In 1892 the magazine was enlarged to hold ten rounds. This also involved widening the body and trigger guard, as the magazine had a staggered double column of cartridges as opposed to a single column.[22]

In an effort to enforce fire control and conserve ammunition and supplies, a sliding plate, which separated the breech from the magazine, was incorporated. This enabled the rifle to be loaded with single shots in the old position yet retaining an ammunition reserve for rapid fire in an operational emergency.

After experiences in the Boer War it was essential to find a method of reloading rapidly.

Lee therefore invented a fire round re-charger clip, which meant that all the rounds could be pushed into the magazine with the thumb. The Mk II corrected many of the failings of the earlier Mk I and Mk I*, being finally declared obsolete in 1926.[23]

Following the introduction of the Mk III SMLE rifle, the Lee-Metford underwent a change allowing it to use charge-loading. Apart from a few minor changes, such as a charger bridge, sights and magazine, the rifle was identical to the Magazine Lee-Metford Mk II, approved in 1893.[24]

Martini-Henry

Length (gun):	48in
Barrel:	33.5in
Weight:	8.6lb
Calibre	:0.45in
Rifling:	7 grooves, L/H
Operation:	Breech Loading
Feed:	Single round manual

---

20 Orr, David R, *Duty Without Glory* (2008).
21 Skennerton, Ian, *The Lee Enfield Story* (1993).
22 Skennerton, Ian, *The Lee Enfield Story* (1993).
23 Skennerton, Ian, *The Lee Enfield Story* (1993).
24 Skennerton, Ian, *The Lee Enfield Story* (1993).

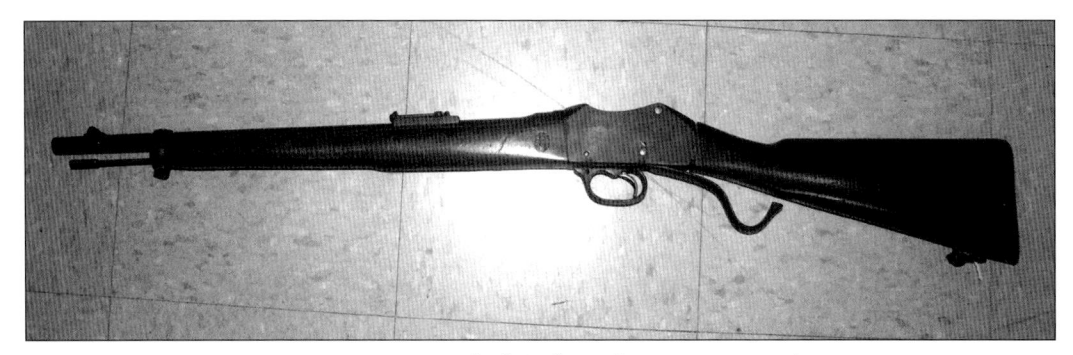

UVF Martini-Metford Carbine. (Somme Museum)

The Martini-Henry was chosen by the British Army as the longer-term solution to converting Enfield rifles with the Snider action. This combination of a Martini breech and Henry barrel ranged from the Mk 1 to the Mk 5 (Mk2 – modified trigger; Mk3 – improved back sight; Mk 4 – general improvements; Mk 5 – took the .303 cartridge, becoming the Martini-Metford).[25]

The Martini-Henry was the first metal cartridge, breech-loading firearm for the British Army, and adopted in 1871. It was also the first bottleneck-type cartridge adopted by the British Army. It became obsolete in the 1890s with the introduction of bolt-action rifles, although large numbers were converted to .303in and some are still in civilian use.[26]

The breechblock is operated by the lever behind the trigger guard. When the lever is depressed the block falls, the firing pin is cocked, the empty case ejected, and the breech exposed for loading. Return the lever and the block rises and is ready for use again.

Martini-Henry variants were used throughout the British Empire for 30 years. Whilst the Snider was the first breechloader firing a metallic cartridge in regular British service, the Martini was designed from the outset as a breechloader and was both faster firing and had a longer range.[27]

Mauser
Model 1888 Commission Rifle

Length:	49in
Barrel:	29in
Weight:	8.5lb
Calibre:	0.317in
Rifling:	4 grooves R/H
Operation:	Breech loading
Feed:	5 round box magazine

Mauser was a German arms manufacturer of a line of bolt-action rifles and semi-automatic pistols from the 1870s to 1995. Their designs were built for the German armed forces since the late 19th and early 20th centuries. Military Mauser designs were also exported and licensed to a number of countries, as well as being a popular civilian firearm.

In 1886 the French Army introduced the Lebel Model 1886 rifle, which used a smokeless powder cartridge. The invention of smokeless powder in the late 19th century immediately rendered all of

---
25   Millar, Ian, *The Illustrated Book of Guns* (2000).
26   Du Quesne-Bird, Nicholas, *The Observer's Book of Firearms* (1978).
27   Martini-Henry <http://en.wikipedia.org/wiki/Martini-Henry> (Accessed 3 October 2014).

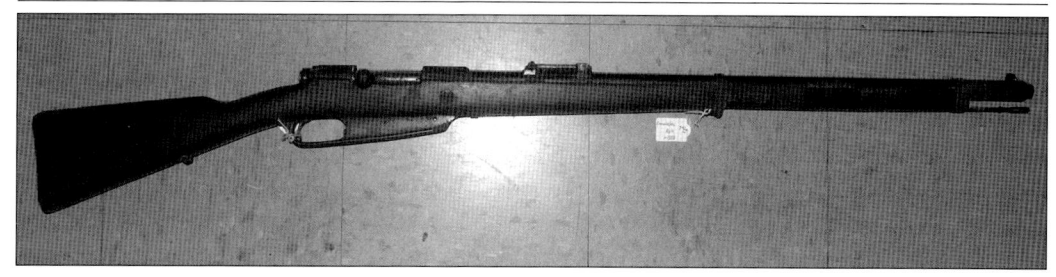

A Model 1888 Commission Rifle used by the UVF. (Somme Museum)

the large-bore black powder rifles then in use obsolete. Smokeless powder allowed smaller diameter bullets to be propelled at higher velocities, with accuracy to 1,000 yards (910 m), making most other military rifles obsolete. Like the Mauser 71/84, its disadvantage was a slow-to-load 8-round tube magazine.

However this advancement by the French led to it becoming another aspect of the arms race between the Germany, France, and Europe in general at the time. It directly caused the Germans to set up a Small Arms Commission in 1888 to chart the way ahead for such a weapon. Perhaps surprisingly for something designed by committee they came up with a very effective and modern weapon officially designated the Model 1888 (Gewehr 88), it later became known as the "Commission Rifle".[28]

They took the best features of the Lebel along with a modified Mauser action, firing the 7.92 × 57 mm Mauser smokeless round and a Mannlicher-style box magazine.[29]

The magazine protruded a short distance below the receiver, but was non-removable. Soldiers were issued their rounds in clips of five which were inserted into the magazine from the top, the empty clip falling through the bottom of the magazine when the fifth round had been fired.[30]

The barrel design and rifling were virtually copied from the French Lebel. It has an odd appearance as the entire barrel is encased in a sheet metal tube for protection.[31] It was also claimed to dissipate heat caused by rapid firing.[32] With the tube removed the rifle looks rather modern. The tube was intended to increase accuracy by preventing the barrel from directly contacting the stock, but in reality it provided a space for water to be trapped if exposed to harsh conditions and increased the risk of rust.[33] It had no wooden forward hand guard.

The Karabiner 88 was the carbine version. Both would be updated in the early 20th century and saw limited use in World War I.[34]

Whilst the Commission Rifle had a few Mauser features, it is incorrect to call it a "Mauser." and Mauser was one of the few major arms manufacturers in Germany that did not produce Gewehr 88s. It was also manufactured in Austria by Steyr.[35]

---

28 Miller, Ian, *The Illustrated book of Guns* (2000).
29 Mauser <http://en.wikipedia.org/wiki/Mauser> (Accessed 2 October 2014).
30 Miller, Ian, *The Illustrated book of Guns* (2000).
31 Gewehr 1988 <http://en.wikipedia.org/wiki/Gewehr_1888> (Accessed 2 October 2014).
32 Miller, Ian, *The Illustrated book of Guns* (2000).
33 Gewehr 1988 <http://en.wikipedia.org/wiki/Gewehr_1888> (Accessed 2 October 2014).
34 Mauser <http://en.wikipedia.org/wiki/Mauser> (Accessed 2 October 2014).
35 Miller, Ian, *The Illustrated book of Guns* (2000).

Vetterli

M1869

Length:	52in
Barrel:	33.1in
Weight:	10.3lb
Calibre:	0.41in
Rifling:	4 grooves, L/H
Operation:	Breech loading
Feed:	12 round tube

The Vetterli rifles were a series of Swiss army service rifles in use from 1869 to circa 1890 which combined the American Winchester Model 1866's tubular magazine with a regular bolt featuring for the first time two opposed rear locking lugs which locked into the recesses in the body. This novel type of bolt was a major improvement over the simpler Dreyse and Chassepot bolt actions.

It had a somewhat unusual safety device which consisted of a small catch below the bolt lever and when this was pushed forward and the breech closed, the catch slipped backwards pulling the striker to half-cock. Full-cock was restored by the simple process of raising and lowering the bolt lever.[36]

This was the first repeating bolt action rifle to feature a self-cocking action and a small caliber bore. As a result of the Swiss Federal Council's decision in early 1866 to equip the army with a breech loading repeating rifle, the Vetterli rifles were, at the time of their introduction, the most advanced military rifles in Europe. It replaced the Amsler-Milbank rifles, which were a metallic cartridge conversion from previous Swiss muzzle loading rifles.[37]

The Italian Army in 1870 adopted a modified Vetterli design, simplified for economy, as a single-shot, designating it the M1870.

With three versions, an infantry rifle (53in barrel), a short rifle (43.1in barrel) and a cavalry carbine (36.8in barrel) it remained the Italian service rifle from 1870-1878, when it was replaced with the M1870/87 Italian Vetterli-Vitali variant. The M1870 was a single-shot bolt action rifle chambered for the 10.4 mm Vetterli centrefire cartridge, at first with black powder and later with smokeless powder.[38]

In 1887 the Italian Military updated the single shot Model 1870 to become the M1870/87 Italian Vetterli-Vitali with a four-round Vitali box magazine.

The Ulster Volunteers were able to purchase them on the international arms market at the bargain price of 5 francs each, including belt and bayonet.[39] Brigadier General Count Gleichen described them as "not good, but weedy and weak."[40]

---

36 Miller, Ian, *The Illustrated book of Guns* (2000).
37 M1870 Vetterli <http://en.wikipedia.org/wiki/Vetterli_rifle#M1870.2F87_Italian_Vetterli-Vitali> (Accessed 2 October 2014).
38 M1870 Italian Vetterli <http://en.wikipedia.org/wiki/M1870_Italian_Vetterli> (Accessed 2 October 2014).
39 Bowman, Timothy, *Carson's Army: Ulster Volunteer Force, 1910-22* (2007).
40 Bowman, Timothy, *Carson's Army: Ulster Volunteer Force, 1910-22* (2007).

A Vetterli rifle used by the UVF. (Somme Museum)

Steyr/Mannlicher
Romanian Mannlicher M1893
Length: 48.3in
Barrel: 28.5in
Weight: 8.8lbs
Rifling: 2 groove R/H

Steyr Mannlicher is a firearms manufacturer based in the city of Steyr, Austria, originally part of Steyr-Daimler-Puch.

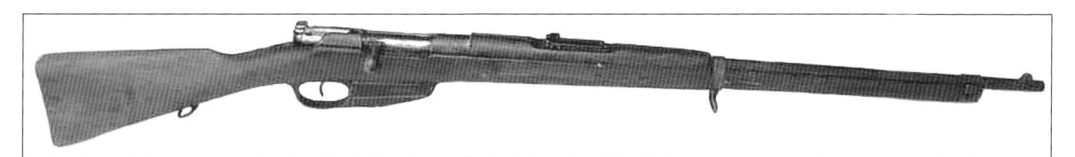

Mannlicher M1904 rifle.

The Mannlicher Repeating Rifle Model 1904 Contract was a large-caliber version of the series that had included the Romanian and Dutch Mannlichers. It had a straight-grip stock, and a handguard which ran from the receiver ring to the barrel band. The magazine case resembled that of the Gewehr 88, but the barrel jacket of the German gun was absent; a bayonet lug was on the right side of the nose cap. The launch of this rifle by Steyr was to use up old stocks of M92/93 Romanian Actions, and in order to capture some of the smaller markets missed by Mauser/DWM.

The Mannlicher 1893 offered by Steyr to Romania was itself a somewhat modernized version of the German Model 1888 that was also known as the Commission Rifle.

At the outbreak of the First World War any undelivered rifles were requisitioned by the Austro-Hungarian Army.

The 12,000 rifles ordered and supplied to the Ulster Volunteers are often referred to as the Irish Mannlicher M1904 Repeating Rifle, though also as the 7.9 mm Repetiergewehr M.93/13. They look very close to the M93 Romanian Mannlicher, but these rifles were produced with left-over parts from the M1892 Romanian Mannlicher. It is therefore not impossible to find a Romanian eagle mark stamped on them along with 5-digit serial numbers.[41]

---

41 Austro-Hungarian Weapons Mannlicher Export Modell Rifles <http://www.hungariae.com/Mann04.htm> (Accessed 21 November 2014).

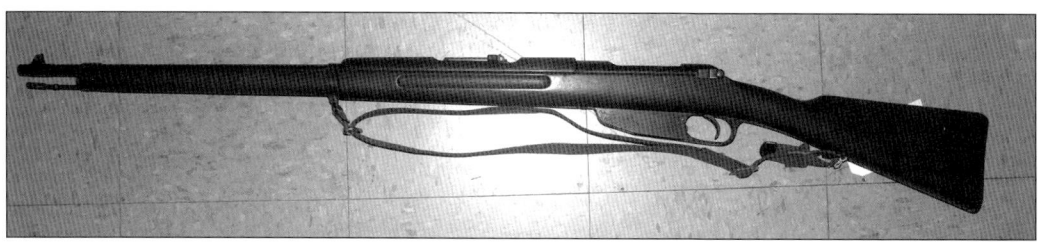

UVF 0038 – A Steyr rifle used by the UVF. (Somme Museum)

During the M1904's rework to 7.9 mm, the M1893 magazine was modified for the use of the 5-round 7.92 mm Gewehr 88 clips and the magazine's outer reinforcement ribs were also eliminated.[42]

The rifles were issued with M1893 type Romanian bayonets with serials not matching the rifles; blade 255 mm, overall 380 mm long. Muzzle ring diameter was 14.5 mm.

In 2011 a gentleman found a package in his attic in a house in Belfast which he believed may be fishing equipment. On closer inspection it turned out to be a Mannlicher M1904 rifle, along with 15 live rounds of ammunition and a small pistol which also had live rounds.[43]

Vickers-Maxim

Calibre:	.303in
Barrel length:	28.4in
Overall length:	43in
Weight:	33lb
Operation:	Recoil
Rifling:	4 grooves R/H
Feed:	250-round belts
Rate of fire:	500 rounds/min
Muzzle velocity:	2,440ft/sec
Maximum range:	4,000yds
Cooling:	Water
Weight of tripod:	50lb

The Vickers machine gun or Vickers gun is a name primarily used to refer to the water-cooled .303 British (7.7mm) machine gun produced by Vickers Limited, originally for the British Army. The machine gun typically required a six to eight-man team to operate: one fired, one fed the ammunition, the rest helped to carry the weapon, its ammunition and spare parts.

It was based on the successful Maxim gun of the late 19th century. When in 1886 Vickers purchased the Maxim Company outright they took the design of the Maxim gun and improved it, reducing its weight by simplifying the action and substituting components made with high strength alloys. A muzzle booster was also added.

---

42 Austro-Hungarian Weapons Mannlicher Export Modell Rifles <http://www.hungariae.com/Mann04.htm> (Accessed 21 November 2014).
43 UVF Mannlicher found in attic <http://www.belfasttelegraph.co.uk/news/local-national/northern-ireland/historic-uvf-rifle-found-in-belfast-attic-28676509.html> (Accessed 21 November 2014).

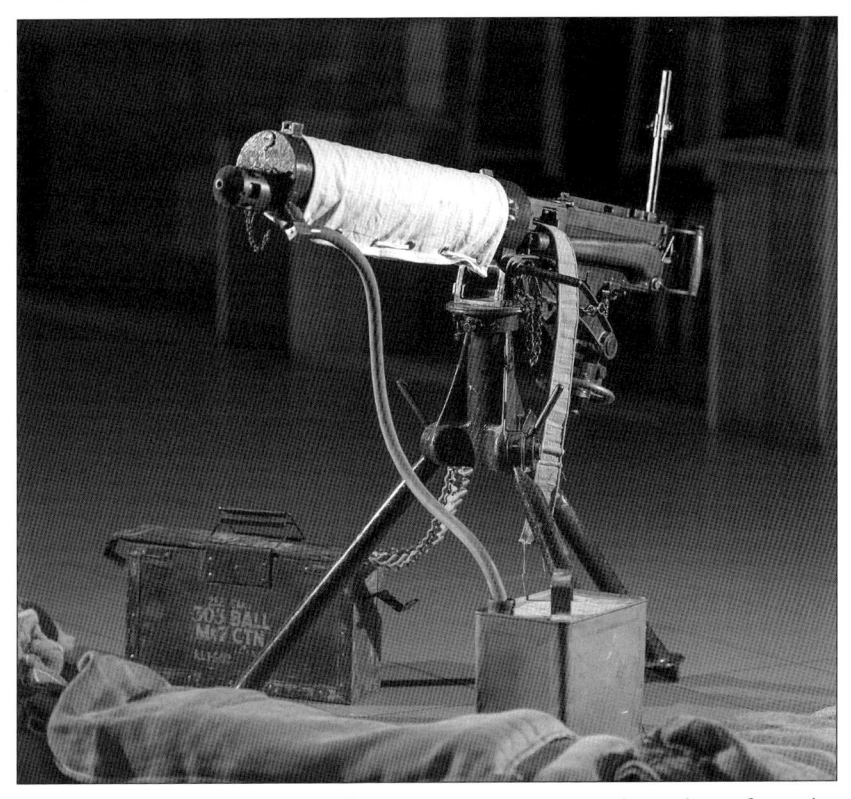

The Vickers machine gun or Vickers gun is a name primarily used to refer to the water-cooled .303 British (7.7 mm) machine gun produced by Vickers Limited, originally for the British Army. (Somme Museum)

On 26 November 1912 the British Army formally adopted the Vickers gun as its standard machine gun, using it alongside their existing Maxims.[44, 45]

During World War One it was considered the standard medium machine-gun of the British Army. When deployed, it was actually mounted on a tripod, and the barrel was water-cooled by means of a jacket around it, fed by a hose from a nearby can.

The gun had a remarkable capacity for sustained fire, despite weather or operational conditions, but this led to obvious problems of wear. The water-cooled jacket had a capacity of about 7 pints, which would begin to boil after 3,000 rounds of steady fire at about 200 rounds a minute. Thereafter the water evaporated steadily at the rate of 1 or 2 pints per thousand rounds, depending on the rate of fire and the climatic conditions. The gun was fitted with a condenser tube leading into an old-fashioned 1 gallon petrol can, and if some water was put into the can first and the steam passed through it, a considerable amount could be used again.[46]

---

44 Vickers-Maxim <http://en.wikipedia.org/wiki/Vickers_machine_gun> (Accessed 3 October 2014).
45 McNab, Chris, *Twentieth Century Small Arms*.
46 Miller, Ian, *The Illustrated book of Guns* (2000).

Appendix IV

An example of orders for a UVF camp of instruction

SHANES CASTLE,
Antrim.

8th April 1914

ADVANCE ORDERS FOR CAMP OF INSTRUCTION.

1. A Camp of Instruction will assemble at Lissanoure Castle on Sunday 19th April, terminating on Saturday evening 25th April.

2. Postal Address: Lissanoure Castle, Killagan
   Telegrams: Cloughmills (porterage 3d)
   Stations: Dunloy, 4 ½ miles
   Ballymoney, 8 miles

3. The contingent from 1st (Mr G Young's) Battalion will assemble at Lissanoure between 4:30 and 6:00 p.m. on the 19th and leave on Wednesday evening the 22nd.

4. The contingent from the 2nd (Colonel Lyle's) Battalion will assemble at Lissanoure between 5:00 and 6:00 p.m. on Wednesday the 22nd, and leave on Saturday evening the 25th.

5. Tickets of admission will be issued to those attending without which no one will be admitted.

6. No liquor will be allowed to be brought into or consumed in camp.

7. No dogs allowed in camp.

8. There will be a doctor appointed who will attend those requiring his services.

9. Camp will be under Military discipline and strict obedience to orders will be enforced.

10. All coming to Camp should bring with them, Great Coats or Mackintoshes, complete change of clothing, extra pair of boots, puttees, soap, towel, hair brush, razor, pillow slip (which will be filled in camp), and the new Volunteer headdress, though an ordinary cap may be brought as well. Bandoliers and Haversacks will not be required. Working clothes should be worn at work as there will be a good deal of lying down, etc.

11. Anyone in possession of a revolver should bring it with about 20 rounds of ammunition, as revolver ammunition cannot be provided in camp.

12. Paillasses and two blankets will be provided for everyone, but men can bring extra rugs if they wish, about 40 tin wash basins will be provided and a drying room.

13. Arrangements for reaching camp will be notified by the Battalion Commander, but in most cases will be by private arrangement.

14. Bicycles can be stored in camp.

15. The first meal will be served in camp at 7pm on the 19th April.

16. On arrival everyone will report himself to the Camp Adjutant, Capt. Stewart Richardson, who will issue a special badge (to be always worn), camp number, and tell off each man to his mess. The payment due by each, about 7/- per three days will be paid to the Camp Adjutant on arrival.

A O'Neill,
Captain,
Camp Commandant[1]

---

1   Advance orders for Easter Camp at Shanes Castle – April 1914.

Appendix V

UVF Special Order Enlistment for Imperial Forces

1. A scheme to form one or more Ulster Volunteer Divisions to join Lord Kitchener's Army has received the approval of the War Office.
2. Each Division will be formed into three Brigades, each of four Service Battalions, of about 1,000 men each.
3. These Service Battalions will be formed out of the existing Regiments and Battalions composing the Ulster Volunteer Force. The Service Battalions will receive Territorial designations as far as possible similar to the designations of their present Ulster Volunteer Force Regiments, and the men from the same Ulster Volunteer Force Regiment will be kept together as far as possible.
4. The service Battalions will be formed at BALLYKINLAR CAMP, and other Camps to be selected and notified hereafter.
5. The conditions of service and pay etc., will be as follows: The men will be enlisted for THREE YEARS, or the DURATION OF WAR. If the war only lasts six months, the men would be discharged as expeditiously as possible at the end of the six months. Age Limits: Men who have not previously served in the Army, Militia or Special Reserve, between the ages of 19 and 36 – ex-soldiers 19 to 43, ex-non-commissioned officer 19 to 50. After discharge the Military authorities will have no further claim in the men.
6. The pay of the men will be 1/- per day, free rations, clothing, and equipment (including Government rifle and ammunition), just the same as any ordinary British soldier of the line.

    Separation allowance for the wives of married men to be 1/1 a day, for the wife, 2d per day for each legitimate child (up to the age of 16); and if the soldier has lost his wife for each legitimate child 4d per day, widows pensions and wound pensions will be as laid down in the Army Regulations for pay and allowances.
7. Officers Commanding Battalions (other than those in the Belfast Division) will parade their respective Battalions in the most convenient manner, and explain the conditions of service to the men, and furnish the number of suitable men anxious to enlist to Headquarters, retaining for their own information the nominal roll of such men.

    On receipt of this information instructions will be sent direct to Battalion Commanders as regards the attestation and Medical examination for the men, and Orders for their destination. (Special orders are being issued on this subject to the OC Belfast Division (UVF.)
8. Non-commissioned officers will be selected, after joining the service battalions, by the Officer Commanding these Battalions.
9. Applications for Commissions, with the recommendations of officers commanding Ulster Volunteer Force Battalions and Regiments, should be submitted to this office, on the proper Military Form (which can be obtained on application) these will be forwarded direct to the War office with the observations of the GOC UVF.

APPENDIX V 399

10. The services of the officers of the Ulster Volunteer Force called away on mobilisation will be restored to the Ulster Division by the War Office as far as the necessities of the Service permit.
11. The General Officer Commanding UVF wishes to call the attention of all ranks to the urgent appeal which has been made by Lord Kitchener which he commends to the members of the UVF.

G HACKET PAIN Colonel
Chief Staff Officer, U.V.F.
Old Town Hall, Belfast
2nd September, 1914

The 13th Service Battalion Royal Irish Rifles (Central Antrim Volunteers) at Clandeboye Camp, County Down, 1914. This is one of their first parades after receiving their 36th (Ulster) Division uniforms, but no equipment as yet. (Somme Museum: 1994-192)

Bibliography

Printed Sources

Abbott, Richard, *Police Casualties in Ireland, 1919-1922* (2000)
Augustein, Joost (ed), *The Irish Revolution, 1913-1923* (2002)
Balfour, Chamberlain, Long, Wyndham, Beresford, Campbell, Sinclair et al., *Against Home Rule, The Case for Union* (1912)
Bartlett, Thomas and Jeffery, Keith (ed), *A Military History of Ireland* (1996)
Batchelor, P and Matson, C, *VCs of the First World War – The Western Front 1915* (1998)
Baguley, Margaret (ed), *The Spender Correspondence, World War I and the Question of Ulster, The correspondence of Lilian and Wilfred Spender* (2009)
Beatty, Jack, *The Lost History of 1914; How the Great War was not Inevitable* (2012)
Bowman, Timothy, *Carson's Army – The Ulster Volunteer Force, 1910-22* (2007)
Callanan, Frank, *T.M. Healy: Rise and Fall of Parnell and the Establishment of the Irish Free State* (1996)
Canning, WJ, *Ballyshannon, Belcoo, Bertincourt* (1996)
Churchill, Winston S, *Great Contemporaries* (1941)
Citizens' Committee to the Ulster Service Men, *The Great War 1914-1918: Ulster Greets her Brave and Faithful Sons and Remembers her Glorious Dead* (1919)
Clark, Wallace, *Guns in Ulster* (1967)
Corrigan, Gordon, *Mud, Blood and Poppycock* (2003)
Cousins, Colin, *Armagh and the Great War* (2011)
Crawford, FH, *Guns for Ulster* (1947)
Crozier, Brig-Gen FP Crozier, CB, CMG, DSO, *A Brass Hat in No Man's Land* (1930)
Crozier, Brig-Gen FP Crozier, CB, CMG, DSO, *Ireland for Ever* (1932)
D'Arcy, Bishop of Down, Connor & Dromore, *Celebrating the Ulster Covenant* (1912)
Denman, Terence, *A Lonely Grave: The Life and Death of William Redmond* (1995)
Denman, Terence, *Ireland's Unknown Soldiers: The 16th (Irish) Division in the Great War* (1992)
Downing, Taylor (ed), *The Troubles* (1990)
Dungan, Myles, *Irish Voices from the Great War* (1998)
Du Quesne-Bird, Nicholas, *The Observer's Book of Firearms* (1978)
Eakins, Arthur, *The Somme – What Happened to the Casualties* (30 Oct 2008)
Falls, Cyril, *History of the 36th (Ulster) Division* (1922)
Fitzpatrick, D (ed), *Ireland and the First World War* (1988)
Foster, RF, *Modern Ireland 1600-1972* (1989)
Grand Orange Lodge of Ireland, *Steadfast for Faith and Freedom, 200 Years of Orangeism* (1995)
Grayson, Richard S, *Belfast Boys – How Unionists and Nationalists fought and died together in the First World War* (2009)
Green, Alice Stopford, *Loyalty and Disloyalty: What it means in Ireland* (1918)
Gregory, Adrian and Paseta, Senia (ed), *Ireland and the Great War 'A War to Unite Us All'?* (2002)
Grob-Fitzgibbon, *Turning Points of The Irish Revolution: The British Government, Intelligence and the Cost of Indifference, 1912-1921* (2007)
Gwynn, Stephen Lucius, *John Redmond's Last Years* (1919)
Haines, Keith, *Fred Crawford: Carson's Gunrunner* (2009)

Harris, HED, *The Irish Regiments in the First World War* (1968)
Hezlet, Sir Arthur, *The 'B' Specials* (1972)
Horne, John (ed), *Our War: Ireland and the Great War* (2008)
Hughes, Dr Gavin, *The Hounds of Ulster* (2012)
Hume, David, *For Ulster and Her Freedom: The story of the April 1914 gunrunning* (1989)
Hyde, H Montgomery, *Carson* (1953)
Ingram, Rev Brett, *Covenant and Challenge* (1989)
Jackson, Alvin, *Home Rule – An Irish History 1800-2000* (2004)
Jeffery, Keith, *Ireland and the Great War* (2000)
Kennedy, Dennis, *The Widening Gulf: Northern attitudes to the independent Irish State 1919-49* (1988)
Kenny, Kevin (ed), *Ireland and the British Empire* (2004)
Lawlor, Pearse, *The Outrages, 1920-1922* (2011)
Leslie, Rose Jane and Quail, Des, *Old Belfast* (2013)
Lewis, Geoffrey, *Carson: The man who divided Ireland* (2006)
Lucy, Gordon, *The Ulster Covenant, An Illustrated History of the 1912 Home Rule Crises* (2012)
McGarry, Ferghal, *The Rising – Ireland: Easter 1916* (2010)
McKenna, John, *A Beleaguered Station: The Memoir of Head Constable John McKenna, 1891-1921* (2009)
McNab, Chris, *Twentieth Century Small Arms* (2001)
McNeill, Ronald, *Ulster's Stand for Union* (1922)
Miller, David, *The Illustrated Book of Guns* (2000)
Mitchell, Gardiner S, *'Three Cheers for the Derrys!'* (2008)
Moore, Steven, *The Irish on the Somme* (2005)
Moore, Steven, *The Chocolate Soldiers: The story of the Young Citizen Volunteers and 14th Royal Irish Rifles during the Great War* (2016)
Muenger, Elizabeth A, *The British Military Dilemma in Ireland: Occupation Politics 1886-1914* (1991)
Orr, David R, *Duty Without Glory: The story of Ulster's Home Guard in the Second World War and the Cold War* (2008)
Orr, Philip, *The Road to the Somme* (1987)
Parkinson, Alan F, *Friends in High Places: Ulster's Resistance to Irish Home Rule, 1912-14* (2012)
Perry, Nicholas (ed), *Major General Oliver Nugent and the Ulster Division 1915-1918* (2007)
Richardson, Neil, *According to their lights: Stories of Irishmen in the British Army, Easter 1916* (2015)
Ryan, AP, *Mutiny at the Curragh* (1956)
Shearman, Hugh, *Not an Inch: A Study of Northern Ireland and Lord Craigavon* (1942)
Skennerton, Ian, *The Lee Enfield Story* (1993)
Stewart, ATQ, *The Ulster Crises* (1967)
Truesdale, David, *'Young Citizen, Old Soldier' From boyhood in Antrim to hell on the Somme* (2012)

Journals

Battle Lines: Journal of The Somme Association.
Bulletin of the Military Historical Society, Vol 45, No.194.
Causeway: Cultural Traditions Journal, Spring 1995 – 'The Myth of the 36th (Ulster) Division' – T Bowman.
History Ireland, Vol.1 No.2 Summer 1993 – 'Irish Artists and the First World War' – Keith Jeffery.
History Ireland, Vol.10 No.1 Spring 2002 'The Ulster Volunteers 1913-14: Force or farce?' – Timothy Bowman.

Irish Historical Studies xxix No. 114 (Nov 1994) – "The red livery of shame": the campaign against army recruitment in Ireland, 1899-1914'.

Men, Women and War: Studies in War, Politics and Society #9 (1993), 'The Great War in Modern Irish Memory" TG Fraser & K Jeffery (eds).

Belfast Covenant Trail – Ulster-Scots Community Network & Ulster Historical Foundation, 'Young Citizen Volunteers: 10 September 1912'.

Donegal Annual – Journal of the County Donegal History Society – No.59 (2007), 'Captain Henry Gallaugher DSO'.

36th Ulster Division Memorial Association, *From the shipyard to the Somme* (2013).

Newspapers

Newtownards Chronicle – 15 May 1915
Newtownards Chronicle – 5 June 1915
Northern Whig, 11 September 1912
Northern Whig & Belfast Post, 13 November 1916
Northern Whig – 11/9/1912
Irish News and Belfast Morning News – 11/9/1912
Northern Whig – 10/9/1912
The Times – 16/4/1914
Irish Times – 18/10/1913
Northern Whig – 2/7/1914
Northern Whig – 25/9/1913
Northern Whig – 13/7/1914
Northern Whig – 29/9/1913
Northern Whig – 16/7/1913
Belfast Evening Telegraph – 25/7/1913
Belfast Evening Telegraph – 20/12/1913
Northern Whig – 23/7/1914
Northern Whig – 14/11/1921
Belfast Weekly News – 21 October 1893
The New York Times – 27 August 1920
Belfast News Letter – 5 August 1915
Irish News – 10 August 1914
Newtownards Chronicle & Co Down Observer – 1 May 2014

Electronic Sources

Spartacus Educational – Frank Percy Crozier <http://www.spartacus.schoolnet.co.uk/FWWcrozierF.htm> (Accessed 6 November 2011)

Kilmarnock Somme Association <???> (Accessed 2011)

South Belfast Friends of the Somme Association – UVF Hospital <http://www.belfastsomme.com/hospital.html> (Accessed 24 December 2012)

The Telegraph – Northern Ireland Catholics are now more unionist than the English. Can the United Kingdom last? <http://blogs.telegraph.co.uk/news/edwest/100095628/northern-ireland-catholics-are-now-more-unionist-than-the-english-can-the-united-kingdom-last/> (Accessed 28 December 2012)

The Easter Rising of 1916 <http://www.bbc.co.uk/history/british/britain_wwone/easter_rising_01.shtml#five> (Accessed 3 October 2014)

Lee-Metford <http://en.wikipedia.org/wiki/Lee-Metford> (Accessed 2 October 2014)

Belfast Telegraph – Is Catholic support for a united Ireland on the wane? <http://www.belfasttelegraph.co.uk/news/local-national/northern-ireland/is-catholic-support-for-a-united-ireland-on-the-wane-16013433.html#ixzz2GNeziqjv> (Accessed 28 December 2012)

School of History and Anthropology, Queen's University Belfast – The development of Unionism before 1912 <http://www.qub.ac.uk/sites/irishhistorylive/IrishHistoryResources/ArticlesandLectures/ThedevelopmentofUnionismbefore1912/> (Accessed 28 December 2012)

School of History and Anthropology, Queen's University Belfast – Ireland and the First World War: the Historical Context <http://www.qub.ac.uk/sites/irishhistorylive/IrishHistoryResources/ArticlesandLectures/IrelandandtheFirstWorldWar/> (Accessed 28 December 2012)

C – Ulster Unionist Council: (Accessed 28 December 2012)

Rootsweb: <http://archiver.rootsweb.ancestry.com/th/read/FERMANAGH-GOLD/2011-08/1314575885> (Accessed 4 December 2011)

Grand Lodge News – March 2013 <http://www.irish-freemasons.org/GLN_pdf_Files/GLI_News_03_10.pdf> (Accessed 8 January 2014)

Ulster Volunteers, January 1913 – Ulster-Scots Community Network <http://www.ulster-scots.com/uploads/901740969819.PDF> (Accessed 5 August 2013)

SS Libau <http://en.wikipedia.org/wiki/SS_Libau> (Accessed 5 May 2014)

The Loyal Dublin Volunteers… a forgotten organisation – Belfast News Letter –<http://www.newsletter.co.uk/features/the-loyal-dublin-volunteers-a-forgotten-organisation-1-3719467> (Accessed 5 February 2014)

Friends School Lisburn – World War One Archive <http://www.friendsschoollisburn.org.uk/ww1/sources.asp?pagehead=tasks#E> (Accessed 2 July 2007)

Great War Forum <http://1914-1918.invisionzone.com/forums/index.php?showtopic=182134&page=2> (Accessed 5 February 2014)

TM Healy <http://indigo.ie/~kfinlay/Tim%20Healy/ First Home Rule Bill (1886) – antrim Militai.htm> (Accessed 24 November 2001)

Eoin MacNeill Stop Order <http://www.bbc.co.uk/news/uk-northern-ireland-26418138> (Accessed 3 March 2014)

An Army With Banners –South Belfast Friends of the Somme Association – <http://www.belfast-somme.com/army_with_banners.htm> (Accessed 18 June 2009) Drumalis <http://www.drumalis.co.uk/Background_and_History.aspx> (Accessed 17 February 2014)

Vickers-Maxin <http://en.wikipedia.org/wiki/Vickers_machine_gun> (Accessed 3 October 2014)

Webley Revolver <http://en.wikipedia.org/wiki/Webley_Revolver> (Accessed 3 October 2014)

Martini-Henry <http://en.wikipedia.org/wiki/Martini-Henry> (Accessed 3 October 2014)

TM Healy <http://www.britannica.com/EBchecked/topic/258243/> (Accessed 18 February 2014)

M1870 Italian Vetterli <http://en.wikipedia.org/wiki/M1870_Italian_Vetterli> (Accessed 2 October 2014)

Mannlicher M1895 <http://en.wikipedia.org/wiki/Mannlicher_M1895> (Accessed 2 October 2014)

Gewehr 1988 <http://en.wikipedia.org/wiki/Gewehr_1888> (Accessed 2 October 2014)

Mannlicher M1888 <http://en.wikipedia.org/wiki/Mannlicher_M1888> (Accessed 2 October 2014)

Ships Nostalgia – John Kelly (Belfast) now Kelly Fuels <http://www.shipsnostalgia.com/showpost.php?p=92891&postcount> (Accessed 20 February 2014)

Dix Noonan Webb – Vice-Admiral F. Martin-Leake <http://www.dnw.co.uk/auction-archive/catalogue-archive/lot.php?auction_id=265&lot_id=88075> (Accessed 23 February 1914)

<http://www.nam.ac.uk/exhibitions/online-exhibitions/dads-army/roberts-family/lord-roberts> (Accessed 11 March 2014)

<http://en.wikipedia.org/wiki/Chlorocardium_rodiei> (Accessed 13 April 2014)

Titanic Village – The sinking of dreams <http://www.bbc.co.uk/news/uk-northern-ireland-17557619> (Accessed 25 May 2014)

<http://www.titanic-nautical.com/RMS-Titanic-Chronology.html> (Accessed 25 May 2014)

Africa Hunting <http://www.africahunting.com/threads/john-henry-patterson-1867-1947.2822/> (Accessed 26/5/2014)

<http://en.wikipedia.org/wiki/Ernest_Clark_%28governor%29> (Accessed 23 June 2014)

Ulster Genealogy <http://ulster.failteromhat.com/defenceunion.htm> (Accessed 5 July 2014)

Vetterli <http://en.wikipedia.org/wiki/Vetterli_rifle#M1870.2F87_Italian_Vetterli-Vitali> (Accessed 2 October 2014)

The Nursing Record and Hospital World, 24 February 1900 http://rcnarchive.rcn.org.uk/data/VOLUME024-1900/page160-volume24-24thfebruary1900.pdf (Accessed 3 September 2014)

The Ulster Volunteer Force Gun Running at Larne, April 1914

By JWT Watters http://www.orangenet.org/gunrun.htm (Accessed 30 November 2011)

Clyde Valley – Gun Running in 1912 http://abalmoralperspective-hma.blogspot.com/2011/04/clyde-valley-gun-running-in-1912.html (Accessed 30 November 2011)

Mauser <http://en.wikipedia.org/wiki/Mauser> (Accessed 2 October 2014)

Austro-Hungarian Weapons Mannlicher Export Modell Rifles http://www.hungariae.com/Mann04.htm> (Accessed 21 November 2014)

UVF Mannlicher found in attic <http://www.belfasttelegraph.co.uk/news/local-national/northern-ireland/historic-uvf-rifle-found-in-belfast-attic-28676509.html> (Accessed 21 November 2014)

1885 General Election <http://en.wikipedia.org/wiki/United_Kingdom_general_election,_1885> (Accessed 23 November 2014)

1886 General Election <http://en.wikipedia.org/wiki/United_Kingdom_general_election,_1886> (Accessed 23 November 2014)

Edward James Saunderson <http://en.wikipedia.org/wiki/Edward_James_Saunderson> (Accessed 24 November 2014

General Election 1892 <http://en.wikipedia.org/wiki/United_Kingdom_general_election,_1892> (Accessed 26 November 2014)

'Signed in blood' claim challenged by scientific test <http://www.bbc.co.uk/news/uk-northern-ireland-politics-19747495> (Accessed 8 November 2014

Journal of the Australian War Memorial – Called to arms: Australian soldiers in the Easter Rising 1916

Jeff Kildea <http://www.awm.gov.au/journal/j39/kildea/> (Accessed 3 January 2015

Roger Casement: How did a hero come to be considered a traitor? <http://www.bbc.co.uk/news/uk-northern-ireland-25017936> (Accessed 3 January 2015

Forgotten Moore was one of the great Irish satirists <http://www.irishidentity.com/extras/famous-gaels/stories/mooore.htm> (Accessed 3 January 2015

Cambridge University Library <http://www.lib.cam.ac.uk/deptserv/rarebooks/200701.html> (Accessed 3 January 2015

Service marks centenary of Covenant signing <http://www.belfastcathedral.org/news/item/460/service-marks-centenary-of-covenant-signing/> (Accessed 6 January 2015

Ulster Covenant: Thousands on centenary parade <http://www.bbc.co.uk/news/uk-northern-ireland-19769191> (Accessed 6 January 2015

Unionist parade to mark Ulster Covenant centenary begins peacefully in Belfast <http://www.telegraph.co.uk/news/uknews/northernireland/9575713/Unionist-parade-to-mark-Ulster-Covenant-centenary-begins-peacefully-in-Belfast.html> (Accessed 6 January 2015

Thousands mark Larne gun-running centenary <http://www.bbc.co.uk/news/uk-northern-ireland-27175185> (Accessed 7 January 2015

26–27 July 2014: Heritage weekend to mark centenary of Kilcoole gun-running, Kilcoole, Co. Wicklow <http://www.decadeofcentenaries.com/26-27-july-heritage-weekend-to-mark-centenary-of-kilcoole-gun-running-kilcoole-co-wicklow/> (Accessed 7 January 2015

Equally audacious: the Kilcoole gun-running <http://www.irishtimes.com/culture/heritage/equally-audacious-the-kilcoole-gun-running-1.1869586> (Accessed 7 January 2015

Massive Ulster Volunteer Force re-enactment marks centenary in West Belfast <http://www.belfasttelegraph.co.uk/news/local-national/northern-ireland/massive-ulster-volunteer-force-reenactment-marks-centenary-in-west-belfast-29619972.html> (Accessed 7 January 2015

In pictures: Parade marks UVF centenary <http://www.newsletter.co.uk/news/regional/in-pictures-parade-marks-uvf-centenary-1-5021355> (Accessed 7 January 2015)

Thousands take part in UVF parade <http://www.u.tv/News/Thousands-take-part-in-UVF-parade/6efcb111-802b-49a6-b879-fdea1f306181> (Accessed 7 January 2015)

Thousands on parade to mark centenary of UVF's founding <http://www.belfasttelegraph.co.uk/news/local-national/northern-ireland/thousands-on-parade-to-mark-centenary-of-uvfs-founding-29212027.html> (Accessed 7 January 2015

10,000 loyalists march in Belfast parade to mark centenary of the Ulster Volunteer Force <http://www.irishcentral.com/news/10000-loyalists-march-in-belfast-parade-to-mark-centenary-of-the-ulster-volunteer-force-204070191-237583821.html> (Accessed 7 January 2015

Thousands at UVF march in Belfast <http://www.u.tv/News/Thousands-at-UVF-march-in-Belfast/909d2c98-38ca-412d-8ead-441f22096b99> (Accessed 7 January 2015

Irish Volunteers launch their own newspaper <http://www.rte.ie/centuryireland/articles/irish-volunteers-launch-their-own-newspaper> (Accessed 11 January 2015

A Most Seditious Lot: The Militant-Separatist Press 1896-1916 <http://theirishrepublic.wordpress.com/tag/the-irish-volunteer/> (Accessed 1 January 2015

South Derry Volunteers: men 'of good courage' <http://www.newsletter.co.uk/news/features/south-derry-volunteers-men-of-good-courage-1-4888311> (Accessed 1 January 2015)

The Ulster Reform Club, http://www.ulsterreformclub.com/our_club.html (Accessed 28 January 2015)

Irish Medals – War of Independence <http://irishmedals.org/r-i-c-d-m-p-k-i-a-.html> (Accessed 4 February 2015)

Belfast parade for 100 years since WW1 march <http://www.bbc.co.uk/news/uk-northern-ireland-32675752> (Accessed 10 May 2015)

WWI commemorative parade in Belfast <http://www.u.tv/News/2015/05/09/WWI-commemorative-parade-in-Belfast-36938> (Accessed 10 May 2015)

'Inniskillings' in Dublin, 1916 <http://www.inniskillingsmuseum.com/inniskillings-in-dublin-1916/> (Accessed 25 January 2016)

PRONI

PRONI D1327/4/3
PRONI D1633/2/19 – Lilian Spender Diary – 6/5/1914
PRONI D1238/178 – UVF Order 74, 18/7/1914
PRONI D.1238/101 – UVF Order 10, 7/2/1914
PRONI D.1238/72 – letter from Gen. Adair to Capt. Hon. A O'Neil – 21/04/1914
PRONI, D/1132/6/17 – Letter from Lord Northland
PRONI, D.1238/115 – UVF Order 18
PRONI, D.1238/115 – UVF Order 20

Somme Museum & Somme Association

UVF Orders	UVF Order 57, 1914
UVF Order 02, 1913	UVF Order 59, 1914
UVF Orders 04, 1913	UVF Order 60, 1914
UVF Orders 05, 1913	UVF Order 61, 1914
UVF Order 07, 1913	UVF Orders 64, 1914
UVF Order 08, 1913	UVF Orders 68, 1914
UVF Order 09, 1913	UVF Order 70, 1914
UVF Order 10, 1913	UVF Order 72, 1914
UVF Order 17, 1913	UVF Order 75, 1914
UVF Order 29, 1913	UVF Order 76, 1914
UVF Order 30, 1913	UVF Order 77, 1914
UVF Order 01, 1914	UVF Order 78, 1914
UVF Order 02, 1914	UVF Order 79, 1914
UVF Order 03, 1914	UVF Order 82, 1914
UVF Order 05, 1914	UVF Order 86, 1914
UVF Order 06, 1914	UVF Order 88, 1914
UVF Order 07, 1914	UVF Order 89, 1914
UVF Order 10, 1914	UVF Order 90, 1914
UVF Order 13, 1914	UVF Order 93, 1914
UVF Order 14, 1914	UVF Orders 106, 1914
UVF Order 15, 1914	UVF Orders 110, 1914
UVF Order 17, 1914	UVF Orders 111, 1914
UVF Order 19, 1914	UVF Orders 121, 1914
UVF Orders 21, 1914	UVF Orders 123, 1914
UVF Orders 22, 1914	UVF Orders 124, 1914
UVF Orders 23, 1914	UVF Orders 128, 1914
UVF Order 24, 1914	UVF Orders 129, 1914
UVF Orders 26, 1914	UVF Orders 133, 1914
UVF Orders 36, 1914	UVF Orders 134, 1914
UVF Orders 47, 1914	UVF Orders 139, 1914
UVF Order 51, 1914	UVF Orders 155, 1914
UVF Orders 53, 1914	UVF Orders 19, 1915
UVF Order 54, 1914	UVF Orders 22, 1915
UVF Order 55, 1914	UVF Orders 35, 1915
UVF Orders 56, 1914	UVF Orders 01, 1916

UVF Circular Memorandum, 18 May 1914
UVF Circular Memorandum 23 May 1914
Letter from County Inspector Morrison, 23 May 1914
Orders – 1st Battalion, North Antrim Regiment – 3 June 1914
Letter from Div Com WT Adair on Voluntary Aid Detachments – 13 June 1914
No134/1914 – North Antrim Regiment – 17 June 1914 – Somme Museum
Letter from General Hacket Pain on the carrying of arms openly – 27 June 1914
UVF Memorandum to OC Battalions Belfast Regiment UVF – 29 Oct 1920
Ulster Volunteer Force – Lieut-Col Young 30 September 1913
Commanding Officer, County Antrim volunteers officers of Antrim Regiments 21 October 1913
Handwritten note to UVF Orders 20 October 1913 by WT Adair
10 January 1914 – Letter from OC 1st North Antrim Regiment

Memo from WT Adair – 14 March 1914
Letter from Lt Col McCammon to Divisional, Regimental and Battalion Commanders – 18 March 1914
Precautionary Period – Lt Col McCammon 19 March 1914
Notes by General Adair of verbal directions of Sir Edward Carson – 22 March 1914
North Antrim Regiment UVF Orders – 23 March 1914
Advance orders for Easter Camp at Shanes Castle – April 1914
Presentation of Colours to 1st Batt, North Antrim Regiment
Orders from OC 1st Batt North Antrim Regiment – 29 April 1914
Orders from OC 1st Batt, North Antrim Regiment – 5 May 1914
Circular Memorandum to Div, Regt and Batt Commders – 7 May 1914
Musketry Instructions – 30 June 1914
Urgent and Special Order for 1st Batt, North Antrim Regiment UVF – 7 July 1914
Memorandum – Refugees – 10 July 1914
Ammunition – 16 July 1914
Scheme Defence of River Bann – General Adair, 25 July 1914
Circular Memorandum – OC 1st Batt, North Antrim Regiment, 3 August 1914
Circular Memorandum – OC 1st Batt, North Antrim Regiment – 7 August 1914
Correspondence between Adair and Hacket Pain – 9 August 1914
Question regarding Status of Lady Signallers – 27 August 1914
Answer regarding Status of Lady Signallers – 28 August 1914
Memo – 3 September 1914
Letter from Sir Edward Carson to Lieutenant-General Richardson – 9 September 1914
Memo No. 160 – Men Enlisting for Imperial Service – 12 September 1914
Memo No. 162 – Antrim Division UVF – 21 September 1914
UVF HQ's note
Memo No.167 – C/O Antrim Division UVF – 2 November 1914
Memo No.170 – Antrim Division, UVF
Memo No. 174 – Registration Motor Cars Foreign Invasion – 2 January 1915
Battalion Orders, 1st Batt North Antrim Regiment – 4 January 1915
Memo No.173 – County Antrim UVF – 12 January 1915
Circular Memorandum from GOC UVF – 13 May 1915
Memo 184 – Enlistment in Irish Defence Corps – Antrim Division UVF – 27 June 1915
Rifle Competition at Loughanmore – paper dated 8 June 1915
Appeal for sandbags for Ulster Division – 26 August 1915
Fund for Supply of Milk to the 12th Batt Royal Ulster Rifles – 10 November 1915
Possible attack on armouries by Sinn Feinners – 23 December 1915
Memo from Adair to Young – Antrim UVF – 31 January 1915
Circular Memorandum – 1 May 1916
Circular Memorandum – 29 May 1916
Ulster Volunteer Force Orders – Message to the Ulster People – 1916
Circular Memorandum – UVF Patriotic Fund – 6 July 1916
Memo from General WT Adair – 7 July 1916
Circular Memorandum – UVF Patriotic Fund from Lieut-Gen Richardson – 20 July 1916
Removing Bolts of Rifles – 28 September 1917
Rifles – Gen Sir WT Adair – 15 August 1918
Billy Gibson, 14th RIR, RIF, WW1 Interview 097
Billy McFadzean, WW1 Interview 103
Jack Christie, WW1 Interview 096

James Colville, WW1 Interview, DOB 25/08/1897, 2010/113(e), DVD conversion from VHS tape 2011-07-13
Tommy Jordan, WW1 Interview, VHS Tape
William Williamson, WW1 Interview 108, DOB 1897
Harry Currie, WW1 Interview

With special thanks to the following individuals and organisations for their willingness to assist with their time and resources

Abbott, Richard
Bain, Mark
Bowman, Timothy
Charley, Col Robin
Elpelt, Aribert
Flowers, Paul
Forrester, Hugh
Gamble, Matthew
Haines, Keith
Henderson, Nigel
Hughes, Dr Gavin
Laverty, Henry
Luke, John
McClimmonds, William
McFarland, Alan
McGurk, Dougie
Metcalfe, Nick
Moore, Steven
Orr, Philip
Rea, Pamela
Robinson, Cameron
Simpson, Norman
Spence, Laura
Walker, Carol
Wylie, Tom, the late
Young, John

Belfast Telegraph
Deputy Keeper of the Records, Public Record Office Northern Ireland
Newtownards Chronicle
Police Museum, Belfast
Royal Ulster Rifles Museum, Belfast
Somme Museum and Somme Association, Conlig
Spectator Newspapers
Ulster Museum, Belfast

Index

INDEX OF PEOPLE

Abercorn, Duchess of 40, 303, 310
Abercorn, Duke of 19-20, 37, 86-87, 102, 155, 230, 249, 381
Acton, Lord 97
Adair, Major-General Sir William 135, 150, 152, 168, 216-217, 219, 241-243, 298, 333, 377, 379
Adams, Hugh James 115, 289
Adgey, Robert 229, 271
Agar-Robartes, T.G.R. 57-59
Agnew, Captain Andrew 208-211, 213-216, 224, 251, 366, 368
Alexander, Lieutenant A.M. 124
Alexander, Bishop William 24
Amery, Leo S. 231
Anderson, Sir John 347, 349
Andrews, John M. viii, 103
Andrews, Thomas 37
Archdale, Ed. 288
Armour, Reverend James 46, 96
Asquith, Herbert Henry 28, 35, 38, 54, 56, 59, 92, 96-97, 175, 178, 186-189, 191, 195-197, 228, 233, 239, 243, 245-246, 250, 259-262, 267, 329-330, 335
Asquith, Margot 259
Asquith, Violet 42
Astor, Waldorf 115

Balfour, Arthur James 21, 23-24, 26, 29-30, 199
Bangor, Viscount 65, 263, 380
Barbour, J. Milne 104
Barr, Mrs Ainsworth 143
Barrie, H.T. 44
Bates, Richard Dawson 79, 157, 215, 288, 308, 319
Beach, Sir Michael Hicks 23
Beaverbrook, Lord 247
Bective, Countess of 255
Bedford, Duke of 51, 115
Bell, Charles 116
Bell, Francis 116
Belshaw, Mrs 166
Bentley, Sergeant 70
Berchtold, Count 262
Beresford, Admiral Lord Charles 63, 81, 83, 199
Bernstorff, Count 280

Birrell, Augustine 43, 113, 181, 189-190, 197, 235, 238
Blacker, Major Stewart 263, 290, 381
Blyth, Hon. Audley 109
Bonar Law, Andrew 24, 29-30, 42, 51-54, 62, 96-97, 117, 129, 167, 183, 186-188, 245-246, 249, 260-261, 337, 339, 356
Bowman, Timothy 125, 356, 361
Boyton, Godfrey 138
Brannigan, Sergeant Major W.J. 160
Bristow, Mr John 293
Brooke, Captain Basil 125, 345, 367
Bruce, Albert 289
Bruce, Miss 305, 307
Budden, Captain H.A. 164-165
Bull, Sir William 164
Bullock, Stephen 200-202, 362
Burke, T.H. 11
Burnside, Miss 320
Butt, Issac 10
Byrne, Inspector General 337-338

Caldwell, Robert 352
Campbell, A.G. 310
Campbell, James Henry Mussen 42-43
Campbell, Joseph 96
Campbell, Lloyd 130, 288
Campbell, Sam 368
Carson, Lady 305, 360
Carson, Lord Sir Edward vii, 12, 24-30, 33, 35-38, 40-42, 45, 48-52, 54, 57-60, 62-65, 72, 78, 80-85, 94-97, 99, 103, 108, 111-112, 117-118, 125-129, 132, 140, 143, 147, 153, 155, 157, 159, 168-170, 172, 174-175, 178, 181-184, 186-187, 191, 194, 197-199, 203, 206, 211-216, 219, 225-226, 228, 231-233, 240, 243-246, 248-249, 251-253, 255, 257-261, 264, 267-269, 272, 279, 283, 288-291, 296-297, 305, 307, 333, 335, 337-339, 341, 346, 349, 353, 356-357, 359-360, 362, 367-368, 370-371, 373
Casement, Sir Roger 96, 236, 280, 292, 326-327, 339
Castlereagh, Lord 9, 63, 83, 101-102, 183, 295
Cavendish, Lord Frederick 11

Cecil, Lord Hugh 63
Cecil, Lord Robert 79, 199
Chaine, William 211, 217
Chamberlain, Austen 29, 187, 199
Chamberlain, Joseph 17, 23-24
Chichester, Colonel R Spencer 70-71, 156, 183-184, 263, 382
Childers, Erskine 236
Christie, Jack 114, 269
Churchill, Lord Randolph vi, 13-15, 18, 23
Churchill, Winston vii-viii, 46-51, 54, 62, 97, 129, 178, 181-182, 185-187, 190, 193-195, 197-198, 225, 228, 248, 260, 349
Clanwilliam, Captain Earl of 263, 295, 380
Clark, H.J. 272, 381
Clark, Harry 61, 272, 381
Clark, S.C. 378, 382
Clarke, Alex 314
Clarke, Sir Ernest 344
Clarke, George 288
Clarke, Harry 61
Clarke, James 239
Clarke, Tom 326
Clements, Canon 362
Coffin, Major-General Clifford 335
Cole, Lord 103
Collins, Michael 341
Colville, James 101
Connolly, James 117, 239, 326-327
Conor, William 311
Convery, J.P. 175
Conway, Sergeant Henry 64
Cooke, Mr 177
Couchman, Colonel G. 108, 181, 216, 263, 377, 381
Couser, Mr 215
Cowser, Richard 330
Craig, Charles C. 115-116, 129, 183
Craig, Captain (later Lieutenant-Colonel) James 27-28, 30, 34, 36, 38-40, 51, 75, 78, 81-83, 89, 130, 139, 143, 159-160, 168, 179, 181-183, 197, 206, 212-214, 224, 240, 245-246, 248, 260-261, 264, 267-268, 271, 274, 280, 287, 314, 347, 349-350, 353, 356-360, 362, 370 373
Craig, John 76
Craigavon, Lord *see* Craig, Captain (later Lieutenant-Colonel) James
Crawford, Major (later Lieutenant-Colonel) Frederick Hugh 20, 23-24, 40, 51, 65, 67, 83-84, 90, 92, 130, 164-165, 168-169, 206-216, 224, 251, 280, 294, 345-346, 356, 366-368, 370
Crawford, Colonel R.G. Sharman 40, 288, 294

Crichton, Major Viscount 113, 147
Crockett, Alex 61
Crosbie, Dr 230
Crozier, Captain (later Major and Brigadier General) Frank Percy 108, 158-159, 161, 181-182, 203, 205, 231, 235, 261, 284, 287, 291, 346, 348, 377
Crozier, William 283
Culhane, Sean 341
Cunningham, James 171
Currie, Harry 368
Curzon, Lord 79, 96, 232
Cushendun, Lord 13

D'Arcy, Charles Frederick 82, 257
D'Arcy Irvine, Major CC 105, 378
Davis, H.O. 130
Davis, Lieutenant-Colonel Robert 130
de Broke, Lord Willoughby 157
de Robeck, Rear-Admiral J.M. 193
de Valera, Éamon 335, 339, 360
Devlin, Joseph 47, 109, 186, 248, 341
Dillon, John 245, 248, 297, 337-338, 360
Dobbs, Captain A.F. 263, 380
Donaghy, Reverend John Lyle 75
Donnelly, Reverend John 61
Downshire, Marquis of 103, 255
Duchess of Somerset 139
Dufferin, Marquis of 365
Dunleath, Lord 112, 225
Dunraven, Lord 24

Eames, Sergeant 89
Edwards, Sergeant Joseph 124, 165
Egerton, Captain A.F. 263
Elgar, Sir Edward 232
Elphick, Sergeant 70
English, Sergeant James 124
Ensell, Staff Sergeant 45
Ensor, Captain 346
Erne, Earl of 37, 147, 203
Ewart, Sir William 19

Faick, Captain Marthin 210
Falls, Charles F. 105, 378
Falls, Cyril 106, 121, 203, 378
Farnham, Major Lord 145, 165, 170, 249, 263, 381
Ferdinand, Archduke Franz 251
Ferguson, General 194
Ferrar, Major 70
Foch, Marshal Ferdinand 363
Forde, Major William George 112

INDEX

Forrest, Colonel 321
Forster, E.M. 46, 49
Fremantle, Admiral Hon. Sir E.R. 79
French, Field Marshal Sir John 122, 167, 190-191, 195, 197, 347
Friend, Major-General 191
Fullerton, S. 217

Gaffikin, Major 367
Gaussen, Captain H.A. 263, 381
Geddes, Fred T. 65-66, 71, 293
George V, King 28, 43, 77, 79, 92, 99, 113, 122, 128, 132, 167, 169, 187-188, 195, 243, 245-246, 260-261, 349, 357, 359
Gibson, Dr William 374, 377
Gibson, William John 68
Gladstone, William Ewart 9-10, 12-13, 17-18, 21, 23, 25
Gleichen, Brigadier General Count 46, 54, 147, 178, 181, 385, 392
Glenavy, Baron 42
Glover, Matthew 160
Godley, Hugh 42
Goodman, Constable 218
Gordon, Acting Sergeant Robert 218
Gough, General Hubert 192-195, 197, 225, 282, 310, 339
Gould, Matilda 367
Goulding, Sir Edward 258
Graves, Alfred 283
Greenwood, Hamar 350
Griffith, Arthur 25, 239, 339

Hacket Pain, G.W. 73, 123, 127, 130, 140, 144, 156, 172, 235, 240, 242, 244, 263, 329, 341, 359, 377
Haig, Lord 370
Hall, Captain Frank 72, 79, 104, 164, 292
Hall, Major Frank 124
Hall, Captain Roger 161
Hall, Sergeant William 124
Hamilton, Gustavus 37
Hamilton, Reverend Dr Thomas 308
Hanna, Sergeant William 89, 268
Harcourt, Sir William 25
Harmsworth, Alfred 247
Harrell, Assistant Commissioner David 236-238
Head, Major R.N. 263, 380
Healy, T.M. 17, 338-339
Hemingway, Ernest 110
Herdman, Captain E.C. 103, 381
Herdman, Ella 154
Hickman, Brigadier General 283

Hickman, Colonel Thomas E. 121, 123, 130, 165, 267
Hill, Sir Henry 239
Hobson, Bulmer 96, 236-237, 240
Holmes, County Inspector 46
Hotzendorff, Conrad von 262
Hughes, Sergeant Patrick 63

Jameson, Leander Starr 25-26, 191
Jones, W.H. 206
Jordan, Tommy 290

Kelly, Samuel 215, 224
Kerley, Florence 166
Ketch, Miss 150
Kipling, Rudyard vii, 52, 54, 115, 232
Kirk, T.S. 307
Kitchener, Lord 262, 267, 270, 273-274, 296, 398-399
Knight, Michael Elliott 174, 381,
Kulhmann, Baron von 257

Lanesborough, Earl of 105, 203, 207, 378, 381
Lansdowne, Lord 29, 245-246
Leach, General Sir E.P. 172
Leitrim, Earl of 177, 200-202, 213, 230, 362, 378
Lenox-Conyngham, Major William 116, 226, 381
Lenox-Cunningham, Mina 226
Leslie, John 328
Lewis, Lt-Col 263
Liddell, Sir Robert 308, 310, 318-320, 365
Lloyd George, David 27, 245, 248-249, 330, 335, 337-338, 349, 356, 360
Londonderry, Lady 29, 37-38, 40, 51, 57, 99, 249
Londonderry, Lord 29, 40, 49, 52, 54, 83, 129, 159, 161, 183, 199, 214, 249, 308
Long, Walter 29, 36, 52, 199, 231-232, 253
Longford, Lord 34
Loreburn, Lord 128
Lowther, Sir Henry Moore 210-211
Lyons, W.H.M. 243
Lyttle, Madeline 139
Lyttle, William Bob 221

MacDonnell, Sir Anthony 24
Mackie, James 67, 311
Mackinnon, General 291
MacMaster, Sergeant-Major William 365
MacNamara, Miss Rose 330
MacNeill, Eoin 54, 175-177, 326
Macready, Major-General Nevil 183, 185, 194, 233, 238, 246-247, 347, 349-350, 356
Madden, Gerald 248

Madden, Major 171
Magill, Andrew 238
Mahon, Lieutenant-General Sir B.T. 385
Mahon, District Inspector J.W. 63-64
Malone, Captain L.E. 263
Maloney, Lord Justice 299
Manning, John 202
Marinan, District Inspector P.A. 128
Martin, Alexander 144
Martin-Leake, Captain Francis 193
Massereene, Lord 217, 380
Massy-Beresford, Monica 225
Mathison, Captain 366
Matthews, Hugh 169
Maultsaid, Jim 287
May, Captain 71
Mayhew, Lieutenant-Colonel R.S. 263
McCalmont, Major-General Sir Hugh 172, 295, 297
McCalmont, Major Robert 203, 217-219, 263
McCammon, Major (later Lieutenant-Colonel) T.V.P. 79, 130, 144, 221, 229, 241
McCann, Mrs Agnes 30
McCann, Alexander 30
McCann, Francis 351
McCartan, Patrick 175
McCarthy, Sergeant Matt 341
McCaughey, Sir Samuel 129
McCurtain, Tomas 341
McDowall, William 'Bill' Hunter 254
McFadzean, Billy 68-69
McFarlane, Sergeant 172
McHugh, Head Constable James 218
McKee, Lily 220
McKee, Malcolm 367
McKenna, John 35
McKissick, Dr 316
McLaughlin, Reverend Mr 290
McMaster, Colonel Henry 44
McMaster, William 365-366
McMeekin, Alexander 112
McMenemy, William 170
McMordie, R.J. 66-67
McNeice, Reverend F.J. 87
McNeill, Ronald 63, 84, 181, 249
Meyer, Kuno 199
Middleton, Lord 30
Miliken, Shaw 366
Milligan, Alice 96
Milner, Lord 191, 199, 231-232, 261
Mitchell, Captain 71
Mitchell, John 9
Monro, General 77

Montgomery, Boughey William Dolling 21, 75, 288
Montgomery, Dr Henry 82
Moore, Francis Frankfort 21
Moore, District Inspector William 26, 218-219
Morley, John 16
Moroney, Detective Sergeant Denis 343
Morrish, G.P. 288
Morrison, Captain 213-214
Morrison, County Inspector 243
Morrison, Miss 70
Murland, Charles 112, 380

Napier, Colonel 9
Nelson, John 257
Nesbitt, Reverend S.T. 82
Nesbitt, Robert 161
Norfolk, Duke of 116
Northcliffe, Lord 247
Northland, Lord 161, 378, 381
Nugent, Colonel (later Major-General) Oliver 145-146, 248, 272, 300, 331, 335

O'Brien, William 338
O'Connell, Daniel 9
O'Connor, Sir James 358
O'Flanagan, Father 358
O'Hea, Bernard 21
O'Leary, Lance-Corporal Michael 299-300
O'Neil, Captain Sean 327
O'Neill, Captain the Hon Arthur 111, 146-147, 367, 381, 397
O'Neill, Eoin 117
O'Neill, Lord 102
O'Neill, Captain Terence 365-367
O'Shiel, Kevin 239
Orr, Captain Robert 279
Orr, Sergeant 225

Page, Captain 282
Paget, Sir Arthur 182, 189-192, 197, 199
Painter, H.E. 228
Paisley, Reverend Ian 369
Parnell, Charles Stewart 10, 12, 338
Patterson, Colonel J.H. 109-110, 377
Pearse, Patrick 117, 175, 236, 239, 326-327
Pearson, Edward 39
Pease, J.A. 262
Penny, Captain A.F. 263
Phill, Captain 101
Pirrie, Lord 46, 96
Pitt the Younger, William 9, 53-54
Pole-Carew, General Sir Reginald 158

INDEX

Porter-Porter, Mr J. 230
Powell, Major-General C.H. 272, 274, 284, 297, 378, 382
Proctor, J.C.B. 377, 380

Ramsay, Sir William 87, 232
Ranfurly, Lord 23
Redmond, John Edward 28, 117, 175, 178, 232, 239, 240, 243, 245-246, 248-249, 259-260, 263-264, 267, 280, 283, 329-330, 335, 337, 360
Redmond, R.S. 161
Redmond, William 'Willie' 11, 28, 32, 47, 57-58, 97, 117-118, 128, 180
Reid, Whitelaw 40
Repington, Colonel Charles à Court 108, 197, 199
Ricardo, Captain Ambrose 34, 38, 154, 156, 249, 263, 271, 381
Ricardo, David 154
Richardson, Lieutenant-General Sir George 121-122, 134, 152, 155, 165, 168, 177, 212, 235, 269, 274, 277, 296, 316, 323-324, 327-328, 344, 377
Riddell, Councillor 71
Ridgeway, Sir Joseph 26
Roberts, Constable Charles 218
Roberts, Field-Marshal Lord 51, 79, 121, 165, 232, 310
Roberts, Sergeant Samuel 160
Rogers, F.H. 160, 380
Rosebery, Lord 13, 59
Rosenzweig, Jennie 92
Ross, Martin 85
Rothschild, Lord 115
Ruffell, Dr Alastair 90

Saddell, Laird of 202
Salisbury, Lord 15, 23
Salvidge, Alderman 95
Saunderson, Colonel Edward James 15, 20, 26-27
Sayers, Andy 143-144, 380
Schiemann, Theodor 199
Sclater, Edward 40, 288
Scriven, Major Jack 125, 140
Seely, Colonel J.E.B. 167, 178, 181, 190, 192, 195, 197-198
Selassie, Emperor Haile 386
Selbourne, Lord 232
Seymour, Sir Edward 79, 232
Shankey, District Inspector 225
Shaw, Colonel Frederick 44
Simon, Sir John 42, 132, 181
Simpson, Robert C. (Roy) 265

Sinclair, Rosabelle 303
Sinclair, Thomas 19, 40, 46, 76, 92, 173
Skeffington, J. 175
Smiley, Lady Elizabeth 253
Smiley, Hugh 253-254
Smith, Deputy Inspector General 349
Smith, F.E. 29, 63-64, 81, 95, 183, 199
Smith, Robert 225
Spence, Gusty 367
Spencer-Chichester, Colonel R. 70
Spender, Captain (later Lieutenant-Colonel) Wilfred Bliss viii, 109, 122, 129-130, 138, 140, 144, 152, 160, 167, 209, 212, 215, 232, 258, 263-264, 272, 274, 332, 346, 352-356, 359
Spender, Lady Lilian 109, 140, 150, 405
Spindler, Captain 280
Spiro, Bruno 206, 209-210
Stamfordham, Lord 169
Stevenson, Mr 70
Stewart, Hugh 104
Stewart-Moore, John Leslie 162, 226, 289
Stoker, Bram 21
Stone, Major L.G.T. 263
Stronge, Sir James 272
Stronge, Sir Norman 370
Saunderson, Major Somerset 249
Swanzy, District Inspector Oswald Ross 341, 343

Templetown, Lord 21-22, 31, 86, 130
Thompson, J.A. 144
Treguiz, Louis 34
Trimble, William Copeland 63-64, 103, 127, 147
Tudor, Major General Henry Hugh 348-350

Wallace, Colonel Robert Hugh 32-34, 40, 43, 80, 112, 119, 252
Ward, Matthew 363
Ward, Samuel 363
Ward, Sergeant Thomas 363
Warden, F.W. 47
Waring, Captain Holt 64, 256, 380
Washington, John 164, 208
Watson, Ensign 80-81
Watt, Captain 43
Watters, John 144, 217
Watton, John 221
Webster, John 345
Weygand, General 363
White, Sir George 46
White, J.C. 305, 310
White, Captain J.R. 46, 96
Whitla, Alexander 129
Wilde, Oscar 36

Wilhelm II, Kaiser 97-98, 200, 247, 280
Williamson, Sergeant 89
Williamson, William 280, 380-381
Wilson, James 319, 378
Wilson, Sir Henry 187, 191, 197, 358, 363
Wilson, Woodrow 335
Workman, Frank 67
Wright, Jack 101

Wright, J.H. 257
Wylie, Mr 349
Wyndham, George 24

Young, Colour-Sergeant 89
Young, Lieutenant-Colonel George C. 106, 144, 243, 396
Young, Sergeant Osbourne 34

INDEX OF PLACES

Abbeylands 172
Aghadowey 147, 377
Ahogill 107
Albert Clock 290
Aldershot 193, 199, 213
Allee du Sacre Coeur 324
Amoy 164
Ampertaine 314
Ancre, River 376
Antrim Castle 149
Antrim (City) 113, 187, 297, 396
Antrim (County) 57, 102, 111, 129, 140, 146-147, 149-152, 162, 168, 197, 216-217, 242-243, 247-248, 273, 333-334, 386
Antrim Hills 84
Ardglass 34
Armagh Barracks 180
Armagh (City) 152, 180-181, 191, 226, 290, 345
Armagh (County) 13, 26, 32, 39, 57, 140-141, 247-248, 272-274, 289, 345, 370, 379, 386
Armoy 149
Ashgrove 132
Australia 88, 118, 129
Austria vii, 169, 239, 246, 258, 261-262, 391, 393
Austria-Hungary see Austria

Bad Homburg 78
Balbrigan 280
Ballaghaderrin 299-300
Ballee 149
Ballinamallard 105, 378
Ballintoy 149
Ballybogey 149
Ballycastle 149, 164, 242, 312, 328
Ballyclare 82, 86, 141, 149, 219, 253
Ballydivity 162
Ballyeaston 86
Ballygawley 141, 177
Ballygomartin Road 171
Ballyholme Bay 214
Ballykinlar 268, 280, 282-284, 305, 329, 398

Ballykinler see Ballykinlar
Ballymacarret 351-352
Ballymena 46, 107, 111, 138, 143, 145, 147, 149, 219, 241, 253, 255, 257, 312-313, 351
Ballymena Castle 111, 255, 257
Ballymoney 46, 149, 289, 312, 396
Ballynafeigh 101
Ballynure 86, 313
Ballyshannon 105-106, 129, 134, 138, 171, 177, 201, 203, 230, 235, 267, 269, 284, 362, 378, 400
Balmoral 51-52, 54, 57, 99, 125-127, 129, 141, 157, 233, 279, 367
Baltic 210-211, 213, 224
Banbridge 141, 147, 221, 312-313, 380
Bangor 86, 95, 111, 140, 191, 204, 221, 223-224, 280, 369-370, 380
Bann, River 241, 407
Bannvale House 314
Bantry 191
Baronscourt 86-87, 102, 155, 230-231
Bay Road 218, 312
Bedford Street 80, 82-83
Belfast viii, 13-16, 18-23, 29-34, 36, 39-40, 43, 46-52, 54, 59, 61-62, 65-69, 71, 73, 77, 79-86, 88, 90, 92, 94-96, 98-99, 101, 103-104, 106, 108-109, 111, 113-114, 116, 121-122, 124-127, 129-131, 136, 138, 140-145, 147, 156, 159-160, 162, 165-166, 169-171, 173-174, 178, 181, 183-187, 190-191, 194, 197, 199, 202, 205-206, 208-209, 211, 213-218, 220-221, 223-224, 226, 229, 233-234, 240, 243-244, 246, 248-249, 251-253, 255, 257-258, 260-261, 266, 268-269, 273-274, 276, 279-280, 282-285, 287-288, 290-293, 295-297, 300, 302-303, 305, 307-311, 314, 317-318, 322-323, 326, 328, 331, 334, 337, 341-347, 349, 351-353, 355, 357-359, 367-368, 371-374, 376-377, 379-380, 382-383, 386, 394, 399
Belfast City Hall 65-66, 81-85, 86, 88, 92, 96, 130, 140, 276, 295-296, 320, 342, 344, 357-358, 376

INDEX

Belfast City Hospital 303
Belfast Distillery 95
Belfast Lough 36, 67, 95, 181, 183, 191, 194, 213, 215, 221
Belgium 140, 258, 260, 271, 280, 307, 310, 363
Belleck 84
Belleek 105, 378
Bergen 208-209, 211
Berlin 169, 198, 206, 257
Bermuda 122
Bessbrook 161
Birmingham 33, 200-202, 229, 231
Blenheim Palace 62
Bogside 343
Botanic Gardens 305
Boyne Bridge 140
Bradford 185-187
The Braid 107
Brighton 23
Bristol 88, 211
Bristol Channel 211
Brookeborough 105, 378
Brownlow House 284-285
Buckingham Palace 195, 243, 245-246, 258, 360
Bundoran 140

Cairo 307
Camberley Staff College 122
Canada 45, 88, 118, 122, 158, 359, 368-369
Carlisle Bridge 343-344
Carlton Club 59, 199
Carnalbanagh 87
Carnlough 35
Carrickblacker House 110, 137
Carrickfergus 95, 149, 172, 178, 180-181, 191, 193-194, 219-220, 228, 253, 329, 369
Carrickmore 124, 175
Carrigart 202
Carrowdore 111
Castle Hume 103, 147, 235
Castle Place 94
Castle Upton 21-22, 86
Castledawson 61
Castlewellan 235
Cavan (County) 12, 20, 42, 113, 145, 165, 248-250, 273, 313, 380-381, 386
Celtic Park 46-50, 62
Ceylon 158
Chaine Memorial Road 365
Chatham 263, 272
China 88
City Cemetery 173, 367

Clandeboye 115, 155, 268, 270, 272, 276-277, 280-282, 284, 290-292, 295, 328-329, 337, 362-363, 399
Clare (County) 52, 189
Clare Park 149
Clifton Street 174, 287
Cliftonville 101
Clonallon Street 352
Clones 171, 174, 380-381
Clontarf 237
Cloreen 251
Clougfern 172
Clough, Co Down 112
Clough, Co Antrim 149
Clyde, River viii, 191, 224
Coleraine 43, 202, 241, 299, 360, 381-382
Comber Street 352
Comber 103, 111, 224
Conlig viii, 111, 408
Constitutional Club 75, 116
Cookstown 141, 147, 257
Copeland 63, 95, 215, 411
Copeland Islands 95, 215
Copenhagen 209-210
Cork 52, 280, 326, 341
Craigavon House 36-40, 43, 58, 78, 108, 133, 139, 142, 144, 158, 160, 171, 178-179, 181-184, 193-194, 196-198, 203, 212, 214-215, 219, 239-240, 242, 314-319, 321-322, 373, 383
Craigwarren 107
Crewe 181
Crossgar 102, 114, 226, 289
Croydon 274
Crumlin 149, 312
Cuinchy 299
Cullybackey 107
Curragh v, 12, 27, 30, 33, 43, 46, 49-54, 56, 59, 61, 64, 77-80, 82, 86, 89-90, 92, 95, 97, 99, 129-130, 139, 165, 169, 178, 180-181, 183, 185, 187, 189-193, 195, 198-199, 206-211, 213-215, 225, 236-237, 239, 245-246, 268, 284, 329, 339, 401, 412
Curran Road 218, 220
Customs House 131

Denmark 209-210
Derry (County) 241, 380
Derry 17, 64, 118, 122, 138, 140, 182, 201, 215, 230, 243, 253, 290, 329, 360, 380
Derrygonnelly 105
Derrygore 203
Dervock 162, 164
The Diamond 13, 343

Donacloney 221, 308
Donaghadee 95, 111, 221-222, 224-225, 228, 370, 373, 375
Donaghmore 175
Donard Lodge 256, 282, 284
Donard Park 103
Donegal vii, 12, 43, 110, 138, 175, 177, 201-202, 249, 268, 273, 284, 287, 313, 344, 379-380, 386
Donegall Pass 280
Donegall Place 85
Donegall Square 85, 130
Down (County) viii, 32, 95, 101-104, 112, 114, 125, 133, 152, 180, 224, 268, 274, 293, 314, 362-363, 378, 399
Downing Street 191
Downpatrick 34, 380
Drogheda 140
Dromore 92, 147, 173, 400
Drumalis 253-254
Drumbeg 251
Drumoolish 140
Dublin vi-vii, 10-12, 18, 24-25, 35-37, 42, 44-45, 58, 82, 86, 88, 117, 140, 162, 165, 167, 170, 175, 180, 182, 184, 191-193, 212, 214, 236-237, 239-241, 248, 250, 280, 283, 287, 289, 294-295, 298-299, 302, 310, 312-313, 326-330, 335, 339-340, 345, 349, 352, 357-359, 367, 371, 384-385
Dublin Castle 24, 45, 110-111, 183, 189, 230, 326, 345, 352, 385
Dunbarton House 314
Duncairn 65, 337
Dundalk 190-192, 328
Dunderave 149
Dundrum 282
Dungannon 141, 162, 170, 312, 381
Dungloe 175
Dunkirk 211, 387
Dunloy 149, 396
Dunmurry 127, 149, 227
Dunseverick 149

East Down 27, 34, 112
East Ham 274
Eaton Place 169, 269
Ebrington Barracks 344
Edinburgh 40, 59, 88, 92, 263
Egypt 12, 252
Elbe, River 209
English Channel 211
Enniskillen 37, 62-63, 105-106, 121, 138, 141, 175, 180-181, 191, 203, 235, 329, 344, 362, 378, 382

Euston 215, 263

Falls Road & District 16, 18, 49-50, 90-91, 159, 173, 351, 367
Fallswater Street 90-91
Fermanagh (County) 11-12, 34-35, 91, 102-103, 105, 113, 125, 138, 141, 171, 175, 177, 184, 225-226, 246, 248, 267, 273, 298, 345, 360, 362, 380, 386
Fernhill House 171, 373
Finner 268-269, 284, 287, 329
Firth of Clyde 191
Fishguard 215
Florencecourt 103, 106, 378
Forth River 59, 171, 205
Fortwilliam 254
Foster Green Hospital 321
Foundry Street 352
Fountain Street 119
Fowler Hall 44, 283, 358
Foyle, River 215, 343
France 9, 71, 88, 239, 249, 254, 258, 262, 264, 272, 280, 304, 307, 310, 324, 331, 391

Galgorm 107, 149
Gallipoli 110
Galwally 307, 314-315, 321
Garvagh 33, 377
Germany 27, 46, 97, 99, 145, 169, 199, 206, 236, 239, 247, 252, 258, 260-262, 280, 327, 335, 337, 391
Gibraltar 181, 191
Gilford 314-315, 318-319, 380, 382-383
Glasgow 88, 92, 95, 158, 201-202, 215, 260, 279, 291, 330, 368
Glaslough 170, 257
Glenarm 212, 218-219
Glenavy 42, 149
Glencairn 159, 311, 373
Glenwherry 107
Glynn 149, 211
Grand Central Hotel 49
Grand Opera House 47
Gravehill 107
Great Yarmouth 211, 215
Greencastle 149
Greenisland 149, 380
Grey Point Fort 95
Greyfriars Churchyard 88
Grosvenor Road 351
Guildhall Square 343

Hamburg 46, 169, 206, 211-213, 224, 330

Hamiltonsbawn 290
Hammersmith 164-165
Harryville 107
Helen's Tower 221, 362-363
Heysham 36
Hilden 104, 321
Hilden House 321
Hill Mount 149
Hillsborough 257, 370, 380
Hollywood Barracks 220
Holyhead 215, 295
Holywood 46, 95, 127, 181, 191, 197, 280, 329
Horse Guards 102, 113, 147, 295
Hotel Cecil 159
Howth 236-241, 253, 258
Hull 122
Hyde Park 186, 199, 231

Iceland 209
India 122, 125, 150, 154, 165, 252
Inglis' Bakery 70
Inverary 202
Irish Sea 178, 181, 215, 233
Irvinestown 105, 378
Islandmagee 366
Isle of Man 138, 229
Italy 35, 88, 206

Kashmir Road 351
Kasr-el-Aini Hospital 307
Kerry (County) 52, 262, 280, 292
Kiel 209-210, 212, 280
Kilcoole 239, 405
Kilkeel 147, 200, 313, 368, 380
Killybegs 84
Killylea 39, 334
Killyleagh Castle 103, 133, 200
Kilmore 312, 334
Kilrea 161, 241, 377
Kilwaughter 211
Kincraig 149
Kingstown 42, 191, 295
Knockballymore 170-171

Lambeg 289, 366, 369
Lamlash 191, 197
Lancaster 369
Larne 13, 50, 52, 75, 141, 149, 152, 208, 211-212, 215-221, 224-225, 228, 231, 239-240, 253-254, 257, 312, 365-366, 369-370, 373
Laxford, Loch 209, 212
Lecale 34
Legan Street 101

Lenaderg 256
Lichfield 199
Lisbellaw 105, 344, 378
Lisburn 35, 101, 104, 127, 141, 149, 226, 243, 257, 266, 280, 289, 293-294, 312, 325, 341, 343, 346, 363, 382
Lisnabreeney 221
Liverpool 40, 88, 92, 94-95, 158, 165, 181, 229, 291, 307
Llandudno Bay 215
Loch Lomond 202
London 9, 12, 21, 23-24, 35-36, 40, 51, 54, 59, 75, 88, 164-165, 169-170, 182, 184, 187, 190-191, 195, 199, 203, 206-207, 212-215, 225, 249, 255-256, 261, 263, 268-269, 274, 291-292, 299-300, 314, 316, 346, 349, 356, 358-359, 362
Londonderry (County) 43, 45, 57, 116, 145, 167, 169, 226, 247-248, 272-273, 299, 359, 380, 386
Londonderry 24, 69, 104, 118, 141, 181, 202, 227, 239, 248, 302, 314, 329, 343, 381-382, 386
Longford, County 34, 109
Lough Erne 103
Loughanmore 298, 379
Loughgall 13, 171, 313
Loughgille 149
Luke's Point 95
Lundy Island 211, 213
Lurgan 200, 274, 284-285, 312-313
Lyric Theatre 371

Macroom 299
Maghera 61, 272, 377
Magherafelt 17, 34, 377
Magheramorne 225
Magilligan Camp 145
Maguiresbridge 105, 314, 378
Maidstone 102
Malone 295, 297
Malta ii, 122
Manchester 42, 88, 92, 165
Mater Infirmorum 303
Meath, County 348
Metropolitan Hall 250
Middle East 110
Monaghan 12, 43, 113, 170-171, 173-174, 180, 227, 248-249, 257, 273, 341, 380, 386
Moneymore 116, 265, 377, 413
Montober 140
Mount Stewart 99
Moyallen 152
Mull of Kintyre 202
Mull of Saddell 202

Mulroy 201
Murlough House 103
Murray-Ker 170

Nanking 88
Narrow Water Castle 124-125, 164
New York 208, 232, 247, 351-352, 402
New Zealand 359
Newbliss 170
Newcastle 34, 103, 208, 256, 280-282, 284, 289, 329
Newry 132, 141, 147, 161, 248
Newtownards 101, 111, 129, 224, 268, 292-293, 312, 329, 352
Newtownbreda 68, 101
Newtownbutler 105, 113, 378, 382
Newtowncunningham 147
Nigeria 158
Norbury 274
North Antrim 106, 295
North Channel 181
North Down 111, 215
North Sea 211-212
Northumberland Street 114
Norway 208

Old Town Hall 129-131, 160, 199, 217, 229, 266, 268-269, 280, 282, 287, 300-302, 323, 380, 399
Omagh 34, 88, 141, 180-181, 191, 263, 265, 290, 313, 362, 380-382
Orange Halls 39, 44, 52, 162, 174, 294
Orlock 221
Ormeau Park 51
Ormiston 156

Paris 198, 367
Pau 303-304
Peking 122
Peter's Hill 229
Pettigo 105, 378
Phoenix Park 11
Pickie Point 95
Piershill Barrack 263
Plymouth 168
Portadown 64, 141, 200, 282, 381
Portglenone 107
Portora Hill 63
Portpatrick 84
Portrush 40, 149, 201, 242, 313
Portugal 191
Princess Gardens Girls School 321
Protestant Hall 143, 362

Randalstown 149, 380
Raphoe 93, 178
Rasharkin 149, 354, 356
Rathmines 340
Reform Club 49, 92, 94, 169, 405
Renfrew 202
Richill 11
Rosapenna Hotel 202
Roscommon 236
Rosslare 214, 224
Rossnowlagh 177, 313
Rotunda, The 117, 175
Royal Albert Hall 24, 59
Royal Avenue 49, 85, 94
Royal Belfast Academical Institution/RBAI 19
Russia 198, 248, 258, 261

Sackville Street 326
Samaritan Hospital 305
Sarajvo 251
Scotland 30, 46, 53, 76, 84, 88, 165, 202, 209, 215, 224, 243-244, 254, 303, 373
Seaforde (Down) 112, 378
Seaforde (Sussex) 295-296
Serbia 239, 246, 258, 261-262
Seville House 36
Seymour Hill House 227
Shane's Castle 102
Shankill 16, 18, 68, 160-161, 171, 205, 229, 269, 285, 287, 367
Shiel Park 95
Sion Mills 34, 38, 43, 103, 154, 381
Soloheadbeg 340
Somme Museum viii
Somme Nursing Home 322
Somme, Battle of 326, 331-332, 334-335, 370
Somme, River 376
South Africa 12, 25, 27, 34, 88, 118, 123, 155
South Wales 214
Springhill 116, 226
St Anne's Cathedral 284, 288, 371
St George's Market 293
St Mary's Hall 47
St Nicholas Parish Church 87
St Stephen's Green 283
Stewart's Yard 160, 282
Stock Exchange 199
Stormont 322, 367, 372
Strabane 141, 304, 312-313
Straid 86
Strandtown 243, 382
Strangford 34
Stranocum 149, 225-226

Sudan 123
Sutherlandshire 209
Svendborg 210
Sydenham 274

Tamlaght 61, 140
Templepatrick 21-22
Tempo 105, 344, 378
Tenby 214
Thiepval 311, 362-363, 365-366
Thronemount 149
Tiger's Bay 345
Tipperary 307, 312, 340
Tobar Mhuire 102
Tobermore 45, 273
Toome 241
Topped Mountain 106
Toronto 45
Transvaal 25-26
Trelleborg 211
Trim 348
Trinity College 36-37, 42, 162, 335, 371
Tullymurry 282
Tynan Abbey 140-141, 272, 312, 370
Tyrella House 34
Tyrone (County) 12, 31, 34, 39-40, 87, 102-103, 138, 141, 175, 180, 220-221, 226, 246, 248, 267, 273, 290, 329, 360, 380-381, 386

Uganda 109
Ulster Club 21, 94
Ulster Hall 13-15, 20, 23, 46-48, 50, 68, 80-81, 83, 85, 96, 252, 288,
Ulster Reform Club 92, 94, 169, 405
United States of America vii, 87-88, 206, 280, 335, 339
University College Dublin 117
Upperlands 272, 314

Victoria Barracks 46, 181, 191
Vulcan Street 352

Waringstown 64, 115, 152, 200
Wattsbridge 174
West Down 256, 315
West Ham 274
Westbourne Presbyterian Church 92
Westminster 9, 12, 15, 23-24, 27-28, 56, 92, 96, 101, 116, 232, 243, 247, 298, 322, 338-340, 350, 356-357, 359
Wexford 214-215
Whiteabbey 149, 172, 313
Whitehall 116, 168, 195, 284
Whitehead 95, 221, 368
Whitehouse 61, 149
Wicklow 44, 239
Willowfield 103, 374
Wolverhampton 123
Woolwich 164

Ye Olde Castle Restaurant 292
York 88, 92, 147

INDEX OF MILITARY FORMATIONS & UNITS

British Army 59, 65, 79, 99, 103, 106, 109, 115, 122-123, 125-126, 140, 158, 165, 189, 193, 195-196, 198, 206, 243, 262, 264, 269, 289, 292, 295, 333, 340, 343, 359, 387, 390, 394-395
British Expeditionary Force 225, 252, 262, 264, 307, 386
British Indian Army 121-123, 274
Irish Citizen Army 117, 327
Irish Republican Army 44, 230, 340-341, 344, 346-347, 349, 352, 356-359, 367, 370

36th (Ulster) Division vi-vii, 106, 112, 268, 270-276, 280-281, 283-284, 288-292, 294-297, 300, 303, 305, 311, 323, 328-329, 331-335, 337, 341-342, 346, 348, 356, 362-363, 365, 370-371, 374, 376, 399
Antrim Division, UVF 271, 288

Belfast Division, UVF 125, 127, 144, 381-382, 398

3 Cavalry Brigade 192
15 Ulster Reserve Infantry Brigade 181, 329
107 (Belfast Brigade) 275, 277

Regiments (listed alphabetically, then numerically by battalion where applicable):
Armagh Regiment 103, 110, 137, 153, 171, 263, 272, 381-382
Belfast Regiment 71, 108-109, 127, 159, 353, 355, 406
Cavan Regiment 380-381
Central Antrim Regiment 203, 257, 380
Derry City Regiment 172, 377, 380, 382
Donegal Regiment 200, 202, 230, 256, 362, 378
1st Battalion Donegal Regiment 177, 378

3rd Battalion Donegal Regiment 177, 380-381
Dorset Regiment 191, 344
Dragoon Guards 109
East Belfast Regiment 120, 156, 233, 255, 282, 374, 377, 382
East Down Regiment 255, 257, 380, 382
Fermanagh Regiment 105-106, 121, 163, 203, 235, 378, 381-382
Irish Guards 171, 263, 299
King's Own Scottish Borderers 237
King's Own Yorkshire Light Infantry 45
King's Royal Rifle Corps 160
16th Lancers 192
Life Guards 147
Monaghan Regiment 174, 257, 328, 381
1st Battalion North Antrim Regiment 60, 107, 120, 137, 143, 162, 185, 242-243, 253, 257, 259, 279, 381
North Belfast Regiment 101, 108, 255-256, 268, 282, 377
North Derry Regiment 377, 380
1st Battalion, North Down Regiment 150, 204, 221, 294
2nd North Down Regiment 224, 255, 331
1st Battalion (North) Tyrone Regiment 250, 381
Norfolk Regiment 284
North Irish Horse 263
Royal Dublin Fusiliers 44, 329
Royal Fusiliers 110, 263
Royal Inniskilling Fusiliers 88, 124, 329
9th Service Battalion, Royal Inniskilling Fusiliers (Tyrone Volunteers) 271, 275, 283-284, 295
10th Battalion, the Royal Inniskilling Fusiliers (Derry Volunteers) 275, 284, 370
11th Royal Inniskilling Fusiliers (Donegal and Fermanagh Volunteers) 362, 275, 279, 284, 362
Royal Irish Fusiliers 20, 275, 277, 281, 284
Royal Irish Regiment 11
Royal Irish Rifles 160, 268, 275, 282, 329
3rd Royal Irish Rifles (North Down Militia) 34, 130
5th Royal Irish Rifles 35, 130, 329
8th Battalion, the Royal Irish Rifles (East Belfast Volunteers) 275, 284, 287, 374
9th Battalion, the Royal Irish Rifles (West Belfast Volunteers) 275, 284-285, 287
10th Battalion, the Royal Irish Rifles (South Belfast Volunteers) 275, 284-285
11th Battalion, Royal Irish Rifles (South Antrim Volunteers) 275, 284, 289, 3631st South Belfast Regiment 127, 255
12th Battalion Royal Irish Rifles (Mid Antrim Volunteers) 254, 284, 289, 301

13th Battalion, the Royal Irish Rifles (1st County Down Volunteers) 275, 284, 399
14th Battalion, the Royal Irish Rifles (Young Citizen Volunteers) 68-69, 72, 233, 275, 279, 284, 286-287
16th Battalion, the Royal Irish Rifles (2nd County Down Volunteers) 275, 284
Saskatchewan Light Horse 158
Somerset Light Infantry 279
South Antrim Regiment 137, 219, 241, 255, 257, 380, 382
South Belfast Regiment 127, 255, 257, 282, 377
2nd Battalion South Belfast Regiment 255, 257, 282
South Derry Regiment 116, 377
South Down Regiment 295, 378
1st Battalion, South Down Regiment 256, 378, 380
2nd Battalion, South Down Regiment 161, 378, 380
South Londonderry Regiment 61, 140, 381
Tyrone Regiment 112, 155, 177, 230, 250, 257, 378, 381-382
2nd Battalion, Tyrone Regiment 381-382
4th (Dungannon) Battalion, Tyrone Regiment 161, 378, 381
West Belfast Regiment 109, 159, 203, 255, 282, 284, 296, 377
West Down Regiment 256, 380, 382

Belfast Defence Corps 293
Belfast Signallers 140, 141
Cavan Volunteer Force (CVF) 145
County Down Volunteers 214, 275, 284
Despatch Riding Corps 106, 127, 138, 140-144, 217, 226, 242, 256
Enniskillen Horse 127-128, 147-148, 235, 274
Fermanagh Volunteers 134, 171, 275, 284
Imperial Yeomanry 34, 64, 109, 130
Indian Medical Service 130
Irish Home Defence Corps 293-294
Louth Militia 32
Loyal Dublin Volunteers 44-45, 250, 283, 298, 328-329, 358
Motor Car Corps 106, 138, 152, 160, 216, 221
Nile Frontier Force 132
North Down Volunteers 114, 216
Officer Training Corps (OTC) 293
Royal Army Medical Corps 273, 275-276, 328
Royal Army Service Corps 274, 346
Royal Artillery 122, 124, 130, 263
Royal Engineers 273, 284
Royal Field Artillery 274-275
Royal Garrison Artillery 265

INDEX 421

Royal Horse Guards 113, 247, 295
Royal South Down Militia 34
Signalling and Despatch Riding Corps (US&DRC) 138
Somerset Light Infantry 263, 279
Special Service Section 120.138
Supplementary Reserve 148
Ulster Home Guard 227, 265
Ulster Volunteer Force vi-viii, 31, 35, 39, 42-45, 47, 53-54, 56-57, 59-62, 64-66, 68, 71-72, 90, 97, 99-100, 103-106, 108, 110-120, 122-125, 127, 129-133, 137-142, 144-148, 150-155, 157-158, 160-163, 165-166, 168-169, 171-174, 177-178, 180, 183-184, 187, 189-191, 193, 196-204, 207, 209, 216-220, 226-227, 231-233, 239-244, 247, 250-261, 263-274, 279, 282-285, 287-292, 294-297, 299-301, 303, 305, 309-311, 316- 318, 321, 323-325, 328-335, 341, 343-344, 346-347, 349, 358, 362, 365- 367, 371, 373, 377, 383, 385-386, 392-393, 398
Volunteer Defence Corps 293-294
Volunteer Training Corps 293-294, 298, 328
West African Frontier Force 158
Zhob Valley Field Force 122
Zionist Mule Corps 119

Royal Navy 27, 143, 178, 184, 191, 197, 213, 236, 260
HMS *Attentive* 181, 191
HMS *Bluebell* 208
HMS *Gibraltar* 191
HMS *Monmouth* 88
HMS *Pathfinder* 181, 191, 193-194
HMS *Royal Arthur* 191-192

INDEX OF GENERAL & MISCELLANEOUS TERMS

Act of Union 9, 13, 23, 87
Ancient Order of Hibernians 61, 189, 211
Anglo-Irish Treaty 359-360
Antrim Iron Ore Company 208
Ark Lodge X 32
Armagh, Archbishop of 24, 42, 82, 99,
Auxiliary Division (ADRIC) 340,348

Bangor Spectator 75, 221
Belfast and County Down Railway 282
Belfast Celtic 62, 95
Belfast City Hospital 303
Belfast Corporation 47, 293, 405
Belfast Technical Institute 318
Belfast, Lord Mayor of 65-66, 68-71, 83-84, 94, 233, 295, 302, 310, 332, 344
Berlin Congress (1878) 21
Black and Tans 340, 348, 351
Boer War (1899-1902) 33, 115, 123, 130, 154-155, 158, 200, 232, 248, 263, 268, 302, 387, 389
Boundary Commission 360
Boxer Rebellion (1900) 122
Boyne Standard 83
Boyne, Battle of the 64, 80-81, 83, 96, 367
Boys' Brigade 39
Brassards 119
British Covenant 231-232
British East Africa Company 109
British Government vi, 40, 75, 97, 198, 208, 211, 237, 259, 271, 335, 346, 351, 353, 356, 359, 366
British League 51, 123, 157-159, 267, 279, 362

British Red Cross Society 303, 311
British South Africa Company 25

Catholic emancipation 9
Certificate of Proficiency 162-163
Church Lads Brigade 114
Clearing Hospital 148-149
Clydeside Steamship Company 368
Committee of Imperial Defence 122, 138, 211, 258, 264
Conservative Party vi, 9-10, 12-13, 17-18, 23, 25- 30, 36, 51-53, 59, 62, 64, 116, 159, 165, 167, 189, 195, 232, 247, 259, 356-357
County Down Railway 280, 282
County Enrolment Book 106, 135
Crime Special Branch 39, 46, 124,126, 228
Crimean War (1853-56) 323
Cumann na mBan 330

Dail Eireann 340
Despatch Riders vii, 127, 138, 140,141, 142, 144, 184, 217, 229, 256,
Detective Branch 124,165
Director of Ordnance 90, 130
Distinguished Service Order 109, 154
Dublin Government 170, 180
Dublin Metropolitan Police 42, 236-237, 329, 349
Dublin Parliament vii, 57-58, 197, 290

Easter Rebellion 249, 280, 326-330, 335, 338

Enniskillen Horse 103, 127-128, 147-148, 235, 274

Fermanagh Vigilance 345
First Aid Corps 150
FM Foyer & Co Ltd 165
Fourth Flotilla 181
Free State Seanad 42
Freemasons 21

General Post Office (Dublin) 326
Gilbey Liquor 109
Gregg and Company 65
Gun Barrel Proof Act 164
Gun-running vii, 84, 152, 168, 206-229

Haldane Reforms 65, 302
Harland and Wolff 18, 20, 46
Harrods 203, 207
Home Rule vi-viii, 9-13, 16-21, 23-32, 35, 37-40, 42-47, 50-53, 56-59, 61-63, 68, 73-79, 82, 86-87, 92, 96-97, 99, 106, 110-112, 116-118, 122, 124, 128-132, 138, 145, 164, 167, 169-170, 174-175, 178, 185-186, 189, 195, 198-199, 203, 209, 231, 240-243, 245-250, 255, 259-260, 264, 266-268, 270-272, 280, 283, 287-288, 291-292, 298, 330-331, 335, 337-339, 349, 351, 357, 360, 366-368, 370-373
Home Rule League 10, 12

Imperial Defence Committee 138
Imperial Government 12, 170, 258-259, 270
Indemnity Guarantee Fund 129
Intelligence Branch 151
Irish Land Act 10, 23
Irish Nationalists 9, 11-13, 16, 18, 23, 25, 27-28, 32, 35, 45, 47, 49, 51, 57, 61, 64, 67, 95, 97, 99, 116-117, 130, 145, 152, 161, 175, 177, 184, 186, 195, 198, 205-206, 221, 233, 235-236, 239-242, 248, 258- 260, 266, 297-299, 329-330, 335, 337-339, 342-344, 352, 355-356, 368
Irish Parliamentary Party 10, 12, 17-18, 23, 25, 117, 176, 241, 246, 326, 329, 335, 337-340
Irish Protestants 9, 15, 165, 263
Irish Republican Brotherhood 117, 326
Irish Unionist Party 15, 20, 27, 36, 52, 140, 255, 340
Irish War of Independence 340, 359

John Ferguson & Co 164, 206

Ladies Imperial Club 199
Lee-Enfield rifle 388-394
Lee-Metford rifle 388-394

Liberal Government 10, 27-28, 33, 46, 56, 178, 247, 260
Liberal Party 9-10, 12, 17-18, 19, 25-28, 32, 40, 47, 51, 56, 92, 152, 169, 185-186, 255, 262, 338
Liberal Unionists 18-19, 23, 25
Lisburn Standard 266, 363
Londonderry Supply Depot 302

MacIlwaine, Lewis and Company Ltd 368
Manchester Guardian 157, 195
Mannlicher rifle 388-394
Martini-Enfield rifle 203
Martini-Henry rifle 388-394
Masonic Lodge 86
Mauser 175, 226, 236, 239, 284, 388-394
Messrs W&G Baird 162
Messrs Workman and Clark 51, 67, 215, 221
Midland Gun Company 32
Midland Railway 50-51
Military Council 99, 129
Moss Bros. 268
Mountjoy II 215, 218, 220-221, 227, 253

National Rifle Association 31, 42
North of Ireland Cricket Ground 368
North of Ireland Rifle Club 23
Northern Railway 290

Operation 'Lion' 206, 225-226
Orange Order 13, 17, 26, 32-33, 35-40, 43-44, 46, 48, 52-53, 62, 73, 79-80, 85, 95-96, 99-100, 111-112, 118-119, 124, 158, 162, 165, 167, 174, 233, 236, 250-251, 253, 294-295, 331, 358, 369
Order of St John of Jerusalem 303, 311, 383

Papal Decree 30
Peep O Day Boys 13
Presbyterian Church 18-21, 30, 35, 40, 46, 51, 56, 59-61, 68, 75, 77, 82, 86-87, 90, 92, 96, 99, 110, 112, 114, 164, 206, 211, 225, 257, 310, 335, 346, 371

Royal Belfast Academical Institution (RBAI) 19
Royal Irish Constabulary vii, 11, 16-17, 23, 31, 35, 39, 41-42, 45, 50, 61-63, 110-111, 113, 117, 124-125, 128, 132, 147, 161, 165, 171, 173, 179-180, 185, 187, 189-190, 197, 211, 219, 228, 230, 233, 235, 243, 280, 290, 299, 329, 337, 340-341, 343-344, 346-349, 351-352, 354-356
Royal Ulster Constabulary (RUC) 212, 321, 322
Royal Victoria Hospital 307, 318

INDEX

Russo-Turkish War (1877-78) 21

Second Anglo-Afghan War (1878-80) 122, 232
Sinn Fein 25, 97, 175, 236, 323, 330, 335, 337-340, 343, 345, 350, 351, 359
South African War (1899-1902) *see* Boer War (1899-1902)
Special Branch 39, 46, 64, 124, 126, 173, 189, 228, 233, 343
Special Emergency Gendarmerie 348
Sphagnum Moss Association 302
SS *Aud* 280, 326
SS *Balmerino* 208, 214
SS *Castro* 211, 280
SS *Clyde Valley* 215-216, 220-221, 224-225, 227-228, 253, 330, 366, 368-369
SS *Fanny* 208-212, 214-215, 224, 252, 370
SS *Graniamore* 201-202
Steyr Rifle 391, 393-394
Suffragettes 40, 49, 92, 156, 172

Tandragee Orange Heroes 295

Ulster Constitution Defence Committee 369
Ulster Convention 19
Ulster Covenant 77-134
Ulster Day 62, 78-79, 82-83, 85, 86, 89, 94-96, 99, 140, 124, 372
Ulster Defence Fund 99
Ulster Defence Scheme 297
Ulster Defence Union 20-21
Ulster Liberal Association 46, 48
Ulster Movement 13, 134
Ulster Patriotic Fund 323-325
Ulster Prisoner of War and Comforts Fund 301-302
Ulster Provisional Government 99, 100, 121, 260,

Ulster Special Constabulary (USC) 265, 328, 343, 345-347, 349-356, 359
Ulster Unionist Council (UUC) 26, 31-32, 36, 40, 48, 51, 78, 87, 99-100, 113, 124, 129, 157, 164, 174, 197, 199, 215, 244, 249, 268-269, 345-346, 350
Ulster Volunteer Nursing Corps 127
Ulster Women's Declaration 92
Ulster Women's Gift Aid 334
Union Defence League 231-232
Unionism 18, 20-21, 29-30, 38, 52, 89, 130, 189
United Irish League 175
UUC *see* Ulster Unionist Council

Vetterli Rifle 388-394
Vickers Maxim machine-gun 394-395
Victoria Cross 68, 299
Voluntary Aid Detachment (VAD) 139, 148, 303, 311

Waffen, Munition and Militar-Effekten 206
War Office 65, 122, 127, 167, 187, 190-192, 197, 268, 272, 298, 302-303, 305, 307-308, 310, 316-317, 398
Webley revolver 387-388
White's Conquerors Flute Band 112
Wigan Coal and Iron Company 368
William Ewart & Son Ltd 70
Workman and Clark 51

York Street Flax Spinning Company 70
Yorkshire Post 152, 157
Young Citizen Volunteers (YCV) 65, 67-68, 70, 72, 109, 156, 233-234, 279, 287
Young Ulster 20, 24

Zulu War (1879) 21